Gothic Antiquity

Gothic Antiquity

History, Romance, and the Architectural Imagination, 1760–1840

DALE TOWNSHEND

OXFORD
UNIVERSITY PRESS

Great Clarendon Street, Oxford, OX2 6DP,
United Kingdom

Oxford University Press is a department of the University of Oxford.
It furthers the University's objective of excellence in research, scholarship,
and education by publishing worldwide. Oxford is a registered trade mark of
Oxford University Press in the UK and in certain other countries

© Dale Townshend 2019

The moral rights of the author have been asserted

First Edition published in 2019

Impression: 3

All rights reserved. No part of this publication may be reproduced, stored in
a retrieval system, or transmitted, in any form or by any means, without the
prior permission in writing of Oxford University Press, or as expressly permitted
by law, by licence or under terms agreed with the appropriate reprographics
rights organization. Enquiries concerning reproduction outside the scope of the
above should be sent to the Rights Department, Oxford University Press, at the
address above

You must not circulate this work in any other form
and you must impose this same condition on any acquirer

Published in the United States of America by Oxford University Press
198 Madison Avenue, New York, NY 10016, United States of America

British Library Cataloguing in Publication Data
Data available

Library of Congress Control Number: 2019934067

ISBN 978-0-19-884566-9

DOI: 10.1093/oso/9780198845669.001.0001

Printed and bound in Great Britain by
Clays Ltd, Elcograf S.p.A.

Links to third party websites are provided by Oxford in good faith and
for information only. Oxford disclaims any responsibility for the materials
contained in any third party website referenced in this work.

Preface

The relationship between Gothic literature—romances, dramas, poetry, chapbooks—and Gothic architecture—the architectural style of the Middle Ages, in both its 'survivalist' and 'revivalist' forms—is something that has long fascinated the Gothic scholarly tradition. No doubt this is because, well beyond the preoccupation with the ruined castles, abbeys, convents, and towers of the Middle Ages that we see throughout the so-called 'first wave' of British Gothic writing (c.1760–1840), the two have been yoked together by that most thoroughly over determined of adjectives: the term 'Gothic' itself.[1] For Clara F. McIntyre in 1921, the fact that an eighteenth-century literary form shared its name with a medieval and 'medievalist' architectural style was more misleading than it was revealing: 'We all know at least a little about a Gothic cathedral,' she wrote, 'but when we find the term given to a novel we are all, I believe, a trifle vague.'[2] While a writer such as Ann Radcliffe, McIntyre continued, certainly populated her fictions with 'Gothic abbeys' and 'Gothic windows', it was to the European Renaissance and not to the 'Gothic' past of the English Middle Ages that the writer's best-known narratives characteristically returned.[3] But McIntyre's reservations are exceptional, and for the vast majority of scholars in the first four decades of the twentieth century, there was something intrinsic, even absolute, about the relationship between eighteenth-century Gothic writing and its architectural namesake, even if they could not always articulate precisely why this was so. For Dorothy Scarborough in 1917, for example, the 'Gothic castle', like the ruined and crumbling abbey, contributed in no small part to the definitive sense of 'mystery and awe' elicited by Gothic fiction, its secret passageways, trapdoors, underground vaults, and dungeons 'a fit setting for the unearthly visitors that haunt it'; the 'horrific romance' in general, she tautologously concluded, 'shows a close kinship with its architecture'.[4] Compounding the identifications between the literary and the architectural that were already in place in the eighteenth century, Edith Birkhead in *The Tale of Terror* (1921) drew attention to what she took to be the startling correspondences between Horace Walpole's *The Castle of Otranto*

---

[1] For the use of the phrase 'first wave' to designate British Gothic writing of the late eighteenth and early nineteenth centuries, see Rictor Norton, ed., *Gothic Readings: The First Wave, 1764–1840* (London: Leicester University Press, 2000).
[2] Clara F. McIntyre, 'Were the "Gothic Novels" Gothic?', *PMLA* vol. 36, no. 4 (Dec. 1921): pp. 644–67 (p. 645).
[3] McIntyre, 'Were the "Gothic Novels" Gothic?', p. 645.
[4] Dorothy Scarborough, *The Supernatural in Modern English Fiction* (New York and London: G. P. Putnam's Sons, 1917), p. 9.

(published late 1764; dated 1765) and William Beckford's *Vathek* (1786) and the authors' architectural work at Strawberry Hill, Twickenham, and Fonthill Abbey, Wiltshire, respectively, thus reinstating an early critical tendency that remains prevalent if not inveterate to this day.[5] Despite what it promised in its title, Eino Railo's *The Haunted Castle* (1927) ultimately had very little to say about the relationship between Gothic fiction and architecture beyond pointing out that the haunted castle was a dominant motif in what he termed the 'horror-romanticism' of Walpole, Matthew Lewis, Walter Scott, and others, one that took its place alongside such other tropes as the criminal monk, the wandering Jew, incest, ghosts, and demonic beings.[6] In his pioneering account of Jane Austen's 'Northanger Novels' of the same year, Michael Sadleir made some important observations regarding the political significance of architectural ruins in post-French Revolutionary Gothic romances published in Britain, if only eventually to dismiss these fictions' architectural preoccupations—the abbeys, castles, and ruins so frequently referenced in their titles—as being one of the many 'fatuities of the school'.[7] J. M. S. Tompkins was similarly attuned to the use—and highly conventionalized overuse—of architecture in her account of Gothic romance in *The Popular Novel in England* (1932), claiming that, since Gothic architecture had suffered from such 'degradation' and 'over-production' in Gothic fiction, it was barely necessary to discuss the matter at all.[8]

In his essay 'Forms of Time and of the Chronotope in the Novel: Notes Toward a Historical Poetics' of 1937, the Russian theorist Mikhail Bakhtin developed his notion of the 'chronotope'—that complex conflation of space and time that lends to a literary genre its singularity—through a brief but important analysis of the architecture of Gothic romance. The Gothic castle, he argued, is 'saturated through and through with a time that is historical in the narrow sense of the word, that is, the time of the historical past';[9] more trenchantly, it was this particular chronotopic arrangement of time and space that was said to lend to Gothic literature its generic specificity. Though Bakhtin's theories have since been fruitfully applied to the analysis of the early Gothic—most notably by Robert Miles in *Gothic Writing 1750–1820: A Genealogy* (1993) and by Jacqueline Howard in *Reading Gothic Fiction: A Bakhtinian Approach* (1994)—the belated translation of his work on the Gothic chronotope into English meant that its

---

[5] Edith Birkhead, *The Tale of Terror: A Study of the Gothic Romance* (London: Constable and Co., 1921), pp. 30, 97.

[6] Eino Railo, *The Haunted Castle: A Study of the Elements of English Romanticism* (London: George Routledge & Sons, 1927), p. vii.

[7] Michael Sadleir, *The Northanger Novels: A Footnote to Jane Austen*, The English Association Pamphlet no. 6 (Oxford: Oxford University Press, 1927), p. 17.

[8] J. M. S. Tompkins, *The Popular Novel in England 1770–1800*, 2nd edn (Lincoln: University of Nebraska Press, 1961), p. 268.

[9] Mikhail Mikhailovich Bakhtin, 'Forms of Time and of the Chronotope in the Novel: Notes toward a Historical Poetics', in Mikhail Mikhailovich Bakhtin, *The Dialogic Imagination: Four Essays*, trans. M. Holquist and Caryl Emerson (Austin: University of Texas Press, 1981), pp. 84–258 (p. 245).

impact upon the Anglo-American critical tradition was slow to take effect. Indeed, though architectural matters were frequently mentioned in earlier criticism, it was really only with the publication of Warren Hunting Smith's *Architecture in English Fiction* in 1934 that they received any sustained critical attention at all. Though Hunting Smith was not solely concerned with Gothic fictional forms, his study remains, to date, unsurpassed in its encyclopedic knowledge of the field, and in its searching examination of the relationship between architecture and literature across a broad range of eighteenth- and nineteenth-century texts and writers. This was followed soon thereafter by the publication of Montague Summers's *The Gothic Quest* in 1938, a study that, though by no means solely concerned with architecture, continuously pondered the question in relation to the countless forgotten romances, dramas, and chapbooks that it brought to light. In his characteristically passionate tone, Summers paused amid a discussion of Walpole and Clara Reeve in order to argue that 'The connexion between the Gothic Romance and Gothic Architecture is, so to speak, congenital and indigenous', that it 'goes deep down to and is vitally of the very heart of the matter'.[10]

Summers's primary objective in *The Gothic Quest* was to recuperate for serious consideration a literary form that had fallen foul of the same cultural biases that, in the first half of the eighteenth century, had dismissed Gothic architecture as crude, uncouth, and barbaric. To this gesture, the reconsideration of architecture in Gothic writing as something of far greater significance than what earlier critics had tended to denounce as conventionalized 'claptrap' or superficial 'paraphernalia' became paramount. The Gothic castle, Summers here and elsewhere insisted, was so central to the Gothic as legitimately to be conceived as a literary 'character' in its own right, invariably functioning, as such, as much more than a vague historical referent or the marker of an atmospheric *mise en scène*.[11] As he put it in a short piece on the relationship between architecture and literature published in the *Architectural Design and Construction* journal in 1931, 'It is the castle which is the protagonist of Walpole's romance; and throughout all Otranto's progeny, whose name is legion indeed, the remote and ruined castle, the ancient manor, the vast fortress, the lone and secret convent, the dark and mysterious monastery, are ever and again the principal features of the tale.'[12] Of all early critical opinions, it was this claim to the personified form and function of architecture in the early Gothic that has proved to be one of the most enduring. As E. J. Clery put it in her Introduction to the Oxford World's Classics edition of *The Castle of Otranto* in 1996, 'Few critics have failed to make the point that the gothic

---

[10] Montague Summers, *The Gothic Quest: A History of the Gothic Novel* (London: The Fortune Press, 1938), p. 189.
[11] See, for instance, Montague Summers's argument in his 'Introduction' to Constable's edition of *The Castle of Otranto and The Mysterious Mother* (London: Constable, 1924), pp. xi–lvii.
[12] Montague Summers, 'Architecture and the Gothic Novel', *Architectural Design and Construction* vol. 2, no. 2 (December 1931): pp. 78–81 (p. 80).

castle is the main protagonist of *Otranto*, and that the story of usurpation, tyranny, and imprisonment could be seen as an extension of the mood evoked by the setting.'[13] More recently, Carol Margaret Davison in *Gothic Literature 1764-1824* (2009) has drawn upon, and extended, such readings of architecture as the Gothic's primary 'protagonist', though leavening this approach with greater sensitivity to the architectural style's historical significations.[14]

In the Introduction that she wrote for Devendra P. Varma's *The Gothic Flame* in 1957, J. M. S. Tompkins signalled the critical sea change effected by what was otherwise a highly derivative study by pointing out that 'what has altered our attitude to Gothic writings is, of course, the application of Freudian psychology to literature and literary periods'.[15] By this way of reasoning, the Gothic castle—'that formidable place, ruinous yet an effective prison, phantasmagorically shifting its outline as ever new vaults extend their labyrinths, scene of solitary wanderings cut off from light and human contact, of unformulated menace and the terror of the living dead'—now presented itself to critics 'as the symbol of neurosis', a textual 'symptom' of anxiety concerning the forces of contemporary political and religious oppression.[16] As Tompkins's careful choice of words suggests, it was in the wake of a critic such as Varma that psychoanalysis became Gothic criticism's dominant metalanguage, if not always in an orthodox Freudian sense, then at least through the deft synthesis of psychoanalysis and Marxism that we encounter in David Punter's *The Literature of Terror* (1980). In Punter's account, matters of architectural interest—from Walpole's Castle of Otranto, through the ruined abbeys of Radcliffe, to Mervyn Peake's *Gormenghast* series (1946-59), and beyond—are never far away. Yet, it was really only with the attention that Anglo-American feminist scholars began to pay Gothic writing from the late 1970s onwards that architecture became an object of critical interest in its own right. Crucial to this feminist turn was Ellen Moers's work on the 'female Gothic' in *Literary Women* (1979), as well as Sandra M. Gilbert and Susan Gubar's feminist critique of Gaston Bachelard's *The Poetics of Space* (1958) in *The Madwoman in the Attic* (1979). Countering Bachelard's exclusive focus upon sites of 'topophilia'—the comforting and 'felicitous' home of childhood experience to which the modern bourgeois subject repeatedly returns in dreams and nostalgic flights of fancy—with their notion of 'topophobia', Gilbert and Gubar drew

---

[13] E. J. Clery, 'Introduction', in Horace Walpole, *The Castle of Otranto*, ed. W. S. Lewis (Oxford: Oxford University Press, 1996), pp. vii–xxxiii (p. xv).

[14] Carol Margaret Davison, *Gothic Literature 1764-1824* (Cardiff: University of Wales Press, 2009), pp. 70-3.

[15] J. M. S. Tompkins, 'Introduction', in Devendra P. Varma, *The Gothic Flame, Being a History of the Gothic Novel in England: Its Origins, Efflorescence, Disintegration, and Residuary Influences* (London: Arthur Barker: 1957), pp. xi–xv (p. xiii).

[16] Tompkins, 'Introduction', *The Gothic Flame*, p. xiii.

attention, primarily through nineteenth-century Gothic fictional examples, to the architectural spaces of gender-based anxiety, terror, and oppression.[17]

Equally central to this second-wave feminist critical endeavour was the architectural topography of the psyche described by Carl Gustav Jung in *Contributions to Analytical Psychology* (1928): the claim that human consciousness could be equated with the upper stories of a nineteenth-century building, the preconscious with the sixteenth-century ground floor, and the unconscious with the antique and pre-antique structures ominously lurking, undiscovered, in the cellar.[18] Thus spatialized, psychoanalytic conceptualizations of subjectivity would further inform the critical reading of architecture in Gothic fiction, particularly in Claire Kahane's influential account of female subject-formation through an encounter with a maternal ghost in womblike subterranean architectural space in the essay 'Gothic Mirrors and Feminine Identity' (1980); in Jerrold E. Hogle's reading of 'cryptonomy' and subterranean space in 'The Restless Labyrinth' (1980); and in Ian Watt's 1986 psychoanalytic reading of the architecture of *The Castle of Otranto*.[19] Eugenia C. DeLamotte paid considerable attention to the function of architecture in Gothic fiction in *Perils of the Night* (1990), most memorably reading the bedchamber of Emily St Aubert, the heroine of Radcliffe's *The Mysteries of Udolpho* (1794), as the physical and sexual boundary of the 'self' that is continuously transgressed, disrupted, and penetrated by a number of unwelcome masculine threats.[20] In her largely Kristevan reading of eighteenth- and nineteenth-century Gothic in *Art of Darkness* (1995), Anne Williams provided an equally influential feminist reading of architecture, qualifying and supplementing Jung's architectural psychic metaphor with gendered insights so as to argue that the Gothic castle, its walls, towers, and ramparts signified consciousness and male-dominated realms of power, and its dungeons, attics, secret rooms, and hidden passages 'the culturally female, the sexual, the maternal, the unconscious'.[21] As in DeLamotte's study, the architecture of Gothic fiction is given gendered, highly politicized meanings in the work of these critics, an inflection that played itself further in such other important feminist readings as

---

[17] See Sandra M. Gilbert and Susan Gubar, *The Madwoman in the Attic: The Woman Writer and the Nineteenth-Century Literary Imagination* (New Haven and London: Yale University Press, 1979), pp. 87–8. For a more recent continuation of this feminist reading of Gothic architectural space, see Carol Margaret Davison, 'Gothic Architectonics: The Poetics and Politics of Gothic Space', *Papers on Language and Literature* vol. 46 (2010): pp. 136–63.

[18] See C. G. Jung, *Contributions to Analytical Psychology*, trans. H. G. and Cary F. Baynes (New York: Harcourt Brace, 1928), pp. 118–19.

[19] See, respectively, Claire Kahane, 'Gothic Mirrors and Feminine Identity', *The Centennial Review* vol. 24, no. 1 (winter 1980): pp. 43–64; Jerrold E. Hogle, 'The Restless Labyrinth: Cryptonomy in the Gothic Novel', *Arizona Quarterly* no. 36 (1980): pp. 330–58; and Ian Watt, 'Time and the Family in the Gothic Novel: *The Castle of Otranto*', *Eighteenth-Century Life* vol. 10, no. 3 (1986): pp. 159–71.

[20] Eugenia C. DeLamotte, *Perils of the Night: A Feminist Study of Nineteenth-Century Gothic* (New York and Oxford: Oxford University Press, 1990), pp. 149–92.

[21] Anne Williams, *Art of Darkness: A Poetics of Gothic* (Chicago and London: University of Chicago Press, 1995), p. 44.

Kate Ferguson Ellis's *The Contested Castle* (1989); Alison Milbank's *Daughters of the House* (1992); Maggie Kilgour's *The Rise of the Gothic Novel* (1995); and Diane Long Hoeveler's *Gothic Feminism* (1998).

These historical, psychoanalytic, and feminist studies of the Gothic constitute only a small sample of the many critical works that have addressed the significance of architecture to Gothic writing of the late eighteenth and early nineteenth centuries. One thinks, too, of Robin Lydenberg's often-overlooked account of the parallels between the responses generated by Gothic architecture and those exploited by early Gothic fiction, or of Linda Bayer-Berenbaum's related attempts in *The Gothic Imagination* (1982) at drawing out the connections between the psychological states elicited by Gothic architecture and those to be found in literary manifestations of the Gothic aesthetic.[22] Other, better-known examples include the brief architectural turn of Victor Sage's *Horror Fiction in the Protestant Tradition* (1988), a study that, in part, sought to read the dark houses of Gothic literature as powerful allegories of larger theological concerns, or, to take a more recent example, Fred Botting's often-cited Foucauldian reading of ruins, graveyards, labyrinths, and other 'heterotopic' spaces in the early Gothic literary tradition.[23] When not reading Gothic architecture through such allegorical or theoretical lenses, critics have expended considerable energy in identifying the 'real' houses that inform some of the well-known architectural piles in the literature, not only in the often-cited parallels between Strawberry Hill and *Otranto* or, more tangentially, between Fonthill Abbey and *Vathek*, but also in, say, Rictor Norton's claim that Haddon Hall, Derbyshire, might well have been the source for Radcliffe's Chateau-le-Blanc in *The Mysteries of Udolpho*.[24] Such critical quests for the 'real' houses behind the novels are all shades of the same endeavour that had so frustrated Nikolaus Pevsner in his work on the houses of Jane Austen's fiction in 1968: try as he might, the twentieth century's greatest topographer and architectural historian was ultimately unable to provide any definitive answers, concluding that Austen 'did not visualize any one thing for any one house or town' when she penned her fictions.[25] Architecture, it turns out, is more the work of the imagination than any mimetic representation of a real-life building. In an important essay of 1998, Stephen Clarke proposed a useful solution to the problem of the relationship between 'real' and 'fictional' Gothic buildings of the eighteenth

---

[22] See Robin Lydenberg, 'Gothic Architecture and Fiction: A Survey of Critical Responses', *The Centennial Review* vol. 22 (1978): pp. 95–109, and Linda Bayer-Berenbaum, *The Gothic Imagination: Expansion in Gothic Literature and Art* (Cranbury, NJ, London, and Mississauga, Ont.: Associated University Presses, 1982), pp. 47–71.

[23] Victor Sage, *Horror Fiction in the Protestant Tradition* (Houndmills: Macmillan Press, 1988), pp. 1–25, and Fred Botting, 'In Gothic Darkly: Heterotopia, History, Culture', in *A New Companion to the Gothic*, ed. David Punter (Oxford: Blackwell, 2012), pp. 13–24.

[24] Rictor Norton, *Mistress of Udolpho: The Life of Ann Radcliffe* (London: Leicester University Press, 1999), p. 209.

[25] Nikolaus Pevsner, 'The Architectural Setting of Jane Austen's Novels', *Journal of the Warburg and Courtauld Institutes* vol. 31 (1968): pp. 404–22 (p. 409).

century by arguing that, though they might occasionally overlap, the 'written Gothic' of authors such as Ann Radcliffe and Jane Austen is fundamentally different from the 'built Gothic' of the early Gothic Revival: while the former traded in the intricacy, mystery, complexity, and obscurity of the sublime, the latter were intended to be light, airy, cheerful, and picturesque.[26]

In post-millennial Gothic criticism, there is barely a monograph on Romantic-era Gothic writing that does not at least gesture towards the term's architectural meanings, or explore the ways in which Gothic architecture is implicated in Gothic writing's broader ideological work.[27] David Punter and Glennis Byron include a short overview of Gothic architecture and the eighteenth-century Gothic Revival in *The Gothic* (2004), while Victor Sage's important essay on Gothic Revivalist architecture, initially published in 1998, was reprinted in the second edition of Marie Mulvey-Roberts's *The Handbook of the Gothic* in 2009.[28] William Hughes, David Punter, and Andrew Smith's *The Encyclopedia of the Gothic* (2013) includes short entries on Gothic architecture, the Gothic Revival, and ruins, and Nick Groom's *The Gothic* (2014) includes a brief but informative overview of Gothic architecture, even as it ranges widely to explore the Gothic's other political, cultural, and literary manifestations across time.[29] In the more extended form of the scholarly monograph, Kerry Dean Carso has addressed the relationship between Gothic architecture and nineteenth-century literature in *American Gothic Art and Architecture in the Age of Romantic Literature* (2014), while David Annwn Jones commences his *Gothic Effigy* (2018), a wide-ranging study of the Gothic aesthetic across several media and forms, with a brief discussion of Gothic Revivalist architecture in eighteenth- and nineteenth-century England, Wales, and America.[30] Most recently, Alison Milbank's *God and the Gothic* (2018) has provided a fascinating account of the ambivalent responses to monastic ruins in eighteenth-century Gothic fiction and their theological relation to the cultural work of the 'Long Reformation'.[31]

---

[26] Stephen Clarke, 'Abbeys Real and Imagined: Northanger Abbey, Fonthill, and Aspects of the Gothic Revival', *Persuasions* 20 (1998): pp. 93–105 (p. 99).

[27] See, for example, Angela Wright's discussion of abbeys and castles in *Britain, France and the Gothic, 1764–1820: The Import of Terror* (Cambridge: Cambridge University Press, 2013), pp. 88–146, and Diane Long Hoeveler's reading of the representation of ruined abbeys in *The Gothic Ideology: Religious Hysteria and Anti-Catholicism in British Popular Fiction, 1780–1880* (Cardiff: University of Wales Press, 2014), pp. 197–246.

[28] See David Punter and Glennis Byron, *The Gothic* (Oxford: Blackwell, 2004), pp. 32–6, and Victor Sage, 'Gothic Revival', in *The Handbook of the Gothic*, 2nd edn, ed. Marie Mulvey-Roberts (Houndmills: Palgrave Macmillan, 2009), pp. 156–69.

[29] See William Hughes, David Punter, and Andrew Smith, eds, *The Encyclopedia of the Gothic*, 2 vols (Oxford: Wiley-Blackwell, 2013), vol. 1, pp. 38–40 and 40–4; vol. 2, pp. 579–81, and Nick Groom, *The Gothic: A Very Short Introduction* (Oxford: Oxford University Press, 2012), pp. 12–23.

[30] David Annwn Jones, *Gothic Effigy: A Guide to Dark Visibilities* (Manchester: Manchester University Press, 2018).

[31] See Alison Milbank, *God and the Gothic: Religion, Romance, and Reality in the English Literary Tradition* (Oxford: Oxford University Press, 2018), pp. 13–61.

From the rise of a scholarly Gothic tradition onwards, then, critics have repeatedly returned to the architectural question, accounting for its presence in the literature variously through psychoanalytic, feminist, or new historicist theoretical lenses, or through the shorter, introductory explications outlined above. However, there remains, to date, no sustained and closely historicized account of Gothic writing in relation to the broader Gothic Revival in architecture with which it was contemporary, and it is this gap in the study of Gothic literature between the years 1760 and 1840 that *Gothic Antiquity* attempts to fill. In this respect, this book aligns itself most closely with work on the architecture/literature relation that has been published over the last four decades in the field of British romanticism, a literary tradition that is closely aligned but not always entirely coterminous with the early Gothic. These include Anne Janowitz's *England's Ruins* (1990); Sophie Thomas's *Romanticism and Visuality* (2008); Nicole Reynolds's *Building Romanticism* (2010); and Tom Duggett's *Gothic Romanticism* (2010). Though neither Reynolds nor Duggett is primarily concerned with the precise forms of 'Gothic' literature that I treat in this book, both studies have been particularly influential in my own thinking on the subject. The same might be said of Lee Morrissey's *From the Temple to the Castle* (1999), a brilliant account of the literature/architecture relation in selected authors who were either practising architects and architectural patrons with considerable involvement in the design process—John Vanbrugh, Alexander Pope, and Horace Walpole—or those whose writings demonstrate abiding architectural preoccupations, such as John Milton and Thomas Gray. Other modern studies of the architecture/literature relationship, including Ellen Eve Frank's *Literary Architecture* (1979) and David Anton Spurr's *Architecture in Modern Literature* (2012), do not treat eighteenth- and nineteenth-century British Gothic in any depth.

If Gothic literary studies have failed adequately to provide a sustained and historically rigorous account of how Gothic writing of the period 1760–1840 participated in the broader architectural impulses of the Gothic Revival, studies of Gothic architecture in the eighteenth and nineteenth centuries have been correspondingly cursory in their treatment of the literary context. In his seminal *A History of the Gothic Revival* (1872), the first scholarly study to define and constitute the movement as such, Charles Locke Eastlake gave writers of Gothic romance short shrift, maintaining that the trivial 'Gothic' productions of Horace Walpole and Ann Radcliffe were as far removed from the splendid, revived 'mediævalism' of Walter Scott as the 'Gothick' frippery of Batty Langley was from the 'authentic' Gothic architecture of William Butterfield.[32] Though arguing that, prior to its architectural manifestations, the revivalism of the late seventeenth and eighteenth centuries was primarily a literary phenomenon, Kenneth Clark in *The Gothic Revival* (1928) cautioned against any meaningful interaction between the architectural and the

---

[32] Charles L. Eastlake, *A History of the Gothic Revival* (London: Longmans, Green, and Co., 1872), p. 113.

literary by insisting that 'it is impossible to show a smooth interaction, or even a close parallel, between eighteenth-century Gothic novels and buildings'.[33] While the 'Gothicness' of popular romance, he continued, 'consisted in gloom, wildness, and fear', revived domestic Gothic architecture 'was too sensible to admit these qualities', striving instead for an atmosphere of 'lightness and variety'.[34]

In *Gothic Antiquity*, I subject Clark's sense of the limited relationship between Gothic literature and Gothic Revivalist architecture to ongoing scrutiny, sometimes disagreeing with it (as in the case of Walpole's self-conscious drawing upon what he understood to be the tradition of 'Gothic story' in his fashioning of Strawberry Hill), and at other times confirming it (as in nineteenth-century Gothic architects' attempts at purging the revived Gothic style of its long-standing relationship with Gothic fiction). Even in such cases, though, I maintain that literature was central to the work of the Gothic Revival, albeit only through an impulse of negative recoil. Other aspects of Clark's *The Gothic Revival* are similarly foundational to my argument. It was in the first chapter of the study that Clark introduced an influential distinction between 'Gothic Revival' and 'Gothic Survival', meaning by the former that self-conscious return to, and revitalization of, the architectural styles of the Middle Ages that we first encounter in the eighteenth century, and by the latter the 'tiny brackish stream' of Gothic architectural practice that persisted, attenuated yet largely unaltered, from the medieval period onwards.[35] Gothic survivalism, he claimed, comprised three closely interrelated elements: the work of Renaissance architects (Christopher Wren, John Vanbrugh, Nicholas Hawksmoor) who occasionally built in a Gothic idiom; the tendency of local builders and craftsmen to cling to older architectural traditions, as in the Oxford colleges that were built in the Gothic style well into the seventeenth century; and the more sentimental approach to the ruined remains of original medieval piles adopted by antiquarian scholars, from shortly after the dissolution of the monasteries during the mid-1530s onwards. While these instances of the persistence or the survival of Gothic, Clark argued, were in some senses quantifiably different from the eighteenth-century Gothic Revival, they nonetheless called for a reflection on the accuracy and applicability of the phrase itself. In his essay 'Gothic Survival and Gothick Revival' of 1948, H. M. Colvin adopted a far more categorical stance in relation to Clark's distinction, claiming that 'Gothic survival and Gothick revival had nothing in common', and foregrounding the difference between these two impulses through the use of the archaic spelling of the term 'Gothick'.[36] Giles Worsley, by contrast, advanced, in the fashion of Clark, a strong argument in favour of Gothic survivalism in "The

---

[33] Kenneth Clark, *The Gothic Revival: An Essay in the History of Taste*, 2nd edn (Harmondsworth: Penguin Books, 1962), p. 33.
[34] Clark, *The Gothic Revival*, p. 33.   [35] Clark, *The Gothic Revival*, p. 1.
[36] H. M. Colvin, 'Gothic Survival and Gothick Revival', *The Architectural Review* vol. 103 (1948): pp. 91–8 (p. 95).

Origins of the Gothic Revival: A Reappraisal' (1993), the essay in which he pointed to a number of sixteenth-century Gothic architectural projects so as to cast doubt on the very nature of an eighteenth-century 'Gothic Revival'.[37] More recent architectural historians have continued to ponder the question. I shall address this and other related matters in the Conclusion to this book, but for now it is important to stress that my interest in Gothic architecture in *Gothic Antiquity* straddles both sides of the revivalist/survivalist divide. That is, I am as interested in drawing attention in this study to the interplay between literature and architecture in such revivalist or 'modern Gothick' structures as Strawberry Hill, Fonthill Abbey, and the new Palace at Westminster as I am in addressing notable instances of Gothic survival in the eighteenth and early nineteenth centuries—the ways in which antiquaries and writers of Gothic fiction, poetry, and drama in the period 1760–1840 responded to the ruined castles, abbeys, and monasteries of what we now term 'medieval' Britain.

Clark's account of the Gothic architecture/literature relation set the terms of the debate for several later scholars. Though he reiterated Clark's claim concerning the literary origins of the Gothic Revival in England, Paul Frankl's treatment of literature in his wide-ranging, pan-European study *The Gothic* (1960) was slight, the argument merely rehearsing the commonplace assumption that Walpole 'was contributing to the popularization of Gothic [architecture] in the widest circles through his novel, *The Castle of Otranto*'.[38] Georg Germann's account of Gothic literature in *Gothic Revival in Europe and Britain* (1972) is even more perfunctory, achieving little more in this regard than reiterating the claim that Strawberry Hill provided the 'inspiration' for *The Castle of Otranto*.[39] Much the same pertains to Michael McCarthy's otherwise pioneering focus upon the work of Thomas Gray, Horace Walpole, and the domestic architecture of the Strawberry Hill architects in *The Origins of the Gothic Revival* (1987): even though his subject matter begs literary questions, this is never a concern that he explores in any depth.

It is true that, with the critical turn towards interdisciplinarity across the arts and humanities in the late twentieth century, more recent accounts of the Gothic Revival in architecture have been less reluctant to engage with literary questions. In *Gothic Revival* (1994), Megan Aldrich was the first scholar to achieve more than a mere gesturing towards the links between Walpole's home and his fiction, citing across her study examples of literary responses to Gothic architectural forms taken from Ann Radcliffe's *The Mysteries of Udolpho* (1794), Jane Austen's *Northanger Abbey* (1818), and even Bram Stoker's *Dracula* (1897). Ultimately, though, Aldrich's attention is more architectural than it is literary, with these and other fictional examples often

---

[37] Giles Worsley, 'The Origins of the Gothic Revival: A Reappraisal: The Alexander Prize Essay', *Transactions of the Royal Historical Society* vol. 3 (1993): pp. 105–50.
[38] Paul Frankl, *The Gothic: Literary Source and Interpretations through Eight Centuries* (Princeton, NJ: Princeton University Press, 1960), p. 392.
[39] Georg Germann, *Gothic Revival in Europe and Britain: Sources, Influences and Ideas*, trans. Gerald Onn (London: Lund Humphries with the Architectural Association, 1972), p. 55.

only marshalled as epigraphs to illustrate broader architectural concerns. Chris Brooks's excellent, more self-consciously interdisciplinary *The Gothic Revival* (1999), by contrast, devotes at least one discrete chapter to the Gothic novel, exploring, in greater detail than any critic before him, the claim that the imaginative possibilities of the Gothic past spread initially not through architecture but through eighteenth-century British and European literature, from the graveyard verse of the 1740s, through the literary antiquarianism of Thomas Percy and Richard Hurd, and into the fictions of Walpole, Radcliffe, Matthew Lewis, Johann Wolfgang von Goethe, Johann Friedrich von Schiller, John Polidori, Mary and Percy Bysshe Shelley, and others.[40] Similarly, Michael Charlesworth's *The Gothic Revival 1720–1820* of 2002, an indispensable three-volume collection of primary resources, includes a number of literary extracts, among them poems by Alexander Pope, William Shenstone, and Lord Byron, and prose descriptions by Radcliffe, Austen, Washington Irving, and Sheridan Le Fanu.[41] Useful though this material is, Gothic literary studies have for the most part failed to take up the challenge that Charlesworth's anthology implicitly wagers—the historicized reading of Gothic fiction alongside the Gothic architectural debates and aesthetics with which it was contemporary, and with which these writers and texts very clearly engaged. Michael J. Lewis's *The Gothic Revival* (2002) of the same year returned to the earlier claims of Clark and Brooks to argue that 'The Gothic Revival began as a literary movement, drawing its impulses from poetry and drama, and translating them into architecture';[42] beyond a few references to graveyard verse, Gray, and Edmund Spenser, however, the matter is never pursued. Having offered a number of revealing architectural–historical readings of select Gothic fictions in his more recent *Georgian Gothic* (2016), Peter N. Lindfield has drawn out the correlations between the efflorescence of the Gothic novel in England between 1770 and 1800 and the rise in the number of scholarly essays by antiquaries on Gothic architecture, sculpture, and fragmentary Gothic remains.[43] The paradox that Lindfield exposes is that, while modes of the Gothic proliferated in later eighteenth-century Britain through such means, the taste for the Gothic in interior design and furnishing in the same period was in some ways waning. Thus, while historians of the eighteenth- and nineteenth-century Gothic Revival in Britain and Europe more broadly have by no means entirely overlooked the matter of literature, it is fair to say that Gothic literature has not been their sole focus. *Gothic Antiquity* is my response to this issue, a historicized reading of Gothic fiction, poetry, and drama that is attuned throughout to literature's close and sometimes complex relations to the surviving and revived architectural style with which it came to share its name.

---

[40] See Chris Brooks, *The Gothic Revival* (London: Phaidon Press, 1999), pp. 105–26.
[41] See Michael Charlesworth, ed., *The Gothic Revival 1720–1870*, 3 vols (Mountfield: Helm Information, 2002).
[42] Michael J. Lewis, *The Gothic Revival* (London: Thames & Hudson, 2002), p. 13.
[43] See Peter N. Lindfield, *Georgian Gothic: Medievalist Architecture, Furniture and Interiors, 1730–1840* (Woodbridge: Boydell Press, 2016), pp. 131–43.

Acknowledgements

This book has benefited immeasurably from the assistance of many individuals and institutions over the decade and more that it has taken me to complete. My greatest debt of gratitude is to the Arts and Humanities Research Council (AHRC) for having awarded me an eighteen-month-long AHRC Leadership Fellowship (June 2015–December 2016) for *Writing Britain's Ruins, 1700–1850: The Architectural Imagination*, the larger research project from which this study derives. Douglas Brodie, then Head of the School of Arts and Humanities at the University of Stirling, provided further support, while Berthold Schoene and Sharon Handley, respectively Head of Research and Knowledge Exchange and Pro-Vice-Chancellor for the Faculty of Arts and Humanities at Manchester Metropolitan University, oversaw the transition of the project to my new institutional home in September 2016, and generously granted me a further period of institutional research leave. AHRC funding also made possible the appointment of Peter Lindfield as the project's Research Assistant, without whose brilliance, efficiency, architectural expertise, and photographic skills this book would have been greatly impoverished. The members of the *Writing Britain's Ruins* research network stimulated and greatly enriched my thoughts on Gothic architecture, antiquarianism, and literature in the late eighteenth and early nineteenth centuries, and I am especially grateful to have worked so closely with such distinguished scholars: Michael Carter; Oliver Cox; Sally Foster; Nick Groom; Marion Harney; James Kelly; Emma McEvoy; Hamish Mathison; David Punter; Fiona Robertson; Rosemary Sweet; Nicola Watson; James Watt; and Angela Wright. Beyond this, Angela Wright has been a good friend and source of Gothic inspiration over the years. Jess Edwards, Head of the Department of English at Manchester Metropolitan University, and Antony Rowland, Head of the Centre for Creative Writing, English Literature and Linguistics, have been the most supportive of managers, while my friends and colleagues in the Manchester Centre for Gothic Studies—Xavier Aldana Reyes; Linnie Blake; Helen Darby; Chloé Germaine Buckley; Sarah Illot; Emma Liggins; and Sorcha Ní Fhlainn—have provided a convivial environment in which to work. Thanks, too, to the many colleagues who read portions of the manuscript in draft form, and to those with whom I've discussed some of the book's ideas over the years, among them Kirstie Blair; Fred Botting; Stephen Bygrave; John Drakakis; Matt Foley; Katie Halsey; Emma McEvoy; Stephen Penn; Jon Stobart; Angus Vine; and Merle Williams. Stephen Clarke has been the most astute and insightful of readers, and I am especially grateful to him for having so generously shared with me his unsurpassed knowledge of Horace Walpole and the early Gothic Revival. Tim Fulford kindly let me read his work on Wordsworth's later poetry prior to the publication of his monograph on the subject, and Norbert Besch helped me to access some rare eighteenth-century Gothic fictions. At a crucial time in the book's genesis, the Trustees of the Lewis Walpole Library, Yale University, awarded me a Lewis Walpole Fellowship, facilitating an intensive period of work on manuscript and archival material to which I would not otherwise have had access. Special thanks are due to Nicole Bouché, the Executive Director of the Lewis Walpole Library, as well as to the assistance, support, and good humour of Kristen McDonald, Scott Poglitsch, Cindy Roman, and Sue Walker. The staff at a number of other research libraries have been similarly indispensable to the researching of this book, and I would like to acknowledge here the help that I have received from the Archives and Special Collections at King's College, London; the Beinecke Rare Book and Manuscript Library, Yale University; the Bodleian Libraries, Oxford; the British Library, London; Cambridge University Library; the Library of the Royal Institute of British Architects, London; the Library of the Society of Antiquaries of London; the National Library of Scotland, Edinburgh; Pembroke College Library, Cambridge; the Research Library and Archive of the Sir John Soane's Museum, London; the Yale Center for British Art, New Haven; and the librarians and interlibrary-loan facilities at Stirling and Manchester Metropolitan Universities. The anonymous readers for Oxford University Press provided much-needed input, guidance, and support, and I am especially grateful to them, and to my editors Jacqueline Norton and Aimee Wright, for their belief in a project that has been so long in the making. Neil Morris copy-edited the typescript with enviable accuracy, care, and attention, and Pauline Hubner has proved, once again, to be a meticulous indexer. My parents, Howard and Shannon Townshend, have always been unstintingly supportive of my academic pursuits, and I am grateful to them, and to my brother Jonathan Townshend, for having tolerated my single-mindedness over the years. Dickens, the adorable RagaMuffin kitten, took up residence in my study in the final year of the project, bringing both distraction and endless delight. Jay Barlow, David Carr, Leora Cruddas, Tracey Farber, Renée Gerritsen, Basil Lawrence, and Stefan Sten Olsson have long been my emotional stalwarts, while Stephen Penn has remained my primary source of laughter and joy throughout. This book is dedicated to him.

Some of the material on William Gilpin in Chapter 1 first appeared in 'Ruins, Romance and the Rise of Gothic Tourism: The Case of Netley Abbey, 1750–1830', *Journal for Eighteenth-Century Studies* vol. 37, issue 3 (2014): pp. 377–94, © 2013, British Society for Eighteenth-Century Studies. An early version of Chapter 4 first appeared as 'Improvement and Repair: Architecture, Romance and the Politics of Gothic, 1790–1817', *Literature Compass* vol. 8, issue 10 (2011): pp. 712–38, © 2011, the author, Literature Compass © 2011 Blackwell Publishing Ltd. I am grateful to the editors and publishers of both articles for permission to use small portions of this work here.

Contents

List of Figures   xxi
List of Abbreviations   xxiii

   Introduction: Gothic Antiquity, Gothic Architecture, Gothic Romance   1

1. Associationist Aesthetics and the Foundations of the Architectural Imagination   45

2. Horace Walpole's Enchanted Castles   89

3. From 'Castles in the Air' to the Topographical Gothic: Locating Ann Radcliffe's Architectural Imagination   131

4. Improvement, Repair, and the Uses of the Gothic Past: Architecture, Chivalry, and Romance   179

5. 'Venerable Ruin' or 'Nurseries of Superstition': Ecclesiastical Architecture and the Gothic Literary Aesthetic   221

6. Antiquarian Gothic Romance: Castles, Ruins, and Visions of Gothic Antiquity   267

   Conclusion: From the Gothic to the Medieval: Historiography, Romanticism, and the Trajectories of the Architectural Imagination   311

Select Bibliography   357
Index   389

List of Figures

0.1.	'Système figuré des connoissances humaines'	21
0.2.	John Carter, *The Entry of Prince Frederick [sic] into the Castle of Otranto*	40
0.3.	George Perfect Harding, illustration to *The Castle of Otranto*	43
1.1.	Sample of Ann Radcliffe's annotations in Alexander Gerard's *An Essay on Taste*	58
1.2.	William Gilpin's drawing of Glastonbury Abbey, Somerset	76
1.3.	William Beckford's editorial marks in *Dreams, Waking Thoughts, and Incidents*	84
2.1.	Willey Reveley, *South West view of the Castle of Otranto, Italy*	95
2.2.	John Carter, *South View of the Castle of Otranto*	95
2.3.	*Castello Di Otranto*, from Jeffery's 1796 edition of the novel	97
2.4.	Diana Beauclerk's illustration to Book III of *The Faerie Queene*	114
3.1.	Richard Bentley's headpiece to Thomas Gray's 'A Long Story'	135
3.2.	Rev. William Warren Porter (1776–1804), *Castle of Udolpho*	148
3.3.	James Nasmyth's etching of the Castle of Udolpho	149
3.4.	Emily's first glimpse of Udolpho, from Limbird's 1824 edition of the novel	151
3.5.	Image of the Chateau-le-Blanc, from Limbird's 1824 edition of the novel	151
3.6.	*The Enchanted Castle*, engraving by William Woollett and François Vivarès	153
3.7.	William Marlow (1740–1813), *Capriccio: St Paul's and a Venetian Canal*	170
5.1.	Conyers Middleton, D.D., Principal Librarian to the University of Cambridge	227
5.2.	Tailpiece for Thomas Gray's 'Ode on a Distant Prospect of Eton College'	239
5.3.	Thomas Rowlandson, *North Entrance of Strawberry Hill with a Procession of Monks*	251
6.1.	Wenceslaus Hollar's title page for William Dugdale's *Monasticon Anglicanum*	297
6.2.	Engraving of Cumnor Place	306
7.1.	Frontispiece to Pugin's *The True Principles of Pointed or Christian Architecture*	356

List of Abbreviations

Correspondence	*The Yale Edition of Horace Walpole's Correspondence*, ed. W. S. Lewis, 48 vols (New Haven: Yale University Press, 1937–83)
GM	*The Gentleman's Magazine: And Historical Chronicle*
Library Edition	*The Library Edition of the Works of John Ruskin*, 39 vols, ed. E. T. Cook and Alexander Wedderburn (London: George Allen; New York: Longmans, Green, and Co., 1903–12)
LWL	The Lewis Walpole Library, Yale University, Farmington, Connecticut
ODNB	Oxford Dictionary of National Biography (Oxford: University Press, 2018), http://www.oxforddnb.com
OED	Oxford English Dictionary (Oxford: Oxford University Press, 2018), http://www.oed.com
RA	Royal Academy of Arts, London
RIBA	Royal Institute of British Architects, London

'Who ever thought of looking for a muse in an old castle?'
    Mr Simpson, in Ann Radcliffe's *Gaston De Blondeville* (1826)

Introduction
Gothic Antiquity, Gothic Architecture, Gothic Romance

In the early months of 1802, the prominent British antiquary and draughtsman John Carter set out from his home in Pimlico, London, for Wales in order to visit, among other sites, the venerable remains of Gothic antiquity at the ruins of White Castle, Monmouthshire. 'I wholly gave into [sic] the impulse of the moment', his subsequent account in *The Gentleman's Magazine* related, 'that I was an adventurous being of old times, about to atchieve [sic] some perilous exploit.'[1] Though armed with nothing but his pen, his ink, and his sketchbook for drawing, Carter styled himself here, as elsewhere across the hundreds of pseudonymous letters and commentaries on architectural and literary matters that he published in *The Gentleman's Magazine* between 1797 and 1817, as a knight in the service of an imperilled maiden, the chivalrous suitor to the vulnerable 'heroine' that was Gothic architecture, and the scourge of the 'MONSTER', as he saw it, that was 'ARCHITECTURAL INNOVATION'.[2] 'Antiquity among us is again threatened, wounded, and reviled,' he would later emotively opine; 'Shall I, then, her zealous votary, her constant knight, remain unconcerned, inactive; sit down in slothful ease; my steely guise, my pencil, and my pen thrown by, all left to rust, and useless grow? Forbid it, my life's dearest hope!'[3] Substituting a suit of armour for a 'steely guise', and the weaponry of lances, swords, and maces for a set of drawing implements, Carter, like many a conservation-minded antiquary of his day, regarded the mere act of observing, documenting, and sketching the material remains of the Gothic past to be as effective a means of 'warfare' as the chivalrous jousts and tournaments of the Middle Ages.

Upon entering the ruins of White Castle in 1802, however, this self-styled crusader of the Gothic faith is overcome by sentiments of an altogether less valiant nature: 'My nerves...soon told me I was no valorous knight; and, full of modern

---

[1] 'An Architect', 'Pursuits xliv', *GM*, 72 (1802), I, pp. 22–4 (p. 22). Although most of Carter's correspondence in *The Gentleman's Magazine* was published anonymously, or under such pseudonyms as 'An Architect', 'An Englishman', 'An Artist and an Antiquary', and 'J.C.', J. Mordaunt Crook has provided an exhaustive list of those that may be safely attributed to Carter in *John Carter and the Mind of the Gothic Revival* (London: The Society of Antiquaries of London, 1995), pp. 80–90.
[2] 'An Architect', 'Pursuits lxvii', *GM*, 74 (1804), I, pp. 28–31 (p. 30).
[3] 'An Architect', 'Pursuits lxvii', p. 30.

Gothic Antiquity: History, Romance, and the Architectural Imagination, 1760–1840. Dale Townshend, Oxford University Press (2019). © Dale Townshend.
DOI: 10.1093/oso/9780198845669.001.0001

fear and trembling, I scrambled up the height I had thus sought to gain.'[4] A 'new fancy' taking hold of him, Carter's self-composure is undone by vivid images of phantoms, ghosts, and monsters that crowd in upon his mind:

> [S]o bewildered and distracted as I was, I pictured to myself that I saw hollow-eyed Envy, pushed on by an unwieldy Arrogance, stalking through the gloomy aperture to end at once my labours and my troubles. Determining, however, (thus apparently deserted) to fight my own cause, I advanced forward to meet the hideous spectres, when, aiming to seize the Furies by their scaly throats, I received such a death-dealing blow from some unseen adversary, that I fell senseless to the ground.[5]

The service of chivalrous action has shaded into something darker and considerably more threatening. Though he enters the ruin as a constant knight, Carter leaves it in the manner of a swooning heroine of Gothic romance, falling senseless to the ground only to be revived by his guide's swift administering of a restorative cordial.

In the architectural journalism of John Carter, this was by no means an isolated incident.[6] Describing his visit to Portchester Castle, Hampshire, in the same year, he noted that 'far other sensations than those allied with Antiquarian pleasures took too fast hold of my attention' as he entered the ruin.[7] Among these 'other sensations', the experiences of horror and terror are paramount, for, surveying the dungeons within the castle, he is reminded of the *cachots*, the notorious underground cells of the Bastille in pre-revolutionary France, an involuntary yoking together of architectural and historical association that is sufficient to rupture his 'Antiquarian pleasures' with a range of more intense and unsettling responses: 'The horrors attendant on review of these objects, which till a short time ago had been the receptacles of those who had forgot their God and King, threw my soul into a shudder; and many a pang of dread and dismay pursued me as I fought my way out of these contaminated mounds.'[8] A similar sense of dreadful sublimity awaited the antiquary at the then ruined Llandaff Cathedral near Cardiff, Wales, in 1803. Entering the church and anticipating within it a few moments of quiet contemplation, he is involuntarily overcome by what he mistakes to be a host of spectral beings. 'The nave suddenly became thronged by a number of people,' he recounts, figures 'who with loud and piercing cries hurried in a frantic manner towards me'. 'The sight was appalling', he confesses, 'and, if ever mortal creatures

---

[4] 'An Architect', 'Pursuits xliv', p. 23.
[5] 'An Architect', 'Pursuits xliv', p. 24.
[6] For a fuller account of this, see Dale Townshend, 'Architecture and the Romance of Gothic Remains: John Carter and *The Gentleman's Magazine*, 1797–1817', in *Gothic and the Everyday: Living Gothic*, ed. Lorna Piatti-Farnell and Maria Beville (Houndmills: Palgrave Macmillan, 2014) pp. 173–94.
[7] 'An Architect', 'Pursuits lix', *GM*, 73 (1803), I, pp. 229–31 (p. 231).
[8] 'An Architect', 'Pursuits lix', p. 231.

were mistaken for beings not of this world, here was an instance the most fearful and hideous. I am under no hesitation in declaring, that I absolutely took them for a company of spectres assembled with the intent of inflicting upon me some mental derangement.'[9] Collapsing in terror, as he did in the ruins of White Castle, Carter only comes to in Cardiff a few days later, none the wiser as to how he got there. As he realizes, his intentions to assemble at Llandaff 'materials for the protection of Antiquity against that host of individuals who are ever on the alert to attack her most precious remains' have been compromised by 'the old delusions worked up in my imagination'.[10]

Brief though they are, Carter's descriptions of his experience at White Castle, Portchester Castle, and Llandaff Cathedral in 1802–3 usefully draw into focus the primary concerns of *Gothic Antiquity: History, Romance, and the Architectural Imagination, 1760–1840*: eighteenth- and early nineteenth-century conceptualizations of the antique Gothic past; the antiquarian interest in that past's Gothic architectural remains; and, especially, the fiction, poetry, and drama that we have since come to identify as the 'Gothic' in a different but related sense of that word. As the received literary-historical narrative goes, Gothic literature, the writing of supernatural horror and terror, arose with, and in the wake of, the publication of Horace Walpole's *The Castle of Otranto* in late 1764. Of these various meanings conjured up by the term 'Gothic', the notion of 'Gothic antiquity' is perhaps the most difficult to define, signifying, as it did, a mythical, vague, and somewhat nebulous sense of the national British past, a broad historical epoch that encompassed what modern historiography has come to identify as the medieval and the Renaissance or early modern periods. This is the sense in which Carter conceptualized Gothic antiquity and the architectural relics that it left behind: a vanished British (though often more narrowly English) history that stretched, roughly, from the fifth through to the sixteenth century. As Angus Vine has argued, 'antiquity' in the early modern period was a fluid and somewhat malleable category that could feasibly imply, at once, the distant past of ancient Roman and Greek civilization as well as the more recent past of the previous generation.[11] The eighteenth century was heir to this semantic imprecision: as Samuel Johnson's *A Dictionary of the English Language* (1755–6) defined it, the noun 'antiquity', derived from the Latin *antiquitas*, meant nothing more particular than 'old times, time past long ago', its people, its works, or, in a more ludicrous sense, 'old age'.[12]

---

[9] 'An Architect', 'Pursuits lxviii', *GM*, 74 (1804), I, pp. 124–7 (pp. 125–6).
[10] 'An Architect', 'Pursuits lxviii', p. 126.
[11] Angus Vine, *In Defiance of Time: Antiquarian Writing in Early Modern England* (Oxford: Oxford University Press, 2010), pp. 17–18.
[12] Samuel Johnson, *A Dictionary of the English Language*, 2 vols (London: Printed by W. Strahan for J. and P. Knapton, and T. and T. Longman; C. Hitch and L. Hawes; A Millar; and R. J. Dodsley, 1755–6), vol. 1.

Though notions of 'antiquity' had previously been the preserve of the classical Greco-Roman worlds, it was Britain's ancient, post-Roman 'Gothic' past and its material relics and immaterial legacy that increasingly came to absorb the antiquarian mind from the mid-seventeenth century onwards.[13] This is not suggest that the interest in Britain's classical past that had begun with the work of humanist scholars in the mid-Tudor period had been entirely eclipsed, and, in many instances, the preoccupation with the nation's Roman and pre-Roman legacies—its ruins, coins, roads, implements, linguistic traces—coexisted with the study of the vernacular Celtic and Gothic. For classicists such as Colen Campbell in *Vitruvius Britannicus* (1715-25) and Isaac Ware in *A Complete Body of Architecture* (1756), as for classical antiquaries, the coupling of 'Gothic' with cherished notions of the 'antique' remained something of an oxymoron. Rosemary Sweet has traced the origins of the interest in Gothic antiquities, in particular, to High Church Toryism and the veneration of the outward forms of religious buildings that we first see in William Dugdale's *Monasticon Anglicanum* (1655) and *The History of St Pauls Cathedral in London* (1658).[14] It was during the 1670s, as H. M. Colvin has argued, that John Aubrey wrote *Chronologia Architectonica*, including in the fourth section the first historical account of English 'Gothick' architecture.[15] As the case of Dugdale suggests, the phrase 'Gothic antiquity' in the long eighteenth century most frequently implied ecclesiastical architectural ruins, though it also extended to the remains of castles and other fortifications: as Noah Heringman explains, the stony remains of the British Middle Ages could be valued as 'antiquities' once they were recognized as architecture, different yet comparable in their way to the ruins of classical antiquity.[16] A spirit of nationalism was certainly one of Gothic antiquarianism's primary driving forces: as Thomas Burgess's *An Essay on the Study of Antiquities* (1780) would later put it, the 'British Antiquary' ought always to demonstrate a 'natural attachment and general partiality to the Antiquities of his own country'.[17] The work of Joan Evans, Stuart Piggott, Martin Myrone and Lucy Peltz, Sweet, Heringman, and others has drawn attention to just how rich and multifaceted the interest in local, British antiquities across the long eighteenth century was, and the extent to which it assumed different and often competing inflections across the

---

[13] For a comprehensive account of the antiquarian interest in the literature, architecture, and culture of the Middle Ages in the long eighteenth century, see Rosemary Sweet, *Antiquaries: The Discovery of the Past in Eighteenth-Century Britain* (London and New York: Hambledon & London, 2004), pp. 231-76.

[14] Rosemary Sweet, 'Gothic Antiquarianism in the Eighteenth Century', in *The Gothic World*, ed. Glennis Byron and Dale Townshend (Abingdon and New York: Routledge, 2014), pp. 15-26.

[15] H. M. Colvin, 'Aubrey's *Chronologia Architectonica*', in *Concerning Architecture: Essays on Architectural Writers and Writing Presented to Nikolaus Pevsner*, ed. John Summerson (London: Allen Lane, 1968), pp. 1-12.

[16] Noah Heringman, *Sciences of Antiquity: Romantic Antiquarianism, Natural History, and Knowledge Work* (Oxford: Oxford University Press, 2013), p. 221.

[17] Thomas Burgess, *An Essay on the Study of Antiquities* (Oxford, 1780), p. 13.

constituent nations of Great Britain.[18] While Welsh, Irish, and Scottish antiquaries tended to locate the origins of their nations in Celtic and Milesian antiquity, English antiquaries often looked towards the Gothic past, the word itself deeply connected, as I show below, to political understandings of the nation's point of genesis. Strongly Anglocentric in orientation, Gothic antiquarianism was often used to assert the political and cultural supremacy of England over Wales, Scotland, and Ireland. What started out as the amateur interests of a few gentleman scholars became, by the early nineteenth century, a mainstream, popular pursuit, its appeal no doubt enhanced by the centrality of ruined Gothic antiquities to the aesthetic of the picturesque. As one of the practical means through which the broader cultural preoccupation with Gothic antiquity between 1760 and 1840 was expressed, the antiquarian interest in Gothic architecture is one of the major preoccupations of this book, particularly in its fascinating, sometimes paradoxical, interactions with the literary cultures of the day.

In an equally imprecise sense, Gothic antiquity was also, as scholars such as Samuel Kliger, J. G. A. Pocock, Glyn Burgess, R. J. Smith, Robert Miles, and Sean Silver have shown, a pervasive political construct that rose to prominence in Britain towards the end of the seventeenth century: in the wake of the Glorious Revolution of 1688 and the vanquishing of the Stuart line of kings, Whig politicians made frequent appeal to ancient 'Gothic' origins in order to validate and defend the virtues of the constitutional monarchy.[19] Pitting the so-called 'Gothic balance'—the democratic distribution of power between Parliament and the sovereign supposedly evidenced in the ancient Anglo-Saxon witenagemot— against the king's absolute powers, such versions of national history mythologized the Goths as a freedom-loving people who had been invited to England by Vortigern in AD 449, when he sought to defend his native Britons, now made vulnerable by the withdrawal of the Romans, from the aggressive incursions of the Scots and Picts who had settled north of Hadrian's Wall. Establishing themselves in England in the seven kingdoms of the heptarchy, it was held that these

---

[18] See Joan Evans, *A History of the Society of Antiquaries* (Oxford: Oxford University Press, 1956); Stuart Piggott, *Ruins in a Landscape: Essays in Antiquarianism* (Edinburgh: Edinburgh University Press, 1976); Martin Myrone and Lucy Peltz, eds, *Producing the Past: Aspects of Antiquarian Culture and Practice, 1700–1850* (Aldershot: Ashgate, 1999); Sweet, *Antiquaries*; Susan Pearce, ed., *Visions of Antiquity: The Society of Antiquaries of London, 1707–2007* (London: The Society of Antiquaries of London, 2007); and Heringman, *Sciences of Antiquity*.

[19] See Samuel Kliger, *The Goths in England: A Study in Seventeenth and Eighteenth Century Thought* (Cambridge, Mass.: Harvard University Press, 1952); J. G. A. Pocock, *The Ancient Constitution and the Feudal Law. A Study of English Historical Thought in the Seventeenth Century, A Reissue with a Retrospect* (Cambridge: Cambridge University Press, 1987); Glyn Burgess, *The Politics of the Ancient Constitution: An Introduction to English Political Thought, 1603–1642* (University Park: Pennsylvania State University Press, 1993); R. J. Smith, *The Gothic Bequest: Medieval Institutions in British Thought, 1688–1863* (Cambridge: Cambridge University Press, 2002); Robert Miles, *Gothic Writing, 1750–1820: A Genealogy* (London: Routledge, 1993); and Sean Silver, 'The Politics of Gothic Historiography, 1660–1800', in *The Gothic World*, ed. Glennis Byron and Dale Townshend (Abingdon and New York: Routledge, 2014), pp. 3–14.

Germanic 'Goths'—from the Venerable Bede's *Historia ecclesiastica gentis Anglorum* (c. AD 731) onwards, a collective, erroneously applied name for the Angles, Saxons, Jutes, and Danes—brought with them to England their democratic systems of government. Despite the Norman Conquest of 1066 and the subsequent imposition of the 'Norman Yoke', the spirit of Saxon or Gothic liberty, it was claimed, remained largely unvanquished, and sought expression, even now, in contemporary political life. Eighteenth-century understandings of this hardy and noble ancient 'Gothic' tribe that, prior to settling in England, had, under the leadership of Alaric, been responsible for the sacking of Rome in AD 410 were largely derived from two sources: the work of the Roman historian Cornelius Tacitus in *Germania* (c. AD 98), and the arguments of the sixth-century Roman bureaucrat of Gothic extraction Jordanes in *Getica* (c. AD 551). In seventeenth- and eighteenth-century Britain, the political 'myth' of Gothic origins circulated in such forms as Richard Verstegan's *A Restitution of Decayed Intelligence* (1605); Nathaniel Bacon's *An Historicall Discourse of the Uniformity of the Government of England* (1647–51); William Temple's essay 'Of Heroick Virtue' (1690) and *An Introduction to the History of England* (1695); James Tyrrell's *Bibliotheca politica* (1692–4) and *The General History of England* (1698); *Winter* (1726), the first part of James Thomson's *The Seasons* (1730), and his lengthy poem *Liberty* (1735–6); Thomas Nugent's translation of Charles de Secondat, Baron de Montesquieu's *The Spirit of Laws* (1750); Gilbert Stuart's *An Historical Dissertation Concerning the Antiquity of the English Constitution* (1768); Thomas Percy's translation of Paul-Henri Mallet's *Northern Antiquities* (1770); John Aikin's translation of Tacitus in *A Treatise on the Situation, Manners, and Inhabitants of Germany* (1777); Edward Gibbon's *The History of the Decline and Fall of the Roman Empire* (1776–89); John Pinkerton's *A Dissertation on the Origin and Progress of the Scythians or Goths* (1787); and especially Sharon Turner's *History of the Anglo-Saxons* (1799–1805).

Strongly Whiggish in political inflection though they were, claims to England's Gothic origins could also be made by prominent Tory politicians of the age: wresting back the ancient constitution from the perversion to which he thought it had been subjected by Sir Robert Walpole's Whig administration, the Tory Henry St John, 1st Viscount Bolingbroke, stealthily perpetuated a 'Gothic' vision of national political origins in his 'Remarks on the History of England, from the Minutes of Humphry Oldcastle, Esq' in *The Craftsman* (1730–1), further making an appeal to the 'Freedom of our *Gothick* Institutions of Government' in a compilation of some of his earlier anti-Walpole journalism in *A Dissertation Upon Parties* (1735).[20] Many discontented, so-called 'Patriot' Whigs in Walpole's

---

[20] Viscount Henry St John Bolingbroke, *A Dissertation Upon Parties; In Several Letters to Caleb D'Anvers* (London: Printed by H. Haines, 1735), p. 102. For more on this, see Isaac Kramnick, *Bolingbroke and His Circle: The Politics of Nostalgia in the Age of Walpole* (Cambridge, Mass.: Harvard University Press, 1968), pp. 111–87, and Edward H. Jacobs, *Accidental Migrations: An*

government followed suit, for the equation of 'Gothic' and 'Whiggish' was a pervasive one: as Robert Molesworth wrote in the translator's Preface that has become known as 'The Principles of a Real Whig' in 1705, 'My Notion of a Whig, I mean of a real Whig (for the Nominal are worse than any Sort of Men) is, That he is one who is exactly for keeping up to the Strictness of the true old Gothick Constitution.'[21] Such correspondences were clearly evidenced in the commonplace assumption that Gothic architecture, in all its apparent resistance to classical rules and precepts outlined in Vitruvius's *De architectura libri decem* (c.15 BC), embodied the freedom-loving spirit of the ancient Goths. The name 'Gothic', in other words, facilitated the conflation of political discourse and architectural style, correspondences that Whiggish poetry of the early to mid-century frequently invoked. Gilbert West's *The Institution of the Order of the Garter* (1742), for example, a masque-like celebration of the spirit of Magna Carta, poetic lyricism, chivalry, and the genius of England that is said to have originated with 'The valiant sons of Poverty, the *Goths*', plays itself out in front of, and inside, the lofty Gothic battlements of 'fair *Windsor's Tow'rs*'.[22] In the Second Epode of William Collins's Pindaric ode 'To Liberty' (1747), a vastly condensed retelling and partial revision of Thomson's earlier *Liberty*, the personified spirit of Gothic freedom, having arrived in Britain, establishes her 'Shrine' in 'an hoary Pile' in 'some religious Wood'. Emerging as if by magic, Liberty's fane, at least initially, is appropriately fashioned in the Gothic style: 'How learn delighted, and amaz'd, / What Hands unknown that Fabric rais'd? / Ev'n now before his favor'd Eyes, / in *Gothic* Pride it seems to rise!'[23] Equally explicit connections between Whiggish political liberties and Gothic architecture were drawn by writers such as Samuel Boyse in 'The Triumph of Nature' (1742) and Edward Lovibond in 'On Rebuilding Combe Neville' (posthumously published in 1785).[24] Perhaps the most well-known expression of Whiggish politics in Gothic architectural form is the Gothic Temple or Temple of Liberty (1744–8) that was designed for Richard Temple, Viscount Cobham, by the Catholic Tory architect James Gibbs for the grounds at Stowe, Buckinghamshire, the long-time seat of the Whiggish Temple-Grenville family and a focal point for a powerful anti-Walpole

Archaeology of Gothic Discourse (Lewisburg: Bucknell University Press; London: Associated University Presses, 2000), pp. 96–122.

[21] Robert Molesworth, *An Account of Denmark, With Francogallia and Some Considerations for the Promoting of Agriculture and Employing the Poor*, ed. and introd. Justin Champion (Indianapolis: Liberty Fund, 2011), p. 174.
[22] [Gilbert West], *The Institution of the Order of the Garter. A Dramatick Poem* (London: Printed for R. Dodsley, 1742), pp. 2, 29.
[23] William Collins, *Odes on Several Descriptive and Allegoric Subjects* (London: Printed for A. Millar, 1747), pp. 29–30. On the relationship between these poems by Thomson and Collins, see William Levine, 'Collins, Thomson, and the Whig Progress of Liberty', *Studies in English Literature, 1500–1900* vol. 34, no. 3 (Summer, 1994): pp. 553–77.
[24] See Kliger, *The Goths in England*, pp. 29–30.

Whig coalition.[25] Over the door of the Gothic Temple was carved a line from Pierre Corneille's *Horace* (1640) that clearly expressed the building's political and stylistic Gothicism: '*Je rends graces aux Dieux de nestre pas Romain*' ('I thank the Gods that I am not a Roman').[26] It is these and other political conceptualizations of Gothic antiquity that I explore across at least two chapters of this book, considering in more depth the perceived relations between political Gothicism and Gothic architecture in Chapter 4, and Ann Radcliffe's radical critique of what she later came to regard as the politically ineffective liberalism of this Whiggish discourse in Chapter 6. My objective, however, is also, in part, to trouble such simple aesthetic and political allegiances: as I show at various points throughout the study, not all liberal Whigs were advocates of Gothic architecture, and the style, in the fashion of Bolingbroke's appropriations of Gothic constitutional origins, could also be appropriated by far more conservative voices—'Old Whig' and Tory—such as John Carter himself.

Whether intentional or not, Carter's descriptions of his experience at White Castle in 1802 also drew strongly on what, by then, had become the recognizable conventions of Gothic romance: the ruined castle, the quest motif, the curiously feminized figure that is overcome by the fanciful terrors of ghosts and other supernatural beings within a gloomy architectural setting. This did not go unnoticed by the magazine's readers. Signing himself 'An Admirer of Don Quixote', one anonymous respondent in 1803 mischievously characterized Carter as the Don Quixote of architectural form: 'Like the knights of former times, whose business it was to roam in quest of persecuted damsels, this Champion of our antient [sic] edifices, in the fervour of his pursuits, makes occasionally some egregious mistakes. To take a windmill for a giant, or a flock of sheep for an army, is certainly not in his way; but, *mutatis mutandis*, the case is the same.'[27] Other comparisons were far less good humoured. Referencing the extreme emotions that Carter had recorded in the dungeons of Portchester Castle, another correspondent in July 1802 cuttingly observed that 'the pleasing descriptions of such authors as Mrs. Radcliffe would do more for our old religious buildings than a thousand anathemas from a violent Antiquary'.[28] As this writer provocatively continued, the romances of Ann Radcliffe and her imitators had done far more to promote the appreciation of Gothic architecture than the indefatigable Carter had achieved across an entire lifetime. As if to underscore the comparison, the same issue of *The Gentleman's Magazine* included 'Verses Addressed to Mrs Radcliffe', a lengthy poem by one G. H. that proudly flaunted Ann Radcliffe's architectural

---

[25] See John Martin Robinson, *Temples of Delight: Stowe Landscape Gardens* (London: George Philip and the National Trust, 1990), pp. 102–3.
[26] Robinson, *Temples of Delight*, p. 103.
[27] Anon., 'Response to John Carter', *GM*, 73 (1803), I, p. 332.
[28] Anon., 'Response to John Carter', *GM*, 72 (1802), p. 623.

achievements: 'Those crumbling arches, those decaying walls, / Each prostrate column former times recalls; / Fancy, forgetful of the lapse of years, / From broken pillars perfect fabricks [sic] rears.'[29]

Of course, at the time of Carter's writing, the fictions of Horace Walpole, Ann Radcliffe, Matthew Lewis, and innumerable other now forgotten writers were not always generically designated as 'Gothic', or at least not in the ways in which the term is used in literary studies today. It is nonetheless true that, even if it was not always named as such, a critical understanding of the 'Gothic' as a singular and distinctive literary mode had already begun to take shape in the early decades of the eighteenth century, and in some instances even before this. In an essay in *The Spectator* in July 1712, for example, Joseph Addison provided a positive assessment of what John Dryden in *King Arthur; or, The British Worthy* (1691) had called 'the fairy kind of writing', tales of the supernatural that 'raise a pleasing kind of horror in the mind of the reader, and amuse his imagination with the strangeness and novelty of the persons who are represented in them'.[30] Epitomized by the plays of Shakespeare, this free and imaginative strain for Addison derived from a native English rather than classical tradition, in some senses the literary and aesthetic equivalent of the political spirit of the Gothic that I have outlined above. However, when Walpole added the term 'Gothic' to his original subtitle to *Otranto* in the second edition of 1765, the phrase 'A Gothic Story' was more a historical marker of the fiction's purported origins in what the Preface to the first edition referred to as 'the darkest ages of Christianity' than an indicator of its ghostly subject matter. While this historical vision necessarily included intimations of horror and terror—the 'principal incidents' of the story, the first Preface reminds its readers, were 'believed' at the time of the text's original composition— the term 'Gothic' in the period 1760–1840 was not, first and foremost, employed to signify a particular literary mode, genre, or style. The same pertains to *The Champion of Virtue*, Clara Reeve's self-proclaimed 'Gothic Story' that was originally published in 1777, and then revised and reissued under the more familiar title of *The Old English Baron: A Gothic Story* in 1778. As Reeve's Preface to the second edition of the novel noted, this was a 'Gothic Story' primarily insofar as it sought to provide 'a picture of Gothic times and manners', thus too making use of 'Gothic' as a category of historical description that included, but was by no means solely restricted to, its supernatural contents.[31] The same might be said of other late eighteenth- and early nineteenth-century fictions that featured the adjective 'Gothic' in their subtitles, including Richard Warner's *Netley Abbey: A Gothic Story* (1795); Isabella Kelly's *The Baron's Daughter: A Gothic Story*

---

[29] G. H., 'Verses Addressed to Mrs. Radcliffe', *GM*, 72 (1802), II, pp. 950.
[30] Joseph Addison, *Critical Essays from The Spectator, With Four Essays by Richard Steele*, ed. Donald F. Bond (Oxford: Clarendon Press, 1970), p. 200.
[31] Clara Reeve, *The Old English Baron*, ed. James Trainer, with intro. and notes by James Watt, 2nd edn (Oxford: Oxford University Press, 2008), p. 2.

(1802); Mary Tuck's *Durston Castle; or, The Ghost of Eleonora. A Gothic Story* (1804); and Eliza Ratcliffe's *The Mysterious Baron; or, The Castle in the Forest, a Gothic Story* (1808). While the 'Gothic' past represented in these texts almost invariably includes depictions of the supernatural, the epithet was employed more as a marker of the texts' historical settings, their evocations of the times and manners of bygone days, than as a name for a ghostly strain in modern literature. Nor were their evocations of the Gothic past any more precise than the antiquarian and political conceptions of Gothic antiquity explored above. As Mary Muriel Tarr has pointed out, the anonymous *Phantoms of the Cloister* (1795) refers to the 'barbarism of the times' when depicting the reign of Henry V; Anne Ker in *Adeline St Julian* (1800) extends the era of 'monkish despotism' well into the seventeenth century; and the action in Sophia Frances's *The Nun of Miserecordia* (1807) commences as late as 1738.[32] Famously, Radcliffe begins *The Mysteries of Udolpho* (1794) in the year 1584, a time that, according to modern historiographic categories, would fall within the Renaissance rather than the 'Gothic' or medieval period. Irrespective of these inconsistencies, Alfred E. Longueil has persuasively argued that it was only through the incessant coupling of scenes of supernaturalism with depictions of ancient 'Gothic' times in these and other fictions that the term eventually came to assume its current literary-critical meanings at all.[33] In their own day, the novels that we now identify as 'Gothic' were more likely to be dismissed by the periodical press as '*hobgobliana*', 'Terrorist Novel Writing', or, as E. J. Clery has noted, simply as 'romances' or 'modern romances'.[34] The finer points of nomenclature aside, several episodes that we find in the journalism of John Carter neatly encapsulate the primary concern of this book: the abiding but still relatively under-explored links between Gothic architecture and manifestations of the 'Gothic' literary imagination in British culture of the late eighteenth and early nineteenth centuries. In writing about the former, it is almost as if Carter has no choice but to make recourse to some of the definitive features of the latter.

But such episodes also point, in a much less overt way, to the ways in which Gothic architecture was central to the work of the literary imagination in the period 1760–1840: though Carter's responses to architectural space were, no doubt, involuntary, identical responses and scenarios were deliberately invoked, courted, and employed by most of the poets, dramatists, and novelists whom we

[32] Mary Muriel Tarr, *Catholicism in Gothic Fiction: A Study of the Nature and Function of Catholic Materials in Gothic Fiction in England, 1762–1820* (Washington: Catholic University of America Press, 1946), pp. 8–9.
[33] Alfred E. Longueil, 'The Word "Gothic" in Eighteenth Century Criticism', *Modern Language Notes* 38, no. 8 (Dec. 1923): pp. 453–60.
[34] See, for instance, the anonymous review of Francis Lathom's *Astonishment!!! A Romance of a Century Ago* (1802) in *Flowers of Literature; for 1803* (London: Printed by J. Swan for B. Crosby and Co., 1804), p. 442; the anonymous article 'Terrorist Novel Writing', in *The Spirit of the Public Journals for 1797* (London: Printed for R. Phillips, 1798), pp. 223–5; and E. J. Clery, 'The genesis of "Gothic" fiction', in *The Cambridge Companion to Gothic Fiction*, ed. Jerrold E. Hogle (Cambridge: Cambridge University Press, 2002), pp. 21–40 (p. 22).

now designate as 'Gothic'. That popular authors of the day routinely sought inspiration in Britain's ruined Gothic piles was a tendency upon which both champions and opponents of the literary Gothic frequently commented. In order to participate in what a reviewer in *Spirit of the Public Journals for 1797* disparagingly referred to as the Radcliffe-inspired system of 'Terrorist Novel Writing' that was plaguing the contemporary literary scene, the reviewer concluded that an author of questionable ability need only proceed with the same levels of thoughtlessness as that required for the rote following of a recipe, one in which architecture was the primary ingredient: three murdered bodies, three skeletons, a murdered old woman, an 'old castle, half of it ruinous', and a 'long gallery, with a great many doors, some secret ones'.[35] In a less critical fashion, others embraced the architectural interests of Gothic writing as the source of the mode's imaginative power. Self-consciously theorizing in the Prologue to his Gothic drama *The Castle Spectre* (performed at Drury Lane in December 1797; published 1798) the Gothic mode's dependence on architectural form, Matthew Lewis personified the type of literary romance exemplified by his earlier fiction *The Monk* (1796) as a fair enchantress who, having retreated from the world, forever roams the dark, ruined aisles and haunted towers of Gothic cathedrals and castles:

> FAR from the haunts of men, of vice the foe,
> The moon-struck child of genius and of woe,
> Versed in each magic spell, and dear to fame,
> A fair enchantress dwells, Romance her name.
> She loathes the sun, or blazing taper's light:
> The moon-beamed landscape and tempestuous night
> Alone she loves; and oft, with glimmering lamp,
> Near graves new-open'd, or 'midst dungeons damp,
> Drear forests, ruin'd aisles, and haunted towers,
> Forlorn she roves, and raves away the hours![36]

Apostrophized by a youth 'who yet has lived enough to know / That life has thorns'—lines that, coming only a year after the public furore over *The Monk*, undoubtedly reference Lewis himself—the personified figure of Romance joins the troubled author near the 'time-bowed towers' of Castle Conwy ('Conway'), North Wales, the haunted castle of the play's title. Urged by Romance to 'renew' the ancient state of the castle's crumbling walls, an eager Lewis '[speeds] the fallen tower to raise', presenting in the drama that follows the product of his architectural musings.[37] In a similar fashion, the Scottish Romantic poet Anne Bannerman

---
[35] Anon., 'Terrorist Novel Writing', p. 225.
[36] M. G. Lewis, *The Castle Spectre: A Drama* (London: Printed for J. Bell, 1798), p. iii.
[37] Lewis, *The Castle Spectre*, pp. iii–iv.

reflected on the imaginative potential of ecclesiastical ruins—what she called those 'dim regions of monastic night'—in the Prologue to *Tales of Superstition and Chivalry* (1802), claiming that it was in such Gothic piles that the 'long-lost Spirit of forgotten times' resided and whence it whispered still into 'Fancy's ear', 'Blending with terrors wild, and legends drear, / The charmed minstrelsy of mystic sound / That rous'd, embodied, to the eye of Fear, / The unearthly habitants of faery ground.'[38] Gothic architectural ruin drove the work of the literary imagination. Thus it was that, looking back on the 'fictitious narratives' of the previous decade, William Godwin in the conclusion to his discussion of fourteenth-century English architecture in *Life of Geoffrey Chaucer* (1804) came to remark upon the extraordinary power of Gothic buildings, both ruined and in a state of repair, to 'seize' the writer's imagination:

> These ancient palaces had also a number of other characteristics, which seize the imagination, and have lately been called up with great success by the inventors of fictitious narratives. Such are their trap-doors for descent; their long-protracted galleries; their immense suite of rooms opening one beyond the other; their chapels constituting a part of the mansion, by means of which the solitary explorer of the building unexpectedly descends among the monuments of the dead and the crumbling memorials of departed religion; and their arras hangings, with ill-contrived and rattling doors concealed behind them.[39]

As will become evident in the course of this book, Godwin's language is strongly Walpolean, a debt that becomes clear in the light of his reliance upon Walpole's discussion of Gothic architecture in *Anecdotes of Painting in England* (1762–71). In a much more satirical spirit, however, the anonymous author of *The Age: A Poem* of 1810 figured the Gothic writer as a 'votaress' of romance, a quasi-religious devotee of highly imaginative literature who seeks inspiration by moonlight at a shrine-like, ivy-covered Gothic edifice:

> She goes with look enthusiastic
> To yonder edifice fantastic,
> Where fancy speaking from its trances
> Gives inspiration of romances.
> Here vot'ries crowd of all conditions
> To view the fleeting exhibitions;
> And, well as crazy brain permits
> Sketch down each vision as it flits:
> While deeper mysteries are brewing

---

[38] Anne Bannerman, *Tales of Superstition and Chivalry* (London: Printed for Vernor and Hood, by James Swan, 1802).
[39] William Godwin, *Life of Geoffrey Chaucer, Early English Poet*, 2nd edn, 4 vols (London: Printed by T. Davison for Richard Phillips, 1804), vol. 1, p. 256.

>   They see at first a gothic ruin.
>   (This seems to be a rule of late.
>   From which none dare to deviate)
>   'Tis castle large with turrets high
>   Intruding always on the sky;
>   And as they're old in place of clothes
>   Around them ivy kindly grows;
>   Somewhat like Adam's coat or Eve's,
>   Except for fig, they're ivy leaves.[40]

As contemporary culture perceived it, the characteristic pose of the Gothic romancer, dramatist, or poet was that of a distracted young woman or epicene young man who sought inspiration for his or her fictions before a ruined Gothic pile. Although Mr Simpson, in that line from the Introduction to Ann Radcliffe's *Gaston De Blondeville* (1826) that I cite as the epigraph to this book, incredulously asks of his interlocutor, 'Who ever thought of looking for a muse in an old castle?', the reality is that countless Gothic writers, not least of all Radcliffe herself, routinely did just that.[41]

The Architectural Imagination

As these opening comments suggest, the primary aim of *Gothic Antiquity* is to describe and articulate the 'architectural imagination' that was at work in British culture of the late eighteenth and early nineteenth centuries. By this I mean not only the fictional, poetic, or dramatic preoccupation with depicting ruined and unruined Gothic architectural space in late eighteenth- and early nineteenth-century British literature, but also and especially the imaginative capacities of Gothic architecture as they were perceived, theorized, and exploited by contemporary poets, romancers, dramatists, and novelists, many of whom deliberately fashioned imaginative responses to architectural form in ways that were remarkably similar to those recorded by John Carter in the ruins at White Castle, Portchester Castle, and Llandaff Cathedral in 1802–3. As I explore in detail in Chapter 1, this architectural imagination was discursively underpinned by the work of British empiricist philosophers and aestheticians who, from the late seventeenth century onwards, sought to account for the imaginative effects of architectural forms, both classical and Gothic, upon the minds of those who

---

[40] Anon., *The Age; A Poem: Moral, Political, and Metaphysical* (London: Printed for Vernor, Hood, and Sharpe, 1810), pp. 202–3.
[41] Ann Radcliffe, *Gaston De Blondeville; or, The Court of Henry III Keeping Festival in Ardenne, A Romance and St Alban's Abbey: A Metrical Tale; With Some Poetical Pieces*, 4 vols (London: Henry Colburn, 1826), vol. 1, p. 47.

perceived them. By the phrase 'architectural imagination', then, I mean, first and foremost, the power and ability of architecture to conjure up in the perceiver ideas, impressions, reveries, and trains of thought, so many mental images that, in accordance with the assumptions of associationist psychology, were said to combine with others so as to constitute the workings of what was described as the faculty of the 'imagination'. As I argue throughout this study, these architectural impressions and associations constituted, appropriately, the 'foundation' of countless Gothic romances, dramas, poems, and chapbooks in the period 1760–1840. By the architectural imagination I thus also necessarily mean the ways in which Gothic architectural form actively fuelled the production of literature and imaginative literary response, be this through the countless topographical poems, fictions, and plays that were written about, to, or in particular historical sites of ruin across Britain, or through poets' and writers' projections of fanciful, romantic visions into wholly imagined architectural structures that disparagingly came to be designated as 'castles in the air'.

The architectural imagination also pertains to the ways in which poets, novelists, dramatists, romancers, and aestheticians between the years 1760 and 1840 often metaphorically conceptualized their creative practice in architectural terms, a tendency that reveals the significance of architecture to those modes of literature that have subsequently become known as the 'Gothic' and the 'Romantic'. It was the Scottish philosopher Alexander Gerard who, in his influential *An Essay on Taste* (1759), claimed that the creative faculty of genius was, itself, metaphorically to be conceived as a 'grand architect' insofar as it constructed out of disparate sensory impressions, and through the workings of association, 'a regular and well-proportioned whole': 'Thus genius is the grand architect, which not only chooses the materials, but disposes them into a regular structure.'[42] This metaphor set the terms for several subsequent discussions of genius and originality in the period. A similar schema, for example, works its way implicitly through Edward Young's *Conjectures on Original Composition* (1759), in which original genius is described as an architect or 'Master-workman' who effects acts of creativity *ex nihilo*, the imitator, by contrast, merely the lowly workman or labourer who 'but nobly builds on another's foundation' with 'pre-existent materials not their own'.[43] In William Duff's *An Essay on Original Genius* (1767), too, literal and metaphorical architectural practices are paramount, not least in his account of the work of original poetic genius. For such a figure, nature initially 'supplies the materials of his composition'; while the sensory impressions that the poet receives from the world of empirical experience are to be thought of as 'under-workmen' or toiling

---

[42] Alexander Gerard, *An Essay on Taste [...] With Three Dissertations on the Same Subject by Mr De Voltaire, Mr D'Alembert, Mr De Montesquieu* (London: Printed for A. Millar; Edinburgh: Printed for A. Kincaid and J. Bell, 1759), p. 176.

[43] Edward Young, *Conjectures on Original Composition, in a Letter to the Author of Sir Charles Grandison* (London: Printed for A Millar, and R. and J. Dodsley, 1759), p. 25, pp. 11–12.

builders, his 'Imagination, like a masterly Architect, superintends and directs the whole', calling into being, via a reference to Shakespeare's *A Midsummer Night's Dream*, 'things that are not' and peopling entire worlds of its own.[44] Gerard returned to his early architectural metaphor in *An Essay on Genius* (1774), here again figuring the faculty of genius as an architect who constructs of often chaotic sensory impressions a noble 'edifice' of a unified idea through associative principles: 'Thus imagination is no unskilful architect; it collects and chuses [sic] the materials; and though they may at first lie in a rude and undigested chaos, it in a great measure, by its own force, by means of its associating power, after repeated attempts and transpositions, designs a regular and well-proportioned edifice.'[45] Derived from the Latin and Greek, the prefix 'archi-' suggested a return to first principles, imbuing the artist-as-architect with powers similar to those of the Greek god Hephaistos (Vulcan or Mulciber in Latin), the angelic architect who, once fallen, fashions from Chaos the sublime classical architecture of Pandaemonium in Book I of John Milton's *Paradise Lost* (1667; 1674). Like the discourse of original genius and the practice of architecture in the eighteenth century itself, this was a highly gendered formulation: while women were more likely to be conceived as the devotees of romance who merely sought their 'inspiration' from pre-existent ruined Gothic piles, such were the architectural powers of male writers that they could call forth and embody these architectural structures themselves. Such architectural conceptualizations of the mind's creative abilities were by no means confined to rarefied aesthetic reflection. In the early nineteenth century, Walter Scott drew upon what, by now, were the commonplace links between architectural construction and the workings of the literary imagination when he anthologized in the first volume of *English Minstrelsy* (1810) the anonymous 'Castle-Building, An Elegy', a lyrical poem that figured the act of literary creation as an exercise in aerial architectural construction. Apostrophizing the faculty of 'Fancy' throughout, the poem celebrates the potential for literary composition to transport both those who create it and those who consume it to a realm of aesthetic pleasure that is beyond the 'smiling tracks of fairy land', the place of 'The gilded spire, arched dome, and fretted vault'.[46]

The perceived continuities between acts of original composition and the architectural design of buildings were facilitated, no doubt, by practical historical conditions pertaining to the architect's cultural position during the long eighteenth century. Mark Crinson and Jules Lubbock have pointed out that, between

---

[44] William Duff, *An Essay on Original Genius; And its Various Modes of Exertion in Philosophy and the Fine Arts, Particularly in Poetry* (London: Printed for Edward and Charles Dilly, 1767), pp. 281–2.

[45] Alexander Gerard, *An Essay on Genius* (London: Printed for W. Strahan; T. Cadell; Edinburgh: W. Creech, 1774), p. 65.

[46] Anon., 'Castle-Building, An Elegy', in *English Minstrelsy. Being a Selection of Fugitive Poetry from the Best English Authors; With Some Original Pieces Hitherto Unpublished*, 2 vols (Edinburgh: Printed for John Ballantyne and Co.; Manners and Miller; and Brown and Crombie; London: John Murray, 1810), vol. 1, pp. 237–42 (pp. 241, 239).

1660 and the professionalization of the practice of architecture that commenced in 1834, the title of 'architect' was freely available to almost any mason, surveyor, carpenter, builder, designer, or even amateur enthusiast who wished to appropriate it, a situation that was underpinned by the lack of clear and established routes of architectural education and training.[47] Such, at least, is the state of affairs bemoaned in *An Essay on the Qualifications and Duties of an Architect* (1773), a tract that, though anonymously published, has sometimes been attributed to the architect, surveyor, and assistant Clerk of Works to the City of London James Peacock: 'The Term Architect is frequently made use of, and misapplied, by some who do not rightly consider its true Meaning; as well as often assumed by others, who either ignorantly, or designedly, assume that which is not their Right.'[48] Bypassing the skills and expertise of others, all gentlemen, others complained, presumed themselves capable of serving as their own architects. Neither the Royal Works nor the Royal Society—institutions with which earlier architects such as Inigo Jones, Nicholas Hawksmoor, and Christopher Wren had worked—imposed upon its craftsmen a regulated theoretical or practical training, favouring, instead, a hands-on involvement in the process of building and construction. If not through such empirical means, architectural pursuits could also be entered into through apprenticeship to such crafts as masonry, bricklaying, and carpentry, or even via such amateur undertakings as painting, drawing, playwriting, and science. Often perceived to be the product of close, visual observation, architectural design could also be practised by propertied men of leisure, or at least those who could afford to travel to sites of classical architectural significance abroad. While, in France, an academy devoted solely to architecture had been established as early as 1671, the establishment of the Royal Academy of Arts (RA), London, in December 1768 made no special allowance for architects, who were to be admitted alongside painters, sculptors, and other artists. As John Wilton-Ely describes it, the late eighteenth and early nineteenth centuries thus marked the epoch of the 'gentleman-architect, the artist-architect, and the craftsman-architect', a state of affairs that persisted until the establishment in 1834 of what would eventually become the Royal Institute of British Architects (RIBA).[49] I shall address this and other significant changes to the identity of the architect in the first four decades of the nineteenth century in the Conclusion to this book, but for the moment it is sufficient to acknowledge that it was the lack of a formal training and professional

---

[47] Mark Crinson and Jules Lubbock, *Architecture: Art of Profession? Three Hundred Years of Architectural Education in Britain* (Manchester: Manchester University Press, 1994), p. 17.

[48] Anon., *An Essay on the Qualifications and Duties of an Architect, &c. With Some Useful Hints for the Young Architect or Surveyor* (London: Printed for the Author, 1773), p. 7.

[49] John Wilton-Ely, 'The Rise of the Professional Architect in England', in *The Architect: Chapters in the History of the Profession*, ed. Spiro Kostof (New York: Oxford University Press, 1977), pp. 180–208 (p. 183).

identity for the architect that allowed writers and literary aestheticians to appropriate his work as a metaphorical description of their own creative practice.

Insights gleaned from Kojin Karatani's analysis of architectural metaphor in the work of René Descartes, Immanuel Kant, Georg Wilhelm Friedrich Hegel, and other Western philosophers are useful in determining just what was at stake in such identifications. The sense that the philosopher was to be conceptualized as an architect, Karatani argues, originated in Plato's *Symposium* (385–370 BC), a text that initiated what he evocatively describes as the *'will to architecture'*, and a compulsion that would characterize philosophical reflection in the West from this moment onwards.[50] The attractions of this are easy to see, for if the philosopher is an architect, he exists always in a position of absolute mastery, arrogating to himself the power of the grand creator and closing off the philosophical system over which he presides from the contingencies introduced by the client, the building's inhabitants, and the builder. Like the architect, the philosopher's realm is the order of 'making' (*poiesis*) and not of 'becoming', while his architectural powers of construction only further encode his ability to realize the impossible and to reassert order and structure in times of great crisis.[51] Plato's Socrates, of course, had banished the poets from his ideal city state in Book X of *Republic* (*c*.380 BC), but when they make their return with the rise of romanticism towards the end of the eighteenth century, they do not, Karatani maintains, seize back the philosopher's power so much as become absorbed by philosophy's greater, more encompassing, work. Like philosophers, then, it is through their self-identification as architects that the poets, artists, and other original geniuses of the late eighteenth century came to assert the full extent of their sovereignty and the limits of their accountability to others.

If the imaginative fabrications of original genius were those sturdy architectural constructions celebrated by the likes of Gerard, Young, and Duff, so illegitimate acts of imaginative creation, both literary and architectural, were to be dismissed as 'folly'. An early instance of the use of the noun 'folly' in the architectural sense of the term illustrates this particularly well. In the third volume of Richard Graves's *The Spiritual Quixote* (1773), a picaresque satire on Methodism, the narrator describes a visit to The Leasowes, Halesowen, the estate of the poet William Shenstone and the site on which he erected the ruined folly of Halesowen Priory in *c*.1750. 'As they walked on,' the narrator notes, 'they saw an object, amidst the woods, on the hedge of the hill; which, upon enquiry, they were told was called "Shenstone's Folly"'; 'This is a name', the narrator continues, 'which, with some sort of propriety, the common people give to any work of taste, the

---

[50] Kojin Karatani, *Architecture as Metaphor: Language, Number, Money*, trans. Sabu Kohso and ed. Michael Speaks (Cambridge, Mass.: MIT Press, 1995), p. xxxii.
[51] See Karatani, *Architecture as Metaphor*, pp. 4–24.

utility of which exceeds the level of their comprehension.'[52] Though this gloss is bound up in a number of assumptions about the relationship between class and architectural taste, it usefully reveals, through the use of the possessive case, contemporary understandings of sham ruins or follies as the expression of the builder's or architect's pleasure-driven, somewhat excessive, or even deranged imagination. But for its detractors, Gothic fiction, too, was the expression of authorial folly. The anonymous and undated poem *The Age of Folly* described the host of 'Lady Authors' who 'compose, in sweet romantic strain, / Whole reams of manuscript for MISTER [William] LANE' of the Minerva Press as 'labourers in folly's cause', before proceeding to condemn the writings of Lewis, Radcliffe, and their followers who 'common scenes of common life discard / Who bounds of probability o'er leap, / And conjure Dæmons, from the vasty deep!':

> How smoothly flows, the mild instructive page,
>   When shades, and spectres, every thought engage:
>   When Daggers, Death, and Inquisitions Dire,
>   Fill the wild brain with energetic fire:
>   When shrouded sprites, with skeletons arise,
>   And *blue-mould candles*, nature's place supplies.[53]

As I elaborate in the Conclusion to this book, the distinction between 'folly' and more legitimate acts of imaginative creation would subsequently be absorbed into, and replaced by, romanticism's theorization of the differences between fancy and the imagination in the first two decades of the nineteenth century. Before that point, the notion of 'folly' was one of the many places where architectural and literary discourses interacted, and merely one example of this book's interest in the extensive metaphorical system that writers of poetry, novels, romance, and drama shared with practising architects in the period. Together with the eighteenth-century revival of the classical notion of the sister arts, this linguistic common ground meant that, at least until the professionalization of the practice of architecture during the mid- to late nineteenth century, literature and architecture enjoyed throughout the long eighteenth century a relationship closer than it had ever been before or, indeed, has been since.

Architecture, Literature, and the Sister Arts

As Carter himself eventually conceded, his writings in the pages of *The Gentleman's Magazine* were those of a 'necromantic pen' insofar as they called up, in the

---

[52] Richard Graves, *The Spiritual Quixote; or, The Summer's Ramble of Mr Geoffry [sic] Wildgoose, A Comic Romance*, 3 vols (London: Printed for J. Dodsley, 1773), vol. 3, p. 23.

[53] Anon., *The Age of Folly: A Poem* (London: Printed for the Author, n.d.), pp. 19, 21.

fashion of many a Gothic romancer, several 'hideous shapes' in order to end the 'baleful strife' of architectural innovation, modernization, and improvement.[54] I shall address the particular forms that, to Carter's mind, these forces of architectural modernization and improvement took in Chapter 4, but for now it is important to reflect upon the extent to which this comment, like much of Carter's writing, seemed to assume that antiquarian architectural practices and literature were conceptually cognate (though by no means entirely compatible) endeavours: in writing about Gothic architecture, this antiquary often wields, no doubt self-consciously, the necromantic pen of the Gothic romancer. The intimate relationship between architecture and literature in the period was formally enshrined by the discourse of the sister arts, an aesthetic that circulated prominently among eighteenth-century visual artists, poets, musicians, and architects, and which ultimately looked back to '*Ut pictura poesis*' ('as is painting, so is poetry'), a phrase from Horace's *Ars Poetica* (*c.*19 BC). As Hildebrand Jacob's *Of the Sister Arts; An Essay* (1734) described it, the notion derived also from the Ciceronian position that all arts were closely related, and from which, Jacob 'safely' concluded, 'Poetry, Painting, and Music are closely ally'd'.[55] With the similarities between poetry, music, and painting rendering the critical discussion of one 'without a mutual borrowing of *Images*, and *Terms*' gleaned from another somewhat of an impossibility, they were best metaphorically to be conceived as 'the *Sister Arts*'; this relationship of 'near Resemblance', in turn, meant that any attempt at explaining the one would also provide 'some Insight into the other at the same Time'.[56] Since all art forms, for Jacob, arose chiefly out of the same principles of imitation and harmony, they remained essentially identical at their points of origin. Beyond this, he explained, 'Almost all the *Parts* of poetry are found in *Painting*', while '*Harmony*, which is the *Essence* of *Music*, is, as it were, the *Dress* or *Cloathing* [*sic*] of Poetry'; by the same principle, painting 'is a kind of *dumb Harmony*, which charms and sooths [*sic*] us thro' our *Eyes*, just as music does thro' our *Ears*'.[57] According to this way of thinking, the individual arts were thought to achieve perfection when they exploited their similarities with those contiguous to them, with poetry thus aspiring to the condition of music, music to painting, and so forth.

Though pervasive, such assumptions did not go unchallenged, and in 1766, the German aesthetician Gotthold Ephraim Lessing would provide in *Laocoön: An Essay on the Limits of Painting and Poetry* a powerful critique of the assumed equivalences between poetry and painting. But before this, and, indeed, well into the nineteenth century, artists and architects in Britain invested much in the concept of the sister arts. While Jacob's essay makes no mention of architecture,

---

[54] 'An Architect', 'Pursuits xxxiv', *GM*, 7 (1801), I, pp. 309–13 (p. 311).
[55] Hildebrand Jacob, *Of the Sister Arts; An Essay* (London: Printed for William Lewis, 1734), p. 3.
[56] Jacob, *Of the Sister Arts*, p. 3.   [57] Jacob, *Of the Sister Arts*, p. 4.

several practising architects and architectural theorists were keen to elevate their amateur gentlemanly pursuit to the condition of art, thus assuring it a place in the aesthetic pantheon alongside poetry, painting, sculpture, and music. Embodying this doctrine in its own form, the lengthy *The Art of Architecture, A Poem* (1742) drew upon the discourse of the sister arts by employing an extended analogy between poetry and the practice of architecture; demonstrating what he took to be the interchangeability between the two roles, this anonymous author identified himself only as 'either as a Poetical ARCHITECT, or an Architectural POET'.[58] Recalling Jacob's belief in the ultimate perfectibility of the artwork, the persona urges students and practitioners of architecture to aspire towards the moments of creative excellence witnessed in the sculptures of John Michael Rysbrack; the portraiture of Giacomo Amiconi; William Hogarth's prints; the paintings and etchings of John Wootton, George Lambert, and Joseph Goupy; the grammatical elegance of Lindley Murray; and the music of George Frideric Handel.[59] Including encomiastic tributes to the work of Inigo Jones, Andrea Palladio, and John Vanbrugh, and critical of the Revivalist 'GOTHICK' architectural style of William Kent and Batty Langley, *The Art of Architecture* is a firm statement of eighteenth-century classicism. Indeed, the discourse of the sister arts was particularly central to the French architectural tradition of the Académie Royale d'Architecture, a strain of classicism epitomized by Jacques-François Blondel's *Cours d'architecture* (1771–7) and the *Encyclopédie ou dictionnaire raisonné des sciences, des arts et des métiers* (1751–72) of Denis Diderot and Jean le Rond d'Alembert. As I shall explore more fully in Chapter 1, however, the discourse of the sister arts in Britain was also strategically appropriated by admirers of the Gothic style. And despite Lessing's argument in *Laocoön*, it continued to enjoy currency in the work of John Soane during the first three decades of the nineteenth century, albeit here largely restored to its classical foundations.

The concept was important to architectural practice in continental Europe, too. The first volume of the French *Encyclopédie* that was published on 28 June 1751 included a fold-out engraving of a tree-diagram of the figurative structure of secular human knowledge, 'Système figuré des connoissances humaines', a taxonomic system inspired, in part, by Francis Bacon's *The Advancement of Learning* (1605) (see Figure 0.1). The diagram divided secular knowledge into the three broad categories of memory, reason, and imagination, relating 'memory' to the practice of history, 'reason' to the realm of philosophy, and 'imagination' to the arts of poetry. Revealingly, it is under the general branch of the 'imagination' that the *Encyclopédie* situates what it terms 'civil architecture', a categorization that renders non-religious architectural endeavours akin to the arts of music, painting,

---

[58] Anon., *The Art of Architecture, A Poem. In Imitation of Horace's Art of Poetry* (London: Printed for R. Dodsley, 1742), p. ii.
[59] Anon., *The Art of Architecture*, p. 15.

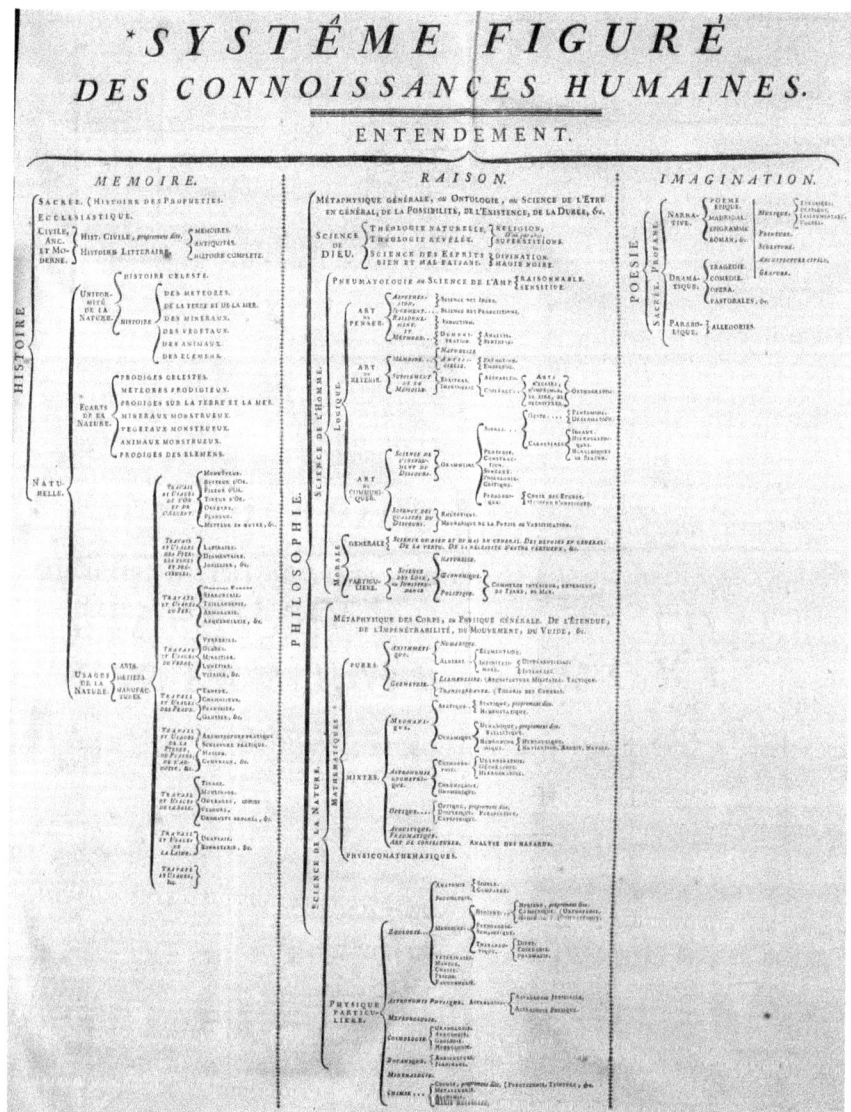

Figure 0.1 'Système figuré des connoissances humaines', from *Encyclopédie, ou dictionnaire raisonné des sciences, des arts et des métiers*, vol. 1 (1751).
Source: Wikimedia Commons.

sculpture, and engraving, all of these, in turn, encompassed by the broader category of 'poetry', which itself is divided into narrative, dramatic, and allegorical strains. As Kevin Harrington has argued, this situating of architecture within the realm of the 'imagination' in the first issue of the *Encyclopédie* was, in itself, a decisive shift, for when it was first published in the *Prospectus* for potential subscribers to the larger project in 1750, the tree-diagram of knowledge had placed civil, naval, and military architecture under the category of 'reason', thus rendering architecture akin to mathematics and natural jurisprudence.[60] However, when conceived under the reworked schema as an imaginative art comparable in its own way to music, painting, and sculpture, architecture, both classical and Gothic, was imbued with the power to move and inspire imaginative reveries within the mind of the spectator to the same degree as the other expressive arts. It was precisely this imaginative power to which John Carter fell victim in the Gothic Cathedral of Llandaff and the Castles of Portchester and White in the early years of the nineteenth century.

History and Romance

In the places where he presumed to discover the material vestiges of history, Carter encountered the powerful lure of romance. Indeed, as indicated in its subtitle, *Gothic Antiquity* engages throughout with the complex nature of the relationship between history and romance, the former the eighteenth-century term for what has since more often been referred to as historical writing or 'historiography', and the latter a cultural shorthand for highly imaginative fiction or an imaginative subjective predisposition more generally. The distinction went as far back as Aristotle's assertion of the differences between history and poetry in *Poetics* (c.335 BC); if, by the eighteenth century, 'history' had come to signify the locale of truth, 'romance', like poetry and other imaginative literature, marked its polar opposite. During the second half of the century, these two opposing forces were drawn into intense confrontation with one another through a number of important developments on both sides. Scholars such as Thomas Preston Peardon, Stephen Bann, Karen O'Brien, Mark Salber Phillips, Ruth Mack, Ben Dew and Fiona Price, and Porscha Fermanis and John Regan have drawn attention to the extraordinary variety of historical writing in Britain over the long eighteenth century, often taking the years between 1760 as 1840 to be the most crucial to the 'invention' of modern historical sensibilities and practices, and charting literature's participation in this process.[61] Peardon, for example, has

---

[60] Kevin Harrington, *Changing Ideas on Architecture in the Encyclopédie, 1750–1776* (Ann Arbor, MI: UMI Research Press, 1985), pp. 21–6.

[61] See Thomas Preston Peardon, *The Transition in English Historical Writing, 1760–1830* (New York: Columbia University Press, 1933); Stephen Bann, *Romanticism and the Rise of History* (New York: Twayne, 1995); Karen O'Brien, *Narratives of Enlightenment: Cosmopolitan History from Voltaire to Gibbon* (Cambridge: Cambridge University Press, 1997); Mark Salber Phillips, *Society and Sentiment: Genres of Historical Writing in Britain, 1740–1820* (Princeton, NJ: Princeton University Press, 2000); Ruth Mack, *Literary Historicity: Literature and Historical Experience in Eighteenth-Century Britain* (Stanford: Stanford University Press, 2009); Ben Dew and Fiona Price, eds, *Historical Writing in Britain, 1688–1830: Visions of History* (Houndmills: Palgrave Macmillan, 2014);

tracked the important changes in historiography that took place between 1760 and 1830, from the Tory rationalism of David Hume, William Robertson, and Edward Gibbon to the sentimental, Whig nationalist histories of the nineteenth century. Expanding on Pearson's point that, far from being a monolith, historical writing was a disparate and multifaceted phenomenon, Phillips has usefully explored the many historiographical genres in circulation in Britain between 1760 and 1830, calling attention, for instance, to the 'philosophical history' of David Hume's *The History of England* (1754–61) and Voltaire's *Essai sur les mœurs et l'esprit des nations* (1756); the 'conjectural history' of Montesquieu's *De l'esprit des lois* (1748), Adam Ferguson's *Essay on the History of Civil Society* (1767), and Henry Home, Lord Kames's *Sketches of the History of Man* (1774); and the 'sentimental history' of Samuel Richardson's *Clarissa* (1748–9) and *The History of Sir Charles Grandison* (1753–4), as well as Adam Smith's *The Theory of Moral Sentiments* (1759). Not only was romance, as Phillips argues, a 'parahistorical' mode, but it was also further removed from the lofty elevation of history on the eighteenth century's hierarchical ordering of the aesthetic. And while history was gendered as masculine, romance, like the world of fiction that it epitomized, was most frequently regarded as a feminine preserve.[62] With its shameless flaunting of acts of creative idealization, romance undoubtedly proved a threat to the conceptualization of historiography as the record of 'Truth, Impartiality, Fidelity, and Accuracy' articulated by Hugh Blair in his *Lectures on Rhetoric and Belles Lettres* (1783).[63]

Yet it was this literary form that became the object of intense cultural interest at precisely that moment during which modern notions of history were being constituted, as if history required an opposite against which to define and constitute itself. Arthur Johnston has provided a solid though gender-biased account of the antiquarian interest in the metrical romances of the Middle Ages over the long eighteenth century, focusing in particular on the editorial and scholarly work of Thomas Percy, Thomas Warton, Joseph Ritson, George Ellis, and Walter Scott.[64] As Nick Groom has shown, Thomas Percy was by far the most influential of late eighteenth-century literary antiquaries, assembling in his three-volume *Reliques of Ancient English Poetry* (1765) the literary vestiges—ballads, songs, sonnets, and romances—of 'Gothic antiquity' in the fashion that other antiquarians collected and studied architectural fragments.[65] To this selection we might add such crucial studies, enquiries, and reassessments as Richard Hurd's *Letters on Chivalry and*

and Porscha Fermanis and John Regan, eds, *Rethinking British Romantic History, 1770–1845* (Oxford: Oxford University Press, 2014).

[62] Phillips, *Society and Sentiment*, p. 12.
[63] Hugh Blair, *Lectures on Rhetoric and Belles Lettres*, 3 vols (Dublin: Printed for Messrs Whitestone, Colles, Burnet, et al., 1783), vol. 3, p. 42.
[64] Arthur Johnston, *Enchanted Ground: The Study of Medieval Romance in the Eighteenth Century* (London: The Athlone Press, 1964).
[65] Nick Groom, *The Making of Percy's Reliques* (Oxford: Clarendon Press, 1999).

Romance (1762); relevant essays by John and Anna Laetitia Aikin in *Miscellaneous Pieces, in Prose* (1773); James Beattie's discussions of fable and romance in *Dissertations Moral and Critical* (1783); Clara Reeve's *The Progress of Romance* (1785); and the practice of literary antiquarianism more generally.[66] The origins of romance, in particular, was a topic that exercised several literary antiquaries. In 'An Essay on Ancient English Minstrels' and 'Essay on the Ancient Metrical Romances' from the *Reliques*, Percy had argued that minstrelsy and romance were of 'Gothic' abstraction, a term by which he meant England's northern, Saxon ancestors. Hurd and Mallet concurred. For others, fictions such as the *Arabian Nights' Entertainments* suggested that romance derived ultimately from Arabic, Saracenic, or 'Eastern' roots, and was then brought to Europe via crusaders' contact with the East, a point that Thomas Warton argued rather forcefully in the first volume of *The History of English Poetry* (1774). The presumed origins of Gothic architecture—whether it was a Northern European or a Saracenic form—were equally disputed. When not seeking to resolve the problem of origins once and for all, writers, aestheticians, and reviewers of the day were often given to debating the larger and more controversial question of the relationship between romance and history, a problem brought to the fore by the bold flouting of the romance/history divide in such fictions as Thomas Leland's *Longsword, Earl of Salisbury: An Historical Romance* (1762) and Sophia Lee's *The Recess; or, A Tale of Other Times* (1783–5).[67] As Ian Duncan has shown, the period rehearsed the perceived tensions between the two to the point of cliché, yet their differences were also strangely constitutive forces in the generation of literature.[68]

There is no clearer illustration of the fraught relationship between history and romance than in the controversy that ensued over Horace Walpole's *Historic Doubts on the Life and Reign of King Richard the Third* (1768), his courageous yet ultimately troubled foray into the writing of history that was published by Dodsley in London in February 1768. Though revealing in its own right, the debacle also has much to tell us about the context in which Gothic fiction in Britain first circulated, bringing to the fore a major preoccupation of this book: the relationship between Gothic antiquarianism, both literary and architectural, and Gothic literature. In his Preface to *Historic Doubts*, Walpole set out his aims to dispel the 'ignorance and misrepresentation' that had accreted around the figure of King Richard III, thereby aligning his interventions with historical truth and all earlier

---

[66] For an overview of the scholarly study of 'Gothic' romance and the literature of the early Gothic Revival more generally, see Peter Sabor, 'Medieval Revival and the Gothic', in *The Cambridge History of Literary Criticism, Vol. IV: The Eighteenth Century*, ed. H. B. Nisbet and Claude Rawson (Cambridge: Cambridge University Press, 1997), pp. 470–88.

[67] See the contemporary reviews of *The Recess* reprinted in E. J. Clery and Robert Miles, eds, *Gothic Documents: A Sourcebook, 1700–1820* (Manchester: Manchester University Press, 2000), pp. 180–2.

[68] See Ian Duncan, *Modern Romance and the Transformations of the Novel: The Gothic, Scott, Dickens* (Cambridge: Cambridge University Press, 1992).

accounts of the monarch with the forces of romance, myth, and fable.[69] More than being composed of 'palpable forgeries' and 'inherited lies', historiography, Walpole claimed, was 'dry', 'superficial', and 'void of information', criticisms seemingly directed at the conjectural historian's characteristic dismissal of empirical, evidence-based modes of reasoning in favour of overarching philosophical supposition.[70] As Abby Coykendall has pointed out, Walpole at moments such as this participated in the Enlightenment's scepticism towards the received narratives of the past even as he turned that same scepticism upon the project of Enlightenment historiography itself.[71] Aware, too, of the political bias that informs all sanctioned versions of the past, Walpole in *Historic Doubts* set out to recover Richard III, the last king of the House of York, from the unflattering treatment that he had received at the hands of Lancastrian historians, all intent, as he believed them to be, upon fashioning the monarch as a monstrous, ruthless murderer of his two nephews Richard of Shrewsbury, Duke of York, and Edward V—the 'Princes in the Tower' of popular renown. Embarking in *Historic Doubts* on an exercise in revisionist history, he proceeded from the basis of certain key 'material facts', 'records', and 'charters' to cast doubt on, among a number of other apparent truisms, the belief that Richard had murdered the two princes, while strongly suggesting that Perkin Warbeck, later executed as an imposter, was, indeed, one of the survivors.[72]

As Sweet has shown, antiquarianism, in the meticulous attention that it brought to bear upon the material remains of local, regional, and national antiquity, was in a number of senses at odds with the sweeping historiographies of Hume and Robertson.[73] In this respect, the methodology informing *Historic Doubts* is more conventionally antiquarian than it is historiographical. With the support of his sponsors Lord Fitzwilliam, Charles Lyttelton, Henry Baker, George Vertue, and Joseph Ames, Walpole had been elected a Fellow of the Society of Antiquaries of London on 19 April 1753. Accordingly, much of the argument in *Historic Doubts* hinges on what Walpole erroneously took to be a 'Coronation Roll', a piece of material evidence that, in his flawed reasoning, indicated that the young Edward V was present—or at least was intended to be present—at Richard's coronation. While he questions the reliability of such historians as Hall, Holinshed, Thomas More, and Hume, Walpole stops short at the figure of Shakespeare, claiming of his dramatic treatment of the events in *Richard III* that 'This indeed is the authority which I do not pretend to combat.'[74] For the rest, received history is a tissue of

---

[69] Horace Walpole, *Historic Doubts on the Life and Reign of King Richard the Third* (London: Printed for J. Dodsley, 1768), p. iii.
[70] Walpole, *Historic Doubts*, p. ix.
[71] See Abby Coykendall, 'Chance Enlightenments, Choice Superstitions: Walpole's Historic Doubts and Enlightenment Historicism', *The Eighteenth Century* vol. 54, no. 1 (spring 2013): pp. 53–70.
[72] Walpole, *Historic Doubts*, pp. xi–xii.   [73] Sweet, *Antiquaries*, p. xiv.
[74] Walpole, *Historic Doubts*, p. 114.

forgeries, half-truths, and untruths, qualities that, as opposed to Walpole's attempt at evidence-based revisionism, render historiography formally and thematically indistinguishable from romance.

The publication of *Historic Doubts* provoked immediate reaction, from the approval of William Cole and the more measured responses of Thomas Gray, through the negative responses of William Guthrie in *The Critical Review* and Edward Gibbon in *Mémoires littéraires de la Grande Bretagne* (1768-9), to the heated attacks of Hume, the Reverend Doctor Jeremiah Milles (Dean of Exeter and President of the Society of Antiquaries), and the Reverend Mr Robert Masters.[75] Milles read a critique of Walpole's work at a meeting of the Society of Antiquaries in March 1770, and in January 1771 Masters followed suit.[76] Masters's address was published as a pamphlet in 1772, and then again in the second volume of *Archaeologia*, the journal of the proceedings of the Society of Antiquaries of London, in 1773.[77] In turn, Walpole responded to his critics in a succession of publications, including his 'Supplement' (1769), 'A Reply to the Observations of the Rev. Dr Milles' (1770), 'Short Observations on the Remarks of the Rev. Mr Masters' (*c*.1773), and the 'Postscript' (1793), all of which—though they exist in earlier forms—were posthumously published in Volume 2 of *The Works of Horatio Walpole* in 1798.[78] What is most notable about the responses to *Historic Doubts* and Walpole's various replies, however, is the way in which they manipulated the same distinction between history and romance that Walpole had brought to bear upon writing it. While dismissing earlier histories of Richard III as romances, Walpole initially offered *Historic Doubts* as an exercise in authentic historical narrative, supplemented and rendered more accurate by the findings of material, antiquarian evidence. But what his critics routinely accused him of having written was what Frederick William Guydickens dismissed as a fiction that was 'ridiculous and inconsistent with probability'.[79] As Masters concluded, Walpole had 'not communicated so much new light to this period of our history' as privileged in his study 'ridiculous tradition' over true, historical fact.[80] A belated

---

[75] See P. W. Hammond, 'Introduction', in *Historic Doubts on the Life and Reign of Richard the Third, Including the Supplement, Reply, Short Observations and Postscript*, by Horace Walpole, ed. P. W. Hammond (Gloucester: Alan Sutton, 1987), pp. vii–xxiii (pp. ix–xiv). For a collection of contemporary responses to *Historic Doubts*, see Peter Sabor, ed., *Horace Walpole: The Critical Heritage* (London and New York: Routledge & Kegan Paul, 1987), pp. 111–28.

[76] See Hammond, 'Introduction' in *Historic Doubts*, p. xiii.

[77] See Robert Masters, *Some Remarks on Mr Walpole's Historic Doubts on the Life and Reign of King Richard the Third* (London: Printed by W. Bowyer and J. Nichols, 1772), and Robert Masters, 'Article XXXI–Some Remarks on Mr Walpole's Historic Doubts', *Archaeologia; Or, Miscellaneous Tracts Relating to Antiquity*, vol. 2 (1773), pp. 198–215.

[78] Walpole's responses, including the early MS version of the 'Postscript', are bound in Horace Walpole, *Historic Doubts on the Life and Reign of King Richard the Third*, LWL, Quarto 49 3909.

[79] F. W. D. [Frederick William Guydickens], *An Answer to Mr Horace Walpole's Late Work, Entitled Historic Doubts on the Reign and Life of King Richard the Third; Or, An Attempt to Confute Him from His Own Arguments* (London: Printed for B. White, 1768), p. 53.

[80] Masters, *Some Remarks on Mr Walpole's Historic Doubts*, p. 20.

respondent in 1791 similarly dismissed *Historic Doubts* as 'the Effusions of a luxuriant and exuberant Fancy' that betrayed the author's 'Romantic turn of Mind', the result being a text that, like *The Castle of Otranto*, might be intended for 'Amusement' only.[81] To write fictions about haunted castles, spectres, and hobgoblins was one thing, but to infect the annals of national history with the same Gothic spells and enchantments was 'such a flagrant Act of Barbarity and Impiety, as Truth must Reprobate, Justice must Condemn, and Humanity must Execrate'.[82]

The consequences of the debacle are well documented. Reluctant to concede defeat to Milles, Walpole did not immediately resign from the Society of Antiquaries. In the summer of 1772, however, he seized his opportunity. In addition to having learned of the publication of Masters's critique in a forthcoming volume of *Archaeologia*, Walpole was now embarrassed to be associated with a Society in which, as Samuel Foote's play *The Nabob* (1772) had satirically shown, even so absurd a topic as the history of Dick Whittington and his cat could become a legitimate point of discussion.[83] Increasingly contemptuous of institutionalized antiquarianism, Walpole in 1772 launched and published at Strawberry Hill the short-lived *Miscellaneous Antiquities*, his rival publication to *Archaeologia*, and in his correspondence from this moment onwards he frequently dismissed the Society and its members as 'boobies', and the practice of antiquarian publication as dull, dry, and unnecessarily arcane.[84] The Preface to the later *Hieroglyphic Tales*, the collection of flagrantly imaginative short fictions that he published in 1785, went so far as to parody the work of the literary antiquarian, claiming to present to the reader for the first time stories written 'a little before the creation of the world'.[85]

Though these instances post-date the *Historic Doubts* affair of the early 1770s, they were all manifestations of the same objective that Walpole, apropos of his method in the first volume of his *Anecdotes of Painting in England*, had described in a letter to Henry Zouch as early as 1762: 'I do not see why books of antiquities should not be made as amusing as writings on any other subject.'[86] As Walpole saw it, the stultifying 'dryness' of antiquarian scholarship demanded acts of imaginative rejuvenation. This is not to suggest that he eschewed antiquarian

---

[81] St. Christopher, *Free and Candid Remarks on Mr Horace Walpole's Historic Doubts on the Reign and Life of Richard the Third* (Basseterre: Printed by Edward L. Low, 1791), p. 62.

[82] St. Christopher, *Free and Candid Remarks*, p. 63.

[83] See Walpole's *Short Notes of the Life of Horatio Walpole, Youngest Son of Robert Walpole, Earl of Orford, and of Catherine Shorter, his First Wife, 1747–1779*, LWL, MSS vol. 149, fol. 18. See, too, R. W. Ketton-Cremer, *Horace Walpole, A Biography*, 3rd edn (Northampton: John Dickens & Co. Ltd, 1964), pp. 248–51. For Foote's presentation of antiquaries in his play, see, in particular, Act III, in which the Nabob of the play's title attends a meeting of the Society of Antiquaries of London.

[84] See, for example, Horace Walpole to William Cole, 14 December 1775, *Correspondence*, vol. 1, p. 384, and 1 September 1778, *Correspondence*, vol. 2, p. 116.

[85] Horace Walpole, *Hieroglyphic Tales* (Strawberry Hill: Printed by Thomas Kirgate, 1785), p. vi.

[86] Horace Walpole to Henry, 20 March 1762, *Correspondence*, vol. 16, p. 52.

activity altogether. On the contrary, and as W. S. Lewis has shown, his life-long endeavours in this regard included extensive collecting; richly documented visits to country houses and churches; acts of building and architectural remodelling; and prolific publication and correspondence.[87] Nonetheless, and as his letters to the Cambridge antiquary William Cole repeatedly show, Walpole self-consciously cultivated a far more imaginative approach to the field. Anticipating Cole's reactions to *The Castle of Otranto* shortly after its publication, Walpole conceded that though he and his antiquarian friend 'love[d] the same ages', Cole ought to 'excuse' the 'worldly' author 'for preferring the romantic scenes of antiquity' in the fiction.[88] As he playfully put it in a letter to Cole in 1782, 'I know I am but a fragment of an antiquary, for I abhor all Saxon doings, and whatever did not exhibit some taste, grace or elegance, and some ability in the artists. Nay, if I may say so to you, I do not care a straw for archbishops, bishops, mitred abbots and cross-legged knights.'[89] Walpole's imaginative, admittedly 'superficial' approach to the Gothic past is best summed up in the strikingly poetic lines of a letter that he had written to George Montagu in 1766:

> Visions, you know, have always been my pasture; and so far from growing old enough to quarrel with their emptiness, I almost think there is no wisdom comparable to that of exchanging what is called the realities of life for dreams. Old castles, old pictures, old histories, and the babble of old people make one live back into centuries that cannot disappoint one.[90]

More than being objects of antiquarian interest in their own right, old castles, pictures, and histories were useful insofar as they facilitated nostalgic and fanciful flights into vanished antique realms. Accordingly, the disparate, seemingly unrelated objects in his collection at Strawberry Hill were linked, as Sean R. Silver has argued, more through taste and implicit chains of association than overarching and coherent historical narratives.[91] His reluctance extended to antiquarian enquiries into national origins, too: 'I am not overjoyed at your wading into the history of dark ages,' he wrote to the Scottish antiquary John Pinkerton in 1785; 'In general,' he continued, 'I have seldom wasted time on the origin of nations, unless for an opportunity of smiling at the gravity of the author, or at the absurdity of the manners of those ages.'[92] His lack of interest in this particular, ideologically driven strand of Gothic antiquarianism extended even to Pinkerton's *An Inquiry into the History of Scotland* (1789), a passionate assertion of Scotland's Gothic

---

[87] Wilmarth S. Lewis, 'Horace Walpole, Antiquary', in *Essays Presented to Sir Lewis Namier*, ed. Richard Pares and A. J. P. Taylor (London: Macmillan, 1956), pp. 178–203.
[88] Horace Walpole to William Cole, 28 February 1765, *Correspondence* vol. 1, p. 85.
[89] Horace Walpole to William Cole, 15 February 1782, *Correspondence* vol. 2, p. 301.
[90] Horace Walpole to George Montagu, 5 January 1766, *Correspondence*, vol. 10, p. 192.
[91] See Sean R. Silver, 'Visiting Strawberry Hill: Horace Walpole's Gothic Historiography', *Eighteenth-Century Fiction* vol. 21, no. 4 (summer 2009): pp. 535–64.
[92] Horace Walpole to John Pinkerton, 30 September 1785, *Correspondence*, vol. 16, p. 282.

origins that was intended to combat the Celticism inspired by James Macpherson's Ossian poems: 'I am so totally unversed in the story of original nations,' the jaded Walpole wrote, and 'always find myself so little interested in savage manners unassisted by individual characters, that, though *you* lead me with a firmer hand than any historian through the dark tracts, the clouds close round me the moment I have passed them, and I retain no memory of the ground I have trod.'[93] Walpole's interest in the Gothic past was more imaginative than strictly antiquarian, his attractions to Gothic architecture, as I shall show in Chapter 1, more aesthetic than deliberately and self-consciously political.

The very public events over *Historic Doubts* also seem to have intensified Walpole's long-standing conviction that received histories such as those by Hume, Gibbon, and More were formally and thematically indistinguishable from fiction. As early as 1758, Hume and Walpole had crossed swords with one another over Walpole's *A Catalogue of the Royal and Noble Authors of England* (1758), with Hume accusing Walpole of certain crucial oversights and Walpole, in turn, accusing the century's most influential historian of not adequately acknowledging his sources.[94] By 1760, this had developed into a strong scepticism towards formal historiography, with Walpole in his letters often confounding the differences between history and romance through self-consciously describing personal experiences and historical events as if they were developments in a fictional narrative.[95] In April 1777, for example, he attempted to justify to Mason his not having read 'one syllable' of Jean-François Marmontel's *Les Yncas* (1777), a history of the religious conquest of Spanish America, by claiming that 'History is romance enough, without purposely perverting it.'[96] In 1783, in a letter that looked back on the controversy around *Historic Doubts*, he again dismissed earlier histories of Richard III as 'nonsensical chimeras', despairingly writing that 'I have often said that *History in general is a Romance that is believed, and that Romance is a History that is not believed.*'[97] This would become somewhat of a Walpolean mantra: in a commonplace book entry of c. February 1783, he wrote that 'History is a Romance that is believed: Romance a history not believed—that is the difference between them'; in the Postscript to *Hieroglyphic Tales*, he claimed that 'There is infinitely more invention in history, which has no merit if devoid of truth, than in romances and novels, which pretend to none.'[98] A slightly

---

[93] Horace Walpole to John Pinkerton, 31 July 1789, *Correspondence*, vol. 16, pp. 302–3.
[94] See Horace Walpole to David Hume, 15 July 1758, and David Hume to Horace Walpole, 2 August 1758, *Correspondence*, vol. 40, pp. 135–42.
[95] See Horace Walpole to Horace Mann, 4 March 1760, *Correspondence*, vol. 21, p. 376, and Horace Walpole to Mary Berry, 10 July 1790, *Correspondence*, vol. 11, p. 86.
[96] Horace Walpole to William Mason, 18 April 1777, *Correspondence*, vol. 28, p. 301.
[97] Horace Walpole to Robert Henry, 15 March 1783, *Correspondence*, vol. 15, p. 173.
[98] Accompanied by a printed transcription, the MS of this commonplace book is bound into W. S. Lewis, ed., *A Note Book of Horace Walpole* (New York: William Edwin Rudge, 1927), p. 49, LWL, 575 927 3 Copy 1; Walpole, *Hieroglyphic Tales*, Postscript.

modified version of these claims worked its way into the 'Detached Thoughts' that were published in Volume 4 of Walpole's *Works*: 'History is a Romance that is believed; romance a history that is not believed.'[99] Formally and thematically indistinguishable from one another, history and romance derived their differences for Walpole not through any inherent quality but only from the varying levels of credibility that their readers invested in each. In his interrogation of the inveterate assumption that romance could never serve the ends of faithful historical enquiry, Walpole thus seems to have pre-empted the better-known arguments around the use and value of historical romances that I address later in this book, among them William Godwin's 'Of History and Romance' (1797) and Walter Scott's 'An Essay on Romance' (1824).

The *Historic Doubts* controversy thus brought to the fore Walpole's scepticism towards formal historiography and institutionalized antiquarianism, throwing into relief his long-held reservations about both and forcing him to retreat more doggedly into some strange, uncharted territory between the two. It was into this liminal place between history and antiquarianism that *The Castle of Otranto* was born, a text that, in its aims to liberate the shackled fancy of contemporary prose fiction through the imaginative capacities of romance, echoed its author's desire to enrich both historiography and antiquarianism with an imaginative supplement. Though paratextually framed in the first Preface as a 'dry' antiquarian discovery, Walpole's 'edited' and 'translated' document was a chronicle of extraordinary wonders. From the moment of its inception, then, Gothic fiction occupied an awkward position in relation to the two major modes of historical enquiry with which it was contemporary. The relationship between Gothic writing and eighteenth-century historiography has recently become a topic of critical interest. As Jonathan Dent has shown, Gothic fictional narratives often tended to expose and foreground that about which formal historiography in the period had little or nothing to say.[100] Fiona Price, meanwhile, has provided an engaging account of the ways in which historical fiction from Horace Walpole to Walter Scott interacted with, and critiqued, the pervasive myth of Gothic liberty and ancient constitutionalism that I outlined above.[101] While portions of *Gothic Antiquity*, too, are devoted to this intriguing question, the argument, in a related but different critical gesture, explores the tense and fractious relationship between Gothic writing and the eighteenth-century antiquarian tradition, both of which were uncomfortably yoked together by a mutual interest in the nation's ancient Gothic past and the description and documentation of its material, architectural remains.

---

[99] Horace Walpole, *The Works of Horatio Walpole, Earl of Orford*, 5 vols (London: Printed for G. G. and J. Robinson, and J. Edwards, 1798), vol. 4, p. 368.
[100] Jonathan Dent, *Sinister Histories: Gothic Novels and Representations of the Past, From Horace Walpole to Mary Wollstonecraft* (Manchester: Manchester University Press, 2016).
[101] Fiona Price, *Reinventing Liberty: Nation, Commerce and the Historical Novel from Walpole to Scott* (Edinburgh: Edinburgh University Press, 2016).

Gothic Antiquarianism, Gothic Romance

Though they often adopted the same architectural ruins as their point of departure, Gothic antiquarianism and Gothic fiction were no easy bedfellows. Indeed, what was particularly ironic about the necromantic turn of John Carter's pen in his journalism of 1802–3 was the antiquary's long-standing antipathy towards the Gothic literary mode. In 'Theatrical Representations', the regular column in *The Gentleman's Magazine* that he devoted to accounts of the contemporary London stage, Carter reviewed performances of such plays as *Feudal Times; or, The Banquet Gallery* by George Colman the Younger (first performed at the Theatre Royal in Drury Lane on Saturday, 19 January 1799); Lewis's *The Castle Spectre* (a performance of which he attended at Drury Lane on 16 May 1799); Lewis's *Adelmorn, the Outlaw* (1801) (which Carter saw shortly after its debut); and, in 1802, Joanna Baillie's *De Montfort*, first anonymously published in the first volume of *Plays on the Passions* in 1798. The note that Carter sounds across all of his reviews is that the sets, properties, costumes, characters, and dialogue of the Gothic stage are uniformly plagued by gross historical inaccuracy. Reviewing Colman's *Feudal Times*, for instance, he complained that the production was so marred by 'monstrous anachronism' that he had no alternative but to write to the theatre manager in order to express his alarm.[102] In his review of *The Castle Spectre*, he observed that, despite the absence of specific dating for the action, one might deduce from references internal to the script that the drama sought to 'hold up to public view the customs and portraits of our ancestors before the fifteenth century'.[103] Having established this point, though, Carter provided a painstaking, scene-by-scene critique of the production's many historical errors, focusing in particular on the anachronisms introduced by the choice of costumes, the stage furniture, action, dialogue, and even the sound effects used. As he facetiously carped, 'I wish to be informed upon what antient [sic] authority the family belonging to this castle are summoned to dinner by the sound of a horn!'[104] Particularly offensive to his antiquarian sensibilities was Lewis's rendition of Gothic architectural space, especially the dramatic use to which the Hall of Conwy Castle in *The Castle Spectre* was put. 'Its architecture in general is taken from our antient [sic] modes of the Saxon and pointed arched works,' he concluded, 'but disposed in a way that does not in the least accord with the arrangement of our castellated structures.'[105] Turning the nation's ruined Gothic piles

---

[102] 'An Artist and an Antiquary', 'Theatrical Representations i', *GM*, 69 (1799), I, pp. 113–16 (p. 114).
[103] 'An Artist and an Antiquary', 'Theatrical Representations ii', *GM*, 69 (1799), I, pp. 468–72 (p. 468).
[104] 'An Artist and an Antiquary', 'Theatrical Representations ii', p. 468.
[105] 'An Artist and an Antiquary', 'Theatrical Representations ii', p. 469.

into a scene of romance and spectacle, the Gothic drama debased and defiled antiquity's hallowed remains.

Indeed, though he was superficially preoccupied with the anachronisms of script and theatrical production, it soon becomes clear that Carter was more concerned with the ways in which the literary Gothic characteristically subjected his sense of the venerable Gothic past to negative and unflattering acts of misrepresentation. For Carter, the Middle Ages marked a time of splendid and since unmatched cultural and political achievement; by contrast, though not without exception, writers of the literary Gothic perpetuated a vision of Gothic antiquity as a time of ignorance, barbarity, Catholic superstition, and feudal oppression—the 'darkest ages of christianity', the 'empire of superstition', or 'those dark ages' invoked in Walpole's first Preface to *Otranto*, and repeated by numerous Gothic romances and dramas written and produced in its wake.[106] Of course, the conviction that the Middle Ages was a particularly 'dark' period in human history was by no means a Gothic-fictional invention, for its origins might be said to lie in the work of Petrarch and other Renaissance humanists of fourteenth-century Italy.[107] Nonetheless, the Gothic constituted one of the ways in which the idea was circulated and popularized in later eighteenth-century Britain. As Carter described them in 1800, his aims in his theatrical reviews were thus to appear before the British public 'as the champion to defend the honour of our antient [*sic*] history against the theatrical despoilers of its fair truth and honour', demolishing, as he did so, the 'dramatic strong-holds' of the theatrical painters, tailors, and machinists who have 'blinded' their audiences with the 'moonstruck' impressions of modern romance.[108] What underpinned these concerns was his conviction that the larger and more significant national past to which Gothic structures attested was as worthy of reverence as the architectural forms themselves. By his own admission, Carter was 'a real Antiquary' insofar as the Gothic fabrics that he surveyed spoke of the great, the warlike, and the good people who once built and inhabited them, architecture thus serving as irrefutable proof of the 'enlightened genius and skill!' of the Middle Ages and their people.[109] For 'if we allow our ancestors to have excelled in the display of their enlightened genius,' he reasoned, that genius that is 'so wonderfully manifested in our antient [*sic*] structures', one is no longer capable of countenancing the belief that they 'were savage, and without any taste for what is called the fine arts'.[110] Ancient architecture for Carter thus ideally functioned as a cultural aide-memoire, reminding the English nation 'of

---

[106] Horace Walpole, *The Castle of Otranto*, ed. Nick Groom (Oxford: Oxford University Press, 2014), pp. 5–6.
[107] See Theodore E. Mommsen, 'Petrarch's Conception of the "Dark Ages"', *Speculum* vol. 7, no. 2 (April 1942): pp. 226–42.
[108] 'An Artist and an Antiquary', 'Theatrical Representations iv', *GM*, 70 (1800), I, pp. 318–21 (p. 318).
[109] 'An Architect', 'Pursuits iii', *GM*, 68 (1798), II, pp. 926–7 (p. 926).
[110] 'An Architect', 'Pursuits viii', *GM*, 69 (1799), I, pp. 189–91 (p. 189).

the sublime genius of their authors', the 'heroic acts of those defenders of their country who brought perfidious France beneath their triumphant swords', and 'our long race of sovereigns, the admiration and dread of surrounding nations'.[111] Though it is Gothic architecture that is Carter's point of departure, it is ultimately towards this broader and more encompassing vision of Gothic antiquity that he is most strongly drawn.

There is nothing particularly unusual about this, for as I show throughout this book, Gothic architecture in the late eighteenth and early nineteenth centuries, both 'survivalist' and 'revivalist', was always much more than a style or fashion for the construction of buildings: strongly linked to, even utterly inseparable from, competing versions of history, it incarnated, for better or for worse, the vanished Gothic past in the modern present. More than this, and as I explore in more detail in Chapter 6, Gothic architecture routinely prompted acts of historical reflection and projection: in the face of buildings both ruined and complete, artists and antiquaries, essayists and romancers, dramatists and poets were frequently compelled to engage in imaginative reconstructions of the anterior past of which these structures were but a trace—another manifestation, that is, of the architectural imagination that this study explores. Writing under the pseudonym of Philistor in *The Gentleman's Magazine* in 1788, John Pinkerton registered as much when he complained that a 'visionary turn' had become 'characteristic of our Antiquaries', identifying within their methods a predilection towards historical 'dreaming' that, he urged, ought to be eradicated through the imposition of 'accurate and precise reasoning' and the prohibition of historical conjecture.[112] The imaginative vision of the Middle Ages to which John Carter, in particular, clings answers to what I term in this study the 'white Gothic', a nostalgic construction of the historical past that is based upon fantasies of chivalry, heroism, and splendour, the liberties enshrined in the Magna Carta, and literal and metaphorical forms of enlightenment. Expressed in such adjectives as 'noble', 'excellent', 'splendid', 'golden', 'venerable', and 'glorious', this vision of the Middle Ages constructed the nation's past as an epoch of unprecedented cultural greatness, one fundamentally opposed to the tyranny, ignorance, and superstition of the 'Dark Ages' figured in Gothic romance and drama.

It was in his path-breaking study *The Literature of Terror* of 1980 that David Punter coined the notion of 'white Gothic', a category through which he sought to distinguish the pleasant and anodyne medievalism of Edmund Spenser, Richard Hurd, and John Keats from the darker, more disturbing 'Gothic' imaginings of a Radcliffe or a Lewis.[113] One of my contentions in *Gothic Antiquity* is that the full

---

[111] 'An Architect', 'Pursuits viii', p. 190.
[112] Philistor [John Pinkerton], 'Letter XI: On the Cultivation of our National History', *GM*, 58 (1788), II, p. 1150.
[113] David Punter, *The Literature of Terror: A History of Gothic Fictions from 1765 to the Present Day* (London and New York: Longman, 1980), p. 101.

implications of Punter's white Gothic, though admittedly mentioned only in passing, have not been fully explored, and that, as a concept, it usefully opens up for reconsideration the plurality by which constructions of Gothic antiquity in the period 1760–1840 were characterized. This is so not only in what would eventually become the critical distinction between the Gothic and the Romantic, but also *within* texts that we might categorize as 'Gothic' too: far from being a monolith, Gothic antiquity as it is imagined by the writers of Gothic fiction is a varied and internally divided category. Mark Madoff was the first critic to explore the plurality of eighteenth-century constructions of the Gothic past in his often-cited article 'The Useful Myth of Gothic Ancestry' (1979), showing how starkly contrasting 'utopian' and 'dystopian' historical visions were used to buttress competing political agendas.[114] James Watt contributed to the debate in *Contesting the Gothic* (1999), drawing attention to the strain of 'Loyalist Gothic' fictions that, in the tradition of Reeve's *The Old English Baron* and as evidenced again in her later *Memoirs of Sir Roger de Clarendon* (1793), tended to construct the Middle Ages in Britain as a period of military valour, patriotism, and fixed social hierarchies—so many conservative, Old Whig retreats into a national 'Gothic' past that served as a welcome alternative to the military defeats, political crises, and American and French revolutionary sentiments of the late eighteenth-century present.[115] Subsequent work on constructions of the past in what has come to be termed the field of 'Romantic Medievalism' has often reached similar conclusions.[116] Yet, despite these critical interventions, the assumption that Gothic writing routinely traffics in 'nightmarish' versions of history is an inveterate one, and often accompanied by the equally inaccurate assumption that these texts were habitually set in the 'dark' and 'barbaric' countries of mainland Catholic Europe. In a sense, *Gothic Antiquity* is an extended meditation on these assumptions, though in place of Madoff's 'utopian' Gothic and the 'Loyalist' Gothic of Watt, and for reasons elaborated upon below, the argument substitutes Punter's notion of the white Gothic.

Indeed, it would appear that, without naming it as such, Carter himself anticipated just such a category. In the manuscript of *Pursuits of Antiquaries*, an unpublished four-part poem that he completed around 1803, Carter maintained that the task of the antiquary was to prove the 'whiteness' of the Gothic remains that were once regarded as 'black'. The British antiquary sings, he writes,

---

[114] Mark Madoff, 'The Useful Myth of Gothic Ancestry', *Studies in Eighteenth-Century Culture* vol. 8 (1979): pp. 337–50.
[115] James Watt, *Contesting the Gothic: Fiction, Genre and Cultural Conflict, 1764–1832* (Cambridge: Cambridge University Press, 1999), pp. 42–69.
[116] See, for instance, Elizabeth Fay, *Romantic Medievalism: History and the Romantic Literary Ideal* (Basingstoke: Palgrave Macmillan, 2002).

> Of churchmen in their spires and towers
> Of castles wide, and painted bowers
> Of tombs thereon lye cross legg'd knights
> Of mouldy vaults, of spectres, sprights,
> Noting inscriptions what [sic] they lack,
> And proving white what erst was black,
> Thus day by day they increase pious store
> Of the right antiquarian lore.[117]

Though they reference the literal antiquarian practice of uncovering the original surfaces and colours of an ancient artefact that have been obscured by the passage of time, the concepts of light and dark, whiteness and blackness invoked in these lines have important metaphorical resonances too: in Carter's own fashion, the antiquarian scholar ought to devote his labours to proving that the so-called 'Dark Ages' were anything but the period of national barbarity, savagery, and darkness that they are commonly taken to be. We get some sense of his understanding of the past in his enthusiastic account of Westminster Abbey in an entry in *The Gentleman's Magazine* in 1799. Lapsing into the simple, immediate present, Carter vividly relives some of the grand historic scenes to which this ancient Gothic pile was once witness:

> I see the eager enthusiastic multitude filling the ailes [sic] and the galleries of the structure; I hear their pious acclamations, and now I see the shrine in possession of its royal saint; ascending clouds of incense, gorgeous vestment, glittering insignia, scriptural banners! Again, the soft breathings of the harmonious choir, wafting on angels [sic] wings the inspired soul to bliss immortal.[118]

Piety, royalty, and lyricism: such is the nature of Carter's Gothic antiquity. Significantly, though, and as the lines from *Pursuits of Antiquaries* cited above indicate, the white Gothic does not preclude the possibility of haunting. In describing his responses to Raby Castle, County Durham, in 1799, Carter once again outlined the turns that his 'fantastic delusion' took: a striking example of 'the romantic turn of former days', the gates, towers, walls, and buttresses of Raby 'well reconcile our minds to give a willing belief to all the stories of warlike knights, of beauteous dames, of gallant tournaments, of noble feasts, of trophied halls, and painted bowers, that fill the pages of our books of chivalry'; 'nay,' he continues, 'we are not insensible to the whispered tales of fairies, giants, ghosts, and spectres', the 'Fantastic delusions of a soul entranced!'[119] While the white Gothic thus makes

---

[117] *Pursuits of Antiquaries, During the Years 1791, 1793, 1794, 1795, 1796, 1797, 1798, 1799. In Four Parts. A Merry Ballad. To the Ancient Tune of 'When we were not over wise'* (c.1803). King's College London, Archives, Leathes MS 7/5.
[118] 'An Architect', 'Pursuits xv', *GM*, 69 (1799), II, pp. 856–61 (p. 861).
[119] 'An Architect', 'Pursuits ix', *GM*, 69 (1799), I, pp. 295–6 (p. 295).

allowance for the supernatural—as I have suggested, the coupling of 'Gothic' with notions of ghostliness reached far back into the eighteenth century—Carter's visions of an imaginary procession of monks within the ruins of Tintern Abbey, Monmouthshire, clearly indicate that these spectres have been divested of their ability to evoke the sublime horrors and terrors of the Gothic-fictional aesthetic: these 'white-robed brethren' merely 'seemed to wave [him] on to the haunted fane, where round each relict doorway, window, arch, or tower, in airy windings or earthly prostrations, they still shewed me what remained of all that once was glorious'.[120] The ghosts of the white Gothic, in other words, exist only in order to point to the vanished splendours of the Gothic past, and, as such, are qualitatively different from the terrifying visions of dark, Gothic romance that had quite undone the valiant knight in the ruins of White Castle, Portchester Castle, and Llandaff Cathedral that same year.

If the English past for Carter was a vanished epoch of unprecedented and subsequently unmatched cultural greatness, neither it nor its architectural remains could be appropriately designated 'Gothic'. Although the work of revivalists such as Walpole, Hurd, Percy, Ritson, Elizabeth Montagu, and numerous other Gothic literary antiquaries had done much to recuperate the adjective as the positive name for a native English tradition of romance, supernaturalism, and cultural taste more generally, the term continued to circulate pejoratively as the sign of all things monstrous, uncouth, tasteless, and uncivilized, particularly where matters of architecture were concerned.[121] In a letter of c.1519 to Pope Leo X concerning the ancient monuments of Rome, Raphael and Baldassare Castiglione described German architecture, purportedly the style of the barbarian Goths, as 'dreadful and completely worthless', juxtaposing its crude forms with the 'beautiful style of that of Rome and of the ancients'.[122] In a similar fashion, Giorgio Vasari in *The Lives of the Artists* (1549–50; 1568) repeatedly dismissed the Gothic art and architecture of the Middle Ages as the 'barbarous German style', again annexing to his aesthetic use of the term its associations with the ancient Germanic tribe, and comparing it unfavourably with the more mannered and refined forms of the Italian Renaissance.[123] John Evelyn's *A Parallel of the Antient Architecture with the Modern* (1664), his English translation of Roland Fréart de Chambray's *Parallèle de l'architecture antique et de la moderne*, glossed 'Gothique' as 'barbarous and unsightly', while in his *An Account of Architects and Architecture* (1706), he

---

[120] 'An Architect', 'Pursuits xlvii', *GM*, 72 (1802), I, pp. 300–3 (p. 301).
[121] For a detailed account of the term's architectural meanings, see E. S. de Beer, 'Gothic: Origin and Diffusion of the Term; The Idea of Style in Architecture', *Journal of the Warburg and Courtauld Institutes* vol. 11 (1948): pp. 143–62.
[122] 'The Letter to Leo X by Raphael and Baldassare Castiglione', in *Palladio's Rome: A Translation of Andrea Palladio's Two Guidebooks to Rome*, by Vaughan Hart and Peter Hicks (New Haven and London: Yale University Press, 2009), pp. 177–92 (p. 184).
[123] Giorgio Vasari, *The Lives of the Artists*, trans. Julia Conaway Bondanella and Peter Bondanella (Oxford: Oxford University Press, 2008), p. 117.

described the architecture of the Rome-sacking Goths as 'a certain Fantastical and Licentious manner of Building' comprising 'Congestions of Heavy, Dark, Melancholy and *Monkish Piles*, without any just Proportion, Use or Beauty, compar'd with the truly *Antient*'.[124] While, for Evelyn, the classicism of Inigo Jones's Banqueting House, Whitehall, was rich, grave, and stately, the Gothic of Henry VII's Chapel at Westminster Abbey was, paradoxically, both 'gross and heavy' and 'miserably trifling', a tasteless assemblage of 'sharp Angles, *Jetties*, Narrow Lights, lame *Statues*, *Lace* and other *Cut-work* and *Crinkle Crankle*'.[125] Later in the century, similar anti-Gothic biases circulated in *Parentalia*, the posthumous biography of the leading seventeenth-century classicist Sir Christopher Wren that was compiled by his son and published in London in 1750. Throughout the *Parentalia*, in fact, 'Gothick' as a term of architectural description becomes a synonym for barbarity and untamed wildness, meanings that are actively exploited by Wren in his Evelyn-inspired references to the 'Gothick Rudeness of the old design' and 'crude Gothick Inventions, far from the good Examples of the Ancients'.[126] The style's associations with the Catholic past only intensified the term's negative associations: for many eighteenth-century Protestants, 'Gothic' implied the superstitions of the Catholic faith that had been hideously memorialized in stone.

Such negative uses of the term persisted throughout the century. In a glossary entry in *The Gentleman's Magazine* in 1801, Carter could thus accurately parse the significations of 'Gothic' as 'A term of reproach, a barbarous appellation, an invidious designation, a vulgar epithet, an ignorant by-word, a low nick-name, given to hold up to shame and ignominy our antient [sic] English Architecture, the pride of human art, and the excellence of all earthly scientific labours'; 'At length the opportunity is arrived', he continues, 'to tear down this rag of prejudice, this scum of Innovation, this word "Gothic," which for a century past has branded with ignominy all our national works.'[127] Instead, Carter maintained that Britain's native architectural tradition should be known and referred to by such neutral terms as 'Norman', 'the pointed style of architecture', or simply 'our antient [sic]' architectural style, merely a few examples of the many interchangeable names for Gothic that he employs throughout his writings. Concluding his contributions to *The Gentleman's Magazine* for the year 1805, he wistfully anticipates a future in which Englishmen will have learned to 'venerate' their own architectural remains

---

[124] John Evelyn, trans., *A Parallel of the Ancient Architecture with the Modern in a Collection of Ten Principal Authors who have Written Upon the Five Orders [...]* (London: Printed by Thomas Roycroft for John Place, 1664), p. 100; John Evelyn, *An Account of Architects and Architecture, Together with an Historical, Etymological Explanation of Certain Terms, Particularly Affected by Architects* (London, 1706), p. 5.
[125] Evelyn, *An Account of Architects and Architecture*, p. 10.
[126] Christopher Wren, Jnr, *Parentalia: Or, Memoirs of the Family of the Wrens* (London: Printed for T. Osborn and R. Dodsley, 1750), pp. 275, 289.
[127] 'An Architect', 'Pursuits xxxv', *GM*, 71 (1801), I, pp. 413–18 (p. 413).

and the splendid 'source from whence such glories spring', jettisoning the term 'Gothic' so as to bring into circulation 'a name descriptive of their merits, and instilling at the same propitious moment into every breast a fervent desire to adopt the grateful appellation'.[128]

Carter was not the only Gothic antiquary to take issue with the very term used to designate his field. In a letter to Charles Lyttelton in 1758, James Bentham had claimed that 'Gothick' was at once too general and too loaded with opprobrious connotations to be used as the name for what he took to be England's national architectural style, further questioning its semantic content, use, and applicability in *The History and Antiquities of the Conventual and Cathedral Church at Ely* (1771).[129] James Essex similarly wrestled with the problem of nomenclature in the manuscript for his proposed history of the Gothic in 1777.[130] Though with considerably less caution, the Catholic John Milner justified his use of the term 'Gothic' in *A Dissertation on the Modern Style of Altering Antient Cathedrals* (1798), explaining in a lengthy footnote that:

> I have used the word *Gothic* throughout the present treatise, for the pointed order of Architecture which obtained in the middle ages, because it is that which is most used in this sense; at the same time that I know it to be improper and ludicrous, being first adopted, in this meaning, by real Goths, the destroyers of the arts and literature of preceding ages, in the 16th century.[131]

Although Edward Gibbon in the final chapter of *The History of the Decline and Fall of the Roman Empire* (1776–88) had argued that, contrary to popular belief, the decay and spoliation of classical Rome was not solely attributable to the invading Gothic tribes, 'Gothic' still connoted architectural destruction and vandalism, and was thus a poor name for what was taken by its supporters to be a noble and tasteful English form.[132] Since it conjured up evocations of a dark, barbaric, and invariably Catholic past, it could not be used by English Protestant antiquaries except reluctantly: as Carter's work shows, synonyms such as 'Saxon', 'Norman', 'Christian', 'English', and 'the pointed style' abound, as do such anxious and convoluted constructions as 'the architectural style most unjustly referred to as "Gothic"'.

---

[128] 'An Architect', 'Pursuits xcii', *GM*, 75 (1805), II, pp. 1191–2 (p. 1192).

[129] See William Stevenson, ed., *A Supplement to the First Edition of Mr Bentham's History and Antiquities of the Cathedral & Conventual Church of Ely* (Norwich: Printed by and for Stevenson, Matchett, and Stevenson, 1817), pp. 57–60, and James Bentham, *The History and Antiquities of the Conventual and Cathedral Church of Ely* (Cambridge: Printed at the University Press, 1771), pp. 35–7. For a discussion of this and other instances, see David Matthews, *Medievalism: A Critical History* (Cambridge: D. S. Brewer, 2015), pp. 51–2.

[130] See Donald R. Stewart, 'James Essex', *The Architectural Review* (November 1950): pp. 317–21.

[131] John Milner, *A Dissertation on the Modern Style of Altering Antient Cathedrals, As Exemplified in the Cathedral of Salisbury* (London: Printed by and For J. Nichols, 1798), p. 44.

[132] For an assessment of Gibbon's argument in relation to the Gothic invasions, see Martin S. Briggs, *Goths and Vandals: A Study of the Destruction, Neglect and Preservation of Historical Buildings in England* (London: Constable, 1952), pp. 1–15.

Of course, the one term that Bentham, Essex, Carter, and Milner did not have at their disposal was 'medieval', the more neutral adjective that, as I explore more fully in the Conclusion to this book, was first carefully and deliberately chosen as an alternative to the injurious 'Gothic' in Thomas Dudley Fosbrooke's *British Monachism* of 1817, the year of Carter's death. Forced either to work with an inappropriate, negatively signifying term or to resort to cumbersome syntactical constructions so as to avoid it, Gothic antiquaries, architects, and enthusiasts turned 'Gothic' against itself by constructing the historical past that it signified as an epoch of literal and metaphorical brightness, whiteness, and light—the white Gothic. While it is in a sense fitting that the literary and antiquarian cultures of the late eighteenth century have often been identified as 'medievalist'—on the most fundamental of levels, these are writers and scholars who devoted their energies to studying the period that we now know as 'medieval'—the term risks obscuring the linguistic battles in which they were engaged. The white Gothic, however, was by no means restricted to antiquarian discourse, and as this book shows, it worked its way into popular Gothic literature of the period too, often within fictions otherwise given over to figuring the Middle Ages as a time of darkness, savagery, and barbarism. The distinction between the white Gothic and its more disturbing opposite is by no means fundamental or absolute, and the two often coexist as different yet complementary representational modes within the same Gothic text. Its contours are clearly laid out in *The Entry of Prince Frederick [sic] into the Castle of Otranto*, one of the two pen-and-wash watercolours of scenes from *The Castle of Otranto* that Carter had painted for Walpole, and which he exhibited at the Royal Academy in 1790 (see Figure 0.2).[133]

It is hardly surprising that Walpole and Carter, the eighteenth century's two most vocal defenders of the Gothic style, were strongly drawn to one another's work. From 1780, and for a period of approximately ten years, Walpole had employed Carter to record the Gothic Revivalist architecture and interiors of Strawberry Hill, Twickenham, the draughtsman and artist in this capacity producing numerous images of, among other rooms, the Hall, Holbein Chamber, Tribune, Armoury, and Library. With Richard Bull, Walpole also commissioned Carter to provide images for capacious, extra-illustrated copies of the second edition of *A Description of the Villa of Mr Horace Walpole* (1784), numerous personalized variations of which remain in collections today.[134] In addition, Carter produced at least three informal sketches of Walpole, as well as watercolours of

---

[133] This image is held at the LWL, SH Contents C323 no. 2. Framed, shelved in LFS Bin 68. *The Death of Matilda* (1791), Carter's second pen-and-wash watercolour based on *Otranto*, is currently held at the British Architectural Library, RIBA, London, Carter John SB52/5. See Crook, *John Carter and the Mind of the Gothic Revival*, pp. 12–13.

[134] See, as only two of several examples, Richard Bull's extra-illustrated copy of Horace Walpole, *A Description of the Villa of Mr Horace Walpole, Youngest Son of Sir Robert Walpole Earl of Orford, at Strawberry-Hill near Twickenham, Middlesex* (Strawberry Hill: Printed by Thomas Kirkgate, 1784), LWL Folio 33 30 Copy 11, as well as the copy in the Huntingdon Library, California, 130368.

40 GOTHIC ANTIQUITY

Figure 0.2 John Carter, *The Entry of Prince Frederick [sic] into the Castle of Otranto* (1790). Courtesy of the Lewis Walpole Library, lwlpr15827.

the printing house, its interiors, and at least two maps of the Strawberry Hill estate.[135] In a reflection of what, at least until their professional relations soured, was the mutual regard between them, Carter dedicated the first volume of *Specimens of Ancient Sculpture and Painting Now Remaining in this Kingdom* (1786) to Walpole, and named the 'late lord Orford' in the manuscript of his unpublished

---

[135] For an account of Carter's work for Walpole, see Stephen Clarke, *The Strawberry Hill Press & Its Printing House: An Account and an Iconography* (New Haven and London: Yale University Press, 2011), pp. 71–5.

autobiography *Occurrences in the Life, and Memorandums Relating to the Professional Persuits [sic] of J. C* (1817) as being among his 'patrons'.[136] Although the precise background to the commissioning of *The Entry of Prince Frederick* is not known, Walpole was clearly enamoured of it, hanging the completed painting in the Little Parlour at Strawberry Hill and itemizing it in his list of further additions to his collection in the 1784 edition of *A Description*. Carter, for his part, recorded that he 'Was paid for it 20 guineas', a considerable sum by contemporary standards.[137]

As the image shows, Carter's Gothic past is one of colour, music, vibrancy, and marvellous chivalric display. The Marquis of Vicenza appears mounted on a richly caparisoned horse, a lengthy train of drum- and trumpet-wielding guards behind him, and a line of attendants carrying his gigantic sword in front. In the foreground appears an assortment of minstrels and musicians—a reflection, no doubt of Carter's abiding sense of the lyricism and imaginative richness of the Middle Ages. Manfred with Isabella beside him occupy the picture's focal point, and behind them appear the sable plumes of the giant helmet of the statue of Alfonso the Good that, falling from the sky, has crushed Conrad, Manfred's son and heir, to death. Crucially, and despite Carter's extensive involvement in documenting Strawberry Hill, the architectural forms that so dominate the image make no reference to Walpole's home. Instead, as Lewis's reading of the image has observed, they seem to allude to King's College Chapel, Cambridge, merely one architectural citation in what for Peter N. Lindfield is an anachronistic combination of several Gothic styles that range from the Romanesque to the Perpendicular.[138] Walpole and Carter also appear in the painting, the former probably represented in the bottom right-hand corner in conversation with a page, and the antiquary in all likelihood the third figure in the focal point beside Isabella.[139] The spectacle of heraldry, chivalry, and minstrelsy, and the staggering sublimity of towering Gothic forms: such are the appeals of Carter's white Gothic, a vanished and ethereal golden age that, as in his journalism, the viewer is able to access through the architectural portal that frames the composition. Were it not for the fact that the word is anachronistic with reference to the 1790s, one might almost be led to describe the scene as 'medieval', at least in the ways that a critic such as Clare A. Simmons has used the adjective in an attempt to differentiate such utopian yet politically

---

[136] John Carter, *Occurrences in the Life, and Memorandums Relating to the Professional Persuits [sic] of J. C*. (1817), King's College London, Archives, Leathes MS 7/4.1.

[137] See Wilmarth S. Lewis, *Rescuing Horace Walpole* (New Haven and London: Yale University Press, 1978), p. 184.

[138] Lewis, *Rescuing Horace Walpole*, p. 184, and Peter N. Lindfield, 'Heraldry and the Architectural Imagination: John Carter's Visualisation of *The Castle of Otranto*', *The Antiquaries Journal* vol. 96 (2016): pp. 291–313.

[139] In Lewis's reading of the image in *Rescuing Horace Walpole*, p. 184, Walpole is the figure to the right of Isabella, but as Lindfield in 'Heraldry and the Architectural Imagination' has shown, this is more likely a representation of Carter himself, with Walpole moved to the lower right-hand side of the painting.

conservative visions of history from their darker, more critical and radical 'Gothic' counterparts.[140] To employ the category that David Matthews has coined in relation to a later, nineteenth-century painting, John Everett Millais's *The Knight Errant* (1870), the world that Carter depicts here is that of the '*romantic* Middle Ages', the time of festivity and feasting, of knights, heraldry, and martial prowess.[141] Its very existence in the painting, though, depends upon a wilful act of repression: not only does Carter exclude from the scene all intimations of the enchantment, the necromancy, and the incestuous horrors and terrors of Walpole's 'darkest ages', but also, more immediately, the hollow irony that underpins the description of the arrival of Frederic in *Otranto*: for all the grandness of the occasion, the Marquis of Vicenza is not the legitimate heir that he at this point in the narrative is taken to be. As Stephen Cheeke's study of ekphrasis has shown, relations between the sister arts of painting, prose, and poetry in the eighteenth century were hardly harmonious, but were often plagued by irreconcilable differences, tensions, and paradoxes.[142] This is especially the case in this image, for while Carter's inclusion of the plumed helmet certainly gestures towards events that occurred in the recent past in *The Castle of Otranto*, the watercolour occludes and silences the future temporal developments in the narrative so as permanently to embalm and enshrine a particular vision of Gothic antiquity: the white Gothic.

Carter was by no means the only artist visually to interpret scenes from Walpole's fiction.[143] Six plates illustrative of *Otranto*, drawn by Anne Melicent Clarke and engraved by Andrew Birrell, were published by E. and S. Harding in July 1793, probably to accompany Bodoni's printing in Parma of J. Edwards's sixth edition of the novel that appeared in 1791; included in Giovanni Sivrac's Italian translation of the novel in 1795, they were then issued again in Edward Jeffery's editions of 1796 and 1800.[144] In addition to Clarke's images, Walpole also knew illustrations of the text by, among others, Anthony Highmore, Johann Wilhelm Meil, and Bertie Greatheed—the latter a 15-year-old amateur who, of his own accord in 1796, produced four illustrations for the novel that Walpole greatly admired.[145] The abiding tone and mood of many of these images might be summed up in one particularly striking illustration by George Perfect Harding, one of the six plates that the artist published in 1793, and which is bound into a unique extra-illustrated copy of Bodoni's Parma edition of the novel of 1791 (see Figure 0.3).[146]

---

[140] See the distinction that Clare A. Simmons draws between the Gothic and the medieval in *Popular Medievalism in Romantic-Era Britain* (New York: Palgrave Macmillan, 2011), pp. 141–65.
[141] Matthews, *Medievalism*, p. 15.
[142] See Stephen Cheeke, *Writing for Art: The Aesthetics of Ekphrasis* (Manchester and New York: Manchester University Press, 2008).
[143] For a comprehensive account of visualizations of Otranto, see Peter N. Lindfield, 'Imagining the Undefined Castle in *The Castle of Otranto*: Engravings and Interpretations', *Image [&] Narrative* vol. 18, no. 3 (2017): pp. 45–62.
[144] A. T. Hazen, *A Bibliography of Horace Walpole* (New Haven: Yale University Press, 1948), p. 61.
[145] Horace Walpole to Bertie Greatheed, Snr, 22 February 1796, *Correspondence*, vol. 42, p. 430.
[146] Horace Walpole, *The Castle of Otranto: A Gothic Story* (Parma: Printed by Bodoni for J. Edwards, London, 1791), LWL 24 17 791P Copy 9.

Fig. 0.3 George Perfect Harding, illustration to *The Castle of Otranto* (1793). Courtesy of the Lewis Walpole Library, 24 17 791P Copy 9.

While Carter's watercolour had attempted to fix in visual form a splendid yet fleeting moment in narrative time, Harding's image seems closer in spirit to the predominant mood of Walpole's fiction. As the first Preface to *Otranto* claims, the story appears to have been written around the same time as the events described therein occurred—that is, between '1095, the æra of the first crusade, and 1243, the date of the last'.[147] The year 1529, apparently the year in which the Italian manuscript was 'printed in the black letter' in Naples, is significant too, marking, as Walpole knew, the publication of John Rastell's *A dyaloge of Syr Thomas More*, a text more commonly known as his *Dialogue Concerning Heresies* and one of his many crucial Counter-Reformation tomes that defended the Catholic practices of saints, images, and pilgrimages against the encroachments of the new Lutheran doctrine. Sensitive to these and other aspects of the text's 'Gothic' setting, Harding's illustration provides a pointedly Protestant rendition of the dark and superstitious past in its realization of that chilling scene in which Frederic, Marquis of Vicenza, is confronted and admonished by the spectre wrapped in a hermit's cowl. The iconic signs of Catholicism are all present here, including clerical habiliments, an oratory, a rosary, an altar, a crucifix, and, crucially, the pointed arches, stained-glass windows, and elaborate tracery of the Gothic architectural style. The Gothic past, this Protestant vision of history suggests, is dominated not by the chivalry and lyricism that Carter foregrounds so much as by the superstitions of the Catholic faith, a benighted belief system that, in its effects, is indistinguishable from the experience of horror and terror.

Bertie Greatheed's four watercolours achieved much the same effect: through his renditions of the foot of the giant in the chamber, the spectre of the hermit, the death of Matilda, and the apparition of Alfonso, the 'Gothic' of the story's subtitle marks a savage epoch of necromancy and enchantment, albeit one that is no less attractive for being so. This, in Matthews's terms, is the '*grotesque* Middle Ages', the assumption that the here aptly named 'Gothic' past was one of barbarism, threat, violence, religious corruption, and perverse sexuality.[148] Their differences in form, medium, and context aside, how starkly this contrasts with Carter's visualization of history in *The Entry of Prince Frederick*. From colour, movement, and vibrancy to gloom, horror, and anxiety: *Gothic Antiquity* tracks the ceaseless shuttling between the poles of the white and the dark Gothic within and between a selection of texts, arguing, in its concluding chapter, that is was through the aesthetic and historiographic developments of the early nineteenth century that the 'Gothic' past of previous centuries was eventually replaced by the category of the 'medieval'. The changes effected within the realm of the architectural imagination between 1800 and 1840, I conclude, were equally profound.

---

[147] Horace Walpole, *The Castle of Otranto*, p. 5.   [148] Matthews, *Medievalism*, p. 15.

1
Associationist Aesthetics and the Foundations of the Architectural Imagination

That architectural forms were capable of conjuring up vivid, imaginative visions in the minds of those who beheld them was an assumption set in place by the aesthetics of associationism, a way of conceptualizing architecture, the imagination, and the relationship between them that, though by no means uncontested, held sway in Britain for much of the eighteenth century. Derived from the empiricist philosophy of John Locke, David Hume, and their followers, associationism enshrined the power and ability of architecture to move and inspire the conscious mind, constituting, as it were, the 'foundation' of the architectural imagination and setting discursively in place the terms that would govern the relationship between architecture and literature in the period. Working systematically through the principles of associationism that run in architectural, philosophical, and aesthetic thought from Locke, through Joseph Addison, Mark Akenside, William Chambers, Alexander Gerard, Horace Walpole, Thomas Gray, and others, into the work of John Soane, this chapter explores the ways in which the long eighteenth century variously celebrated and censured the imaginative capacities of what were invariably taken to be the opposing Gothic and classical styles. John Summerson has argued that it is a 'great mistake' to consider the two 'as *opposites*': 'they are very different but they are not opposites and they are not wholly unrelated'.[1] For the eighteenth century, however, the Gothic and the classical were antagonistic architectural modes, the perceived differences between them occasioning and structuring much theoretical reflection. Associationism, I demonstrate, also informed theories of the sublime and the picturesque, though the extent of its uptake in these discursive fields varied considerably. While the landscaping techniques of Steven Switzer, Thomas Whately, William Shenstone, and others drew strongly on the imaginative powers of Gothic ruins, William Gilpin countered this association-based tradition with his particular version of the picturesque. As I show towards the end of the chapter, however, the architectural imagination constituted far more than an empiricist understanding of

---

[1] John Summerson, *The Classical Language of Architecture* (London: Methuen & Co., 1963), p. 8.

Gothic Antiquity: History, Romance, and the Architectural Imagination, 1760–1840. Dale Townshend, Oxford University Press (2019). © Dale Townshend.
DOI: 10.1093/oso/9780198845669.001.0001

the mind as the imaginative yet ultimately passive receptacle for the sensory impressions emanating from structures external to it: though a writer and architectural enthusiast such as William Beckford took associationism as his point of departure, he eventually moved well beyond this and into a far more creative, generative, even idealist conceptualization of the architectural imagination.

Architecture and Associationism

As John Archer's searching genealogy of architectural associationism has pointed out, a seventeenth-century writer such as Sir Henry Wotton theorized in *The Elements of Architecture* (1624) a limited form of association in proposing what he termed a 'due *Respect* betweene [*sic*] the *Inhabitant*, and the *Habitation*', a principle derived from Vitruvius's account of a building's 'character' in the first book of *De architectura*.[2] Vitruvian architectural principles, Anthony Vidler has argued, frequently installed such an analogy between the building and the body, although this was to be replaced when, with the rise of sublime aesthetics in the eighteenth century, architecture came to be perceived as objectifying and eliciting various mental states.[3] While the bodily analogy employed by Wotton and other seventeenth-century architectural theorists was tacitly informed by an associationism of sorts, the conjuring up of impressions and images in the mind of the beholder was not yet, in itself, regarded as a legitimate or desirable aspect of architectural practice.

Indeed, it was only in the fourth edition of John Locke's *An Essay Concerning Humane [sic] Understanding* (1690) of 1700 that the phrase 'the association of ideas' was coined. Locke's discussion of this concept in the chapter that he added to the end of Book II of the revised *Essay* proceeds by way of a distinction between those ideas that have a 'natural Correspondence and Connexion' with one another and those that are owing merely 'to Chance or Custom'.[4] While the former fall well within the 'Office and Excellency of Reason', the latter remain of the order of 'wanton Phancies' or 'madness'.[5] Maintaining that, once acquired, the connections between an object and conscious ideas 'not at all of kin' to it are 'very hard to

---

[2] John Archer, 'The Beginnings of Association in British Architectural Esthetics', *Eighteenth-Century Studies* vol. 16, no. 3 (spring 1983): pp. 241–64 (p. 244); Henry Wotton, *The Elements of Architecture* (London: Printed by John Bill, 1624), p. 119.

[3] Anthony Vidler, *The Architectural Uncanny: Essays in the Modern Unhomely* (Cambridge, MA, and London: MIT Press, 1992), pp. 69–72. For an account of the importance of Vitruvian notions of 'character' to eighteenth-century architectural debates, see John Archer, *The Literature of British Domestic Architecture, 1715–1842* (Cambridge, MA, and London: MIT Press, 1985), pp. 46–54.

[4] John Locke, *An Essay Concerning Humane Understanding. In Four Books* (London: Printed for Awnsham and John Churchill; and Samuel Manship, 1706). This 1706 edition is a verbatim reprint of the fourth edition of 1700.

[5] Locke, *An Essay Concerning Humane Understanding*, pp. 279–81.

separate', Locke demonstrates his claim with reference to a telling example: though there is no absolute connection between darkness and a childish fear of the supernatural, the link between them, once set in place by the superstitious tales of a servant girl, is likely to endure well into adult life.[6] Ghosts, by this way of reasoning, were the preserve of working-class women, a repetition of the links between supernaturalism and the ghostly tales of old wives that we encounter in Shakespeare and other early modern dramatists. These claims would later be reiterated in the fifth, expanded version of Locke's *Some Thoughts Concerning Education* (1693) that was posthumously published in 1705: once established by the negligent servant's tales of the supernatural, the irrational connection between darkness and an incapacitating fear of ghosts and spirits will, in all likelihood, persist throughout adulthood.[7] Though Locke's critique of the learned links between one object and another makes little mention of architecture, his scepticism towards associationism in general meant that architectural theorists of the early eighteenth century were reluctant to engage with associationist principles in any sustained fashion. As Archer maintains, this wariness was only intensified by the prevailing Palladian style's emphasis upon order and uniformity, and its accompanying discouragement of fanciful or imaginative viewer response.

Joseph Addison, however, made a number of important contributions to associationist thought in the eleven essays that he published on 'Taste and the Pleasures of the Imagination' in *The Spectator* in 1711 and 1712. Breaking free of the shackles of Locke's anti-associationist position, Addison's account of 'fancy' or the 'imagination'—terms, he reminds his readers, that he uses 'promiscuously' or interchangeably throughout—turns upon a crucial distinction between 'primary' and 'secondary' pleasures.[8] By the imagination's primary pleasures Addison means the delight and gratification that the subject experiences through acts of visual perception, those pleasures 'which entirely proceed from such objects as one before our eyes'; secondary pleasures, by contrast, are those that flow 'from the ideas of visible objects, when the objects are not actually before the eye, but are called up into our memories, or formed into agreeable visions of things that are either absent or fictitious'.[9] It is through this secondary but by no means less important category that Addison recuperates as a source of aesthetic pleasure that which Locke had dismissed as 'wanton fancies'. Indeed, courting precisely those trains of association that Locke had rejected as 'madness', Addison boldly advocated in an essay of June 1712 that the spectator look 'beyond' the rational and sensory realm of nature so as to indulge in the rich world of association to which the empirical world ultimately pointed. Not insignificantly, his vouching for the

---

[6] Locke, *An Essay Concerning Humane Understanding*, pp. 280–2.
[7] John Locke, *Some Thoughts Concerning Education*, 5th enlarged edn (London: Printed for A. and J. Churchill, 1705), pp. 223–24.
[8] Addison, *Critical Essays from The Spectator*, p. 176.
[9] Addison, *Critical Essays from The Spectator*, p. 176.

imagination's secondary pleasures is couched in the language of romance: 'In short, our souls are at present delightfully lost and bewildered in a pleasing delusion, and we walk about like the enchanted hero of a romance, who sees beautiful castles, woods and meadows; and at the same time hears the warbling birds, and the purling streams.'[10] Associationism for Addison marked the realm of imaginative fiction, the conscious, mental experience of heightened flights of fancy from which romance narrative ultimately derived. The observer's return to the primary pleasures of visual perception, by contrast, ends the 'secret spell' of romantic reverie; the 'fantastic scene' of association disperses, and the 'disconsolate knight' finds himself 'on a barren heath, or in a solitary desert'.[11]

Although the theory of the imagination that Addison thus far had advanced was concerned more with the perception of natural objects than with architectural form per se, he turned to consider architecture in an article published in *The Spectator* on Thursday, 26 June 1712. Assigning the visual perception of architecture to the realm of primary pleasure, Addison here stresses the importance of architectural grandeur, scale, and majesty to its effects, for 'everything that is majestic', he argues, 'imprints on the mind of the beholder, and strikes in [*sic*] with the natural greatness of the soul'.[12] The examples of grandeur that he cites, however, are primarily classical in style, and eventually he is led to disclose his preferences for the grandeur of ancient Greek and Roman architecture over the mere 'vastness' of the Gothic:

> Let any one reflect on the disposition of mind he finds in himself, at his first entrance into the Pantheon at Rome, and how his imagination is filled with something great and amazing; and, at the same time, consider how little, in proportion, he is affected with the inside of a Gothic cathedral, though it be five times larger than the other; which can arise from nothing else, but the greatness of the manner in the one, and the meanness in the other.[13]

Drawing upon the argument that Roland Fréart de Chambray had advanced in *Parallèle de l'architecture antique avec la moderne* (1650), Addison's privileging of the classical over the Gothic here is based upon the conviction that grandeur resides in something more than a building's size and proportion. Even as he expressed his appreciation of select manifestations of Gothic architecture on the Continent, he voiced a similar predilection for classicism in his responses to St Peter's Basilica, Rome, in *Remarks on Several Parts of Italy* in 1705:

> The Proportions [are] so very well observ'd, that nothing appears to an Advantage, or distinguishes itself above the rest. It seems neither extremely high, nor

---

[10] Addison, *Critical Essays from The Spectator*, p. 182–3.
[11] Addison, *Critical Essays from The Spectator*, p. 183.
[12] Addison, *Critical Essays from The Spectator*, p. 188.
[13] Addison, *Critical Essays from The Spectator*, p. 188.

long, nor broad, because it is all of them in a just Equality. As on the contrary in our *Gothic* cathedrals, the Narrowness of the Arch makes it rise in Height, or run out in Length; the Lowness often opens it in Breadth, or the Defectiveness of some other Particular makes any single Part appear in greater Perfection.[14]

Addison's architectural observations, here, seem difficult to reconcile with his political Whiggism: apparently unswayed by the commonplace Whiggish tendency to perceive in Gothic architecture the embodiment of native poetic and political liberties, he privileges the classical over the Gothic style.[15] Indeed, in Addison's hands, classicism could be as effective a means of propagating Whiggish principles as the Gothic was for other writers, for his appreciation of Italian classical architecture seems inseparable from the republication spirit of liberty that he celebrates throughout the *Remarks*. In his later *Cato, A Tragedy* (written 1712; performed 1713), too, he would explore the Whiggish principles of liberty, republicanism, and the heroic resistance to sovereign tyranny through classical rather than through Shakespearean or 'Gothic' dramatic forms. Such political considerations aside, Addison effectively circumvented Locke's caution regarding mental association by placing it at the heart of his conceptualization of the imagination's secondary pleasures.

A more particular engagement with the imaginative capacities of the Gothic occurs in the essay 'No. 110', Addison's celebrated reflection on ecclesiastical ruins, the supernatural, Locke, and mental association that he had published earlier in *The Spectator* in July 1711. Recounting a visit to his fictional friend, the landed, High Church Tory Sir Roger de Coverley, in Worcestershire, the narrator describes a night-time walk to the Gothic ruin of an apparently haunted abbey that lies a short distance from Sir Roger's house. Despite the warnings of ghostly activity in and around the abbey that he receives from his host's servants, the narrator, presumably Addison himself, will not be daunted, and goes on to describe, in an extremely influential passage, the 'supernumerary horrors' that are conjured up in his mind within the Gothic ruin through the workings of association:

> The ruins of the Abbey are scattered up and down on every side, and half covered with ivy and elder bushes, the harbors of several solitary birds which seldom make their appearance till the dusk of the evening. The place was formerly a church-yard, and has still several marks in it of graves and burying-places. There is such an Echo among the old ruins and vaults, that if you stamp but a little

---

[14] Joseph Addison, *Remarks on Several Parts of Italy, &c. in the Years 1701, 1702, 1703* (London: Printed for Jacob Tonson, 1705), pp. 174–5.

[15] On Addison's politics, and the claim that the essays in *The Spectator* transcend the differences between Whig and Tory, see Lawrence E. Klein, 'Joseph Addison's Whiggism', in *'Cultures of Whiggism': New Essays on English Literature and Culture in the Long Eighteenth Century*, ed. David Womersley, assisted by Paddy Bullard and Abigail Williams (Newark: University of Delaware Press, 2005), pp. 108–26 (p. 113).

louder than ordinary, you hear the sound repeated. At the same time the walk of elms, with the croaking of the ravens which from time to time are heard from the tops of them, looks exceedingly solemn and venerable. These objects naturally raise seriousness and attention: when the night heightens the awfulness of the place, and pours out her supernumerary horrors upon every thing in it, I do not at all wonder that weak minds fill it with spectres and apparitions.[16]

In its references to echoing graves and tombs, the passage knowingly alludes to both the 'bare ruin'd choirs' of Shakespeare's Sonnet 73 and to Act V, scene iii, of John Webster's *The Duchess of Malfi* (1613–14), that moment in which Delio and Antonio, unaware of the fact that the Duchess is dead, hear ghostly echoes of her voice throughout the ruined abbey in which they are conversing. With darkness obscuring the sense of vision, a train of imaginative associations—those secondary, non-visual pleasures of the imagination—spontaneously develops in the mind of Addison's narrator, in stark contradiction of the imaginative paucity of the Gothic that he would later theorize. Although he links them in the passage with a certain cognitive weakness, Addison nonetheless countenances precisely those associations between darkness and the supernatural that Locke had dismissed, crucially adding to this coupling of ghosts and darkness a third term: ruined Gothic architectural space. Immediately thereafter, his argument turns to consider the implications of Locke's 'Of the Association of Ideas' from the *Essay*, and, having cited the philosopher's example of the child's irrational fear of the dark that is acquired through the supernatural stories of women servants, Addison tacitly proves the great empiricist wrong. For, not only has Addison in the dark ruin come to understand the superstitions of the working classes, but he has not been entirely immune to the 'supernumerary horrors' of a weak mind himself. 'I should not have been thus particular upon these ridiculous horrors,' he concludes, 'did not I find them so very much prevail in all parts of the country.'[17] 'At the same time,' he continues, 'I think a person who is thus terrified with the imagination of Ghosts and Spectres much more reasonable, than one who contrary to the reports of all Historians sacred and profane, ancient and modern, and to the traditions of all nations, thinks the appearance of Spirits fabulous and groundless.'[18] Addison would rather entertain the possibility of the existence of the spirit-world than resign himself to the implications of rationalist and materialist philosophy. But in the process Gothic architecture is imbued with the imagination's secondary pleasures: with the visual sense frustrated by the darkness, the ruin is charged with the ability to conjure up in the narrator's mind powerful associations of ghosts, revenants, and other supernatural beings. In another seeming contradiction of

---

[16] Joseph Addison, *The Works of the Late Right Honourable Joseph Addison, Esq*, 4 vols (Birmingham: Printed by John Baskerville for J. and R. Tonson, 1761), vol. 3, p. 33.
[17] Addison, *The Works of the Late Right Honourable Joseph Addison* vol. 3, p. 34.
[18] Addison, *The Works of the Late Right Honourable Joseph Addison*, vol. 3, p. 34.

his claims to the Gothic's relative affective weakness in 1712, Addison would undertake a similar task in *The Drummer; or, The Haunted House* (1716), a drama about the Tedworth ghost that explored to light-hearted, satirical effect the popular associations between the supernatural and houses erected in the ancient 'Gothick Way of Building'.[19]

With hindsight, it is clear to see that Addison's essay marked a key moment in the instantiation of the architectural imagination of eighteenth-century Gothic writing. At the very least, his phrasing in the piece consolidated the post-Reformation tendency to construct ecclesiastical piles for the remainder of the century as Ovidian *loci terribiles*, places of supernatural horror and terror, an impulse that was already present in *The Duchess of Malfi* and other early modern texts. In a direct reference to Addison, Robert Blair employed the phrase 'supernumerary horror' in *The Grave* (1743) when, by the light of a flickering taper, the persona in the darkened churchyard perceives an assortment of morbid objects, including sculls, coffins, epitaphs, worms, ghosts, and funereal Yew trees: 'The sickly Taper / By glimmering thro' thy low-brow'd misty Vaults, / (Furr'd round with mouldy Damps, and ropy Slime,) / Lets fall a supernumerary Horror, / And only serves to make thy Night more irksome.'[20] Taken together, Addison and Blair presage what we might term the 'spatiality' of eighteenth-century Gothic writing, that is, its intimate association with the architecture of ecclesiastical ruin, a feature that I shall explore in greater depth in Chapter 5. Over eight decades later, the scenario that Addison had outlined in essay 'No. 110' would still be very much in place, when Nathan Drake in 'The Abbey of Clunedale', a Gothic fragment that was initially published in *Literary Hours* (1798), described one Edward De Courtenay's night-time visit to a ruined Gothic abbey and his falling prey therein to a host of superstitious horrors and terrors.[21] Robert Southey's 'Poor Mary, The Maid of the Inn', a supernatural ballad anthologized in Walter Scott's *An Apology for Tales of Terror* (1799), rehearsed a similar scenario.[22] Just as Addison did much earlier, eighteenth-century Gothic writing tirelessly explores the 'supernumerary horrors' generated by the associations of Gothic ecclesiastical ruin. Well beyond the example of ruined monasteries, abbeys, and convents, in fact, Gothic romance, drama, short fiction, and poetry are nothing if not the writing of Gothic-architectural association, an imaginative, self-consciously 'romantic' response to architecture that, for all his classicism, Addison had effectively legitimized, and upon which Matthew Lewis, William Godwin, Anne Bannerman, and the other

[19] Joseph Addison, *The Drummer; or, The Haunted House, A Comedy* (London: Printed for Jacob Tonson, 1716), Act I, scene i, p. 12.
[20] Robert Blair, *The Grave: A Poem* (London: Printed for M. Cooper, 1743), p. 4.
[21] Nathan Drake, 'Number XX ["The Abbey of Clunedale"]', in *Literary Hours; or, Sketches Critical and Narrative*, 3 vols (London: Printed by J. Burkitt, 1798), vol. 1, pp. 325–44.
[22] See Robert Southey, 'Poor Mary, The Maid of the Inn', in *An Apology for Tales of Terror*, ed. Walter Scott (Kelso: Printed at the Mail Office, 1799), pp. 19–26.

contemporary commentators that I surveyed in the Introduction frequently reflected. So inveterate had the links between Gothic architecture, associationism, and Gothic fiction become that a minor Gothic novelist such as Frances Clifford could only hope to distinguish herself by setting her four-volume romance *The Ruins of Tivoli* (1810) in and around the classical ruins of Tivoli's Temple of the Sybil, though extracting from these the associations of haunting and other 'gloomy ideas' that were more habitually reserved for Gothic architecture.[23] Addison's views were influential in architectural practice, too. As Vaughan Hart has shown, John Vanbrugh absorbed Addison's ideas through personal acquaintance with the author, through his subscription to the original 1712 collected quarto edition of *The Spectator*, and through their republication in a collected quarto edition of 1721.[24] Though he did not participate in the arch-classicist's condemnation of the Gothic style, Vanbrugh drew upon the essays on 'Taste and the Pleasures of the Imagination' for his work in 'the Castle Air' at Kimbolton Castle, Cambridgeshire, and on his own buildings at Greenwich.

Nonetheless, Addison was not primarily a theorist of architecture, and influential though it was, his revision of Locke did not immediately bring about a wide-scale embrace of associationist principles in early eighteenth-century architectural theory and practice. In *An Essay on the Nature and Conduct of the Passions and Affections* (1728), Francis Hutcheson brought a more orthodox version of Locke to bear on the principles of moral philosophy. Though Hutcheson conceded to the necessity of association as the basis for the workings of memory and language, he remained, like Locke, of the opinion that acquired associations between an object and a set of unrelated ideas 'raise the Passions into an extravagant Degree, beyond the proportion of real Good in the Object', and then 'commonly beget some secret Opinions to justify the Passions'.[25] As in Locke, these learned connections are so insuperable that they persist even when they defy the strictures of rational knowledge; 'Persons, who by reasoning have laid aside all Opinions of *Spirits being in the dark* more than in the light', Hutcheson, echoing Locke, argues, 'are still uneasy to be alone in the dark.'[26] By contrast, David Hume's claim in *A Treatise of Human Nature* (1739) that all human knowledge and mental life were based upon the principles of association did much to promote the appropriation of associationist thought by mid-century architectural theorists and aestheticians. In his chapter 'Of the connexion or association of ideas' in the first volume of the *Treatise*, Hume argued that it was the faculty of 'fancy' or

---

[23] Frances Clifford, *The Ruins of Tivoli; A Romance*, 4 vols (London: J. F. Hughes, 1810), vol. 1, p. 3.
[24] Vaughan Hart, *Sir John Vanbrugh: Storyteller in Stone* (New Haven and London: Yale University Press, 2008), pp. 86–8.
[25] Francis Hutcheson, *An Essay on the Nature and Conduct of the Passions and Affections. With Illustrations on the Moral Sense*, 2nd edn (London: Printed for James and John Knapton and John Crownfield et al., 1730), p. 94.
[26] Hutcheson, *An Essay on the Nature and Conduct of the Passions and Affections*, p. 95.

'imagination'—the terms, as in Addison, interchangeable with one another—that served to forge connections between otherwise discrete mental ideas. For Hume, the synthesizing effects of the imagination proceeded according to three 'universal principles', namely 'RESEMBLANCE, CONTIGUITY in time or place, and CAUSE AND EFFECT', the most effective of which, he claimed, was the latter.[27] More than just a system for comprehending the formation and movement of ideas within human consciousness, Hume's theory was also a way of accounting for the relationship between the external world of objects and the inner world of the mind: while ideas were bound together by relations of resemblance, contiguity, and causation, sensory impressions were joined with one another only by the principle of resemblance.[28] Although the *Treatise* makes occasional recourse to architectural examples in the process of explaining the workings of mental and sensory association, Hume's study was not, primarily, a treatise on architectural associationism. Nonetheless, its claim that association was the fundamental principle governing human consciousness, knowledge, and learning was extremely influential, and one that was put to more narrowly aesthetic and architectural use in Mark Akenside's *The Pleasures of Imagination* (1744), John Baillie's *Essay on the Sublime* (1747), and in the anonymous *An Enquiry into the Origin of the Human Appetites and Affections* (1747).[29]

The first edition of Akenside's anonymously published *The Pleasures of Imagination*, for one, drew upon both Hume and Addison in seeking to illustrate in poetic form the imaginative pleasures referenced in its title. Conceptualizing, like Hume, the imagination as that which mediates between the material world of sensory perception and the immaterial world of the mind, Akenside, here following Addison, theorized the secondary pleasures of the imagination as deriving from the resemblance between an artistic representation of an object and the original object in nature. Architectural metaphors, images, and tropes figure consistently throughout the poem's three books, to the extent that, as in Young's later *Conjectures on Original Composition* and Duff's *An Essay on Original Genius*, what eventually emerges is a notably architectural conceptualization of the imaginative faculty. Undoubtedly, aspects of the poem are keen to acknowledge the pleasures of what we now term 'the Gothic imagination', those tales of ghosts, goblins, and sprites that Addison, for all his classical leanings, had positively appraised in an essay published in *The Spectator* in July 1712.[30] Akenside's poem goes so far as to rewrite Addison's account of the Gothic imagination in his

---

[27] David Hume, *A Treatise of Human Nature: Being an Attempt to Introduce the Experimental Method of Reasoning into Moral Subjects*, 3 vols (London: Printed for John Noon, 1739–40), vol. 1, pp. 27, 29.
[28] Hume, *A Treatise of Human Nature*, vol. 2, p. 16.
[29] See Archer, 'The Beginnings of Association in British Architectural Esthetics', pp. 258–9.
[30] See the essay for Tuesday, 1 July 1712, in Addison, *Critical Essays from The Spectator*, pp. 199–201.

well-known description of the village matron at her fireside who 'suspends the infant-audience' gathered about her with her tales of 'evil sprites' and chain-rattling 'unquiet souls / Ris'n from the grave'.[31] And yet, as this image of the enraptured child-listener suggests, Akenside encourages his readers to move beyond this scene of early oral enchantment towards the 'mature' enjoyment of a more moral, beautiful, and truthful source of imaginative pleasure. The persona's 'chearful [sic] song', he claims, 'With better omens calls you to the field', a sentiment that in a subsequent passage amounts to a call for an act of Gothic renunciation:

> And leave the wretched pilgrim all forlorn
> To muse, at last amid, the ghostly gloom
> Of graves, and hoary vaults, and cloister'd cells;
> To walk with spectres thro' the midnight shade,
> And to the screaming owl's accursed song
> Attune the dreadful workings of his heart;
> Yet be you not dismay'd.[32]

Evoked in the architectural images of graves, vaults, and cloistered cells, the Gothic imagination is the stuff of 'monkish horrors', all to be dispelled, the persona promises, by the illuminations of his 'gentler star'.[33] Urged to 'tune to Attic themes, the British lyre', the poem's readers are exhorted to turn away from 'the reluctant shades of Gothic night'—the paraphernalia of Blair, Thomas Gray, and other graveyard poets of the 1740s and early 1750s—towards the beauty, truth, and genius of the classical style.[34] This, it soon becomes clear, is primarily an act of architectural aspiration and transcendence, one teleologically driven away from the 'mossy roofs' of native Gothic antiquity towards the 'eternal vault', 'The princely dome', 'the columns and the arch', and the 'breathing marbles and the sculptur'd gold' of ancient Greece and Rome.[35] In the light of Akenside's Whiggish political leanings—sentiments clearly legible in this edition of the poem in its spirited defence of liberty against the powers of tyranny—this is a significant move: like Addison before him, he breaks with the tendency to figure the Gothic style as the architectural embodiment and material representation of liberty.[36]

---

[31] Mark Akenside, *The Pleasures of Imagination. A Poem in Three Books* (London, 1744), Book I, ll. 255–70.
[32] [Mark Akenside], *The Pleasures of Imagination* (1744), Book I, ll. 395–401.
[33] [Akenside], *The Pleasures of Imagination*. Book I, ll. 401–7.
[34] [Akenside], *The Pleasures of Imagination*, Book I, l. 604.
[35] [Akenside], *The Pleasures of Imagination*, Book I, ll. 276, 514; Book III, ll. 583–4.
[36] For a reading of Akenside's relation to Whiggish politics, and the political differences between the 1744 and 1757 editions of *The Pleasures of Imagination*, see Michael Meehan, *Liberty and Poetics in Eighteenth Century England* (London and Sydney: Croom Helm, 1986), pp. 52–63, and Adam Rounce, 'Akenside's Clamours for Liberty', in *'Cultures of Whiggism': New Essays on English Literature and Culture in the Long Eighteenth Century*, ed. David Womersley, assisted by Paddy Bullard and Abigail Williams (Newark: University of Delaware Press, 2005), pp. 216–33.

Drawing together Addison's celebration of classical architecture in *Remarks on Several Parts of Italy* with his essays on the pleasures of the imagination from *The Spectator*, Akenside subtly nuances the metaphor of the genius-as-architect in order to render the imaginative faculty as the architect of, specifically, august classical forms.

With David Hartley's *Observations on Man, his Frame, his Duty, and his Expectations* (1749), association became the fundamental principle governing the human appreciation of beauty. But even in the wake of Hartley, the associations that architectural forms, in particular, were deemed capable of exciting were somewhat limited, for neoclassical aesthetics demanded 'a uniformity of response among viewers that association could not guarantee, especially if designs were meant to suggest aspects of politics, history, or society with which the viewer was not necessarily familiar'.[37] For instance, even as he subscribed to a Humean notion of sympathy, Edmund Burke, in the first edition of *A Philosophical Enquiry into the Origin of Our Ideas of the Sublime and Beautiful* (1757), echoed Locke in rejecting the associationist paradigm on the basis of its distracting from certain natural and innately sublime and beautiful objects. And yet, his argument remains obliquely critical of Locke in places, too. In Section XIV of the *Enquiry*, 'Locke's opinion concerning darkness, considered', Burke, with all due 'deference' to the philosopher, argues that the 'universal' fear of the dark derives not from the learned associations between night-time and the nursemaid's supernatural tales, but rather from the fundamental sublimity of the night itself, its essential ability to inspire terror, danger, and fear.[38] If the fear of night is pervasive across all cultures and historical periods, this is because darkness is 'originally an idea of terror' that is only afterwards 'chosen as a fit scene for such terrible representations' in stories of goblins and ghosts.[39]

The year 1759 was particularly significant for architectural associationism, marking, as it did, the publication of Alexander Gerard's *An Essay on Taste* and William Chambers's *A Treatise on Civil Architecture*. Alexander Gerard, Professor of Moral Philosophy and Logic at Marischal College at the University of Aberdeen, had been awarded a prize by the Edinburgh Society for the Encouragement of Arts, Sciences, Manufacturers, and Agriculture for an unpublished version of his essay in 1756. In its published form of 1759, the *Essay* seeks to account for the faculty of taste, dividing it up into the separate senses of novelty, sublimity, beauty, imitation, harmony, ridicule, and virtue, with each chapter devoted to considering the respective functions of each. When these senses fruitfully combine, '*good taste*', Gerard maintains, is the inevitable result.[40] In effect, taste is Gerard's

---

[37] Archer, 'The Beginnings of Association in British Architectural Esthetics', p. 260.
[38] Edmund Burke, *A Philosophical Enquiry into the Origin of Our Ideas of the Sublime and Beautiful* (London: Printed for R. and J. Dodsley, 1757), p. 141.
[39] Burke, *A Philosophical Enquiry into the Origin of Our Ideas of the Sublime and Beautiful*, p. 142.
[40] Gerard, *An Essay on Taste*, p. 2.

synonym for the imagination, that creative faculty that links together chains of association in the mind of the beholder at the moment of sensory perception, mediating thus between the bodily senses and the perceiver's rational and moral functions. Accordingly, the imaginative powers of association are central to Gerard's discussions of each of taste's composite elements; as the *Essay* concludes, 'The sentiments of taste depend very much on *associations*' that have been augmented by the power of custom.[41] The quality of novelty, for instance, is said to 'exalt and enliven the frame of mind', making it 'receive a strong impression from them' and rendering those objects that possess it 'in some measure agreeable' to the observer.[42] Furthermore, if largeness and grandeur are central to the generation of sublime effect, Gerard, contra Burke, claims that it is association more than the size of an object per se that renders it so: 'in order to comprehend the whole extent of the sublime, it is proper to take notice that objects, which do not themselves possess that quality, may nevertheless acquire it, by *association* with such as do'.[43] That is, association for Gerard supplements what might be lacking within the sublime object, particularly in the case of architecture, where it is more often a building's associations with scenes of grandeur than any inherent quality within the structure itself that imbue it with its sublimity: 'the principal source of grandeur in architecture', he thus reasons, 'is *association*, by which the columns suggest ideas of strength and durability, and the whole structure introduces the sublime ideas of the riches and magnificence of the owner'.[44]

Though accurate in its assessment of the significance of Gerard to theories of architectural associationism, Archer's sense of the 'unlimited speculation' set in place by the *Essay* requires careful qualification.[45] First, as an aesthetic of taste, its applicability was limited solely to the appreciation of classical form, with the Gothic consistently relegated to the category of bad or immature taste. Deeming proportion to be central to the sense of beauty, for example, Gerard dismisses Gothic architecture as being 'crowded with minute ornaments' that fall 'as much short of perfect beauty' by 'their disproportion' as 'by their deviation from simplicity'.[46] Sublimity, too, seems to be an effect exclusive to classicism, an assumption that is implicit in his celebration of the 'separate pleasures' arising from those classical elements—'the beauty, proportion, fitness, and ornaments of the parts'—that serve to 'heighten' the architectural sublime.[47] While the 'profusion of ornament' that one finds in '*Gothic* structures' may 'please one who has not acquired enlargement of mind', Gerard maintains that the perceiver, having

---

[41] Gerard, *An Essay on Taste*, p. 112.   [42] Gerard, *An Essay on Taste*, p. 5.
[43] Gerard, *An Essay on Taste*, p. 20.
[44] Gerard, *An Essay on Taste*, p. 23. For an insightful account of the importance of association in the work of Gerard and other writers of the Scottish Enlightenment, see Rachel Zuckert, 'The Associative Sublime: Gerard, Kames, Alison, and Stewart', in *The Sublime: From Antiquity to the Present*, ed. Timothy M. Costelloe (Cambridge: Cambridge University Press, 2012), pp. 64–76.
[45] Archer, 'The Beginnings of Association in British Architectural Esthetics': p. 264.
[46] Gerard, *An Essay on Taste*, p. 37.   [47] Gerard, *An Essay on Taste*, p. 82.

achieved a certain aesthetic maturity, will observe 'superior elegance in the more simple symmetry and proportion of *Grecian* architecture'.[48] Secondly, given that an observer's susceptibility to the powers of association requires what Gerard terms a certain 'sensibility of heart' or 'delicacy of passion', its pleasures are by no means universal, for as he claims, 'The souls of men are far from being like susceptible of impressions of this kind.'[49] Neither are all participants in the aesthetic encounter necessarily in possession of the 'good sense' that is the 'indispensable ingredient in true taste', that faculty of sound judgement that facilitates the 'accurate perception of things as they really are'.[50]

As this suggests, the workings of association are subjected to a rigorous process of regulation, limitation, and control in Gerard, and this often through the censuring of unrestrained imaginative reverie in language that recalls Locke's condemnation of the excesses of association-driven 'romance'. 'When reason is weak,' Gerard claims, 'it loses itself in a long and intricate demonstration; it cannot retain the connection of the whole; it sees nothing but confusion; and contains neither conviction nor delight.'[51] Compromising the refinement that is necessary to good taste, false refinement for Gerard 'is extravagantly touched with the chimeras of its own creation'.[52] Though the imaginative powers that confer upon perceived objects certain mental associations might appear to be 'fictitious or chimerical' by nature, Gerard insists that all associations be linked by an imaginative power that is, in the end, governed by a faithfulness to things 'as they really are', thereby reining in a seemingly 'wild and lawless' fancy with relations of resemblance, custom, proximity, coexistence, or causation.[53] Through the application of principles derived from Hume's discussion of the role of resemblance, contiguity in time or place, and relations of cause and effect in his *Enquiry*, Gerard regulates and controls the wild flights of the romantic imagination by subjecting them to a strongly mimetic imperative.

It was for these and other reasons that Gerard's *Essay* provoked a critical reaction from none other than Ann Radcliffe, the unsurpassed 'romancer' of Gothic-architectural association in the period. A crucial but critically overlooked source, here, is her personal copy of the second, 1764 edition of *An Essay on Taste*. Several pages of manuscript annotations in Radcliffe's distinctive hand indicate the closeness—and strong sense of disagreement—with which she engaged with Gerard's arguments (see Figure 1.1).[54] I shall return to discuss Radcliffe's responses to Gerard in the margins of his text in Chapter 3. For the moment it

---

[48] Gerard, *An Essay on Taste*, pp. 122–3.   [49] Gerard, *An Essay on Taste*, pp. 86–9.
[50] Gerard, *An Essay on Taste*, p. 90.   [51] Gerard, *An Essay on Taste*, p. 121.
[52] Gerard, *An Essay on Taste*, p. 133.   [53] Gerard, *An Essay on Taste*, pp. 167–8.
[54] See Radcliffe's MS annotations in Alexander Gerard, *An Essay on Taste. The Second Edition, with Corrections and Additions. To Which are Annexed, Three Dissertations on the Same Subject, by Mr De Voltaire, Mr D'Aembert, and Mr De Montesquieu* (London: Printed for A. Millar; Edinburgh: Printed for A. Kincaid and J. Bell, 1764), pp. 12–16. Beinecke Library, Yale University, Osborn pc127.

58 GOTHIC ANTIQUITY

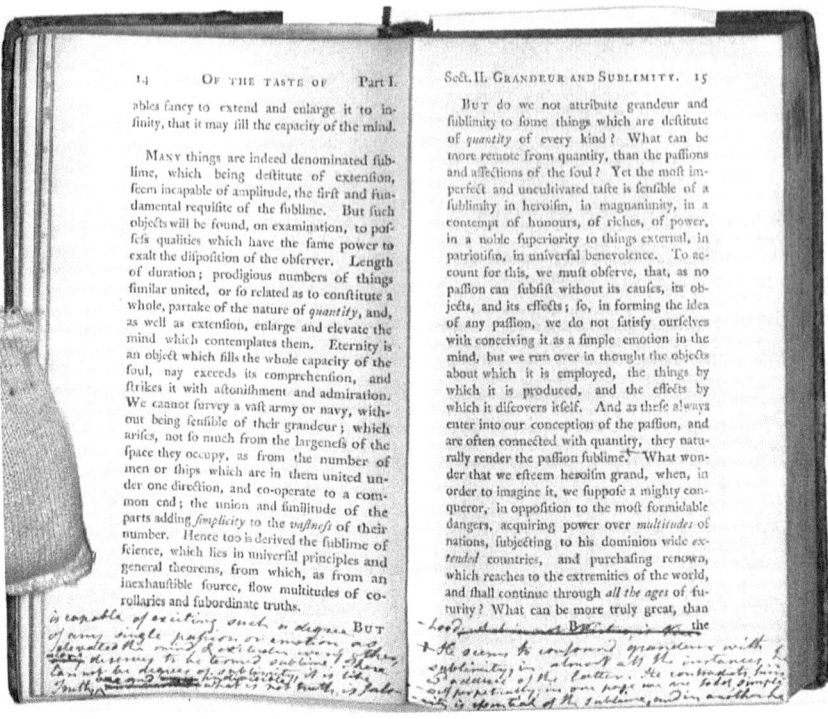

Figure 1.1 Sample of Ann Radcliffe's annotations in the second edition of Alexander Gerard's *An Essay on Taste* (1764). Courtesy of The James Marshall and Marie-Louise Osborn Collection, Beinecke Rare Book and Manuscript Library, Yale University, Osborn PC127.

is sufficient to make the point that, while extremely influential, the *Essay* did not receive unqualified support from those who sought to cultivate in relation to Gothic architecture a far more imaginative, sublime, and self-consciously 'romantic' response.

The restrictions that Gerard placed upon a perceiver's associative responses are equally pronounced in William Chambers's *A Treatise on Civil Architecture*, an influential account of architectural aesthetics that was published in the same year and then reworked as *A Treatise on the Decorative Part of Civil Architecture* in 1791.[55] Drawing, like Gerard, upon the doctrine of the sister arts, Chambers stresses throughout his study the claim that architecture, like poetry, has the power to move the viewer by exciting in him 'unbounded' mental associations: 'Materials in Architecture are like words in Phraseology; which singly have little or

---

[55] For an account of the two editions of Chambers's text, see Robin Middleton, 'Chambers, W. "A Treatise on Civil Architecture", London 1759', in *Sir William Chambers*, ed. Michael Snodin (London: V&A Publications, 1996), pp. 68–76.

no power, and may be so arranged as to excite contempt; yet when combined with Art, and expressed with energy, they actuate the mind with unbounded sway.'[56] Like Gerard, it is ultimately an aesthetic of pleasure that Chambers is committed to advancing, that is, the pleasure to be derived from the associations brought to mind in those 'judicious spectators' or 'persons of more enlightened conceptions' who are 'desirous of being enabled to judge the Beauties of a building, without entering into the detail of it's [sic] Construction'.[57] Even as he provides in the *Treatise* a detailed account of the five orders of classical architecture—the Doric, Ionic, Corinthian, Tuscan, and Composite—it is 'the imagination of the beholder' of the building with which he is most concerned.[58] However, and predictably for the architect who, in 1776, would design Somerset House, London, in the classical style, Chambers's schema remains resolutely classicist in bias; in illustrating his claims through reference to the examples of Vitruvius, Palladio, Vincenzo Scamozzi, Inigo Jones, and Christopher Wren, his account consistently marginalizes Gothic form. As in Gerard, this often amounts to a censuring of the imaginative excesses with which Gothic architecture is implicitly associated: though caryatids, he claims, might well grace a Grecian structure, they ought never to resemble the 'indecent attitudes, distorted features, and all kinds of monstrous and horrid productions, of which there are such frequent instances in the works of the Goths'.[59] By no means 'unbounded', then, the architectural imagination that emerges in Chambers's account of the associations called to mind by classical form is ordered, rational, and self-consciously chaste.

Horace Walpole's Architectural Imagination

As Stephen Clarke has pointed out, Horace Walpole's architectural tastes were complex, varied, and, for one so deeply invested in the Gothic style at Strawberry Hill, invariably surprising.[60] While one might expect Walpole to have been as enamoured of Elizabethan and Tudor architecture as he was of the earlier styles of the Middle Ages, his discussions of architecture in *Anecdotes of Painting in England* (1762–71) and elsewhere reveal his distaste for their 'barbarous mixtures', an expression of his misgivings about architectural hybridity and the merging of different styles that may be identified throughout his correspondence and

---

[56] William Chambers, *A Treatise on Civil Architecture, in which the Principles of that Art are Laid Down, and Illustrated by Plates, Accurately Designed, and Elegantly Engraved by the Best Hands* (London: Printed for the Author by J. Haberkorn, 1759), p. ii.
[57] Chambers, *A Treatise on Civil Architecture*, pp. 18, 84.
[58] Chambers, *A Treatise on Civil Architecture*, p. 74.
[59] Chambers, *A Treatise on Civil Architecture*, p. 37.
[60] Stephen Clarke, 'Horace Walpole's Architectural Taste', in *Horace Walpole: Beyond The Castle of Otranto*, ed. Peter Sabor (New York: AMS Press, 2009), pp. 233–44.

published work.[61] He expressed equally strong reservations about the 'modern Gothic' combinations of classical and Gothic forms in the work of William Kent and Batty Langley, while the excesses of Vanbrugh's baroque architecture at Castle Howard, Yorkshire, provoked particular censure.[62] More peculiarly, as both Clarke and John Wilton-Ely have shown, Walpole expressed ambivalent and even contradictory responses to the neoclassicism of Robert Adam, an architect whom he in 1766 would commission to work on the interiors of the Round Drawing Room at Strawberry Hill, but then later, from 1775 onwards, vociferously critique for his work at Grosvenor Square and Carlton House, London.[63] For all his Gothic undertakings, Clarke observes, Walpole remained ultimately wedded to the rules of architectural decorum and stylistic purity, one instance of the solid bedrock of classicist values that underpins much of his architectural writing.

More than being overly preoccupied with the finer details of architectural periodicity and style, however, Walpole's architectural tastes remained, in the end, fundamentally imaginative. Certainly, it was with contemporary accounts of the architectural imagination as set out by theorists of associationism that he engaged with the publication of the first volume of his *Anecdotes of Painting in England* in 1762. Although, in the Preface to the first edition, Walpole describes Chambers's treatise as 'the most sensible book and the most exempt from prejudice that ever was written on that science', his chapter on the 'State of Architecture to the end of the Reign of Henry VIII' turns upon a subtle but marked inversion of *A Treatise on Civil Architecture*.[64] Reversing Chambers's privileging of the classical over the Gothic style, Walpole, in what has become the book's best-known passage, privileges the imaginative properties of the Gothic over those of the Grecian:

> It is difficult for the noblest Grecian temple to convey half so many impressions to the mind, as a cathedral does of the best Gothic taste—a proof of skill in the architects and of address in the priests who erected them. The latter exhausted their knowledge of the passions in composing edifices whose pomp, mechanisms, vaults, tombs, painted windows, gloom and perspectives infused such sensations of romantic devotion; and they were happy in finding artists capable of executing

---

[61] Clarke, 'Horace Walpole's Architectural Taste', pp. 234–6.
[62] Clarke, 'Horace Walpole's Architectural Taste', p. 237.
[63] Clarke, 'Horace Walpole's Architectural Taste', pp. 238–9. See, too, John Wilton-Ely, 'Gingerbread and sippets of embroidery': Horace Walpole and Robert Adam', *Eighteenth-Century Life* vol. 25, no. 2 (spring 2001): pp. 147–69, and 'Style and Serendipity: Adam, Walpole and Strawberry Hill', *The British Art Journal* vol. 11, no. 3 (spring 2011): pp. 3–14.
[64] Horace Walpole, *Anecdotes of Painting in England; With Some Account of the Principal Artists; And Incidental Notes on Other Arts; Collected by the Late Mr George Vertue; and Now Digested and Published from His Original MSS*, 4 vols (Strawberry Hill: Printed by Thomas Farmer, 1762–71 [1780]), vol. 1, p. xiii.

such machinery. One must have taste to be sensible of the beauties of Grecian architecture; one only wants passions to feel Gothic.[65]

Juxtaposing classical taste with Gothic passion, Walpole celebrates the Gothic for its ability to provoke in the viewer not only powerful imaginative response, but an intense and 'passionate' level of emotional engagement too: though 'stripped of it's [sic] altars and shrines', Westminster Abbey is 'nearer converting one to popery than all the regular pageantry of Roman domes'; 'Gothic churches inspire superstition', he asserts, the Grecian, mere 'admiration'.[66] No marker of anti-Catholicism, superstition, here, becomes the sign of the intensely imaginative engagement that the Gothic fosters. In more narrowly literary terms, he would argue much the same in his attempts at defending Shakespeare from the criticisms of Voltaire and other French critics in the Preface to the second edition of *The Castle of Otranto* in 1765: though they failed to conform to the rules of Aristotelian poetics, the tragedies of the 'Gothic' Bard were imaginatively superior to the dry and moribund neoclassicism of Pierre Corneille and Jean Racine. So central would these convictions be to Walpole's literary and architectural thought that he would rework them as a pithy epigram for the 'Detached Thoughts' that were posthumously published in the fourth volume of his *Works* in 1798: 'A Gothic cathedral strikes one like the enthusiasm of poetry; St Paul's, like the good sense of prose.'[67]

As Clarke and Marion Harney have pointed out, this passage from the *Anecdotes* is also Walpole's direct riposte to Addison's insistence upon the superiority of Roman taste to the Gothic in his essays on 'Taste and the Pleasures of the Imagination'.[68] It is true that Walpole was a lifelong reader of Addison, and his manuscript annotations in the nine-volume edition of *The Spectator* that he owned is evidence of him having worked closely through all of the essays.[69] In addition to Addison's *Miscellaneous Works, in Verse and Prose* (1726), Walpole also owned a copy of the third edition of his *Remarks on Several Parts of Italy* (1726), and as an early letter to Thomas Gray reveals, he was sufficiently well acquainted with its contents as to pen a witty parody of it in a description of his travels in and around London in October 1735.[70] As the parodic tone of this letter implies, Walpole remained critical in several respects of Addison's literary and architectural classicism. As he put it in his second *Book of Materials* (c.1775), 'Addison is a glaring proof that pedantry and servility to rules tend [to] dishabilitate a man of Genius. Compare his Cato and Shakespeare's Julius Caesar.

---

[65] Walpole, *Anecdotes of Painting*, vol. 1, pp. 107–8.
[66] Walpole, *Anecdotes of Painting*, vol. 1, p. 108.
[67] Walpole, *The Works of Horatio Walpole*, vol. 4, p. 368.
[68] Clarke, 'Horace Walpole's Architectural Taste', pp. 231–2; Marion Harney, *Place-making for the Imagination: Horace Walpole and Strawberry Hill* (Farnham: Ashgate, 2013).
[69] *The Spectator*, 10th edn, 9 vols (London: Tonson, 1729), LWL, 49 1860, v. 1–9.
[70] Horace Walpole to Thomas Gray, c.15 October 1735, *Correspondence*, vol. 13, pp. 85–90.

There is as much difference between the soul of Julius and the timidity of Addison.'[71] Thus, despite his claim in the *Anecdotes* that he 'certainly' did not mean 'by this little contrast' between the classical and the Gothic to make any unfavourable comparison between the 'rational beauties of regular architecture' and the 'unrestrained licentiousness of that which is called Gothic', Walpole ends up, in effect, doing precisely that: the 'persons who executed the latter', he claims, 'had more taste, more genius, and more propriety than we chuse [sic] to imagine'.[72]

Several other manuscript sources indicate that Walpole's views on the superlative imaginative potential of Gothic architecture had been theoretically taking shape since at least 1759, and practically ever since he had commenced the 'Gothicizing' of Twickenham's Strawberry Hill, to use his own awkward coinage, in the late 1740s.[73] Although there is no reference to the *Essay on Taste* in either Walpole's published oeuvre or across his correspondence, Allen T. Hazen's *A Catalogue of Horace Walpole's Library* indicates that Walpole owned a copy of Chambers's *Treatise* and kept it in the Round Tower at Strawberry Hill.[74] His nephew, George Walpole, 3rd Earl of Orford, is listed as one of the subscribers to the original volume, while, in a letter to William Cole on 10 January 1771, Walpole wrote that 'I am slightly acquainted with Mr Chambers the architect, and have a good opinion of him.'[75] He also owned a copy of Chambers's *A Dissertation on Oriental Gardening* (1772), a text that exerted a considerable influence on his conceptualization of the irregularity of the Gothic style and the affinities that it shared with chinoiserie. As if in a direct attempt at refuting Chambers's classicism, however, Walpole's *Book of Materials* from *c*.1759 argued that:

> If two architects of equal Genius & Taste, or one man professing both, & without the least degree of partiality was ordered to build two buildings, (& supposing him unlimited in expense) one in the Grecian & one in the Gothic style, I think, the Gothic would strike most at first, the Grecian would please the longest.[76]

Gothic 'strikes' or seizes the imagination more than does classical form. While the 'pleasure' of the classical resides in its associations with ancient Greek and Roman civilization, these are likely to be rivalled by those with a nationalistic, historical partiality to 'old knights, Crusades, the wars of York and Lancaster'. While men who 'think by rote' might, in accordance with the mainstream fashions of the day, be inclined to favour the Grecian and Roman, those who 'think for themselves'

---

[71] Horace Walpole, *Book of Materials, 1775*, LWL, 49 2615, fol. 10.
[72] Walpole, *Anecdotes of Painting*, vol. 1, p. 108.
[73] Walpole first used the verb 'Gothicizing' in a letter of 1750. See Horace Walpole to Horace Mann, 1 September 1750, *Correspondence*, vol. 20, p. 185.
[74] Allen T. Hazen, *A Catalogue of Horace Walpole's Library. With Horace Walpole's Library by Wilmarth Sheldon Lewis*, 3 vols (New Haven and London: Yale University Press, 1969), vol. 3, p. 129.
[75] Horace Walpole to William Cole, 10 January 1771, *Correspondence*, vol. 1, p. 212.
[76] Walpole, *Book of Materials, 1759*, LWL, 49 2615, fol. 52.

will inevitably express a predilection for the Gothic. The ending to this note in the *Book of Materials* comes by way of a telling disclosure of Walpole's commitment to the associative richness of the Gothic: 'I, who have great difficulty of not connecting every inanimate thing to the idea of some person, or of not affixing some idea of imaginary persons to whatever I did see, would prefer that building that furnished me with most ideas, which is not judging fairly of the merit of the buildings abstractedly.' Though, in 'abstract' terms, it fell short of classical rules, Gothic architecture for Walpole was the most effective 'furnisher' of mental associations, 'And for this reason,' he concluded, 'I believe, the gloom, ornaments, magic of the hardiness of the building, would please me more in the Gothic than the simplicity of the Grecian.'[77] These views would be reworked into his celebration of Gothic 'passion' over Grecian 'taste' in the first volume of the *Anecdotes* three years later, and extended beyond theoretical abstraction into his own architectural practice at Strawberry Hill from the late 1740s onwards. As another manuscript source dated 31 August 1772 reads, 'Great effects may be produced by the disposition of a House, & by studying lights & shades, and by attending to a harmony of colours. I have practiced all these rules in my house at Strawberry hill [*sic*] and have observed the impressions made on Spectators by these arts.'[78] Written in what appears to have been a moment of reflection upon his own architectural practice, this source draws attention to the ways in which, for Walpole, Gothic architecture was primarily intended to call up 'impressions' in the mind of the beholder, from the feelings of 'awe', 'Devotion', and 'sobriety' in the Chapel, through to the evoking of a 'gothic tone' in the rest of the house.[79]

As Walpole recorded in the manuscript of his autobiographical *Short Notes of the Life of Horatio Walpole* (c.1746–79), his account of Gothic architecture in the *Anecdotes* angered William Warburton, the Bishop of Gloucester and religious controversialist who, in a revised edition of *The Works of Alexander Pope* (1751) of 1760, had provided a brief and remarkably positive account of the Gothic style.[80] Glossing in a footnote a line from Pope's Epistle IV, 'To Richard Boyle, Earl of Burlington' (1731), Warburton had sought to divide the category of 'Gothic architecture' into its constituent parts, distinguishing between what he referred to as the 'Saxon'—a style, he claimed, that was brought to England by the Crusaders' contact with Palestine—and the more noble 'Gothic' or 'Norman' style, the signature vaulted ceilings and pointed arches of which he, like Sir James Hall in *Essay on the Origin and Principles of Gothic Architecture* (1797) and *Essay on*

---

[77] Walpole, *Book of Materials, 1759*, fol. 52.
[78] A transcription of MS13-1947 from the Fitzwilliam Museum, Cambridge, is included as an appendix to Michael Snodin, ed., with the assistance of Cynthia Roman, *Horace Walpole's Strawberry Hill* (New Haven and London: Yale University Press, 2009), p. 348.
[79] See Matthew M. Reeve, '"A Gothic Vatican of Greece and Rome": Horace Walpole, Strawberry Hill, and the Narratives of Gothic', in *Tributes to Pierre du Prey: Architecture and the Classical Tradition, from Pliny to Posterity*, ed. Matthew M. Reeve (New York: Harvey Miller, 2014), pp. 185–98.
[80] See Walpole, *Short Notes of the Life of Horatio Walpole*, fol. 19.

the Origin, History and Principles of Gothic Architecture (1813) several years later, would argue were designed to resemble groves and avenues of trees.[81] Believing that he had 'exhausted the subject' in his three-page note, Warburton, as Walpole was to learn from Bishop Lyttelton, felt slighted by Walpole's refusal to engage with, or even acknowledge, his arguments in the *Anecdotes*. Claiming ignorance of the discussion, Walpole in *Short Notes* dismissed Warburton's objections as 'impertinent self-conceit', yet what the dispute brings to the fore is Walpole's reluctance to make absolute distinctions between different historical and stylistic manifestations of the Gothic, and, consequently, his tendency to treat it as if it were a homogeneous and internally undifferentiated category that was to be valued primarily for its imaginative effects. Tellingly, the outline of the contributions that he was likely to make to James Essex's proposed history of Gothic architecture is cursory and impressionistic, a reflection, perhaps, of his earlier claim in the *Anecdotes* that 'it was difficult to ascertain the periods when one ungracious form' of Gothic—Danish, Saxon, Norman—'jostled out another'.[82] '[T]he plan I think should lie in a very simple compass,' he wrote in a letter to William Cole in August 1769, but would conceivably stretch from the end of Saxon architecture; encompass the introduction and decoration of round Roman arches; address that moment at which the 'beautiful Gothic' arrived at its perfection; and then track its demise in the 'bastardized' and 'barbarous' Gothic forms built during the reigns of Henry VIII, Elizabeth I, and James I.[83] For the remaining parts of the proposed history, Walpole was happy to defer to others who were better placed: the antiquarian Cole, he advised, should determine the 'chronologic period of each building', while the architect Essex should cover observations on the 'art, proportions and method of building'.[84]

This is a point worth pausing over, since the historicizing and internal ordering of Gothic architecture was a matter that troubled enthusiasts of the Gothic in the period, and one that, despite several earlier attempts, would only really be settled with the publication of Thomas Rickman's *An Attempt to Discriminate the Styles of English Architecture* in 1817. Batty Langley, for example, had sought to merge the orders of classical architecture with the features of the 'Gothick' style in his and his brother Thomas's *Ancient Architecture Restored, and Improved* (1741–2), claiming in the prefatory 'Dissertation' to have recovered through over twenty years of diligent observation 'The Rules by which the ancient Buildings of this Kingdom were erected and adorned'.[85] Despite the fact that both Horace Walpole

---

[81] See William Warburton, ed., *The Works of Alexander Pope, Esq*, 9 vols (London: Printed for A. Millar, J. and R. Tonson, et al, 1760), vol. 3, pp. 327–30.

[82] Walpole, *Anecdotes of Painting*, vol. 1, p. 107.

[83] Horace Walpole to William Cole, 11 August 1769, *Correspondence*, vol. 1, pp. 190–2.

[84] Horace Walpole to William Cole, 11 August 1769, *Correspondence*, vol. 1, p. 191.

[85] Batty and Thomas Langley, *Ancient Architecture, Restored and Improved, by a Great Variety of Grand and Usefull Designs, Entirely New, in the Gothick Mode for the Ornamenting of Buildings and Gardens* (London, 1742).

and his father, Sir Robert, are listed as subscribers to the first edition, Horace later cuttingly responded to Langley's attempts at articulating the five 'orders' of Gothic, implying that his system was little more than a strategic, fanciful 'invention', his work in the Gothic mode more generally tantamount to the massacre and desecration of 'that venerable species' of architecture.[86] To dissect the style, as Langley had done, was, in effect, to murder it. This contempt for regulating what, for Walpole, was an essentially rule-free architectural form followed through to 1762, the year in which Thomas Warton, in the second edition of his *Observations on the Fairy Queen of Spenser* (1754), sought to subject the Gothic to the same kinds of analytical attention that classical architecture had enjoyed in the work of Vitruvius, Sebastiano Serlio, and Giacomo Barozzi da Vignola, that is, the distinguishing within ancient Greek and Roman architecture the five classical orders. Glossing Spenser's reference in Book IV, Canto x, of *The Faerie Queene* to 'stately pillours framd after the doricke guise', Warton in Section XI of the *Observations* digressed to provide an influential account of Gothic architecture, internally dividing the category of the 'old gothic style' into four chronologically sequenced variations or 'orders', from the Anglo-Saxon period up to the reign of Henry VIII: Gothic Saxon, Absolute Gothic, Ornamental Gothic, and Florid Gothic.[87]

As Nathan Drake would later observe, Warton's endeavours here 'gave birth to that spirit of enquiry into our Gothic Remains which has since been so widely diffused'.[88] Motivated by their mutual interests in Gothic architecture, Warton sent a copy of his study to Walpole shortly after it had been published, a gift to which Walpole duly responded.[89] That Walpole had indeed read Warton's volumes 'very attentively' is attested to by the minute corrections with which he annotated his personal copy.[90] Struck by the differences between his cursory treatment of the Gothic in the *Anecdotes* and the rigour and detail of Warton's own, Walpole flatteringly responded with a proposition: 'I have scarce skimmed the subject; you have ascertained all its periods. If my *Anecdotes* should ever want another edition, I shall take the liberty of referring the readers to your chronicle of our buildings.'[91] He did not make good on his promise, though, for the second edition of the four-volume *Anecdotes* that was published in 1765 lacked all reference to Warton's typology. Almost doggedly so, the Gothic, for Walpole, remained an internally undifferentiated category, the appropriate response to which was imaginative rather than archaeological. But as he explained in his

---

[86] Walpole, *Anecdotes of Painting in England*, vol. 4, p. 107.
[87] See Thomas Warton, *Observations on The Fairy Queen of Spenser*, 2nd edn, 2 vols (London: Printed for R. and J. Dodsley; Oxford: Printed for J. Fletcher, 1762), vol. 2, pp. 184–98.
[88] Nathan Drake, *Essays, Biographical, Critical, and Historical, Illustrative of the Rambler, Adventurer, and Idler [...]*, 2 vols (London: Printed by J. Seeley for W. Suttaby, 1810), vol. 2, p. 190.
[89] Horace Walpole to Thomas Warton, 21 August 1762, *Correspondence*, vol. 40, p. 253.
[90] Horace Walpole to Thomas Warton, 21 August 1762, *Correspondence*, vol. 40, p. 254. See Walpole's personal copy of Warton's book at the LWL, 48 1840.
[91] Horace Walpole to Thomas Warton, 21 August 1762, *Correspondence*, vol. 40, p. 254.

first *Book of Materials*, it was precisely the apparent rulelessness of the style, its resistance to dissection and internal ordering along classical lines, that enhanced its imaginative potential: 'Rules prevent faults but they prevent improvement too. The moment the Romans settled the rules of the five orders, they were afraid to invent'; the 'Gothic architects', by contrast, 'had never been told that they must not pass such & such lines', and therein lay the source of their imaginative power.[92] Revealingly, the history of 'the beautiful Gothic' on which Walpole, Essex, and Cole were to collaborate was never to be realized.[93] Like the political myth with which it shared a name, the architectural Gothic for Walpole primarily implied freedom and imaginative liberty on both the architect's and the perceiver's behalves, a style of building and a set of associative responses that proudly defied the strictures of system, ordering, and classification. Though he appears not to have been consciously preoccupied with the political meanings of Gothic architecture, Walpole thus situated himself within a strongly Whiggish tradition of sublime, imaginative liberty, a poetic strain that, as Abigail Williams has shown, reached back through Anthony Ashley Cooper, 3rd Earl of Shaftesbury, John Dennis, and Addison to the work of Longinus.[94]

No doubt Walpole would have differed from the Tory Warton's approach to the Gothic style in another respects, too, for as the later *Verses on Sir Joshua Reynolds's Painted Window at New-College Oxford* (1782) reveals, Warton remained, in the end, somewhat critical of the Gothic, and, as his classicism-derived typology of Gothic architecture in the *Observations* suggests, an advocate of the 'barbarous mixture' of styles that Walpole routinely jettisoned.[95] The immediate occasion of Warton's poem was the insertion in 1782 of painted glass into the west window of the antechapel of Oxford's New College. Prepared by Thomas Jervais between 1778 and 1785, these stained-glass images of stylized, classical forms were based on paintings by Sir Joshua Reynolds, the founder and first president of the Royal Academy of Arts and, in his series of Discourses delivered at the RA between 1769 and 1790, one of the century's staunchest advocates of neoclassical aesthetics. Like Akenside in *The Pleasures of Imagination*, Warton initially provides a stirring account of the late fourteenth-century Chapel as 'faithless truant to the classic page'.[96] Celebrating it as the realm of 'minstrel-harps' and 'sabling rime', the persona, through marked allusions to

---

[92] Walpole, *Book of Materials*, fol. 53.
[93] See Nikolaus Pevsner, 'Walpole and Essex', in *Some Architectural Writers of the Nineteenth Century*, by Nikolaus Pevsner (Oxford: Clarendon Press, 1972), pp. 1–8 (p. 2).
[94] See Abigail Williams, *Poetry and the Creation of a Whig Literary Culture* (Oxford: Oxford University Press, 2005), pp. 173–203.
[95] For an account of Warton as a 'warm Tory', see Richard Mant, *The Poetical Works of the Late Thomas Warton, BD, Volume I*, 5th edn (Oxford: Printed at the University Press, for W. Hanwell and J. Parker; London: F. and C. Rivington, 1802), p. ix.
[96] Thomas Warton, *Verses on Sir Joshua Reynolds's Painted Window at New-College Oxford* (London: Printed for J. Dodsley, 1782), p. 3.

John Milton's 'Il Penseroso' (1645), takes particular delight in the imaginative lure of Gothic architecture, even if that implies a succumbing to the powers of Catholic superstition:

> But chief, enraptur'd have I lov'd to roam,
> A lingering votary, the vaulted dome,
> Where the tall shafts, that mount in massy pride,
> Their mingling branches shoot from side to side;
> Where elfin sculptors, with fantastic clew,
> Oer [sic] the long roof their wild embroidery drew;
> Where SUPERSTITION, with capricious hand
> In many a maze the wreathed window plann'd,
> With hues romantic ting'd the gorgeous pane,
> To fill with holy light the wonderous fane;
> To aid the builder's model, richly rude,
> By no Vitruvian symmetry subdued;[97]

But no sooner have the delights of this 'mystic pile' been sung than Warton dismisses these very lines as the 'mistaken strain' of a 'pensive bard'. Turning swiftly away from the scene of dubious Gothic enchantment, the persona now endeavours to aspire to the realm of truth and beauty epitomized by Reynolds's images, rejecting as he does so the 'sombrous imagery' and deceptive charms of the Gothic in favour of the truth and beauty of classicism: 'No more the Sacred Window's round disgrace, / But yield to Grecian groups the shining space.'[98] Unlike Akenside's act of Gothic renunciation in *The Pleasures of Imagination*, however, Warton's poem closes on a note of imaginative, stylistic, and, no doubt, political hybridity, praising Reynolds's images as a laudable instance of the reconciliation of the otherwise opposed classical and Gothic styles:

> Artist, tis thine, from the broad window's height,
> To add new lustre to religious light:
> Not of it's [sic] pomp to strip this antient shrine,
> But bid that pomp with purer radiance shine:
> With arts unknown before, to reconcile
> The willing Graces to the Gothic pile.[99]

A Gothic-architectural purist at heart, Walpole could only have taken exception to Warton's paean to the stylistic intermingling of classical and Gothic modes.

Walpole differed markedly, too, from the more scholarly approach to Gothic architecture adopted by Thomas Gray, his erstwhile fellow Etonian and Cambridge

---
[97] Warton, *Verses on Sir Joshua Reynolds's Painted Window at New-College Oxford*, p. 3.
[98] Warton, *Verses on Sir Joshua Reynolds's Painted Window at New-College Oxford*, p. 7.
[99] Warton, *Verses on Sir Joshua Reynolds's Painted Window at New-College Oxford*, p. 8.

undergraduate with whom he, to somewhat disastrous effects, had set out on the grand tour in 1739. Looking back on Gray's lifelong architectural preoccupations in his memoir of the poet in 1775, William Mason paused amid a discussion of his subject's antiquarian interests to add that 'I must not omit to mention his great knowledge of Gothic architecture', one that he derived not from extant 'written accounts' but from 'that internal evidence which the buildings themselves give of their respective antiquity', and which allowed him to 'pronounce, at first sight, on the precise time when every particular part of any of our cathedrals was created'.[100] While on the Continent, Barrett Kalter has pointed out, Gray routinely expressed a predilection for the Gothic cathedrals of Paris, Amiens, and Rheims over, say, the baroque style of the Palace of Versailles, yet it is really only in his three-volume manuscript *Commonplace Book* (c.1736–71) that his attention becomes historically and stylistically refined.[101] In 1758, Gray commenced the serious and systematic study of Gothic architectural antiquities, recording in 'Ecclesiae', a section in the second volume of his *Commonplace Book*, detailed antiquarian information that he had acquired first-hand from numerous cathedrals across England and Wales, among them Lincoln, Ely, York, Durham, Carlisle, Lichfield, Hereford, Worcester, Bristol, Wells, Exeter, and Salisbury.[102] In 'Gothica Architectura', an essay included in the third volume of the *Commonplace Book* but not published until T. J. Mathias's two-volume *The Works of Thomas Gray* in 1814, Gray paid careful attention to what, following Christopher Wren, he termed 'Saxon' or 'old Norman' architecture, a style characterized by 'great solidity, heaviness, & rude simplicity' and one that was 'better adapted' to castles, walls of cities, and other places of defence than 'to the purposes of habitation, magnificence, or religious worship'.[103] Observing that it appeared to have been copied from the Roman style 'in that degenerate state', Gray noted that traces of this architectural mode were visible across all parts of the Roman Empire, but in England it persisted from the time of the Norman Conquest of 1066 to approximately 1256.

It is when Gray begins to enumerate the characteristic features of this specific manifestation of the Gothic that his essay assumes particular interest: the 'semi-circular, or round-headed arch'; 'the massy Piers, or Pillars, either of an octagonal, round, or elliptical form on which the arches rise'; the squares, octagons, and other 'uncouth forms & innovations' that decorate the capitals; the flat ceilings lacking in vaulting; and zigzag or chevron ornamental mouldings in front of the arches, along the walls, or beneath the windows. As Marion Roberts has noted, Gray

---

[100] Thomas Gray, *The Poems of Mr Gray. To Which are Prefixed Memoirs of his Life and Writings by W. Mason, M.A.* (York: Printed by A. Ward, 1775), pp. 338–9.
[101] Barrett Kalter, 'DIY Gothic: Thomas Gray and the Medieval Revival', *ELH* vol. 70, no. 4 (winter 2003): pp. 989–1019 (p. 996).
[102] Thomas Gray, *Thomas Gray's Commonplace Book* (c.1736–71), 3 vols, Pembroke College Library, Cambridge, CB1–3, vol. 2, fols 891–932.
[103] Thomas Gray, 'Gothica Architectura', in *Thomas Gray's Commonplace Book*, vol. 3, fols 943–6 (fol. 943).

tellingly turned his back here on the architectural controversy that preoccupied so many of his contemporaries—that is, the distinctions between the round arches of so-called 'Saxon Gothic' and the pointed arches of the 'Norman' style—pioneeringly in order to articulate the definitive characteristics of what we now term Romanesque architecture (in Europe) or Norman architecture (in Britain).[104] In the process, he fashioned for himself a specialized architectural vocabulary through the use of such terms as 'chevron', 'zig-zag', and 'nebule', some of these imported from the study of heraldic notation.[105] Differentiating a particular 'Gothic' style, dating it, and methodologically describing its ornamental features, Gray presages the move towards archaeological rigour and accuracy that we see in antiquarian and architectural writing of the early nineteenth century. Though the effects of this are evident in Thomas Pitt's subsequent study of the Gothic, it was James Bentham's use of Gray's work in *The History and Antiquities of the Conventual and Cathedral Church of Ely* (1771) that brought his theories to a wider audience.[106] Such a precise, technical, and closely historicized strategy might seem strange in one who, in his poetry, relied upon a far more associative approach to Gothic architecture and architectural ruin, not only in *Elegy Written in a Country Churchyard* (1751), but in 'Ode on a Distant Prospect of Eton College' (1747) and 'A Long Story' (1753) too. The difference between his methodology in the *Commonplace Book* and that of his friend Horace Walpole is equally marked: while Gray set about the disciplined, empirical recording of the early Gothic's specific forms and variations, Walpole tended to celebrate a free and internally undifferentiated architectural mass primarily for its imaginative effects.

Walpole's interests in the Gothic style's imaginative capacities extended long after the 'Gothicizing' of Strawberry Hill had been completed with the late addition of the Beauclerk Closet in 1774. Having gratefully acknowledged in a letter to Mrs Alison in January 1790 the receipt of the gift of her husband the Reverend Archibald Alison's *Essays on the Nature and Principles of Taste* (1790), the ageing Walpole warmly responded to the treatise a few weeks later: 'I can say with truth that it has pleased me much: there is a great deal of ingenuity, and the subject seems to have been meditated intensely.'[107] Supplementing an otherwise strongly Burkean account of the sublime and the beautiful with principles derived from Hartley, Alison's *Essays* became the first major appropriation of associationist psychology by British aestheticians in the period. The key terms of the argument are taste; the 'emotions' of the sublime and the beautiful; the imagination; and pleasure: simply put, taste is that faculty which allows us to experience the emotions of sublimity and beauty through the work of the imagination, the

---

[104] Marion Roberts, 'Thomas Gray's Contribution to the Study of Medieval Architecture', *Architectural History* vol. 36 (1993): pp. 49–68 (p. 56).
[105] Roberts, 'Thomas Gray's Contribution to the Study of Medieval Architecture', p. 57.
[106] Roberts, 'Thomas Gray's Contribution to the Study of Medieval Architecture', p. 62.
[107] Horace Walpole to Mrs Alison, 18 February 1790, *Correspondence*, vol. 42, p. 273.

effects of which, for Alison, are invariably pleasurable. As it was for Gerard, the imagination is little more than the sum total of mental associations, the formation of interlinked trains of ideas and mental images that arise in response to aesthetic objects. Upon seeing a sublime or beautiful object, he argues, 'Trains of pleasing or solemn thought arise spontaneously within our minds, our hearts swell with emotions, of which the objects before us seem to afford no adequate cause.'[108] Contrary to Burke's position in the *Enquiry*, then, sublimity and beauty are not qualities that inhere within the objects themselves; instead, they are the products of the imaginative reveries that they provoke in the perceiver's mind. Equally, taste becomes more than a simple matter of sensory perception, since, as Alison reasons, we only experience the sublimity or beauty presented to us by our senses 'when our imaginations are kindled by their power, when we lose ourselves amid the number of images that pass before our minds, and when we waken at last from this play of fancy, as from the charm of a romantic dream'.[109] Given that objects acquire beauty and sublimity only through association, it is imperative for Alison that the imagination remain 'free and unembarrassed' and not in any way 'restrained'.[110]

At first glance, Alison's account of Gothic architecture in the *Essays* seems to accord with Walpole's views. 'The Sublimest of all the Mechanical Arts', he wrote, 'is Architecture', its productions themselves sublime 'in proportion to their Antiquity, or the extent of their duration'. It thus follows that, of all architectural styles, 'The Gothic castle is still more sublime than all', since, as Alison reasoned, 'besides the desolation of Time, it seems also to have withstood the assaults of War'.[111] As it was for Walpole, association was key to the style's sublimity. While generally admiring of Alison's argument, Walpole in his second letter to Mrs Alison also disclosed an important point of disagreement: 'May I venture to ask if Mr A. does not confound taste and subsequent imagination too much? and does he not attribute too much to the association of ideas, and thence destroy the simplicity of ideas? Methinks he does so, particularly in architecture, on which I differ with him the most.'[112] Alison had seemingly overemphasized the Gothic's imaginative power. If Walpole's objections read as a move away from the associationist paradigm, it is important to remember that what was really at stake was his belief in the innate and absolute tastefulness of Gothic architecture, a conviction that ran counter not only to Alison, but, beyond that, to Allan Ramsay, a painter and writer whom Walpole otherwise greatly admired. As Ramsay had put it in *A Dialogue on Taste* (1755; 1762), the beauties of Gothic architecture 'have no

---

[108] Archibald Alison, *Essays on the Nature and Principles of Taste* (London: Printed for J. J. G. and G. Robinson; Edinburgh: Bell & Bradfute, 1790), p. 3.
[109] Alison, *Essays on the Nature and Principles of Taste*, p. 3.
[110] Alison, *Essays on the Nature and Principles of Taste*, pp. 6–7.
[111] Alison, *Essays on the Nature and Principles of Taste*, pp. 226–7.
[112] Horace Walpole to Mrs Alison, 18 February 1790, *Correspondence*, vol. 42, p. 274.

deeper foundation than fashion' or 'habit formed upon caprice', an argument that was informed by Joshua Reynolds's critique of the effects that custom and the association of ideas had on the perception of absolute beauty in an essay published in *The Idler* in 1759.[113] Reluctant to attribute its beautiful and sublime qualities solely to custom or to the associations that it incites, however, Walpole, against the likes of Ramsay and Alison, stressed the Gothic style's inherent qualities without abandoning his earlier associationist stance, and reaffirming, in this way, the point that he had made in his *Book of Materials* in c.1759: so intrinsic are the beauties of the Gothic that they have no option but to 'strike most at first' the mind of any 'unbiased' architect who perceives them, powerfully seizing the imaginations of those who have never been prejudiced by the prevailing taste for classicism. While Gothic certainly drives the work of the imagination, it is by no means dependent on the mental associations of its perceivers for its charms.

Walpole's stance becomes clearer still when it is contrasted with the later work of John Soane, the architect who, having been a disciple of William Chambers at the Royal Academy, became one of the major exponents of associationist aesthetics in the first four decades of the nineteenth century.[114] Appointed as Professor of Architecture at the Royal Academy in March 1806, Soane was required to deliver six public lectures on architectural matters per year. The first series of lectures commenced in 1809–10, and ran intermittently until 1819; in the 1830s, once Soane's eyesight had begun to fail him, his scripts were publicly read by Henry Howard, the secretary to the Royal Academy.[115] Invoking, in his first lecture, the doctrine of the sister arts, Soane impressed upon his audience the notion that architecture's affinities with other creative forms lay primarily in its powers to affect the mind of the observer.[116] Turning, in his fifth lecture, to the matter of Gothic, he argued that Gothic architecture was inseparable from the Catholic faith, observing that 'the early works of the Saxons and Normans are particularly calculated to increase that gloom and melancholy which entered so powerfully into the devotion and bigotry of monkish times'.[117] Beyond the devious effects that Gothic places of worship exerted upon the minds of fearful and superstitious Catholic devotees, the associations that they bring to mind, in the present, nonetheless instil an admiration for those who built them: 'The amazing extent, astonishing height, and the interesting effects produced by the continuity of the

---

[113] See Allan Ramsay, *A Dialogue on Taste*, 2nd edn (London, 1762), p. 48. For Joshua Reynolds's claims, see Joshua Reynolds and Edmond Malone, 'The True Idea of Beauty', in *The Works of Sir Joshua Reynolds: Containing his Discourses, Idlers, A Journey to Flanders and Holland (Now First Published), and his Commentary on Du Fresnoy's 'Art of Painting'* (Cambridge: Cambridge University Press, 2014), pp. 357–62.

[114] For an account of Chambers's influence on the young Soane, see Gillian Darley, *John Soane: An Accidental Romantic* (New Haven and London: Yale University Press, 1999), p. 15.

[115] See David Watkin, ed., *Sir John Soane: The Royal Academy Lectures* (Cambridge: Cambridge University Press, 2000), p. 21.

[116] Watkin, ed., *Sir John Soane*, p. 29. [117] Watkin, ed., *Sir John Soane*, p. 120.

vaulted roofing and other features of these buildings, create in every mind awe and respect for those whose piety, genius, and talents raised such mighty structures.'[118] Walpole had made a similar point about the 'genius' of Gothic architects in the *Anecdotes*. However, further reservations enter into Soane's account of Gothic associationism in a passage from the same lecture that follows immediately thereafter: as the eye of the observer wanders through the lofty nave, the extensive aisles, the choir, the sanctuary, and the chapel, his mind, having been quite 'satiated' with this 'rich banquet', falls under the spell of the 'delirium' that has been produced by 'such a blaze of effect'.[119] As his use of the word 'delirium' indicates, there remained something deeply unsettling for Soane about the Gothic's associative potential, the same imaginative power that he no doubt harnessed and exploited in the crypt-like Monk's Parlour at his home at Lincoln's Inn Fields, London: its effects upon the modern and ancient perceiver alike, he claims, are, like fictional romance, 'calculated to dazzle the eyes and astonish the minds of the multitude'.[120] Though arguing much the same point, Walpole had been far more approving of the Gothic's imaginative capacities. Turning to a consideration of the classical, moreover, Soane proclaims the Gothic to be 'inferior to the Grecian', particularly where matters of association are concerned.[121] When compared with the imaginative richness of the Pantheon, the temples at Paestum, the ruins of the Temple of Minerva, and other classical sites, the Gothic seems practically moribund. Soane inverts the claims of Walpole just as Walpole had inverted those of Addison. Thus it was that when, in his first lecture, he celebrated 'the splendid effects of architecture, and its power to affect the mind', Soane was referring not to the Gothic but specifically to the classicism of ancient Greece and Rome.[122] Over the course of the long eighteenth century, associationism was enlisted by both sides of the classical/Gothic divide in an early manifestation of what, in the next century, would be formalized and known as the 'Battle of the Styles'.

Picturesque Visions

When situated in relation to the aestheticians who both preceded and followed him, Walpole, in his belief in the extraordinary imaginative potential of the Gothic, appears to have been a lone voice in the wilderness. Certainly, not all contemporary aestheticians agreed with his position. In *Dissertations Moral and Critical* (1783), for instance, James Beattie had voiced the opinion of many in claiming that while 'Gothick buildings' may, upon certain occasions, be 'very

---

[118] Watkin, ed., *Sir John Soane*, p. 120.
[119] Watkin, ed., *Sir John Soane*, p. 120.
[120] Watkin, ed., *Sir John Soane*, p. 121.
[121] Watkin, ed., *Sir John Soane*, p. 123.
[122] Watkin, ed., *Sir John Soane*, p. 39.

sublime', sublimity was, on the whole, a quality reserved for the Grecian style.[123] As I suggested above, however, Walpole was joined in his convictions by the succession of Whiggish aestheticians who had long praised the imaginative liberties of the Gothic. William Temple had enthusiastically celebrated 'Gothick Wit' and the extraordinary poetic achievements of this 'visionary Tribe' in his essay 'Of Poetry'.[124] In *The Advancement and Reformation of Modern Poetry* (1701), John Dennis had ambivalently celebrated the barbarous creativity of 'our Gothick Cathedrals' over the classicism of St Peter's in Rome, even as his argument ultimately came out in favour of ancient Greek and Roman rules, order, and regularity. In *Characteristicks of Men, Manners, Opinions, Times* (1711), Shaftesbury with similar ambivalence had valorized the crude but noble spirit of Gothic politics and architecture alongside his defence of a native English strain of poetry, a cultural form that had laboured to throw off the 'horrid Discord of jingling Rhyme' so as to assert 'antient Poetick Liberty'.[125] Furthermore, several eighteenth-century theorists and practitioners of picturesque landscape gardening drew upon the associative potential of ruined Gothic architecture in their design and conceptualization of picturesque vistas. In *The Nobleman, Gentleman, and Gardener's Recreation* (1715), Stephen Switzer had advocated the ornamental use of architectural ruin as a means of courting the viewer's mental associations, not least among them the melancholy suggestion that, like the perceived object itself, she or he, too, will die and decay.[126] Like Walpole, Henry Home, Lord Kames, argued strongly in favour of the imaginative superiority of Gothic over classical architectural ruin in his account of landscape gardening in *Elements of Criticism* (1762), one of the most important aesthetic applications of associationist thought in the period; William Mason, Walpole's friend and correspondent, would later make much the same claim in his poem *The English Garden* (1772–81). In his 'Unconnected Thoughts on Gardening' of 1764, the poet and landscape gardener William Shenstone maintained that a Gothic ruin, such as an ornamental castle or an abbey, might be put to great imaginative effect in a landscape so long as it were appropriately situated. Gothic ruins, he argued, 'derive their power of pleasing' not only from their picturesque 'irregularity', but also for 'the latitude they afford

---

[123] James Beattie, *Dissertations Moral and Critical* (London: Printed for W. Strahan and T. Cadell; Edinburgh: Printed for W. Creech, 1783), p. 618.

[124] William Temple, *Miscellanea: The Second Part. In Four Essays*, 2nd edn (London: Printed by J. R. for Ri. and Ra. Simpson, 1690), p. 320.

[125] John Dennis, *The Advancement and Reformation of Modern Poetry. A Critical Discourse. In Two Parts* (London: Printed for Richard Parker, 1701), dedicatory epistle; Anthony Ashley Cooper, Earl of Shaftesbury, *Characteristicks of Men, Manners, Opinions, Times*, 3 vols (London: Printed by John Darby, 1711), vol. 1, pp. 217–18.

[126] See Stephen Switzer, *The Nobleman, Gentleman, and Gardener's Recreation; or, An Introduction to Gardening, Planting, Agriculture, and Other Business and Pleasures of a Country Life* (London: Printed for B. Barker and C. King, 1715), pp. 149–50.

the imagination'.[127] In *Observations on Modern Gardening* (1770), Thomas Whately similarly maintained that Gothic ruins preserved the memory of the times and manners in which they were built, and were thus capable of inciting 'certain sensations of regret, of veneration, or compassion' in the perceiver.[128] And so this tradition continued through the latter part of the eighteenth into the early nineteenth century. Uvedale Price wrote of the 'Gothic' ideas of 'fairies and chivalry' brought to mind by the sight of a fifteenth-century castle in *An Essay on the Picturesque* (1794); Richard Payne Knight provided a poetic celebration of the imaginative power of ruined Gothic abbeys and castles in *The Landscape* (1794) and in his theoretical account of the same in *An Analytical Inquiry into the Principles of Taste* (1805); and Humphry Repton asserted the value of Gothic over classical ruins in *Observations on the Theory and Practice of Landscape Gardening* (1805) and elsewhere.[129]

Similar claims made their way into literary-critical discourse too. When William Hazlitt reviewed John Black's English translation of August Wilhelm Schlegel's *A Course of Lectures on Dramatic Art and Literature* (1815) in *The Edinburgh Review* in February 1816, he was as intent upon clarifying Schlegel's distinction between the classical and the Romantic—the conceptual division that, in the course of the nineteenth century, would partially displace that between the classical and the Gothic—as he was asserting, against figures such as Soane, that the imaginative power of Gothic ruins far outreached the classical: 'A Grecian temple... is a classical object; it is beautiful in itself, and excites immediate admiration. But the ruins of a Gothic castle have no beauty or symmetry to attract the eye; and yet they excite a more powerful and romantic interest from the ideas with which they are habitually associated.'[130] In clarifying Schlegel's notion of the 'romantic', Hazlitt turned to the example of a richly associative Gothic ruin in order to illustrate his point. William Gilpin's particular version of picturesque aesthetics, by contrast, approached the imaginative properties of Gothic architecture with a discernible sense of caution. Gilpin had begun to formalize his understanding of the picturesque—the examination, description, adaptation, and appreciation of the national British landscape as it 'would appear to advantage on canvas'—in *An Essay on Prints* (1768), and later developed it throughout his

---

[127] William Shenstone, 'Unconnected Thoughts on Gardening', in *The Works in Verse and Prose, of William Shenstone, Esq.*, 2 vols (London: Printed for R. and J. Dodsley, 1764), vol. 2, pp. 125–47 (p. 131).

[128] Thomas Whately, *Observations on Modern Gardening, Illustrated by Descriptions* (London: Printed for T. Payne, 1770), p. 132.

[129] See Dale Townshend, 'The Aesthetics of Ruin', in *Writing Britain's Ruins*, ed. Michael Carter, Peter N. Lindfield, and Dale Townshend (London: British Library Publishing, 2017), pp. 83–115.

[130] [William Hazlitt], 'Art. IV. *Lectures on Dramatic Literature.* Translated from the German, by John Black, Esq. 2 vol. Baldwin & Co. 1815', *The Edinburgh Review or Critical Journal* vol. xxvi (February 1816): pp. 67–107 (p. 70).

publications of the 1780s, 1790s, and early 1800s.[131] Unlike the stationary, more 'domestic' picturesque of Payne Knight and Price, Gilpin's picturesque was, as Vivien Jones describes it, a 'peripatetic' mode, the natural object of so many ambulatory tours through parts of England, Scotland, and Wales.[132] As he would argue in *Three Essays* (1792), it was the roughness, ruggedness, and irregularity of Britain's native Gothic ruins that differentiated the picturesque object from the smoothness and neatness of Burkean notions of the beautiful.[133] Accordingly, his writing is replete with appeals to the inherently picturesque qualities of ruined Gothic structures: the 'picturesque eye' delights in 'the ruined tower, the Gothic arch, the remains of castles, and abbeys', for they are 'consecrated by time' and, as such, almost as deserving of 'veneration' as the works of the natural world itself.[134]

Thus far, Gilpin's claims seem indistinguishable from those writers in the tradition of picturesque landscaping that I have surveyed above, but where he differed from the likes of Shenstone and Whately was in the increasing scepticism with which he came to regard the workings of architectural association. This depended, first, upon Gilpin's lack of interest in—even vehement rejection of—history, that is, his disregard for any aspect of a Gothic ruin that did not immediately pertain to its visual, picturesque appeal in the present. There are several examples of this across Gilpin's oeuvre, but it is most clearly illustrated in an image from the draft manuscript of what would be published as *Observations on the Western Parts of England, Relative Chiefly to Picturesque Beauty* in 1798 (see Figure 1.2). This drawing of Glastonbury Abbey, Somerset, like the accompanying sketch in the manuscript of Netley Abbey, Hampshire, indicates that Gilpin's interest in Gothic ruin was strictly visual, the Roman numerals at the apexes of the triangles that dissect the floor plan indicating little more than the positions from which the architectural remains could be perceived to their most picturesque advantage. In his poem *The Tour of Dr Syntax in Search of the Picturesque* (1812), William Combe would satirize the picturesque tourist's disregard for history when his eponymous protagonist pauses before a ruined Gothic

---

[131] William Gilpin, *Observations on the River Wye, and Several Parts of South Wales, &. Relative Chiefly to Picturesque Beauty; Made in the Summer of the Year 1770* (London: Printed for R. Blamire, 1782), p. 40.

[132] Vivien Jones, '"The coquetry of nature": Politics and the Picturesque in Women's Fiction', in *The Politics of the Picturesque: Literature, Landscape and Aesthetics Since 1770*, ed. Stephen Copley and Peter Garside (Cambridge: Cambridge University Press, 1994), pp. 120–44 (p. 120). On the differences between Gilpin, and Price and Knight, see Kim Ian Michasiw, 'Nine Revisionist Theses on the Picturesque', *Representations* no. 38 (spring 1992): pp. 76–100. For an account, in turn, of the differences between Price's and Knight's accounts of the picturesque, see Andrew Ballantyne, 'Genealogy of the Picturesque', *British Journal of Aesthetics* vol. 32, no. 4 (October 1992): pp. 320–9.

[133] William Gilpin, *Three Essays: On Picturesque Beauty; On Picturesque Travel; And On Sketching Landscape: To Which is Added A Poem, On Landscape Painting* (London: Printed for R. Blamire, 1792), p. 6.

[134] Gilpin, *Three Essays*, pp. 27, 46.

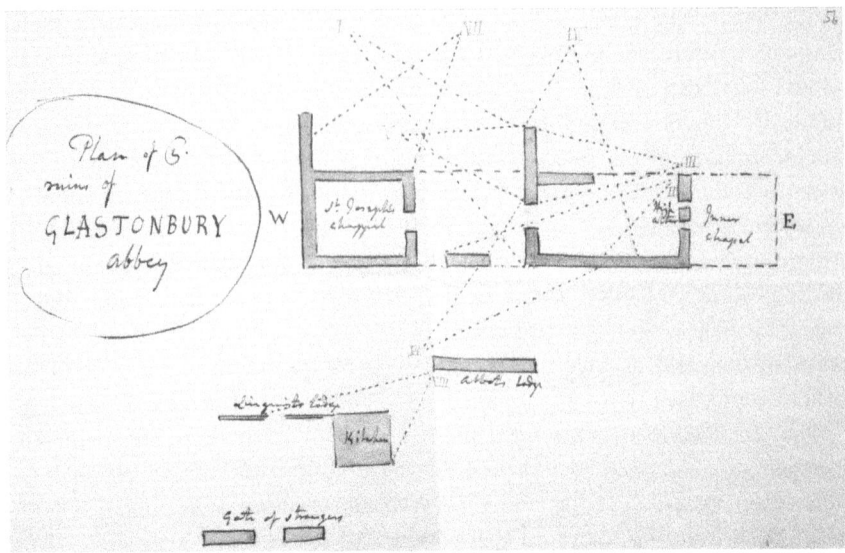

Figure 1.2 William Gilpin's drawing of Glastonbury Abbey, Somerset, from the manuscript draft of *Observations on the Western Parts of England* (1798). Courtesy of The Bodleian Libraries, The University of Oxford, MS.Eng.misc.d.558, fol. 56.

castle to celebrate its visual qualities over any potential historical significance that the structure might bear: 'But now, alas! no more remains / Than will award the painter's pains: / The palace of the feudal victor / Now serves for nought but a picture.'[135] Divested of their relations to historical time, Gothic ruins in Gilpin became the objects of two-dimensional picturesque representation, robbed, as such, of the associative potential that they were accorded in the work of Alison, Whately, Price, and other landscape designers.

Secondly, Gilpin's resistance to associationist thought extended to the claim that the qualities of the picturesque resided not in the mind of the beholder but in the qualities particular to the Gothic ruin itself, an argument that precluded the viewer's mental cerebrations from making any considerable contribution to the scene. Thirdly, and echoing Locke before him, Gilpin actively legislated against architecture's ability to excite in the viewer imaginative chains of association by distinguishing the picturesque from what he termed a tendency towards the 'romantic'. If the picturesque was the ordered, rule-bound subject of representation, the romantic, like its literary namesake, occasioned a 'riot' of the imagination, precisely those chains of association that Shenstone and Whately, in the tradition inaugurated by Addison, had tended to celebrate; while the former was the desirable aesthetic response, the latter was overly imaginative to the point of

---

[135] William Combe, *The Tour of Dr Syntax in Search of the Picturesque: A Poem* (London: R. Ackermann's Repository of Arts, 1812), p. 70.

being whimsical. The distinction between the picturesque and the romantic would receive its most sustained elaboration in Gilpin's essay 'On Picturesque Travel' from his *Three Essays*. Having outlined the various pleasures to be derived from the traveller's 'pursuit' of a scene of picturesque beauty, Gilpin turns to consider the ultimate objective of the picturesque expedition, namely the accurate visual rendition of the natural scene in an impressionistic sketch generated on-site through the use of the Claude glass, that requisite 'knick-knack' through which eighteenth-century domestic tourists viewed, and then sketched or painted, the picturesque landscape.[136] Although allowing for something more than a mere slavish copying of nature, Gilpin legislates here against the unpoliced excesses of association via a telling choice of metaphor: 'The imagination becomes a camera obscura, only with this difference, that the camera represents objects as they really are; while the imagination, impressed with the most beautiful scenes, and chastened by rules of art, forms it's [sic] pictures, not only from the most admirable parts of nature; but in the best taste.'[137] Thus, if fancy has any part to play in the genesis of a picturesque composition at all, it is the limited or curtailed fancy of a camera obscura. As Jonathan Crary has argued, the camera obscura, that popular optical device used for the projection of an image onto a screen, served, in the rationalist and empiricist philosophies of Gottfried Wilhelm Leibniz, René Descartes, Isaac Newton, and John Locke as a metaphor for the accuracy, veracity, and truth of the subject's visual perceptions.[138] Distinguished later in the eighteenth century from the phantasmagoria or magic-lantern show, this device claimed to offer visible truths in the place of imaginative fiction, realism in the place of romance. Gilpin's insistence that the picturesque tourist commit him- or herself to the representation of objects 'as they really are' accords well with these imperatives. Having limited the imaginative potential of the picturesque vista by metaphorically describing it as a camera obscura, Gilpin turns to a revealing rejection of the riotous extremes of romantic fiction. 'It is thus in writing romances,' he claims: 'The correct taste cannot bear those unnatural situations, in which heroes, and heroines are often placed: whereas a story, *naturally*, and of course *affectingly* told, either with a pen, or a pencil, tho known to be a fiction, is considered as a transcript from nature; and takes possession of the heart.'[139] While the marvellous 'disgusts the sober imagination', the sober heart and mind are 'gratified only with the pure characters of nature'.[140] Like the realist novel, picturesque representation was to be governed by the laws of verisimilitude, keeping forever at bay the marvellous excesses of imaginative fiction.

---

[136] See Malcolm Andrews, *The Search for the Picturesque: Landscape Aesthetics and Tourism in Britain, 1760–1800* (Aldershot: Scolar Press, 1990), pp. 67–73.
[137] Gilpin, *Observations on the River Wye*, p. 52.
[138] Jonathan Crary, *Techniques of the Observer: On Vision and Modernity in the Nineteenth Century* (Cambridge, Mass., and London: MIT Press, 1992), p. 27.
[139] Gilpin, *Three Essays*, p. 53.   [140] Gilpin, *Three Essays*, p. 53.

Perhaps predictably, Gilpin's resistance to associationist aesthetics centred ultimately upon the figure of the ghost, architecturally inspired intimations of the supernatural that, as I have argued in this chapter, had played an important role in associationist thought at least since Addison's critique of Locke in 1711. Gilpin's responses to the ruined Gothic castle at Donnington, Berkshire, in his *Observations on the River Wye* occasioned musings on the place of the supernatural within picturesque composition more generally. Through reference to the *Aeneid* (29-19 BC), he argued that classical culture made recourse to the supernatural and other 'awful imaginings' only as a way of compensating for a building's profound lack of original beauty. 'In Virgil's days', the argument goes, 'the Tarpeian rock was graced by the grandeur of the capitol', and both were 'sufficiently enobled [sic]'.[141] Prior to this, however, the scene 'wanted something to give it splendor [sic]', and as if as a means of supplementing this lack of picturesque potential, Virgil 'therefore has judiciously added a few ideas of the awful kind; and has contrived by this machinery to impress it with more dignity in it's [sic] rude state, than it possessed in its adorned one'.[142] The tawdry thrills of the sublime, in other words, mask, but also in their very presence disclose, the absence of true picturesque beauty. Ghosts, spectres, and other such phantoms thus have no place within the frame of a scene that is truly and authentically picturesque, for as Gilpin unequivocally puts it, 'Of these imaginary beings the painter, in the mean time, makes little use. The introduction of them, instead of raising, would depreciate his subject.'[143] The camera obscura ought to remain clearly differentiated from the magic-lantern show: while the former was the empirically reliable means through which one could appreciate and then pictorially render the Gothic ruins in a picturesque landscape, the latter, like modern romance, was a dangerous technology designed for the conjuring up of ghosts, goblins, and other phantasmagorical beings.

William Beckford's Architectural Imagination

Of all writers on architectural matters in the late eighteenth and early nineteenth centuries, it was undoubtedly William Beckford who occupied the most complex, vexed, and often surprising relation to the aesthetics of architectural associationism. From his early travel writing of the late 1770s through to his later publications of the mid-1830s, Beckford's oeuvre attests to a number of notable shifts and unexpected turns whenever matters of the architectural imagination are concerned. Though he was profoundly influenced by the associationist paradigm,

---

[141] Gilpin, *Observations on the River Wye*, p. 97.
[142] Gilpin, *Observations on the River Wye*, p. 97.
[143] Gilpin, *Observations on the River Wye*, p. 97.

he also effected a crucial shift away from the empiricism of eighteenth-century aesthetics towards a more creative, active, and generative understanding of the architectural imagination. This coincided with a lifelong process in which Beckford eventually came to decry, censure, and censor the imaginative reveries of his youth, a process that relied in part upon a rejection of Gothic-architectural fancy and the embrace of the more 'mature' visions of the classical style.

In response to the observation that his work at Lansdown Tower, Bath, attested to his skills as an 'able architect', Beckford, in conversation with an unnamed friend towards the end of his life, famously replied, 'I ought to know something about it... for I was a pupil of Sir W. Chambers when he had been building Somerset House.'[144] This posthumously recollected detail was subsequently written into Beckfordian biography, and, in *The Life and Letters of William Beckford of Fonthill* (1910), Lewis Melville noted that, in addition to having been tutored by Mozart, the adolescent Beckford enjoyed the architectural instruction of William Chambers.[145] Although James Lees-Milne doubted the veracity of these claims in *William Beckford* (1976), Robert J. Gemmett has recently vouched for the relationship between the two men, founding his claims on the presentation copy of Chambers's *Dissertation on Oriental Gardening* that Beckford owned.[146]

What is less debatable is the extent to which the young Beckford, like Ann Radcliffe later, defied the chaste and rational classicism of aestheticians such as Gerard and Chambers in seeing in the Gothic ruins and edifices of England's cathedrals extraordinary potential for associative reverie. His early manuscript *Fragments of an English Tour* (1779), a diary of the tour through parts of England that he made with his tutor John Lettice in the summer of that year, includes a compelling description of his flight of fancy within the darkened interior of York Minster, York, in September 1779.[147] 'Seized', bewildered, and 'lost' in the vastness and architectural detail of the darkened cathedral, Beckford in his description recalls Walpole's account of the imaginative powers of Gothic architecture in the *Anecdotes*: Beckford too is 'absorbed' in 'a train of legendary Ideas' and 'quite transported' beyond the present 'to those Regions inhabited by the Saints whose Images appeared glowing between every Arch and terminating every Aile [sic]'.[148] His attention 'fixed' by the sight of the cathedral's Great East Window, he is even more astonished by the 'apparition' that the window's reflection casts upon the

---

[144] Anon., 'Conversations with the Late W. Beckford, Esq. No. V', *The New Monthly Magazine and Humorist*, part 3 (1844): pp. 418–27 (p. 419).

[145] Lewis Melville, *The Life and Letters of William Beckford of Fonthill* (London: William Heinemann, 1910), p. 18.

[146] Robert J. Gemmett, *William Beckford's Fonthill: Architecture, Landscape and the Arts* (Oxford and Charleston, SC: Fonthill Media Limited, 2016), p. 24.

[147] William Beckford, *Fragments of an English Tour* (1779), Bodleian Library, Oxford, MS Beckford d.3, fols 10–18 (fol. 10).

[148] Beckford, *Fragments of an English Tour*, fol. 10.

screen. Standing alone in the gloom, it would appear that Beckford has no alternative but to abandon himself to reveries involving not religious awe and devotion but visions of the ghosts of the cathedral's founders:

> There was some thing so strange and mysterious in these Galleries that I almost imagined the holy Spirits of the Founders of the Pile still loved to linger in their Recesses. Impressed with this Idea I remained a long while beneath the Tower wishing every Instant some Form might look over the Parapet of the Galleries or some Voice be heard calling to me from their Shades.[149]

Though he receives neither intelligence nor admonition from these imagined beings, Beckford leaves York Minster convinced of the fact that 'they reigned profoundly throughout the whole Structure'; retreating 'under some sense of unworthiness', he leaves the ghostly 'revered Founders' to 'sleep in peace'.[150]

This is by no means the only scene of architectural reverie in *Fragments of an English Tour*. Yet it was in his printed but subsequently suppressed travelogue *Dreams, Waking Thoughts, and Incidents* (1783) that Beckford gave full and somewhat audacious expression to his predisposition towards imaginative architectural response. The often-quoted opening to *Dreams* figures the young author as one who is habitually lost within a miasma-like cloud of waking fancy: 'Shall I tell you my dreams?—To give an account of my time, is doing, I assure you, but little better. Never did there exist a more ideal being. A frequent mist hovers before my eyes, and, through its medium, I see objects so faint and hazy, that both their colours and forms are apt to delude me.'[151] As it turns out, these delusions come most frequently to the fore when Beckford responds to buildings in states of both completion and ruin, a tendency that makes of the entire travelogue a record of the architectural associations that the young man indulged in on his grand tour from England, through Holland and Germany, to Italy. As he later declared, this attitude towards architecture was somewhat of a self-consciously cultivated pose, one that, as in the case of Walpole, was defiantly opposed to the dry, scientific pretensions of the antiquarian method: 'I absolutely will have no antiquary to go prating from fragment to fragment,' he expostulated in Rome; 'The thought alone is quite distracting, and makes me resolve to view nothing at all in a scientific way; but struggle and wander about, just as the spirit chuses [*sic*].'[152] Accordingly, the language of associationism permeates the travelogue throughout, whether in his references to his 'visionary way of gazing' at buildings, the 'phantoms', 'exotic fancies', and 'extravagant reveries' that they provoke, or the 'train of romantic

---

[149] Beckford, *Fragments of an English Tour*, fols 12–13.
[150] Beckford, *Fragments of an English Tour*, fol. 13.
[151] William Beckford, *Dreams, Waking Thoughts, and Incidents, In a Series of Letters, from Various Parts of Europe* (London: Printed for J. Johnson and P. Elmsly, 1783), p. 1.
[152] Beckford, *Dreams, Waking Thoughts, and Incidents*, p. 204.

associations' set in play in his mind by his perceptions of architectural space, both at home and abroad.[153]

As these phrases suggest, Beckford seemed to be flouting his tutor Chambers's advice concerning the moderation and chastity of imaginative architectural response. Indeed, the first recorded reverie in *Dreams* not only returns to the wild, Gothic reverie of his earlier *Fragments of an English Tour*, but also appears defiantly to delight in precisely those 'indecent attitudes, distorted features, and all kinds of monstrous and horrid productions' that Chambers had identified 'in the works of the Goths'.[154] Visiting Canterbury Cathedral in June 1780 prior to setting off for the Continent, Beckford claims that 'I have always venerated its lofty pillars, dim ailes [sic], and mysterious arches.'[155] Within its deserted interiors, he engages in a flight of fancy that is characterized here, as at York, more by terrifying thoughts of ghosts than any sombre act of religious contemplation. Looking over his shoulder, he thinks of 'spectres that have an awkward trick of syllabling men's names in dreary places', imagining a 'sepulchral voice' that intones the Catholic creed of saints' relics.[156] As he is well aware, these visions are nothing but the 'horrors' that the 'deep-vaulted tombs, and pale, though lovely figures extended upon them' have incited.[157] Still, they provide some measure of defence against the tribulations of European travel, and later in the journey Beckford, bored and unstimulated by the architecture of Germany, consoles himself with his mind's abilities to people even the most uninspiring of landscapes and buildings with 'phantoms'.[158]

Beckford's *Dreams, Waking Thoughts, and Incidents* contains several notable dismissals of the Gothic style, a fact that seems difficult to reconcile with the Gothic turn that his tastes would take at Fonthill Abbey from 1796 onwards. In Verona, for instance, he juxtaposes the 'gothic violence' of architectural demolition with the elegance of classical antiquities, while later he rejects the Italian architecture of the Middle Ages in favour of Renaissance classicism.[159] If Gothic fortresses were the shameful testament to violence and tyranny, so the 'antient gothic buildings' of an ecclesiastical function 'were nothing but long, dark, and massive vaults, without the least ornament, or beauty'.[160] Accordingly, the text is eloquent on the beauties of Italian classical architecture, splendours that range from the 'genius' of Palladio and Sansovino at Venice, through the 'variety of pillars, of pediments, of mouldings, and cornices' of the city in general, to the façade of San Giorgio Maggiore, 'by far the most perfect and beautiful edifice any

---

[153] Beckford, *Dreams, Waking Thoughts, and Incidents*, pp. 2, 3, 18, 41, 75.
[154] Chambers, *A Treatise on Civil Architecture*, p. 37.
[155] Beckford, *Dreams, Waking Thoughts, and Incidents*, p. 2.
[156] Beckford, *Dreams, Waking Thoughts, and Incidents*, pp. 2–3.
[157] Beckford, *Dreams, Waking Thoughts, and Incidents*, p. 3.
[158] Beckford, *Dreams, Waking Thoughts, and Incidents*, p. 56.
[159] Beckford, *Dreams, Waking Thoughts, and Incidents*, pp. 139, 273.
[160] Beckford, *Dreams, Waking Thoughts, and Incidents*, p. 273.

eyes ever beheld'.[161] But this is not to suggest that the travelogue is structured by that insuperable distinction between the classical and the Gothic that informed the architectural writings of most of his contemporaries. Instead, Beckford's early architectural imagination relies upon a more general and accommodating difference between classical and 'non-Classical' styles, the latter a particularly capacious category that included the Gothic, the Chinese, and the Oriental more generally.

An architectural enthusiast of particular versatility, Beckford in the *Dreams* is stirred by buildings and ruins in both the classical and Gothic styles. The Venetian Gothic of the Doge's Palace in Venice, for instance, provokes an associative train that, with hindsight, reads like a mental 'romance' in the tradition of Radcliffe. Contemplating the gruesome modes of imprisonment and torture that the notorious Council of Ten were reputed to impose, Beckford imagines beneath the Palace 'secret recesses of punishment' sunk deep beneath the city's canals, 'damp and gloomy caverns, whose inhabitants waste away by painful degrees, and feel themselves whole years a dying'.[162] Overcome by the 'Horrors and dismal prospects' conjured up by his imagination, he hastily returns to his place of residence, yet still 'haunted by fancy' he takes his pencil in hand, as if under a strange compulsion, to draw images of 'chasms and subterraneous hollows, the domain of fear and torture, with chains, rocks, wheels, and dreadful engines in the style of Piranesi'.[163] Beckford's associative responses to the Doge's Palace are informed by his familiarity with Giovanni Battista Piranesi's *Le Carceri d'Invenzione* (1750), a sixteen-print series of *capriccios* detailing entirely imaginary prisons. But he is equally stirred by the 'beautiful symmetry' of classical form, such as he encounters at the colonnade of St Peter's Square before the Basilica in Rome.[164] Within St Peter's by night, he marvels at the accoutrements of Catholic worship not in any religious sense, but is rather imaginatively 'transported' through them to a place he 'knew not where'.[165] A similar secular and aesthetic response to elements of originally religious significance characterizes his 'An Excursion to the Grand Chartreuse, in the Year 1778', the travelogue appended to *Dreams*. Seeking to enhance the imaginative appeal of the Basilica of St Peter's, Beckford contemplates refurnishing its interiors through the addition of transparent curtains of yellow silk for the windows, and innumerable lanterns in the Chinese style. So absorbed is he in the construction and embellishment of this 'imaginary palace' that he declares himself to have 'no spirits left for the Pantheon', the next stop on his Roman itinerary.[166] At the Pantheon, though, he is effortlessly transported back 'into antiquity', a time when 'the Pagan gods were in their niches' and the saints of

---

[161] Beckford, *Dreams, Waking Thoughts, and Incidents*, pp. 91, 87, 90.
[162] Beckford, *Dreams, Waking Thoughts, and Incidents*, p. 106.
[163] Beckford, *Dreams, Waking Thoughts, and Incidents*, p. 107.
[164] Beckford, *Dreams, Waking Thoughts, and Incidents*, p. 200.
[165] Beckford, *Dreams, Waking Thoughts, and Incidents*, p. 200.
[166] Beckford, *Dreams, Waking Thoughts, and Incidents*, p. 202.

Catholicism 'out of the question'.[167] Predictably, it is in the Colosseum that Beckford's associative imagination is particularly engaged, for here 'Many stories of antient Rome thronged into my mind,' he writes, the ruins calling up associations of elaborate scenes of triumph and despair, victory and defeat, as warriors, loaded with all manner of strange spoils, return from Parthian expeditions to great acclamation and praise.[168] As they do later at Pompeii, the associations that accrete for Beckford in Italy are gleaned primarily from a familiarity with classical myth and literature. In the potential for imaginative reverie that it extracts from both the classical and the Gothic styles, Beckford's architectural imagination is far more versatile than that of Walpole.

The architectural reveries of *Dreams, Waking Thoughts, and Incidents* were not to be published until many years after Beckford's death, and critics have long conjectured as to the reasoning behind the last-minute suppression of the text. As Brian Fothergill has observed, the motion was spearheaded by the once-supportive Lettice and endorsed by Beckford's mother and other members of the family, who held that the young man's bold descriptions of his waking dreams were inappropriate for one who was destined for a career in politics.[169] This, together with the rumours surrounding Beckford's inappropriate relationships with the young William Courtenay and his married cousin Louisa Beckford, demanded urgent intervention. Preoccupied at this time with the writing of what would become known as *Vathek*, Beckford duly capitulated and was hastily ushered into a marriage with Lady Margaret Gordon. Much later in life, though, he published a thoroughly edited, expurgated, and revised account of his grand tour in the two-volume *Italy; With Sketches of Spain and Portugal* (1834). An image from the opening page of Beckford's own copy of *Dreams* indicates the ruthlessness with which he approached the process of editing while reworking the earlier text for publication (see Figure 1.3).

What is notable about *Italy* is the pains that it takes to censure, discipline, and control the architectural imagination of the younger man, a faculty, he now claims, that belonged to 'the bloom and heyday of youthful spirits and youthful confidence, at a period when the old order of things existed with all its picturesque pomps and absurdities'.[170] Substituting romance for the more objective 'delineations of landscape', the first volume of *Italy* is stripped of all the architectural reveries of *Dreams*, including, most notably, the flight of fancy in the darkened interiors of Canterbury Cathedral at the outset of his grand tour.[171] The few waking dreams that remain in the second volume, a collection of letters that

---

[167] Beckford, *Dreams, Waking Thoughts, and Incidents*, p. 202.
[168] Beckford, *Dreams, Waking Thoughts, and Incidents*, pp. 204–5.
[169] Brian Fothergill, *Beckford of Fonthill* (London: Faber & Faber, 1979), pp. 146–7.
[170] William Beckford, *Italy; With Sketches of Spain and Portugal*, 2 vols (London: Richard Bentley, 1834), vol. 1, p. i.
[171] Beckford, *Italy*, vol. 1, p. ii.

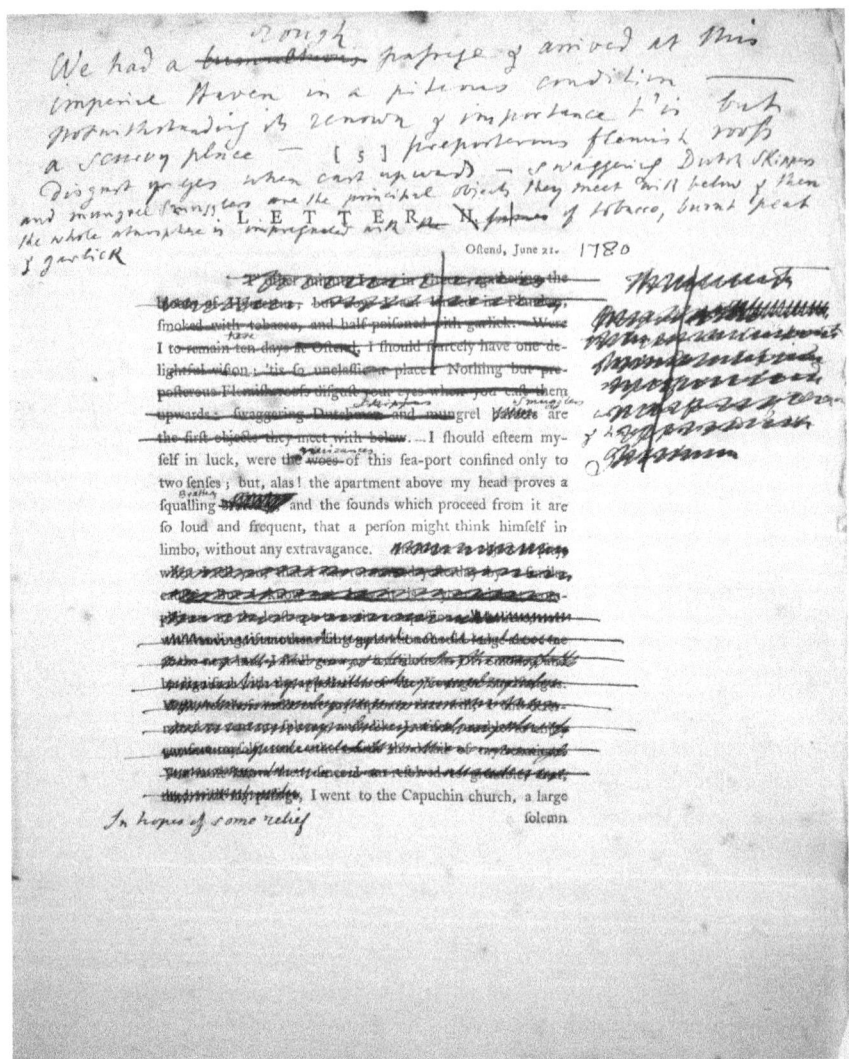

Figure 1.3 William Beckford's editorial marks in his personal copy of *Dreams, Waking Thoughts, and Incidents* (1783). Courtesy of The Bodleian Libraries, The University of Oxford, MS.Beckford.C.41, p. 5.

Beckford had written during a trip to Portugal and Spain in 1787, appear, against the earlier work, to be circumscribed by a strict adherence to the rules of rationality and decorum. For example, although, having observed a Gothic monastery in Belém, Lisbon, Beckford may enthusiastically declare that 'Nothing can be more beautiful as a specimen of elaborate gothic sculpture' than such a 'complicated enamelled mass of flying buttresses and fretted pinnacles', the pile provokes in him no associative flight of fancy—or none, at least, that he chooses to record here.[172] The same applies to his documented experiences of the architecture of Spain. Having drawn a link between architectural association and the juvenile visions of a much younger man, the older Beckford subjects his architectural imagination in *Italy* to a rigorous act of expurgation.

That this was a deliberate and calculated act on Beckford's behalf is clear: the journals from his tour of Portugal and Spain in 1787–8—editions of which Boyd Alexander first published as late as 1954—contain many details that do not feature in the published version. The journal, for instance, records Beckford's reading of Frances Brooke's *The History of Lady Julia Mandeville* (1763), a proto-Gothic tale of suffering and lost love that brings to mind his loss of his wife, Margaret, the year before. 'My imagination soon ceasing to prey on these imaginary horrors', he writes, 'took its flight to Fonthill, and pictured to itself the pale image of my Margaret.'[173] Though he realizes that 'no power can recover' the peaceful hours that he and his wife passed at Vevey, his imagination transports him to Fonthill Splendens as a means of redressing the loss.[174] Some four months later, the same faculty assumes more disturbing, Gothic proportions as his sleep in Portugal is disturbed by a terrifying nightmare:

> I fancied my dear mother was no more, and that a phantom, seizing me by the hair, was transporting me through the clouds to Fonthill, where I beheld her breathless body extended in a gloomy vault. I thought also that my eldest infant lay strangled on the steps which lead down to its dark abode.[175]

Tellingly, not one of these architectural reveries features in the version of the Spanish and Portuguese tour that Beckford published in 1834. This process is repeated in *Recollections of an Excursion to the Monasteries of Alcobaça and Batalha* (1835), a compilation of notes and memories from a trip that Beckford had made to Portugal in June 1794. Here, though, Beckford presents his younger self as one whose tendencies towards Gothic-architectural reverie were continuously thwarted by the demands of a more pressing, not to say quotidian, reality. While, at first sight, the 'regal monastery' of Alcobaça is said to be so 'imposing' as to inspire in the viewer 'a sense of oppression', this response is 'relieved', he claims, by the picturesque scene of its surrounds.[176] Though, like the cathedrals of Canterbury and York, the interior of Alcobaça is candle-lit, gloomy, and pregnant with imaginative potential, he is reminded here, or so the mature writer claims, only of the fact that the Catholic worshippers seemed engaged in the act 'of

---

[172] Beckford, *Italy*, vol. 2, pp. 56–7.
[173] Boyd Alexander, ed., *The Journal of William Beckford in Portugal & Spain, 1787–1788*, 2nd edn (Stroud: Non Such Publishing, 2006), p. 151.
[174] Alexander, ed., *The Journal of William Beckford in Portugal & Spain, 1787–1788*, p. 151.
[175] Alexander, ed., *The Journal of William Beckford in Portugal & Spain, 1787–1788*, p. 164.
[176] William Beckford, *Recollections of an Excursion to the Monasteries of Alcobaça and Batalha* (London: Richard Bentley, 1835), p. 35.

adoring the real Presence'.[177] During a visit to the 'solemn recess' of the monastery's sepulchral Chapter, the architectural associations of the young Beckford return, but 'Just as I was giving way to the affecting reveries which such an object could not fail of exciting in a bosom the least susceptible of romantic impressions,' he writes, 'in came the Grand Priors hand in hand, all three together.'[178] His trance disturbed, Beckford is promptly summoned to the kitchen.

In the more recognizably Gothic surroundings of Batalha, Beckford later in life recalled with obvious fondness 'its rich cluster of abbatial buildings, buttresses, and pinnacles, and fretted spires, towering in all their pride, and marking the ground with deep shadows that appeared interminable'.[179] In these lines alone, he displays a far more refined vocabulary for the description of Gothic architecture than that available to Horace Walpole in the previous century, and one that was seemingly informed by a familiarity with Rickman's work in *An Attempt to Discriminate the Styles of English Architecture*. Throughout, in fact, the *Recollections* are marked by a sophisticated use of architectural terminology, such as in his references to the 'curiously-groined vaulted hall', 'a pierced parapet of the purest Gothic design', or a row of arches that are 'fretted and pinnacled and crocketed in the best style of Gothic at its best period'.[180] While Beckford does recall some of the reveries that Batalha inspired—among them the 'strange jumble of ideas and recollections' that 'fermented in my brain' while he visited there—these are not primarily inspired by Gothic architecture, but rather through such events as the 'spectre-like form' and portentous ravings of the old man in the garden that echo eerily through the monastery's vaults and arches.[181] Not even a performance of a play by Batalha's monks is capable of rousing the romantic predispositions of his youth, a fact that seems all the more surprising in view of the plot's Gothic details: an act of double infanticide, a vision of a ghost, and, in the fifth act, the sentiments of 'horror and terror' being 'worked up to the highest pitch'.[182] Beckford looks on with wry detachment as those around him are moved to tears. Looking back, he remembers at Batalha one potentially imaginative moment when visiting the tombs of King Alfonso V, his grandson Prince Alfonso, and the Infanta of Castile, but here again his guide 'would not allow me even one moment to ruminate and moralize upon vicissitudes and bereavements—they quite urged me along'.[183] As in his revisions to *Dreams, Waking Thoughts, and Incidents* in *Italy*, Beckford excludes an account of his architectural imagination from his final publication. The *Recollections* even register a bold movement away from the appreciation of

---

[177] Beckford, *Recollections of an Excursion to the Monasteries of Alcobaça and Batalha*, p. 36.
[178] Beckford, *Recollections of an Excursion to the Monasteries of Alcobaça and Batalha*, p. 37.
[179] Beckford, *Recollections of an Excursion to the Monasteries of Alcobaça and Batalha*, p. 66.
[180] Beckford, *Recollections of an Excursion to the Monasteries of Alcobaça and Batalha*, pp. 18, 82, 85.
[181] Beckford, *Recollections of an Excursion to the Monasteries of Alcobaça and Batalha*, pp. 71–3.
[182] Beckford, *Recollections of an Excursion to the Monasteries of Alcobaça and Batalha*, p. 113.
[183] Beckford, *Recollections of an Excursion to the Monasteries of Alcobaça and Batalha*, p. 90.

the Gothic style that, as critics have often argued, inspired his Gothic works at Fonthill Abbey: by 1835, Beckford is keen to resist the 'cult' of Batalha by articulating not only some reservations about the Gothic of Don Emanuel's celebrated mausoleum, but also with James Murphy's effusive tribute to it in his *Travels in Portugal* of 1795.[184] Having sold Fonthill and relocated to Bath and the neoclassical designs of Henry Goodridge's Lansdown Tower, the 74-year-old Beckford now cites John Evelyn to reduce the Gothic of Batalha to 'the quips, and cranks, and wanton wiles' of a corrupt, meretricious architecture, to 'Saxon crinklings and cranklings', and 'preposterous long and lanky marrow-spoon-shaped arches of the early Norman' style. Aspiring now towards the classical, Beckford had effected the act of Gothic-architectural renunciation advocated by Akenside in *The Pleasures of Imagination* and, more complexly, Warton in *Verses on Sir Joshua Reynolds's Painted Window at New-College Oxford*.

Perhaps the singularity of Beckford's architectural imagination, then, lies in his remarkable ability to cast up, imagine, and fashion architectural forms that, as the early writings continuously assert, have no concrete existence in the physical, workaday world of reality at all, but which remain, of necessity, bound within the order of the imagination. There are certainly strong intimations of these fantasies in such early works as 'The Long Story', a text that was published as *The Vision* in 1930, and written by the then 17-year-old Beckford for his friend and tutor Alexander Cozens in *c*.1777 while he was abroad in Switzerland. It is during a trip to the mysterious centres of the earth that the first-person narrator, at one point identified as 'William', encounters the weird, unfathomable architecture of the Halls of the Glorious, a strange yet sublime compound of nature and art, but neither fully one nor the other, and comprising a dazzling colonnade of crystal pillars that 'supported neither frieze nor Cornice, nor any ornament in the least degree consistent with the rules of Architecture we observe on the surface of the earth, but sustained on the airy Capitals a variety of glistening Garlands composed of Sparrs and intermixed like the branches which form our Bowers'.[185] 'Figure to yourself', he advises Cozens,

> a variety of marble agates jaspers and other stones some of which you are utterly unacquainted with, all painted by the hand of nature with an infinity of elegant veins, all gleaming with the polish of a Mirror and reflecting every object in the same manner. Mark how the pavement, like a Lake of marble extends amongst this spacious Labyrinth of Columns as far as your Eye can reach, deny, if you are able the beauty of the Scene.[186]

---

[184] On the importance of Batalha to the early Gothic Revival, see John Frew and Carey Wallace, 'Thomas Pitt, Portugal and the Gothic Cult of Batalha', *The Burlington Magazine* vol. 128, no. 1001 (August 1986), pp. 579–85.
[185] William Beckford, *The Long Story* (*c*.1777), Bodleian Library, Oxford, MS. Beckford *c*. 46, fol. 35.
[186] Beckford, *The Long Story*, fol. 35.

This, like all the architectural structures in 'The Vision', is pure architectural fantasy: fanciful, fantastical, and physically impossible, it is a jarring assemblage of strange components 'as no human Language can describe'.[187] There are other examples of such imaginary architectures in Beckford's early work, the most well known of which occurs in his unpublished 'The Transport of Pleasure' of c.1777–8, the manuscript that Boyd Alexander entitled 'Fonthill Foreshadowed' in his study *England's Wealthiest Son* of 1962.[188] Similarly addressed to Cozens, it details a fantasy of pleasurable intellectual and sensual seclusion in a luxurious, hill-poised Gothic tower situated alongside an adjoining, highly orientalized house. Like 'The Vision', it prophetically anticipates the turns that the author's architectural imagination would take, not only in the Gothic–Oriental hybrid of *Vathek*, but also his work with James Wyatt at Fonthill. Similar references to imaginary orders of architecture that are yet to be conceived, identified, and named as such run throughout *Vathek*, particularly in the unfathomable and imposing Halls of Eblis, and in the accompanying *Episodes*.[189] Keen, from its earliest manifestations, to move beyond the empiricist underpinnings of associationist aesthetics and into what Immanuel Kant in the *Critique of Pure Reason* (1781) would call the 'productive imagination', Beckford's architectural idealism is a faculty that, like Shakespeare's Prospero in *The Tempest*, is capable of conjuring up 'cloud-capped towers' and 'gorgeous palaces' out of nothing.[190] It is to the charting of a similar movement in the literary and architectural work of Horace Walpole that the next chapter turns.

---

[187] Beckford, *The Long Story*, fol. 51.
[188] See William Beckford, *Fonthill Foreshadowed* (c.1777–8), Bodleian Library, Oxford, MS Beckford d. 9.
[189] For more on this, see Peter N. Lindfield and Dale Townshend, 'Reading *Vathek* and Fonthill Abbey: William Beckford's Architectural Imagination', in *Fonthill Recovered: A Cultural History*, ed. Caroline Dakers (London: UCL Press, 2018), pp. 284–301.
[190] Immanuel Kant, *The Critique of Pure Reason*, trans. and ed. Paul Guyer and Allan W. Wood (Cambridge: Cambridge University Press, 2000), pp. 238–40.

2
Horace Walpole's Enchanted Castles

Given the vehemence with which Horace Walpole extolled the vast imaginative potential of Gothic architecture, it seems surprising that *The Castle of Otranto, A Story*, his literary experiment that was first published anonymously by Thomas Lowndes in London on 24 December 1764, contains very little by way of architectural description at all. Instead, with the adjective 'Gothic' absent not only from the novel's title but from the body of the text, too, the first edition of *Otranto* required of its readers a gesture of architectural association, one that sutured the word 'Castle' in the title to the evocations of an ancient, benighted, or 'Gothic' past in such phrases from the Preface as 'the darkest ages of christianity', 'the empire of superstition', and the 'ancient errors and superstitions' of the 'artful priest'.[1] Through this process of prompted association, together with subsequent references in the narrative to a chapel, a vault, subterraneous passages, an oratory, a black tower, a postern gate, battlements, an oriel window, and other features of the architecture of the Middle Ages, the Castle of Otranto assumes 'Gothic' properties, but beyond this, architectural description in *The Castle of Otranto* is scant. Perhaps, as Walpole saw it, these markers of the Gothic were sufficient to provoke in the reader the rich imaginative associations that he had praised elsewhere. Though the narrative references an assortment of rooms, chambers, courtyards, passages, vaults, galleries, and adjoining ecclesiastical buildings, these never ultimately combine into a coherent and easily navigable sense of space. Within Walpole's fictional castle, we might say, the architecture is as fractured and lacking in coherence as the body of the giant that comes to inhabit it.

This aspect of the novel amounted to a literary manifestation of what Walpole termed '*Sharawaggi*', the principle of irregularity and asymmetry that he identified in Chinese architecture and landscape gardening more generally. Explaining the virtues of the Gothic style to a resistant Horace Mann in February 1750, Walpole, through recourse to the familiar classical/Gothic divide, glossed '*Sharawaggi*' as the 'Chinese want of symmetry, in buildings, as in grounds or gardens'.[2] In England, the concept went as far back as William Temple's account of '*Sharawadgi*', the

---

[1] Walpole, *The Castle of Otranto*, p. 5.
[2] Horace Walpole to Horace Mann, 25 February 1750, *Correspondence*, vol. 20, p. 127. For an account of Walpole's turning away from fashionable chinoiserie in favour of the Gothic, see David Porter, 'From Chinese to Goth: Walpole and the Repudiation of Chinoiserie', *Eighteenth-Century Life* vol. 23, no. 1 (February 1999): pp. 46–58.

Gothic Antiquity: History, Romance, and the Architectural Imagination, 1760–1840. Dale Townshend, Oxford University Press (2019). © Dale Townshend.
DOI: 10.1093/oso/9780198845669.001.0001

beauty of studied irregularity in Chinese gardening practices, in his essay 'Upon the Gardens of Epicurus' (1685);[3] during the eighteenth century, it was invoked by such writers on architecture and landscape gardening as William Shenstone, Alexander Pope, and Walpole himself. For Matthew M. Reeve, this 'want of symmetry' in *The Castle of Otranto*'s architecture found its real-life counterpart in the 'double' that was Walpole's architectural project at Strawberry Hill, a structure that, like the fiction that it is often said to have inspired, deliberately trafficked in the ambiguous, the unfamiliar, and the labyrinthine as an assault upon, and refreshing alternative to, the clear lines and symmetries of the prevailing Palladian style.[4] Certainly, and as Marion Harney has pointed out, Walpole seemed particularly dissatisfied with his father's Palladian house at Houghton Hall, Norfolk, a structure to which he repeatedly referred in tones of 'contempt and disdain' in his letters.[5] Other critics, such as Timothy Mowl, George E. Haggerty, and Reeve elsewhere have identified in Walpole's attraction to the irregularity of the Gothic intimations of a complex and non-normative sexuality, seeing, as Lytton Strachey did, something decidedly 'queer' about his architectural tastes.[6] 'He liked Gothic architecture, not because he thought it beautiful', wrote the knowing Strachey, 'but because he found it queer; and accordingly the Gothic castles (whether of Otranto or of Strawberry) which he himself constructed, were more remarkable for their queerness than for their beauty.'[7] House and novel are yoked together as mutually compatible yet no doubt highly encoded expressions of non-heteronormative sexuality. Walpole himself certainly conceptualized architecture in gendered if not overly sexual terms. As he argued in the fourth volume of *Anecdotes of Painting in England* (dated 1771; published 1780), 'Architecture indeed, has in a manner two sexes; its masculine dignity can only exert its muscles in public works and at public expense: its softer beauties come better within the compass of private residence and enjoyment.'[8] A feminine 'private residence' built in the masculine style of castles, abbeys, and other 'public works', Strawberry Hill, by Walpole's own definition, was androgynous and indeterminate, simultaneously male and female though neither fully one nor the other.

What I wish to revisit in this chapter is the long-held critical assumption—one certainly initiated and fostered by Walpole and one still present in a number of

---

[3] See Temple, *Miscellanea*, p. 132.
[4] See Matthew M. Reeve's argument in '"A Gothic Vatican of Greece and Rome": Horace Walpole, Strawberry Hill, and the Narratives of Gothic', pp. 185–209.
[5] Harney, *Place-making for the Imagination*, pp. 22–3.
[6] For such queer-theoretical readings of Walpole's interest in the Gothic style, see Timothy Mowl's argument in *Horace Walpole, the Great Outsider* (London: John Murray, 1996); George E. Haggerty, 'Strawberry Hill: Friendship and Taste', in *Horace Walpole's Strawberry Hill*, ed. Michael Snodin with the assistance of Cynthia Roman (New Haven and London: Yale University Press, 2009), pp. 75–85; and Matthew M. Reeve, 'Gothic Architecture, Sexuality, and License at Horace Walpole's Strawberry Hill', *Art Bulletin* 95, no. 3 (September 2013): pp. 411–39.
[7] Lytton Strachey, *Characters and Commentaries* (New York: Harcourt, Brace and Co., 1933), p. 39.
[8] Walpole, *Anecdotes of Painting in England*, vol. 4, p. vi.

recent studies—that the Castle of Otranto as it features in Walpole's Gothic narrative is, indeed, based on the author's Gothic Revivalist architectural work at Strawberry Hill. The matter is of such significance because it lies at the heart of how critics have most often accounted for the relationship between Gothic architecture and Gothic fiction in the eighteenth century. Though apparently natural and self-evident, these presumed links between the textual and the architectural have a complex history. At the very least, the tendency to tie a writer and his or her works back to the house in which they were produced is, as Susan Bernstein has argued, one of the 'unexamined fantasies of historicism', the residual trace of a Romantic criticism that seeks to return the work of literature to the original genius that produced it, as if this act of architectural attribution were somehow capable of mastering the play of unruly textuality.[9] As I seek to show, however, Walpole's real and fictional houses relate to one another not through any simple process in which the architectural patron-turned-author 'wrote' the real Strawberry Hill into the imaginary architecture of Otranto, nor how *The Castle of Otranto* might be explained in and through reference to Walpole's house, but rather, less directly, through the author's lifelong investment in the architecture of romance that influenced and determined the creation of both fiction and home. That is, while there is certainly much to be said about the relationship between Strawberry Hill and the fictional Otranto as architectural structures, this derives, I argue below, not from any simple return of the architecture of the house in the architecture of the novel, but rather from the romance-derived trope of the enchanted castle that featured so prominently in the literature and correspondence that were generated in relation to both.

Otranto's Shifting Foundations

The question of the 'real' castle behind *The Castle of Otranto* has long engaged readers and critics in a game of ever-shifting origins. In early January 1765, George Montagu suggested as much when, in a letter of thanks for the copy of the text that Walpole had sent him on the day on which *Otranto* had famously lost its 'maidenhead', he wrote, 'Let me hear what is said of it; it will puzzle and must please.' The puzzle, it is clear, pertained partly to the fiction's relation to Walpole's home, for as Montagu, having recently read the narrative, continued, 'I fancy you found your own castle of Strawberry very cold and comfortless.'[10] Montagu's sense of puzzlement had good cause, for, while protecting Walpole's anonymity and maintaining his guise as the translator William Marshal, the Preface to the first

---

[9] Susan Bernstein, *Housing Problems: Writing and Architecture in Goethe, Walpole, Freud, and Heidegger* (Stanford, CA: Stanford University Press, 2008), p. 3.
[10] George Montagu to Horace Walpole, 3 January 1765, *Correspondence*, vol. 10, p. 146.

edition of the novel teased its readers with the suggestion that the Castle of Otranto was based upon a 'real' and 'particular' architectural structure. 'The scene', Marshal in that well-known passage writes,

> is undoubtedly laid in some real castle. The author seems frequently, without design, to describe particular parts. *The chamber*, says he, *on the right hand; the door on the left hand; the distance from the chapel to Conrad's apartment*: these and other passages are strong presumptions that the author had some certain building in his eye.[11]

Like the device of the discovered document, the suggestion that a castle 'like' Otranto actually existed added to the fiction an air of antiquarian authenticity. Following Walpole's disclosure of his authorship of the text merely through the inclusion of the initials 'H. W.' beneath the dedicatory sonnet to Lady Mary Coke in the second edition of *The Castle of Otranto, A Gothic Story* in April 1765, the first Preface's claim to the fictional castle's 'real' and 'particular' antecedents inevitably pointed readers directly to Walpole's own 'Gothic Castle' at Strawberry Hill, the residence that he had been conscientiously Gothicizing since buying the lease to Chopp'd Straw Hall in 1749. Such was Walpole's literary and architectural fame by 1765 that readers could not but connect the fiction and the house with one another.

Although the Preface to the second edition of *Otranto* does not pursue the matter of the 'real' structure behind the Castle of Otranto any further, visitors to Strawberry Hill after 1765 frequently claimed to see in its towers and battlements the real-life inspiration for Walpole's novel. As Emma McEvoy has pointed out, the literary meanings of the building, though certainly in place earlier, 'changed' considerably following Walpole's disclosure of authorship, with Strawberry Hill from this moment onwards entering into 'an interesting symbiotic relationship' with the novel that it was thought to have inspired.[12] Frances Burney's description of a visit that she and her father made to Strawberry in September 1785 is perhaps the most illustrative of these presumed correspondences: the 'deep shade in which some of his antique portraits were placed', Burney notes, 'and the lone sort of look of the unusually shaped apartments in which they were hung', brought to the mind of the visitors 'striking recollections' of 'his Gothic story of the Castle of Otranto'.[13] Walpole playfully entered into the spirit in letters to his close friends, writing from Strawberry Hill to Horace Mann in November 1771 that 'I myself

---

[11] Walpole, *The Castle of Otranto*, p. 7.
[12] Emma McEvoy, *Gothic Tourism* (Basingstoke: Palgrave Macmillan, 2016), p. 43.
[13] Madame d'Arblay [Frances Burney], *Memoirs of Doctor Burney, Arranged from his own Manuscripts, from Family Papers, and from Personal Recollections*, 3 vols (London: Edward Moxon, 1832), vol. 3, p. 66. Burney, here, misremembers the year that she and her father visited Strawberry Hill, claiming that it was in 1786. However, a letter from Walpole to Charles Burney on Tuesday, 6 September 1785, makes clear the actual year. See Walpole's *Correspondence*, vol. 42, pp. 149–50.

expect a treasure tomorrow, a complete suit of armour of Francis the First, which I have bought out of the Crozat collection. It will make a great figure here at Otranto.'[14] Satirically figured by Thomas Chatterton as 'Baron Otranto' in *The Town and Country Magazine* in 1769, Walpole, his Gothic story, and his Gothic Revival home at Strawberry Hill became synonymous with one another in the last three decades of the eighteenth century.[15]

As the increasing levels of reference to *Otranto* perceivable across the 1774 and 1784 editions of *A Description of the Villa of Horace Walpole* indicate, Walpole himself, over time, came to emphasize the connections between his 'real' and fictional castles.[16] Apart from a reference in the appendix to Lavinia Bingham's picture of a young lady reading *Otranto* to her companion, the first edition of *A Description* contains no other reference to Walpole's narrative.[17] To the second, expanded, and illustrated edition of 1784, however, Walpole added a Preface that included a wry and defensive jibe directed at those 'who might be disposed to condemn the fantastic fabric' of Strawberry Hill, as, at once, the 'very proper habitation of' and the 'scene that inspired' the author of *The Castle of Otranto*.[18] In addition to listing Bingham's picture, the second edition of *A Description* annotated, here for the first time, Marcus Gheeraerts the Younger's portrait (c.1603) of Henry Cary, 1st Viscount Falkland, that hung in the Gallery at Strawberry Hill with the note that 'The idea of the picture walking out of its frame in the Castle of Otranto was suggested by this portrait.'[19] In a supplement entitled 'Curiosities added since this Book was compleated [*sic*]', the 1784 edition also included mention of Lady Craven's gift, 'A view of the Castle of Otranto as it really exists, a washed drawing', and in a section entitled 'More Additions', the watercolour 'Procession in Castle of Otranto, by J[ohn] Carter' that I addressed in the Introduction.[20] As Stephen Clarke has pointed out, *A Description*, while printed, was never published, was not distributed to visitors to Strawberry Hill, and did not, strictly speaking, serve as a guidebook to the house at all.[21] Instead, it

---

[14] Horace Walpole to Horace Mann, 18 November 1771, *Correspondence*, vol. 23, p. 350.

[15] See the satirical portrait of Walpole in 'Baron Otranto and Mrs Heidelburgh' in *The Town and Country Magazine; or, Universal Repository of Knowledge, Instruction, and Entertainments* I (December 1769), pp. 617–20.

[16] For an exacting account of the complex bibliographic history of Walpole's *Description*, see Stephen Clarke, '"Lord God! Jesus! What a House!": Describing and Visiting Strawberry Hill', *Journal for Eighteenth-Century Studies* vol. 33, no. 1 (2010): pp. 357–80.

[17] Horace Walpole, *A Description of the Villa of Horace Walpole, Youngest Son of Sir Robert Walpole Earl of Orford, at Strawberry-Hill, Near Twickenham. With an Inventory of the Furniture, Pictures, Curiosities, &c.* (Strawberry Hill: Printed by Thomas Kirgate, 1774), p. 131.

[18] Horace Walpole, *A Description of the Villa of Horace Walpole, Youngest Son of Sir Robert Walpole Earl of Orford, at Strawberry-Hill, Near Twickenham. With an Inventory of the Furniture, Pictures, Curiosities, &c.*, 2nd edn (Strawberry Hill: Printed by Thomas Kirgate, 1784), p. iv.

[19] Walpole, *A Description of the Villa of Horace Walpole* (1784), p. 51. Walpole erroneously attributes this portrait to Paul van Somer.

[20] Walpole, *A Description of the Villa of Horace Walpole* (1784), pp. 94–5.

[21] Clarke, '"Lord God! Jesus! What a House!"', pp. 358–60.

was a text such as the unique Eton copy, entitled *Catalogue for Shewing [sic] the House* and written in Thomas Kirgate's hand, that in all likelihood was consulted by Walpole's servants when guiding ticket-holding visitors through carefully selected portions of Strawberry Hill.[22] By contrast, *A Description* was produced partly as a gift for a select group of friends, but also as a means of ordering, curating, and preserving for posterity the record of Walpole's collections; as such, it had a surprisingly limited circulation during Walpole's lifetime. Nonetheless, it did urge those for whom it was intended to engage with the building through the fictional lens of *The Castle of Otranto*, pointing out references to the novel in the structure and contents of house as it did so. Such were the commonplace associations between the writer's 'Gothic Story' and his 'little Gothic Castle' that were canonized in the slightly amended reprint of the 1784 edition of *A Description* that was published in Walpole's posthumous *Works* in 1798.[23]

That the southern Italian town of Otranto, Lecce, was, and still is, home to an imposing eleventh-century Gothic castle, the Castello di Otranto, initially seemed to have escaped the fiction's author and earliest readers alike. When, as late as November 1786, Lady Elizabeth Craven presented him with a watercolour of the south-west view of the Castle of Otranto in Italy, a 271-by-511-mm painting that had been rendered on site by Willey Reveley in 1785, a delighted but also partly embarrassed Walpole acknowledged the gift with a startling disclosure: 'I did not even know that there was a Castle of Otranto'; 'When the story was finished, I looked into the map of the kingdom of Naples for a well-sounding name, and that of Otranto was very sonorous' (see Figure 2.1).[24] In January 1788, some fourteen months later, Walpole wrote to Sir William Hamilton, the British ambassador to the Spanish court at Naples, to ascertain whether the picture was merely a case of flattery on Lady Craven's behalf, or whether a castle at Otranto corresponding 'so very well with the circumstances of the narrative' did, indeed, exist. Hamilton's reply was unambiguous and curt: 'Dear Sir, You may be very sure that the Castle of Otranto does exist and is not a castle in the air.'[25] Initially located in the 'real' and 'particular' Gothic castle at Strawberry Hill, the foundations of the text had been swiftly displaced by an image that suggested a different, though, given Walpole's ignorance about its existence, ultimately improbable, point of origin in the Castello di Otranto in southern Italy.

Reveley's painting was subsequently copied by John Carter in the watercolour *South View of the Castle of Otranto with the Acroceraunian Mountains of Epirus in the Distance* (see Figure 2.2). Copies of Carter's image, in turn, were included in

---

[22] See Anna Chalcraft and Judith Viscardi, *Visiting Strawberry Hill: An Analysis of the Eton Copy of 'The Description of the Villa'* (Wimbledon: Chalcraft & Viscardi, 2005).
[23] Walpole, *The Works of Horatio Walpole*, vol. 2, p. 396.
[24] Horace Walpole to Lady Craven, 27 November 1786, *Correspondence*, vol. 42, p. 178.
[25] William Hamilton to Horace Walpole, 19 February 1788, *Correspondence*, vol. 35, p. 438.

HORACE WALPOLE'S ENCHANTED CASTLES 95

Figure 2.1 Willey Reveley, *South West view of the Castle of Otranto, Italy; rough stone walls dividing fields in foreground with massive walls of castle beyond, overlooking sea to left*, March 1785. Pen, grey ink, and watercolour. British Museum 1927,0712.8. © Trustees of the British Museum.

Figure 2.2 John Carter, *South View of the Castle of Otranto*. Courtesy of the Lewis Walpole Library, lwlpr15797.

Richard Bull's personal copy of *Otranto* and in his extra-illustrated edition of *A Description*.[26] Walpole retrospectively bound a coloured engraving based on Carter's copy of Reveley into his personal copy of the second edition of *Otranto* (1765), tellingly entitling it *A View of the Real Castle of Otranto on the Eastern Coast of the Kingdom of Naples*.[27] An untitled, engraved reproduction of Carter's image with the addition of two figures in the foreground by 'Barlow, sculp.' features again in the London-based publisher J. Edwards's sixth edition of *The Castle of Otranto* that was printed by Bodoni in Parma in 1791, an edition that, at least in some surviving copies, also features Andrew Birrell's engravings of the illustrations to the novel that were executed by Anne Melicent Clarke.[28] A version of this image of the castle, here entitled *The Castle of Otranto, From an Original Drawing as it now exists in the Kingdom of Naples*, was used as the frontispiece for the reprinting of *Otranto* in the second volume of Walpole's posthumous *Works*.[29] As Peter N. Lindfield's analysis of the many illustrated editions of the novel has insightfully concluded, none made any attempt to draw architectural links between the castle at Otranto and Strawberry Hill.[30]

The materiality of a number of early editions of *Otranto* substantially intensified the ruse concerning the 'real' building behind Walpole's fictional castle. Those editions that included fore-edge paintings—decorative scenes painted on the edge of the book opposite the spine and gilded over so as to render them invisible when the book was closed—are a case in point. While some included scenes of the dark, subterranean recesses beneath Otranto—structures that have no equivalence in the architecture of Strawberry Hill—others made variously accurate and inaccurate attempts at representing the author's iconic house, as if to draw the two structures together.[31] Other illustrated editions of the novel complicated matters even further. Jeffery's edition of 1796, for instance, included in the front matter a coloured plate of the castle that, despite being titled *Castello Di Otranto* after the 'real' Italian pile, is an entirely imaginary Italianate building. The scene from the

---

[26] See Richard Bull's copy of the first edition of *Otranto* (1765), LWL, 24 17 765 Copy 2. For Bull's extra-illustrated copy of the second edition of Walpole's *A Description* (1784), see LWL, Folio 33 30 Copy 11.

[27] See Walpole's personal, annotated copy in the British Library, London, c.40. C. 24.

[28] Anne Melicent Clarke produced six plates for the first Italian translation of the novel, *Il castello di Otranto. Storia Gotica*, trans. Giovanni Sivrac (London: Molini, Polidori, Molini and Co., 1795). These plates were later engraved by Andrew Birrell and included in Edward Jeffery's edition of *Otranto* in 1796. For a copy of J. Edwards's 1791 edition containing Clarke's drawings, see LWL, 24 17 791P Copy 4. These images do not appear in the copy of the same edition that Walpole gave to G. Birch, 24 17 791P Copy 6, probably because they were only published by E. and S. Harding in July 1793. For an account of these images, see Hazen, *A Bibliography of Horace Walpole*, p. 61.

[29] Walpole, *The Works of Horatio Walpole*, vol. 2, p. 1. For a detailed account of the circulation of this and other images of the Castle at Otranto, see Lindfield, 'Imagining the Undefined Castle in *The Castle of Otranto*'.

[30] Lindfield, 'Imagining the Undefined Castle in *The Castle of Otranto*'.

[31] For a fore-edge painting of the dark, labyrinthine dungeons beneath the Castle of Otranto, see LWL, 24 17 769 Copy 1. For two attempts at representing Strawberry Hill on the illustrated fore-edge, see LWL, 24 17 782 Copy 3 and LWL, 24 17 719P Copy 15.

Figure 2.3 *Castello Di Otranto*, from William Beckford's personal copy of Jeffery's 1796 edition of the novel. Courtesy of the Lewis Walpole Library, 24 17 796.

novel that it depicts is the entry of Frederic, Marquis of Vicenza, to Otranto, the same episode that had inspired John Carter's watercolour of 1790 (see Figure 2.3). One extra-illustrated copy of Edwards's edition even included, among a host of other contradictory clues, a fold-out copy of a map to the Italian region of Otranto, thus seeking to anchor the text in real-life architectural space.[32] In late eighteenth-century editions of *The Castle of Otranto*, paratextual markers directed readers in search of the 'actual' castle in divergent, vastly opposing directions, a characteristic of the text's convoluted publication history that seems very much to have been part of Walpole's and his publishers' game.

Scholars of the early twentieth century, however, routinely followed the leads suggested by the first Preface and the 1784 edition of *A Description* in linking the architecture of *Otranto* closely to Strawberry Hill itself. For this school of thought, W. S. Lewis's argument in 'The Genesis of Strawberry Hill' (1934) has proved to be particularly influential: 'It is something more than a cliché of criticism to say', Lewis reasoned, 'that the Castle of Otranto and Strawberry Hill are one and the same.'[33] Here, Lewis painstakingly set out to identify Otranto's gallery as the State Apartment (or Gallery) at Strawberry Hill; the chamber to the right of this as the Tribune; Isabella's chamber as Strawberry's Blue Bedchamber; Matilda's apartment as the Holbein Chamber; the top of the black tower where Theodore is

---

[32] Horace Walpole, *The Castle of Otranto, A Gothic Story*, 6th edn (Parma: Printed by Bodoni for J. Edwards, 1791), LWL, 24 17 719P Copy 9.
[33] W. S. Lewis, 'The Genesis of Strawberry Hill', *Metropolitan Museum Studies* vol. 5, no. 1 (August 1934): pp. 57–92 (p. 90).

rescued by Matilda as the Plaid Bedroom adjacent to Walpole's own; and so on.[34] Rigorous and scholarly though the argument is, there remain aspects of Otranto's architecture that defy Lewis's attempts: 'The "subterraneous passage" with the trapdoor', he concludes, 'is a fiction'; the 'little chamber beneath' where Theodore lay, though in all likelihood a reference to Strawberry's Little Cloister or Oratory, is not, strictly speaking, 'on' the stairs; and while the Great Hall of Otranto is seemingly Strawberry Hill's Paraclete, it has been 'expanded considerably from its actual size of about fourteen feet square' in the novel.[35] In attempting to map the architecture of Otranto on to that of Strawberry Hill, Lewis continuously comes up against aspects of the fiction for which he simply cannot account. As he concedes, 'It is not clear which is the Great Council Chamber', although, merely by a process of elimination, it 'must be either the Refectory or the library', in much the same way that 'The only room left for the unhappy Conrad' is Strawberry's Beauty Room.[36] Even by Lewis's own admission, the identification of specific references to the architecture of Strawberry Hill in *Otranto* is, at times, strained and unconvincing: if the 'little chamber' where Theodore lay is, indeed, Strawberry's Little Cloister, the 'circumstance of its being the room where the great astrologer, Conrad's tutor, drowned himself' only lends further 'color to the belief', for it was here, in a large vase kept in the Cloister, that Walpole's cat, Selima, was drowned. 'It is not beyond the creative powers', Lewis somewhat dubiously concludes, 'to transmute a cat named Selima into a great astrologer.'[37]

It is difficult not to read in Warren Hunting Smith's insistence that 'It is incorrect...to infer that the Castle of Otranto *is* Strawberry Hill' in his *Architecture in English Fiction* of the same year a direct riposte to Lewis's claims.[38] As Smith elaborated, 'There are many things in Walpole's imaginary castle which do not appear in his real one', not least an enclosed courtyard, a great hall with latticed gallery, and a subterranean passage leading to a church; 'Walpole's literary creation, therefore, is more authentic in its details than his real castle, and certainly more formidable.'[39] Thus wrote a critic who, in addition to being an important scholar of eighteenth-century architecture and fiction in his own right, had worked alongside W. S. Lewis as Associate Editor on the *Yale Edition of Horace Walpole's Correspondence* since 1934. Later, Lewis would pay touching tribute to 'Warren' in his autobiographical *One Man's Education* (1968), claiming that 'For thirty years he has chaperoned the Edition through the press, quietly vigilant, mindful of the infinite number of small details of editing, the mishandling

---

[34] Lewis, 'The Genesis of Strawberry Hill': pp. 89–90.
[35] Lewis, 'The Genesis of Strawberry Hill': p. 90.
[36] Lewis, 'The Genesis of Strawberry Hill': p. 90.
[37] Lewis, 'The Genesis of Strawberry Hill': p. 90.
[38] Warren Hunting Smith, *Architecture in English Fiction*, Yale Studies in English, Vol. LXXXIII (New Haven: Yale University Press; Oxford: Oxford University Press, 1934), p. 79.
[39] Smith, *Architecture in English Fiction*, pp. 79, 80.

of any one of which is a blemish.'⁴⁰ In 1934, however, these two redoubtable Walpoleans were engaged in a doubtless gentlemanly dispute over the architectural antecedents to the 'real' building behind Walpole's fictional pile.

Both seem to have been partially won round to the other's position, and in May 1936 Smith published 'Strawberry Hill and Otranto', a short but important letter to the editor of *The Times Literary Supplement* that outlined their points of compromise. While mutually at work on the Yale Edition of Walpole's *Correspondence*, 'Mr W. S. Lewis and I', Smith writes, 'have become convinced that all discrepancies between Otranto and Strawberry Hill'—obstacles encountered by Lewis and foregrounded by Smith—'are explained by Walpole's letter to Mme du Deffand, January 27th, 1775.' An English translation of the letter in question reads as follows:

> Two or three years after [having written *The Castle of Otranto*], I was going to Cambridge University, where I had spent three years of my youth. In entering one of the colleges I had entirely forgotten about, I found myself precisely in the courtyard of my castle. The towers, the doors, the chapel, the great hall, everything matched with the utmost accuracy. After all, the idea [meaning 'image'] of this college had been unconsciously in the back of my mind, and I had used it to create the plan of my castle, without being aware of it, and in a way that I firmly believed I had entered Otranto.⁴¹

Proceeding according to the evidence suggested here, Smith now claimed that the 'real' building behind Otranto, while conceding that it was partly Strawberry Hill, was an unnamed college at Cambridge—not Walpole's alma mater King's College, but one that he and Lewis, through careful reasoning, took to be Trinity.⁴² Though Walpole was 'unconscious' of its influence when he wrote *Otranto* in 1764, Smith and Lewis concluded that Cambridge provided the author with the architectural elements that were lacking at Strawberry Hill, including a courtyard, a great hall with latticed gallery, an oriel window, and even a subterranean passage leading to a nearby church. This revised position was reflected in the edition of *The Castle of Otranto* that Lewis prepared for Oxford University Press in 1964: the architecture of Otranto, he here argued, 'was thus compounded of Strawberry Hill and probably Trinity' at Cambridge.⁴³

With several recent critics and editors of the novel following the lead of Walpole, Lewis, and Smith, the assumption that Strawberry Hill, or at least parts of it, received fictional representation in *The Castle of Otranto* has become

---

⁴⁰ Wilmarth Sheldon Lewis, *One Man's Education* (New York: Alfred A. Knopf, 1968), p. 279.
⁴¹ Warren Hunting Smith, 'Strawberry Hill and Otranto', *The Times Literary Supplement*, Saturday, 23 May 1936, p. 440.
⁴² Horace Walpole to Madame du Deffand, 27 January 1775, *Correspondence*, vol. 6, p. 145. I am grateful to Fanny Lacôte for having provided this translation.
⁴³ W. S. Lewis, 'Introduction', in *The Castle of Otranto, A Gothic Story*, by Horace Walpole, ed. and introd. W. S. Lewis (London: Oxford University Press, 1964), pp. vii–xvi (p. xi).

somewhat of a critical orthodoxy, working its way into most modern editions of the text.[44] Elaborating on Dianne S. Ames's argument concerning the 'subjunctive' mode of Strawberry Hill's architecture, Lee Morrissey has creatively linked Walpole's text and house together through the concept of 'folly' that is crucial to both.[45] One notable exception to this coupling is Bernstein's argument in *Housing Problems*, a study in which she argues that Strawberry Hill and *Otranto* are 'off balance', and that Walpole's house and fiction are in no way coeval with one another, and by no means the products of 'a single cause'.[46] Apart from such exceptions, criticism has tended to regard the two as being inseparably linked. There is undoubtedly a degree of merit in this. As Walter Scott pointed out in the critical introduction that he wrote for James Ballantyne's 1811 edition of the novel, the connections between *Otranto* as narrative and Strawberry Hill as building are manifold: in the former, 'Mr Walpole resolved to give the public a specimen of the Gothic style adapted to modern literature, as he had already exhibited its application to modern architecture.'[47] Just as Walpole the architect had taken care to combine the requirements of modern convenience with 'the rich, varied, and complicated tracery and carving of the ancient cathedral', so, in *Otranto*, it was his aim to combine the 'imposing tone of chivalry' and 'marvellous turn of incident' of the ancient romance with the 'accurate exhibition of human character' to be found in the modern novel.[48] To read *Otranto*, Scott concluded, was to experience the same degree of supernatural awe and terror that one felt when spending a solitary night in an old, tapestry-strewn Gothic mansion. Walpole's ingenuity lay in his extracting in *Otranto* the sensations of melancholy and supernatural awe that, though easily elicited in truly ancient piles, were 'almost impossible' to evoke in 'such a modern Gothic structure' as Strawberry Hill, thus 'attaining in composition, what, as an architect, he must have felt beyond the power of his art'.[49]

The connections between house and novel do not end there. *Otranto*, Walpole wrote to William Mason in April 1765, was 'begun without any plan at all', and 'though in the short course of its progress I did conceive some views, it was so far

---

[44] See, for example, Frederick S. Frank, ed., *The Castle of Otranto and The Mysterious Mother, A Tragedy* (Peterborough, Ont.: Broadview, 2003), p. 61; Michael Gamer, ed., *The Castle of Otranto* (London: Penguin, 2001), pp. xxiii–xxv; E. J. Clery, ed., *The Castle of Otranto* (Oxford: Oxford University Press, 1996), p. 117; and Groom, ed., *The Castle of Otranto*, p. 116.

[45] For Ames's original argument, see Dianne S. Ames, 'Strawberry Hill: Architecture of the "As If"', *Studies in Eighteenth-Century Culture* 8 (1979): pp. 351–63. See, too, Lee Morrissey, *From the Temple to the Castle: An Architectural History of British Literature, 1660–1760* (Charlottesville and London: University Press of Virginia, 1999), pp. 108–30.

[46] Bernstein, *Housing Problems*, pp. 49–50.

[47] [Walter Scott], 'Introduction', in *The Castle of Otranto; A Gothic Story*, by Horace Walpole (Edinburgh: Printed by James Ballantyne and Co; London: Hurst, Rees, Orme, and Brown, 1811), pp. iii–xxxvi (p. xii).

[48] Scott, 'Introduction', pp. xii–xiii.   [49] Scott, 'Introduction', pp. xx–xxi.

from being sketched out with any design at all'.[50] The 'unplanned' process of composition that Walpole brought to bear on his fiction was mirrored in the construction of Strawberry Hill, a building that too seemed to grow, albeit at a considerably slower pace, through a series of largely unanticipated accretions. We might also bear in mind that, much like the architectural spaces in *Otranto*, Strawberry Hill, as I intimated above, was neither a military nor a clerical building, not a castle nor an abbey nor a monastery. As Walpole wrote to Horace Mann in 1759, the house was both fortified and ecclesiastical in design: 'I...am going to make great additions to my castle; a gallery, a round tower, and a cabinet, that is to have all the air of a Catholic chapel—bar consecration!'[51] The house, as Michael Snodin has put it, thus came to represent 'two highly evocative types of historical building', the Gothic monastery or convent, on the one hand, and the Gothic castle on the other.[52] In a similar fashion, the castellated architecture in *The Castle of Otranto* continuously veers towards the ecclesiastical, with the castle bordering on, and eventually becoming indistinguishable from, the chapel, the 'convent', and the 'cathedral', the Church of Saint Nicholas with which it is 'contiguous'.[53] It is important to remember, too, that, however playfully, both fiction and house looked to biblical precedents as a legitimizing foundation of sorts. 'I could wish [the author] had grounded his plan on a more useful moral than this,' Marshal in the first Preface claims, 'that *the sins of fathers are visited on their children to the third and fourth generation*', parsing biblical verses from the Books of Exodus, Numbers, and Deuteronomy to this effect. Similarly, Walpole's earliest known reference in a letter of 1749 to the process of 'Gothicizing' Strawberry Hill appropriated, no doubt ironically, a verse from Deuteronomy as its authorizing injunction: 'Did I tell you that I have found a text in Deuteronomy, to authorize my future battlements? *When thou buildest a new house, then shalt thou make a battlement for thy roof, that thou bring not blood upon thy house, if any man fall from thence.*'[54]

'Filled with Gothic Story'

The castle in Walpole's fiction, however, also draws upon a number of other sources for its layout, its structure, and even its eventual crumbling into ruin, literary constructions of architectural space, I want to argue, that are located in the

---

[50] Horace Walpole to William Mason, 17 April 1765, *Correspondence*, vol. 26, p. 6.
[51] Horace Walpole to Sir Horace Mann, 8 July 1759, *Correspondence*, vol. 21, p. 306.
[52] Michael Snodin, 'Going to Strawberry Hill', in *Horace Walpole's Strawberry Hill*, ed. Michael Snodin, with the assistance of Cynthia Roman (New Haven and London: Yale University Press, 2009), pp. 15–57 (p. 15). See, too, Harney, *Place-making for the Imagination*, p. 132.
[53] Walpole, *The Castle of Otranto*, p. 26.
[54] Horace Walpole to George Montagu, 28 September 1749, *Correspondence*, vol. 9, p. 102.

tradition of what literary antiquaries such as Richard Hurd and Walpole himself termed 'Gothic story'. In exploring these fictional antecedents, it is worth returning to two well-known but hitherto only partially scrutinized Walpolean sources: the first, the teasing statements that directly precede and follow William Marshal's claim that 'The scene is undoubtedly laid in some real castle' in the first Preface, and the second, Walpole's often-quoted letter to the Reverend William Cole of 9 March 1765, in which he recounted the dream that prompted the feverish writing of *Otranto* in the summer of the previous year.

'Though the machinery is invention, and the names of the actors imaginary,' Marshal the editor maintains, 'the ground-work of the story is founded on truth', thus pre-empting, through the use of the architectural metaphor of the 'ground-work', his claim that the castle in which the action is set is 'particular' and 'real' in origin.[55] But no sooner has he vouched for historical authenticity than he undercuts it with an emphasis upon the structure's fictional foundations: 'Curious persons, who have leisure to employ on such researches, may possibly discover in the Italian writers the foundation on which our author has built.'[56] Despite the prevailing sense of untruth in the first Preface, this reference to Italian literature is less misleading than it would at first appear: in *Short Notes of the Life of Horatio Walpole*, Walpole claimed that he had learned Italian under the tutorship of 'Signor Piazza' (Girolamo Bartolomeo Piazza) during the four years that he spent at King's College, Cambridge, between March 1735 and early 1739; he had also spent a considerable amount of time in Italy while on the grand tour between 1739 and 1741.[57] Coming immediately after the discussion of the 'real' Castle of Otranto, and extending the architectural metaphor through reference to another 'foundation' upon which the castle has been 'built', these closing lines to the first Preface issue the 'curious' or 'leisured' reader with a challenge: though apparently 'founded' on the truthful 'ground-work' of a real castle, the 'foundation' is as literary as it is historical, and it falls to the task of those readers who are so inclined to 'discover' the 'Italian writers' on whom both the Castle of Otranto (as structure) and *The Castle of Otranto* (as narrative or text) are based.

Walpole's letter to Cole proceeded in a similar fashion to provide the fiction with several competing points of origin. Hoping that Cole's professed 'partiality' to Strawberry Hill might incline him to 'excuse the wildness of the story', Walpole underscored the claim in the first Preface that the foundations of the castle lay in some 'real' castle, here his own at Strawberry Hill, with the comment, 'You will even have found some traits [in the Castle of Otranto] to put you in mind of this place.' What is striking here is his non-committal tone. Directly thereafter, moreover, Walpole confounds this by foregrounding the text's origins in a dream, and, beyond this, in the realms of what he describes as 'Gothic story':

---

[55] Walpole, *The Castle of Otranto*, p. 7.   [56] Walpole, *The Castle of Otranto*, p. 7.
[57] See Walpole, *Short Notes of the Life of Horatio Walpole, Youngest Son of Sir Robert Walpole*, fol. 1.

Shall I even confess to you what was the origin of this romance? I waked one morning in the beginning of last June from a dream, of which all I could recover was, that I had thought myself in an ancient castle (a very natural dream for a head filled like mine with Gothic story) and that on the uppermost bannister of a great staircase I saw a gigantic hand in armour.[58]

The architectural origin that is Strawberry Hill retreats, and gives way here to dream and Gothic story, two more illusory points of genesis. In what seems to be a reference to the armoury and the nearby 'uppermost bannister' at Strawberry Hill, Walpole's dream of June 1764 is reworked in the novel when Bianca the terrified servant claims to have seen 'upon the uppermost bannister of the great stairs a hand in armour as big, as big—I thought I should have swooned'.[59] While Walpole's dream has received considerable psychoanalytic attention, what has not been sufficiently interrogated is Walpole's indebtedness to this realm of 'Gothic story', an indebtedness that was acknowledged in his reference to the 'foundational' functions of the 'Italian writers' in the first Preface, and one which opens up the architectural origins of the Castle of Otranto to further speculation.[60]

As Richard Hurd's *Letters on Chivalry and Romance* (1762) indicates, the phrase 'Gothic story' referred for the mid-eighteenth-century literary antiquary to, among other fictions, the romances of Torquato Tasso and Ludovico Ariosto in the Italian tradition, and to selected works by Edmund Spenser, William Shakespeare, and John Milton in the English. As one of the few remaining traces of chivalry, 'Gothic' romance, for Hurd, the literature of the so-called dark and 'barbarous' ages, was that 'spark' that kept that glorious institution alive: if 'The spirit of Chivalry' was 'a fire which soon spent itself', 'Romance, which was kindled at it, burnt long, and continued its light and heat even to the politer ages.'[61] Arguing throughout his *Letters* for the reassessment and contemporary recuperation of romance, Hurd asserted the imaginative richness of the 'Gothic' past over the 'paganism' of classical Greek and Roman civilization. We feel 'very sensibly' this 'difference' between Gothic and classical poets, he argued, when we compare Horace's witch Canidia with the witches in Shakespeare's *Macbeth*; equally, the blood-dripping myrtles from Virgil's *Aeneid* cannot be compared with the delights of the enchanted forest in Tasso's *La Gerusalemme liberata*. And so Hurd throughout the *Letters* continues, systematically juxtaposing the Cyclopses, Bacchuses, and Theseuses of the classical tradition with their 'exact' but imaginatively superlative 'counter-parts' in the 'Gothic' writings of Shakespeare,

---

[58] Horace Walpole to Rev. William Cole, 9 March 1765, *Correspondence*, vol. 1, p. 88.
[59] Walpole, *The Castle of Otranto*, p. 95.
[60] For a psychoanalytic reading of Walpole's dream, see Anne Williams, 'Reading Walpole Reading Shakespeare', in *Shakespearean Gothic*, ed. Christy Desmet and Anne Williams (Cardiff: University of Wales Press, 2009), pp. 13–36.
[61] Richard Hurd, *Letters on Chivalry and Romance* (London: Printed for A. Millar; Cambridge: Printed for W. Thurlbourn and J. Woodyer, 1762), pp. 3–4.

Milton, Tasso, and Ariosto.[62] In all respects, he maintains, literary fictions, their characters, and their scenarios are 'the more poetical for being Gothic'; just as Shakespeare 'is greater when he uses Gothic manners and machinery' than 'when he employs classical', so Gothic objects and traditions in general possess, 'by their nature and genius, the advantage of the [classical] in producing the *sublime*.'[63] As I argued in the previous chapter, Walpole rehearsed a similar argument concerning the imaginative superiority of Gothic architecture over the classical style in the first volume of *Anecdotes of Painting*, in his letters, and in other manuscript sources.

The principle of aesthetic relativism is key to Hurd's argument. Commenting on English writers' apparent disregard for the Aristotelian Unities, Thomas Rymer in *The Tragedies of the Last Age Consider'd and Examined by the Practice of the Ancients* (1678) had drawn an unflattering parallel between the literature and the architecture of the Gothic past, claiming that 'I have thought our Poetry of the last Age was as rude as our Architecture.'[64] But if, for Hurd, the literature of Gothic antiquity appeared to lack the order, regularity, and unity of the classical writers, this only pointed to the necessity of approaching Gothic romance on its own terms, a criticism that he directed not only at Rymer, but at Thomas Warton's reading of Spenser in his expanded and revised *Observations on the Fairy Queen of Spenser* (1762) that was published earlier the same year. Hurd employs an important architectural example in order to argue his point: 'When an architect examines a Gothic structure by Grecian rules, he finds nothing but deformity. But the Gothic architecture has it's [*sic*] own rules, by which when it comes to be examined, it is seen to have it's [*sic*] merit, as well as the Grecian.'[65] 'The question is not', Hurd thus reasons, 'which of the two is conducted in the simplest or truest taste', but rather 'whether there is not sense and design in both, when scrutinized by the laws on which each is projected.'[66] In the case of *The Faerie Queene*, Spenser's purpose 'was not to write a classic poem' so much as 'to adorn a gothic story', one founded, despite Warton's claims to the contrary, on the unity of the quest motif.[67] John Hughes had argued much the same in 1715, observing of *The Faerie Queene* that 'It ought rather to be consider'd as a Poem of a particular kind', and that 'to compare it therefore with the Models of Antiquity' would be tantamount to 'drawing a Parallel between the *Roman* and the *Gothick* Architecture': while 'there is doubtless a more natural Grandeur and Simplicity' in the former, we find in the latter 'great

---

[62] Hurd, *Letters on Chivalry and Romance*, p. 31.
[63] Hurd, *Letters on Chivalry and Romance*, pp. 55, 60.
[64] Thomas Rymer, *The Tragedies of the Last Age Consider'd and Examin'd by the Practice of the Ancient, and by the Commonsense of All Ages* (London: Printed for Richard Tonson, 1678), p. 142.
[65] Hurd, *Letters on Chivalry and Romance*, p. 61.
[66] Hurd, *Letters on Chivalry and Romance*, p. 61.
[67] Hurd, *Letters on Chivalry and Romance*, p. 75.

Mixtures of Beauty and Barbarism, yet assisted by the Invention of a Variety of inferior Ornaments'.[68] Gothic literature, like Gothic architecture, had to be assessed according to criteria peculiar to itself. Alexander Pope had made the same point in his figuring of Shakespeare's plays, in all their irregularity, as 'an ancient majestic piece of *Gothick* Architecture' in his Preface to *The Works of Shakespear* (1725): when 'compar'd with a neat Modern building' built in the 'elegant and glaring' classical style, they are 'more strong and solemn', displaying 'the greater variety' and a series of 'much nobler apartments'; while 'we are often conducted to them by dark, odd, and uncouth passages', Pope punningly concedes, the whole cannot fail 'to strike us with greater reverence, tho' many of the Parts are childish, ill-plac'd, and unequal to its grandeur'.[69] Similarly articulated through a series of seemingly unbreachable oppositions between the classical and the Gothic architectural styles, Hurd's argument in the *Letters* finally leaves its readers in no uncertainty as to what the category of 'Gothic story' comprises: among the writers and texts to which his defence of the imaginative impulses of the Gothic continuously returns are French translations of the European romance *Amadis of Gaul* (first published in 1508); Tasso's *La Gerusalemme liberata* (1581); Ariosto's *Orlando Furioso* (1516); Spenser's *The Faerie Queene* (1590–6); some of Shakespeare's plays (particularly *Macbeth* [c.1606], *Hamlet* [c.1600], and *A Midsummer Night's Dream* [c.1594–6]); and Milton's *Comus* (1634). That is, though Milton would later become apostate to the Gothic cause with his use of the classical epic form in *Paradise Lost* (1667; 1674), the poet remained, in Hurd's estimation, forever 'fond' of 'Gothic fictions'.[70] The one notable omission, of course, is Geoffrey Chaucer. Although Hurd gives *The Canterbury Tales* passing mention, and despite the moderate interest that John Dryden, Alexander Pope, Thomas Percy, and Thomas Warton had expressed in the writer's work, it was really only in the early decades of the nineteenth century that Chaucer became a key figure in the revival of interest in the literature of the Gothic past.[71]

---

[68] John Hughes, ed., *The Works of Mr Edmund Spenser*, 6 vols (London: Printed for Jacob Tonson, 1715), vol. 1, pp. lx–lxi.

[69] Alexander Pope, ed., *The Works of Shakespear*, 6 vols (London: Printed for Jacob Tonson, 1725), vol. 1, pp. xxiii–xxiv. For a discussion of the use of such architectural metaphors in the work of Hughes, Pope, and Hurd, see Nicole Reynolds, 'Gothic and the Architectural Imagination', in *The Gothic World*, ed. Glennis Byron and Dale Townshend (Abingdon and New York: Routledge, 2014), pp. 85–97.

[70] Hurd, *Letters on Chivalry and Romance*, p. 117.

[71] See Peter Sabor's argument in 'Medieval Revival and the Gothic'. Walpole himself had limited interest in Chaucer. Believing himself early on in life to be descended from Chaucer, his interest in Chaucer's work was as genealogical as it was literary, although there is evidence of him later being familiar with Dryden's Chaucerian adaptations and with Thomas Tyrwhitt's edition of *The Canterbury Tales* (1775–8). See Horace Walpole to George Montagu, 11 August 1748, *Correspondence*, vol. 9, p. 68; Horace Walpole to William Mason, 13 November 1781, *Correspondence*, vol. 29, p. 165; and Horace Walpole to William Mason, 14 April 1775, *Correspondence*, vol. 28, p. 191.

Horace Walpole made no secret of his intolerance of Richard Hurd and his account of the art and literature of the Gothic ages. In a belated reply to a letter in which the Reverend Henry Zouch had candidly expressed his negative responses to Hurd's *Moral and Political Dialogues* (1759), Walpole in 1760 described Hurd as 'a most disagreeable writer!'[72] Though it is 'impossible', he conceded, 'not to own that he has sense and great knowledge', this scholarship was 'couched in so hard a style' that Walpole declared himself as having 'no patience to read him'.[73] These views seem to have persisted well into Walpole's later life.[74] Even so, Hurd's *Letters on Chivalry and Romance* are useful in providing insight into what Walpole in both his letter to Cole and in the subtitle to the second edition of *Otranto* in 1765 meant by the phrase 'A Gothic Story'. In *Jerusalem Delivered*, Tasso reserves the term 'Goth' as a means of referring to the ancient barbarian tribe; in the first edition of *Otranto*, Walpole could not make use of the adjective 'Gothic'—a largely eighteenth-century, and thus anachronistic, appellation that referred, in part, to that which was of the ancient 'Gothic' past—without revealing his text's modern origins.[75] Having done so, however, Walpole in 1765 was now content to apply to it the descriptor of 'A Gothic Story', declaring in the process *Otranto*'s affinities with what contemporary literary antiquaries such as Hurd took to be the 'Gothic stories' of Shakespeare, Milton, Spenser, Ariosto, Tasso, and other British and European writers and romancers of the 'dark' or 'barbarous' past. After all, Walpole's professed aim, as the second Preface to *Otranto* put it, to rejuvenate 'the strict adherence to common life' in the modern realist novel with the 'imagination and improbability' of ancient romance, was, despite himself, one that was thoroughly in accordance with Hurd's own.[76] In turning to the literature of Gothic antiquity, both Hurd and Walpole sought to revivify a moribund mimetic, realist, and classicist tradition in contemporary art and literature with the vital imaginative supplement that was 'Gothic romance'.[77] More trenchantly, Hurd's elaboration of the category of 'Gothic story' in the *Letters* takes us closer to identifying those unnamed 'Italian writers' to which Walpole in the first Preface cryptically refers—writers and fictions, he argues, that constitute the 'foundation' upon which the writer has 'built', and which, in their characteristic concerns with enchanted castles, reveal another important antecedent to the architectural details of *The Castle of Otranto*.

[72] Horace Walpole to Rev. Henry Zouch, 9 January 1760, *Correspondence*, vol. 16, p. 33.
[73] Horace Walpole to Rev. Henry Zouch, 9 January 1760, *Correspondence*, vol. 16, p. 33.
[74] See Walpole's *Correspondence*, vol. 29, pp. 117, 35, 309.
[75] In referring to the ancient Gothic tribe, a line from Book 17 describes the term '*Goth*' as 'a rude destructive name'. See Torquato Tasso, *Jerusalem Delivered; An Heroic Poem: Translated from the Italian of Torquato Tasso, by John Hoole*, 2 vols (London: Printed and sold by J. Dodsley, P. Vaillant, T. Davies et al.; Oxford: D. Prince; Cambridge: W. Thurlbourn and J. Woodver, 1763), vol. 2, Book 17, l. 473.
[76] Walpole, *The Castle of Otranto*, p. 9.
[77] See Horace Walpole to Jean-Baptiste-Jacques Élie de Beaumont, 18 March 1765, *Correspondence*, vol. 40, p. 379.

Enchanted Castles

Urged by an anxious Manfred in *The Castle of Otranto* to inform him of what terror-inducing sights he and Diego have witnessed behind the door of the castle's great chamber, the reluctant Jaquez, speaking on his petrified friend's behalf, describes Diego's witnessing of an armour-clad foot and leg 'as large as the helmet below in the court', as if the 'giant' to which it belonged had been laid out on the chamber's floor.[78] 'Before we could get to the end of the gallery,' Jaquez breathlessly continues, 'we heard the door of the great chamber clap behind us, but we did not dare turn back to see if the giant was following us.'[79] Overcome by terror at the spectacle, and bewildered by his superior's own anxieties concerning other mysterious happenings in the castle, Jaquez implores Manfred for urgent intervention: 'But for heaven's sake, good my lord, send for the chaplain and have the castle exorcized, for, for certain, it is enchanted.'[80] To this plea, the other servants enthusiastically lend their voices, threatening to leave Manfred's employ if the infernal magic at Otranto is not laid immediately to rest. Though Manfred dismisses these 'dotards' with his characteristic sense of flippancy, the truth that Jaquez has brought to light at this moment cannot be so easily repressed: Otranto is an enchanted castle in which Manfred seeks to beguile, imprison, and seduce his subjects, the true nature of which the villain himself, though bent upon the concealment of this truth, unwittingly exposes when, in pursuit of Isabella shortly before this confrontation, he is overheard as saying, 'I tell you she must be in the castle; I will find her in spite of enchantment.'[81] As such, Otranto is akin to those architectural piles found in countless 'ancient' romances of sixteenth-century Europe, sources that considerably complicate its long-presumed origins in the 'real' castle at Strawberry Hill and that point, instead, to its fictional and imaginative antecedents in the 'Gothic stories' of sixteenth-century Italy and France. In a direct paralleling of these scenes of enchantment later on in the narrative, Bianca replies to her mistress with the expostulation that 'This castle is certainly haunted!'[82] As Nick Groom's edition of *The Castle of Otranto* points out, this line is strongly Shakespearean in its associations, bringing to mind both the haunted Castle of Elsinore in *Hamlet* and the King's references to spectral activity before Barkloughly Castle, Wales, in Act III, scene iii, of *Richard II*.[83] While Walpole's appropriation of the 'haunted' castles of Shakespeare in *Otranto* has been critically explored, his fiction's relation to the 'enchanted' castles of the European romance tradition has rather escaped consideration.[84]

---

[78] Walpole, *The Castle of Otranto*, p. 32.
[79] Walpole, *The Castle of Otranto*, p. 33.
[80] Walpole, *The Castle of Otranto*, p. 33.
[81] Walpole, *The Castle of Otranto*, p. 29.
[82] Walpole, *The Castle of Otranto*, p. 39.
[83] See Nick Groom's editorial gloss of Bianca's lines in Walpole, *The Castle of Otranto*, p. 124.
[84] On Walpole's use of *Hamlet* in *Otranto*, see Yael Shapira, 'Shakespeare, *The Castle of Otranto*, and the Problem of the Corpse on the Eighteenth-Century Stage', *Eighteenth-Century Life* vol. 6, no. 1 (winter 2012): pp. 1–29.

Walpole may well have been exposed to the capacious body of medieval romance as early as 1727, the year in which he went to Eton. A letter from Henry Seymour Conway of April 1745 provides a picture of the young Walpole as being thoroughly enamoured of the seventeenth-century French romances of Madeleine de Scudéry and Gauthier de Costes, as well as the sixteenth-century story of *Amadis of Gaul*, possibly in one of its many Spanish, Italian, German, French, and Portuguese variations: 'I remember you buried in romances and novels; I really believe you could have said all the *Grand Cyrus*'s, the *Cleopatra*'s, and *Amadis*'s in the world by heart, nay, you carried your taste for it so far that not a fairy tale escaped you.'[85] Although Conway, registering in 1745 a change in Walpole's early disposition and reading habits, notes that 'it's a long time since you were romantic', his subsequent claim that his cousin has 'laid up a vast stock of romance' is one that is easily corroborated.[86] As Allen T. Hazen's *A Catalogue of Horace Walpole's Library* (1969) reveals, Walpole's library at Strawberry Hill contained, among other romances, a copy of de Coste's *Cléopâtre*, and at least two versions, one in French and one in English, of the *Amadis of Gaul* narrative.[87]

The 'Italian writers' most likely to have provided the 'foundation' for Walpole's enchanted Castle of Otranto, however, are Ariosto in *Orlando Furioso* and Tasso in *La Gerusalemme liberata*. In Canto 12 of Ariosto's epic romance, the hero Orlando pursues a figure whom he takes to be his beloved Angelica, carried in the arms of another knight, into a splendid and luxuriously furnished palace built of 'various marbles'.[88] Encountering within the building not his lover but a number of other disillusioned knights, Orlando joins the imprisoned throngs of those who have been led there in similar, fruitless pursuit of their objects of desire: 'It does so seem the thing to all conspire, / For which each one does wish, and must desire.'[89] This 'wond'rous palace', it turns out, is the construct of the wizard Atlante, and is intended as a means of preventing the fulfilment of the prophecy concerning the death of his protégé Ruggier, who, through similarly magical means, has entered the castle in pursuit of a giant.[90] Made invisible by her magic ring, Angelica, too, has been beguiled into Atlante's enchanted domain, so 'That he might those vermillion cheeks persue [sic], / Those golden locks and those fine eyes so black'.[91] Posing as the site for the consummation of sexual and romantic desire, this 'dome

---

[85] Henry Seymour Conway to Horace Walpole, 18 April 1745, *Correspondence*, vol. 37, p. 189.
[86] For a further comment on what Conway took to be Walpole's declining taste for romance, see Henry Seymour Conway to Horace Walpole, *Correspondence*, vol. 37, p. 203.
[87] See Hazen, *A Catalogue of Horace Walpole's Library*, vol. 1, p. 326; vol. 2, p. 465.
[88] These and other references to Ariosto's poem in this chapter are taken from the expanded and annotated 1757 edition of William Huggins's translation of the text, first published in 1755. See Ludovico Ariosto, *Orlando Furioso, By Ludovico Ariosto. Translated from the Italian, by William Huggins, Esq.*, 2nd edn, 2 vols (London: James Rivington and James Fletcher; Surrey: John Cook, 1757), vol. 1, p. 161.
[89] Ariosto, *Orlando Furioso*, vol. 1, Canto 12, stanza 20, p. 162.
[90] Ariosto, *Orlando Furioso*, vol. 1, Canto 12, stanza 13, p. 162.
[91] Ariosto, *Orlando Furioso*, vol. 1, Canto 12, stanza 33, p. 166.

magnificent' in *Orlando Furioso* is the architectural embodiment of all human longing.[92] When strife between Orlando and Ferrau, King of Circassia, ensues over the love of Angelica, both contenders for her affection eventually escape from Atlante's enchanted pile. Confronting one another in a duel shortly thereafter, Ferrau swears never to wear a helmet in conflict until such time as he may don that of Orlando, his rival. Like the magic sword Durendal, Orlando's helmet once belonged to Almontes, one of Ferrau's kinsmen. The remainder of the action of Canto 12 rapidly descends into farce. With Orlando having removed his helmet so as to duel with Ferrau, the still-invisible Angelica attempts to defuse the conflict by running away with it and hanging it on the branch of a tree beside a nearby river. Recognizing the helmet as belonging to Orlando, a momentarily triumphant Ferrau eagerly seizes it, fulfilling his earlier oath as he places it proudly on his head. With this objective met, his only remaining quest is for the figure of Angelica herself. Riding off into the distance, Ferrau will be killed by Orlando in a later canto of the poem, while Orlando, in time, will come to replace his helmet with another.

Prophesies, oaths, giants, enchanted helmets, and magical swords: there is much in *Orlando Furioso* that recalls the plot and paraphernalia of *The Castle of Otranto*. Manfred's castle is a variant of the enchanted palace of Atlante in Ariosto. Both buildings are the sites of seemingly inexplicable supernatural phenomena, and in both, architectural space is enlisted in the villains' libidinous pursuit of a vulnerable heroine, Angelica in *Orlando* and Isabella in *Otranto*. Walpole's indebtedness to the work of Tasso in *La Gerusalemme liberata* is even more pronounced. Walpole owned several versions of this romance, including an Italian edition of 1735 and a 1792 reprint of John Hoole's English translation, *Jerusalem Delivered*, of 1763.[93] Though he was clearly enamoured of Tasso's poem from a very young age—his early unpublished story 'Patapan; or, The Little White Dog: A Tale from Fontaine' (1749) invoked it through the familiar trope of the enchanted castle—Walpole was particularly preoccupied with *Jerusalem Delivered* in the years leading up to his writing of *The Castle of Otranto*.[94] In a letter of May 1762, he claimed that his ideal romance, were he ever to write one, would include a man of 'propriety and dignity' similar to Tasso's Rinaldo, though one who was 'insensible to all the arts and enchanting allurements of Armidas and Calypsos, and their maids of honour'.[95] One year later, on a tour of parts of England with Cole in July 1763, Walpole and his

---

[92] Ariosto, *Orlando Furioso*, vol. 1, Canto 12, stanza 29, p. 165.
[93] Hazen, *A Catalogue of Horace Walpole's Library*, vol. 2, p. 223; vol. 1, p. 422. The copy of *La Gerusalemme liberata* (Urbino, 1735) that Walpole owned and kept in the main Library at Strawberry Hill is kept at the LWL, Quarto 49 2066. Given its temporal proximity to the writing and publication of *The Castle of Otranto* in 1764, all references to Tasso's poem in this chapter are taken from the first edition of Hoole's two-volume English translation of 1763. Walpole kept the second, 1792 edition of Hoole's translation in the main Library at Strawberry Hill.
[94] See 'Patapan; or, The Little White Dog: A Tale from Fontaine' (1749), LWL, Folio 49 2616 II MS, fols 93–112. See a transcript of Walpole's manuscript in Appendix I, *Correspondence*, vol. 30, pp. 287–306.
[95] Horace Walpole to Lady Henrietta Cecilia West, 4 May 1762, *Correspondence*, vol. 40, p. 245.

travelling companion visited Burleigh (or 'Burghley House'), the seat of the Earl of Exeter near Peterborough. Here, the figure of Armida loomed large. Walpole's journal entry in what would eventually be published as *Visits to Country Seats* (1928) lists among the many artworks to be seen within this 'noble Pile' a painting referred to as '*Armida enchanting the Sword of Rinaldo, Gennaro*'.[96] Even though Walpole and Cole alike misidentify one of the paintings at Burleigh as Benedetto Gennari II's *Rinaldo and Armida* (1676–9)—while the Earl had, indeed, assembled a sizeable collection of works by Gennari, there is no evidence of him ever having owned this particular piece—the collection included two paintings entitled *Rinaldo and Armida*, the first now attributed to the Studio of Domenichino, and the second now catalogued as being 'After Annibale Carracci and Antonio Maria Panico'.[97] Walpole also encountered Tasso's popular narrative in other forms, including George Frideric Handel's *Armida* (1711), an opera, with a libretto by Giacomo Rossi, with which we know he was familiar.[98]

Whatever the precise sources of the story, Walpole's debt to Tasso is considerable. The invocation with which *Jerusalem Delivered* opens prefigures Walpole's aims in *Otranto* 'to blend the two kinds of romance, the ancient and the modern' so as to produce through this act of imaginative regeneration what the second Preface described as 'a new species of romance': 'Forgive me, if with truth I fiction join, / And grave verse with other charms than thine.'[99] Across twenty cantos, the narrative recounts the Christian recovery of Jerusalem from the Saracens during the Crusades (1096–9), a time scheme that, in itself, echoes Walpole's setting of his narrative 'between 1095, the æra of the first crusade, and 1243, the date of the last'.[100] United under the leadership of Godfrey of Bouillon, the Christian corps comprises many a 'sabled knight' drawn from England, France, the Netherlands, Italy, Germany, and Greece;[101] Aladine, the tyrant leader of the Saracens, is, at once, Godfrey's foil, his counterpart, and his arch-enemy at war. In this respect, *Otranto* looks directly to *Jerusalem Delivered* for the trajectory of its plot: just as *Otranto* involves the eventual vanquishing and expulsion of a tyrant-ruler from a castle, so *Jerusalem Delivered* details the removal of the tyrant Aladine from the castle-like structure that is the old, walled city of Jerusalem.

Of particular significance to *The Castle of Otranto*, though, is the use to which Tasso puts the forces of magic and enchantment. Enlisting a range of supernatural

---

[96] Horace Walpole, 'Horace Walpole's Journals of Visits to Country Seats', in *The Sixteenth Volume of the Walpole Society, 1927–1928*, ed. Paget Toynbee (Oxford: Printed for the Walpole Society by John Johnson at the University Press, 1928), p. 59.
[97] I am grateful to Jon Culverhouse, Curator at Burghley, for assistance and clarification in these matters.
[98] See Horace Walpole to Horace Mann, 4 August 1757, *Correspondence*, vol. 21, p. 121.
[99] Walpole, *The Castle of Otranto*, pp. 9, 13; Tasso, *Jerusalem Delivered*, vol. 1, Book 1, ll. 15–16.
[100] Tasso, *Jerusalem Delivered*, vol. 1, Book I, l. 22. Walpole, *The Castle of Otranto*, p. 5.
[101] See the reference to 'each sabled knight' of the Christian forces in Tasso, *Jerusalem Delivered*, vol. 1, Book 1, l. 399.

forces in its defence, the Saracen army has at its disposal the assistance of Hidroates, the magician who presides over Damascus, as well as his niece, the redoubtable sorceress Armida, who, among other objects of enchantment, is in possession of a magic wand that is capable of turning men into fish; 'to her', the poem relates, 'was ev'ry art of magick known, / And all the wiles of womankind her own'.[102] Bearing similarities to the figures of Circe and Medusa, Armida seeks to sabotage the success of the Christian army by wooing its most heroic warriors into her clutches. In Book 7, she beguiles Tancred, a Christian knight in quest of his beloved Clorinda, into her enchanted castle, a structure that is set upon an equally magical island. Tasso's description of the pile owes much to Ariosto's depiction of the wizard Atlante's enchanted castle in *Orlando Furioso*:

> And now they came to where, amidst a flood
> Obscene with filth, a stately castle stood;
> What time the sun withdrew his fearful light,
> And sought the sable caverns of the night,
> At once the courier blew a sounding blast,
> And sudden o'er the moat the bridge was cast.[103]

Armida's castle is 'Impregnable by art and nature made', and, entirely unawares, Tancred is duly imprisoned there, detained as if by a 'strange enchantment'.[104] What renders this structure particularly impervious to Christian attack is that, as the sage warns them, its interiors are labyrinthine to the point of being impenetrable:

> Within, high walls with winding paths surround
> The secret dwelling, and the search confound:
> Maze within maze distracts the doubtful sight;
> A map shall guide your wand'ring steps aright.
> Amidst the lab'rynth lies the magick grove,
> Where ev'ry leaf impregnate seems with love.[105]

This architecture works its way directly into Walpole's fiction: if the Castle of Otranto is a 'labyrinth of darkness', this is because it takes its inspiration not, as Lewis eventually realized, from Strawberry Hill, but from Armida's enchanted castle in *Jerusalem Delivered*.[106]

---

[102] Tasso, *Jerusalem Delivered*, vol. 1, Book 4, ll. 183–4.
[103] Tasso, *Jerusalem Delivered*, vol. 1, Book 7, ll. 206–211.
[104] Tasso, *Jerusalem Delivered*, vol. 1, Book 7, ll. 217, 336.
[105] Tasso, *Jerusalem Delivered*, vol. 2, Book 14, ll. 553–8.
[106] Walpole, *The Castle of Otranto*, p. 26. As Groom's edition notes, another literary source for Otranto's labyrinth is the subterranean space beneath the palace in the Happy Valley in Samuel Johnson's *The History of Rasselas, Prince of Abissinia* (1759). It is also the labyrinth-like palace or bower in which Rosamond is imprisoned in several versions of the tale of Henry II's love for Rosamond Clifford. See Horace Walpole to William Cole, 9 March 1765, *Correspondence*, vol. 1, p. 91.

In Book 15, the Christian army, having gained ground in their assault upon Jerusalem, takes up arms against Armida and her sorcery, and, having been informed of her whereabouts by the Christian sage, arrives before her magical abode. In the interim, she has succeeded in capturing Rinaldo, another Christian knight renowned for his prowess and bravery, wooing him, as she did Tancred earlier, into her domain, and holding him a love-struck prisoner in a 'sumptuous garden' within the castle's walls.[107] When the Christians set out to free Rinaldo, they are as confounded by the ever-shifting spatial arrangements within the castle as Armida's prisoner himself. With Rinaldo eventually delivered by the knights from the temptress's powers, however, the enraged enchantress destroys her castle. The poem ends on a note of haunting, with Armida articulating both her plans for suicide and the threat that she will return to plague each of those who have injured her in life.

Although Marshal, Walpole's editorial persona in *The Castle of Otranto*, is quite particular about the 'Italian' nationality of the writers on whom the text was based—at the very least, it is consonant with the claim that the story was an English translation of the 'Original Italian of Onuphrio Muralto, Canon of the Church of St Nicholas at Otranto'—it is clear that Walpole also drew upon the romances of a number of other national traditions in the fashioning of his fictional castle. Richard Hurd had cited Thomas Hobbes in his reply to the author in William Davenant's *The Preface to Gondibert, An Heroick Poem* (1650) to argue that 'inchanted [*sic*] castles' recurred tirelessly in Gothic romances from across the European continent.[108] Through her mouthpiece, Euphrasia, Clara Reeve would argue the same point in *The Progress of Romance* (1785): 'enchanted palaces', together with 'delicious gardens' and 'endless labyrinths', were some of the most distinguishing characteristics of that 'species' or 'Genus' of writing that was ancient romance.[109] Accordingly, Walpole would also have encountered the convention in *Amadis of Gaul*, a French translation of which he later owned, as well as in certain versions of the Bevis of Hampton and Guy of Warwick narratives in the English tradition.[110] The sheer bathos underpinning Walpole's story also suggests that he approached the romance mode in *Otranto* through Cervantes's satirical treatment of it in *Don Quixote* (1605–15), particularly in the ludicrous event of the falling helmet that opens the narrative and its allusions to the affair of the 'enchanted' helmet in Cervantes's satire. Equally significant is Walpole's

---

[107] Tasso, *Jerusalem Delivered*, vol. 2, Book 14, l. 3.

[108] See Hurd's quoting of Hobbes in Hurd, *Letters on Chivalry and Romance*, p. 100. For Hobbes's original comments, see 'The Answer of Mr Hobbes to Sir Will. D'Avenant's Preface Before Gondibert', in *The Preface to Gondibert, An Heroic Poem* (Paris: Chez Matthieu Guillemot, 1650), pp. 129–64 (p. 147).

[109] Clara Reeve, *The Progress of Romance, Through Times, Countries, and Manners; With Remarks on the Good and Bad Effects of It, On Them Respectively; In a Course of Evening Conversations*, 2 vols (Colchester: Printed by W. Keymer, 1785), vol. 1, p. 54.

[110] See Hazen on Walpole and the old French *Amadis de Gaule* (1779) in *A Catalogue of Horace Walpole's Library*, vol. 2, p. 465.

lifelong fascination with Edmund Spenser's *The Faerie Queene* (1590–6), another epic romance to which the enchanted castle at Otranto alludes, and to which Walpole in his correspondence about Strawberry Hill continuously referred. As David Fairer has argued, it was *The Faerie Queene* that, more than any other fiction, facilitated the eighteenth century's engagement with the imaginative possibilities of Gothic romance.[111] Although Walpole did not approve of the thirty-two illustrations that the architectural designer William Kent produced for it, he owned and kept a copy of Kent's illustrated three-volume *The Faerie Queene* (1751), a collation of the original editions of 1590 and 1596, in the main Library at Strawberry Hill.[112]

In the 'Legend of Britomartis', the allegorical tale of chastity as it is recounted in Book III, Britomart abandons her quest for her destined husband, Artegall, in order to assist the despairing knight Scudamour in the recovery of his lady, Amoret, from imprisonment in the enchanted castle of Busirane. Walpole appears to have been particularly struck by this narrative of enchantment, figuring himself in 1762 in a letter to Lady Mary Coke, to whom he would later dedicate *Otranto*, as the Scudamore to her Amoret.[113] Approaching Busirane's castle, Britomart and Scudamour perceive the vast wall of fire that surrounds it, one of the many 'enchauntments' that the magician has employed to render the structure impregnable.[114] Undeterred, Britomart succeeds in penetrating this wall of flame, but finds within the castle's walls opulent interiors of an equally enchanting nature, a visual impression of which is afforded by one of the five large, highly evocative watercolours of scenes from Books I, III, and VI of *The Faerie Queene* that Diana Beauclerk painted in c.1781 (see Figure 2.4).[115] Surrounded by luxurious arrases of silk and gold that recount tales from Ovid's *Metamorphoses*, not even the noble Britomart is invulnerable to the enchanter's assault upon her senses. Forced to witness an erotically charged Masque of Cupid, Britomart in Busirane's abode finds herself in a castle that is as enchanted as that at Otranto: the signs on the lintels provide contradictory advice, and doors mysterious open and close, while a vision somewhat resembling Walpole's skeleton in a hermit's cowl is only one of the ghastly spectacles that passes, ghostlike, before her eyes. Apprehending Busirane, however, Britomart forces the enchanter to reverse his spells, eventually releasing Amoret from her imprisonment. With his enchantments brought to an

---

[111] David Fairer, 'The Faerie Queene and Eighteenth-century Spenserianism', in *A Companion to Romance: From Classical to Contemporary*, ed. Corinne Saunders (Oxford: Blackwell Publishing, 2007), pp. 197–215 (p. 197).

[112] Allen T. Hazen, *A Catalogue of Horace Walpole's Library* (1969), vol. 1, p. 99. For Walpole's responses to Kent's illustrations, see Horace Walpole to George Montagu, 13 June 1751, *Correspondence*, vol. 9, p. 116.

[113] Horace Walpole to Lady Mary Coke, 30 June 1762, *Correspondence*, vol. 31, p. 26.

[114] Edmund Spenser, *The Faerie Queene. By Edmund Spenser [...] Adorn'd with thirty-two Copper-Plates, from the Original Drawings of the late W. Kent, Esq; Architect and principal Painter to his Majesty*, 3 vols (London: Printed for J. Brindsley and S. Wright, 1751), vol. 2, Book III, Canto XI, stanza xiii.

[115] These drawings are now held at the LWL, B373 no. 6+ to 10+.

Figure 2.4 Diana Beauclerk's illustration to Book III of *The Faerie Queene* (c.1781). Courtesy of the Lewis Walpole Library, lwlpr31144.

end, so the luxurious rooms in the castle decay and then mysteriously disappear, seemingly without a trace: 'Returning back, those goodly roomes, which erst / He saw so rich and royally arayd, / Now vanisht utterly.'[116]

As Warton argued in the second edition of *Observations on the Fairy Queen of Spenser*, the disappearance of the enchanted castle in the poem demonstrated Spenser's indebtedness to that 'species of literature' that 'emerged from the depths of Gothic ignorance and barbarity'.[117] Though it may feature most prominently in *Orlando Furioso*, the 'vanishing of an enchanted palace or garden after some knight has destroyed the enchanter', Warton observed, is 'common to all ancient romances in general'.[118] Certainly, if there is one consistent feature across the depictions of enchanted castles in the romance tradition it is that, once the enchanter has been vanquished, his or her enchanted abode dissolves, collapses, disappears, or falls spectacularly to the ground. The fall of Atlante's

---

[116] Spenser, *The Faerie Queene*, vol. II, Book III, Canto XII, stanza xlii.
[117] Warton, *Observations on the Fairy Queen of Spenser*, vol. 1, p. 1.
[118] Warton, *Observations on the Fairy Queen of Spenser*, vol. 1, p. 17.

castle in *Orlando Furioso* illustrates this particularly well. In Canto 22, the knight errant Astolf is led, as if by fate, to the magician's pile. Gaining entrance, he consults the book of enchantments that he acquired in India, a tome that contains a spell that is capable of breaking the wizard's hold over his prisoners. Pitting his own magic against that of Atlante, Astolf blows his horn; 'In smoke and clouds away the palace flew', the enchanted castle thus disappearing as spontaneously as did Busirane's in *The Faerie Queene*.[119] *Jerusalem Delivered* includes a similar scene of architectural destruction, but here, not by an heroic vanquisher so much as at the hands of the enchantress Armida herself. With the assistance of 'Three hundred Deities from deepest Hell', Armida destroys her enchanted palace in so wrathful and passionate an act of magic that not even a vestige of ruin remains:[120]

> No longer now the stately walls appear'd;
> No trace remain'd where once the pile was rear'd.
> Like cloudy vapours of the changing skies,
> Where tow'rs and battlements in semblance rise,
> That fleet before the winds or solar beam:
> Like idle phantoms of a sick man's dream:
> So vanish'd all the pile, and nought remain'd
> But native horrours 'midst a rocky land![121]

True to its textual foundations, Manfred's castle at Otranto is destroyed at just that moment in which Theodore is revealed to be its true and legitimate heir: 'the walls of the castle behind Manfred were thrown down with a mighty force, and the form of Alfonso, dilated to an immense magnitude, appeared in the centre of the ruins'.[122] However, unlike the castles of Armida, Atlante, and Busirane that disappear without any remainder, Walpole's enchanted pile persists as an architectural ruin, with the disconsolate characters retiring to the 'remaining part of the castle' in the closing paragraph of the narrative.[123] As I argue below, it is this aspect of *The Castle of Otranto* that resonated most deeply with Walpole's architectural project at Strawberry Hill.

The Romance of Strawberry Hill

To the same extent that he drew upon the enchanted castles of Ariosto, Tasso, and Spenser in his fashioning and eventual destruction of the Castle of Otranto, so

---
[119] Ariosto, *Orlando Furioso*, Canto 22, stanza 23, p. 359.
[120] Tasso, *Jerusalem Delivered*, vol. 2, Book 16, p. 168, l. 87.
[121] Tasso, *Jerusalem Delivered*, vol. 2, Book 16, p. 168, ll. 500-7.
[122] Walpole, *The Castle of Otranto*, p. 103.   [123] Walpole, *The Castle of Otranto*, p. 105.

Walpole employed the language and conventions of 'Gothic' romance in much of his correspondence around the remodelling of Strawberry Hill from the late 1740s onwards.[124] In other words, the relationship between the two buildings resides not simply in the author having 'represented' his home in his fiction, but rather through his self-conscious references to the features of Gothic romance in relation to both. Contrary to Kenneth Clark's claims, literature was crucial to the eighteenth-century Gothic Revival. As early as January 1761—that is, several years before the Gothicizing of Strawberry Hill had been completed or *The Castle of Otranto* written and published—Walpole, in a clear expression of what Barrett Kalter has described as his abiding interest in evanescence, intimated that Strawberry Hill was neither a permanent structure nor one that was necessarily built to last, claiming in a letter to Horace Mann that 'my castle is built of paper' and the Walpolean 'empire' in general most likely 'to vanish as rapidly as it has advanced'.[125] As several critics have pointed out, this sense of a 'paper castle' was more than mere rhetorical flourish on Walpole's behalf, for as the 1784 edition of *A Description* makes clear, much use was made of paper in the decoration of Strawberry Hill.[126] In addition to Thomas Bromwich's moulded papier mâché fan-vaulting of the State Apartment, the Staircase Hall was hung with 'gothic paper, painted by one Tudor, from the screen of Prince Arthur's tomb in the cathedral at Worcester', and the Refectory 'with paper in imitation of stucco'.[127] At Strawberry Hill, painted paper formed the basis for the many Gothic *trompe l'œil*, and was used in several of the curiosities and artworks that Walpole displayed there, including a paper mosaic of flowers by Mrs Delany in the Breakfast Room, paper cut-outs of Walpole's parents in the Green Closet, and a paper-cut owl and a flower in paper mosaics in the Passage.[128] Brightly coloured paper was also used to line the house's interiors, with blue paper used in the Breakfast Room; wallpaper of vivid crimson and blue in the Red and Blue Bedchambers respectively; green paper in the Tea Room; and purple paper in the Holbein Chamber. The 'paper house' also referenced the Strawberry Committee's reliance on antiquarian

---

[124] For the dating of the beginnings of, and various stages within, Walpole's modifications to Strawberry Hill, see Michael Snodin and Cynthia Roman's *Horace Walpole's Strawberry Hill*, pp. xiv–xv. For further accounts of the building and its progress, see W. S. Lewis, 'The Genesis of Strawberry Hill'; Peter Guillery and Michael Snodin, 'Strawberry Hill: Building and Site', *Architectural History* 38 (1995): pp. 102–28; and Michael McCarthy, *The Origins of the Gothic Revival* (New Haven and London: Yale University Press, 1987), pp. 63–86.

[125] For a discussion of Walpole's interest in evanescence, see Barrett Kalter, *Modern Antiques: The Material Past in England, 1660–1780* (Lewisburg: Bucknell University Press, 2012), pp. 154–6; Horace Walpole to Horace Mann, 27 January 1761, *Correspondence*, vol. 21, p. 471.

[126] For a reading of the significance of paper at Strawberry Hill, see Ruth Mack, 'Paper Castle, Paper Collection: Walpole's Extra-Illustrated Copy of the Description of Strawberry Hill', in *Horace Walpole's Strawberry Hill*, ed. Michael Snodin with the assistance of Cynthia Roman (New Haven and London: Yale University Press, 2009), pp. 107–15. See, too, Anna Chalcraft's elaboration upon this metaphor in *A Paper House: Horace Walpole at Strawberry Hill* (London: Highgate Publications, 1998).

[127] Walpole, *A Description of the Villa of Mr Horace Walpole* (1784), p. 3.

[128] Walpole, *A Description of the Villa of Mr Horace Walpole* (1784), pp. 22, 26, 71, 72.

engravings of Gothic architectural details for their designs, sources that included Francis Sandford's *A Genealogical History of the Kings of England* (1677), William Thomas's *A Survey of the Cathedral Church of Worcester* (1737), and William Dugdale's *The History of St Pauls Cathedral in London* (1658). The metaphor of the 'paper house' would also no doubt have referred to Walpole's extensive and ever-growing collection of books, to his commissioning of numerous drawings and paintings of the house and gardens, as well as to the private printing press that he established there in 1757.[129] As a carefully staged spectacle of colour and light, Strawberry Hill depended largely on paper and the images and words recorded on paper for the generation of its associations, impressions, and effects.

Unlike the durability of stone, however, paper, as Walpole's letter to Mann registered, was also worryingly ephemeral, a consideration that, in Walpole's own mind, applied as much to his writings as to his architectural works. Indeed, as concerned with notions of posterity as his letters at times are, Walpole in his correspondence repeatedly dwelt on what he took to be the inevitable fall, downfall, or disappearance of Strawberry Hill and the Walpolean ancestral genealogy that it was designed to monumentalize, giving expression to fantasies of death and obliteration that were often reminiscent of the traceless vanishing of the enchanted castles in the 'Gothic stories' of Ariosto, Tasso, and Spenser. In a letter of 1771 that is fraught with all manner of anxiety concerning the survival and preservation of his literary, epistolary, and architectural legacy, Walpole wrote to Henry Seymour Conway that 'My buildings are paper, like my writings, and both will be blown away in ten years after I am dead; if they had not the substantial use of amusing me while I live, they would be worth little indeed.'[130] Similar intimations of impermanence, death, and the eventual disappearance of the literal and metaphorical 'house' of Walpole feature prominently in a letter that he wrote to Mann in May 1775. Having expressed the sense of 'joy' that he anticipates in showing his friend his work at Strawberry Hill, Walpole breaks off to consider the impossibility of this ever happening. Not only is Mann, the English diplomat abroad, a long-time resident of far-off Florence, but Strawberry Hill, itself, is an imaginary 'castle in the air', a toy, or a trifling architectural fantasy, one that is unlikely to endure beyond the roles of amusement and distraction that it fulfils for Walpole in the present:

> One passes away so soon, and worlds succeed to worlds, in which the occupiers build the same castles in the air. What is ours but the present moment? and how many of mine are gone! and what do I want to show you? A plaything-vision, that

---

[129] See Anna Chalcraft and Judith Viscardi's extended discussion of the use of paper at the house in *Strawberry Hill: Horace Walpole's Gothic Castle* (London: Frances Lincoln Ltd, 2007).

[130] Horace Walpole to Henry Seymour Conway, 5 August 1771, *Correspondence*, vol. 38, p. 110.

has amused a poor transitory mortal for a few hours, and that will pass away like its master!'[131]

Of course, if his home was a 'plaything', this was partly because it had been modelled on the rural cottage, Chopp'd Straw Hall, that Walpole had leased from the London toy-seller Elizabeth Chenevix in April 1747.[132] Walpole returned to this concern with the impermanence of paper and the transience of human existence in a letter to Lady Ossory in 1778, abruptly changing direction during a discussion of poetic fame and the imaginative appeal of the Gothic ruins at Netley Abbey, Hampshire, so as to express an arresting vision of personal and architectural obliteration even more intense than that in the earlier letter to Conway: 'I sometimes dream, that one day or other somebody will stroll about poor Strawberry and talk of Lady Ossory—but alas! I am no poet, and my castle is of paper, and my castle and my attachment and I, shall soon vanish and be forgotten altogether!'[133] A modern Gothic structure so heavily dependent upon paper, Strawberry Hill, Walpole feared, would not endure, but eventually disappear without leaving so much as a ruin in its place. Here, as elsewhere, he was patently aware of the differences between 'surviving' and 'revived' Gothic architectural forms. Lacking in the safeguard against oblivion inscribed in the very materiality of architectural ruin at Netley or in the name, works, and poetic reputation of Alexander Pope, Walpole may thus bequeath to posterity little more than his voluminous collection of papers—so many letters, he claims, that are the 'remnant of an useless life' and which he touchingly dedicates here to his 'friends'. In the earlier letter, not even Walpole's papers provided much by way of a defence against death and the passage of time; here, they ensure the posthumous remembrance for which Walpole towards the end of his life had hoped in bequeathing copies of his books to his friends, and the careful selection and arrangement of his papers for posthumous publication in the five-volume *The Works of Horatio Walpole, Earl of Orford* in 1798.[134]

Walpole returned to the impermanence of Strawberry Hill in the second edition of *A Description* in 1784. By this time, bitter experience at Houghton Hall, the paternal 'House of Walpole' that contained the vast collection of paintings that had been painstakingly documented and catalogued in *Aedes Walpoliana* (1747), had taught him that a home and its contents were anything but secure and permanent fixtures. So as to defray the debts incurred by the profligate lifestyle of Horace's nephew George, 3rd Earl of Orford, Sir Robert's collection of art had

---

[131] Horace Walpole to Horace Mann, 17 May 1755, *Correspondence*, vol. 24, p. 103.
[132] See Snodin, 'Going to Strawberry Hill', pp. 15–57.
[133] Horace Walpole to Lady Ossory, 11 August 1778, *Correspondence*, vol. 33, p. 43.
[134] For an example of Walpole's bequeathing of copies of his own works to his friends, see his note on the paper wrapping of a copy of *Hieroglyphic Tales* (Strawberry Hill: Printed by Thomas Kirgate, 1785): 'A Strawberry edition to be delivered on my death to Thomas Barrett, Esq., of Lee in Kent. HW', LWL, 33 32 Copy 1.

been sold off in 1779 to Catherine the Great of Russia, and permanently moved to the Hermitage, Saint Petersburg. Five years later, Walpole was still smarting at this act of disrespect towards his father's collection, yet he now read in the events further premonitions concerning the future of his own 'paper fabric' and the valuable collections that it housed: it would be 'a total insensibility to the pride of family', he writes, to expect the work of so 'insignificant' a man as himself to 'last or be treated with more veneration and respect than the trophies of a palace deposited in it by one of the best and wisest Ministers that this country has enjoyed'.[135] A figment, a mirage, a paper house, a castle in the air: Strawberry Hill, Walpole repeatedly expressed, was likely to dissolve with the speed at which the enchanted castles disappeared in the romances of Tasso, Ariosto, and Spenser. The collapse of the castle in the closing moments of *Otranto* thus uncannily enacts the future that Walpole projected for his own 'Gothic castle'. And yet, we may surely detect in the references to the 'remaining part of the castle' in the fiction's final paragraph a conscious sense of wish fulfilment on the author's behalf: the obdurate, architectural ruins that persist once the tyrant has been vanquished offer a certain security against the traceless vanishing that Walpole feared awaited his own 'paper Fabric'.[136]

The 'romance' of Strawberry Hill was pervasive, and extended to the use that Walpole made of Edmund Spenser in his correspondence around the house. Thanking Warton for the gift of a copy of the second edition of the *Observations* in a letter of August 1762, Walpole invited the author to join him at Twickenham, where, he claimed, 'You might play at fancying yourself in a castle described by Spenser.'[137] In strictly poetic terms, Walpole seems not to have been overly enamoured of Spenser, even describing the poet's distinctive appropriation of the sonnet and its rhyme schemes as 'rugged, uncouth, and unmusical' in later life.[138] Nonetheless, he repeatedly drew on Spenserian reference when writing about Strawberry Hill, even if the lines that he believed Spenser to have penned were often the result of egregious misattribution. The most notorious of these is his description of 'Strawberry' as the fruit of its namesake in a letter to Montagu in July 1763. Referring to the progress made on the Gallery, Walpole writes that 'Strawberry is growing sumptuous in its latter day; it will scarce be any longer like the fruit of its name, or the modesty of its ancient demeanour', both qualities, he continues, that 'seem to have been in Spenser's prophetic eye' when he wrote the lines, 'the blushing strawberries, / Which lurk, close-shrouded from high-looking eyes, / Shewing that sweetness low and hidden lies'.[139] Unattributed in W. S. Lewis's edition of the letters, these lines are not Spenserian at all, but

---

[135] Walpole, *A Description of the Villa of Mr Horace Walpole* (1784), p. i.
[136] Walpole, *The Castle of Otranto*, p. 105.
[137] Horace Walpole to Thomas Warton, 21 August 1762, *Correspondence*, vol. 40, p. 255.
[138] See Horace Walpole to William Roscoe, 4 April 1795, *Correspondence*, vol. 15, p. 261.
[139] Horace Walpole to George Montagu, 1 July 1763, *Correspondence*, vol. 10, pp. 84–5.

come rather from Canto IV, stanza 1 of *The Purple Island; or, The Isle of Man* (1633) by Phineas Fletcher, the English poet who published as least one of his poems with Spenser's name on the title page. Other examples of Spenserian misattribution occur in his correspondence, to the extent that we might deduce that, irrespective of their accuracy, Walpole at Strawberry Hill considered Spenser, the celebrated writer of 'Gothic story', to be a guiding and authenticating poetic presence of sorts.[140]

Accordingly, Strawberry Hill became an enchanted castle built upon 'enchanted ground', the eighteenth-century phrase, as Arthur Johnston has pointed out, that denoted any territory in a romance that was subject to the workings of a magician, including the enchanted wood in Tasso, the enchanted wood in Bunyan's *The Pilgrim's Progress* (1678), or in numerous responses to the presentation of topographical and architectural space in *The Faerie Queene*.[141] It was precisely upon this imaginative literary tradition that Walpole drew when, in a letter to Mann in June 1753, he eventually realized his dream of sending his distant friend a folded-up image of his 'paper house'. Including in his letter a now-lost drawing of the south side of Strawberry Hill, Walpole wrote that 'The enclosed enchanted little landscape then is Strawberry Hill', accompanying the picture with a detailed description of its prospects, its paper-based illusions and effects, its contents, and its furnishings, yet stressing all the while the house's 'diminutiveness'.[142] Mann clearly appreciated the force of literary allusion behind the gift, and in his reply expressed his admiration for the drawing and the home that it represented as, indeed, an 'enchanted little landscape' with its 'venerable little castle, so Gothic and so venerably gloomy' in effect.[143] To Walpole and his circle, Strawberry Hill was a 'Gothic story' cast in paper and stone, the real and fictional piles fashioned by its inhabitant linked with one another not through mimetic representation but through the language and architecture of imaginative fiction.[144]

Walpole, Sweet Enchanter

'My whole castle was illuminated, and the palace of Armida was not more enchanting,' wrote Walpole to Lady Ossory in October 1778, describing a splendid assembly that he had hosted at Strawberry Hill for his three nieces Waldegrave, Anna Maria Keppel, and Laura Keppel earlier that month.[145] If Strawberry Hill

---

[140] For another example of this, see Horace Walpole to Mary Berry, 4 September 1798, *Correspondence*, vol. 11, pp. 62–8.
[141] Johnston, *Enchanted Ground*, pp. 7–9.
[142] Horace Walpole to Horace Mann, 12 June 1753, *Correspondence*, vol. 20, pp. 379–84.
[143] Horace Mann to Horace Walpole, 13 July 1753, *Correspondence*, vol. 20, pp. 387–7.
[144] Horace Mann to Horace Walpole, 13 July 1753, *Correspondence*, vol. 20, pp. 386–7.
[145] Horace Walpole to Lady Ossory, 21 October 1778, *Correspondence*, vol. 33, p. 61.

was Armida's castle, Walpole himself was, by implication, the enchanter. This correspondence, however, necessarily placed him in a compromising position: Armida was a female, Circe-like temptress of demonic sexual prowess, and the enchanters Atlante, Archimago, and Busirane, the most likely male equivalents from *Orlando Furioso* and *The Faerie Queene*, ruthless villains intent on the seduction of vulnerable young women. Nor did the figure of Comus from Milton's masque of that name present a viable alternative: coaxing the bewildered Lady into what she believes to be a rustic cottage, the sorcerer leads her to his enchanted palace in the labyrinthine woods, restraining her there on an enchanted chair, and repeatedly subjecting her to his unwelcome advances. Walpole could not entertain the fantasy of having built an enchanted castle at Strawberry Hill without heaping upon himself the ignominy, dubious sexual appetite, and sheer moral turpitude that such literary identifications set in place. More than this, and as Fairer has pointed out, opposition to the rule of the Whig Prime Minister Sir Robert Walpole earlier in the century had often appropriated *The Faerie Queene* to satirical effect, frequently rendering Horace Walpole's father as Spenser's Archimago, the evil enchanter of the British realm.[146] In *The Castle of Indolence* (1748), perhaps the best-known poem about an enchanted castle in the period, James Thomson similarly put the trope to satirical use, presenting, like Spenser, Tasso, and Ariosto before him, the magical abode into which the 'false Inchanter Indolence' lures his victims as the place of unbridled luxury, self-gratification, and self-indulgence.[147] As Christine Gerrard has shown, the flattery, sycophancy, indulgence, vanity, and excess that thrive within Thomson's enchanted pile all replay the criticisms that writers of the Opposition had levied against Sir Robert, to the extent that the castle serves as an allegory of his political administration.[148] It is only with the arrival of Selvaggio, the Knight of Industry and Arts, that the wily enchanter, his castle, and his troop of drugged and slothful supporters are vanquished, and this, significantly, by the 'Gothic' system of power-sharing between sovereign and Parliament for which the Knight stands, and which Sir Robert was thought by the Tory Bolingbroke, Thomson, and other malcontented Patriot Whigs to have compromised: 'Whenas the Knight had fram'd, in BRITAIN LAND / A matchless Form of glorious Government; / In which the sovereign Laws alone command, / Laws stablish'd [sic] by the Public free Consent, / Whose Majesty is to the Sceptre lent.'[149] Within the context of what Gerrard has described as the 'political

---

[146] Fairer, '*The Faerie Queene* and Eighteenth-century Spenserianism', p. 202.

[147] James Thomson, *The Castle of Indolence: An Allegorical Poem. Written in Imitation of Spenser* (London: Printed for A. Millar, 1748), Canto 1, stanza 1, p. 41.

[148] Christine Gerrard, '*The Castle of Indolence* and the Opposition to Walpole', *The Review of English Studies* vol. 41, no. 161 (Feb. 1990): pp. 45–64. For another excellent account of literary satire in the age of Sir Robert Walpole, see Bertrand A. Goldgar, *Walpole and the Wits: The Relation of Politics to Literature, 1722–1742* (Lincoln and London: University of Nebraska Press, 1972).

[149] Thomson, *The Castle of Indolence*, Canto 2, stanza xxiv, p. 53.

Spenserianism' of the eighteenth century and its tendency to attack Sir Robert as a wily magician, Walpole's magical avatar had to be carefully selected.[150]

It was thus with the figure of the more benign enchanter, Prospero, that Horace Walpole self-consciously identified, the magician in Shakespeare's *The Tempest* (c.1611) who wields a more benevolent form of magic and who exercises powers of enchantment that, though not entirely free of cruelty, are ultimately more salutary than destructive in nature.[151] In contrast to the cruel and violent enchantments of the witch Sycorax, Prospero's power is tellingly characterized by an ability to call forth fanciful architectural visions as evanescent as Walpole's own. As he informs Ferdinand and Miranda in the wake of the appearance and then sudden vanishing of the fairies Iris, Ceres, and Juno in Act IV, scene i:

> These our actors,
> As I foretold you, were all spirits, and
> Are melted into air, into thin air;
> And like the baseless fabric of this vision,
> The cloud-capped towers, the gorgeous palaces,
> The solemn temples, the great globe itself,
> Yea, all which it inherit, shall dissolve;
> And, like this insubstantial pageant faded,
> Leave not a rack behind.[152]

Equally possessed by an acute awareness of the transience of writing, visions, architecture, and life itself, Walpole could not help but be drawn to the figure of Prospero. It is surely Prospero's 'baseless fabric of this vision' speech that he alluded to in his arresting reference to Strawberry Hill as a 'fantastic fabric' in the closing lines of the Preface to the 1784 edition of *A Description*.[153] More poignantly, on the front paste-down of his personal copy of the second edition of *Otranto* Walpole pasted a cut-out of 'To the Hon. and Ingenious Author of the Castle of Otranto', a sixteen-line poem that was initially published in *The St James's Chronicle* in June 1765, a few months after the public disclosure of

---

[150] For a discussion of 'political Spenserianism' and the opposition to Sir Robert Walpole, see Christine Gerrard, *The Patriot Opposition to Walpole: Politics, Poetry, and National Myth, 1725-1742* (Oxford: Clarendon Press, 1994), pp. 150–84.

[151] Although there is no indication that Walpole was aware of it, Thomas Duffet had brought Shakespeare and the trope of the enchanted castle together in *The Mock Tempest; or, The Enchanted Castle* (1674), a parody not of Shakespeare's original but of John Dryden and William D'Avenant's adaptation of Shakespeare in *The Tempest; or, The Enchanted Island* (1667).

[152] *The Tempest*, Act IV, scene i, ll. 148–56, in William Shakespeare, *The Norton Shakespeare, Based on the Oxford Edition*, 2nd edn, ed. Stephen Greenblatt, Walter Cohen, Jean E. Howard, and Katharine Eisaman Maus, with an essay by Andrew Gurr (New York and London: W. W. Norton & Co., 2005), p. 3104. In Alexander Pope's *The Works of Shakespear* (1725), one of the editions of Shakespeare that Walpole owned, Prospero's speech, with a few differences in wording and punctuation, occurs in Act IV, scene iv, of volume 1.

[153] Walpole, *A Description of the Villa of Horace Walpole* (1784), p. iv.

Walpole's authorship.[154] Signed only by the pseudonym 'Philotrantus', the poem has often been attributed to Thomas Gray; Walpole, however, annotated his copy with the line, 'by Mr Birch'. Without mentioning its author, William Cole transcribed the poem by hand into his copy of the first edition of *The Castle of Otranto*.[155] When it appears again, in print, in Edwards's edition of 1791, it is noted as being by 'G. Birch', but the copy of this edition of *Otranto* that Walpole sent to one 'G. Birch' bears no clues to the poet's identity beyond the small correction that, presumably, Birch himself makes in pencil to one of the poem's lines.[156] Hazen's *Bibliography of Horace Walpole*, however, identifies the author as George Birch, presumably the minor eighteenth-century poet of that name and author of the slim volume *Love Elegies* (1775).[157] Although W. S. Lewis's discussion of Cole's copy of *Otranto* in *Rescuing Horace Walpole* does not pursue the question of authorship any further, it does make the important point that, in the identifications that it draws between Walpole and Shakespeare, the poem would undoubtedly have delighted Walpole in his professed aims in the second Preface to defend Shakespeare from the criticism he had received from Voltaire and other French neoclassicists.[158]

The relevance of Birch's poem to Walpole, I would suggest, might be even more crucial in the connection that it draws between the author of *Otranto* and the magician Prospero. 'Thou sweet Enchanter! at whose Nod / The airy Train of Phantoms rise', the poem opens, directly recalling the work of Shakespeare's gentle magician in Act IV. 'By thee decoy'd, with curious Fear / We tread thy *Castle*'s dreary Round; / Though horrid all we see and hear, / Thy Horrors charm while they confound.' It is in the final stanza that the analogies between Walpole and Prospero become especially pronounced, as Shakespeare is presented as looking down favourably upon Walpole, the living embodiment of both Prospero and himself alike:

> Again his [i.e. Shakespeare's] Manners he may trace,
> Again his Characters may see,
> In soft Matild [*sic*], Miranda's Grace,
> And his own Prospero in thee.

Within a context in which Walpole and his novel were frequently the subject of poetic effusion and praise—without being any more specific, Ann Yearsley's 1784 poem about *Otranto* had also apostrophized the author as a 'great Magician' and a

---

[154] Philotrantus, 'To the Hon. and ingenious Author of The Castl [*sic*] of Otranto', *The St James's Chronicle; or, the British Evening Post*, 18–20 June 1765, Issue 670.

[155] *The Castle of Otranto, A Story* (London: Printed for Thomas Lowndes, 1764), LWL, 24 17 765 Copy 1.

[156] Birch cancels through underlining the word 'horrid' in the line 'Though horrid all we see and hear', substituting it for 'Horror'. See LWL, 24 17 791P Copy 6.

[157] Hazen, *A Bibliography of Horace Walpole*, p. 52.

[158] Lewis, *Rescuing Horace Walpole*, p. 183.

'noble Sorcerer'—it is surely significant that it was this particular text that Walpole chose to paste into his personal copy of his fiction.[159] In Walpole's hands, however, the supernaturalism of Prospero has been considerably attenuated. As Simon During has shown, enchantment underwent a fundamental shift towards the end of the eighteenth century, moving away from the occultic supernaturalism of earlier periods and into the secular realm of spectacle, dramatic special effects, and stage-managed wonders.[160] Strawberry Hill is testament to precisely such a process, for the enchantments that the building offered were not, in the end, the treacherous supernatural allurements of an Armida, a Comus, an Atlante, or a Busirane, but rather the salutary, less threatening pleasures of imagination, taste, and female genius as represented by the paintings of Lady Diana Beauclerk and the sculptures of Anne Damer. As Lady Burrell's 'Lines Sent to Mr Walpole' of 1790 put it, '*Here* Fancy needs no airy visions paint; / For Taste *supplies*, whate'er the eye can want, / The gay Enchantress waves her magic Wand, and Sculpture triumphs by a *female* hand.'[161] At Walpole's enchanted castle, the wily seduction of visitors had been replaced by a carefully managed sense of serendipity, that making of discoveries 'by accidents and sagacity, of things which they were not in quest of'.[162] If the Castle of Otranto was the place of horror, terror, and supernatural enchantment, Strawberry Hill was intended as the place of light, delight, and carefully orchestrated wonder. Each incarnated a different version of the Gothic past: the 'darkest ages of Christianity' at Otranto, the white Gothic— quite literally, with the house's whitewashed roughcast lime plaster exteriors—at Strawberry Hill. In Clarke's terms, the gloomy architecture of the 'written Gothic' was, from the start, placed in a relation of tension with the 'built Gothic' of the eighteenth-century Gothic Revival.[163] The heir to the milder magic of Shakespeare and Prospero, Walpole finally assumes his rightful place in the illustrious tradition of 'Gothic Enchanters' that Hurd had celebrated in his *Letters on Chivalry and Romance*. Abjuring his 'rough magic' and threatening to break his magical staff, Prospero exits Shakespeare's play on a note of despair, anticipating in his final speech a return to Naples, the site, perhaps not coincidentally, at which Walpole's enchantments in *The Castle of Otranto* begin. Across Horace Walpole's architectural, literary, and epistolary oeuvre, though, we continuously encounter the

---

[159] See Ann Yearsley, 'To the Honourable H—E W—E, on Reading *The Castle of Otranto*. December 1784', in *Poems on Several Occasions*, 3rd edn (London: Printed for T. Cadell, 1785), pp. 66–73.

[160] See Simon During, *Modern Enchantments: The Cultural Power of Secular Magic* (Cambridge, Mass., and London: Harvard University Press, 2002), pp. 1–73.

[161] Lady Burrell's poem is included in, among other places, Richard Bull's extra-illustrated copy of Walpole's 1784 edition of *A Description of the Villa of Mr Horace Walpole*, LWL, Folio 33 30 Copy 11.

[162] Walpole defines 'serendipity', his coinage, in a letter to Horace Mann, 28 January 1754, *Correspondence*, vol. 20, p. 408. For an application of this to the visitor's experience to Strawberry Hill, see John Iddon, *Strawberry Hill & Horace Walpole: Essential Guide* (London: Scala, 2011), p. 9.

[163] Clarke, 'Abbeys Real and Imagined: Northanger Abbey, Fonthill, and Aspects of the Gothic Revival'.

image of an enchanter who forever eschewed the dull turns of the quotidian in favour of the intoxicating enchantments of the faerie realm.

Enchanted Castles after Walpole

As an enchanter, Horace Walpole arrogated to himself the ability to call up 'gorgeous palaces' and 'solemn temples' in the Gothic style, often regarding his work at Strawberry Hill as the primary inspiration for a number of other contemporary Gothic Revivalist buildings, remodellings, and architectural designs. As McCarthy has argued, traces of Strawberry Hill, both faint and more pronounced, may be identified in John Chute's work for James Pettit Andrews at Donnington Grove, Berkshire; at Chute's family home, The Vyne, in Hampshire; in Richard Bentley's unexecuted plan and elevation for a farmhouse for Sir Thomas Seabright in Herefordshire; and in the Gothic conversions of Richard ('Dickie') Bateman's Grove House into The Priory, Old Windsor.[164] Walpole's responses to these and other manifestations of domestic Gothic architecture reveal the extent to which he regarded himself, in Matthew M. Reeve's terms, as the veritable 'arbiter of the Gothic taste' with 'Strawberry Hill as its paradigm'.[165] His responses to James Wyatt's Gothic remodelling of Thomas Barrett's Lee Priory, Kent, are probably the most exemplary: as Walpole wrote to Barrett in June 1788, Lee Priory was 'finished by a great master', his 'paper house' at Strawberry Hill, by contrast, 'but a sketch by beginners'.[166] In 1794, Walpole would praise Lee Priory as 'a child of Strawberry prettier than the parent', as the issue or offspring of Strawberry Hill that contained 'a delicious closet'—Wyatt's Strawberry Room—that Walpole deemed 'so flattering to me!'[167] These metaphors of filiation are revealing: as Reeve and Lindfield have argued, Lee Priory, aspects of Chute's The Vyne, Bateman's villa at Old Windsor, and Donnington Grove were seen to constitute a 'second generation' of Gothic country houses, a familial relation that not only placed Walpole in the role of single, reproductive parent, but which also implicitly laid down the terms of a queer family romance between Walpole, his male friends and designers, and their Gothic 'offspring'.[168] With its Gothic designs by Richard Bentley and Johann Heinrich Müntz, both of whom had been involved in the work at Strawberry Hill, Bateman's villa at Old Windsor, too, was ripe for Walpolean appropriation. As he claimed in a letter to the Earl of Strafford in

---

[164] McCarthy, *The Origins of the Gothic Revival*, pp. 92–115.
[165] Matthew M. Reeve, 'Dickie Bateman and the Gothicization of Old Windsor: Gothic Architecture and Sexuality in the Circle of Horace Walpole', *Architectural History* 56 (January 2013): pp. 97–131 (p. 97).
[166] Horace Walpole to Thomas Barrett, 5 June 1788, *Correspondence*, vol. 42, pp. 220–1.
[167] Horace Walpole to Mary Berry, 27 September 1794, *Correspondence*, vol. 12, p. 111.
[168] Matthew M. Reeve and Peter N. Lindfield, '"A Child of Strawberry": Thomas Barrett and Lee Priory, Kent', *The Burlington Magazine*, CLVII, December 2015, pp. 836–42 (p. 836).

June 1781, Walpole was 'proud' of 'having converted Dicky [*sic*] Bateman from a Chinese to a Goth'; 'I preached so effectually', he wrote, 'that his every pagoda took the veil.'[169] As he had written to Mann several years earlier, 'I did not doubt but you would approve Mr Bateman's [Gothicized villa] since it has changed its religion; I converted it from Chinese to Gothic.'[170] That these claims were, strictly speaking, disingenuous only underscores the vehemence with which Walpole identified with the enchanter's powers of architectural creation: The Grove at Old Windsor, far from being a building in the 'pure' Chinese style, had included hybridized forms of Gothic elements before its 'conversion' from 1758 onwards, revealing Bateman's affinity with the Gothic that characterized his work at Shobdon in Herefordshire, too.[171]

Walpole the enchanter adopted a similar position in relation to his literary endeavours, keeping an extremely close eye on contemporary responses to his novel and painstakingly recording in his own hand, on a blank page towards the end of his own copy of the text, a non-chronological list of some of the numerous reprintings, adaptations, appropriations, and critical responses that *Otranto* was to enjoy, from the early 1780s up until two years before his death. Among these are 'Mr Jephson's Tragedy of the Count of Narbonne', a play 'taken from this story';[172] particular 'scenes in a Pantomime called the [*sic*] Enchanted Castle' that was 'acted at the Theatre in Covent garden [*sic*] in 1787';[173] an abridged French translation of the novel that was printed in Amsterdam in 1767;[174] the 'two chapters in praise of the Castle of Otranto as a moral story' in Ellenor Fenn's 'Female Guardian printed in 1784';[175] an Italian edition of the novel that was printed 'by Bodoni, at Parma' in 1791;[176] another unspecified and undated edition 'published in Ireland';[177] a 'very

---

[169] Horace Walpole to the Earl of Strafford, 13 June 1781, *Correspondence*, vol. 35, p. 359.
[170] Horace Walpole to George Montagu, 24 September 1762, *Correspondence*, vol. 10, p. 43.
[171] Reeve, 'Dickie Bateman and the Gothicization of Old Windsor', pp. 110–11.
[172] A reference to Robert Jephson's *The Count of Narbonne, A Tragedy* that was performed at the Theatre Royal, Covent Garden, London, in 1781. For a printed version of the script, see Robert Jephson, *The Count of Narbonne. A Tragedy. As it is Acted at the Theatre Royal in Covent Garden* (London: Printed for T. Cadell, 1781).
[173] A reference to Miles Peter Andrews's unpublished pantomime that, though called *The Castle of Wonders* in manuscript form, was entitled *The Enchanted Castle* when its songs and recitatives were published separately in 1786. Contrary to Walpole's dating of the play to 1787, it was actually performed in Covent Garden in late 1786. See the announcement of the play's debut on Tuesday, 18 December, in *The Public Advertiser*, Monday, 17 December 1786, Issue 16404. See, too, Miles Peter Andrews, *The Songs, Recitatives, Airs, Duets, Trios, and Choruses, Introduced in the Pantomime Entertainment of the Enchanted Castle, as Performed at the Theatre-Royal, Covent-Garden* (London: Printed for the Author, 1786).
[174] *Le Château d'Otrante, histoire gothique, par. M. Horace Walpole, traduit sur la seconde édition angloise par M.[arc Antoine] E.[idous]* (Amsterdam and Paris: Prault le jeune, 1767).
[175] See A Lady [Ellenor Fenn], *The Female Guardian* (London: Printed and Sold by John Marshall and Co., 1784).
[176] Though printed in Italy, this was an English edition of the text, and entitled *The Castle of Otranto, A Gothic Story* (Parma: Bodoni for J. Edwards, 1791).
[177] Walpole was probably referencing one of the two unauthorized reprintings of the first edition of *Otranto* that were published in Dublin in 1765, the first by J. Hoey and the other by E. Watts.

neat' English-language edition, illustrated with woodcuts, that was published in Berlin in 1794;[178] an expanded, Italian translation that was published in London 1795, 'with cuts by Edwards in Pall Mall' that were 'signed by Miss Clarke, niece of Sir Charles Radcliffe';[179] and two smaller editions published in London 'in collections of Novels', 'one by Wenman, and the other by C. Cooke'.[180]

Of all of these, it was with Jephson's *The Count of Narbonne* (1781) that Walpole was particularly delighted, a play that, in both its plot and its architectural setting, is as much indebted to *The Mysterious Mother* (1768) as it is to *Otranto*. Walpole had collaborated with the Irish playwright earlier in his career when, in 1775, he was persuaded by Jephson's friend, the lawyer Edward Tighe, to write a short epilogue for Jephson's tragedy *Braganza* (1775). Walpole was a great admirer of Jephson's work, and even confessed at one point to being 'jealous' of his poetic fame and ability.[181] While suggesting certain changes to plot and diction, and declining Jephson's invitation to write either a prologue or an epilogue for the piece, Walpole responded warmly to a manuscript draft of *The Count of Narbonne* in January 1780.[182] Making 'a great deal more' than he 'thought possible out of the skeleton of a story', *The Count of Narbonne*, in Walpole's estimation, dispensed with 'the marvellous' and put his 'extravagant materials into an alembic', as if to extract from them 'only what was rational'.[183] It also returned *Otranto* to the dramatic form to which, in the estimation of both William Warburton and Walpole himself, his 'Gothic Story' was really best suited.[184] The play was duly produced and performed at the Theatre Royal in Covent Garden in 1781, and in its printed form included a fulsome dedication to Walpole. Walpole, in turn, bound Jephson's presentation copy of *The Count of Narbonne* into a copy of the fourth edition of *Otranto*, a gesture that indicates something of the esteem in which he held it.[185]

In the same letter of January 1780 in which he praised Jephson for his work in *The Count of Narbonne*, Walpole took care to list a number of other fictions that

---

[178] Walpole is referring here to *The Castle of Otranto, A Gothic Story* (Berlin: C. F. Himbourg, 1794), which includes four woodcuts by J. W. Meil.

[179] This was the first Italian translation of the novel, and entitled *Il Castello di Otranto. Storia Gotica*, trans. Giovanni Sivrac (London: Molini, Polidori, Molini and Co., 1795). The 'Miss Clarke' to whom Walpole here refers is Anne Melicent Clarke.

[180] Respectively, *The Castle of Otranto: A Gothic Story. A New Edition* (London: Printed for Wenman and Hodgson, 1793) and the edition of the novel that was printed by J. Wright for the publisher C. Cooke in London in 1794.

[181] Horace Walpole to Robert Jephson, 13 July 1777, *Correspondence*, vol. 41, p. 363.

[182] See Horace Walpole to Robert Jephson, 25 January 1780, *Correspondence*, vol. 41, pp. 406–9.

[183] Horace Walpole to Robert Jephson, 25 January 1780, *Correspondence*, vol. 41, p. 406.

[184] See Walpole's Preface to the first edition of *The Castle of Otranto*, in which William Marshal claims that 'It is a pity that [the author] did not apply his talents to what they were evidently proper for, the theatre' (Walpole, *The Castle of Otranto*, p. 7). For Warburton's comments on the tragic and dramatic aspects of *Otranto*, see *The Works of Alexander Pope, Esq., Vol. IV. Containing His Satires, etc.*, ed. William Warburton (London: Printed for C. Bathurst, W. Strahan, J. and F. Rivington et al., 1770), pp. 166–7.

[185] See the copy at the LWL, 49 3730.2.

he believed his Gothic story to have inspired, among them 'Sir Bertrand: A Fragment', the short Gothic fiction that, though here misattributed by Walpole to Anna Laetitia Aikin, is now generally thought to have been written by her brother John as a companion piece to his sister's essay 'On the Pleasure Derived from Objects of Terror' that was published in the siblings' collaborative *Miscellaneous Pieces, in Prose* in 1773.[186] John Aikin illustrated in 'Sir Bertrand' his sister's sense of the 'terrible joined with the marvellous' in the Gothic and Eastern romance traditions, figuring the ruined architectural pile in which much of the action occurs as one of those enchanted castles of ancient romance.[187] Recalling the architectural hybridity of *Otranto*, this ruined pile is as much haunted as it is enchanted. Though he was flattered by 'Sir Bertrand', Walpole was less pleased with Clara Reeve's attempts at rectifying what she took to be the imperfections of *Otranto* in *The Champion of Virtue* (1777), another 'offspring' of the text that was republished under the more familiar title of *The Old English Baron* in 1778. 'I cannot compliment the author of *The Old English Baron*,' wrote Walpole of Reeve's narrative; 'It was totally void of imagination and interest', he continued, and 'though it condemned the marvellous', it paradoxically 'admitted a ghost'.[188] In part, Reeve's solution to what she saw as the bathetic 'disenchantments' of *Otranto* in *The Old English Baron* was to leave the Castle of Lovel, the part-haunted, part-enchanted palace around which much of the action revolves, very much in place at the narrative's end. As Edmund Lovel (the newly restored legitimate heir) and his entourage approach the castle, they watch as 'the outward gates flew open'; entering the courtyard, the great folding doors leading to the hall are 'opened without any assistance', and when Edmund enters the hall, 'every door in the house' mysteriously 'flew open'.[189] As Warton had observed in 1762, scenes 'such as that of blowing a horn, at the sound of which the gates of a castle fly open' were a standard feature of romance narrative, recalling in this particular instance the mysterious opening and closing of the doors in the palaces of Atlante in *Orlando Furioso* and Busirane in *The Faerie Queene*. Reeve's narrative thus sustains the wonders that she deemed to have been compromised by the ending of *Otranto* through letting her own enchanted Lovel Castle persist, as it were, beyond the close of the story, presiding over a succession of marriages, births, and future narrative developments.

Ellenor Fenn's favourable response to *Otranto* in her conduct book *The Female Guardian* (1784) was significant not only because it promoted the narrative as

---

[186] For an account of the controversy surrounding authorship and attribution, as well as the claim that 'Sir Bertrand' is a fragment of a larger, more complete piece, see Luke R. J. Maynard, 'A Forgotten Enchantment: The Silenced Princess, the Andalusian Warlord, and the Rescued Conclusion of "Sir Bertrand"', *Eighteenth-Century Fiction* vol. 23, no. 1 (Fall 2010): pp. 141–62.
[187] J. and A. L. Aikin, *Miscellaneous Pieces, in Prose* (London: Printed for J. Johnson, 1773), p. 126.
[188] Horace Walpole to Robert Jephson, 27 January 1780, *Correspondence*, vol. 41, p. 410.
[189] Reeve, *The Old English Baron*, p. 115.

a suitably moral and instructive fiction for young ladies, but also because it underscored the extent to which the architecture of the castle in *Otranto* looked ultimately to the conventions of romance for its foundations. Significantly, for Fenn, Walpole's use of the trope of the enchanted castle in his fiction meant that it lacked all reference to his 'real' castle at Strawberry Hill:

> When the 'ancient castle,' in which [Walpole's] imagination had placed him during the night, was 'like the baseless fabric of a vision,' dissolved in air, he amused himself with raising this delightful structure, where we may truly say, all is *enchantment!* Can one refrain from wishing that the elegant gothic scenes at *Strawberry-hill* had been pictured by the masterly hand of their owner.[190]

Citing Prospero's speech in Act IV, scene i, of *The Tempest*, Fenn, like Birch's poem discussed above, figures Walpole as Shakespeare's mild Enchanter who, far from simply representing Strawberry Hill in his text, fashioned Otranto out of material no more substantial than a romance or a dream. Miles Peter Andrews's pantomime *The Castle of Wonders* (c.1786), another source included in Walpole's list, achieved much the same thing, successfully restoring the architecture of Walpole's fictional castle to its 'Gothic' literary sources. While Andrews's lyrics for the music that William Shield wrote for the pantomime, here entitled *The Enchanted Castle*, were published in 1786, its original script exists today only in manuscript form.[191] Set, at least partly, on an enchanted island situated off the coast of India—a realm strongly suggestive of Prospero's enchanted isle—the action recounts the capturing of Columbine by an evil necromancer, and her imprisonment in his enchanted castle; within, she is surrounded by the monstrous forms of advocates, lawyers, and other middle-class professionals whom the magician, a masculine equivalent to Tasso's Armida, has turned into beasts. When Zany and Columbine's suitor Harlequin are shipwrecked on the island, they are assisted by the Genius of the Wood, a figure seemingly derived from the attendant spirit that assists the imperilled Lady in *Comus*. Following a range of bizarre set changes that include a musical interlude on the High Street of contemporary Boston, the magician and his castle are eventually vanquished, and the lovers Harlequin and Columbine happily restored to one another at the play's end.

Thus Walpole fashioned himself as a magician who was capable of calling up 'cloud-capped towers' and other 'baseless' literary and architectural fabrics. But his manuscript list of responses to, and adaptations of, *Otranto* is just as revealing for what it leaves out as for what it includes. One such omission is William Beckford's *The History of the Caleph Vathek*, the Oriental fiction that was translated by Samuel Henley and published without the author's knowledge or consent

---

[190] A Lady [Ellenor Fenn], *The Female Guardian*, p. 95.
[191] See Miles Peter Andrews, *The Castle of Wonders* [1786?], M.S. Larpent Collection, No. 752. Henry E. Huntington Library and Art Gallery, California.

as *An Arabian Tale* in 1786. If Walpole seems not to have regarded *Vathek* as belonging to the 'new species of romance' instantiated by *Otranto*, this might well have been because, as Henley's scholarly notes to the unauthorized translation made clear, the enchanted architecture of the tale looked not to 'Gothic' antecedents so much as to the Oriental magic and wonder of *The Arabian Nights' Entertainment*. Though Walpole certainly perceived continuities between the Eastern tradition of romance and Gothic architecture—'the *Arabian Nights* and King's [College] Chapel [Cambridge]', he wrote in 1789, are alike insofar as both are 'above all rules'—the heightened fancy and lawlessness of the former seemed even for this committed advocate of the imagination somewhat excessive.[192] His most notable omission, though, must surely be the work of Ann Radcliffe, the most successful writer of Gothic romance in the last decade of the eighteenth century. Famed and successful in Walpole's lifetime though she was—dying in March 1797, Walpole lived right through her staggering successes of the 1790s—Radcliffe seems only once to have been the subject of direct and specific mention across Walpole's works and letters, while there is no evidence of him ever having owned or kept any copies of her novels at Strawberry Hill. In a letter to Lady Ossory on 4 September 1794—that is, some four months after the publication of *The Mysteries of Udolpho*—the aged enchanter made the following comment: 'I have read some of the descriptive verbose tales, of which your ladyship says I was the patriarch by several mothers. All I can say for myself, is, that I do not think my concubines have produced issue more natural for excluding the aid of anything marvellous.'[193] This is a clear yet dismissive reference to Radcliffe's penchant for natural description and her signature technique of the explained supernatural. The irony behind Walpole's reluctant acknowledgement of literary paternity, though, is that it was in Ann Radcliffe's fiction that his enchanted castles most securely came to establish themselves, an aspect of Radcliffe's architectural imagination that I shall explore more fully in the next chapter.

---

[192] Horace Walpole to Mary Berry, 30 June 1789, *Correspondence*, vol. 11, p. 22. For Walpole's sense of the overbearing 'wildness' of *The Arabian Nights' Entertainment*, see Horace Walpole to William Mason, 3 February 1781, *Correspondence*, vol. 29, p. 101.

[193] For the dating of the publication of *Udolpho* to Thursday, 8 May 1794, see Norton, *Mistress of Udolpho*, p. 93. For Walpole's letter, see Horace Walpole to Lady Ossory, 4 September 1794, *Correspondence*, vol. 34, p. 204.

3
From 'Castles in the Air' to the Topographical Gothic
Locating Ann Radcliffe's Architectural Imagination

It is nothing new to say that Ann Radcliffe was the 'Great Enchantress' to the majority of readers and critics of her day. In the one-volume reissue of the four-part *The Pursuits of Literature* of 1798, the otherwise anti-Gothic T. J. Mathias paid tribute to 'the mighty magician of THE MYSTERIES OF UDOLPHO, bred and nourished by the Florentine Muses amid the paler shrines of Gothic superstition and in all the dreariness of Inchantment [*sic*]', while, in a revised edition of *Confessions of an English Opium-Eater* in 1856, Thomas De Quincey looked fondly back upon his youth to describe Radcliffe as the 'great enchantress of that generation'.[1] While these and other such encomiums to the writer's 'magical' abilities are well known, critics have perhaps overlooked the architectural contexts in which they were first uttered.[2] For Mathias, Radcliffe was a poetess 'whom Ariosto would with rapture have acknowledged', a claim that he underscored by citing two lines from *Orlando Furioso*: like Armida in her enchanted castle, Radcliffe's powers of enchantment were primarily architectural in nature. If women were to be admitted to architecture's masculine realms at all, they could only do so as destructive enchantresses. Nonetheless, Radcliffe's romances for Mathias remained infinitely superior to the work of other women writers who penned 'Inscriptive nonsense in a fancied Abbey'.[3] Several decades later, De Quincey made much the same point: in describing Radcliffe as the 'great enchantress', he was referring specifically to the effects that her description of the ruined Furness Abbey in *A Journey Made in the Summer of 1794* (1795) had exerted over his own tour of the English Lake District in the late 1790s.[4] If Radcliffe possessed an Armida-like power to call up imaginary enchanted piles in her fictions, she was

---
[1] T. J. Mathias, *The Pursuits of Literature: A Satirical Poem in Four Dialogues. With Notes*, 8th edn (London: Printed for T. Becket, 1798), p. 58; Thomas De Quincey, *The Works of Thomas De Quincey, Vol. II: Confessions of an English Opium-Eater, 1821–1856*, ed. Grevel Lindop (London: Pickering & Chatto, 2000), p. 147.
[2] See, for example, Robert Miles, *Ann Radcliffe: The Great Enchantress* (Manchester: Manchester University Press, 1995), and Dale Townshend and Angela Wright, 'Gothic and Romantic Engagements: The Critical Reception of Ann Radcliffe, 1789–1850', in *Ann Radcliffe, Romanticism and the Gothic*, ed. Dale Townshend and Angela Wright (Cambridge: Cambridge University Press, 2014), pp. 3–32.
[3] Mathias, *The Pursuits of Literature*, p. 58.
[4] De Quincey, *The Works of Thomas De Quincey, Vol. II*, p. 147.

Gothic Antiquity: History, Romance, and the Architectural Imagination, 1760–1840. Dale Townshend, Oxford University Press (2019). © Dale Townshend.
DOI: 10.1093/oso/9780198845669.001.0001

also capable of changing 'real-life' architectural ruins into objects of speculation and wonder. As William Hazlitt confessed in *Lectures on the English Comic Writers* in 1819, 'part of the impression with which I survey the full-orbed moon shining in the blue expanse of heaven, or hear the wind sighing through autumnal leaves, or walk under the echoing archways of a Gothic ruin, is owing to repeated perusal of the Romance of the Forest and the Mysteries of Udolpho'.[5] The power of Radcliffe's writings was such that they imbued Gothic buildings with a new set of literary associations, and therein was thought to lie the proof of her original genius, a faculty that Edward Young in *Conjectures on Original Composition* had illustrated through reference to Armida the Enchantress and her magic wand.[6]

Mathias, De Quincey, and Hazlitt were by no means the only critics to celebrate Radcliffe's powers to influence, determine, and ineradicably alter her readers' perceptions of architectural space. As compelling as they were enduring, the evocative descriptions of Gothic architecture offered across Radcliffe's oeuvre were the subject of frequent critical reflection, both in her own time and in the retrospective appraisals of the writer and her work that appeared after her death in 1823. Some three years before her demise, and six years before he prefaced the posthumously published *Gaston De Blondeville* with his 'Memoir of the Life and Writings of Mrs Radcliffe' in 1826, Thomas Noon Talfourd paid a 'tribute of gratitude' to Radcliffe for her 'wild and wondrous tales', claiming that when we read them, 'we breathe only in an enchanted region', one in which 'mouldering castles rise conscious of deeds of blood, and the sad voices of the past echo through deep vaults and lonely galleries'.[7] If Radcliffe, for Talfourd, was capable of casting 'spells' that were 'truly magical' in effect, this was largely because of her ability imaginatively to transport her readers to, and immerse them deeply within, the vaults and galleries of the Gothic piles so graphically figured in her fictions.[8] Citing a phrase from John Cosens's poem *The Economy Of Beauty* (1772–3), Anna Laetitia Barbauld similarly maintained that the 'genius' of the writer resided in the 'gloomy forests, and abrupt precipices, and the haunt of banditti' that occur in her novels set abroad, and in the '"time-shook towers," vast uninhabited castles, winding staircases, long echoing aisles' that abounded in her writings set in Britain.[9] Frequently celebrated in the language of building, design, and construction, Ann

---

[5] William Hazlitt, *Lectures on the English Comic Writers* (London: Printed for Taylor and Hessey, 1819), p. 250.

[6] Young, *Conjectures on Original Composition*, p. 10.

[7] T. D. [Thomas Noon Talfourd], 'On British Novels and Romances, Introductory to a Series of Criticisms on the Living Novelists', *The New Monthly Magazine, and Universal Register* vol. XIII, no. 73 (1 Feb. 1820): pp. 205–9 (pp. 208–9).

[8] T. D. [Thomas Noon Talfourd], 'On British Novels and Romances, Introductory to a Series of Criticisms on the Living Novelists', p. 209.

[9] Mrs Barbauld [Anna Laetitia Barbauld], 'Mrs Radcliffe', in *The British Novelists, With An Essay, and Prefaces Biographical and Critical, Vol. XLIII* (London: Printed for F. C. and J. Rivington et al., 1820), pp. i–viii (p. i).

Radcliffe's imagination became, for the nineteenth century, a thoroughly architectural affair. As Leigh Hunt put it in 1849, it was precisely Radcliffe's architectural imagination—what he termed her 'discovery of the capabilities of *an old house or castle* for exciting a romantic interest'—that raised her art above the 'feudal dilletante-ism [sic]' of Horace Walpole.[10] The magical abilities of the Great Enchantress had quite eclipsed those of Walpole's Prospero.

It was thus in some senses fitting that some of Radcliffe's less forgiving readers would employ architectural metaphors to articulate their more ambivalent responses to her work. In his *Biographical and Critical History of the British Literature of the Last Fifty Years* (1834), Scottish poet and songwriter Allan Cunningham maintained, rather generously at first, that, more than any of her forebears, Radcliffe had provided 'a rusty key of a gothic pattern' to an ancient Gothic castle, opening its 'unwilling doors' and leading her readers 'through the terrific domains of superstitious dread and fear'.[11] In figuring the reading of a Radcliffean romance as an experience akin to being led through a portal and into the labyrinthine interiors of a Gothic pile, Cunningham may well have been alluding to the metaphor that Walter Scott had employed in his 'Prefatory Memoir to Mrs Ann Radcliffe' that was published in Ballantyne's one-volume reprinting of five of Radcliffe's novels in 1824. Using the Prologue to *The Italian* (1797) as his example, Scott here claimed that 'This introductory passage may be compared to the dark and vaulted gateway of an ancient castle', an entirely appropriate point of entry, he claimed, to the 'corresponding' tale of mystery and terror that follows it.[12] Of course, the architectural metaphors of both Cunningham and Scott may have been prompted by the trope that Radcliffe herself had employed in the epigraph that features on the title page of *The Mysteries of Udolpho* (1794): 'Fate sits on these dark battlements, and frowns, / And, as the portals open to receive me, / Her voice, in sullen echoes through the courts, / Tells of a nameless deed.'[13] To begin reading *Udolpho* was to pass like its resident heroine through the foreboding threshold of an ancient Gothic castle. In itself, there is nothing particularly unusual about this: as Warren H. Smith has shown, the title-page vignettes of several novels and romances published after 1750 in Britain show a distinct trend towards the use of Gothic or pseudo-Gothic architectural images.[14] Most pertinently, the title page to Percy's *Reliques* (1765),

[10] Leigh Hunt, *A Book for a Corner; or, Selections in Prose and Verse from Authors the Best Suited to that Mode of Enjoyment* (London: Chapman & Hall, 1849), p. 103.

[11] Allan Cunningham, *Biographical and Critical History of the British Literature of the Last Fifty Years* (Paris: Baudry's Foreign Library, 1834), p. 122.

[12] Walter Scott, 'Prefatory Memoir to Mrs Ann Radcliffe', in *The Novels of Mrs Ann Radcliffe [...] Complete in One Volume. To Which is Prefixed, A Memoir of the Life of the Author* (London: Hurst, Robinson, and Co.; Printed at Edinburgh by James Ballantyne and Co., 1824), pp. i–xxxix (p. xii).

[13] See the title page of the first edition of the novel, Ann Radcliffe, *The Mysteries of Udolpho, A Romance; Interspersed with Some Pieces of Poetry*, 4 vols (London: G. G and J. Robinson, 1794).

[14] Warren H. Smith, *Architectural Design on English Title-Pages* (London: The Bibliographical Society, 1933), p. 295.

the three-volume anthology of 'Gothic' literary antiquities that Radcliffe certainly knew, included Charles Grignion the Elder's engraving of Samuel Wale's image of a lyre set among an English oak tree and three fragments of Gothic architectural ruin. What is notable about *Udolpho*, though, is that Radcliffe chose to adopt this publishing convention not visually but through her characteristic use of poetic ekphrasis or 'word-painting'.

Though these seem like positive assessments on Cunningham's and Scott's behalf, they both came by way of a prelude to the articulation of more trenchant criticisms: for Scott, famously, Radcliffe's narrative gateways, portals, and antechambers ultimately led the reader to disappointment, the contrivances resorted to in the process of the explained supernatural in danger of evoking 'censure' in that which once 'so keenly interested' the reader.[15] As John Dunlop, punning heavily on the meanings of 'passage' as both an architectural structure and a unit of prose, had put it earlier, the technique of the explained supernatural meant, in short, that 'we may say not only of Mrs Radcliffe's castles, but of her works in general, that they abound in "passages that lead to nothing"'.[16] The quoted line comes from the second stanza of Thomas Gray's 'A Long Story', a semi-autobiographical poem about sexual desire and poetic identity that, through the interventions of Horace Walpole, was first published in *Designs by Mr R. Bentley, for Six Poems by Mr T. Gray* in 1753:

> In Britain's Isle, no matter where,
> An ancient pile of building stands:
> The Huntingdons and Hattons there
> Employ'd the power of Fairy Hands.
>
> To raise the cieling's [sic] fretted height,
> Each panel in achievements cloathing [sic],
> Rich windows that exclude the light,
> And passages, that lead to nothing.[17]

As Bentley's explanation points out, the illustrated headpiece to the poem pictures a view of the house that 'formerly belonged to the earls of Huntingdon and lord keeper Hatton', a detail that identifies the pile that is said to be magically conjured up by 'Fairy Hands' as the Manor House at Stoke Park, Buckinghamshire. Bentley's headpiece (see Figure 3.1) was based on a rough sketch of Stoke Manor House that

---

[15] Scott, 'Prefatory Memoir to Mrs Ann Radcliffe', p. xii.
[16] John Dunlop, *A History of Fiction: Being a Critical Account of the Most Celebrated Prose Works of Fiction, from the Earliest Greek Romances to the Novels of the Present Age*, 3 vols (London: Longman, Hurst, Rees, Orme, and Brown, 1816), vol. 1, p. 475.
[17] Thomas Gray, 'A Long Story', in *Designs by Mr R. Bentley, for Six Poems by Mr T. Gray* (London: Printed for R. Dodsley, 1753), pp. 14–23 (p. 14).

FROM 'CASTLES IN THE AIR' TO THE TOPOGRAPHICAL GOTHIC   135

Figure 3.1 Richard Bentley's headpiece to Thomas Gray's 'A Long Story' (1753). Courtesy of the Lewis Walpole Library, lwlpr16189.

Gray himself had produced.[18] Though in Bentley's image the building is more Elizabethan than Gothic in style, it is rendered distinctly Gothic in Gray's verse in the references to its antiquity, painted glass, gloomy interiors, and labyrinthine passages, all of which are appropriated by Dunlop so many years later as a metaphor for Radcliffe's fictional technique. Cunningham's assessment becomes even more negative when he proceeds to argue that, grand and impressive though they were, the textual-cum-architectural structures of the writer 'could not last—they were not of God, and so they failed'.[19] Like an Armida or a Prospero witnessing the disappearance of an enchanted palace, 'The authoress lived long enough to see the fabric which she had reared melt away, and Nature resume her reign with the same ease and quietness that the moon succeeds the tempest.'[20]

Damning though it is, Cunningham's criticism demands closer attention: enormously successful though she undoubtedly was, there is, indeed, something evanescent, temporary, and impermanent about Ann Radcliffe's Gothic castles. Focusing on the castles that feature in *The Castles of Athlin and Dunbayne* (1789), *A Sicilian Romance* (1790), *The Mysteries of Udolpho*, and *A Journey Made in the Summer of 1794* (1795), this chapter charts the genesis, development, and eventual modification of Radcliffe's architectural imagination over the most active years

---

[18] For Gray's original sketch, see *Mr Gray's Original Drawing of Stokehouse*, LWL, lwlpr15920. For a reading of Bentley's illustrations to Gray's poems, see Loftus Jestin, *The Answer to the Lyre: Richard Bentley's Illustrations from Thomas Gray's Poems* (Philadelphia: University of Pennsylvania Press, 1990).
[19] Cunningham, *Biographical and Critical History*, p. 124.
[20] Cunningham, *Biographical and Critical History*, p. 124.

of her career. Bypassing, for the moment, the abbeys, monasteries, and other ecclesiastical buildings that occur across her romances, and reserving an account of the architecture of *Gaston De Blondeville* for Chapter 6, this chapter explores the transition from imaginary Gothic architectural forms—those proverbial 'castles in the sky'—to those 'real-life' Gothic castles and fortifications frequently described in contemporary histories and antiquarian topographies. Broadening the focus out beyond the particular case of Radcliffe, the argument explores an overarching, more general sense of cultural transition in the late eighteenth and early nineteenth centuries, one that resulted in a marked cultural turn away from fake ruins, follies, and fictional 'castles in the air' and a movement into the more 'authentic', grounded, and antiquarian impulses of what I term the 'topographical Gothic'.

Ann Radcliffe's Castles

Radcliffe's debut on the late eighteenth-century publishing scene came by way of an assertion of not only her place within the emergent Gothic fictional tradition, but also of the architectural preoccupations that would come to dominate her entire oeuvre. Anonymously published by Thomas Hookham in London in one volume on Saturday, 30 May 1789, *The Castles of Athlin and Dunbayne; A Highland Story* at once declared its affinities with Walpole's *The Castle of Otranto* and foregrounded its architectural concerns in the modifications that it made to its primary source text, John Home's *Douglas: A Tragedy* of 1756.[21] Though first performed in Edinburgh some nine years before Radcliffe's birth, Home's play was enthusiastically revived on the London stage in the last three decades of eighteenth century; in the period 1770–1800, the script ran to over fifteen reprintings, and in 1784 the famed Sarah Siddons, whom Radcliffe greatly admired, played the role of Home's leading character, Lady Matilda Randolph, in a production of the play at the Theatre Royal in Covent Garden, London.[22]

Set in medieval Scotland, the plot details several sources of conflict: initially, in the play's Prologue, with its gesturing towards the historical tensions between the English and the Scots; secondly, in the ongoing war between the Danes and the

---

[21] For the precise date of publication of the novel, see the column 'On This Day is Published', *The Times*, Saturday, 30 May 1789, issue 1168, p. 2. For an account of Home's play as a major source for the novel, see Alison Milbank, 'Introduction', in *The Castles of Athlin and Dunbayne* by Ann Radcliffe, ed. Alison Milbank (Oxford: Oxford University Press, 1995), pp. vii–xxiv (p. ix); and Alison Milbank, 'Ways of Seeing in Ann Radcliffe's Early Fiction: *The Castles of Athlin and Dunbayne* (1789) and *A Sicilian Romance* (1790)', in *Ann Radcliffe, Romanticism and the Gothic*, ed. Dale Townshend and Angela Wright (Cambridge: Cambridge University Press, 2014), pp. 85–99.

[22] See the list of 'Dramatis Personae' in John Home, *Douglas. A Tragedy. By Mr Home. Marked with the Variations in the Manager's Book, at the Theatre Royal in Covent Garden* (London: Printed for T. Lowndes, T. Nicholl, and S. Bladon, 1784).

Scots that serves as the background to the more immediate action; thirdly, in the age-old rivalries between the Houses of Malcolm and Douglas; and finally, in the differences between Glenalvon, Lord Randolph, and Matilda that are internal to the Malcolm dynasty itself. Radcliffe, however, silences several of these tensions in *Athlin and Dunbayne*, instead focusing her narrative exclusively on the enmity that plays out between two architectural structures and dynastic 'houses', the two castles of the fiction's title. Indeed, as they are in such later texts as *The Mysteries of Udolpho* and *The Italian*, relations of difference and opposition are key to Radcliffe's architectural imagination in this romance, her first utilization of what Angela Wright has called the 'two-castle model', a commonplace thematic and structural principle employed in several Gothic narratives written by women in the late eighteenth century.[23] Athlin Castle, a pile 'venerable from its antiquity, and from its Gothic structure', is said to be 'more venerable from the virtues which it enclosed', while the 'lofty towers' and 'Gothic magnificence' of the edifice of Dunbayne Castle are said to 'frown' down in 'proud sublimity' from the rocky outcrop on which it is built.[24] If Athlin encloses virtue and domestic happiness, Dunbayne marks its opposite, since it is only 'Misery' that dwells there, for 'there the virtues were captive, while the vices reigned despotic'.[25] As this indicates, notions of spatial accessibility and enclosure are particularly important in the novel, for while Athlin is more open than closed, serving throughout the narrative as an architectural space through which characters may freely pass, the Castle of Dunbayne, with the 'subterranean labyrinths' beneath it and the 'horrible dungeon' in one of its towers, is disorientating, inaccessible, and the place of torturous confinement and imprisonment.[26] When John Cross adapted Radcliffe's fiction as *Halloween; or, The Castles of Athlin and Dunbayne*, a 'New Grand Scotch Spectacle' that was produced at the New Royal Circus, London, in September 1799, he exploited the differences between architectural containment and openness set up in his source text: the stage directions for the printed script of 1809 reveal that most of the scenes set in Athlin depicted the sublime exteriors of this Gothic pile, while, at Dunbayne, most of the scenes occurred within the dungeon in which Osbert is imprisoned.[27]

Crucially, each of the two castles in Radcliffe's narrative embodies a particular mode of political power, with what Radcliffe terms 'the superior advantages of an

---

[23] Angela Wright, 'The Gothic', in *The Cambridge Companion to Women's Writing in the Romantic Period*, ed. Devoney Looser (Cambridge: Cambridge University Press, 2015), pp. 58–72 (p. 66).
[24] Ann Radcliffe, *The Castles of Athlin and Dunbayne*, ed. Alison Milbank, (Oxford: Oxford University Press, 1995), pp. 3, 13.
[25] Radcliffe, *The Castles of Athlin and Dunbayne*, p. 39.
[26] Radcliffe, *The Castles of Athlin and Dunbayne*, pp. 29, 21.
[27] For the printed version of the script, see J. C. Cross, 'Halloween; or, The Castles of Athlin and Dunbaye', in *Circusiana; or, A Collection of the Most Favourable Ballets, Spectacles, Melo-Dramas, &c. Performed at the Royal Circus, St George's Field*, 2 vols (London: Lackington, Allen, and Co., 1809), vol. 2, pp. 185–230.

equitable government' in operation at Athlin, and the tyrannous reign of a despotic overlord presiding at Dunbayne.[28] The Gothic style, here, is used to represent and embody two contrasting political regimes: a more liberal system at Athlin, and an oppressive, feudal arrangement at Dunbayne. At Athlin, consequently, the Earl may bestow well-deserved preferment upon the servant classes, while at Dunbayne relations between the ruling powers and those who serve them are governed by intimidation, oppression, and fear. Not insignificantly, it is the former system that will prevail at the narrative's end, and Radcliffe, replacing the tragedy of *Douglas* with the felicitous endings of romance, has her hero Osbert, in a politically revealing move, order that the gates of Athlin Castle be 'thrown open' to the sounds of 'universal rejoicings' in the closing moments.[29] Architectural Gothicism here begins to assume meanings that accord well with what Rictor Norton has shown to be Radcliffe's political background of radical Dissent.[30] Indeed, the description reverberates strongly with revolutionary overtones: in opening up the Gothic pile, in all its associations with aristocratic privilege, power, and authority, to universal occupation and possession, the narrative ends upon a note that, after the fall of the Bastille in Paris not even six weeks after the text's original publication, could only have been construed as a politically radical move. Although Radcliffe was read by T. J. Mathias and Richard Polwhele, among others, as a conservative writer who was quite distinct from Mary Wollstonecraft, Anna Laetitia Barbauld, Mary Robinson, Charlotte Smith, Helen Maria Williams, and other 'unsex'd females', the use to which she puts Gothic architecture in her fiction suggests that she harboured equally politically progressive sympathies. From its earliest manifestations, then, Radcliffe's architectural imagination was avowedly radical: as William Hazlitt, citing a phrase from Milton's description of Gothic architecture in 'Il Penseroso', would later observe, 'Mrs Radcliffe's "enchantments drear," and mouldering castles, derived part of their interest, no doubt, from the supposed tottering state of all old structures at the time.'[31]

Radcliffe continued to fashion architectural structures charged with political meaning and significance in *A Sicilian Romance*, her second, two-volume fiction that was published by Thomas Hookham in London in 1790. In this post-revolutionary narrative, the fall of the Bastille is symbolically replayed in Radcliffe's description of the Abbey of St Augustin. The 'rude manners, the boisterous passions, the daring ambition, and the gross indulgences which formerly characterized the priest, the nobleman, and the sovereign' begin to yield to the light of rationality and learning that dawns gradually upon the abbey's edifice; 'Thus', she writes, 'do the scenes of life vary with the predominant passions of mankind, and

---

[28] Radcliffe, *The Castles of Athlin and Dunbayne*, p. 75.
[29] Radcliffe, *The Castles of Athlin and Dunbayne*, p. 112.
[30] See Norton, *Mistress of Udolpho*, pp. 13–25.
[31] Hazlitt, *Lectures on the English Comic Writers*, p. 244.

with the progress of civilization. The dark clouds of prejudice break away before the sun of science, and gradually dissolving, leave the brightening hemisphere to the influence of his beams.'[32] Radcliffe's sanguine embrace of the rhetoric of the French Revolution is subtle but clear.

As in *Athlin and Dunbayne*, Radcliffe fashioned the castles in this narrative on the 'foundations' provided by other writers and texts. If the architectural metaphor seems cheap, it is important to recall that this is precisely how the period conceptualized acts of literary appropriation: when George Manners published his dramatic adaptation of *Athlin and Dunbayne* as *Edgar; or, Caledonian Feuds* in 1806, he explained how he, a modest 'architect', had 'erected' the play on the 'basis' or sound foundation of Radcliffe's plot, avoiding all the while any charge of having plagiarized both Radcliffe and her ultimate 'foundations' in Home's *Douglas*.[33] As in Young's *Conjectures*, original genius is an architect who performs acts of creativity *ex nihilo*, the adaptor merely the lowly workman who is content to build upon pre-existent foundations. But the same charge, of course, could also be applied to Radcliffe herself, for her primary source for historical and topographical information about Sicily seems to have been Henry Swinburne's *Travels in the Two Sicilies*, the first, two-volume edition of which had been published between 1783 and 1785, and the second, four-volume edition issued in 1790.[34] The 'Two Sicilies' of Swinburne's title refer to the Kingdoms of Naples and Sicily, which had been politically united since the fifteenth century. Containing only a few dismissive references to the presence of a 'benighted' Gothic architectural style in Sicily, however, Swinburne's antiquarian interests are firmly classicist: the 'venerable relicks of remote antiquity' in which this traveller so delights are the Doric ruins at Selinunte ('Selinus') and the splendid remains of Grecian architecture at Syracuse.[35] Another likely source for Radcliffe's novel, one that is more cognate with the writer's own fictional vision, is Patrick Brydone's *A Tour Through Sicily and Malta* (1773), an epistolary travelogue composed of letters that Brydone had written to his friend and erstwhile travelling companion, William Beckford of Somerley.[36] While Brydone's letters, too, are not without a classicist interest in the remains of Greek and Roman antiquity, he merges this with a heightened poetic sensibility to Sicily's 'Gothic' qualities: 'since the revival of arts and agriculture', he opines, 'perhaps of all Europe this is the spot that has

---

[32] Ann Radcliffe, *A Sicilian Romance*, ed. Alison Milbank, (Oxford: Oxford University Press, 1993), p. 116.
[33] George Manners, *Edgar; or, Caledonian Feuds. A Tragedy* (London: Printed for Tipper and Richards, 1806), pp. 5–6.
[34] See Alison Milbank, 'Introduction', in *A Sicilian Romance* by Ann Radcliffe, ed. Alison Milbank (Oxford: Oxford University Press, 1993), pp. viii–xxviii (p. xv).
[35] Henry Swinburne, *Travels in the Two Sicilies, by Henry Swiburne, Esq. in 1777, 1778, 1779, and 1780*, 2nd ed., 4 vols (London: Printed by J.Nichols, for T. Cadell and P. Elmsly, 1790), vol. 3, p. 373.
[36] See Norton, *Mistress of Udolpho*, p. 72; Mark Bennett, 'Gothic Travels', in *Romantic Gothic: An Edinburgh Companion*, ed. Angela Wright and Dale Townshend (Edinburgh: Edinburgh University Press, 2016), pp. 224–46 (pp. 234–5).

profited the least', with Sicily thus 'retaining still, both in the wildness of its fields and ferocity of its inhabitants, more of the Gothic barbarity than is to be met with any where [sic] else'.[37] This is the vision of Sicily that seems closest to Radcliffe's own, the land of the mythical Scylla and Charybdis, romance and superstition, kindly nuns immured in convents, and fearsome banditti secreted in the landscape.

Radcliffe's sources in *A Sicilian Romance* are as literary as they are locodescriptive. Like Ellinor and Matilda, the imaginary daughters of Mary, Queen of Scots, in Sophia Lee's *The Recess* (1783–5), the apparently motherless heroines Emilia and Julia have been raised within the 'large irregular fabric' of their father, Ferdinand, 5th Marquis of Mazzini; 'veiled in obscurity' in this pile according to the marquis's inscrutable demands, the young women are said never to have 'passed the boundaries of their father's domains', a claim that assumes both literal and figurative significance when the strictures placed on these 'domains' become clear.[38] Primarily preoccupied, like Walpole's Manfred, with the aristocrat's laws of primogeniture and alliance, the marquis makes of his son Ferdinand the 'sole object' of his paternal pride and concern.[39] However, this is no safeguard against the arbitrary exercise of patriarchal authority that the narrative explores, the severity of which prompts Ferdinand the Younger, Emilia, and Julia to laudable acts of defiance. In a move that will become characteristic of what critics have termed the 'female' tradition in early Gothic writing, Julia, though romantically betrothed to Hippolitus, is coerced by her father into a loveless but politically advantageous alliance with the Duke de Luovo; he is thus a father who, as Hippolitus is quick to point out, exercises his authority against 'the liberty of choice'.[40] If the members of the younger generation are to assert their freedom at all, they must flee the father's castle, the architectural space in which arbitrary patriarchal authority is most intensely exercised. But as his children are soon to realize, the iron will of the father is not so easily circumvented: Ferdinand, like Osbert in the Castle of Dunbayne before him, is imprisoned in a dungeon beneath the Castle of Mazzini, while Julia, anticipating refuge in the Abbey of St Augustin, is made subject there to the equally imperious demands of the paternalistic abbot. Even as they impose upon the heroine their two incompatible agendas, the castle and the abbey, institutions both secular and religious in function, together collude in the oppression of women in what becomes Radcliffe's radical vision of a world of continuous and generalized imprisonment.

As in *Athlin and Dunbayne*, Gothic architecture in *A Sicilian Romance* is highly politicized, though here it is a politics based more upon gender than class

---

[37] Patrick Brydone, *A Tour Through Sicily and Malta. In A Series of Letters to William Beckford, Esq.*, 2 vols (London: Printed for W. Strahan and T. Cadell, 1773), vol. 1, p. 43.
[38] Radcliffe, *A Sicilian Romance*, pp. 5, 7, 6.   [39] Radcliffe, *A Sicilian Romance*, p. 10.
[40] Radcliffe, *A Sicilian Romance*, p. 61.

relations. This castle, it later turns out, is also the site for the incarceration of the children's mother and the first wife of the marquis, Louisa Bernini, and it is her containment within the ruined, underground apartments beneath it—a secret existence gestured towards for much of the narrative only in mysterious footsteps and low, hollow groans—that is eventually revealed to be the source of its apparent haunting. Until this moment, the marquis's servants believe the southern parts of the castle to be inhabited by a 'supernatural power', a claim that, together with the Shakespearean epigraph on the title-page—'I could a tale unfold'—lends to Radcliffe's Sicilian castle associations with the haunted battlements of Elsinore in Shakespeare's *Hamlet*.[41] *A Sicilian Romance*, then, is notable insofar as it marks the first appearance of the haunted—or, at least, seemingly haunted—castle in Radcliffe's oeuvre, a trope that she would realize to greater effect in *Udolpho*. As Louisa recounts her history to her children, however, so the myths and legends that have accumulated around the hauntings at Mazzini systematically unravel: 'The narrative of her sufferings, upon which she now entered, entirely dissipated the mystery which had so long enveloped the southern buildings of the castle.'[42] No ghost, this, so much as the voice of an enraged and mournful woman who has been abused by her tyrant of a husband; to unveil the mysteries of the castle is also to expose the cruel workings of patriarchal power. Even in its earliest manifestations, the Radcliffean technique of the explained supernatural is put to political usage, a move that, as I elaborate in the next chapter, was shared by her contemporary Charlotte Smith.

As the narrative repeatedly stresses, Gothic architecture in *A Sicilian Romance* has played a crucial role in the marquis's violent and repressive schemes: when Ferdinand explores the ruined, underground apartments of Mazzini, he notices that they contain windows that are 'high and gothic' in design; 'An air of proud sublimity, united with singular wildness', the narrator reiterates, 'characterized the place, at the extremity of which arose several gothic arches, whose dark shade veiled in obscurity the extent beyond.'[43] Throughout the narrative, in fact, the Gothic style is coterminous not with a splendid, mythical past but with gender-based violence and incarceration: as Louisa describes it, her ruined apartment has been nothing less than a 'horrid abode' or a 'recess of horror', an architecturally 'Gothic' structure that seems painfully appropriate to a life that has been a 'labyrinth of misfortunes'.[44] And yet, what is perhaps the most significant aspect of the novel is its sense that, far from possessing any innately 'horrid', 'strange', or 'fearful' qualities, the meaning of Gothic architecture is only ever circumstantial and conditional, and wholly contingent upon the mental and sentimental associations that those who perceive it bring to bear upon it. Like their mother, Emilia and Julia initially see in the Castle of Mazzini only the 'gloom and desolation'

---

[41] Radcliffe, *A Sicilian Romance*, p. 10.
[42] Radcliffe, *A Sicilian Romance*, p. 175.
[43] Radcliffe, *A Sicilian Romance*, p. 46.
[44] Radcliffe, *A Sicilian Romance*, pp. 190, 176, 181.

and 'melancholy stillness' that reign there.[45] No sooner have these negative associations been established, though, than the heroines' stepmother, Maria de Vollorno, arrives with her retinue in tow: at this moment, the castle's courts and halls, 'whose aspect so lately expressed only gloom and desolation', now 'shone with sudden splendour, and echoed the sounds of gaiety and gladness'.[46] Mazzini begins to assume a different aspect for Emilia and Julia, too, when they shortly thereafter celebrate their brother Frederick's coming of age. Home to a magnificent entertainment comprising banquets, music, and spectacular displays, the once horrid pile instantly shifts for all those who inhabit it into a place of enchantment and delight, 'as if the hand of a magician had suddenly metamorphosed this once gloomy fabric into the palace of a fairy'.[47] It is during these celebrations that Julia first meets Hippolitus, an experience that has the power further to transform the once-cheerless Mazzini into a palace of romantic delight, as if from 'a gloomy desert into a smiling Eden'.[48] When Hippolitus suddenly leaves Sicily for Naples, however, Julia's architectural perceptions instantaneously alter, the castle duly changing from a scene 'which so lately appeared enchanting to her eyes' to the wretched place in which she now finds herself to be 'solitary and dejected'.[49] The 'scene of dissension and misery' that predominates after the imprisonment of Ferdinand and the elopement of Julia persists up until the discovery of the children's incarcerated mother.[50] With Mazzini having served so long as 'the theatre of a dreadful catastrophe', the only alternative is to abandon it, but not because, as Radcliffe seems to insist, Gothic architecture is inherently and inevitably the marker of patriarchal oppression in a dark and savage past, but only because of the painful associations that the sight of it 'would have revived in the minds of the chief personages connected with it'.[51] When the unnamed narrator of the Prologue stumbles across the ruins of the Castle of Mazzini some 200 years later, he is oblivious to their personal and historical associations, discovering there not the stony relics of tyranny but the 'magnificent remains' of a prospect that is both 'beautiful and picturesque': the ruins now emit 'an air of ancient grandeur' that impresses upon the traveller a sense of 'awe and curiosity'.[52] Appropriating this scene of ruin as a memento mori, the traveller must be reminded that his way of reading the building is, of necessity, historically contingent: a venerable stranger steps into the frame to claim that, as picturesque to the present moment as they may appear, 'These walls...were once the seat of luxury and vice.'[53] Mysteriously metamorphosing over the course of the narrative from gloom to enchantment to suffering to picturesque beauty and back again, Gothic architecture possesses no inherent qualities beyond the various meanings with

---

[45] Radcliffe, *A Sicilian Romance*, pp. 15, 5.
[46] Radcliffe, *A Sicilian Romance*, p. 15.
[47] Radcliffe, *A Sicilian Romance*, p. 17.
[48] Radcliffe, *A Sicilian Romance*, p. 24.
[49] Radcliffe, *A Sicilian Romance*, p. 24.
[50] Radcliffe, *A Sicilian Romance*, p. 97.
[51] Radcliffe, *A Sicilian Romance*, p. 198.
[52] Radcliffe, *A Sicilian Romance*, p. 1.
[53] Radcliffe, *A Sicilian Romance*, p. 1.

which it is imbued by the historically situated perceiver. More radically, in fact, the Castle of Mazzini seems to have no material existence outside of the structuring effects of conscious perception at all, a consideration that, as in William Beckford's architectural fantasies that I discussed in Chapter 1, takes Radcliffe's architectural imagination in *A Sicilian Romance* beyond the empiricist underpinnings of associationist aesthetics and into the subjective idealism of a thinker such as George Berkeley.

Radcliffe would deepen her exploration of the powers of subjective association in the perception, comprehension, and even the structuring of Gothic architectural space in *The Mysteries of Udolpho*, her longest and best-known fiction that combined the architectural interests of *Athlin and Dunbayne* with the Italianate setting of *A Sicilian Romance*. Long before she arrives in Italy, Madame Montoni anticipates 'in imagination the splendour of palaces and the grandeur of castles, such as she believed she was going to be mistress of at Venice and in the Apennine, and she became, in idea, little less than a princess'.[54] Insignificant though they might seem, these fantasies set up an important distinction between palaces and castles, Venice and the Apennines in the narrative, a distinction that is eventually superimposed upon the broader differences between the classical and Gothic styles. The differences between Udolpho and the Chateau-le-Blanc are thus complemented by another set of distinctions in the text—those between the Gothic and the classical, the sublime and the beautiful, respectively. Approaching Venice, Emily St Aubert and Madame Montoni encounter the islands, palaces, and towers of the city seemingly 'rising out of the sea', as if they had been 'called up from the ocean by the wand of an enchanter'—although it is the fact that Montoni's splendid Venetian home is, in reality, an enchanted castle in all the negative, violently seductive associations of that trope that Madame Montoni fails to recognize.[55] The 'airy yet majestic fabrics' that present themselves to view are all classical in style and design: light reflects elegantly on the 'marble porticos and colonnades of St Mark', and the palazzos situated on the Grand Canal alongside Montoni's own reflect the 'beauty' and 'grandeur' of '[Jacopo] Sansovino and [Andrea] Palladio'.[56] As Bonamy Dobrée has pointed out, this is a factual error on Radcliffe's behalf, for Palladio, the Venetian Republic's best-known sixteenth-century architect, did not design or build any palazzos on the Grand Canal.[57] Instead, Radcliffe is simply repeating the erroneous account of Venetian architecture that Hester Piozzi had provided in *Observations and Reflections Made in the Course of a Journey through France, Italy and Germany* (1789), the travel narrative

---

[54] Ann Radcliffe, *The Mysteries of Udolpho, A Romance; Interspersed with Some Pieces of Poetry*, ed. Bonamy Dobrée, intro. and notes by Terry Castle (Oxford: Oxford University Press, 1998), p. 166.
[55] Radcliffe, *The Mysteries of Udolpho*, pp. 174, 175.
[56] Radcliffe, *The Mysteries of Udolpho*, pp. 175, 175, 175, 176.
[57] See Dobrée's editorial note in Radcliffe, *The Mysteries of Udolpho*, p. 684.

that, as Clara Frances McIntyre first observed in 1920, is one of Radcliffe's primary sources for the text.[58] Like Piozzi's, Radcliffe's architectural vocabulary is replete with references to the classical style throughout the Venetian sections, her narrative perspective taking care to mention the city's 'colonnades', 'lofty porticos and arcades', and an 'open cupola' that is 'supported by columns';[59] from a barge on the River Brenta, Emily takes particular notice of the 'grandeur of Palladian villas that adorn these shores' and the play of light and shade on their 'porticos and long arcades'.[60] Though Venice seems for the heroine 'almost to realize the romance of fairy land', this is ground that bespeaks more the 'delights' of classicism and classical mythology than the 'enchantments' of old Gothic romance.[61]

Like her aunt, Emily harbours preconceived architectural associations long before she arrives at Udolpho. As she well knows, the 'gloomy and sequestered scenes' of a Gothic building will eventually become accessories to Montoni's attempts 'to terrify her into obedience', imposing upon her and her aunt an 'unlimited authority' that, as he uncomfortably reminds his ward, is founded upon nothing less arbitrary than his personal whim.[62] These pre-existing associations are only confirmed when, in an iconic moment, the heroine catches a glimpse of Montoni's castle for the first time: 'the gothic greatness of its features, and its mouldering walls of dark grey stone, rendered it a gloomy and sublime object'.[63] 'Silent, lonely and sublime', the Castle of Udolpho seems 'to stand the sovereign of the scene, and to frown defiance on all, who dared to invade its solitary reign'.[64] In place of the classical beauty of Venice, Udolpho is the locale of Gothic sublimity. In foregrounding the castle's sublimity, Radcliffe is ventriloquizing James Beattie's account of the sublimity of Gothic architecture in *Dissertations Moral and Critical* (1783), Archibald Alison's views on the sublimity of Gothic castles in *Essays on the Nature and Principles of Taste*, as well as Hester Piozzi's sense of the differences between the classical and Gothic styles in Italy as expressed through the associations evoked by each:

> Gothic and Grecian architecture resembles Gothic and Grecian manners, which naturally do give their colour to such arts as are naturally the result of them. Tyranny and gloomy suspicion are the characteristics of the one, openness and

---

[58] See McIntyre's argument in *Ann Radcliffe in Relation to her Time* (New Haven and London: Yale University Press, 1920), pp. 58–60. For a more recent account of the complex relationship between Radcliffe and Piozzi, see Marianna D'Ezio, '"As like As Peppermint Water is to Good French Brandy": Ann Radcliffe and Hester Lynch Salusbury (Thrale) Piozzi', *Women's Writing* vol. 22 no. 3, (July 2015): pp. 343–54.
[59] Radcliffe, *The Mysteries of Udolpho*, pp. 187, 188, 211.
[60] Radcliffe, *The Mysteries of Udolpho*, p. 209.
[61] Radcliffe, *The Mysteries of Udolpho*, p. 176.
[62] Radcliffe, *The Mysteries of Udolpho*, pp. 224, 216.
[63] Radcliffe, *The Mysteries of Udolpho*, pp. 226–7.
[64] Radcliffe, *The Mysteries of Udolpho*, p. 227.

sociability strongly mark the other—when to the gay portico succeeded the sullen drawbridge, and to the lively corridor, a secret passage and a winding staircase.[65]

It is also in Emily's experiences of the sublimity of Udolpho that Radcliffe's critique of Alexander Gerard that I mentioned in Chapter 1 comes into its own. The annotations in her personal copy of the second, expanded edition of *An Essay on Taste* of 1764 engage closely and critically with Gerard's argument, offering, in the transcribed passage below, an important qualifier to the aesthetician's claim that, in the experience of the sublime, the perceiving mind 'finds such a difficulty in spreading itself to the dimensions of its object'. 'When the mind is filled with the true sublime,' Radcliffe writes,

> all consideration of self is excluded, and almost [consciousness?] is lost. The <u>one</u> object of our sense alone appears to us, the one sensation it excites alone possesses us. It is this <u>one</u> which peculiarly belongs to the sublime; if our sensations are mingled, if the object we behold is capable of exciting at the same instant two different kinds of sensation it may be called grand, magnificent, surprising any thing but sublime. Any object which is capable of exciting such a degree of any single passion or emotion, as elevates the mind & excludes every other, [is] alone deserving to be termed sublime. There cannot be degrees of sublimity, it is like truth, one and indivisible. What is not truth, is false.[66]

For Gerard, the mind struggles to accommodate the sheer vastness of the sublime object; for Radcliffe, by contrast, an object that is truly sublime wholly eclipses and consumes the consciousness of the perceiver—shades of the argument that she would rehearse in the excerpted, posthumously published essay 'On the Supernatural in Poetry' (1826). The sublimity of an architectural mass such as Udolpho is thus always, for Radcliffe, much more than a matter of size and scale: glossing Gerard's claim that 'we take in with ease one entire conception of a simple object, however large', she writes that 'He seems to confound grandeur with sublimity, in almost all the instances he would advise us of the latter.' And while he claims that 'simplicity is essential of the sublime' on one page, 'in another he enumerates the <u>various circumstances or considerations</u>, which conspire to form the sublime;—as in heroism'.

Radcliffe's sense of the architectural sublime at Udolpho merges seamlessly with the proto-feminist consciousness of her heroine. Thoughts of tyranny and suspicion certainly overwhelm Emily's mind: passing through the portal, her heart sinks, 'as if she was going into her prison'; painfully alive to Gothic architecture's associations with feudal and patriarchal oppression, 'her imagination, ever awake

---

[65] Hester Lynch Piozzi, *Observations and Reflections Made in the Course of a Journey through France, Italy, and Germany*, 2 vols (London: Printed for A. Strahan and T. Cadell, 1789), vol. 1, p. 126.
[66] See Radcliffe's annotations in Alexander Gerard, *An Essay on Taste* (1764), pp. 12–16, Beinecke Library, Yale University, Osborn pc127.

to circumstance, suggested even more terrors, than her reason could justify'.[67] Ideas of 'long-suffering and murder' crowd in upon her consciousness, while another 'of those instantaneous and unaccountable convictions, which sometimes conquer even strong minds' impresses upon her the presentiments of 'horror'.[68] Only intensified when Emily enters 'an extensive gothic hall', these associations are particular to the Gothic architectural style in *Udolpho*, and wholly distinct from the sentimental meanings with which Whiggish politicians, writers, and aestheticians had imbued the Gothic throughout the eighteenth century. Such associations also exist in stark contrast to the pleasant, moderate, and controlled mental impressions provoked by the classical architecture of Venice.[69] Indeed, as Peter Otto has argued, Emily's experience of Udolpho's architecture is quite unlike that at Venice and La Vallée before it: if, at her family home in Gascony, perceptions are governed by the natural order, restraint, and providentialism of 'a single cosmic architecture', it is at Udolpho that such simple impressions are thrown into labyrinthine disarray of unlimited imaginative associations.[70] Though she was no champion of what, for her, were the Gothic style's conservative political associations with feudal and patriarchal oppression, Radcliffe, like Walpole, clearly celebrated the Gothic over the classical for its ability to seize, strike, and inspire the workings of the perceiver's imagination.

Visualizing Udolpho

Taking her cue from Piozzi's references to sullen drawbridges, secret passages, and winding staircases, Radcliffe's descriptions of Udolpho make extensive use of the vocabulary of Gothic architecture, from its 'gigantic' gateway and the 'massy walls of the ramparts' to the 'pointed arch of a huge portcullis' and the 'two round towers, crowned by over-hanging turrets'.[71] To these are added such other style-specific references as a 'lofty vault'; vaulted ceilings; 'pillars' and 'pointed arches'; winding passages and tapestry-hung galleries; the 'rich fret-work of the roof'; and 'a painted window, stretching nearly from the pavement to the ceiling of the hall'.[72] Called into being by such terms, however, Udolpho as a structure possesses no distinct form beyond the characteristic vocabulary of the Gothic that is used to refer to it. That is, like the Castle of Otranto, Udolpho is without a rational and coherent ground plan, layout, or structure that might be clearly perceived and

---

[67] Radcliffe, *The Mysteries of Udolpho*, pp. 227–8.
[68] Radcliffe, *The Mysteries of Udolpho*, p. 228.
[69] Radcliffe, *The Mysteries of Udolpho*, p. 228.
[70] Peter Otto, '"Where am I, and what?"—Architecture, Environment, and the Transformation of Experience in Radcliffe's *The Mysteries of Udolpho*', *European Romantic Review* vol. 25, no. 3 (2014): pp. 299–308 (pp. 182–3).
[71] Radcliffe, *The Mysteries of Udolpho*, p. 227.
[72] Radcliffe, *The Mysteries of Udolpho*, p. 228.

understood by either the heroine or the novel's readers; the 'mysteries' of the novel's title pertain as much to the spatial layout of the castle as to the events that occur therein. 'Beyond these', the narrator's piecemeal description notes, 'all was lost in the obscurity of evening'.[73] Radcliffe's use of the word 'obscurity', here, demonstrates an indebtedness to a Burkean conceptualization of the sublime. But if Udolpho is, indeed, to serve as a 'sublime object', it is crucial that it remain shrouded in obscurity, glimpsed only in fragments, and never fully rendered, seen, or described. It is seemingly to these aesthetic ends that Emily is only ever given the occasional glimpse of the castle's towers and battlements from the outside, and even then, only when they are partly concealed by woods and the fall of evening. With its unlockable door, not even the heroine's bedchamber is completely known and familiar to her, and forever unable to comprehend the castle as a finite space, she fears 'that she might again lose herself' in its unfathomable 'intricacies'.[74]

Comparing Radcliffe's novels with those of Charlotte Smith, Walter Scott noted that while Smith's landscapes effortlessly lent themselves to clear representation by visual artists, Radcliffe's seemed to be covered by a 'haze' and 'enveloped in mystery'; though certainly generative of sublime effect, her descriptions, Scott claimed, never communicate 'any absolute precise or individual image to the reader'.[75] This is particularly the case in the 'beautiful descriptions' of the Castle of Udolpho: 'It affords a noble subject for the pencil,' he concedes, 'but were six artists to attempt to embody it upon canvass, they would probably produce six drawings entirely dissimilar to each other, all of them equally authorized by the painted description.'[76] For Scott, the willed obscurity of Radcliffe's architecture was both a boon and a hindrance to visual representation: prompted by the fragmentary descriptions, readers of *Udolpho* themselves became architects insofar as they constructed from the textual fragments a consistent architectural structure. A survey of contemporary images, however, suggests that painters and illustrators were more daunted than excited by the challenge of rendering Udolpho in pictorial form. It is true that visual responses to Radcliffe were commonplace in the period: artists such as J. C. Denham, Henry Singleton, Mary Lloyd, and S. Drummond all produced paintings inspired by *Udolpho* in the 1790s, and many of these were exhibited at the Royal Academy.[77] As Kerry Dean Carso has pointed out, *Udolpho* also captured the imagination of the American Romantic painter, friend of Samuel Taylor Coleridge, and occasional Gothic romancer Washington Allston.[78] What is noteworthy about these and

---

[73] Radcliffe, *The Mysteries of Udolpho*, p. 227.
[74] Radcliffe, *The Mysteries of Udolpho*, p. 258.
[75] Scott, 'Prefatory Memoir to Mrs Ann Radcliffe', p. xxx.
[76] Scott, 'Prefatory Memoir to Mrs Ann Radcliffe', p. xxx.
[77] Rictor Norton, 'Ann Radcliffe, The Shakespeare of Romance Writers', in *Shakespearean Gothic*, ed. Christy Desmet and Anne Williams (Cardiff: University of Wales Press, 2009), pp. 37–59.
[78] Kerry Dean Carso, *American Gothic Art and Architecture in the Age of Romantic Literature* (Cardiff: University of Wales Press, 2014), pp. 29–50.

Figure 3.2 Rev. William Warren Porter (1776–1804), British, *Castle of Udolpho*, undated. Watercolour, graphite, and grey wash on medium, slightly textured, cream wove paper, Yale Center for British Art, Gift of Edward Porter Street, Jr, Yale BE 1945W.

other renditions, though, is just how few of them attempted to visualize the eponymous castle itself.[79]

The few visualizations of Udolpho that do remain rather confirm Scott's point. It was apparently during the late 1790s that the Reverend William Warren Porter rendered the Castle of Udolpho in a watercolour and accompanying sketch (see Figure 3.2). A Fellow of St John's College, Oxford, who died in June 1804 at only 28 years old, Porter was a keen amateur sketcher of picturesque Gothic architecture in Oxford and its surrounds. The images that were posthumously published as *Engravings from Drawings of the Late Rev. William Warren Porter* in 1806 include archaeologically accurate renditions of the ruins of the Castles of Warwick and Kenilworth, Warwickshire.[80] As his watercolour of the Castle of Udolpho indicates, he was equally enamoured of the imaginary piles that he encountered in Radcliffe's romance, rendering it in the rounded arches and heavy, thick ramparts of what the period referred to as the 'Saxon Gothic' style; a graphite sketch on the recto, apparently a scene from the funeral of Emily's father in the Villerois family tomb, includes the Gothic style's more familiar pointed arches. In the image of Udolpho, the obscurity of Radcliffe's text is replayed in the way in which only a

---

[79] See, for instance, Nathaniel Grogan's *Lady Blanche Crosses the Ravine Guided by the Count and Saint Foix* (c.1796–8), National Gallery of Ireland, NGI.4323.

[80] See *Engravings from the Drawings of the Late Rev. William Warren Porter, Fellow of St. John's College, Oxford* (London: Printed by J. Tyler, 1806).

FROM 'CASTLES IN THE AIR' TO THE TOPOGRAPHICAL GOTHIC   149

Figure 3.3 James Nasmyth's etching of the Castle of Udolpho, 1854. Courtesy of Archives, Institution of Mechanical Engineers (ref NAS/4/5).

portion of the castle appears as one detail of a picturesque sketch that is largely dominated by wild, mountainous landscape.

Long enamoured of Radcliffe and her works, the industrial engineer James Nasmyth, too, produced an etching of Udolpho in May 1854 (see Figure 3.3). As he later described it in his autobiography, 'Now and then I drew upon my fancy, and with pen and ink I conjured up "The Castle of Udolpho"', a claim that suggests that this and other acts of illustration were more of the order of fabrication than representation.[81] Nasmyth subsequently had his drawings printed, and sent copies of them to his friends and acquaintances, including Washington Irving and the Duke of Argyll. In his letter of thanks and acknowledgement, the Duke of Argyll claimed that he had shown the picture of 'Udolpho Castle' to the Duchess of Sutherland, who was 'enchanted with the beauty of the architectural details, and wishes she had seen them before Dunrobin [Castle, Highlands,] was finished; for hints might have been taken from bits of your work'.[82] Flattering though this is, Nasmyth's rendition is more a fantastic assemblage of Gothic architectural details, all of which seem to vanish into the clouds above, than a precise and workable architectural design. More tellingly, it reveals no similarities with the Udolpho of

---

[81] James Nasmyth, *James Nasmyth, Engineer: An Autobiography*, ed. Samuel Smiles (London: John Murray, 1883), pp. 323–4.
[82] Nasmyth, *James Nasmyth, Engineer*, p. 344.

William Warren Porter, at once a testament to Scott's point and a manifestation of the obscurity that clouds the fictional pile.

Bound up in sublime obscurity, Radcliffe's most famous castle remained materially and visually unrealizable, a characteristic that extended to illustrated editions of the novel, too. While the 1798, 1808, and 1869 French translations of the novel were all illustrated, none of them contained any image of Udolpho other than the few architectural details to be glimpsed in some of the interiors.[83] Though the frontispieces of each of the four volumes of the fourth edition of *Udolpho* that was published by George Robinson in London in 1799 include a copperplate illustration, not one of these attempts to depict Montoni's castle itself; the three images that illustrate aspects of the plot that occur within the castle provide little more than the vaguest gesture towards a 'Gothic' interior, with a barest hint, in Volume 4, of a dungeon and a pointed arch.[84] The frontispieces to a two-volume Dutch translation of the novel from 1823 both contain the same illustration of Emily's encounter with the figure behind the black veil, without any architectural detail.[85] Indeed, it was only when John Limbird published a one-volume edition of the novel 'embellished with numerous engravings on wood' in 1824 that Udolpho received formal illustrative representation, first as an image to accompany Emily's first glimpse of, and subsequent entry into, the castle (see Figure 3.4), and, secondly, during the moment of her eventual escape.[86] Even here, though, the woodcuts seem more intent upon amplifying the contrasts between a gloomy, umbrageous Udolpho and the brightness and light of the Chateau-le-Blanc than providing a clear representation of the castle itself. The latter is depicted twice in Limbird's edition, the most detailed of which shows its white exteriors, battlements, and large windows (see Figure 3.5). As the differences in darkness and light between these illustrations indicate, the 'two-castle model' of Radcliffe's earlier fictions features prominently in *Udolpho*, too, the narrative juxtaposing Montoni's gloomy, Italian abode with the more delightful, romantic, and 'enchanting' aspects of the 'white Gothic' at the Chateau-le-Blanc, Languedoc.

---

[83] See *Les Mystères d'Udolphe, par Anne Radcliffe: traduit de l'Anglois sur la troisième édition, par Victorine de Chastenay* (Paris: chez Maradan, 1798). This edition was republished by Maradan with the same illustrations in 1808. For the illustrated edition of 1869, see *Les Mystères d'Udolphe, par Anne Radcliffe, edition illustrée par J.-A. Beaucé* (Paris: Librairie R. Visconti, 1869).

[84] See Volumes 2, 3, and 4 of Ann Radcliffe, *The Mysteries of Udolpho, a Romance; Interspersed with Some Pieces of Poetry*, 4th edn, illustrated with copper plates, 4 vols (London: Printed for G. G. and J. Robinson, 1799). For a discussion of early illustrations of Ann Radcliffe's fiction, see Teri Doerksen, 'Framing the Narrative: Illustration and Pictorial Prose in Burney and Radcliffe', in *Book Illustration in the Long Eighteenth Century: Reconfiguring the Visual Periphery of the Text*, ed. Christina Ionescu (Newcastle upon Tyne: Cambridge Scholars Publishing, 2011), pp. 463–500.

[85] See *De Geheimen van Udolpho. Naar het Engelsch. Van Anna Radcliffe*, 2 vols (Amsterdam: J. C. van Kesteren, 1824).

[86] See Ann Radcliffe, 'The Mysteries of Udolpho', in *Limbird's Edition of the British Novelist; Forming a Choice Collection of the Best Novels in the English Language, Embellished With Engraving*, Vol. I (London: J. Limbird, 1826), pp. 1–328.

Figure 3.4 Emily's first glimpse of Udolpho, from John Limbird's 1824 edition of the novel. Courtesy of The Bodleian Libraries, The University of Oxford, VET. A6 e.844.

Figure 3.5 Image of the Chateau-le-Blanc, the castle of 'whiteness' and light, from John Limbird's 1824 edition of the novel. Courtesy of the Bodleian Libraries, The University of Oxford, VET. A6 e.844.

As in the earlier fictions, Radcliffe's architectural imagination took inspiration for the Chateau-le-Blanc from other texts and sources, for this particular French building—though plausibly based, as Norton has argued, on Haddon Hall in Derbyshire—is also an ekphrastic rendering of *Landscape with Psyche Outside the Palace of Cupid* (1664), a painting by the French baroque painter and draughtsman Claude Gellée (called Le Lorrain, Claude Lorrain, or Claude).[87] Initially included in his *Liber Veritatis* series, the painting was produced for Claude's patron Prince Lorenzo Onofrio Colonna, Grand Constable of the Kingdom of Naples, and depicted a scene from Books IV–VI of Apuleius's *Metamorphoses* or *The Golden Ass* (c. late second century AD). Though it had been present in England since the late 1720s, the painting was only first publicly exhibited in Britain at the 'Old Masters' exhibition at the British Institution, London, in 1819.[88] It was thus only through a subsequent engraving, and not through Claude's original, that the image received such broad circulation in England during the period in which Radcliffe was writing.[89] Following the death of the London-based French landscape engraver François Vivarès in 1780, the British printmaker William Woollett completed an engraving of it for Vivarès's widow, Susanna Vivarès, who published the image in London on 12 March 1782 under the title of *The Enchanted Castle*, the name by which it is still best known today (see Figure 3.6). Thus inaccurately named, the painting was cut free of its classical moorings in Apuleius and reinscribed in the tradition of 'Gothic' romance. The catalogue for the sale of the painting at Bryan's Gallery in 1795 not unreasonably assumed that the image depicted 'the Departure of Rinaldo', a scene from *Jerusalem Delivered*;[90] the error was repeated in 1807 when the catalogue for the Troward sale described the subject as 'Rinaldo and Armida or the Enchanted Castle'. Of the six catalogue listings of the image between 1790 and 1848, it was only in the last of these that the figure in the foreground was correctly identified as Psyche.[91] For the rest, this pensive woman, relocated from the left of the castle in the original to the right in the engraving, was taken to be Circe, or, most frequently, Tasso's mournful and melancholic enchantress Armida, seated before her enchanted castle having been left bereft by the disappearance of her

---

[87] See Michael Levey's mooting of this suggestion in '"The Enchanted Castle" by Claude: Subject, Significance and Interpretation', *The Burlington Magazine* vol. 130, no. 1028 (November 1988), pp. 812–20.
[88] See Leslie Parris, *The Loyd Collection of Paintings and Drawings at Betterton House, Lockinge near Wantage, Berkshire* (London: Bradbury Agnew Press, 1967), pp. 7–10. Having attended the exhibition in the early summer of 1819, John Keats famously alluded to the painting in the penultimate stanza of 'Ode to a Nightingale' that was published in July of that year. See Michael Levey, '"The Enchanted Castle" by Claude: Subject, Significance and Interpretation', p. 820.
[89] See Michael Wilson, *Claude, The Enchanted Castle* (London: The National Gallery, 1982).
[90] Wilson, *Claude, The Enchanted Castle*, p. 14. For the original catalogue to the exhibition, see Michael Bryan, *A Catalogue of that Superlatively Capital Assemblage of Valuable Pictures [...] Sold by Private Contract, at Mr Bryan's Gallery, in Savile Row, on Monday the 27th Day of April, 1795, and Following Days* (London: Printed by S. Low, 1798), p. 17.
[91] Wilson, *Claude, The Enchanted Castle*, p. 14.

Figure 3.6 *The Enchanted Castle* (1782), an engraving by William Woollett and François Vivarès, after Claude Lorrain's *Liber Veritatis* no. 162 or *Landscape with Psyche Outside the Palace of Cupid* (1664). © The Trustees of the British Museum.

lover. By dint of its assumed title alone, Michael Wilson conjectures that the image may also well have conjured up thoughts of Shakespeare's Miranda, pensively seated before the 'baseless fabric of a vision' on her father Prospero's enchanted isle.[92] The Castle of Udolpho, the Chateau-le-Blanc's architectural double, was an equally fictional and imaginative construct, another 'castle in the air' that could not be actualized, realized, or seen in the immediate, physical present.

Undoubtedly, this sublime yet mysterious lack of architectural specificity only enhanced Udolpho's grip upon the cultural imagination. The fiction having been redacted and retold in chapbooks such as *The Veiled Picture; or, The Mysteries of Gorgono,* (1802), and adapted for the stage in such dramas and dramatic operas as Miles Peter Andrews's *The Mysteries of the Castle* (1795), John Bayliss's unperformed melodrama *The Mysteries of Udolpho; or, The Phantom of the Castle* (1804), and the anonymous *The Castle of Udolpho: An Operatic Drama in Five Acts* (1808), the castle of Radcliffe's title achieved nothing less than iconic status. However, even when the romance was adapted as a dramatic spectacle, Udolpho

---

[92] Wilson, *Claude, The Enchanted Castle*, p. 14.

remained in certain senses unrepresentable as a composite architectural object: the stage directions to *The Mysteries of the Castle* required that the scenery merely hint at individual architectural details—large gates, a hall, a turret door, and a subterranean passage all wearing 'an appearance of great antiquity'—none of which ever cohere into a unified structure or rational sense of space.[93] Nonetheless, Radcliffe and her castle, like Walpole and Otranto before her, became closely identified with one another—Mathias's 'mighty magician of THE MYSTERIES OF UDOLPHO', T. J. Horsley Curties's '*Udolpho*'s mighty Foundress', and Matilda Betham's Armida-like 'Enchantress! Whose transcendent powr's / With ease, the massy fabric raise'.[94] English-language emulations and plagiarisms abounded, and the novel was translated into German, French, and Italian; by the end of 1795, *The Mysteries of Udolpho* had been published in both Ireland and America, while, between the years 1794 and 1824, it ran to some thirteen new editions and reprintings in London alone. The titles of novels such as T. J. Horsley Curties's *The Monk of Udolpho* (1807) sought to cash in on the novel's success, while fictions such as Francis Lathom's *The Castle of Ollada* (1795) sought to cultivate in their titles a Radcliffean appeal. To write about Gothic castles was always in some way to pay tribute to Radcliffe's splendid construction, even to the point of trespassing on the enchantress's literary domains. Posing, like Walpole did, as the 'translator' of his own fiction, the Reverend James Douglas, in *The History of Julia d'Haumont* (1797), paused to defend himself against any accusation of plagiarism when he described the 'ponderous towers' and drawbridge of an ancient Gothic castle in his narrative: since 'As many castles have draw-bridges as well as the Castle of Udolpho,' he reasoned, 'the passage was suffered to remain as it stands in the original; more especially as the translator is assured the author never perused that romance.'[95] The term 'castle' became ubiquitous in the titling of new fictions after *Udolpho*: the c.1795 catalogue for the Minerva Press's circulating library in Leadenhall Street, London, includes over twenty romances and dramas that contained the word.[96] Though Walpole had inaugurated it in fiction, the Gothic architectural imagination came into its own in the work of Ann Radcliffe. As a review of the anonymous *Austenburn Castle* (1796) in *The Critical Review* opined, 'Since Mrs Radcliffe's justly admired and successful romances, the

---

[93] Miles Peter Andrews, *The Mysteries of the Castle: A Dramatic Tale, in Three Acts* (London: Printed by W. Woodfall for T. N. Longman, 1795).

[94] T. J. Horsley Curties, *Ancient Records; or, The Abbey of Saint Oswythe*, 4 vols (London: Printed at the Minerva Press, 1801), vol. 3, p. vi; Matilda Betham, 'Lines to Mrs Radcliffe, on First Reading *The Mysteries of Udolpho*', in *Poems*, by Matilda Betham (London: Printed for J. Hatchard, 1808), pp. 11–14 (p. 11).

[95] James Douglas, *The History of Julia d'Haumont: or, The Eventful Connection of the House of Montmelian with that of d'Haumont*, 2 vols (London: Printed for G. Cawthorn, 1797), vol. 1, p. 123.

[96] See *A Catalogue of the Minerva General Library, Leadenhall Street, London* (London: Minerva Literary Repository, c.1795).

press has teemed with stories of haunted castles', so much so that 'criticism is at a loss to vary its remarks'.[97]

Castles in the Air

Ironically signing himself 'A Jacobin Novelist', a deeply conservative critic in *The Monthly Magazine* in 1797 argued that the taste for Gothic romance was a form of cultural revolution akin to the 'terrors' of post-revolutionary France. Bemoaning the dearth of originality in contemporary literature, this critic turned to an important architectural metaphor to make the point: 'What has [the writer] to do', he reasoned, 'but build a castle in the air, and furnish it with dead bodies and departed spirits?'[98] In elaborating the form that such a 'castle in the air' might take, the critic disclosed a deep familiarity with the architectural conventions of the very mode that he so despised: '*an old castle, formerly* of great magnitude and extent, built in the Gothic manner, with a great number of hanging towers, turrets, and pinnacles', one half of it, at least, in ruins, and filled with all manner of 'dreadful chasms', 'gaping crevices', and the requisite '*subterraneous passages*' through which its heroine must pass—but all, of course, as insubstantial as air.[99] It is difficult to overemphasize the importance of the phrase 'castles in the air' to literature, architecture, and the relationship between them in the late eighteenth and early nineteenth centuries. As the *OED* notes, the idiom denotes a 'visionary project or scheme', a 'day-dream', or an 'idle fancy', the formation of 'unsubstantial or visionary projects' metaphorically rendered as an impossible task of architectural construction (*OED*, 11). In earlier periods, it was often varied and used interchangeably with the French '*chateaux en Espagne*', a phrase translated into English as 'castles in Spain', and an idiom based on the once-prevalent but now questionable assumption that there were, indeed, no castles to be found there.[100] Its first recorded usage in Old French is 'Lors feras chastiaus en Espaigne' in *The Romaunt of the Rose* (c.1400), a line that Chaucer translated literally as 'Thou shalt make castels thanne in Spayne', and of which he seemed to be aware in *The House of Fame* (c.1379–80).[101] Both variations of the expression came into common usage from about 1575, after which it occurs in, among other places, Robert

---

[97] Review of *Austenburn Castle*, in *The Critical Review; or, Annals of Literature* no. 16 (Feb. 1796): p. 222.
[98] A Jacobin Novelist, 'Terrorist System of Novel-Writing', *The Monthly Magazine*, vol. IV, no. xxi (August 1797): pp. 102–4 (p. 102).
[99] A Jacobin Novelist, 'Terrorist System of Novel-Writing', p. 103.
[100] For an account of how this metaphor applied to Romantic perceptions of Spain and Spanish architecture in the Romantic period, see Diego Saglia, *Poetic Castles in Spain: British Romanticism and Figurations of Iberia* (Amsterdam and Atlanta, GA: Rodopi, 2000).
[101] See Roland M. Smith, 'Chaucer's "Castle in Spain"', *Modern Language Notes* vol. 60, no. 1 (January 1945): pp. 39–40.

Greene's *The Historie of Orlando Furioso* (1594) and Richard Burton's *Anatomy of Melancholy* (1621). Traces of the idiom even work their way into Prospero's evocations of enchanted castles in Act IV of *The Tempest*, those 'cloud-capped towers', 'gorgeous palaces', and 'solemn temples' that, in dissolving, constitute 'the baseless fabric of a vision', as well as in the 'gay Castles in the Clouds that pass' in Thomson's *The Castle of Indolence*.[102] Undoubtedly, the popularity of Cervantes's *Don Quixote* in eighteenth-century Britain did much to reinforce the expression's currency, for it is while wandering with Sancho Panza around the Spanish countryside that the eponymous self-styled Knight makes of a landlord's plain daughter in a run-down inn a beauteous maiden in need of rescue from a Gothic castle. To indulge in the fantasies of romance and chivalry, Cervantes's text suggests, is to see castles simultaneously 'in the air' and 'in Spain', that is, in places where patently none actually exist.

As the above review indicates, 'castles in the air' was a phrase that was often employed in negative critical responses to Gothic fiction in the 1790s. 'In truth', remarked a review of John Palmer's *The Haunted Cavern* (1795), 'we are almost weary of Gothic castles, mouldering turrets, and "cloud inveloped [*sic*] battlements".'[103] 'Another castle!' carped a reviewer of *Arville Castle* (1795) in *The Analytical Review*; 'But in a "castle in the air"', the disgruntled writer continued, 'what should we fear? and a castle built before the days of Boadicea, and inhabited by a *baron*, long before barons, or even thanes, were known, can be only "the baseless fabric of a vision," conjured up by that wondrous power, which gives even to airy nothings a local habitation and a name.'[104] Appropriating lines from *The Tempest* and *A Midsummer Night's Dream*, this critic regarded the enchanted palaces of the Gothic as insubstantial 'follies' called up by all too numerous a romancer. While damning, the assessment was fair. Though apparently set in first-century Britain, 'when Baodicea headed a considerable army against the Romans, commanded by the General Suetonius', *Arville Castle* compromised its historical vision through depicting the social and kinship structures of the Middle Ages, as well as through egregious architectural anachronism.[105] Despite the use of Ovid, Homer, Pope, and other classical and neoclassical sources in the chapter epigraphs, and for all the novel's attempt at substituting for the ubiquitous Catholics of the Gothic mode the pre-Christian figure of the Druid, it is around two Gothic architectural structures that the narrative plays itself out, the first the

---

[102] *The Tempest* (2005), Act IV, scene i, ll. 148–56; and James Thomson, *The Castle of Indolence* (1748), stanza VI, p. 4.

[103] Review of John Palmer's *The Haunted Cavern: A Caledonian Tale* (1795), *The Critical Review; or, Annals of Literature* vol. 15 (December 1795): p. 480.

[104] Review of *Arville Castle; An Historical Romance* (1795), *The Analytical Review; or, History of Literature* vol. 23, no. 1 (Jan. 1796): p. 55.

[105] Anon., *Arville Castle: An Historical Romance*, 2 vols (London: Printed for B. Crosby and T. White, 1795), vol. 1, p. 1.

'Gothic' Castle of Despair owned by the villain Dunstan, and the second the 'ancient manor, in the West of England' of the novel's title.[106]

Some Gothic writers proudly embraced the epithet, with T. J. Horsley Curties, for instance, describing all romance writers in the wake of Radcliffe as 'humble architects' who ought to be allowed 'to build our airy castles, or mine our subterranean caverns, unmolested'.[107] Others echoed the rhetoric of the Gothic's fiercest critics, and sought to jettison the aerial architecture of their forebears in favour of a more grounded, less overworked idiom. In the 'Avis Au Lecteur' that prefaced the second volume of *The Banished Man* (1794), Charlotte Smith expressed her sense of dismay at 'the imaginary castles which frown in almost every modern novel'.[108] As much a rebuke of her contemporaries as the articulation of a shift towards realism in her own literary practice, Smith recorded here her sense of exhaustion at having laboured so hard to construct the fictional castles of her earlier novels through reference to those illusory castles in Spain:

> For my part, who can now no longer build chateaux even en Espagne, I find that Mowbray Castle, Grasmere Abbey, the castle of Rock-March, the castle of Hauteville, and Rayland Hall, have taken so many of my materials to construct, that I have hardly a watch tower, a Gothic arch, a cedar parlour, or a long gallery, an illuminated window, or a ruined chapel, left to help myself.[109]

As Smith well knew, her 'ingenious contemporaries' were, indeed, ransacking 'every bastion and buttress—of every tower and turret—of every gallery and gateway', not least in so bold a plagiarism of the plot and architectural concerns of her novel *Emmeline* (1788) in a fiction such as Mrs Harley's *The Castle of Mowbray* (1788).[110] As this example indicates, castles in the air were likely to spawn further aerial architecture. Like Smith, Elizabeth Bonhôte justified her setting of her Gothic fiction *Bungay Castle* (1796) in the 'real' ruins of Bungay, Suffolk, by expressing her dissatisfaction with the 'wonderful tales of wonderful castles' witnessed in much modern fiction.[111] 'Castle-building', she claimed, 'appears to have been the passion of all ages'; 'while some have been raising their fabrics on the most solid and lasting foundations', other writers 'have been forming them in the air, where the structure has been erected with infinitely less

---

[106] Anon., *Arville Castle*, vol. 1, p. 1.
[107] Curties, *Ancient Records*, vol. 3, p. vii.
[108] Charlotte Smith, *The Banished Man, A Novel*, 4 vols (London: Printed for T. Cadell Jnr and W. Davies, 1794), vol. 2, p. iv.
[109] Smith, *The Banished Man*, vol. 2, p. iii–iv. For an account of the shift in Smith's fiction, from sentimental Gothic towards a more historically and politically aware form of writing, see Antje Blank, 'Things as They Were': The Gothic of Real Life in Charlotte Smith's *The Emigrants* and *The Banished Man*', *Women's Writing*, vol. 16, issue 1 (2009): pp. 78–93.
[110] See [Mrs M. Harley], *The Castle of Mowbray, An English Romance* (London: Printed for C. Stalker and H. Setchell, 1788).
[111] Elizabeth Bonhôte, *Bungay Castle: A Novel*, 2 vols (London: Printed for William Lane at the Minerva Press, 1796), vol. 1, p. vii.

trouble, as their own invention led them to wish, and very pleasant, no doubt, was the delusion of the moment'.[112] Seeing no reason why Bungay Castle 'should not be as good a foundation for a novel as any other edifice within or without the kingdom', Bonhôte resolved to set her fiction in the 'venerable ruins' situated a mere 20 yards from her home.

From the late 1790s onwards, the expression 'castles in the air' drove and justified the writers' turn towards setting their fictions set in existent Gothic ruins of Britain. The title page of Jane Harvey's *The Castle of Tynemouth* (1806), a two-volume romance set in the extant ruined Northumbrian castle of the novel's title and the nearby Benedictine Priory, featured a poetic fragment that expressed the author's turning away from imaginary castles towards more self-consciously historical and antiquarian subject matter: 'No air-built castles, and no fairy bowers, / But thou, fair Tynemouth, and thy well-known towers, / Now bid th' historic muse explore the maze / Of long past years, and tales of other days.'[113] Albeit to more political intent, Mary Wollstonecraft metaphorically followed suit in the opening paragraph of *The Wrongs of Woman; or, Maria* (1798):

> Abodes of horror have frequently been described, and castles, filled with spectres and chimeras, conjured up by the magic spell of genius to harrow the soul, and absorb the wondering mind. But, formed as such stuff as dreams are made of, what were they to the mansions of despair, in one corner of which Maria sat, endeavouring to recall her scattered thoughts![114]

Behind these lines lurks Ann Radcliffe who, once again in the guise of the enchantress Armida, effortlessly calls up 'Abodes of horror' by the 'magic spell' of her genius. Designed to 'harrow [up] the soul', Radcliffe's castles, Wollstonecraft suggests, looked directly to Shakespeare's haunted battlements of Elsinore for their justification. Against such redoubtable edifices, though, Wollstonecraft pits the imaginary castles of Prospero: the Gothic castles of Radcliffean romance are merely 'such stuff as dreams are made [on]', and considerably removed from the real 'mansions of despair'—asylums, workhouses, ordinary bourgeois homes—that the women of contemporary England inhabit. Maria Edgeworth undertook a similar task in *Castle Rackrent* (1800): even as the title of her fiction courted the imaginary castles of the modern romance tradition, she turned this convention to political ends, exploring through it the politics of the 1800 Acts of Union and the debt underpinning Anglo-Irish estates.

In the period 1760–1840, the expression 'castles in the air' became bound up in the emergent discourse of the literary imagination: while true, authentic, and

---

[112] Bonhôte, *Bungay Castle*, vol. 1, p. vii.
[113] Jane Harvey, *The Castle of Tynemouth. A Tale*, 2 vols (London: Printed for Longman, Hurst, Rees, & Orme; and Vernor, Hood, and Sharp, 1806).
[114] Mary Wollstonecraft, *Mary and The Wrongs of Woman*, ed. Gary Kelly (Oxford: Oxford University Press, 1998), p. 75.

legitimate imaginative acts were the sturdy architectural structures in Alexander Gerard's, William Duff's, and Edward Young's conceptualization of original genius, frivolous, playful, impractical, or overly fanciful imaginative schemes, both architectural and literary, were to be a written off as 'folly', as 'castles' variously 'in the air', 'in the sky', or 'in Spain'. Clara Reeve, in *The Progress of Romance* (1785), consequently had her mouthpiece Euphrasia employ the metaphor as a means of ordering the varying levels of 'truth' to be discerned in the 'fairy land' of romance:

> In this faery land are many Castles of various Architecture.—Some are built in the air, and have no foundation at all,—others are composed of such heavy materials, that their own weight sinks them into the earth, where they lie buried under their own ruins, and leave not a trace behind,—a third sort are built upon a real and solid foundation, and remain impregnable against all the attacks of Criticism, and perhaps even of time itself.[115]

While romances lacking in all vestiges of historical and moral truth are castles in the air, those demonstrating too close an allegiance to truth and common sense are weighed down and eventually 'ruined' by the heaviness of this responsibility. The expression had implications for the reader of Gothic romance, too. In the Appendix to *A Treatise of Human Nature*, David Hume referenced 'the loose and indolent reveries of a castle-builder' to describe those who were more drawn to fiction than empirical truth.[116] Following Hume, the author of 'The Female Castle-Builder', a short essay that was published in *Flowers of Literature for 1801 and 1802*, gently caricatured the female reader of romance as one who followed 'architectural plans, in upper regions', resulting in a worrying susceptibility to romantic love and the neglect of her domestic duties. Yet, 'If these chimeras keep her mind from stagnating, and bestow on it an artificial, though a fallacious, happiness,' the writer concluded, 'I do not see that any invader has a right to rob her of her aerial demesnes.'[117]

So inveterate were the associations between fiction-writing, reading, and the work of aerial architecture that not even novelists of a more historically self-aware persuasion completely escaped implication. When Maria Edgeworth visited Walter Scott's Abbotsford in 1823, she drew upon the commonplace associations between romance-writing and the building of castles in the sky when she ambivalently observed of Scott's home that 'All the work is so solid you would never guess it was by a castle-building romance writer & poet.'[118] But Scott, himself, would make use

---

[115] Reeve, *The Progress of Romance*, vol. 1, pp. 109–10.
[116] Hume, *A Treatise of Human Nature*, vol. 3, p. 287.
[117] Anon., 'The Female Castle-Builder. A Picture from Real Life', *Flowers of Literature for 1801 and 1802*, vol. 1 (1803): pp. 215–17.
[118] Quoted in Gary Kelly, *English Fiction of the Romantic Period, 1789–1830* (London and New York: Longman, 1989), p. 139.

of the analogy: in an imaginative interchange between an autobiographical author figure and an attendant Genie in a journal entry of 1829, the aged author described his own engagements with romance as an exercise in 'aerial architecture': 'Do you approve of Castle Building as a frequent exercise?' the author figure asks the Genie; 'Life were not life without it,' the Genie duly replies, prior to citing two lines from 'Castle-Building, An Elegy', that anonymous poetic figuring of the creative faculty as an exercise in architectural design and construction that Scott had included in *English Minstrelsy*, and to which I referred in the Introduction.[119] 'I reckon myself one of the best aerial architects now living and *Nil me penitet hujus ausi* [I do not repent of this undertaking],' Scott continues, a claim to which the Genie responds with '*Nec est cur [te] peniteat* [Nor is there any reason for you to repent]; most of your novels have previously been subject for airy castles.'[120] As Henry Liddell's poem 'The Wizard of the North' (1833) made clear, at least part of Scott's associations with wizardry and enchantment resided in his ability to call up both actual and fictional castles in the air in the fashion of Ariosto's Atlante.[121] Looking back on her life in the Author's Introduction to the Standard Novels edition of *Frankenstein* in 1831, Mary Shelley, too, claimed that her greatest childhood pleasure was 'the formation of castles in the air—the indulging in waking dreams—the following up trains of thought, which had for their subject the formation of a succession of imaginary incidents'.[122] Her point of reference, here, is the demonic architect who fashions from Chaos the classical architecture of Pandaemonium in *Paradise Lost*: 'Invention', Shelley humbly admits, 'does not consist in creating out of void, but out of chaos; the materials must, in the first place, be afforded.'[123] Through the frequent rehearsal of this expression, architectural metaphor became further entrenched in Romantic conceptualizations of the imagination.

The expression 'castles in the air' had important implications for architectural aesthetics and practice too. As I argued in the previous chapter, Walpole made frequent use of it in his correspondence around the remodelling of Strawberry Hill, often using it to express his anxieties over the impermanence of his 'paper house'. But, in architectural practice, its most obvious point of application was in relation to the follies of eighteenth-century landscape gardening, 'folly' in this instance being a popular name 'for any costly structure considered to have shown folly in the builder' (*OED*, 5a) and serving, as I suggested in the Introduction, as

---

[119] Walter Scott, Journal Entry for Wednesday, 18 March 1829, in *The Journal of Sir Walter Scott*, ed. and introd. W. E. K. Anderson (Edinburgh: Canongate Books, 1998), pp. 600–1 (p. 601).

[120] Walter Scott, Journal Entry for Wednesday, 18 March 1829, *The Journal of Sir Walter Scott*, p. 601.

[121] See Henry Liddell, *The Wizard of the North; The Vampire Bride; and Other Poems* (Edinburgh: William Blackwood; London: T. Cadell, 1833), pp. 1–27.

[122] Mary Shelley, *Frankenstein; or, The Modern Prometheus: The 1818 Text*, ed. Nick Groom (Oxford: Oxford University Press, 2018), p. 173.

[123] Shelley, *Frankenstein*, p. 175.

another key point at which literary and architectural aesthetics in the period overlapped: it was through the notion of 'folly' that both literary and architectural discourse approached the playful and whimsical excesses of the imaginative faculty. As David Watkin has observed, the first artificial Gothic ruins to be built in eighteenth-century Britain, dating to c.1730, were those of John Freeman at Fawley Court, Buckinghamshire, and Alfred's Hall, built for the first Earl of Bathurst at Cirencester Park, Gloucestershire; shortly before 1750, Sanderson Miller constructed a ruined Gothic castle at Hagley Park, Gloucestershire, while in 1750, Randle Wilbraham built Mow Cop Castle, Cheshire, in the Gothic style.[124] The numerous classical, Gothic, Chinese, and Egyptian follies, ornaments, and artificial ruins designed by John Vanbrugh and William Kent for Lord Viscount Cobham's gardens at Stowe, Buckinghamshire; the sham Gothic ruins built from 1762 onwards for Henry Fox, Lord Holland, at Kingsgate, Isle of Thanet, Kent; and the artificial ruins of a Gothic castle at Wimpole Hall, Cambridgeshire, designed by Sanderson Miller in 1749 and built and completed between 1767 and 1772 by James Essex and Lancelot 'Capability' Brown: these are merely a few other notable examples of the widespread bourgeois and aristocratic taste for follies and sham ruins in eighteenth-century England.[125] David Garrick and George Colman the Elder wittily satirized the rage for fake ruins in *The Clandestine Marriage* (1766), having Mr Sterling quip that 'It has just cost me a hundred and fifty pounds to put my ruins in thorough repair.'[126] Whimsical, fanciful, and impractical to boot, these structures, too, were castles in the sky, but they were also, as Nicholas Halmi has reminded us, 'Ruins Without a Past', imaginary sites of architectural dereliction that, having been dislocated from history, served as objects of aesthetic pleasure and moral reflection in the present.[127]

Professional architects made use of the expression too. John Soane, for instance, tacitly invoked it in his retrospective account of his having faked the discovery of the ruined remains of an ancient Roman temple beside the kitchen of his country home, Pitzhanger Manor, Ealing, in 1802.[128] Parodying antiquarian letters to *The Gentleman's Magazine*, Soane and the architect James Spiller had collaborated on

---

[124] David Watkin, 'Built Ruins: The Hermitage as a Retreat', in *Visions of Ruin: Architectural Fantasies and Designs for Garden Follies, with 'Crude Hints Towards a History of My House' by John Soane* (London: The Soane Gallery, 1999), pp. 5–14 (p. 8). For more on Fawley Court as perhaps the earliest artificial Gothic ruin in England, see Geoffrey Tyack, 'The Folly and the Mausoleum', *Country Life* vol. 183, issue 16 (20 April 1989): pp. 215–20.

[125] For a fuller account of follies in eighteenth-century Britain, see Barbara Jones, *Follies & Grottoes*, 2nd edn (London: Constable and Co., 1974), and Gwyn Headley and Wim Meulenkemp, *Follies: A National Trust Guide* (London: Jonathan Cape, 1986).

[126] George Colman and David Garrick, *The Clandestine Marriage, A Comedy* (London: Printed for P. Becket and P. A. De Hondt; R. Baldwin; and T. Davies, 1766), Act II, p. 24.

[127] Nicholas Halmi, 'Ruins Without a Past', *Essays in Romanticism* vol. 18 (2011): pp. 7–27.

[128] See Christopher Woodward, *In Ruins* (London: Vintage, 2002), pp. 165–8, and 'Scenes from the Future', in *Visions of Ruin: Architectural Fantasies and Designs for Garden Follies, with 'Crude Hints Towards a History of My House' by John Soane* (London: The Soane Gallery, 1999), pp. 15–50.

a number of manuscripts announcing the ruins' 'discovery', one of which offered them as a refreshing alternative to the prevailing antiquarian interest in Gothic architecture.[129] Like so many decorative Gothic ruins in the period, these classical ruins were fake, and cleverly modelled by Soane on the temple at the sacred spring of Clitumnus, Umbria, as a means of accounting for the depth at which the pillars appeared to have been submerged beneath the ground. Soane urged his students, artists, and several other visitors to look beyond the remains so as to imagine and then sketch the building in its former condition, activities that were 'sources of amusement' to the numerous persons visiting Pitzhanger and a 'perpetual source of intellectual enjoyment' to Soane himself.[130] As his *Plans, Elevations, and Perspective Views, of Pitzhanger Manor-House* (1833) attests, Soane himself produced images of the building in its 'original' state.[131] The practice culminated in July 1804, when the Ealing Fair was held on the green in front of the manor, and several friends and other tourists flocked to the area. Soane's description of these events in his *Memoirs of the Professional Life of an Architect* (1835) makes much of the centrality of the imaginative faculty in these acts of reconstruction: the arched entrances of the building opened 'a wide field for speculation', and yet, with the aid of 'perseverance and a *warm imagination*', the entire edifice 'was restored in some degree of its ancient magnificence' in the sketches, drawings, and hypotheses of the 'romantic enthusiasts' who viewed them.[132] As he later confessed, his motivation for the hoax was to expose 'those fanciful architects and antiquarians who, finding a few pieces of columns, and sometimes only a few single stones, proceeded from these slender data to imagine magnificent buildings'.[133] Imaginatively converting 'small fragments of tessellated pavements' into 'splendid remains of Roman grandeur', architects and antiquaries for Soane were guilty of erecting castles in the air through an over-reliance upon conjecture, an accusation that, as Christopher Woodward has argued, was in all likelihood aimed at Samuel Lysons's method in his *Remains of Two Temples and Other Roman Antiquities Discovered at Bath* (1802).[134]

In other, less satirical contexts, Soane would invoke the idiom, via Shakespeare, to accompany exhibitions of his own work, particularly his architectural designs

---

[129] This manuscript is bound with Soane's *Crude Hints Towards a History of My House* in the John Soane's Museum Archive, Soane Case 31. For other manuscripts associated with the hoax, some of them in the hand of James Spiller, see John Soane's Museum Archive MS 7/G/4/2–MS 7/G/4/5.

[130] John Soane, *Memoirs of the Professional Life of an Architect, Between the Years 1768 and 1835. Written by Himself* (London: Privately printed by James Moyes, 1835), p. 66.

[131] John Soane, *Plans, Elevations, and Perspective Views, of Pitzhanger Manor-House, of the Ruins of an Edifice of Roman Architecture, Situated on the Border of Ealing Green, with a Description of the Ancient and Present State of the Manor-House, in a Letter to a Friend* (London: J. Moyes, 1802). Although this publication is dated 1802, it was published only in 1833.

[132] Soane, *Memoirs of the Professional Life of an Architect*, p. 65.

[133] Soane, *Memoirs of the Professional Life of an Architect*, p. 66.

[134] Soane, *Memoirs of the Professional Life of an Architect*, p. 66; Woodward, 'Scenes from the Future', pp. 30–1.

that were realized by Joseph Michael Gandy, the 'English Piranesi' whom Soane took into his employ in 1798. Gandy produced several aerial perspectives for ideal, imaginary royal palaces for Soane during the 1820s, including *Bird's-Eye View of a Design for a Royal Residence* (1821), *Bird's-Eye View of a Design for a Royal Palace* (1828), and *View in the Portico for a Royal Residence* (1827).[135] Even as these were dismissed by Soane's critics as 'flimsy piles' that 'rise and fall at the nod of caprice', so Soane and Gandy accompanied their designs in the exhibition catalogues of the Royal Academy for 1825 and 1826 with lines of poetry that defiantly flaunted the analogy.[136] Such were the fleeting architectural fantasies that Soane tied explicitly back to Prospero's 'baseless fabric of a vision' speech when he included these lines from *The Tempest* in the catalogue entry for Gandy's *Architectural Ruins—a Vision* in 1832.[137] Soane cited Prospero's speech at least twice in his public lectures at the Royal Academy, and in his first and eighth lectures pitted the obdurate, glorious remains of Egyptian antiquity against the intimations of vanishing in Shakespeare's 'baseless fabric of a vision' line.[138] As Alison Shell has shown, Soane's home at number 13 Lincoln's Inn Fields also included numerous visual allusions to Prospero's speech; as Sean Sawyer has observed, the architect again invoked the 'baseless fabric of a vision' speech to express a melancholic sense of the disappearance of all of his artwork in his *Description of Three Designs for the Two Houses of Parliament, made in 1779, 1794, and 1796* (1835).[139]

Ann Radcliffe's Gothic *Capriccios*

In a context in which Gothic fictions and architectural fancies were denounced as imaginary, phantasmatic constructions without any anchorage in empirical reality, it is surely significant that *The Mysteries of Udolpho*, like *The Castle of Otranto* before it, generated at least a modicum of debate concerning its 'real' architectural antecedents. In the second part of his *Peak Scenery* in 1819, for example, Ebenezer Rhodes included in his description of Haddon Hall the observation that, as 'a native of Derbyshire', Mrs Radcliffe regularly visited this country house, and that 'some of the most gloomy scenery of her "Mysteries of Udolpho" was studied

---

[135] See Brian Lukacher, *Joseph Gandy: An Architectural Visionary in Georgian England* (New York: Thames & Hudson Inc., 2006), pp. 142–54.
[136] This anonymous review from *Arnold's Library of the Fine Arts* (1833) is cited in Lukacher, *Joseph Gandy*, p. 142.
[137] See Lukacher, *Joseph Gandy*, pp. 152–4, 165.
[138] Lukacher, *Joseph Gandy*, p. 208, n. 7. See David Watkin, ed., *Sir John Soane: The Royal Academy Lectures*, pp. 36, 176.
[139] Alison Shell, 'John Soane, Bardolater', in *'The Cloud-Capped Towers': Shakespeare in Soane's Architectural Imagination* (London: The Sir John Soane's Museum, 2016), pp. 19–27; Sean Sawyer, '"The Baseless Fabric of a Vision": Civic Architecture and Pictorial Representation at Sir John Soane's Museum', in *The Built Surface, Vol. I: Architecture and the Pictorial Arts from Antiquity to the Enlightenment*, ed. Christy Anderson (Aldershot: Ashgate, 2002), pp. 260–77.

within the walls of this ancient structure'.[140] Walter Scott, however, dismissed Rhodes's suggestion as 'absurd', arguing with some assurance that, though the place 'could hardly have been seen by her without suggesting some of those ideas in which her imagination naturally revelled', the writer 'never saw Haddon House'.[141] Instead, Scott put forward his own theory concerning the relationship between Radcliffe's fictional architecture and actual topographical place, advancing what we now know to be the erroneous claim that she found her inspiration for Udolpho in the castles that she encountered on the banks of the Rhine during a trip to Germany in 1793.[142] Other theories concerning the 'real' topographical antecedents to *Udolpho* were posited too: three months after Radcliffe's death in 1823, an article in *The Edinburgh Review* claimed that Radcliffe's husband, William, accompanied by his wife, had served as a British diplomat in Italy during the early 1790s, and that it was here that 'she imbibed that taste for picturesque scenery, and the obscure and wild superstitions of mouldering castles, of which she has made so beautiful a use in her Romances'.[143] In his *Poetics* (1812), George Dyer included an influential essay in which he undertook to account for the use that 'poetry'—a synonym for literature in general—might make of 'real' geographical place and architectural space.[144] The topographical poet, he controversially argued, need not actually have visited or seen the places described in order to render them accurately, a point that he made through the revealing example of 'a modern ingenious novelist, justly admired for her descriptive talents', one who 'relied on the representations of travellers and tourists' but whose fiction was no less topographically accurate for being so.[145] Without mentioning her by name, Dyer thus invoked Ann Radcliffe as an example of the topographical spirit in contemporary literature: even after having visited Europe herself for the first time in 1794, she made it to neither France nor Italy, the countries that she described in her major fictions. So as to differentiate the work of the Great Enchantress from the 'castles in the air' of all those who tried to emulate her, it was imperative that Radcliffe's architectural imagination be critically anchored in an authentic, locatable, and 'real' sense of architectural space.

Despite such allowances, the reality, as I have shown in this chapter, is that Radcliffe's castles remained the stuff of fantasy, airy architectural formations erected upon the scanty foundations of drama, poetry, picturesque description,

---

[140] Ebenezer Rhodes, *Peak Scenery; or, The Derbyshire Tourist*, 2nd edn (London: Printed for Longman, Hurst, Rees, Orme, Brown, and Green, 1824), p. 147. As Norton has shown, the associations between Haddon Hall and the Castle of Udolpho were in place by at least 1812, and actively peddled by the Duke of Rutland, the Hall's owner, well into the 1820s. See Norton, *Mistress of Udolpho*, pp. 210–11.

[141] Scott, 'Prefatory Memoir to Mrs Ann Radcliffe', p. xxv.

[142] Scott, 'Prefatory Memoir to Mrs Ann Radcliffe', p. vi.

[143] Anon., 'The Periodical Press', *The Edinburgh Review* vol. 38, no. 76 (May 1823): pp. 349–78 (p. 351).

[144] George Dyer, 'On the Use of Topography in Poetry', in *Poetics; or, A Series of Poems, and Disquisitions on Poetry*, 2 vols (London: Printed for J. Johnson and Co., 1812), vol. 2, pp. 112–23.

[145] Dyer, 'On the Use of Topography in Poetry', p. 118.

and the writings of others who had visited the regions that she set out to describe. To these sources it is important to add the paintings of Claude, Salvator Rosa, and Nicolas Poussin, the three painters with whom critics frequently compared her, and with whom Radcliffe herself was clearly familiar. 'Whate'er *Lorrain* lighttouched with softening Hue / or savage *Rosa* dash'd, or learned *Poussin* drew': as these lines by Thomson indicate, the three artists were thought to derive from different yet compatible landscape traditions.[146] Based neither upon accurate topographical description nor upon an empirical engagement with 'real' architectural space, Radcliffe's ruined castles were castles in the air, literary equivalents, perhaps, of the *capriccio* frequently found in seventeenth and eighteenth-century landscape painting and architectural practice.

Though the term had important musical implications in the period too, *capriccio* was a discrete subgenre of landscape painting that characteristically featured invented or impossible buildings, fanciful renditions of monumental ruin, and architectural structures of fantastical proportion and elevation at the centre of the composition. It was during the eighteenth century that *capriccio* became an extremely popular form, a fact that is often attributed to the cultural prominence of the grand tour: in an attempt at meeting tourists' demands for visual representations of the Continent's most valued antiquities, painters, etchers, and engravers often turned to the manufacturing of *capriccios*, whether in the form of visual representations of non-existent, entirely imaginary scenes of ancient architecture and ruin, or of highly unlikely hybrid combinations of existent archaeological sites and architectural details. Here, relations of tension, opposition, and juxtaposition are paramount, for the individual elements out of which the *capriccio* is composed seldom, if ever, relate rationally, naturally, or harmoniously to one another. As an art form, *capriccio* is characterized by jarring and disparate assemblages of archaeological and architectural detail that provoke a sense of ambiguity, tension, and speculation, and which serve to generate in the viewer multiple possible readings and interpretations.[147] Unlike the realist imperatives underpinning the *veduta* tradition in European landscape painting, *capriccio* flew flagrantly in the face of mimetic ideals, celebrating, instead, the generative powers of the imagination in the painter's or engraver's fashioning of architectural monument, space, and ruin. Neither Canaletto's Venice nor Giovanni Paolo Panini's Rome, for example, is mimetically represented; though, too, a medium for the visualization of architecture, *capriccio* eschews the documentary drives of the antiquarian topographer of ancient monuments.[148] The tendencies towards idealization that we see in, say, Canaletto's *Capriccio Palladiano* (*c*.1756–9)—an ideal city based on

---

[146] Thomson, *The Castle of Indolence*, stanza 37, p. 20.
[147] Michael Graves, 'Foreword', in *The Architectural Capriccio: Memory, Fantasy and Invention*, ed. Lucien Steil (Farnham: Ashgate, 2014), pp. xxxix–l (p. xlvi).
[148] See David Mayernick, 'Meaning and Purpose of the *Capriccio*', in *The Architectural Capriccio: Memory, Fantasy and Invention*, ed. Lucien Steil (Farnham: Ashgate, 2014), pp. 5–16.

the designs of Palladio—were offset against *capriccios* of a much more sombre tone, such as in John Martin's apocalyptic visions of ruined cities. Indeed, at its most dystopian, *capriccio* was given over to imagining present cities and buildings as the architectural ruins of the future.

Much literary and epistolary writing of the period shared in the *capriccio*'s gloomy forebodings of ruin, from the intimations of the collapse of London in the letters of Horace Walpole in the 1770s, through the poetry of Thomas Lyttleton in 1780 and the comte de Volney's *Les Ruines* (1791), and into Anna Laetitia Barbauld's apocalyptic vision of national ruin and catastrophe in *Eighteen Hundred and Eleven* (1812).[149] With its impossible combination of classical and Gothic architectural forms, Barbauld's poem demonstrates clearly the relations of contrast and juxtaposition that dominate the *capriccio*.[150] In his *Crude Hints Towards an History of My House in Lincoln's Inn Field* (1812), John Soane produced an extraordinary vision of his own home in ruins, a random and puzzling assemblage of architectural fragments to be visited and speculated upon by some imaginary antiquary of the future.[151] An admirer and collector of the works of Charles-Louis Clérisseau, Soane himself sketched and painted several *capriccios*, while Gandy produced of Soane's realized architectural designs vivid and apocalyptic images depicting the master's buildings in a future state of ruin; his *A Bird's-Eye View of the Bank of England* (1830) and *Architectural Ruins—a Vision* (*Bank of England in Ruins*, 1798–1832) are probably the best-known examples.[152] As these examples suggest, *capriccio* was by no means confined to the visual and decorative arts: as a working method for practising architects, it continued—and still continues—to be crucial to the architect's conceptualization and design of idealized architectural space, often serving as a medium through which the architect communicates to the patron or client glimpses of his initial creative vision, or even as a simple, unbridled expression of the architect's otherwise controlled, disciplined, or frustrated creativity.[153]

---

[149] See David Skilton, 'Tourists at the Ruins of London: The Metropolis and the Struggle for Empire', *Cercles* vol. 17 (2007): pp. 93–119. For a fuller account of eighteenth-century poems of ruin and national disaster, see Suvir Kaul, *Poems of Nation, Anthems of Empire: English Verse in the Long Eighteenth Century* (Charlottesville and London: University Press of Virginia, 2000), pp. 85–130.

[150] For an engaging account of the economic and political significance of architectural ruin in Barbauld's poem, see E. J. Clery, *Eighteen Hundred and Eleven: Poetry, Protest and Economic Crisis* (Cambridge: Cambridge University Press, 2017).

[151] Soane's manuscript for *Crude Hints* has been edited by Helen Dorey and published in *Visions of Ruin: Architectural Fantasies & Designs for Garden Follies, with 'Crude Hints Towards a History of My House'* (London: The Soane Gallery, 1999), pp. 53–78.

[152] For recent accounts of the role of *capriccio* in the relationship between Gandy and Soane, see Brian Lukacher, *Joseph Gandy: An Architectural Visionary in Georgian England* (2006), pp. 132–67; and William Palin, 'J. M. Gandy's Composite Views for John Soane', in *The Architectural Capriccio: Memory, Fantasy and Invention*, ed. Lucien Steil (Farnham: Ashgate, 2014), pp. 99–115. For a good account of Gandy's images of architectural ruin, see Woodward, 'Scenes from the Future', p. 28.

[153] For an account of the significance of *capriccios* to modern and contemporary architectural practice, see Alireza Sagharchi, 'Introduction', in *The Architectural Capriccio: Memory, Fantasy and Invention*, ed. Lucien Steil (Farnham: Ashgate, 2014), pp. lxv–lxxiv.

Though they were regularly generated in the process of design, it is important to remember that, by definition, *capriccios* were and are unrealizable as workable plans for plausible architectural structures in the physical world. Even in its negative forms in the *Grotteschi* (1750) and the *Carceri d'invenzioni* (1750) of Piranesi, *capriccio* is pure architectural fantasy, the expression of the architectural imagination in its freest and most uncompromising of forms. And while the example of Piranesi suggests that eighteenth-century *capriccios* were almost uniformly classical in style, a few Gothic examples from the period exist, such as the *capriccios* of Scottish castles that the young Robert Adam produced in the 1780s, including his six *Picturesque Compositions* of Gothic castles set in Italianate landscapes from 1782. Clearly influenced by Adam's friendship with the landscape painter Paul Sandby and the prints of Salvator Rosa that Adam copied from the library at Blair Adam, these were imaginary castles of the first order.[154] In *A Landscape Fantasy Showing Castles and a Domed City* (c.1777–87), Adam juxtaposed a shadowy Gothic castle with a spectral classical city, setting these jarring elements within an equally unfitting Scottish landscape.[155] The dislocation of recognizable architectural signs from their usual contexts is central to the *capriccio* tradition.

It is revealing to situate Ann Radcliffe's fictional architectural forms within this practice, particularly with regard to her placement of what most of her contemporary readers would have taken to be an exclusively British architectural style in the foreign landscapes of Italy and France. Although several tourists identified aspects of Gothic on the Continent, eighteenth-century Britons were largely of the opinion that Gothic architecture was a peculiarly British—or even more narrowly English—phenomenon. That is, the distinction between the classical and the Gothic was often rearticulated in the eighteenth century in national terms, with the former consigned to Europe and the latter to England. Even those who, in the tradition of Wren, attributed it to Saracenic origins held that, even if it was not originally British, it was in Britain that the Gothic style was most perfectly and maturely manifested. Claims to the 'Englishness' of Gothic were particularly prominent in the latter half of the century, from William Gilpin's arguments in *Observations Relative Chiefly to Picturesque Beauty* (1786), through the work of John Carter and John Milner, and into John Britton's *Architectural Antiquities of Great Britain* (1807–27).[156] The frequently reprinted *Essays on Gothic Architecture* (1800), a compilation of previously published work by Thomas Warton, John Bentham, Francis Grose, and John Milner, emphasized the Englishness of the style throughout. As the Preface succinctly put it, 'This style of architecture may

---

[154] Stephen Astley, *Robert Adam's Castles* (London: The Soane Gallery, 2000), pp. 9–10.
[155] See Neil Bingham, Clare Carolin, Peter Cook, and Rob Wilson, *Fantasy Architecture, 1500–2036* (London: Hayward Gallery Publishing, 2004), p. 85.
[156] See Simon Bradley, 'The Englishness of Gothic: Theories and Interpretations from William Gilpin to J. H. Parker', *Architectural History* vol. 45 (2002): pp. 325–46.

properly be called English architecture, for if it had not its origin in this country, it certainly arrived at maturity here.'[157] Tensions with Napoleonic France from 1803 onwards only intensified the urgency of the nationalistic agenda: to identify superlative examples of the Gothic outside of Britain was, in some senses, tantamount to cultural treason.

Rosemary Sweet has charted that process by which British grand tourists from around 1780 onwards gradually came to acknowledge manifestations of the Gothic on the Continent, particularly in Italy.[158] The Reverend G. D. Whittington addressed the sensitive matter of the Gothic's national origins in his posthumously published *An Historical Survey of the Ecclesiastical Antiquities of France* of 1809, claiming not only that earlier—and far better—examples of the Gothic could be found in France, but also that, far from being an exclusively English style, the Gothic had been brought to Europe during crusaders' contact with the East.[159] Unsurprisingly, his thesis attracted considerable criticism, not least from Gothic nationalists such as John Carter. During May and June 1809, the antiquary Thomas Kerrich read a series of provocative papers on the Gothic's national origins at the Society of Antiquaries, and subsequently published them in *Archaeologia* in 1812 as 'Some Observations on the Gothic Buildings Abroad, Particularly those of Italy, and on Gothic Architecture in General'.[160] Kerrich's claim was that the Gilpinian assumption that the Gothic was a peculiarly English style was inaccurate and misinformed, and patently the belief of one who had never left the country. Like Whittington earlier, he attempted to counter this conviction through pointing to a broad range of Gothic architectural examples across the nations of Europe, including the Low Countries, France, Germany, and Italy. Though Kerrich attempted to discredit the nationalist stance, the vehemence of his rhetoric is a useful indicator of just how entrenched the nationalist position was. Indeed, it was really only with the end of the Napoleonic Wars in 1815 and, with that, the resuming of travel to Europe that antiquaries and gentleman scholars of the Gothic came to accept that the style was not exclusively English but, rather, differently inflected in the national architectures of Europe.[161]

To find, then, as we do in Radcliffe's romances of the 1790s, so many ruined Gothic piles in France and Italy was, at least for those who readers not au fait with rarefied antiquarian debate, to experience the same degree of dislocation and

---

[157] *Essays on Gothic Architecture, by the Rev. T. Warton, Rev. J. Bentham, Captain Grose, and the Rev. J. Milner* (London: Printed by S. Gosnell for J. Taylor, 1800), p. iii.

[158] Rosemary Sweet, *Cities and the Grand Tour: The British in Italy, c. 1690–1820* (Cambridge: Cambridge University Press, 2012), pp. 235–66.

[159] See G. D. Whittington, *An Historical Survey of the Ecclesiastical Antiquities of France; With a View to Illustrate the Rise and Progress of Gothic Architecture in Europe* (London: Printed by T. Bensley for J. Taylor, 1809).

[160] Thomas Kerrich, 'Some Observations on the Gothic Buildings Abroad, Particularly those of Italy, and on Gothic Architecture in General', *Archaeologia* vol. XVI (1812): pp. 292–325.

[161] Sweet, *Cities and the Grand Tour*, p. 265.

spatial disorientation in which the *capriccio* tradition characteristically traded. This is particularly the case with the ruined Gothic abbey, a building that plays such an important role in a fiction such as *The Romance of the Forest*: though relocated in this narrative to France, the ecclesiastical ruin was a quintessentially British phenomenon, and spoke of the nation's historical transition from 'benighted' Catholicism to 'enlightened' Protestantism via the dissolution of the monasteries, a point that I shall explore more fully in Chapter 5. Not even an antiquary such as Andrew Coltée Ducarel, who sought to identify connections between French and English manifestations of Gothic in his *Anglo-Norman Antiquities Considered* (1767), would have been able to account for structures such as these. In *Udolpho*, Radcliffe goes so far as to identify instances of what she terms the 'Saxon-gothic style'—for her, that early form of Gothic brought to England by the Anglo-Saxon 'Goths', though what today in a European context would be termed 'Romanesque'—in the remains of a ruined fortress that Lady Blanche and St Foix encounter in the Pyrenees:

> Many parts of it, however, appeared to be still entire; it was built of grey stone, in the heavy Saxon-gothic style, with enormous round towers, buttresses of proportionable strength, and the arch of the large gate, which seemed to open into the hall of the fabric, was round, as was that of a window above.[162]

Transported to a Continental landscape, Saxon Gothic, the architecture of England's ancient Anglo-Saxons, has furnished a castle in Spain. William Marlow undertook a comparable act of national and architectural dislocation in his *Capriccio: St Paul's and a Venetian Canal* (c.1795), relocating St Paul's Cathedral, an iconic fixture on the London skyline, to the canals of Venice (see Figure 3.7). Like other examples in the mode, Marlow's *capriccio* thrives on the relocation of familiar buildings to unfamiliar territories, and it is in this process that the building, its original, and its new surrounds are defamiliarized and rendered strange. Radcliffe's architecture is of the same order: imaginary and fantastical visions of ruin in which relations of juxtaposition, tension, and disjunction predominate over any sense of 'real' or 'plausible' space. At least one reader suspected as much: the reviewer in *The Spirit of the Public Journals* carped that the writer affected 'in the most disgusting manner a knowledge of languages, countries, customs, and objects of art of which she is lamentably ignorant'.[163] 'She suspends *tripods* from the cieling [sic] by chains,' the reviewer continued, 'not knowing that a *tripod* is a utensil standing upon three feet', covering 'the kingdom of Naples with India figs because *St Pierre* has introduced those tropical plants in his tables, of which the scene is laid in India—and she makes a convent of monks a

---

[162] Ann Radcliffe, *The Mysteries of Udolpho*, p. 606.
[163] Anon., 'Terrorist Novel Writing', p. 223.

Figure 3.7 William Marlow (1740–1813), *Capriccio: St Paul's and a Venetian Canal* (*c.*1795), Oil paint on canvas, support: 1295 × 1041 mm. © Tate, London 2018.

necessary appendage to a monastery of nuns'.[164] Samuel Taylor Coleridge was more pointed in his criticisms. 'The manners do not sufficiently correspond with the aera the author has chosen', he wrote, and while, in Radcliffe's depiction of 'the latter end of the sixteenth century' in *Udolpho* there is 'no direct anachronism', the text abounds with 'modern manners' that are never entirely 'counter-balanced by Gothic arches and antique furniture'.[165] As misplaced as her Gothic arches and antique furniture, the India figs in the Neapolitan landscape, or the elephants that Emily St Aubert imagines in the Italian Alps, Radcliffe's architectural imagination was a Gothic *capriccio* ekphrastically rendered in prose, an untenable assemblage of disparate Gothic architectural details invariably joined with parts that, as in the architecture of the Chateau-le-Blanc and Claude's Palace of Cupid, were not uniformly Gothic: as Blanche observes, 'the edifice was not built entirely in the gothic style', but 'had additions of a more modern date'.[166]

---

[164] Anon., 'Terrorist Novel Writing', p. 223.
[165] [Samuel Taylor Coleridge], Review of Ann Radcliffe's *The Mysteries of Udolpho*, *The Critical Review; or, Annals of Literature* (August 1794): pp. 361–72 (p. 362).
[166] Radcliffe, *The Mysteries of Udolpho*, p. 467.

Towards the Topographical Gothic

Ann Radcliffe was unusually responsive to the reception of her work and steered the trajectory of her mid-to-late career very much with critical reactions to her earlier fictions in mind.[167] This almost certainly accounts for the shift across her writing from the overtly imaginative landscapes of her first four novels into the more topographical subject matter of her *Journey*, through the less loco-descriptive turns of *The Italian*, and into the self-consciously antiquarian impulses of the posthumously published *Gaston De Blondeville* and 'St Alban's Abbey, A Metrical Tale' (1826). Seemingly in response to Coleridge's criticisms that the 'Gothic arches and antique furniture' of *Udolpho* were thoroughly out of keeping with the modernity of the tale, Radcliffe elided her signature descriptions of Gothic architecture from *The Italian* altogether, moving her narrative well into the eighteenth century and focusing it instead on the classical ruins of Rome that, as many of her readers would have concurred, were more appropriate to the fiction's Italian setting:

> At intervals, indeed, the moon, as the clouds passed away, shewed, for a moment, some of those mighty monuments of Rome's eternal name, those sacred ruins, those gigantic skeletons, which once enclosed a soul, whose energies governed a world! Even Vivaldi could not behold with indifference the grandeur of these reliques, as the rays fell upon the hoary walls and columns, or pass among these scenes of ancient story, without feeling a melancholy awe, a sacred enthusiasm, that withdrew him from himself.[168]

The word 'Gothic' excluded from the text, Radcliffe's challenge in *The Italian* was to extract from classical architecture associative powers at least as powerful as the Gothic. I shall consider how she achieved this in more detail in Chapter 5. What I wish to consider in the remainder of this chapter and throughout Chapters 5 and 6, though, is the ways in which Gothic fiction after *Udolpho*—in Radcliffe, Walter Scott, and a selection of lesser-known Gothic romancers too—attests to a distinct movement away from those 'castles in the air' with which the mode had become synonymous, and into the realms of what we might call the 'topographical Gothic'. Breaching the divide between antiquarianism and Gothic romance that opened up with Horace Walpole and the *Historic Doubts* debacle of the early 1770s, Gothic fiction of the later 1790s slowly came to share certain objects of architectural interest with the antiquarian topographical tradition. Set no longer in imaginary ruins but in the real, empirical architectural remains that were to be seen across the British landscape, the topographical Gothic, however spuriously, prided itself

---

[167] For a development of this argument, see Townshend and Wright, 'Gothic and Romantic Engagements: The Critical Reception of Ann Radcliffe, 1789–1850', pp. 3–32.
[168] Ann Radcliffe, *The Italian; or, The Confessional of the Black Penitents, a Romance*, ed. Frederick Garber (Oxford and New York: Oxford University Press, 1992), p. 195.

on a greater sense of accuracy and historical authenticity; what resulted, though, was a curious hybrid in which the age-old tensions between romance and history became even more pronounced.

It would be disingenuous to suggest that it was Ann Radcliffe who single-handedly ushered in the vogue for Gothic fictions set in extant or 'real' British castles and abbeys. In fact, the origins of the topographical Gothic predated the rise of Gothic fiction by over a century, and might be said to lie in the tradition of topographical poetry that is often traced back to seventeenth-century texts such as Michael Drayton's *Poly-Olbion* (1612; 1622) and John Denham's *Cooper's Hill* (1642), the former a lengthy illustrated poetic journey through England and Wales and the latter a shorter poem in which Denham described the prospect in and around his country seat at Egham, Surrey.[169] After Denham, topographical poetry, the poetic description of actual place and space, became a recognizable subgenre; Samuel Johnson in his essay on Denham in *The Lives of the Most Eminent English Poets* (1779–81) termed it *'local poetry'*, glossing its 'fundamental subject' as 'some particular landscape, to be poetically described, with the addition of such embellishment as may be supplied by historical retrospection, or incidental meditation'.[170] The movement into topographical Gothic was an extension of this earlier tradition, and, to a certain extent, coeval with the development of the early Gothic itself. An often overlooked aspect of Clara Reeve's censuring of the imaginative extremes of *Otranto*, for instance, was her decision to model the Castle of Lovel in *The Old English Baron* on what Walpole had called a 'real' or 'particular' building—Minster Lovell Hall, Oxfordshire—a fact that nineteenth-century commentators never tired of pointing out.[171] Subsequently published fictions in what James Watt has called the tradition of 'Loyalist Gothic' followed suit, with a novel such as James White's *Earl Strongbow; or, The History of Richard de Clare and Beautiful Geralda* (1789) set in and around Chepstow Castle, Monmouthshire. Sophia Lee set portions of *The Recess* in Kenilworth Castle, an important site of literary production that I consider in more detail in Chapter 6. Nor did the popularity of topographical Gothic fictions in the 1790s entirely displace the vogue for tales set in imaginary Gothic piles: the self-consciously fictional piles evoked in titles such as *The Castle of Wolfenbach* (1793) by Eliza Parsons, *The Haunted Castle* (1794) by George Walker, or *The Haunted Palace* (1801) by Mrs Yorke continued to proliferate. It is important, too, to acknowledge the influence of the early novels of Charlotte Smith on the rise of the topographical Gothic. Though Mowbray Castle, the ruined Gothic pile in Pembrokeshire that is

---

[169] For an excellent account of this tradition, see Robert Arnold Aubin, *Topographical Poetry in Eighteenth-Century England* (New York: Modern Languages Association of America, 1936).

[170] Samuel Johnson, *The Lives of the Most Eminent English Poets; With Critical Observations on their Works*, 2nd edn, 4 vols (London: Printed for C. Bathurst et al, 1783), vol. 1, pp. 110–11.

[171] See, for example, 'Antiquarian Researches', *The Gentleman's Magazine and Historical Review* (July 1857), pp. 67–80 (p. 76).

at the heart of the dispute over the heroine's right to own property in *Emmeline*, is a fictional construct, Smith's Welsh setting, like the domestic British settings of her later novels, did much to validate local British antiquities as the subject of more self-consciously 'Gothic' fictions.

And yet it was Ann Radcliffe who spearheaded the movement into the topographical Gothic. Upon its publication in 1795, her *A Journey Made in the Summer of 1794* was critically hailed as an exercise in picturesque and topographical description. *The Critical Review* remarked that, while Mrs Radcliffe's pen had become renowned for 'a peculiar felicity in the description of objects of fancy', the genre of the travel memoir required that her talents be 'necessarily employed to delineate the grandeur, beauty, or sublimity of real scenery'.[172] Commending Radcliffe on having eschewed the 'creations of her own fancy' of her earlier fictions in favour of 'elaborate accuracy' and 'just discrimination', this reviewer noted that the only regrettable omission in the *Journey* was visual illustration, 'for what might not have been expected from the mutual aid of the pen and pencil!'[173] *The Analytical Review* argued much the same point: praising Radcliffe's move into 'less laboured and artificial diction' than that found in her novels, the reviewer identified in the *Journey* a generic shift away from romance towards factual description.[174] The critic in the first of a three-part review in *The English Review* summed up this shift from romance to topography with the observation that, 'In her romances she paints fancy-pieces; here she draws from nature.'[175] Though the *Journey* was not without its faults, the critical consensus was that it stood as a proud testament to Radcliffe's versatility as a writer: as *The European Magazine* noted, 'Without bearing a comparison with her former writings, which were of a very different cast, this volume must contribute to enlarge her literary reputation, and to place her in a very high rank among our celebrated female writers.'[176]

Shrewd though these contemporary responses are, they do beg the question of just how absolute a generic shift Radcliffe's *Journey* constituted. Modern critical opinion has varied greatly in this respect. For Dorothy McMillan, the *Journey* marks a distinct stylistic transition insofar as it attests to Radcliffe's growing disillusionment with her earlier creative practices.[177] Angela Wright, by contrast, identifies continuities between the *Journey* and Radcliffe's later work, arguing that the writer's nuanced presentations of Catholicism in the former directly manifest

---

[172] Review of Ann Radcliffe's *A Journey* (1795), *The Critical Review; or, Annals of Literature* vol. 14 (July 1795), pp. 241–55 (p. 241).

[173] Review of Ann Radcliffe's *A Journey* (1795), *The Critical Review* (July 1795), p. 242.

[174] Review of Ann Radcliffe's *A Journey* (1795), *The Analytical Review; or, History of Literature* vol. 22, no. 4 (October 1795): pp. 349–55 (p. 350).

[175] Review of Ann Radcliffe's *A Journey* (1795), *The English Review* (July 1795), pp. 1–5 (p. 1).

[176] Review of Ann Radcliffe's *A Journey* (1795), *The European Magazine, and London Review* vol. 28 (October 1795): pp. 257–61 (p. 261).

[177] Dorothy McMillan, 'The Secrets of Ann Radcliffe's English Travels', in *Romantic Geographies: Discourses of Travel, 1775–1844*, ed. Amanda Gilroy (Manchester: Manchester University Press, 2000), pp. 51–67.

themselves in *The Italian* of 1797.[178] Seeing few if any correspondences between the travel memoir and the fiction, JoEllen DeLucia, on the other hand, has described the *Journey* as 'surprisingly "ungothic"'.[179] One way of addressing the issue is to return to the presentation of Gothic ruins, architecture, and Radcliffe's architectural imagination as it is expressed in the domestic tour narrative that complements and completes the European parts of *Journey*, that is, the account of Ann and her husband William's return from the Continent and their travelling from Dover, to London, through Derbyshire, Manchester, and Lancaster, and into the English Lake District.

Radcliffe's architectural imagination was first stimulated on the English leg of the tour when she and her husband visited Hardwick Hall, Derbyshire, the Elizabethan country house that was built by Elizabeth Talbot, Countess of Shrewsbury, to the designs of Robert Smythson during the 1590s. Erroneously believing that Mary, Queen of Scots, had been imprisoned at Hardwick by Queen Elizabeth, Radcliffe's mind is involuntarily overcome by vivid images of the persecuted queen; reduced to a 'spectre of herself', Mary seems to haunt Hardwick Hall and its apartments like a ghost.[180] Albeit less vividly so, similar imaginative promptings are engendered by the castles at Lancaster, Kendal, and Penrith. But it is her descriptions of the visit to the ruins of Brougham Castle and Furness Abbey, then respectively situated within the counties of Westmorland and Lancashire, that best exemplify the transition in Radcliffe's architectural imagination from romance to topography.[181] In his *Survey of the Lakes of Cumberland, Westmorland, and Lancashire* (1789), James Clarke had advanced the erroneous claim that Sir Philip Sidney had resided with the Countess of Pembroke at Brougham Castle while composing portions of *Arcadia*, and it is the pile's literary associations that initially engage Radcliffe's attention.[182] However, while giving a thorough account of the castle's history and how it came to exist in its present state of ruin, Radcliffe momentarily shifts into the topographical mode, describing in detail its layout, its structure, and even the thickness of its walls. Though claiming that Brougham's remains 'show nothing of the magnificence and gracefulness, which so often charm the eye in gothic ruins', her subsequent observations fail to sustain this impartiality, and involve instead an emotive reflection on the

---

[178] Angela Wright, 'Inspiration, Toleration and Relocation in Ann Radcliffe's *A Journey Made in the Summer of 1794, Through Holland and the Western Frontier of Germany* (1795)', in *Romantic Localities: Europe Writes Place*, ed. Christoph Bode and Jacqueline Labbe (London: Pickering & Chatto, 2010), pp. 131–43.

[179] JoEllen DeLucia, 'Transnational Aesthetics in Ann Radcliffe's *A Journey Made in the Summer of 1794* (1795)', in *Ann Radcliffe, Romanticism and the Gothic*, ed. Dale Townshend and Angela Wright (Cambridge: Cambridge University Press, 2014), pp. 135–50 (p. 137).

[180] Radcliffe, *A Journey*, p. 375.

[181] In 1974, the northern parts of Lancashire, including the Furness Peninsula, were merged with Cumberland and Westmorland to form the county of Cumbria.

[182] James Clarke, *A Survey of the Lakes of Cumberland, Westmorland, and Lancashire* (London: Printed for the Author, 1789), p. 10. For Radcliffe's responses, see *A Journey*, p. 426.

politics of Gothic architecture identical to that explored in her earlier fictions: such buildings, she writes, 'exhibit symptoms of the cruelties, by which their first lords revenged upon others the wretchedness of the continual suspicion felt by themselves'.[183] Here again, Radcliffe, like Addison earlier, flatly refuses the liberal, Whiggish meanings with which the period frequently imbued the Gothic style, and with its foreboding dungeons, secret passageways, and iron rings, Brougham Castle is imaginatively transformed into a hybrid of the fictional Castles of Udolpho and Mazzini. The description soon shades into an even darker Gothic romance as Radcliffe explores the ruin further: seeing a narrow staircase winding to a turret in which 'prisoners were probably secured', she fashions in her mind's eye 'the surly keeper descending through this door-case', hearing him rattling the keys of chambers above, and listening with indifference to 'the clank of chains and to the echo of that groan below, which seemed to rend the heart it burst from'.[184] The ruins of the 'great dungeon', now only home to serpents and other venomous reptiles, inspire further horrid imaginings: 'insulted' by the 'gothic elegance' of its architecture, the phantasmatic prisoners who once inhabited this 'hideous vault' would no doubt have languished there, without refreshment or respite.[185] Like Hardwick, Brougham is haunted by those who once lived there: at the 'transforming hour of twilight', the 'superstitious eye' might well mistake the vegetation that adorns it 'for spectres of some early possessor of the castle, restless from guilt, or of some sufferer persevering from vengeance'.[186]

Susceptible not only to the associative powers of ruined castles, Radcliffe's architectural imagination in the *Journey* is equally excited by scenes of ecclesiastical ruin. There is no clearer example of this than in her celebrated account of the ruins of Furness Abbey.[187] Thomas Gray had very little to say about Furness in his *Journal of A Visit to the Lake District in 1769*, which had been anonymously published in 1775. Highly indebted, instead, to the Jesuit priest and antiquary Thomas West's topographical study *The Antiquities of Furness* (1774), Radcliffe begins with a description of 'these venerable ruins', including the 'roof of beautiful gothic fretwork', the nave, the arches and casements, and the remains of the library, scriptorium, cloisters, and refectory.[188] Pausing to rest within the ruin, however, she is involuntarily overcome by 'images' and the 'manners' of past times in a synaesthetic reverie that is as much visual as it is auditory:

> The midnight procession of monks, clothed in white and bearing lighted tapers, appeared to the 'mind's eye' issuing to the choir through the very door-case, by

---

[183] Radcliffe, *A Journey*, p. 427. [184] Radcliffe, *A Journey*, p. 428.
[185] Radcliffe, *A Journey*, p. 430. [186] Radcliffe, *A Journey*, p. 431.
[187] For a discussion of Radcliffe's responses to Furness in the context of other contemporary responses, see Jason Wood, 'Furness Abbey: A Century and a Half in the Tourists' Gaze', in John K. Walton and Jason Woods, eds, *The Making of a Cultural Landscape: The English Lake District as a Tourist Destination, 1750–2010* (Farnham: Ashgate, 2013), pp. 220–40.
[188] Radcliffe, *A Journey*, pp. 487–9.

which such processions were wont to pass from the cloisters to perform the matin service, when, at the moment of their entering the church, the deep chanting of voices was heard, and the organ swelled a solemn peel. To fancy, the strain still echoed feebly along the arcades and died in the breeze among the woods, the rustling leaves mingling with the close.[189]

Though they are more pleasing than horrid, there is little to distinguish these ghostly associations from those recorded by Addison in his essay in *The Spectator* in 1711. More pertinently, the associations that Gothic architecture at Furness provokes are a direct reiteration of her descriptions of the ruined monastery of St Claire as Blanche and her father first experience it in *Udolpho*. While Blanche, we remember, gazes with admiration upon this 'venerable pile', a sound 'of many voices, slowly chanting, arose from within':

> The monks were singing the hymn of vespers, and some female voices mingled with the strain, which rose by soft degrees, till the high organ and the choral sounds swelled into full and solemn harmony. The strain, soon after, dropped into sudden silence, and was renewed in a low and still more solemn key, till, at length, the holy chorus died away, and was heard no more.[190]

The 'train of friars, and then of nuns, veiled in white' that issue from the cloisters and then pass before Blanche's eyes into the woods are the same white-robed monks that Radcliffe later imagines at Furness. Imaginary Gothic ruin gives rise to romance, but, in turn, romance colours and shapes the experience of real Gothic architecture. The possibility also remains that neither episode is entirely of Radcliffe's own devising, for both descriptions repeat the associations that were commonly attached to ecclesiastical piles in much ruin poetry of the eighteenth century. The persona of Thomas Warton's *The Pleasures of Melancholy* (1747), for example, pauses within 'yon' ruin'd Abbey's moss-grown piles' at the 'twilight hour of eve', imagining before him the 'ghostly shape' of the 'cloyster'd brothers' who once inhabited it, and hearing again 'The taper'd choir, at midnight hour of Pray'r' that once resounded 'thro'' the Gothic vaults'.[191] Thomas Gray, too, had sutured Gothic architecture to auditory memory and hallucination in his 'Ode for Music' (1769). Radcliffe's literary rendition and empirical experience of Gothic ruin is conditioned by the poetry that preceded her, to the extent that her descriptions become intertextually haunted. Though apparently wielding the pencil of the topographer in the *Journey*, Radcliffe finds it difficult to relinquish the romancer's necromantic pen.

Topographical Gothic is the result: an antiquarian and topographical interest in extant British Gothic antiquities coupled with the imaginative capacities of

---

[189] Radcliffe, *A Journey*, pp. 490–1.
[190] Radcliffe, *The Mysteries of Udolpho*, p. 483.
[191] Thomas Warton, *The Pleasures of Melancholy. A Poem* (London: Printed for R. Dodsley, 1747).

romance. Beyond the examples of Brougham Castle and Furness Abbey, the domestic sections of the *Journey* as a whole rendered England, its landscapes, and its ruins as 'enchanted ground', the place of ancient romance. The Lakeland scenery near Patterdale, for example, resembles 'one of those beautifully fantastic scenes, which fable calls up before the wand of the magician', while Radcliffe describes the fells around Keswick and Borrowdale as 'the very region, which the wild fancy of a poet, like Shakespeare, would people with witches, and shew them at their incantations, calling spirits from the clouds and spectres from the earth'.[192] Derwentwater seems 'the very abode for Milton's Comus', and Eamont Bridge brings to mind associations with 'Arthur's Round Table'.[193] If these seem particularly English points of reference, it is important to acknowledge that the effect of the *Journey* is ultimately to erase the differences between the European landscapes of Radcliffe's fictions and the English landscapes that she describes, a move that, in the context of British fears of the predominantly Catholic Continent, was of progressive political consequence and a reflection of the writer's cosmopolitan leanings.[194] Like the Rousseauvian peasants of Languedoc, for instance, the rural poor of the Lake District sing merrily as they gather their crops into sheaves, wholly untainted by the luxuries and vices of London society. Seeing thundering cataracts at the Lodore Falls, tremendous chasms at Skiddaw, and even the 'solemn alps' round Helvellyn, Radcliffe in the Lakes appears to be traversing the French and Italian alpine scenery of *Udolpho*.[195] At the same time, Skiddaw is said to resemble a 'volcano', with the 'cloudy vapours ascending from its highest point, like smoke, and sometimes rolling in wreathes down its sides', a description that recalls the account of Mount Etna in *A Sicilian Romance*.[196] In *The Mysteries of Udolpho*, Radcliffe had paraphrased William Gilpin's citation of a remark made by Charles Avison, writing that 'This landscape with the surrounding alps did, indeed, present a perfect picture of the lovely and the sublime, of "beauty sleeping in the lap of horror"'.[197] Returning Gilpin's account of Avison's responses to Derwentwater to its English origins, the *Journey* constructs the English landscape as a mixture of pleasure and horror, beauty and sublimity.

---

[192] Radcliffe, *A Journey*, pp. 416, 440.   [193] Radcliffe, *A Journey*, pp. 452, 424.
[194] For an account of how Radcliffe minimizes the cultural differences between Europe and Britain in *The Italian*, see Katarina Gephardt, *The Idea of Europe in British Travel Narratives, 1789-1914* (Farnham: Ashgate, 2014), pp. 48–59. For a reading of Radcliffe's cosmopolitanism, see Evan Gottlieb, 'No Place Like Home: From Local to Global (and Back Again) in the Gothic Novel', in *Representing Place in British Literature and Culture, 1660-1830: From Local to Global* (Aldershot: Ashgate, 2013), pp. 85–102.
[195] Radcliffe, *A Journey*, p. 415.   [196] Radcliffe, *A Journey*, p. 446.
[197] Radcliffe, *The Mysteries of Udolpho*, p. 55. Gilpin records Avison as having remarked that '*Here is beauty indeed—Beauty lying in the lap of Horror* [sic]'. See William Gilpin, *Observations, Relative Chiefly to Picturesque Beauty, Made in the Year 1772, on Several Parts of England; Particularly the Mountains, and Lakes of Cumberland and Westmoreland*, 2 vols (London: Printed for R. Blamire, 1786), vol. 1, p. 183. Radcliffe renders Avison's 'lying' as 'sleeping'.

Thomas De Quincey was by no means the only Romantic-era visitor to the Lake District to register Radcliffe's determinative topographical presence, and the *Journey* was approvingly cited in such publications as John Housman's *A Descriptive Tour, and Guide to the Lakes, Caves, Mountains, and other Natural Curiosities* (1800); John Robinson's *A Guide to the Lakes* (1819); Samuel Leigh's *Guide to the Lakes and Mountains of Cumberland, Westmoreland and Lancashire* (1832); and Allison's frequently reissued *Northern Tourist's Guide to the Lakes* (1837). In 1810, Wordsworth anonymously published an early version of what, following three intervening editions, would eventually become *A Guide Through the District of the Lakes* in 1835. Before, and in some instances even after, the Lake District became known as 'Wordsworthshire', however, the region was presided over by the Great Enchantress.[198] Through Radcliffe, the British landscape had become the space and place of Gothic romance, the ruins of castles and abbeys that populated it wholly amenable to fictional treatment—despite Walter Scott's claim, that is, that her narratives were such that they 'could not, without great violation of truth, be represented as having taken place in England'.[199]

---

[198] See Edward Thomas, *A Literary Pilgrim in England* (Oxford: Oxford University Press, 1980), p. 261. See, too, the various chapters in John K. Walton and Jason Wood, eds, *The Making of a Cultural Landscape: The English Lake District as a Tourist Destination, 1750–2010* (Farnham: Ashgate, 2013).
[199] Scott, 'Prefatory Memoir to Mrs Ann Radcliffe', p. xxiii.

4
Improvement, Repair, and the Uses of the Gothic Past
Architecture, Chivalry, and Romance

Jane Austen was sufficiently au fait with the conventions of the Gothic to include in her spirited parody of the mode in *Northanger Abbey* (written 1798–9; published late 1817; dated 1818) an account of her 'well-read' heroine's rich inner life of architectural fantasy.[1] Even before she gets to Northanger, Catherine Morland is the dupe of her own architectural imaginings. Hoping to see at Blaise ('Blaize') Castle, near Bristol, an ancient and ruinous architectural site such as one reads about in romances, she makes of what is really a modern Gothic folly in full repair 'an edifice like Udolpho' in her mind's eye, an imaginary castle replete with the requisite towers and long galleries, 'broken promises and broken arches, phaetons and false hangings, Tilneys and trap-doors'.[2] As elsewhere in the novel, architectural folly generates foolishness or 'folly' in the psychological sense of the term too, a pun on the word that Austen knowingly exploits. The proposed trip to Blaise called off, however, the disconsolate heroine, her brother James, and the siblings John and Isabella Thorpe make their way back to Bath. Her architectural desires unrealized, Catherine is later especially delighted to accept the Tilneys' invitation to Northanger Abbey, Gloucestershire, for 'Her passion for ancient edifices', we are told, 'was next in degree to her passion for Henry Tilney – and castles and abbies [*sic*] made usually the charm of those reveries which his image did not fill.'[3] As in her anticipations of Blaise, Catherine's fantasies about Northanger are informed by the architectural conventions of the 'horrid' fictions with which she is deeply familiar: 'Its long, damp passages, its narrow cells and ruined chapel', she muses, 'were to be within her daily reach, and she could not entirely subdue the hope of some traditional legends, some awful memorials of an injured and ill-fated nun.'[4] Here, too, it is the anticipation of architectural ruin at Northanger that she finds especially pleasurable, and despite the information that she gleans to the contrary, nothing can dissuade her from the conviction that the abbey exists even now in a state of picturesque disrepair, with 'a large portion of the ancient

---

[1] Jane Austen, *Northanger Abbey, Lady Susan, The Watsons, and Sanditon*, ed. John Davie and introd. Terry Castle (Oxford and New York: Oxford University Press, 1990), p. 145.
[2] Austen, *Northanger Abbey*, p. 65.   [3] Austen, *Northanger Abbey*, p. 110.
[4] Austen, *Northanger Abbey*, p. 110.

Gothic Antiquity: History, Romance, and the Architectural Imagination, 1760–1840. Dale Townshend, Oxford University Press (2019). © Dale Townshend.
DOI: 10.1093/oso/9780198845669.001.0001

building still making a part of the present dwelling although the rest was decayed, or of its standing low in a valley, sheltered from the north and east by rising woods of oak'.[5] Henry Tilney's fuelling of these fancies is as deliberate as Thorpe's had been earlier: suggesting to the jejune heroine that Northanger is, indeed, just such a building as 'what one reads about' in novels, he encourages her romantic ideations with intimations of gloomy passages and chambers, sliding panels, and tapestry, not to mention the terrifying prospect of her sleeping in this structure entirely unattended.[6] It is thus especially bathetic that, when Northanger Abbey finally draws into view, Catherine glimpses through the trees not the ancient turrets of a Castle of Udolpho but a squat and unprepossessing building with no 'antique chimney' to be seen anywhere at all.[7]

Catherine's anticipations of sublime grandeur at Northanger founder painfully yet comically in the face of a very different architectural reality. Not only is the abbey, despite the ancient connotations of its name, of decidedly 'modern appearance', it is also fundamentally incapable of inducing in the heroine architectural associations anything like those experienced by Radcliffe's Emily St Aubert, not 'one awful foreboding of future misery', that is, nor 'one moment's suspicion of any past scenes of horror being acted within the solemn edifice'.[8] Several architectural theorists of the period had argued that the imaginative powers of Gothic architecture were invariably enhanced and intensified by a building's pre-existing literary associations. As William Hazlitt put it, 'If...we are told that this is Macbeth's castle, the scene of the murder of Duncan, the interest will be instantly heightened to a sort of pleasing horror.'[9] Archibald Alison had argued much the same in *Essays on the Nature and Principles of Taste*, claiming that the most powerful associations of 'Gothic Halls and cathedrals' are, by nature, literary, or generated 'from many beautiful Compositions both in Prose and Verse'.[10] In the face of the architectural reality with which Austen's heroine is confronted, however, such aesthetic principles become difficult to sustain. As Catherine to her disappointment learns, Northanger has been furnished in 'all the profusion and elegance of modern taste', with 'modern' here in all likelihood a synonym for the classical style. The ancient hearth has been fitted with a Rumford fireplace of the latest design, and the large, capacious windows are hardly the gloom-refracting Gothic patterns of her imaginings.[11] 'To be sure,' Catherine concedes, 'the pointed arch was preserved – the form of them was Gothic – they might be even casements –', but these fall short of her romantic expectations of time-worn masonry, dirt, and cobwebs; 'the difference', she observes, 'was very distressing'.[12] The carpeted and wallpapered interiors of the cheerful, well-appointed bedroom to which she is led,

---

[5] Austen, *Northanger Abbey*, p. 111. [6] Austen, *Northanger Abbey*, p. 124.
[7] Austen, *Northanger Abbey*, p. 127. [8] Austen, *Northanger Abbey*, p. 127.
[9] [William Hazlitt], 'Art. IV. Lectures on Dramatic Literature', p. 70.
[10] Alison, *Essays on the Nature and Principles of Taste*, p. 393.
[11] Austen, *Northanger Abbey*, p. 128. [12] Austen, *Northanger Abbey*, p. 128.

moreover, contain nothing of the velvets and moth-eaten tapestries that Henry had described. Turning out, contrary to all expectations, to be 'so modern, so habitable', the abbey has been subjected to a far-reaching process of alteration, repair, and modernization, all carried out according to the expensive tastes of General Tilney, one of Austen's 'distasteful improvers', in Marilyn Butler's words, of the same ilk as the Rushworths of Sotherton in *Mansfield Park* (1814).[13] Though initially a Catholic religious establishment given over to the abstemious life of contemplation, the abbey has been converted into a comfortable domestic habitation, complete with a billiard room, bookcases, coat hooks, and a range of other modern conveniences. Most acutely, portions of the ancient structure have been demolished and replaced by modern, in all likelihood classical, architectural additions that are at odds with the original Gothic style of the place: 'The new building was not only new, but declared itself to be so; intended only for offices, and enclosed behind by stable-yards, no uniformity of architecture had been thought necessary.'[14] For a self-appointed heroine such as Catherine, the effects of these changes are somewhat disappointing, irrespective of the domestic comfort that they have brought. With all traces of the Gothic past having been erased by Tilney's programme of refurbishment, Catherine's Gothic fantasies have no alternative but to fixate on the two romantic objects that remain: the large chest that stands in the corner of her apartment, and the figure of General Tilney himself.

Though it is easy to perceive Austen's refusal to gratify the architectural follies of her heroine as part of her fun-loving parody of the 'paraphernalia' of the Gothic mode, her gesture seems, ultimately, directed more to political than aesthetic ends.[15] As Henry's sobering reflections point out, the Gothic horrors that Catherine anticipates are not to be encountered in so modern and Christian a country as England, characterized, as it is, by transparency and self-policing mutual suspicion: 'Remember the country and age in which we live,' he exhorts her; 'Remember that we are English, that we are Christians.'[16] Her architectural imagination challenged, Catherine muses internally on the politics of her own suspicions: charming though the works of Mrs Radcliffe and her imitators might be, their horrors pertain exclusively to the Alps and the Pyrenees, to Italy, Switzerland, and the South of France, and not to the Midland counties of England in which she finds herself. In England, her thoughts continue, 'there was surely some security for the existence even of a wife not beloved, in the laws of the land, and the manners of the age', and while other nationalities might exhibit a natural predisposition towards villainy,

---

[13] Austen, *Northanger Abbey*, p. 137. For a comprehensive account of the modern conveniences at the Tilney residence, see Marilyn Butler, 'Introduction', in *Northanger Abbey*, by Jane Austen, ed. Marilyn Butler (London: Penguin, 2003), pp. xi–l (p. xxxiv).
[14] Austen, *Northanger Abbey*, p. 147.
[15] See, for instance, Roger E. Moore, *Jane Austen and the Reformation: Remembering the Sacred Landscape* (Abingdon and New York: Routledge, 2016), pp. 79–134.
[16] Austen, *Northanger Abbey*, p. 159.

'in England it was not so'.[17] The architectural modifications effected at the abbey underscore this political point: though of ancient Gothic origins, the English nation has been as modernized and 'improved' as the Tilney residence itself. 'Improvement' is, indeed, the novel's keyword, and one that, as Alistair M. Duckworth has pointed out, lies at the heart of Austen's fictional universe, be that in relation to her exploration of the moral dilemmas surrounding improvement in contemporary landscape-gardening practices—Lancelot 'Capability' Brown and Humphry Repton versus Uvedale Price and Richard Payne Knight—or the debate around political improvement that raged between Edmund Burke and William Godwin during the 1790s.[18]

As I argue in this chapter, similar ideological patterns may be identified in architectural debates of the period, for, well beyond the example of Austen's fictional pile, the renovation of ancient Gothic buildings in late eighteenth- and early nineteenth-century Britain was a politically charged act. Architectural debates, I show, became the site of a politically fraught debate between Tories and conservative Whigs, similarly bent upon the maintenance of ancient Gothic precedents, and more progressive Whigs, intent upon modernizing 'Gothic' structures, architectural and otherwise, to suit present needs. The revolution in France presented political discourse in Britain with a third possibility: in the wake of the storming of the Bastille in Paris in July 1789, British radicals became enthused by the prospect of architectural obliteration and ruin. Despite these differences, all sides of the debate were united in their tendency to figure the British constitution in architectural images, a pervasive metaphorical system that reached back far into the earlier eighteenth century and beyond. As I demonstrate in the final sections of this chapter, it was also through their perceptions of the architectural remains of Gothic antiquity that political essayists, aestheticians, and novelists staged particular attitudes towards the Middle Ages, negotiating, through their architectural preoccupations, the legacy of the nation's Gothic inheritance—what R. J. Smith has influentially termed the 'Gothic bequest'—while interrogating its possible uses in the present.[19]

Fictional Improvements

Nikolaus Pevsner, as I argued in the Preface to this book, encountered all manner of difficulty in his attempts at identifying the 'real' architectural structures behind the many houses, mansions, estates, and cottages to be found in Jane Austen's fiction.[20]

---

[17] Austen, *Northanger Abbey*, p. 161.
[18] Alistair M. Duckworth, *The Improvement of the Estate: A Study of Jane Austen's Novels* (Baltimore and London: The Johns Hopkins University Press, 1971).
[19] See Smith, *The Gothic Bequest*.
[20] See Pevsner, 'The Architectural Setting of Jane Austen's Novels'.

Claire Lamont's reading of Austen's domestic architecture has expressed similar difficulties: while Stoneleigh Abbey, Warwickshire, the Cistercian abbey that was substantially rebuilt and remodelled as a domestic dwelling between 1714 and 1726 and then again between 1813 and 1836, might have been a model for Northanger, the novel, Lamont notes, is thought to have been 'substantially written' before Austen visited Stoneleigh in 1806.[21] More recently, Janine Barchas has read the scenes at Northanger in relation to the 'genuine' history of the buildings on the Farleigh Hungerford estate near Bath, which included Farleigh Hungerford Castle, the medieval Hinton Abbey, and a country house built with the stones of its ruins.[22] It is clear, though, that Austen need not have had a particular building or topographical site in mind when writing her fiction, for detailed accounts of acts of architectural improvement had often featured in Gothic romances of the 1790s, most notably in Ann Radcliffe's bestselling *The Romance of the Forest* (1791). As Diane Long Hoeveler has pointed out, the architectural influence of Radcliffe's third novel was considerable and can be traced across such later fictions as George Moore's magazine serial *Grasville Abbey* (1793–7); John Palmer's *The Haunted Cavern; A Caledonian Tale* (1795); Elizabeth Carver's *The Horrors of Oakendale Abbey* (1797); and several other romances and dramatic adaptations.[23] The narrative commences with the fortuitous crossing of paths of the heroine Adeline and Pierre de la Motte and his wife. Their shared status as fugitives binds the members of the party together, and they travel as a group southwards across France to the forest of Fontanville. Here, La Motte perceives in the shadows the 'Gothic remains of an abbey', the greater parts of which appear 'to be sinking into ruins';[24] in need of a place of refuge, the travellers resolve to pass the night in the most habitable part of the structure. Exploring the ruin as night falls, La Motte and Peter the servant discover a spacious apartment in one of the abbey's towers, a modern architectural improvement that, 'from its stile [sic] and condition, was evidently of a much later date than the other part of the structure'.[25] The alterations to be seen in a second set of apartments into which they move are, to the consternation of both, similarly 'incongruous' with the mouldering walls that they have left behind: 'The room', the narrator notes, 'appeared to have been built in modern times upon a Gothic plan', but La Motte remains sceptical about its stylistic authenticity, wryly observing to Adeline that its style is 'not strictly Gothic'.[26] Climbing the staircase, La Motte

---

[21] Claire Lamont, 'Domestic Architecture', in *Jane Austen in Context*, ed. Janet Todd (Cambridge: Cambridge University Press, 2005), pp. 225–33 (p. 233).

[22] Janine Barchas, *Matters of Fact in Jane Austen* (Baltimore: Johns Hopkins University Press, 2012), pp. 93–126.

[23] See Diane Long Hoeveler, 'The Heroine, the Abbey and Popular Romantic Textuality', in *Ann Radcliffe, Romanticism and the Gothic*, ed. Dale Townshend and Angela Wright (Cambridge: Cambridge University Press, 2014), pp. 100–16.

[24] Ann Radcliffe, *The Romance of the Forest*, ed. Chloe Chard (Oxford: Oxford University Press, 1986), p. 15.

[25] Radcliffe, *The Romance of the Forest*, p. 20.

[26] Radcliffe, *The Romance of the Forest*, p. 20.

discovers further evidence of architectural renovation in the form of a spacious gallery, another product of poor architectural improvement, 'which, from its present condition, seemed to have been built with the more modern part of the fabric, though this also affected the Gothic mode of architecture'.[27] With additions and modern improvements to ancient Gothic piles thus established as the marker of incongruity, inauthenticity, and stylistic affectation, La Motte and his party will limit their work to the renovation and repair of the abbey's already improved apartments: as Peter sanguinely observes, 'when one sees the place by day light, it's none so bad, but what a little patching up would make it comfortable enough'.[28] Peter is dispatched to the nearby town of Auboine in order to purchase the necessary materials, and the work of architectural repair is commenced.

La Motte's and Peter's repairs are intended to render the inhospitable locale 'not only habitable, but comfortable'.[29] Attesting to the success of their ventures, even the initially reluctant Madame La Motte comes to regard the once-melancholy building as 'a domestic asylum, and a safe refuge from the storms of power'; with the arrival of La Motte's son, Pierre, the building, 'so lately the mansion of despair, seemed metamorphosed into the palace of pleasure, and the walls echoed only to the accents of joy and congratulation'.[30] The repairs have, indeed, brought about a radical change in purpose, from ruinous ecclesiastical pile to secular place of domestic asylum. As Alison Milbank has argued, this scene comprises a notable shift in religious functions, too, for La Motte, regarding the abbey as the place where Catholic 'superstition' once lurked, responds to the ruins in the manner of a notional Protestant reformer.[31] Radcliffe's narrative also reverberates at this point with the idiomatic expression that the English jurist Edward Coke coined in *The Third Part of the Institutes of the Laws of England* (1644) in his account of an Englishman's right under common law to domestic freedom, privacy, and autonomy: 'A mans [*sic*] house is his castle, & *domus sua cuique est tutissimum refugium* [his house to him is his safest refuge]; for where shall a man be safe, if it be not in his house?'[32] Ventriloquizing the idiom, La Motte expresses his determination to 'consider this place as my castle', for when compared with such notorious Parisian institutions as the Bicêtre and the Bastille, the apartments in the abbey are to him, as to others, 'also a palace'.[33] In all aspects, the Catholic, superstitious past has been altered and literally 'inhabited' by bourgeois, quasi-Protestant modernity.

---

[27] Radcliffe, *The Romance of the Forest*, p. 20. [28] Radcliffe, *The Romance of the Forest*, p. 23.
[29] Radcliffe, *The Romance of the Forest*, p. 32.
[30] Radcliffe, *The Romance of the Forest*, pp. 34, 66.
[31] See Milbank, *God and the Gothic*, pp. 16–17.
[32] Edward Coke, *The Third Part of the Institutes of the Laws of England: Concerning High Treason, and Other Pleas of the Crown, and Criminall Causes* (London: Printed by M. Flesher, for W. Lee and D. Pakerman, 1644), p. 162.
[33] Radcliffe, *The Romance of the Forest*, pp. 70, 57.

Echoing and elaborating upon this scene, T. J. Horsley Curties devoted most of the first volume of *Ancient Records; or, The Abbey of Saint Oswythe* (1801) to a detailed description of the renovations carried out under the supervision of Sir Alfred St Oswythe, the father of the heroine Rosaline, at the imaginary abbey of the fiction's subtitle. Having fled Scotland beneath a pall of mysterious circumstances, Sir Alfred, Rosaline, and their servants have travelled southwards on horseback over the course of six days, arriving eventually in the forest of St Oswythe, a fictionalized locale near the equally fictional village of Urbandine that is situated somewhere in the English Midlands. As night begins to fall, the fugitives take shelter in the 'turreted ruins' of the 'Gothic Abbey', the destination to which Sir Alfred inscrutably has led them.[34] Though, in ages past, the abbey had been dedicated to the memory of Saint Catherine, it also carries with it a history that is considerably less pious in import. For during the reign of Edward I, the haughty and proud Baron of St Oswythe, a distant relative of Sir Alfred and Rosaline, had, on pain of disclosing the sexual indiscretions of one Sister St Anna, blackmailed the abbey's nuns and monks into resigning to him all of their institutional wealth and reserves. Crippling the community of clerics with his extortionate designs, the baron subsequently imposed upon King Edward to cede the Abbey of St Catherine to his possession, ambitiously taking up residence in this grander structure while letting his castle, his former abode, fall into ruin and neglect. The disrepair of the baron's castle contrasts sharply with the architectural renovations that he oversees at his new home shortly after moving there: 'The Abbey was in itself an immense pile of superior Gothic structure, and, by the wealth of its own coffers, was soon converted to a magnificent and kingly abode.'[35] This secularization of a consecrated building is accompanied by a telling linguistic shift, for, in a reflection of the baron's hubris, the Abbey of St Catherine is renamed Abbey of St Oswythe.

The distinction that Curties, like Radcliffe before him, draws between the baron's disregard for the 'necessary repairs' at his castle and the luxurious 'conversions' that he carries out at the abbey is significant. As John M. Frew has pointed out, the antiquarian preoccupation with architectural restoration in the late eighteenth century was founded upon a similar distinction: that between 'necessary repairs'—interventions necessary to the strength, safety, and security of the building—and cosmetic 'improvements', more far-reaching structural changes that were often undertaken with a range of less urgent practical ends in mind.[36] Most frequently used in the pejorative sense in relation to the destructive landscaping endeavours of Lancelot 'Capability' Brown, 'improvement' had, by the end of the eighteenth century, come to serve in certain circles as a byword for

---

[34] Curties, *Ancient Records*, vol. 1, p. 14.   [35] Curties, *Ancient Records*, vol. 1, p. 21.
[36] John M. Frew, 'Richard Gough, James Wyatt, and Late 18th-Century Preservation', *The Journal of the Society of Architectural Historians* vol. 38, no. 4 (Dec. 1979): pp. 366–74 (p. 368).

unwelcome interference and destruction, the cipher of a distasteful deviation from an ancient building's original style, and a practice wholly at odds with the priorities that antiquaries such as Richard Gough and John Carter increasingly came to afford the work of architectural preservation.[37] Curties's investment in such antiquarian values in *Ancient Records* is clear. The Baron St Oswythe, we are told, had altered the building by turning what was originally the monastery into the Grand Hall of his residence. More gauche improvements than necessary structural repairs, the baron's additions to the pile appear, even so many years later, to be at odds with its original Gothic style, for as Sir Alfred observes, the columns of the Hall 'had doubtless undergone their present altered appearance from those of the church, by the instruction of Sir Alfred's great ancestor, who, he was now convinced, had added that wing of the building to the ancient site'.[38] Unlike the indelible remains of abbey, the baron's work seems far from permanent: the 150 years that have passed between his death and the arrival of Sir Alfred have rendered his constructions themselves in need of necessary repair.

What was originally a temporary shelter soon becomes for Sir Alfred and his party a permanent domestic abode. Surveying the remains of the structure by the light of morning, Sir Alfred discovers within the abbey's precincts the ruins of a church, churchyard, monastery, convent, and chapel. Observing aspects of the building that appear to have been 'beautified in a superior style of magnificence', he passes through a 'double row of heavy Gothic pillars of the Saxon order' and a series of Gothic columns, arches, portals, doors, and stairways, all in various states of disrepair.[39] While exploring the ruin's upper reaches, he discovers the series of interconnecting apartments that had been improved by his ancestor the baron so many years before, decorated and furnished 'in all the sumptuous magnificence of the thirteenth century'.[40] Despite their silent, deserted, and ruinous state, Sir Alfred is heartened to find that these rooms 'might again be rendered habitable, and, in a little time, even convenient and comfortable'.[41] Accordingly, he immediately puts into action his plan of making the abbey habitable, converting the ruined fabric into a place of domestic residence by restoring the apartments in its upper reaches to a state of 'comparative comfort and convenience'.[42]

Although the terms 'repair' and 'improvement' are used interchangeably in the early sections of *Ancient Records*, it soon becomes clear that the repairs undertaken by Sir Alfred are fundamentally different from the vulgar and insensitive architectural improvements effected by the baron so many years before. Sir Alfred delights more in architectural preservation than improvement and addition, intending, as he does, to restore the abbey to 'a slight degree of its former

---

[37] Frew, 'Richard Gough, James Wyatt, and Late 18th-Century Preservation', pp. 371–2.
[38] Curties, *Ancient Records*, vol. 1, p. 59.   [39] Curties, *Ancient Records*, vol. 1, pp. 55, 50.
[40] Curties, *Ancient Records*, vol. 1, pp. 57, 58.   [41] Curties, *Ancient Records*, vol. 1, pp. 56–7.
[42] Curties, *Ancient Records*, vol. 1, p. 61.

splendour' instead of radically modifying its structure to suit his party's needs.[43] Norman Clare, a journeyman, is sent for from the nearby village, and in less than a fortnight the interiors of the ruin begin to wear a very different aspect: 'the west front was soon made habitable, and even comfortable; the chief apartments were stripped of their melancholy remnants of tattered furniture, which being cleaned and mended, such as would bear the operation, with the addition of some auxiliary purchases, were soon put in tolerable order for present use'.[44] These internal refurbishments are accompanied by a thorough process of external structural repair, interventions undertaken, in marked distinction from the evil baron's improvements, in the spirit of both safety and preservation.[45] Throughout, in fact, Sir Alfred is sensitively guided by a vision of the building's original state: the suites in the upper apartment receive 'only sufficient reparation to preserve them from decay, and were left unfurnished, and nearly in their original desolation'.[46] Even those ruins 'such as had not yet fallen' to the south of the church are 'suffered to remain in their latest state', with the only demolition that Sir Alfred will countenance being of those parts of the building 'whose mouldering hand had long since seized their aged forms, and needed only one rude blast to whelm them into nothing'.[47] The processes of improvement and repair in *Ancient Records* are morally weighted in favour of the practice of architectural preservation.

Architectural Improvement and the Gothic Revival

Although *The Romance of the Forest* is set in mid-seventeenth-century France and *Ancient Records* in mid-fourteenth-century England, both fictions are strongly inflected with architectural practices that were contemporary to Britain in the eighteenth and early nineteenth centuries. As Chris Brooks has argued, the earliest manifestations of the Gothic Revival during the 1740s and 1750s were largely domestic in orientation, not least in the stylistic reworking of earlier medieval ecclesiastical buildings as country houses.[48] The best-known example of the conversion of an ecclesiastical pile into a place of modern domestic residence was at Lacock Abbey, Wiltshire, where Sanderson Miller remodelled the thirteenth-century Augustinian convent, already transformed into a country house by William Sharington from 1540 onwards, into a private home in the Gothic style for John Ivory Talbot and his family between 1754 and 1757. Richard Goddard recommended Miller to Talbot in 1753. In the correspondence that passed between the two men, Talbot frequently expressed his commitment to effecting all the improvements in the 'Gothick Taste'; 'the Beauty of Gothick architecture', he opined,

---

[43] Curties, *Ancient Records*, vol. 1, p. 112.
[45] Curties, *Ancient Records*, vol. 1, p. 109.
[47] Curties, *Ancient Records*, vol. 1, p. 111.
[44] Curties, *Ancient Records*, vol. 1, pp. 108–9.
[46] Curties, *Ancient Records*, vol. 1, p. 112.
[48] See Brooks, *The Gothic Revival*, pp. 75–7.

'consists, like that of a Pindarick Ode, in the Boldness and Irregularity of its Members'.[49] Miller produced designs for the gateway and the staircase, but his greatest achievement at Lacock was the Great Hall, an addition with which Talbot was delighted.[50] William Henry Fox Talbot would subsequently continue this programme of restoration and Gothicizing when he moved to Lacock in 1827, and later, his son Charles would further restore the building and, with the assistance of the architect Sir Harold Brakspear, remove many of Ivory Talbot's Gothic additions.[51] The remodelling of monastic buildings as domestic residences continued throughout and beyond the sixteen-year period between the publication of *The Romance of the Forest* and *Northanger Abbey*: Combermere Abbey, Cheshire, was altered in 1795 by Sir Robert Cotton and Gothicized between 1814 and 1821 by Stapleton Cotton; and Nether Winchendon, Buckinghamshire, was reworked by Scrope Bernard between 1798 and 1803.[52] From 1808 onwards, Byron would oversee the ongoing Gothic modification at Newstead Abbey, Nottinghamshire, a process begun by his forebears a century earlier; later examples of the domestic remodelling of ecclesiastical buildings include Conishead Priory at Ulverston, Cumbria, and Toddington Manor, Gloucestershire.

In these and other instances, the challenges of reconciling the architectural style of the Middle Ages to the requirements of modern comfort and convenience were paramount, and well beyond Walpole's determination not to exclude 'convenience, and modern refinements in luxury' from his Gothicizing of Strawberry Hill.[53] Henry Home, Lord Kames, tacitly came out in favour of the Gothic as the style best suited to the ends of modern domestic habitation by figuring 'internal convenience' and 'external regularity'—a byword for Palladian classicism—as 'two incompatibles': for Kames, one could not secure the one without compromising the other.[54] While the air-admitting openness of the classical style might be particularly suited to the hot climates of Greece and Italy, it was not appropriate for domestic architecture in a cold and inclement Britain. William Gilpin, by contrast, held that convenience was a quality peculiar to country houses erected in the Grecian style, claiming that it was the sheer capaciousness of Gothic piles that rendered them 'incumbered [sic]'. 'We are amused with looking into these mansions of antiquity, as objects of curiosity,' he wrote, 'but should never think of comparing them in point of convenience with the

---

[49] See *An Eighteenth-Century Correspondence [...] to Sanderson Miller, Esq. of Radway*, ed. Lilian Dickins and Mary Stanton (London: John Murray, 1910), pp. 298–310 (p. 303).

[50] See Talbot's letter to Miller on 7 September 1754 in *An Eighteenth-Century Correspondence*, p. 306.

[51] For a useful account of the architectural history of Lacock Abbey, see Kathryn Ferry, *Lacock, Wiltshire* (Swindon: The National Trust, 2013).

[52] See Brooks, *The Gothic Revival*, p. 160.

[53] Walpole, *A Description of the Villa of Horace Walpole* (1784), p. iii.

[54] Henry Home, Lord Kames, *Elements of Criticism*, 3 vols (London: Printed for A. Millar; Edinburgh: A. Kincaid and J. Bell, 1762), vol. 3, p. 326.

great houses of modern taste.'⁵⁵ Humphry Repton grappled with similar concerns in *Fragments on the Theory and Practice of Landscape Gardening* (1816), arguing, like Kames, that the architecture of ancient Greece and Rome was unsuited to the poor British weather. The problem that presented itself, however, was that when architects working in the Gothic mode turned to vernacular forms as sources for their designs, they encountered no viable domestic examples but only the many castles, cathedrals, abbeys, colleges, and other such civic buildings that had already been converted into 'dwelling houses' in the reviled 'modern Gothic' style.[56] As sceptical of 'spurious' classical architecture as he is of the 'modern Gothic', Repton articulated the desire for an authentic, genuine, pure, or grounded architectural idiom, and this even in a building that, though erected in the style of the Middle Ages, was really of modern provenance.

The primary difficulty with which Repton grappled was the relationship between a building's outside and its inside, the challenge of reconciling a Gothic exterior with a comfortable and convenient interior.[57] He was not alone in this predicament. As Lindfield has pointed out, several architects and aestheticians of the period expressed similar concerns, with Richard Payne Knight resolving to combine a Gothic exterior with a Grecian interior at his own Gothic country house at Downton Castle, Herefordshire, and Elizabeth Montagu insisting upon the coupling of Gothic exteriors and neoclassical interiors at Sandleford Priory, Berkshire.[58] Radcliffe's and Curties's presentations of the conversions of Gothic ecclesiastical piles into places of domestic habitation resonate with all of these contemporary debates, for their characters, too, encounter the challenge of reconciling an ancient Gothic building to the ways of modern, bourgeois existence. That they all succeed in this endeavour, with Radcliffe's La Motte triumphantly making a 'castle' of his new home and Curties's Sir Alfred seeking to inhabit a structure that is only moderately repaired, is ultimately a matter of political significance. As I explore further below, these architectural practices were relatively superficial cultural manifestations of a much deeper and far more pressing political preoccupation with the 'uses' to which Gothic antiquity and its material and immaterial remains could be put in the modern, enlightened present: whether they should be returned to and literally 'inhabited', slightly modified or 'improved' so as to ensure their currency, or violently razed to the ground. In order to explore this, it is necessary to return to the ways in which Gothic architecture was politically codified earlier in the eighteenth century.

---

[55] Gilpin, *Observations on the Western Parts of England*, p. 127.
[56] Humphry Repton, with the assistance of John Adey Repton, *Fragments on the Theory and Practice of Landscape Gardening. Including Some Remarks on Grecian and Gothic Architecture, Collected from Various Manuscripts* (London: Printed by T. Bensley and Son for J. Taylor, 1816), pp. 2–3.
[57] See Repton, *Fragments on the Theory and Practice of Landscape Gardening*, p. 16.
[58] Lindfield, *Georgian Gothic*, pp. 144–5.

The Politics of Gothic Architecture

As I have argued at various points throughout this book, the Gothic architectural style, in all its resistance to the rule-bound orders of classicism, was closely associated with the call to ancient constitutional liberty that had been championed by Whiggish thinkers and politicians in Britain from the time of the Glorious Revolution onwards. So long as it was believed that the ancient Goths had built in stone and any other materials more durable than wood—a point that antiquaries and architects, from Batty Langley onwards, continuously debated—it was possible for the Whig oligarchy to draw a fairly uncomplicated connection between Gothic architecture and 'Gothic' in the political implications of that term. The metaphorical figuring of the ancient constitution as a Gothic pile was commonplace, and reached back to the seventeenth century. The often-quoted observations of an anonymous correspondent that were first published in *Common Sense* in December 1739, and reprinted in *The Gentleman's Magazine* shortly thereafter, clearly disclosed the link between architectural and political Gothicism, the writer seeing in an ancient 'Gothick hall' traces of the Gothic constitution's checking of absolute royal prerogative:

> Methinks there was something respectable in those old hospitable *Gothick* Halls, hung round with the Helmets, Breast-Plates, and Swords of our Ancestors: I entered them with a Constitutional Sort of Reverence, and look'd upon those Arms with Gratitude, as the Terror of former Ministers, and the Check of Kings. Nay, I even imagin'd that I here saw some of those good Swords that had procur'd the Confirmation of *Magna Charta*, and humbled *Spencers* and *Gavestons*.[59]

Accordingly, the early eighteenth century witnessed the clear expression of Whiggish principles in the erection of James Tyrrell's Gothic Temple at Shotover Park near Oxford (1716–17), a defiant commemoration of the Hanoverian triumph over the Stuart cause in the wake of the defeat of the first Jacobite uprising of 1715.[60] In celebration of the defeat of the second Jacobite uprising in 1745, John Yorke in c.1746 built an octagonal Gothic structure, the Culloden Tower, on his estate at Richmond, North Yorkshire, as a monument to Whig and Hanoverian politics alike; the Duke of Cumberland himself would build a triangular Gothic tower at Windsor and add a Gothic façade to Cumberland Lodge in commemoration of his victory.[61] As David Stewart has pointed out, several of the Gothic follies erected in England after the '45—including those by Miller at Radway Grange, Edge Hill; at George Lyttleton's Hagley estate; at Lord Hardwicke's estate at Wimpole; and Shenstone's ruined priory at The Leasowes, Halesowen—all commemorated the defeat of the Young Pretender, and were to some extent

---

[59] Anon., '*Common Sense*, Dec. 15, no. 150', *GM* vol. 9 (Dec. 1739): pp. 640–2 (p. 641).
[60] Brooks, *The Gothic Revival*, p. 51.   [61] Brooks, *The Gothic Revival*, pp. 51–3.

intended as architectural attacks on England's Catholic, baronial past.[62] Other examples of eighteenth-century Whiggish Gothic architecture include Castle Howard in Yorkshire (1726); the Tower at Whitton Park, Middlesex, built for Archibald Campbell (1734–5) by Roger Morris; and, perhaps most famously, the Gothic Temple or Temple of Liberty (1744–8) at Stowe, Buckinghamshire.[63] As Brooks in this regard has observed, early Revivalist Gothic was 'ideology embodied as style'.[64] Thus it was that the Tory playwright and poet William Whitehead came to reflect on the links between what he took to be the somewhat depraved taste for Gothic architecture and interiors and popular Whiggish politics, pseudonymously commenting in the periodical *The World* in March 1753 that there was something 'congenial' in the Gothic to the Whiggish appeal to 'our old Gothic constitution'; 'I should rather think to our modern idea of liberty,' he dyspeptically added, 'which allows every one the privilege of playing the fool, and of making himself ridiculous in whatever way he pleases.'[65]

Despite these correspondences, however, a Whiggish political stance did not necessarily imply a penchant for Gothic architecture: as I showed in Chapter 1, the ardent Whig Joseph Addison, for the most part a classicist in literary and architectural tastes, was no champion of the Gothic, while Mark Akenside's otherwise strongly Whiggish *The Pleasures of Imagination* called for a forthright rejection of Gothic in favour of classical literary and architectural forms. Though, politically, a staunch Whig, the 'Architect Earl' Richard Boyle, 3rd Earl of Burlington, was a stalwart classicist, sponsoring the publication of William Kent's *The Designs of Inigo Jones* (1727) and providing the original drawings that Isaac Ware would reproduce in his *The Four Books of Andrea Palladio's Architecture* (1738). In c.1716–18, Boyle would commission Colen Campbell partially to remodel his Palladian home at Burlington House, Piccadilly, this rigorously classicist architect a replacement for the freer, baroque classicism of James Gibbs. Sir Robert Walpole, meanwhile, perhaps the century's most influential Whig statesman, had his country house, Houghton Hall, Norfolk, built between 1722 and 1735 in the fashionable Palladian style, and even if his embrace of imaginative freedom unwittingly recast in aesthetic terms the political liberties of the ancient Goths, Horace Walpole seemed more drawn to the Gothic for its imaginative properties than for any overt Whiggish political meaning that it might have connoted. With their Grecian Valley and Elysian Fields, the gardens at Stowe, the most overt display of political Whiggism in garden architecture and

---

[62] David Stewart, 'Political Ruins: Gothic Sham Ruins and the '45', *Journal of the Society of Architectural Historians* vol. 55, no. 4 (December 1996): pp. 400–11. For a further discussion of these and other follies, see Megan Aldrich, *Gothic Revival* (London: Phaidon Press, 1994), pp. 49–52.
[63] See Robinson, *Temples of Delight*, pp. 102–3.
[64] Brooks, *The Gothic Revival*, p. 36.
[65] H. S. [William Whitehead], 'Number 12. Thursday March 22, 1753', *The World*, 3 vols (1761): vol. 1, pp. 67–72 (p. 69). For discussions of this, see Groom, *The Gothic*, p. 62, and Kalter, *Modern Antiques*, p. 123.

landscaping in the eighteenth century, were largely classical in style: William Kent's Temple of Ancient Virtue was based on the Temple of Vesta at Tivoli but built on Ionic principles and juxtaposed with the nearby sham ruin, the Temple of Modern Virtue, that purportedly (though by no means conclusively) contained a statue of the headless torso of Sir Robert Walpole.[66] Furthermore, Gothic could also be appropriated by prominent Tories of the age, not least at Cirencester Park, Gloucestershire, where the Tory Lord Bathurst erected a castellated Gothic lodge known variously as Alfred's Hall and King Arthur's Castle.[67] Sir Roger Newdigate, MP for Oxford University after 1751, is perhaps the best-known High Church Tory to have worked in the Gothic mode. From c.1748 onwards, and over a period of more than fifty years, he rebuilt and remodelled his family seat at Arbury Hall, Warwickshire, in a Gothic idiom that partly alluded to Strawberry Hill, employing the architects Sanderson Miller, Henry Keene, and Henry Couchman to realize his visions.[68] Between 1766 and 1768, and again in collaboration with Keene, he also renovated the Dining Hall of University College, Oxford, his use of the Gothic there designed to court associations with the college's apparent founding by King Alfred.[69] Though largely Whiggish, the political meanings of Gothic architecture were thus far from settled, and, as I argued in Chapter 3, the style could be used to represent and embody a tyrannous system of gendered and economic oppression in the romances of Ann Radcliffe.

Less open to dispute, though, was the perceived politics of architectural improvement, perhaps no more legibly so than in John Carter's responses to the work of James Wyatt, the assiduous yet controversial champion of both Gothic and classical styles of architecture who is best remembered today as the architect of Beckford's Fonthill Abbey. As the designer of the Pantheon that opened on London's Oxford Street in January 1772, Wyatt established his reputation not in the 'modern Gothic' idiom with which his name would become synonymous, but in a neoclassical style related to that of the brothers Robert and John Adam. As John Martin Robinson has pointed out, the favourable reception of Wyatt's work at the Pantheon did much to eclipse the celebrity of Robert Adam, inaugurating an intense rivalry between the two architects that raged throughout the remainder of the decade.[70] Wyatt's success at the Pantheon was confirmed by his election to the Royal Academy in 1785; as his reputation grew, so he enjoyed a number of increasingly prestigious commissions. Appointed as Surveyor to the Fabric of Abbey and College at Westminster Abbey in 1776, Wyatt would undertake

---

[66] Robinson, *Temples of Delight*, pp. 87–90.   [67] Brooks, *The Gothic Revival*, p. 55.
[68] See Lindfield, *Georgian Gothic*, pp. 161–2, and Michael McCarthy, 'Sir Roger Newdigate: Drawings for Copt Hall, Essex, and Arbury Hall, Warwickshire', *Architectural History* vol. 16 (1973): pp. 26–88.
[69] Oliver Cox, 'An Oxford College and the Eighteenth-Century Gothic Revival', *Oxoniensia* vol. 77 (2012): pp. 117–35.
[70] John Martin Robinson, *James Wyatt: Architect to George III* (New Haven and London: Yale University Press, 2011), pp. 37–57.

much work there from the 1780s onwards. George III commissioned Wyatt to oversee the restoration of St George's Chapel, Windsor, from 1787; between 1800 and 1814, £150,000 was spent on Gothicizing the interiors and exteriors of Windsor's State Apartments, a task that would later be taken up and completed by his nephew Jeffry Wyatville.[71] From 1790 onwards, Wyatt enlarged and modernized Frogmore, Berkshire, for Queen Charlotte, and in 1796 he succeeded William Chambers as Surveyor General and Comptroller of the Office of Works, a civic role that often overlapped and conflicted with the private commissions that he undertook for the king. In this official capacity, he would superintend, decorate, restore, and repair all of the buildings, residences, and properties of the royal household, continuing to enjoy close associations with the Hanoverian court until his death in 1813.

Despite such signs of success, Wyatt's reputation, at least in some circles, was sullied by the numerous 'improvements' that he oversaw at Gothic buildings across England between 1787 and 1797, including five cathedrals (Lichfield, Salisbury, Hereford, Durham, and Ely); three churches (St Michael's, Coventry; Mongewell Church, Oxfordshire; Lincoln's Inn Chapel, London); three Oxford college chapels (New College, Magdalen, and Balliol); and two abbeys (Westminster, London and Milton Abbey, Dorset).[72] Wyatt's first project of architectural improvement, completed by 1795, was at Lichfield Cathedral. Here, his work included the partial rebuilding of two of the cathedral's spires; the alteration of the choir; the replacement of broken columns; the erection of buttresses; and the raising of portions of the roof. Motivated more by the desire to impose cosmetic and aesthetic changes than to undertake necessary structural repairs, Wyatt's improvements often relied upon the addition of classical features to originally Gothic forms, a characteristic feature of the hybrid 'modern Gothic' style for which he was both applauded and censured. The overwhelming tenor of his programme, however, was one of demolition: at Lichfield, he removed altar screens, gravestones, and monuments, while at Hereford he destroyed large portions of monumental masonry. It was his work at Durham Cathedral that was the most invasive, involving, as it did, the destruction of the choir-screen and altarpiece, the Bishop's throne, and the Galilee Porch. His commissions at churches such as Milton Abbey, Dorset; Bishop Auckland Chapel, Durham; and the chapels of several Oxford colleges all similarly involved radical architectural improvements, often to the neglect of necessary repairs. His nineteenth-century reputation as 'the Destroyer' seems to have been well deserved, although it is important to remember that more recent work by scholars such as John Martin

---

[71] See Mark Girouard, *The Return to Camelot: Chivalry and the English Gentleman* (New Haven and London: Yale University Press, 1981), p. 24.
[72] See Robinson, *James Wyatt*, p. 224.

Robinson and Megan Aldrich has provided a more balanced assessment of Wyatt's architectural legacy.[73]

Nonetheless, for many of his contemporaries Wyatt's work was indistinguishable from the architectural vandalism wrought by the ancient Goths during the sacking of Rome. Although Horace Walpole was an admirer of Wyatt's work at Lee Priory, described himself as being 'amazed' by the sight of the Pantheon, and in 1789 engaged Wyatt to work on the Offices at Strawberry Hill, he was deeply concerned by Wyatt's improvements at Salisbury Cathedral.[74] Well beyond Walpole, in fact, Wyatt's work came to be regarded by some of the most prominent antiquaries of the day, including Richard Gough, John Milner, and John Carter, as destructive and meddlesome acts of architectural 'improvement' that were indistinguishable, in effect, from controlled acts of vandalism that constituted a vulgar disrespect for the material remains of the nation's Gothic past.

The story of the antiquarian opposition to Wyatt has often been recounted.[75] As Robinson has shown, the debacle revolved anxiously around notions of 'Reformation', according to which Catholic or at least pro-Catholic antiquaries such as Miller and Carter accused Wyatt of re-enacting the architectural destruction of the dissolution of the monasteries.[76] Undoubtedly, the most sustained and public form of opposition was the correspondence that Carter published in *The Gentleman's Magazine* between 1797 and 1817, the lengthy series of pseudonymous articles that I addressed in the Introduction to this book. As Mordaunt Crook describes it, Carter had taken up residence at Durham during the summer of 1795, with the expressed intention of executing drawings of the cathedral and monitoring the direct course of Wyatt's improvements.[77] Witnessing, first-hand, the drastic nature of these undertakings, Carter was compelled to respond, but despite the reservations that he expressed in his report on the matter, the Society of Antiquaries was reluctant to intervene. The concerns expressed by Gough and Milner about Wyatt's work at the cathedrals at Lichfield, Hereford, and Salisbury were similarly ignored. When Wyatt was first nominated as a Fellow of the Society of Antiquaries of London in November 1795, Carter stepped in to oppose the motion, heading up a group of Fellows that were mutually united in their opposition to 'the Destroyer'. While Wyatt enjoyed the favour of the king, as

---

[73] See Megan Aldrich, 'Gothic Sensibility: The Early Years of the Gothic Revival', in *A.W.N. Pugin: Master of Gothic Revival*, ed. Paul Atterbury (New Haven and London: Yale University Press, 1995), pp. 13–30.

[74] See Horace Walpole to Horace Mann, 26 April 1771, *Correspondence*, vol. 23, p. 298, and Horace Walpole to Richard Gough, 24 August 1789, *Correspondence*, vol. 42, pp. 259–60.

[75] See Crook, *John Carter and the Mind of the Gothic Revival*, pp. 33–41; Frew, 'Richard Gough, James Wyatt, and Late 18th-Century Preservation': pp. 366–74; John M. Frew, 'Some Observations on James Wyatt's Gothic Style 1790–1797', *The Journal of the Society of Architectural Historians* vol. 41, no. 2 (May 1982): pp. 144–9; Antony Dale, *James Wyatt, Architect: 1746–1813* (Oxford: B. Blackwell, 1936); Sweet, *Antiquaries*, pp. 276–307; and Robinson, *James Wyatt*, pp. 227–9.

[76] See Robinson, *James Wyatt*, p. 227.

[77] Crook, *John Carter and the Mind of the Gothic Revival*, pp. 23–7.

well as the internal support of figures such as Joseph Farington and Samuel Lysons, his admission to the Society was resisted by Gough, Milner, the Duke of Norfolk, and Henry Charles Englefield, an anti-Wyatt cabal spearheaded by Carter himself. In June and July 1797, two similar attempts at Wyatt's election to the Society failed. But the gravity of royal preferment eventually prevailed in his favour, and he was admitted as a Fellow on 7 December 1797. Henceforth, it was ironically Carter, and not the controversial Wyatt, who became the ostracized party within antiquarian circles: as he bitterly lamented in 1801, 'from that moment until the present hour, I have lain under the interdict of certain men in the Society, so as by their censures I am deemed unworthy of countenance'.[78]

Carter's reaction to the debacle involved an impassioned turn to journalism, initially in *The Builder's Magazine*, and then in *The Gentleman's Magazine*, a publication to which he contributed regularly and consistently until his death. Self-consciously inspired by T. J. Mathias's archly conservative critique of contemporary culture in *The Pursuits of Literature* (1794–7), Carter in *The Gentleman's Magazine* commenced a regular column entitled 'The Pursuits of Architectural Innovation', a serialized commentary on the national thirst for architectural 'innovation' that was informed by as reactionary a politics as Mathias's own. Carter's journalism is of such significance because it reveals the extent to which acts of architectural renovation such as those consistently figured in Gothic fiction were, perhaps inevitably, ideologically inflected, or inscribed within a broader network of political discourses in which Gothic buildings, their preservation, and renovation served a variety of competing political interests. His preoccupation with educating his readership in matters of architectural taste was scant disguise for a Tory political agenda fashioned around the principles of royalism, nationalism, and anti-French sentiment. As they did for many antiquaries, the physical remains of the Gothic past bore testament for Carter to a faded age of glory that demanded the nation's utmost veneration and respect. Within the context of Britain's war with post-revolutionary France, the embrace of England's monumentalized past became a matter of national urgency, for, as he argued, a return to, and re-evaluation of, history's material vestiges could serve as the best possible defence against the threat of French democracy:

> In a day like the present, when 'the infernal dispensers of liberty and equality' are spreading their destroying power over so many realms... It behoves every Eng lishman to come forward in the general cause, to protect his King and country, each in a way his ability enables him to perform, either by his person, his contributions, or his mental faculties; and I know of no way that I can so well aid the general cause, as to stimulate my countrymen to think well of their own

[78] John Carter, 'Appeal on St Stephen's Chapel', *GM*, 71 (1801), II: pp. 613–15 (p. 614).

national memorials, the works of art, of antient [sic] times, and not hold up any foreign works as superior to our own; and, in particular, the name of *France* should never be introduced, but to raise ideas of terror and destruction!'[79]

Antiquity's remains ought to remain untouched by the 'iron hand of architectural innovation', but rather be left to exist in their original states as potent reminders of the 'sublime genius' of their authors;[80] the 'heroic acts of those defenders of their country who brought perfidious France beneath their triumphant swords'; and our duties to both our king and our God alike.[81]

Indeed, while Carter's observations were provoked by the improvements of Wyatt, they soon assumed broader, more apocalyptic, architectural and political overtones. Writing at that moment in European history that he evocatively describes as 'this dread hour, when the "new order of things" is making its desolating way through the world's trembling space', Carter is poignantly aware of the events in post-revolutionary France.[82] Here, too, improvement was the order of the day: as Leora Auslander's account of the transformation of everyday material culture in the new French Republic has pointed out, 'revolutionary' architecture initially consisted largely in the modification and repurposing of the buildings and designs of the *ancien régime*, at least before the classically inspired works of such republican architects as Étienne-Louis Boullée, Claude-Nicolas Ledoux, and Jean-Jacques Lequeu.[83] This was coupled with an extensive programme of architectural demolition, particularly in the deliberate destruction of the ecclesiastical, monastic, royal, and noble monuments and edifices of the old order.[84] In a gesture of counter-revolutionary recoil, then, Carter's work in *The Gentleman's Magazine* aimed to instil in his readers nothing less than 'the fear of God, the honour due to our Sovereign, and the preservation of our Constitution from the inroads of democratic principles'; 'Innovation, in whatever form it may appear,' he concluded, 'is at this hour dangerous and full of suspicion.'[85] With a set of correspondences between innovation and revolution, architectural improvement and political radicalism set firmly in place, Carter set out to combat the dangerous sensuality that, he feared, would eventually engulf England. By contrast, a retreat into a preserved, unaltered past—Carter's sense of the white Gothic—serves as a bulwark against the political turmoil of the present, just as the blaze of his 'animated pen', like that of John Milner's before him, 'shews to

---

[79] 'An Architect', 'Pursuits viii', *GM*, 69 (1799), I, pp. 189–91 (p. 190).
[80] 'An Architect', 'Pursuits i', *GM*, 68 (1798), II, pp. 764–6 (p. 764).
[81] 'An Architect', 'Pursuits viii', p. 190.
[82] 'An Architect', 'Remembrance to the Dean and Chapter of Westminster', *GM*, 71 (1801), I, p. 328.
[83] Leora Auslander, *Cultural Revolutions: Everyday Life and Politics in Britain, North America, and France* (Berkeley: University of California Press, 2009), pp. 132–5.
[84] See Auslander, *Cultural Revolutions*, p. 133.
[85] 'J. C.', 'Milner's Winchester', *GM*, 69 (1799), II, pp. 749–50 (p. 749).

the world the majesty of our forefathers, and drives into boding darkness the hood-winked phalanxes of innovation and democratic principles'.[86]

Architectural Metaphor and Political Discourse

Though particular in his preoccupations with Wyatt and the French Revolution, Carter, it would seem, was simply the mouthpiece for a broader set of concerns, for well beyond his contributions to *The Gentleman's Magazine*, architectural improvement served as the cipher of political progressiveness in the eighteenth and early nineteenth centuries, becoming, as such, one of most important metaphors of British political life. Half a century before Carter commenced his column, improvement had received political inflection when the same correspondent in *The Gentleman's Magazine* who commended 'those old hospitable *Gothick* Halls' for their ability to evoke in the Whig sympathizer 'a Constitutional Sort of Reverence' paused to reflect on the contemporary rage for alteration and modernization:

> And when I see these thrown by, to make Way for some tawdry Gilding and Carving, I can't help considering such an Alteration as Ominous even to our Constitution. Our old *Gothick* Constitution had a noble Strength and Simplicity in it, which was well enough represented by the bold Arches, and the solid Pillars of the Edifices of those Days. And I have not observed that the modern Refinements in either have in the least added to their Strength and Solidity.[87]

As this comment suggests, architectural improvement brought to mind improvement in the political sense, too, a coupling of terms that depended upon the metaphorical figuring of 'Our old *Gothick* Constitution' as an ancient 'Gothick Hall' that I addressed above. It is just such a metaphor upon which Sir William Blackstone would draw in Book the Third of his *Commentaries on the Laws of England* (1768), his study of common law in which he figured the English legal system as a dark and labyrinthine Gothic castle that has been converted by its present heirs in their attempts at turning it into an inhabitable abode.

> We inherit an old Gothic castle, erected in the days of chivalry, but fitted up for a modern inhabitant. The moated ramparts, the embattled towers, and the trophied halls, are magnificent and venerable, but useless. The inferior apartments, now converted into rooms of convenience, are chearful [*sic*] and commodious, though their approaches are winding and difficult.[88]

---

[86] 'J. C.', 'Milner's Winchester', p. 750.
[87] Anon., 'Common Sense, Dec. 15, no. 150', *GM* vol. 9 (Dec. 1739): p. 641.
[88] William Blackstone, *Commentaries on the Laws of England. Book the Third* (Oxford: Printed at the Clarendon Press, 1768), pp. 620–42 (p. 628).

Though time has rendered its exteriors 'magnificent and venerable', this ancient castle is barely suited to modern habitation, an image that expresses Blackstone's reservations with current legal affairs, and utterly in accordance with his aim rationally to order the unruly, madness-inducing 'romance' of English law across the *Commentaries* more generally.[89]

Wilfrid Prest has brilliantly explored this and other architectural matters across Blackstone's work, drawing attention to his lifelong interest in architecture that spanned his early letters; his synthesizing of the theories of John Evelyn, Henry Wotton, James Gills, Ephraim Chambers, and Roland Fréart de Chambray in the manuscript of his *An Abridgment of Architecture* (1743) and the subsequently revised *Elements of Architecture* (1746–7); his initiation and supervision of the completion of the interior of Nicholas Hawksmoor's Codrington library at All Souls College, Oxford, in the late 1740s and early 1750s; and his Gothic Revivalist collaborations with the architect Robert Taylor at St Peter's Church, Wallingford, and elsewhere in Oxfordshire.[90] Blackstone's attempts at articulating the rules of classical architecture, Prest concludes, is mirrored in his desire to establish in the *Commentaries* the rational 'foundations' of English common law. Carol Matthews, too, has traced Blackstone's extensive involvement in the theory and practice of architecture between the 1740s and the 1770s, intriguingly drawing attention to his strong antipathies towards the Gothic and his routine privileging of the symmetry and rationalism of the classical style.[91]

It is precisely such a disdain for feudal or 'Gothic' law that is obliquely expressed in the well-known 'Gothic castle' metaphor from the *Commentaries* cited above. Pitting the virtues of order, light, and elegance against their dark and unruly 'Gothic' and 'romantic' opposites, Blackstone the Tory jurist and architect reveals himself to be more drawn to the classical than the Gothic style. At the very least, he would have endorsed the metaphor that his close friend and fellow Tory, the Gothic Revivalist Sir Roger Newdigate, had earlier employed to describe the English constitution in his 'Essays on Party' (*c.*1760): an architectural construction that originated in 'immemorial time', as 'rude and unformed' as the columns that supported 'the temples of remote antiquity', yet 'massive and solid and of such wonderful substance as to stand through various ages the shocks of civil and foreign wars, anarchy and confusion'. Though Newdigate's English constitution is one of 'Gothic majesty', it is one that has been 'polished even to Corinthian elegance', resulting in a pleasing combination of both ancient Gothic

---

[89] Sue Chaplin, *Gothic and the Rule of Law, 1764–1820* (Basingstoke and New York: Palgrave Macmillan, 2007), pp. 37–54.
[90] Wilfrid Prest, 'Blackstone as Architect: Constructing the *Commentaries*', *Yale Journal of Law and the Humanities* vol. 15 (2003): pp. 103–33.
[91] Carol Matthews, 'Architecture in Blackstone's Life and *Commentaries*', in *Blackstone and his Commentaries*, ed. Wilfrid Prest (Oxford and Portland, OR: Hart Press, 2009), pp. 15–34.

and classical forms.[92] The metaphor referenced the combination of Saxon and Roman law in the nation's legal system. Albeit in a gesture that, at least superficially, was more aesthetic than political, the 'warm Tory' Thomas Warton would advocate a similar fusion of classical and Gothic styles in *Verses on Sir Joshua Reynolds's Painted Window at New-College Oxford* (1782). But Whiggish writers could embrace such political hybridity, too. Writing against the drive towards Gothic purity that we see in 'The PALACE OF THE LAWS' at the end of the fourth part of Thomson's *Liberty*, William Collins had argued for a fusion of classical and Gothic politics in his otherwise strongly Whiggish ode 'To Liberty' (1742): though erected with '*Gothic* Pride', Liberty's fane is enjoined with '*Græcia*'s graceful Orders [to] join', the resulting structure becoming more 'Majestic thro' the mix'd design'.[93]

Less observed is the way in which Blackstone's metaphor also functions as a politically acute appropriation of the discourse of improvement and repair, those architectural practices, as I have argued thus far, that were crucial to the mid-to-late-eighteenth-century Gothic Revival. The immediate context in which the trope occurs is his discussion of the extent to which the legal structures of the Gothic past might ever serve the needs of the present. From the outset, Blackstone articulates the difficulties that he perceives with acts of legal and constitutional creation *ex nihilo*. Insisting instead that the nation build upon the foundations of those structures that are already in place, he makes pointed use of the metaphors of alteration and remodelling: 'But who, that is acquainted with the difficulty of new-modelling any branch of our statute laws (though relating but to roads or to parish settlements) will conceive it ever feasible to alter any fundamental point of the common law, with all it's [*sic*] appendages and consequents, and set up another rule in it's [*sic*] stead?'[94] When, in ages past, it became apparent that the feudal systems of tenure 'were ill suited to that simple and commercial mode of property which succeeded the former', the architects of English law 'wisely avoided soliciting any great legislative revolution in the old established forms'.[95] The gradual modification of the common law over time, he continues, is a 'much better' way of proceeding than what could ever be achieved through 'any great fundamental alteration'.[96] Resisting drastic and unprecedented change in favour of a subtle process of maintenance, Blackstone presents his ideal Gothic castle of the law as the product of ongoing architectural improvement across time. The political implications of this are clear: as R. J. Smith has observed, the jurist

---

[92] Peter D. G. Thomas and Roger Newdigate, 'Sir Roger Newdigate's Essays on Party, c.1760', *The English Historical Review* vol. 102, no. 403 (April 1987): pp. 394–400 (p. 396).
[93] Collins, *Odes on Several Descriptive and Allegoric Subjects*, p. 30.
[94] Blackstone, *Commentaries on the Laws of England. Book the Third*, p. 267.
[95] Blackstone, *Commentaries on the Laws of England. Book the Third*, p. 268.
[96] Blackstone, *Commentaries on the Laws of England. Book the Third*, p. 268.

approached even 'cosmetic change' to the law's 'architecture' with caution.[97] Improvement, then, is Blackstone's favoured mode, for while they are little short of 'useless' in their original state, the 'moated ramparts, the embattled towers, and the trophied halls' of the Gothic castle might be 'converted into rooms of convenience' through strategic acts of modification.[98]

The object of his critique in the *Commentaries* is thus not the process of legal-cum-architectural improvement per se so much as the inelegant ways in which these changes have been executed. This is certainly the sentiment informing the architectural metaphor on which much of the argument of Book the First (1765) depends:

> The common law of England has fared like other venerable edifices of antiquity, which rash and unexperienced [sic] workmen have ventured to new-dress and refine, with all the rage of modern improvement. Hence frequently it's [sic] symmetry has been destroyed, it's [sic] proportions distorted, and it's [sic] majestic simplicity exchanged for specious embellishments and fantastic novelties.[99]

Blackstone returned to the same trope in the closing of Book the Fourth (1769). Wrested from the hands of what he now referred to as 'unskilful' improvers, the improvement and repair of the admittedly 'defective' English constitutional castle ought to be entrusted to the gentry, the nobility, and the peerage: 'To sustain, to repair, to beautify this noble pile, is a charge intrusted [sic] principally to the nobility, and such gentlemen of the kingdom, as are delegated by their country to parliament.'[100]

Such architectural metaphors did not go unchallenged. Jeremy Bentham's critique of Blackstone in *A Fragment on Government* (1776) astutely observed that, in figuring the law as a Gothic castle, Blackstone had effected a linguistic version of the very process of '"fundamental" reparation' that he sought in other respects to oppose: for Bentham, the law might become a Gothic castle only through a radical process of rhetorical alchemy.[101] As such, the image strains under the weight of metaphorical conversion, for as Bentham writes, Blackstone 'should have considered, that it is not easier to [sic] *him* to turn the Law into a Castle, than it is to the imaginations of impoverished suitors to people it with Harpies'.[102] If one was to persist in conceiving the Gothic constitution as a castle,

---

[97] Smith, *The Gothic Bequest*, p. 94.
[98] Blackstone, *Commentaries on the Laws of England. Book the Third*, p. 268.
[99] William Blackstone, *Commentaries on the Laws of England. Book the First* (Oxford: Printed at the Clarendon Press, 1765), p. 10.
[100] William Blackstone, *Commentaries on the Laws of England. Book the Fourth* (Oxford: Printed at the Clarendon Press, 1769), p. 436.
[101] Jeremy Bentham, *A Fragment on Government; Being an Examination of what is Delivered, on the Subject of Government in General, in the Introduction to Sir William Blackstone's Commentaries* (London: Printed for T. Payne, P. Elmsly, and E. Brooke, 1776), p. xxxiv.
[102] Bentham, *A Fragment on Government*, p. xxxiv.

it was a structure that was haunted by the mythological monsters of popular superstition. The weight of historical precedent bore heavily upon the present in Bentham's radical utilitarianism, a negative form of historical influence that was indistinguishable from a terror-inducing act of haunting.[103] Proceeding from the basis of these two images, Frances A. Chiu has persuasively demonstrated the extent to which both progressive and conservative political discourses in England during the period 1777–1800 relied upon the metaphor of the Gothic castle.[104] While conservative Whigs such as Edmund Burke, like the Tory Blackstone before him, tended to perceive the past as a Gothic building in need, at worst, of only minor repair, progressive thinkers such as Mary Wollstonecraft, Anna Laetitia Barbauld, Vicesimus Knox, Joseph Priestley, and John Thelwall were more inclined to figure Gothic antiquity as a terrifying, outmoded, and frequently haunted architectural structure, the only legitimate response to which was abandonment and demolition.

The Architecture of Revolution

Though Chiu's observation is a shrewd one, it overlooks the fact that, couched in architectural metaphors though they were, political debates in England during the 1790s were often more preoccupied with the politics of architectural improvement than with Gothic architecture per se. Much like Blackstone, for instance, Edmund Burke's defence of precedent and tradition in *Reflections on the Revolution in France* (1790) made consistent use of metaphors of architectural improvement and repair. Addressing himself to a nation in the throes of revolutionary turmoil, Burke mourned the French failure both to build upon ancient, established foundations and to tend to those parts of the constitutional 'fabric' that were most in need of repair: 'Your constitution, it is true, whilst you were out of possession, suffered waste and dilapidation, but you possessed in some parts the walls, and in all the foundations of a noble and venerable castle. You might have repaired those walls; you might have built on those old foundations.'[105] Though it draws upon that familiar coupling of political constitutions and Gothic architecture that reached at least as far back as the 1730s, Burke's reference here to France's 'noble and venerable castle' also obliquely refers to a much more immediate, topical event: the storming of the Bastille in Paris in July 1789, that iconic historical occurrence that soon thereafter became the symbol of, and perceived

---

[103] Smith, *The Gothic Bequest*, p. 133.
[104] Frances A. Chiu, 'Faulty Towers: Reform, Radicalism and the Gothic Castle, 1760–1800', *Romanticism on the Net* no. 44 (Nov. 2006): https://www.erudit.org/fr/revues/ron/2006-n44-ron1433/013996ar/ (accessed 5 June 2017).
[105] Edmund Burke, *Reflections on the Revolution in France, and on the Proceedings in Certain Societies in London Relative to that Event* (London: Printed for J. Dodsley, 1790), p. 50.

point of origin for, the French Revolution.[106] The event impacted upon the architectonics of political discourse in significant ways, bequeathing to it a graphic image system of architectural vandalism, demolition, and deliberate ruination.

Certainly, the cataclysmic events in Paris in July 1789 were first communicated to Britons in rousing images of architectural ruin: when the news of the storming of the Bastille on 14 July broke in London a few days later, British newspaper reports made much of the acts of architectural assault and demolition that had ensued at the hands of the enraged mob.[107] As Gillian Russell has pointed out, the event soon translated itself onto the London stage, primarily in the form of the short, spectacular theatrical entertainments that were produced as accompaniments to lengthier featured dramas.[108] Nothing less than a 'Bastille war' ensued between rival London theatres in late July and August 1789, as managers of the minor companies competed to stage theatrical spectacles that detailed events in the French capital. *The Triumph of Liberty; or, The Destruction of the Bastille* debuted at Hughes's Royal Circus on 5 August; Philip Astley staged *Paris in an Uproar; or, the Destruction of the Bastille* on 17 August at Astley's Amphitheatre near Westminster Bridge; and *Gallic Freedom; or, Vive la liberté* was staged at Sadler's Wells on 31 August. John Dent's *The Bastille: A Musical Entertainment of One Act*, the printed script of *The Triumph of Liberty*, presents the destruction of the Bastille as the ultimate goal and end point of the revolution:

> Rejoice, ye men of virtue! ye men of honour! ye men of wisdom! The patriotism of France is no longer *prejudice*, it is now founded in reason, it is now fixed on *truth*. The abominable and inhuman engine of unrelenting despotism is destroyed—the Bastille is annihilated, and the wretch who governed it, and who was worthy of his trust, is now no more.[109]

The *ancien régime* appears to have been destroyed in one passionate act of architectural demolition. Notwithstanding the fact, historically, that the full

---

[106] Lüsebrink and Reichardt have tracked the process through which the Bastille, initially a generic technical term for the municipal towers built in southern France during the Middle Ages, came to be associated with the particular architectural edifice on the eastern outskirts of Paris, and, beyond that, a particular political regime. See Hans-Jürgen Lüsebrink and Rolf Reichardt, *The Bastille: A History of a Symbol of Despotism and Freedom*, trans. Norbert Schürer (Durham and London: Duke University Press, 1997).

[107] See, among several other examples, the announcements of the fall of the Bastille in 'French Revolution!!!', *English Chronicle or Universal Evening Post* (18–21 July 1789, Issue 1535); 'French Bastille', *Oracle Bell's New World* (Monday, 20 July 1789, Issue 43); and 'The Bastile [sic]', *London Chronicle* (28–30 July 1789, Issue 5120). For a comprehensive account of these newspaper reports, see Norbert Schürer, 'The Storming of the Bastille in English Newspapers', *Eighteenth-Century Life* vol. 29, no. 1 (Winter 2005): pp. 50–81.

[108] See Gillian Russell, *The Theatres of War: Performance, Politics, and Society, 1793–1815* (Oxford: Clarendon Press, 1995), pp. 67–8. For another account of the fall of the Bastille on the London stage, see George Taylor, *The French Revolution and the London Stage, 1789–1805* (Cambridge: Cambridge University Press, 2000).

[109] John Dent, *The Bastille: A Musical Entertainment of One Act*, 2nd edn (London: Printed for W. Lowndes, 1790), p. 21.

dismantling of the Bastille took as long as six months to effect,[110] Britons figured its fall as the spontaneous, traceless disappearance of an enchanted castle, making of the event a Gothic romance in the tradition of Ariosto, Tasso, Spenser, and Walpole. In place of applauding the triumph of French democracy, however, the final scene of the play is given over to the celebration of a native British sense of liberty. As a stirring anthem is played, the personified figure of Britannia, seated in her triumphal car and supporting '*two grand transparent Portraits of the King and Queen of Great Britain*', descends from the gods, addressing the newly liberated French with the following lines:

> Amidst the thousand joys that inward glow,
> Your freedom to yourselves and me you owe.
> From Britannia you caught the Patriot flame,
> On Britain's plan then build your future fame.
> Let liberty and reason rule each part,
> And form the Magna Charta of the heart.
> Nor had your city e'er with blood been stain'd,
> Had Virtues like our George and Charlotte's reign'd.[111]

Liberty, here, is presented as an originally and exclusively 'Gothic' prerogative, one that the French might import into their recently liberated country only through a careful emulation of the English example. Burke, by contrast, feared the consequences of national emulation in the other direction: while the British establishment was metaphorically conceived as a Gothic pile, it was vulnerable to the same revolutionary destruction as that enacted by the mob on the Parisian prison. Anxious to avoid this, Burke, through the example of France, proposes for Britain nothing more fundamental than an ongoing process of moderate improvement and repair over time.

Few of Burke's more liberal respondents were sympathetic to this programme. Francis Stone, for one, argued that it masked nothing other than a desire to leave the legal and political status quo in Britain essentially unchanged.[112] William Belsham, similarly, maintained that the moderate changes that Burke proposed to the old 'Monkish institutions, and Gothic modes of education' would be too slow to bring about any effective reform, to the extent that 'every idea of reformation or improvement' in the *Reflections* was merely 'chimerical and absurd' in nature.[113] And yet, while it is indeed easy to caricature Burke as the most conservative and backward-looking of 'old Whigs', his use of the metaphors of improvement in the *Reflections* suggests otherwise. The British constitution, he

---

[110] Lüsebrink and Reichardt, *The Bastille*, p. 1.   [111] Dent, *The Bastille*, pp. 22–3.
[112] See Francis Stone's argument in *An Examination of the Right Hon. Edmund Burke's Reflections on the Revolution in France* (London: Sold by G. C. J. and J. Robinson, J. Johnson, et al., 1792).
[113] William Belsham, *Historic Memoir on the French Revolution* (London: Printed for C. Dilly, 1791), p. 94.

maintains, is passed down, through precedent, from generation to generation in ways that are synonymous with the transmission of property. While this would seem to imply that the past always dominates the present as a heavy and burdensome remainder—a version of the *mortmain* or 'dead hand' of tradition that he discusses elsewhere in the *Reflections*—Burke is keen to emphasize that its return ought always to be moderated and qualified by the forces of progress and improvement. Like any old establishment, the 'original project' of Britain's 'primitive constitution' ought continuously to be 'improved' upon through the lessons of lived experience.[114] 'By adhering in this manner and on those principles to our forefathers,' he argues, 'we are guided not by the superstition of antiquarians, but by the spirit of philosophic analogy.'[115] Unlike the antiquary, who seeks to revive through architectural relics an unchanged Gothic past, the enlightened politician is an architect who remains ever mindful of the need to improve upon antique structures in accordance with present needs and concerns. Burke's argument is informed by a distinction between architects and antiquaries that was often employed in the eighteenth century: in his Preface to *Westmonasterium* (1723), his antiquarian study of the Abbey Church of St Peters, John Dart had claimed that the primary difference between the historian and the antiquary was that while the former 'first builds a new Fabrick, (which, if he's skilful, he may do regularly, having the Materials provided him)', the latter is most characteristically found 'gathering the broken and irregular Fragments of an old one'.[116] But in Burke's system, the ideal politician combines the conservationist imperatives of the antiquary with the architect's flair for creative improvement: 'A disposition to preserve, and ability to improve, taken together, would be my standard of a statesman. Every thing else is vulgar in the conception, perilous in the execution.'[117] The revolutionaries of republican France, by contrast, are marauding vandals who presume to clear away the rubble of the past and erect in its place a 'castle in the air', a fanciful, evanescent, and imaginary political structure that is lacking in both precedent and ancient foundations.

For his opponents, however, it was precisely Burke's antiquarian veneration of the Gothic past that was cause for concern. Belsham dismissed him as an 'obsequious and devoted admirer of antiquity', while the radical Catharine Macaulay cannily pointed out that his taste for ancient Gothic edifices, both literal and symbolic, was by no means universal: 'The leaders of the French Revolution, and their followers', she shrewdly opined, 'see *none of those striking beauties* in the old

---

[114] Burke, *Reflections on the Revolution in France*, pp. 253–4.
[115] Burke, *Reflections on the Revolution in France*, pp. 48–9.
[116] John Dart, *Westmonasterium; or, The History and Antiquities of the Abbey Church of St Peters, Westminster* (London: Printed and Sold by James Cole, et al., [1723]), Preface.
[117] Burke, *Reflections on the Revolution in France*, p. 231. For a discussion of this interplay between improvement and preservation in the *Reflections*, see David Bromwich, 'Burke, *Reflections on the Revolution in France*', in *The Cambridge Companion to British Literature of the French Revolution in the 1790s*, ed. Pamela Clemit (Cambridge: Cambridge University Press, 2011), pp. 16–30.

laws and rules of the Gothic institutions of Europe, which Mr Burke does. They do not profess to have any of the spirit of antiquarians among them.'[118] As David Duff has observed, Burke's veneration of the Gothic past was subject to frequent satirical treatment, with the politician often caricatured as a delusional hero of romance, a Don Quixote-like figure committed to defending both the French queen and civilization itself.[119] Paramount to the response to the *Reflections* was Burke's refusal to confront the Bastille, the Gothic pile that symbolically lay at the heart of revolutionary events, in anything but the most oblique of terms. As Thomas Paine in the first part of *Rights of Man* (1791) would claim, 'Through the whole of Mr Burke's book I do not observe that the Bastille is mentioned more than once, and that with a kind of implication as if he were sorry it is pulled down, and wished it were built up again.'[120] The only two other faint references to it that Paine identifies seemed to express Burke's regret at its demolition. 'From his violence and his grief,' Paine concludes, 'his silence on some points, and his excess on others', it is difficult not to conclude 'that Mr Burke is sorry, extremely sorry, that arbitrary power, the power of the Pope, and the Bastille, are pulled down'.[121] Part of Paine's objective, then, was to offer a corrective to such oversights. Well beyond the role that it played as a prison, the Bastille, he argues, functions as a metaphor for the workings of power in both France and the sovereign states of Europe more generally, for the tyranny of sovereignty proliferates throughout society, multiplying Bastille-like structures and rendering its people the subjects of generalized and perpetual imprisonment: 'Every place has its Bastille, and every Bastille its despot,' he stirringly writes; 'The original hereditary despotism resident in the person of the King, divides and subdivides itself into a thousand shapes and forms, till at last the whole of it is acted by deputation.'[122] Attempting to trap Burke in his own rhetorical web, Paine subversively presents his opponent himself as a likely prisoner: for all the support that he purports to offer the sovereign, it is not inconceivable that he too will end up in the Bastille, a victim to the king's fickle and arbitrary power. Making of the French Revolution a sentimental tragedy of kingship, the *Reflections*, for Paine, relied too heavily upon literary convention; mourning the extinction of the flame of chivalry across Europe, the text was generically indistinguishable from romance, a 'rhapsody' of the imagination that refused to accept that 'the Quixote age of chivalry nonsense is gone'.[123]

---

[118] Belsham, *Historic Memoir on the French Revolution*, pp. 94–5; Catharine Macaulay, *Observations on the Reflections of the Right Hon. Edmund Burke, on the Revolution in France, in a Letter to the Right Hon. The Earl of Stanhope* (London: Printed for C. Dilly, 1790), p. 34.

[119] David Duff, 'Burke and Paine: Contrasts', in *The Cambridge Companion to British Literature of the French Revolution in the 1790s*, ed. Pamela Clemit (Cambridge: Cambridge University Press, 2011), pp. 47–70 (pp. 52–5).

[120] Thomas Paine, *Rights of Man: Being an Answer to Mr Burke's Attack on the French Revolution* (London: Printed for J. Johnson, 1791), p. 23.

[121] Paine, *Rights of Man*, p. 24.   [122] Paine, *Rights of Man*, p. 19.

[123] Paine, *Rights of Man*, p. 22.

Like other radicals of her day, Mary Wollstonecraft remained unpersuaded by Burke's programme of gradual constitutional improvement. In *A Vindication of the Rights of Men* (1790), she accused Burke of mourning the 'empty pageant' of a vanished past, further criticizing him for his mawkish sentimentalism 'for the idle tapestry that decorated a gothic pile, and the dronish bell that summoned the fat priest to prayer'.[124] Charging Burke's architectural idiom with the ruination witnessed in the storming of the Bastille, Wollstonecraft's treatise announced an urgent call for the abandonment of the Gothic structures of the past, advocating instead the building of newer, simpler structures based solely upon the foundations of reason and empirical experience:

> Why was it a duty to repair an ancient castle, built in barbarous ages, of Gothic materials? why were they obliged to rake amongst heterogeneous ruins; or rebuild old walls, whose foundations could scarcely be explored, when a simple structure might be raised on the foundation of experience, the only valuable inheritance our forefathers can bequeath?[125]

As her pejorative use of the term indicates, the structures of 'Gothic' antiquity had no legitimate use or function for Wollstonecraft in the present; instead, they were the vestiges of a past of darkness, tyranny, and oppression, to be rejected outright in favour of new structures and institutions. The 'venerable vestiges of ancient days,' Wollstonecraft claims, all conform to 'gothic notions of beauty—the ivy is beautiful, but, when it insidiously destroys the trunk from which it receives support, who would not grub it up?'[126] The debate between Burke and his opponents ultimately pivoted on the difference between utopian and dystopian conceptualizations of Gothic antiquity.[127]

Wollstonecraft continued her interrogation of the possible uses of the Gothic past in her subsequent work, critiquing in particular the enslaving effects of romance—Richard Hurd's 'spark' that kept the 'flame' of glorious chivalry alive—upon female subjectivity in *A Vindication of the Rights of Woman* (1792) and its fictional expression in *Maria; or, The Wrongs of Woman* (1798). When, in the latter text, she has her heroine claim that 'Marriage had bastilled me for life'— a metaphorical appropriation of the same 'horrible prison' that Wollstonecraft had described in *An Historical and Moral View of the Progress of the French Revolution* (1794)—it is clear that her experience of conjugal oppression is partly

---

[124] Mary Wollstonecraft, *A Vindication of the Rights of Men; in a Letter to the Right Honourable Edmund Burke; Occasioned by his Reflections on the Revolution in France* (London: Printed for J. Johnson, 1790), p. 152.
[125] Wollstonecraft, *A Vindication of the Rights of Men*, pp. 95–6.
[126] Wollstonecraft, *A Vindication of the Rights of Men*, p. 10.
[127] Madoff, 'The Useful Myth of Gothic Ancestry'.

attributable to the delusions fostered in women by the uncritical consumption of romance.[128] Her critique of the taste for Gothic architecture in *Maria* is equally pointed. Even when viewed through a picturesque lens, the architectural remains of Gothic antiquity for Wollstonecraft were beyond the prospect of political and aesthetic recuperation, and wholly unworthy of any act of cultural revival. On the contrary, they necessitated urgent acts of rejection, disavowal, and abandonment. Though localizing her discussion to France, Catharine Macaulay argued much the same point, claiming, against Burke, that the French, who had previously been '*enslaved to misery*', were under no obligation 'to make use of these old materials in the structure of their new constitution, which they suppose to have been of an injurious tendency'.[129] Instead, she praised the builders and architects of the new French Republic for having 'chosen a simple rule for the model of their new structure', while regulating it 'with all that art and design which the experience of ages affords to the wisdom of man'.[130]

Wollstonecraft's and Macaulay's investment in the revolutionary potential of architectural ruin was strongly informed by Constantin-François de Chassebœuf, comte de Volney's *Les Ruines: ou Méditations sur les révolutions des empires* (1791), a radical reflection on the cyclical nature of history and revolution that was translated into English by William Godwin's close friend James Marshall, and published in London by the politically progressive publisher Joseph Johnson in 1792. Reverberating with echoes of the fall of the Bastille, *The Ruins: Or A Survey of the Revolutions of Empires* (1792) extracted from its descriptions of the ruins of ancient Palmyra important historical lessons concerning the impermanence of despotism, the vulnerability of tyranny, and the expression of revolutionary disquiet in acts of architectural demolition. Though Volney, initially deputy and then secretary to the French National Assembly, later distanced himself from revolutionary politics, *The Ruins* in Britain inspired the radical call for the ruination of the 'Gothic' institutions of the past.[131] Similarly under Volney's influence, John Thelwall would articulate an urgent call for the demolition and abandonment of ancient Gothic structures in the first part of *The Rights of Nature, Against the Usurpations of Establishments* (1796), his response to Burke's *Thoughts on the Prospect of a Regicide Peace* of 1796. Elaborating upon the architectural metaphors used in the *Reflections*, Burke in the later text characterized the laws and

---

[128] Wollstonecraft, *Mary and The Wrongs of Woman*, p. 155; Mary Wollstonecraft, *An Historical and Moral View of the Progress of the French Revolution*, 2 vols (London: Printed for J. Johnson, 1794), vol. 1, p. 188.
[129] Macaulay, *Observations on the Reflections of the Right Hon. Edmund Burke*, p. 34.
[130] Macaulay, *Observations on the Reflections of the Right Hon. Edmund Burke*, p. 34.
[131] See Sonja Perovic, 'Lyricist in Britain; Empiricist in France: Volney's Divided Legacy', in *Historical Writing in Britain, 1688-1830: Visions of History*, ed. Ben Dew and Fiona Price (Houndmills: Palgrave Macmillan, 2014), pp. 127-44, and Alexander Cook, 'Reading Revolution: Towards a History of the Volney Vogue in England', in *Anglo-French Attitudes: Comparisons and Transfers between English and French Intellectuals Since the Eighteenth Century*, ed. Christophe Charle, Julien Vincent, and Jay Winter (Manchester: Manchester University Press, 2007), pp. 125-46.

political systems of most modern European countries, including England, as having derived from ancient Gothic structures, cultural and legal foundations that, though of antique origins, have benefited from the forces of improvement ever since: 'The whole of the polity and œconomy of every country in Europe have been derived from the same sources. They were drawn from the old Germanic or Gothic custumary [sic]; from the feudal institutions which must be considered as an emanation from those customs; and the whole has been improved and digested into system and discipline by the Roman law.'[132] In *The Rights of Nature*, however, Thelwall interrogated the 'tropes, and metaphors, and allegories' of his opponent's Whiggish discourse, focusing in particular upon the architectural metaphor invoked in Burke's sense of 'the old Germanic or Gothic customary' as national 'foundation':

> Are these the institutions which Mr. B. wishes to support? Are these the perfect models of social jurisprudence which it is blasphemy to approach with the unhallowed finger of innovation or reform? Are these (in their effects) the regular and orderly fabrics of the ancient legitimate government of states, whose plans and materials were 'drawn from the old Germanic or Gothic custumary,' [sic] and of which those famous architects, 'the civilians, the jurists, and the publicists,' have given us such flattering draughts, ground plots and elevations?[133]

Like Wollstonecraft before him, Thelwall calls for the demolition of all the ancient Gothic institutions that remain. Of no perceivable use to the present, and by no means the remains of a '*venerable* antiquity', the legal and political structures of history are variously described as 'Bastilles of the intellect', 'Augean stables', 'temples of oppression and injustice', and 'insulting mausoleums of buried rights', so many ancient Gothic edifices that, wholly beyond improvement and repair, might only be resisted through wholescale destruction.[134] His argument recalls Bentham's critique of Blackstone in *A Fragment on Government*: if the English law is, indeed, an old Gothic castle, it is one that is profoundly haunted, though here primarily by the spectres of the labouring poor whom it has consistently marginalized. Opposing the violent exorcisms of the 'wandering ghost of popular discontent' imposed by William Pitt the Younger with a ghostly call to arms, Thelwall exhorts the spectres of labour to present themselves.[135] Until such a moment, the English castle will remain a 'tumbling nuisance' in chronic disrepair, a dilapidated Gothic pile with its beams 'disjointed' and its 'foundations gone'.[136]

---

[132] Edmund Burke, *Thoughts on the Prospect of a Regicide Peace, in a Series of Letters* (London: Printed for J. Owen, 1796), pp. 48–9.
[133] John Thelwall, *The Rights of Nature, Against the Usurpations of Establishments*, 2nd edn (London: Published by H. D. Symonds and J. March, Norwich, 1796), pp. 60, 17.
[134] Thelwall, *The Rights of Nature*, pp. 17–18.
[135] John Thelwall, *Rights of Nature, Against the Usurpations of Establishments. Part the Second* (London: Published by H. D. Symonds and J. March, Norwich, 1796), pp. 30–1.
[136] Thelwall, *Rights of Nature, Against the Usurpations of Establishments. Part the Second*, p. 20.

In their impassioned rejections of Gothic architecture, chivalry, and romance, British radicals of the post-revolutionary decade opposed everything that the eighteenth-century Gothic Revival had laboured so hard to resurrect. For such thinkers, the Revival marked the persistence or the return of an oppressive and tyrannous Gothic past, and demanded, as such, urgent acts of renunciation and disavowal. Perhaps their fears were well founded, for as Mark Girouard has pointed out, George III's interests in the Middle Ages—his commissioning of Wyatt's work in the Gothic style at Windsor Castle mentioned above, as well as his support for the painter Benjamin West's splendid depictions of chivalry—were informed by a backward-looking, deeply conservative politics.[137] The threat that the rhetoric of 1790s radicalism posed to the establishment is clear to see. Writing under the pseudonym of 'Will Chip, A Country Carpenter', Hannah More in 1792 put the radical call for the demolition of all antique institutions to counter-revolutionary use in *Village Politics*, a sixteen-page tract addressed 'To All the Mechanics, Journeymen, and Day Labourers, in Great Britain'. Published initially in London, and aimed at the same labouring masses to whose defence Thelwall would spring in *The Rights of Nature*, this archly conservative tract was republished across Britain throughout the 1790s. Its plot concerns an imaginary dialogue between Jack Anvil, a blacksmith, and Tom Hod, a stonemason. Having read Paine's *Rights of Man*, Tom is infused with revolutionary fervour, desiring wide-scale national reform and the establishment of rights and liberties in his native England similar to those recently achieved across the Channel. Alarmed by Tom's radicalism, however, Jack Anvil illustrates the importance of maintaining the status quo through the use of architectural metaphor, an analogy, that is, that the mason might best be able to comprehend. Far from requiring demolition, the constitution for the more moderate Jack is an ancient castle that requires, at most, only minor repair: 'so now and then they mend a little thing, and they'll go on mending, I dare say, as they have leisure, to the end of the chapter, if they are let alone. But no pull-me-down works.'[138] Persuaded by the analogy, and suitably chastened by Jack's apocalyptic vision of the likely destruction of the nation's venerable edifices, Tom abandons his radical ideals in order to join Jack in a toast to Old England.

Political Gothic Fiction and the Legacy of the Gothic Past

Perhaps inevitably, the fictional scenes of architectural improvement with which I began this chapter resonate strongly with these political debates. In Austen's

---

[137] Girouard, *The Return to Camelot*, pp. 22–5.
[138] Will Chip [Hannah More], *Village Politics. Addressed to all the Mechanics, Journeymen, and Day Labourers, in Great Britain*, 2nd edn (London: Printed for and Sold by F. and C. Rivington, 1792), pp. 8–9.

narrative, modern-day England, like Northanger itself, is no haunted Gothic abbey but a venerable pile that has been penetrated by the forces of rationality and light. Horsley Curties, for his part, issued from an auspicious line of High Church Tories, and between 1805 and 1839 held the position of Exon of the Guard in the courts of George III, George IV, William IV, and even the young Queen Victoria.[139] His professional identity in this respect was founded on a commitment to keeping Burke's dwindling flame of chivalry burning brightly; in recognition of his lengthy service to the Hanoverian court, he was dubbed Knight Bachelor at the coronation of William IV in 1831. In his first novel, *Ethelwina* (1799), Curties, like John Carter and many other conservative antiquaries of the day, made of the 'illustrious reign' of Edward III a white Gothic romance, encountering in his return to fourteenth-century England not the vestiges of a dark, oppressive, and superstitious past but a golden age of unmatched cultural and political achievement. Insofar as it nostalgically figures the structures of feudalism, sovereignty, chivalry, and romance as favourable alternatives to the chaos of the present, the white Gothic is an inherently conservative fantasy. The architectural preoccupations of Curties's later *Ancient Records* are part of the same historiographic vision, and express a backward-looking commitment to preserving or even returning to the feudal and hierarchical social and political structures of the Middle Ages.

Ann Radcliffe's attitude towards history, by contrast, has been usefully summed up by James Watt as one of 'abandonment': a dark patriarchal nightmare, Gothic antiquity is characterized by the physical, sentimental, and economic exploitation of women, the only legitimate response to which is urgent abandonment, escape, and flight.[140] Not insignificantly, this becomes in most of her works a matter of her modern, bourgeois heroine's eventual relation to architectural form: though certainly an instance of Brooks's 'ideology embodied as style', the Gothic is also chronotopic, that is, historical time—the Gothic past—embodied as architectural space. For all Montoni's repairs to his castle, Emily's actions construct Gothic antiquity as that from which one should flee. Even though, following their tribulations, Radcliffe's heroines are habitually led to other houses of symbolic import—La Luc's rustic yet enlightened retreat at Savoy in *The Romance of the Forest*, or the Chateau-le-Blanc, the place of literal light and symbolic enlightenment, in *Udolpho*—it is still vital that they leave even these reconstituted versions

---

[139] See Dale Townshend, 'Royalist Historiography in T. J Horsley Curties's *Ethelwina; or, The House of Fitz-Auburne (1799)*, *Gothic Studies* vol. 14, no. 1 (May 2012): pp. 57–73, and Dale Townshend, 'T. I. Horsley Curties, Romance, and the Gift of Death', *European Romantic Review* vol. 24, issue 1 (2013): pp. 23–42.

[140] James Watt, 'Gothic', in *The Cambridge Companion to English Literature, 1740–1830*, ed. Thomas Keymer and Jon Mee (Cambridge: Cambridge University Press, 2004), pp. 119–37 (pp. 123–4). For another account of Radcliffe's feminist historiography, see JoEllen DeLucia, 'From the Female Gothic to a Feminist Theory of History: Ann Radcliffe and the Scottish Enlightenment', *The Eighteenth Century* vol. 50, no. 1 (spring 2009): pp. 101–15.

of Gothic antiquity behind them, retreating finally, as Emily does in her return to La Vallée, into an intensely private world of memory and sentiment. In this move, Radcliffe's radicalism, as Watt has pointed out, seems to give way to political quietism, although, as I shall show in Chapter 6, Radcliffe would take up the radical cause again in her later antiquarian romance *Gaston De Blondeville*.[141]

The architectonics of political discourse also worked their way into much more self-consciously political fiction of the 1790s, perhaps no more so than in the novels of Charlotte Smith. As Loraine Fletcher has argued, Smith's fictional castles reverberate strongly with topical political reference.[142] Her Jacobin epistolary novel *Desmond* (1792), for example, distinguishes between the radical and conservative politics ventriloquized in the narrative through architectural metaphor. Even before Lionel Desmond leaves England for post-revolutionary France, he encounters at the home of Mrs Fairfax the counter-revolutionary General Wallingford, one who, in a conservatism even more exacting than that of Edmund Burke, expresses the wish that all revolutionaries be put to death and the newly established National Assembly be razed to the ground. Equally dismissive of the revolution is Mr Sidebottom. In keeping with the sentiments expressed at the end of Dent's *Bastille*, Sidebottom takes liberty to be an exclusively English virtue, presuming to see in the fall of the Bastille the French nation's belated but fortunate reversion to what Dent's play had called 'the Magna Charta [sic] of the heart': 'if they [the French] will have liberty,' he observes, 'give them a little taste of the liberty of us Englishmen; for, of themselves, they can have no right notion of what it is—and, take my word for it, its [sic] the merest folly in the world for them to think about it.—No, no; none but Englishmen, freeborn Britons, either understand it or deserve it.'[143] Desmond, however, rejects Sidebottom's complacency, and writes off such easy recourse to the myth of the liberty-loving Goth as 'mere cant which we have learned by rote, and repeat by habit'.[144] Refusing to bestow upon the British constitution such 'unlimited praise', Desmond will wager the suggestion that if 'a greater portion of happiness' is, indeed, 'diffused among the subjects of the British government' more than among any other nation, this is only because of the sheer wretchedness of those with whom Britons have been compared, and not due to the inherent perfection of the system itself.[145] It is this perceived 'defectiveness' of the British constitution that informs much of Desmond's politics, and one that drives the process of architectural-cum-constitutional repair for which he advocates.

---

[141] See James Watt's argument in 'Ann Radcliffe and Politics', in *Ann Radcliffe, Romanticism and the Gothic*, ed. Dale Townshend and Angela Wright (Cambridge: Cambridge University Press, 2014), pp. 67–82.
[142] See Loraine Fletcher, 'Charlotte Smith's Emblematic Castles', *Critical Survey* vol. 4, no. 1 (1992): pp. 3–8.
[143] Charlotte Smith, *Desmond*, ed. Antje Blank and Janet Todd (Peterborough, ON: Broadview Press, 2001), p. 80.
[144] Smith, *Desmond*, p. 341.   [145] Smith, *Desmond*, p. 342.

Arriving in Paris in time for the celebration of the first anniversary of the Bastille's fall, Smith's hero is filled with the fervour of the young William Wordsworth, enthusiastically seeing in the ruins of the notorious prison the literalization of 'the levelling principle which the revolutionists have pursued'.[146] Despite his noble birth and title, the Marquis de Montfleuri, Desmond's friend, mentor, and guide to French society, is 'one of the steadiest friends of the people', embracing the abolition of all distinctions in France as the 'subject nearest to his heart', and maintaining, in a direct riposte to Burke, that the 'antiquity of titles' is by no means 'an irrefragable proof of their utility'.[147] If Burke's flame of chivalry has, indeed, been snuffed out, this, for Montfleuri, is a cause for celebration rather than regret, for as his responses to the old edifices of Paris reveal, he sets no store by the relics of Gothic antiquity. Ancient monasteries and cathedrals, as he perceives them, are little more than a sop to the guilty conscience of the aristocracy, built and endowed as penance for their sins and cemented with the blood of the labourers who constructed them. As such, the clerics who inhabit such buildings are the preservers of an antiquated system of superstition and oppression, one that should have been vanquished in the Dark Ages.

Accordingly, Montfleuri's house bears few traces of the Gothic past. In an act of far-reaching architectural modification, modernization, and improvement, Montfleuri has removed from his chateau every fixture that is not of use to him in the present, eradicating its 'gothic gloom' and remodelling it in the fashion of a moderate, bourgeois English dwelling.[148] But if his refurbishments suggest a vulgar disrespect for the past, Smith makes it clear that the jettisoning of outdated political structures need not amount to an insensitivity to antiquity's aesthetic charm: despite his rejection of his ancestors' political legacy, Montfleuri has endeavoured to preserve the large, ruined religious edifice that stands perched on a nearby hill. His sensibilities, here, align themselves closely with Desmond's own, for he, too, advocates a Bastille-like destruction of the oppressive regimes of the past even as he claims to value that past's aesthetic remains: 'I, who love, you know, every thing ancient unless it be ancient prejudices, have entreated my friend to preserve this structure in its present state—than which, nothing can be more picturesque.'[149] In endowing her hero with a picturesque sensitivity to Gothic ruins and landscaping, Smith installs a careful distinction between Gothic politics and Gothic art, suggesting that a radical dismantling of ancient political systems need not mean a vulgar disrespect for antiquity's aesthetic legacy.

Montfleuri's modernized and improved chateau is juxtaposed with the home of his maternal uncle, the Comte d'Hauteville, 'a residence, where mortified and discomfitted [sic] tyranny seems to have taken up its sullen station; and with

---

[146] Smith, *Desmond*, p. 88.   [147] Smith, *Desmond*, pp. 87, 135.
[148] Smith, *Desmond*, p. 112.   [149] Smith, *Desmond*, p. 113.

impotent indignation to colour with its own gloomy hand every surrounding object'.[150] Desmond is struck by the differences between the two dwellings, contrasting 'the chearful [sic] abode of Montfleuri, where every countenance beamed with pleasure and content' with the 'mournful residence' of his uncle, the one the site of enlightened benevolence, the other of a heavy, melancholic atmosphere.[151] The Chateau d'Hauteville, it is clear, is a fitting emblem of its owner's conservative politics: a firm believer in the powers of distinction, privilege, and ancient tradition, d'Hauteville is the diametrical opposite of his nephew. This aspect of the novel's architecture demands closer consideration. Though, as I have argued, the Gothic style was primarily Whiggish in ideological import, it was often read by Jacobin writers of the 1790s as a symbol of archly conservative, oppressive regimes, and mythologized as the sign of power even more crushing than that wielded by Pitt. As Helen Maria Williams's 'The Bastille, A Vision' (1790) indicates, it was British radicals' perceptions of the Parisian prison that sealed for them Gothic architecture's fate: though she never makes use of the term, it is quite clear that the Bastille is 'Gothic' in style, the embodiment of a larger and more threatening 'Gothic' regime that thrives on torture, immolation, and live burial. In Williams's 'To Dr Moore' (1792), the associations between Gothic architecture and feudal oppression and tyranny become even more pronounced: here, 'Those Gothic piles, the works of ages past' become coterminous with 'feudal governments', 'obtrusive reason', 'danger', 'horror', and the power that a resident 'tyrant' wields over his 'slaves'.[152] No simple paean to Whiggish notions of liberty, Smith's Gothic architecture is charged with similar meanings, an intensification of the associations with which Ann Radcliffe had imbued the Gothic style in the same decade.

A supporter of the counter-revolution, Smith's Comte seeks to flee a country that has become threatening, reading in the revolutionaries' destruction of the Bastille a sign of the impending destruction of his own home. Once inside the chateau, Desmond is struck by 'that damp and musty smell' that runs through the 'cold and half-furnished rooms', and this atmosphere of Gothic gloom, together with the chimney of blood-coloured marble and blue velvet furnishings, renders it 'one of the most funereal apartments' that he remembers ever having seen.[153] Having rescued Geraldine from the freebooters and banditti, Desmond makes a return to the abandoned chateau towards the novel's end. The count has fled, and the place has been inhabited by counter-revolutionary troops and ruffians. Imprisoning them in its subterranean dungeons, Desmond and his servants mete out to the supporters of the *ancien régime* a suitable punishment,

---

[150] Smith, *Desmond*, p. 124.   [151] Smith, *Desmond*, p. 124.
[152] Helen Maria Williams, 'To Dr Moore', in *Romantic Women Poets, 1770–1838: An Anthology*, ed. Andrew Ashfield (Manchester and New York: Manchester University Press, 1998), pp. 74–6 (ll. 54–62).
[153] Smith, *Desmond*, p. 129.

conveying them 'to a room in the most ancient part of the castle, which was, when the feudal system was in all its force, a place of confinement for the wretched vassals, over whom those barbarous customs gave the *seigneur*, the power of life and death'.[154] Fleeing the castle, Desmond leaves it to fall into disrepair at the narrative's close—a cipher in Smith, as in Radcliffe, of antiquity's limited relevance and applicability to the present.

And yet, while the novel proposes the abandonment and demolition of the Gothic structures of France, it surprisingly seems to advocate, in relation to England's own 'Gothic castle' of the law, a far more moderate process of repair. Desmond directly invokes Blackstone when he characterizes the English constitution as a defective, partly ruined Gothic edifice that, if not promptly attended to, is likely to crush those who inhabit it:

> If these prejudices are enforced and continued—if every attempt to repair what time has injured, or amend what is acknowledged to be defective, is opposed as dangerous, and execrated as impious; let us go on till the building falls upon our heads, and let those who escape the ruins, continue to meditate on the prodigious advantage of this holy reverence, and to boast of the happiness of being Englishmen!'[155]

Although Desmond claims that the 'very foundation' of English constitutional law is 'defective', it is not its demolition but the repair of these faults that, in the end, lies at the heart of his politics.[156] As he later writes to Mr Bethel, 'I think that our form of government is certainly the best—not that can be imagined—but that has ever been experienced'; accordingly, 'it would be most absurd to dream of destroying it on [sic] theory'—almost as absurd, in fact, as asking a builder to demolish a perfectly good house with only 'some inconveniences about it'.[157] In the end, then, minor repair triumphs over the more radical practice of architectural demolition, a detail that suggests the sense of disillusion with the French Revolution that Smith would explore more fully in the poem *The Emigrants* (1793).

The novel's final embrace of romance seems equally compromising of its revolutionary potential. In keeping with Paine's argument that Burke's *Reflections* had made of 'glorious' Gothic times a sentimental fiction, *Desmond*, like Wollstonecraft's *Maria* and other political Gothic fictions, operates on one level as a critique of the narcotic effects of romance. When confronted with the fiction of the Gothic past defended by Montfleuri's uncle, Desmond advocates a rational scrutinizing of these fantasies so as to expose, once and for all, the 'deformed' politics that underpins them: 'Surely then it is time to recall our imaginations from these wild dreams of fanaticism and heroism—time to remove the gorgeous trappings, with which we have drest up folly, that we might fancy its glory.'[158] Yet there remains at least one

---

[154] Smith, *Desmond*, p. 397.
[155] Smith, *Desmond*, pp. 208–9.
[156] Smith, *Desmond*, p. 209.
[157] Smith, *Desmond*, p. 343.
[158] Smith, *Desmond*, p. 138.

sense in which Desmond himself is susceptible to romantic delusion: founded upon distance, prohibition, and platonic devotion, his love for Geraldine Verney is a courtly-love scenario replayed in the modern present. The task of showing up Desmond's romantic susceptibility for what it is often falls to Mr Bethel: a love set in fanciful 'castles in the sky' and filled with the trappings of 'ancient story', a sentimental complicity in the very Gothic structures that he otherwise so despises.[159] Perhaps, though, this is the consequence of Smith's commitment in *Desmond* to separating out the politics of Gothic antiquity from its aesthetic legacy, the effect of her attempt to revive the form of 'Gothic' romance without its attendant political meanings.

Other writers were far more sceptical of any attempt to draw a distinction between the aesthetic and the political aspects of the Gothic bequest. In its title alone, William Godwin's *Caleb Williams; or, Things as They Are* (1794) foregrounded its commitment to problematizing the romances of the Middle Ages, confrontationally presenting its readers not with an idealized vision of 'things as they ought to be' but with a powerful, realist indictment of modern existence 'as it really is'. Falkland's risible behaviour, it is clear, is governed by a lifelong commitment to the reading of romance. Having drunk deeply 'of the fountain of chivalry', he poses as 'a man of gallantry and virtue', and allows these values to dictate his course of action in relation to his rival, Barnabas Tyrrel.[160] Styling himself as a member of 'the regiment of the old English votaries of beef and pudding', Tyrrel, too, is a supporter of ancient chivalric codes; while Falkland appears to be the more refined of the two, Tyrrel is belligerent and boorish, inflicting a 'rural tyranny' on the tenants of his estate.[161] Like the warring factions in a tournament, both men fashion themselves as 'leaders in the field of chivalry', an engagement that implicates them in a jousting to the death, but when Tyrrel dies, Falkland's code of action becomes even more insubstantial than it originally was.[162] Unable to avenge himself, the 'idle and groundless romances of chivalry' unravel in the hands of this 'true knight', the lack of a suitable opponent reducing them to 'an unintelligible chimera'.[163] More the source of mutual destruction than testament to a noble Gothic past, the romance of chivalry becomes, in the end, a poisoned chalice: as Caleb in the closing moments of his tale notes, Falkland, having imbibed 'the poison of chivalry with [his] earliest youth', has misguidedly pursued 'the phantom of departed honour' to the grave.[164] It thus seems particularly notable that Godwin would offer up so positive an account of the feudalism, chivalry, and romance of the Middle Ages in his *Life of Geoffrey Chaucer* (1804): in

---

[159] Smith, *Desmond*, p. 196.
[160] William Godwin, *Caleb Williams; or, Things as They Are*, ed. and introd. Maurice Hindle (London: Penguin Books, 1988), pp. 13, 18.
[161] Godwin, *Caleb Williams*, pp. 22, 68. [162] Godwin, *Caleb Williams*, p. 23.
[163] Godwin, *Caleb Williams*, pp. 101–2. [164] Godwin, *Caleb Williams*, p. 337.

radical circles of the 1790s, these were all reviled 'Gothic' practices.[165] For Godwin, at least, romance retained one important function: the provision of narrative and character to the work of the historian, without which history would be merely an unintelligible assemblage of desultory, meaningless facts. This is the argument of his 'Of History and Romance' (1797), an essay that asserted not only the historian's necessary reliance upon fictional technique, but also romance's superiority to history. If romance were to be revived at all, it had to be put to work in the service of ethical and political responsibility.

Charlotte Smith returned to her concerns with architecture, improvement, and the uses of chivalry and romance in *The Old Manor House* (1794), attempting to avoid the conservative critical reactions provoked by *Desmond* by setting her novel in and around the War of American Independence (1775–83). This act of temporal distancing, however, does little to disguise the fact that she is again primarily concerned here with assessing the legacy of the Gothic past and its possible uses in the England of the 1790s. Gothic antiquity in the narrative is given physical embodiment in the form of Rayland Hall, the titular 'old manor House' that is situated 'in one of the most southern counties of England', and displaying all the turrets, casements, stained-glass windows, and old fortifications of the Gothic style. Never having received 'the slightest alteration, either in its environs or its furniture' since it was embellished in 1698, Rayland Hall marks the presence of the past as it has persisted, wholly unchanged, into the present, a locale governed by customs and traditions all dating back to 'time immemorial'.[166] The hierarchical distributions of power, the regular feasts of the tenants, and the syncopated turns of social interaction in general render life at Rayland barely distinguishable from that under feudalism; the Royalist factions harboured within it during the English Civil War and at other crucial moments in its history align the Hall with a conservative, backward-looking politics. As in *Desmond*, Gothic architecture in the text signifies an outdated system of political power.

Guided by the same 'antediluvian notions' as those monumentalized in her home, Mrs Grace Rayland looks with disdain on the improvements carried out by Stockton at the nearby Carloraine Castle, a fine old estate that borders her property.[167] While under the ownership of Lord Carloraine, the castle was a testament to the powers of noble blood and inherited wealth, as its owner purchased all the remaining land in the area as a defence against the encroaching tide of bourgeois domestic aspiration. But when he dies, the upstart Stockton, a merchant made rich by his entrepreneurship during the French and Indian War (1754–63), purchases Carloraine and embarks upon a vulgar programme of

---

[165] See Angela Wright's argument in 'The Fickle Fortunes of Chivalry in Eighteenth-Century Gothic', *Gothic Studies*, vol. 14, no. 1 (May 2012): pp. 47–56.
[166] Charlotte Smith, *The Old Manor House*, ed. Jacqueline M. Labbe (Peterborough, ON: Broadview Press, 2002), pp. 40, 201.
[167] Smith, *The Old Manor House*, p. 265.

improvement, presuming 'under the auspices of modern taste, to new model everything'.[168] Having 'no respect for the hitherto inviolate manors, nor for the preserved grounds around Rayland Hall', he turns Carloraine Castle, much to Mrs Rayland's disgust, into a monstrous testament to modern, bourgeois taste.[169]

In contrast to these crass improvements, Mrs Rayland embraces the traditionalist values enshrined in the transmission of property through the powers of blood and noble birthright. Tenacious of her power, and jealous of every attempt 'to encroach on her property', she regards all instances of social mobility as detestable, but particularly the ascendant bourgeoisie's appropriation of the titles, houses, and symbols of the illustrious past as vehicles for their own self-expression—Belgrave, for instance, is dismissed as 'one of the new-made baronets' that, like the host of 'new-created lords', 'spring up like mushrooms, from nobody knows where every year'.[170] In their inhabiting of improved Gothic structures, the merchants, tradesmen, and other members of the ascendant middling classes that surround her are responsible in her eyes for a vulgar and ostentatious display of wealth; what is at stake is nothing less than the worrying democratization—and bastardization—of the hallowed Gothic past, a revolutionary act similar to that demonstrated in the La Motte family's inhabiting of the ruined abbey in *The Romance of the Forest*. The political implications of this are clear. In his *Reflections*, Burke had invoked the virtues of a traditional notion of landed property against the troubling spectre-like incursions of modern economy and capital finance; Mrs Rayland's system of values involves a similar privileging of inherited property against the instantaneous, somewhat ephemeral, conjurations of money. If a hierarchical social order based upon the privileges of property and birth are, to her, the source of virtue, money— the spoils of modern commerce—remains the source of all evil. But while Burke had mourned the passing of the age of chivalry, for Mrs Rayland 'the age of chivalry did not seem to be passed', and perceiving Orlando to bear 'a spark' of that 'martial and dauntless spirit' that had run in her ancestral line, she positions him as a valiant knight in her own service, encouraging his military exploits abroad as much as the re-enactment of ancient chivalrous codes in his duel with Sir John Belgrave.[171] Consequently, a conflict between two competing conceptualizations of romance plays itself out at Rayland Hall: while the house and its owner support martial action that is scripted according to the old codes of chivalry, they frustrate rather than facilitate the expression and consummation of modern sentimental romance, especially when it becomes a private, emotional alternative to the aristocratic codes of ancient alliance. Desiring that Orlando abandon all romantic pretensions in favour of a politically and materially expedient marriage, Mrs Rayland ensures that the Hall halts the smooth progress of love, even to the extent that 'no knight of romance ever

---

[168] Smith, *The Old Manor House*, p. 68.   [169] Smith, *The Old Manor House*, p. 69.
[170] Smith, *The Old Manor House*, pp. 42, 125.
[171] Smith, *The Old Manor House*, pp. 265, 157.

had so many real difficulties to encounter in achieving the deliverance of his princess, as Orlando had in finding the means merely to converse with the little imprisoned orphan'.[172] When metaphorically deployed as a Gothic mansion, the past in *The Old Manor House* persists in the present as an intransigent obstacle to the forces of progress and enlightenment, an architectural detail that once again aligns Smith with the oppressive political meanings of the Gothic explored by Radcliffe.

In both *Desmond* and *The Old Manor House*, Smith's interrogation of the persistence of the Gothic past in the social, political, and economic structures of the present is accompanied by a politicized critique of the supernatural. Bentham's response to Blackstone, as I have shown, turned upon a phantasmatic projection of ghosts, spectres, and ghouls into the Gothic mansion of Blackstone's metaphorical figuring, while Thelwall would imagine in the Gothic pile of the English nation the swarming spectres of popular discontent. In *Desmond*, the enlightened Montfleuri had cited Voltaire in order to argue that the superstitious monsters evoked by such Gothic structures constitute no grounds for their veneration: 'Are you not sensible, that what is just, clear, and evident, must be naturally attended to—and that chimeras cannot always be held in veneration?'[173] In *The Old Manor House*, similarly, Smith populates Rayland Hall with a host of apparently spectral beings: the rumours and superstitions of the servants construct it as a space of supernatural activity, while Monimia believes it to be haunted by the restless spirit of one of the ladies Rayland. If traces of the Gothic past persist in the present at all, they only do so for Smith through a terror-inducing act of haunting. However, as in *Desmond*, Smith radically pushes beyond Bentham's haunted Gothic castle in order to show up the ideological nature of this very fantasy: the assumption that old Gothic buildings are haunted only serves to mythologize them, rendering the undesirable political and economic systems that they encode even more redoubtable. Orlando continuously exposes the extent to which Monimia at Rayland Hall, in entertaining such superstitious fancies, has become subject to the workings of power, astutely pointing out to her that, by bringing in 'supernatural aid', Mrs Rayland has 'taken care to fetter you in as much ignorance as possible'.[174] For Smith, however, the inequalities of class and gender that combine in real life in the invidious position of the orphan are far more terror-inducing than any supernatural entity will ever be. Grounding Monimia's fears in the more urgent forces of lived social and political reality, Orlando demystifies the Gothic pile and everything for which it stands. In time, the heroine's apprehensions decrease 'in proportion as her reason, aided by her confidence in him, taught her that there was in reality little to fear from the interposition of supernatural agency'.[175]

---

[172] Smith, *The Old Manor House*, p. 61.
[173] Smith, *Desmond*, p. 101.
[174] Smith, *The Old Manor House*, p. 75.
[175] Smith, *The Old Manor House*, p. 81.

At once Shakespeare's love-struck comic hero and the titular character of Ariosto's *Orlando Furioso*, however, Smith's Orlando, like Desmond earlier, can never be entirely immune to the seductions of romance. Jacqueline M. Labbe has evocatively described the fancies that preoccupy him as the 'romance of property', the all-consuming hope that at least some part of the Rayland wealth and property—an 'enchanted castle' of the romance genre—might one day devolve to him.[176] In Orlando's mental universe, sentimental romance—the hero's love for the heroine—prevails as much as does the romance of inherited property, to the extent that his love for Monimia becomes inseparable from his material ambitions. Positioned as a knight-in-training by Mrs Rayland, Orlando acts out the aspirations demanded of his name, even while other characters in the fiction, including Warwick and his brother Philip, continuously expose his pretensions. Unswayed, he embarks upon his own version of a chivalrous crusade when he takes up the Hanoverian cause against the American revolutionaries. Ultimately, though, the glorious scripts of fealty that govern his actions prove to be unsustainable, as he returns to England to find Monimia, Mrs Rayland, and Rayland Hall, the three interrelated objects of his quest, respectively absent, dead, and in a state of disrepair. Peering into the dilapidated manor house through a broken window, he succumbs again to the spectral fantasies of a romantic heroine, including the hallucination of the corpse of Mrs Rayland laid out on the bed of a mausoleum-like room and visions of 'Hideous spectres' that seem 'to beckon to him from the other end of it, and to menace him from the walls'.[177] In this teasing play of ghostliness, Orlando himself becomes a spectre, a revenant from the future that returns to haunt the crumbling remains of the past. The romance of the enchanted castle has been ruptured by death, loss, and ruination, and, much to Orlando's disappointment, Rayland Hall has passed into the hands of the Archdeacon Hollybourn.

Even once the contents of Mrs Rayland's will have been disclosed and Orlando named as the Hall's true heir, the prospect of the hero's and heroine's simple return to the structures of the Gothic past is complicated by an important yet surprising architectural detail: prior to inhabiting it, Orlando has to submit the old manor house to a process of moderate refurbishment, gathering around him 'every comfort and every elegance of modern life', yet 'without spoiling that look of venerable antiquity for which it was so remarkable'.[178] The structures of Gothic antiquity are able to meet the needs of the present once they have been altered so as to ensure their comfort and convenience. This recalls the strange recourse to moderate architectural and political 'improvement' at the end of *Desmond*. Carloraine Castle is duly 'sold, pulled down by the purchaser, and the

---

[176] Jacqueline M. Labbe, 'Introduction', in *The Old Manor House,* by Charlotte Smith, ed. Jacqueline M. Labbe (Peterborough, ON: Broadview Press, 2002), pp. 9–29 (p. 19).
[177] Smith, *The Old Manor House*, p. 401.   [178] Smith, *The Old Manor House*, p. 521.

park converted into farms' in the narrative's closing moments, as if the gaucheness of Mr Stockton ought no longer to be countenanced.[179] In this, though, the novel ends on a politically disappointing note: in demolishing the houses of an emergent bourgeois modernity while subjecting the Gothic halls of antiquity to what is really only moderate cosmetic refurbishment, the narrative of *The Old Manor House* eventually aligns itself with the conservatism of a Blackstone or a Burke, a political retreat on Smith's behalf that becomes even more pronounced in *The Banished Man* (1794). While one might have expected of a radical writer such as Smith a sympathy for the acts of abandonment and demolition advocated by the likes of Wollstonecraft, Macaulay, and Thelwall, it is the redoubtable Gothic piles of antiquity that, having been only moderately refurbished, are allowed to remain standing.

---

[179] Smith, *The Old Manor House*, p. 521.

5
'Venerable Ruin' or 'Nurseries of Superstition'
Ecclesiastical Architecture and the Gothic Literary Aesthetic

The representation of Catholicism in Gothic writing has long been the subject of critical interest. It was J. M. S. Tomkins who, in *The Popular Novel in England, 1700–1800* (1932), was the first to address the anti-Catholicism of the mode, an aspersion to which the Gothic bibliophile, Catholic convert, and self-ordained Catholic priest Montague Summers, in *The Gothic Quest* (1938), was quick to respond.[1] For the defensive Summers, early Gothic writing attested not to 'any militant protestantism' on the novelists' behalves so much as an innocuous appropriation of Catholicism's abbots, convents, friars, nuns, rosaries, and cloisters that was motivated merely by an interest in their 'exotic', 'mysterious', and 'romantic' properties.[2] Without always foregrounding the anti-Catholic nature of her sources, Sister Mary Muriel Tarr, in *Catholicism in Gothic Fiction* (1946), undertook to address the function of 'Catholic materials' in Gothic romances published between 1762 and 1820, ranging across such topics as the presentation of the sacraments, the Gothic preoccupation with convents and monasteries, and the representation of monks and abbesses.[3] Though the issue was frequently raised in academic studies in the intervening years, it was not until Victor Sage's *Horror Fiction in the Protestant Tradition* of 1988 that the anti-Catholic nature of Gothic writing received sustained critical attention. Consulting a broad range of Gothic fictions, Sage here advanced the important argument that the rise and currency of the literary Gothic was closely related to the ever-strengthening campaign for Catholic emancipation from the 1770s through to the Catholic Emancipation Act of 1829, an exploration of the first wave of Gothic that he also extended into the nineteenth and twentieth centuries.[4] More recently, the differences in opinion between Tomkins and Summers have repeated themselves in a critical contretemps between Maria Purves and Diane Long Hoeveler. Seeking to counter the

---

[1] See Tompkins, *The Popular Novel in England, 1770–1800*, pp. 274–6.
[2] Summers, *The Gothic Quest*, pp. 195–6.   [3] Tarr, *Catholicism in Gothic Fiction*.
[4] Sage, *Horror Fiction in the Protestant Tradition*, p. 29. For Sage's full exploration of the anti-Catholicism of the mode, see pp. 26–69.

Gothic Antiquity: History, Romance, and the Architectural Imagination, 1760–1840. Dale Townshend, Oxford University Press (2019). © Dale Townshend.
DOI: 10.1093/oso/9780198845669.001.0001

long-held assumption that eighteenth-century Gothic was a vehicle for rabid anti-Catholicism, Purves's *The Gothic and Catholicism* (2009) has drawn attention to the positive, at times sympathetic, representations of Catholics and monastical existence in a range of canonical and lesser-known Gothic poems and fictions.[5] Diane Long Hoeveler's *The Gothic Ideology* (2014), by contrast, has responded to Purves by outlining, through an exhaustive analysis of the representation of nuns, monks, priests, tribunals, and ruined abbeys in Gothic between the years 1780 and 1880, the concept named in her book's title: an intense and vociferously anti-Catholic ideological bias that was perpetuated in Gothic fictions from the mid-eighteenth through to the late nineteenth century.[6]

While returning to similar critical territory, I wish in this chapter to consider the issue from a different, specifically architectural, perspective. Ranging across antiquarian studies, executed architectural projects, romances, letters, essays, and topographical writing, I seek to show how the Gothic fictional aesthetic, in both its pro-Catholic and anti-Catholic extremes, was merely an expression of the broader discourse on ecclesiastical Gothic architecture and architectural ruin in the long eighteenth century. Though architectural matters have not been entirely overlooked in accounts of Catholicism and the Gothic—Hoeveler's study, for one, includes a lengthy analysis of ruined abbeys, a topic that has also been explored in important work by Deborah Kennedy, Michael Charlesworth, and Ana M. Acosta—it is fair to say that these have been limited to a concern with the ways in which abbeys, convents, and other monastical institutions are 'represented' in the fiction.[7] In the account that follows, by contrast, I seek to move beyond a concern with the representation of fictional Gothic abbeys, monasteries, and convents in order to articulate the broader and deeper architectural discourses that made their cultural existence possible, and this in a period in British history that is now not insignificantly often referred to as the 'long Reformation'.[8] That is, continuing to grapple with the original terms and subsequent consequences of Henry VIII's break from Rome, British culture of the eighteenth and early nineteenth centuries remained deeply preoccupied with the Catholic questions of the fifteenth and sixteenth centuries. As Alison Milbank has recently shown, this ongoing sense of theological and political dispute was crucial to the rise of

---

[5] Maria Purves, *The Gothic and Catholicism: Religion, Cultural Exchange and the Popular Novel, 1785–1829* (Cardiff: University of Wales Press, 2009).

[6] Hoeveler, *The Gothic Ideology*, p. 5.

[7] See Deborah Kennedy, 'The Ruined Abbey in the Eighteenth Century', *Philological Quarterly* vol. 80, no. 4 (Fall 2001): pp. 503–20; Michael Charlesworth, 'The Ruined Abbey: Picturesque and Gothic Values', in *The Politics of the Picturesque: Literature, Landscape and Aesthetics Since 1770*, ed. Stephen Copley and Peter Garside (Cambridge: Cambridge University Press, 1994), pp. 63–79; and Ana M. Acosta, 'Hotbeds of Popery: Convents in the English Literary Imagination', *Eighteenth-Century Fiction* vol. 50, no. 3–4 (July 2003): pp. 615–42.

[8] See Nicholas Tyack, ed., *England's Long Reformation, 1500–1800* (Abingdon and New York: Routledge, 1998), and Peter G. Wallace, *The Long European Reformation: Religion, Political Conflict, and the Search for Conformity, 1350–1750*, 2nd edn (Houndmills: Palgrave Macmillan, 2012).

Gothic fiction, a mode in which monastical buildings—those castles of 'Caym' (or Cain) denounced by the proto-reformer John Wyclif, or the 'Bare, Ruined Quires' (or choirs) of Shakespeare's Sonnet 73—play a thematic and theologically significant role, often becoming the objects of a profound and melancholic nostalgia.[9] As in the next chapter, I seek to show how Gothic architecture, particularly the architecture of ecclesiastical ruin, prompted imaginative reconstructions of the nation's Gothic past, an age not only characterized by Catholic 'darkness' and 'superstition', but one also felicitously inhabited by 'enlightened' English Catholics. In this sense, this chapter, like the work of Milbank, is a response to both Purves and Hoeveler: articulating the architectural discourses that made the vacillation between pro-Catholic sympathy and the 'Gothic ideology' possible, it also provides a genealogy of ruined ecclesiastical piles as they come to manifest themselves in first-wave Gothic writing. In traversing this terrain, I explore not only some of the well-known instances of the 'survival' of Gothic architecture in the period— the cultural attitudes towards Gothic ruins that have been addressed in several other studies—but some notable instances of Gothic 'revival' too: the deliberate recuperation of a Catholic architectural style in the work of eighteenth-century Protestants and Catholics alike.

Venerable Ruin/Monkish Piles

Cultural perceptions of ecclesiastical ruin in the long eighteenth century were situated on a discursive fault line, one in which antiquarians' habitual evocations of their 'venerable' nature existed alongside the commonplace, more popular conviction that these were the architectural remains of a shameful and benighted Catholic past. In *Monasticon Anglicanum* (1655–73), his paean to the abbeys, monasteries, cathedrals, and collegiate churches of England, Wales, Scotland, and Ireland that had fallen with Henry VIII's dissolution of the monasteries (1536–41), William Dugdale described ecclesiastical ruins as the 'venerable Fabricks we behold at this day';[10] similar uses of the adjective 'venerable' appear in eighteenth-century English translations of *Monasticon Anglicanum*, the first major study of ecclesiastical institutions and architecture in Britain and Ireland.[11] If not Dugdale's or his translator's innovation, the application of the adjective 'venerable' to the description of inanimate architectural objects appears to have

---

[9] See Milbank, *God and the Gothic*, pp. 1–110.
[10] Originally written in Latin in 1655, *Monasticon Anglicanum* was first translated into English in 1693. See William Dugdale, *Monasticon Anglicanum; or, The History of the Ancient Abbies, and other Monasteries, Hospitals, Cathedral and Collegiate Churches in England and Wales. With Divers French, Irish, and Scotch Monasteries formerly Relating to England*, 3 vols (London: Printed for Sam Keble, 1693), vol. 1.
[11] See, for example, William Dugdale, *Monasticon Anglicanum*, 3 vols (London: Printed by R. Harris for D. Browne and J. Smith, 1717), vol. 1, p. 16.

been a mid-seventeenth-century phenomenon, for such usages do not occur in, say, Philemon Holland's English translation of William Camden's *Britannia* (1610), nor in Thomas Browne's *Hydriotaphia, Urne-Buriall; or, A Discourse on the Sepulchrall Urnes Lately Found in Norfolk* (1658). When, in Webster's *The Duchess of Malfi*, Antonio, walking among the ruins of an ancient abbey, claims that 'I do love these ancient ruins: / We never tread upon them, but we set / Our foot upon some reverend history', it is the noble past for which they stand more than the ruins in and of themselves that becomes the subject of veneration.[12] Indeed, as the etymology offered in the *OED* suggests, 'venerable' before the mid-seventeenth century was more likely to be applied to persons than objects, most famously in the case of the Anglo-Saxon historian, the Venerable Bede. After Dugdale, though, the examples of its application to architectural objects proliferate: Browne Willis too described ecclesiastical ruins in *An History of the Mitred Parliamentary Abbies, and Conventual Cathedral Churches* (1718–19) as 'the most venerable Remains of our ancient Piety', proceeding to cite St Albans Abbey, Hertfordshire, among many other examples, as 'the most venerable Monument of its kind extant in *England*'.[13] In fact, throughout eighteenth-century antiquarian accounts of Britain's ecclesiastical ruins, phrases such as 'venerable piece of antiquity', 'venerable fabric', 'venerable ruin', 'venerable Gothic pile', and 'venerable monuments of our own country' abound, perhaps even to the point of cliché. If these structures were venerable, their architectural remains could be regarded as 'relics' in all the Catholic, religious associations of that word. Citing instances of the use of the adjective in the translations of John Dryden and Edward Fairfax, the first edition of Samuel Johnson's *Dictionary* (1755) defined 'venerable' as 'To be regarded with awe; to be treated with reverence', a gloss that encapsulates well the attitude of deferential respect that the word commanded.[14]

The antiquarian discourse of venerable ruin, however, circulated alongside an equally popular, if not more pervasive, cultural perception of ecclesiastical ruin as the obdurate remainder—and unwelcome reminder—of the Protestant nation's shameful Catholic history, material relics of what David Lowenthal has evocatively described as the 'grievous' and 'menacing' past.[15] It was the seventeenth-century writer, diarist, and translator John Evelyn who was one of the first Englishmen to dismiss the Gothic style as 'Monkish Piles', not in his earlier-discussed *A Parallel of the Antient Architecture with the Modern* (1664) but in the first edition of *An Account of Architects and Architecture*, his influential treatise that, though

---

[12] John Webster, *The Duchess of Malfi*, ed. Elizabeth M. Brennan (New York: W. W. Norton & Co., 1986), Act V, scene iii, ll. 9–11.
[13] Browne Willis, *An History of the Mitred Parliamentary Abbies, and Conventual Cathedral Churches*, 2 vols (London: Printed by W. Bowyer for R. Gosling, 1718–19), vol. 1, 13.
[14] Johnson, *A Dictionary of the English Language*, vol. 2.
[15] See David Lowenthal, *The Past is a Foreign Country, Revisited* (Cambridge: Cambridge University Press, 2015), pp. 136–44.

completed earlier, was published in 1706 and reissued again in 1723. The Goths, Vandals, and other barbarian tribes, Evelyn here argues, destroyed the elegant architecture of ancient Rome, introducing in its stead 'a certain Fantastical and Licentious manner of Building, which we have since call'd Modern (or *Gothic*) rather'.[16] Evelyn's Protestant biases come to the fore in his dismissal of Gothic architecture as 'Congestions of Heavy, Dark, Melancholy and *Monkish Piles*, without any just Proportion, Use or Beauty, compar'd with the truly Antient': not only was the Gothic aesthetically unappealing to the classical eye, it was also inherently Catholic and inextricably bound up with, and tainted by, what British Protestants took to be the superstitions of the old faith.[17] If classical architecture was 'Rich, Grave, and Stately', the Gothic was 'gross and heavy, or miserably trifling', an echo of Evelyn's rejection of the Gothic as the light and frivolous '*Cutwork* and *Crinkle Crankle*' that I discussed in the Introduction to this book.[18]

Evelyn's turn of phrase would be frequently repeated by Protestant opponents of Gothic architecture throughout the century. Christopher Wren, for instance, approvingly cited it in his dismissive account of the Gothic in *Parentalia* (1750).[19] The Church of England clergyman and author Conyers Middleton gave expression to a related and equally influential epithet when, in his biography of Cicero in *The History of the Life of M. Tullius Cicero* (1741), he recorded his dismay at discovering that the orator's house in Arpinum, Naples, 'is now possessed by a convent of Monks, and called the Villa of St Dominic'.[20] 'Strange revolution!' he remarks, 'to see Cicero's porticoes converted to *Monkish cloisters*! the seat of the most refined reason, wit, and learning, to a nursery of superstition, bigotry, and enthusiasm!'[21] The seat of classical learning had become a 'nursery of superstition', shades of the argument concerning the inescapably pagan, heretical origins of Roman Catholicism that Middleton had controversially advanced in his earlier *A Letter from Rome* (1729).

Following a bitter dispute with Richard Bentley—the Master of Trinity College, Cambridge, and the father of the member of Walpole's Strawberry Committee of the same name—Middleton had travelled to Rome in 1723, where, in a series of letters to his friends back in England, he had sought to show 'the *source* and *Origin* of the *Popish Ceremonies*, and the exact *Conformity* of them with those of their *Pagan Ancestors*'.[22] A compilation of this correspondence, *A Letter from Rome*

---

[16] Evelyn, *An Account of Architects and Architecture*, p. 5.
[17] Evelyn, *An Account of Architects and Architecture*, p. 5.
[18] Evelyn, *An Account of Architects and Architecture*, p. 27.
[19] Wren, Jnr, *Parentalia*, p. 308.
[20] Conyers Middleton, *The History of the Life of M. Tullius Cicero*, 3 vols (London: Printed for W. Innys and R. Manby, 1741), vol. 1, p. 5.
[21] Middleton, *The History of the Life of M. Tullius Cicero*, vol. 1, p. 6.
[22] Conyers Middleton, *A Letter from Rome, Showing an Exact Conformity between Popery and Paganism; or, The Religion of the Present Romans to be Derived Entirely from that of Their Heathen Ancestors* (London: Printed for W. Innys, 1729), p. 14.

pays particular attention to the ecclesiastical antiquities that the writer encountered: though setting out in search of the famed 'Classical Ground' of Cicero, Livy, Horace, and others, Middleton in Rome is appalled to discover that it is upon 'Pagan Ground' that he now treads.[23] Though notionally in the service of two different and opposing faiths, St Peter's, in effect, is indistinguishable from the Pantheon of heathen antiquity; throughout modern-day Rome, in fact, the 'Heathen Temples' of the pre-Christian past have simply been reconsecrated 'to the Popish Worship'.[24] The same applies to Catholic ceremonies and practices in general: like the large numbers of altars to be seen within Catholic cathedrals, the use of incense, perfumes, healing charms, talismans, holy water, the doctrine of transubstantiation, and the idol-like powers invested in the saints all attest to the '*Conformity of the Romish with the Pagan Worship*'.[25] As in his biography of Cicero and in the work of many other eighteenth-century writers, the key term in Middleton's exposé of Roman Catholicism is 'superstition', his aim here being to demonstrate the persistence of the 'old Superstition' of paganism in the theology and practice of modern Catholicism.[26] As the treatise concludes, Italian Catholics are 'worshipping at this Day in the *same Temples*; at the *same Altars*; sometimes the *same Images*; and always with the *same Ceremonies*, as the *old Romans*'.[27]

An avid classical scholar, Middleton would assemble an impressive collection of Roman antiquities during his sojourn in Italy; later, in 1744, these were sold to none other than Horace Walpole.[28] A mutual interest in antiquities, however, was not the sole point of connection between the two men: they were also affiliated through their mutual friend, the Cambridge-based antiquary William Cole, and Middleton and Horace himself had corresponded with one another from the late 1730s to the late 1740s. Albeit unsuccessfully, Sir Robert and Horace Walpole had both campaigned for Middleton's preferment in the Church in the late 1730s. While abroad in France in 1739, Walpole had collected from British expatriates in Paris subscriptions towards the publication of Middleton's *The History of the Life of M. Tullius Cicero*, a draft of which he had seen while at Cambridge;[29] upon publication, Middleton's biography drew between the Roman statesman and Sir Robert Walpole a number of favourable and thinly disguised comparisons that his son could only have admired.

The influence of Middleton on Walpole's perceptions of Catholicism, Gothic architecture, and the insuperable connections between them was considerable. In a letter to Middleton in November 1742, Walpole described himself as a 'friend

---

[23] Middleton, *A Letter from Rome*, p. 49.
[24] Middleton, *A Letter from Rome*, p. 36.
[25] Middleton, *A Letter from Rome*, p. 21.
[26] Middleton, *A Letter from Rome*, p. 36.
[27] Middleton, *A Letter from Rome*, p. 70.
[28] John A. Dussinger, 'Middleton, Conyers (1683–1750)', *ODNB*, http://www.oxforddnb.com/view/article/18669 (accessed 16 March 2017).
[29] See Horace Walpole to Conyers Middleton, 1 September 1739, *Correspondence*, vol. 15, pp. 6–7.

Figure 5.1 Conyers Middleton, D.D., Principal Librarian to the University of Cambridge, engraved by John Faber in 1751 from an original in the collection of the Honourable Horace Walpole. Courtesy of the Lewis Walpole Library, lwlpr15525.

and professed admirer' of the writer and his works;[30] Allen T. Hazen's *A Catalogue of Horace Walpole's Library* indicates that Walpole kept several titles by Middleton at Strawberry Hill, including his *Miscellaneous Works* (1752), a precis of *A Letter from Rome* in a tract entitled *Popery Unmask'd* (1744), and thirteen bound volumes of shorter tracts by Middleton as well as the numerous published responses that they elicited.[31] From 1740 onwards, Walpole also compiled the lengthy 'Anecdotes Relating to Dr Conyers Middleton' in his commonplace book, and displayed in the Bedchamber at Strawberry Hill John Giles Eccardt's portrait of Middleton that he had commissioned in 1746, John Faber's 1751 engraving of which appears in Figure 5.1.[32] The *Sermon on Painting* that Walpole delivered

---

[30] Horace Walpole to Conyers Middleton, 23 November 1742, *Correspondence*, vol. 15, p. 10.
[31] Hazen, *A Catalogue of Horace Walpole's Library*, vol. 1, pp. 97, 366.
[32] This manuscript has been published in Walpole's *Correspondence*, vol. 15, pp. 291–304.

before his father at Houghton in 1742 was a direct application of Middleton's principles: here, too, Catholicism is said to be of pagan origins insofar as it invests ordinary objects with religious significance—icons, images of the saints, the Madonna, and idols in canvas or stone.[33] In an earlier letter to Middleton on 22 November 1741, Walpole had expressed his admiration for *A Letter from Rome*, a copy of which he had recently received; 'The most natural proof of admiration', Walpole continued, 'is imitation', and so as to show his correspondent the sheer extent of his regard, Walpole enclosed a copy of a poem, 'An Epistle from Florence, to Thomas Ashton, Esq. Tutor to the Earl of Plimouth [sic]', that he had first drafted in Florence in 1740.[34] This flattering act of emulation, though, was accompanied by an earnest request: that Middleton refrain from letting copies of his poem 'slip about the University', since 'any zeal against popery', he reasoned, 'is not so meritorious with our clergy, as any liberty taken with priests of whatsoever profession, is heinous'.[35]

Walpole's sense of caution is understandable, for 'An Epistle from Florence' is, indeed, as vehemently anti-Catholic in tone as Middleton's *Letter*. First published in Richard Dodsley's *A Collection of Poems in Three Volumes* (1748), Walpole's 'Epistle' was later included in the first volume of his posthumous *Works* (1798). Like James Thomson's *Liberty*, the poem is a Whiggish celebration of the spirit of the goddess Liberty as she traverses centuries and continents from ancient Rome into modern Georgian Britain. Like Middleton, Walpole presents Catholicism as a crafty assimilation of ancient pagan beliefs, a doctrine that involves a powerful collusion between the powers of Church and State, and which results in the dreadful oppression of its devotees. Walpole is particularly suspicious of Catholic miracle-working in the poem, seeking, as did Middleton, to expose the chicanery and subterfuge that informs it: here, priests mumble utterances 'somewhat 'twixt a charm and pray'r', and 'squeeze out on the dull idol-board / A sore-eyed gum of tears'.[36] But what is particularly notable is his drawing upon Middleton's sense of ecclesiastical buildings as 'nurseries of superstition'. Walpole's vision of how the temples of pagan Italy have been seamlessly converted into sites of Catholic worship directly replays the argument of *A Letter from Rome*:

> Each temple with new weight of idols nods,
> And borrow'd altars smoke to other gods.
> PROMETHEUS' vulture MATTHEW'S eagle proves,
> And heav'nly cherubs sprout from heathen loves;

---

[33] See Horace Walpole, *Sermon on the Use and Abuse of Painting* (1742), LWL, Folio 49 2616 II MS.
[34] Horace Walpole to Conyers Middleton, 22 November 1741, *Correspondence*, vol. 15, p. 9.
[35] Horace Walpole to Conyers Middleton, 22 November 1741, *Correspondence*, vol. 15, p. 9.
[36] Horace Walpole, 'An Epistle from Florence, to Thomas Ashton, Esq. Tutor to the Earl of Plimouth [sic]', in *The Works of Horatio Walpole* (1798), vol. 1, pp. 4–16.

> Young GANYMEDE a winged angel stands
> By holy LUKE, and dictates God's commands:
> APOLLO, tho' degraded, still can bless,
> Rewarded with a sainthood, and an S.[37]

Though built according to classical, Italianate principles, the Catholic buildings of Rome assume architecturally 'Gothic' proportions. Described variously as 'cloister'd monkeries', fanes to 'FEAR', 'dark cloisters', and the 'darkling cell' of reason, the cathedrals, convents, monasteries, and other architectural structures that Walpole describes disclose their affinities with Middleton's 'monkish cloisters'.[38]

Of course, such anti-Catholic sentiments were not peculiar to Middleton, and in many ways he was only one exponent of what scholars have long described as the broader and more pervasive discourse of anti-Catholicism in eighteenth-century Britain.[39] Even so, it is difficult not to see in Walpole's literary works beyond the example of this particular poem direct echoes of Middleton. In *The Castle of Otranto*, for instance, Matilda is urged by her mother to offer 'orisons' to a portrait of Alfonso the Good that hangs in the castle's gallery, an obligation that, since 'he is no saint by the almanack', is unfathomable to her.[40] As in Middleton, and in keeping with Walpole's sentiments in the *Sermon on Painting*, Catholicism in *Otranto* arbitrarily makes idols of ordinary, unconsecrated objects. More trenchantly, when the portrait of Manfred's ancestor leaves its frame, and, later, when three drops of blood issue from the nose of the statue of Alfonso in a 'miraculous indication' that 'the blood of Alfonso will never mix with that of Manfred', Walpole appears to be drawing upon Middleton's argument concerning the false miracles of Catholicism in *A Letter from Rome*: 'Nothing is more common among the *Miracles of Popery*, than to hear of *Images* that on certain Occasions had *spoken*, or *shed Tears*; or *sweat*, or *bled*.'[41] As he does throughout the tract, Middleton traces these and other intimations of the miraculous in Catholic worship back to pagan sources: the weeping statue of Apollo and the bleeding statues and images of idols in the Temple of Juno in Livy.[42] Walpole's

---

[37] Walpole, 'An Epistle from Florence', p. 10.
[38] Walpole, 'An Epistle from Florence', pp. 5, 6, 11, 6.
[39] See, for example, Colin Haydon, *Anti-Catholicism in Eighteenth-Century England, c. 1714-80: A Political and Social Study* (Manchester and New York: Manchester University Press, 1993); S. J. Barnett, *Idol Temples and Crafty Priests: The Origins of Enlightenment Anticlericalism* (New York: St Martin's Press, 1999); Mark Canuel, *Religion, Toleration and British Writing, 1790-1830* (Cambridge: Cambridge University Press, 2002); Michael Mullett, *Catholics in Britain and Ireland, 1558-1829* (London: Macmillan, 1988); and E. R. Norman, *Anti-Catholicism in Victorian England* (London: Allen & Unwin, 1968).
[40] Walpole, *The Castle of Otranto*, pp. 38-9.
[41] Walpole, *The Castle of Otranto*, p. 89; Middleton, *A Letter from Rome*, p. 57. See, too, Milbank, *God and the Gothic*, pp. 71-2, for a discussion of Walpole's indebtedness in *Otranto* to Middleton's critique of miracles in *A Free Inquiry into the Miraculous Powers which are Supposed to have Subsisted in the Christian Church* of 1749.
[42] Middleton, *A Letter from Rome*, p. 57.

vision of the work of the 'artful priest' and the 'empire of superstition' over which he presides in *Otranto* looks directly to Middleton for inspiration.[43] Gothic architecture serves as the literal 'theatre' to the crimes, mysteries, and superstitions of the Catholic faith in *The Mysterious Mother* (1768) too. As Florian observes, the Castle of Narbonne, where the once-Catholic yet newly reformed Countess has secluded and surrounded herself with a host of clerical attendants, has become 'a theatre of holy interludes / And sainted frauds', its Gothic ramparts even now home to 'masses, mummings, goblins and processions'.[44] As Walpole in the subsequently published Postscript to the play pointed out, the villainy of Father Benedict in the piece was entirely consistent with the 'dark and superstitious age' in which it was set, and utterly in keeping with 'the crimes committed by Catholic churchmen' when the onset of the Reformation 'not only provoked their rage, but threatened them with total ruin'.[45] In this sense, *The Mysterious Mother* was an extension of Walpole's interest in what, in *Otranto*, William Marshal had described as the 'darkest ages of Christianity'.

The Work of Protestant Recuperation

If, as Linda Colley has argued, the very existence of 'Great Britain' from the passing of the Acts of Union in 1707 onwards depended upon a shared sense of Protestant identity between its constituent nations, Gothic architecture's associations with a dark and superstitious Catholic past presented nascent notions of national and cultural 'heritage' with a number of challenges.[46] Simply put, it was difficult for a nation that self-consciously identified, defined, and constituted itself as Protestant to harness what was taken to be an originally Catholic architectural style to its nationalist ideological agenda. Thomas Burgess registered as much in *An Essay on the Study of Antiquities* (1780), a tract that, like so many other antiquarian studies of its day, urged Britons to turn away from the pursuit of classical antiquities abroad so as to cultivate an attitude of 'attachment and generous partiality to the Antiquities of his own country'.[47] 'In surveying the proud monuments of feudal splendour and magnificence exhibited in the remains of ANTIENT CASTLES,' he argued, antiquaries might see 'amidst the venerable ruins' their associations with 'the many exercises of knighthood' and 'the very

---

[43] Walpole, *The Castle of Otranto*, p. 5.
[44] Horace Walpole, 'The Mysterious Mother: A Tragedy', in *Five Romantic Plays, 1768-1821*, ed. Paul Baines and Edward Burns (New York: Oxford University Press, 2000), pp. 1-69, Act V, scene i, ll. 125-32.
[45] Walpole, *The Mysterious Mother*, p. 69.
[46] See Linda Colley's argument in *Britons: Forging the Nation 1707-1837*, 2nd edn (New Haven and London: Yale University Press, 2005).
[47] Thomas Burgess, *An Essay on the Study of Antiquities* (Oxford, 1780), p. 13.

genius of Chivalry'.[48] If ruined castles were 'venerable', this was because they stood as patriotic testament to 'the generous virtues which were noursed [sic] in those schools of fortitude, honour, courtesy, and wit'; once 'the mansions of our ancient nobility', ruined castles were the 'vestiges of former Hospitality and munificence, the pride and ornament of England'.[49] Monastical ruins, by contrast, necessitated a far more cautious response, one in which the fair-minded antiquary ought rationally and diligently to separate out any vestige of cultural value from a site of antiquity otherwise given over to Catholic licentiousness, indolence, and ignorance. As Burgess writes,

> There is another part of British Antiquities, in the prosecution of which we cannot sufficiently admire the indefatigable diligence and extensive learning employed in collecting the immense treasure of records contained in our MONASTIC antiquities. Though the history of these religious institutions exhibit too many instances of licentiousness, indolence, and ignorance; yet we ought with gratitude to remember that though the inhabitants of the Cloyster [sic] were themselves, for the most part, lost to all good taste, they prevented the surrounding barbarism of those dark Ages from entirely extinguishing the light of classical learning; and that to them was owing the preservation of the most valuable ancient authors, the various discourses of which constitute so interesting a part in the history of Learning.[50]

While the antiquary might, at first sight, be swayed by a monastic ruin's associations with darkness, barbarity, and superstition, he ought to suspend these judgements and actively recall the positive role that abbeys, monasteries, and convents played in the nurturing of classical scholarship. Situated at the limits of the discourse of venerable ruin, the appreciation and valuing of ecclesiastical piles depended upon willed and deliberate acts of reassessment.

Several writers of the period demonstrate just how self-conscious such acts of aesthetic, antiquarian, and political recuperation could be. Ultimately, nothing less than the precise nature of Gothic antiquity was at stake: while 'venerable ruins' incarnated a past of piety and spiritual virtue, 'monkish piles' implied a dark history of ignorance and superstition; as I have suggested throughout this book, Gothic architecture in the eighteenth century was always much more than a matter of style. In 'On Monastic Institutions', an essay that she had published in her and her brother John's collaborative collection *Miscellaneous Pieces, in Prose* (1773), Anna Laetitia Aikin described a walk to 'the venerable ruins of an old Abbey' in an unspecified location in the English countryside.[51] Drawing strongly

---

[48] Burgess, *An Essay on the Study of Antiquities*, p. 16.
[49] Burgess, *An Essay on the Study of Antiquities*, pp. 16–17.
[50] Burgess, *An Essay on the Study of Antiquities*, p. 17.
[51] A. L. Aikin, 'On Monastic Institutions', in *Miscellaneous Pieces, in Prose*, by J. and A. L. Aikin (London: Printed for J. Johnson, 1773), pp. 88–118 (p. 88). That this piece was written by Anna Laetitia

upon the aesthetics of architectural association, Aikin's piece begins by describing how she indulged before the pile in 'a train of ideas relative to the scene', initially regarding, in the fashion of many a 'good protestant' before her, the mere sight of ruin as the 'secret triumph' of the Reformation over the 'haunts of ignorance and superstition'.[52] Her references to associationism and Protestantism within the essay's opening moments are especially revealing: as Isobel Grundy has observed, associationist aesthetics were central to the literary cultures of rational Dissent to which Aikin and her circle belonged.[53] With 'venerable' ruin already placed under considerable strain, though, the essay continues to describe the associations that the pile provokes, a concatenation of negative impressions summed up in Evelyn's splenetic notion of 'Monkish Piles':

> Ye are fallen, said I, ye dark and gloomy mansions of mistaken zeal, where the proud priest and lazy monk fatten'd upon the riches of the land, and crept like vermin from their cells to spread their poisonous doctrines through the nation, and disturb the peace of kings. Obscure in their origin, but daring and ambitious in their guilt![54]

With its stained-glass windows, dark recesses, and gloomy arches, Gothic architecture for Aikin becomes the style that is best suited to the theological contrivances of the Catholic faith, a point that, as I argued in Chapter 1, is consonant with Thomas Warton's sensitivities to the 'superstitions' evoked by the Gothic in *Verses on Sir Joshua Reynolds's Painted Window at New-College Oxford*, and the same religious associations on which John Soane would comment in his fifth lecture at the Royal Academy so many years later. For Aikin, at least initially in the essay, the 'pure light' of heaven is 'clouded' by the 'dim glass' of the arched windows and 'stained' with 'monkish tales and legendary fiction', all fitting emblems of how 'reluctantly' the Catholics who worshipped there 'admitted the fairer light of truth amidst these dark recesses, and how much they have debased its genuine lustre!'; 'far from impressing on the mind the idea of the God of truth and love', the sublime obscurity of the Gothic abbey—its 'low cells, the long and narrow aisles, the gloomy arches, the damp and secret caverns which wind beneath the hollow ground'—are 'only fit for those dark places of the earth in which are the habitations of cruelty'.[55] The general sense of approbation informing Walpole's claim in

---

and not her brother John is attested to by its inclusion in *The Works of Anna Laetitia Barbauld, with a Memoir by Lucy Aikin*, 2 vols (London: Printed for Longman, Hurst, Rees, Orme, Brown, and Green, 1825), vol. 2, pp. 195–213.

[52] Aikin, 'On Monastic Institutions', pp. 88–9.
[53] Isobel Grundy, 'Anna Letitia Barbauld: A Unitarian Poetics?', in *Anna Letitia Barbauld: New Perspectives*, ed. William McCarthy and Olivia Murphy (Lewisburg: Bucknell University Press, 2014), pp. 59–81.
[54] Aikin, 'On Monastic Institutions', p. 89.
[55] Aikin, 'On Monastic Institutions', pp. 89–90.

the *Anecdotes of Painting* that 'Gothic churches inspire superstition', the Grecian style mere 'admiration', has been replayed here to greater anti-Catholic effect.

Mistaken zeal, poisonous doctrines, labyrinthine passages, and sybaritic monks and priests: these Gothic-architectural associations accord well with what Colin Haydon has identified as the vociferously anti-Catholic strain in eighteenth-century Dissent, though embodied here in responses to architectural ruin. Even though the arch-Dissenter Joseph Priestley wished to extend the principles of religious toleration to disenfranchised Catholics, he and other Unitarians opposed the authority of Rome on a number of accounts, including its reliance upon scriptural authority, its uncritical embrace of the Trinity, and its slavish commitment to precedent and historical tradition.[56] John Aikin had articulated an almost identical set of associations in the important essay on the contemporary aesthetic, imaginative, and antiquarian 'passion' for ruins that he published in 1793.[57] Prompted by his son's visit to the 'celebrated ruins' of an unnamed English abbey, an unsentimental Aikin is eventually led to dismiss the associations generated by 'the relics of antiquity in this country' as 'trifling effects on the heart', the ideas that Gothic ruins inspire 'offering nothing dignified or pleasing to the mind'.[58] Though his convictions are well illustrated in his account of the tyrannous political practices of the past that are called to mind by the ruins of a 'castellated mansion', it is his denunciation of the awful associations of ecclesiastical ruins that is of particular interest:

> And if we look back to the original state of our ordinary monastic remains, what shall we see, but a set of beings engaged in a dull round of indolent pleasures, and superstitious practices, alike debasing to the heart and understanding? We are rejoiced that their date is past; and we can have little inducement to recal [sic] them from that oblivion into which they are deservedly sunk, and which best accords with their primitive insignificance.[59]

If Gothic is the architecture of reviled popery, its ruins might only occasion in self-identifying Protestants the triumphant expression of delight: 'Farewel [sic], ye once venerated seats!' Anna Laetitia cries; 'enough of you remains, and may it always remain, to remind us from what we have escaped, and make posterity for ever [sic] thankful for this fairer age of liberty and light'.[60]

What is notable about 'On Monastic Institutions', however, is the way in which its anti-Catholicism gradually cedes to a much more measured and considered approach. '[I]t is cruel to insult a fallen enemy,' Aikin claims, as she begins to chart

---

[56] Haydon, *Anti-Catholicism in Eighteenth-Century England, c. 1714–80*, pp. 61–4.
[57] John Aikin, 'Letter XXIV. On Ruins', in *Letters from A Father to His Son, on Various Topics, Relative to Literature and the Conduct of Life, Written in the Years 1792 and 1793* (London: Printed for J. Johnson, 1793), pp. 262–73.
[58] Aikin, 'Letter XXIV. On Ruins', p. 270.   [59] Aikin, 'Letter XXIV. On Ruins', pp. 270–1.
[60] Aikin, 'On Monastic Institutions', p. 90.

a marked transition in her mental associations from those just described to an altogether 'different train of thought'.[61] Though undoubtedly productive of 'much mischief and superstition', monastic institutions ought to be credited for having spread 'the glimmering of a feeble ray of knowledge, through that thick night which once involved the western hemisphere'.[62] Homer and Aristotle, among others, took shelter there from 'the rage of gothic ignorance', while even the foundational structures of Roman law, and hence the modern system of jurisprudence, were preserved only through monkish efforts. Monks, Aikin continues, were also important chroniclers of their times, and though their histories are 'interwoven with many a legendary tale, and darkened by much superstition', they nonetheless saved civilization from a more dreadful fate: the prospect of having 'no histories at all'.[63] Aikin is particularly preoccupied with the rich literary cultures of the Middle Ages, and pays warm tribute to the important role that monasteries played in the production and appreciation of literature. Fostering the arts of statuary, painting, and rhetoric, monasteries and convents were the sites of intense creativity, and thus 'the Muses, with their attendant arts (in strange disguise indeed, and uncouth trappings) took refuge in the peaceful gloom of the convent'.[64] Other aspects of this renewed vision of Gothic antiquity in the essay accord well with the politics of rational Dissent: it was the Church's contact with Rome, Aikin claims, that served to 'temper' the severities of absolute monarchical government, the Church's congress with the Pope having exposed England to the scientific and intellectual developments of continental Europe.[65] Her sense of the morality of monasticism, too, fits well with Calvinist principles: dependent on the practices of chastity, obedience, poverty, and self-denial, convents and monasteries 'were schools of some high and respectable virtues'—a far cry from the indolence and debauchery of monastic life later denounced by her brother.[66] And prior to the advent of hospitals, monasteries administered medical help to those in need, and sustained the indigent through extraordinary acts of kindness. Seats of learning, art, industry, hospitality, and charity: these are just some of the many virtues of monastic institutions that Aikin in the essay comes to celebrate.

Though initially evocative of the negative associations enshrined in the phrase 'Monkish Piles', Aikin's ruined abbey eventually comes to occupy the nostalgic antiquarian's territory of 'venerable ruin'. This act of architectural reframing brings with it a reconfiguration of her perceptions of Gothic antiquity, from an epoch of untold savagery and darkness to one of charity, learning, and enlightenment. But this has not been achieved without effort, for as a writer such as Burgess had noted, monastical ruins could not be construed as 'venerable ruins' in any simple or straightforward way. What becomes apparent throughout Aikin's

---

[61] Aikin, 'On Monastic Institutions', p. 90.
[62] Aikin, 'On Monastic Institutions', p. 91.
[63] Aikin, 'On Monastic Institutions', p. 94.
[64] Aikin, 'On Monastic Institutions', p. 99.
[65] Aikin, 'On Monastic Institutions', p. 101.
[66] Aikin, 'On Monastic Institutions', p. 106.

piece, in fact, is just how concerted the recuperation of Gothic ruin as a relic of a noble, national religious tradition has been, for, in place of mental ideas spontaneously conjured up through the aesthetic of architectural association, it is only through a deliberate act of rational cogitation, one that resists and works against associative chains, that she is eventually able to bring to mind some of the positive functions that such institutions fulfilled 'during the barbarous ages in which they flourished'.[67] Even so, the essay ends on a careful qualification: though not without their merits, monastic institutions ultimately remained keen to 'exclude' the 'fuller day of science' just as it began to dawn, content merely that 'the dim lamp might still glimmer in their cell'.[68] 'After all that can be said,' Aikin concludes, 'we have reason enough to rejoice that the superstitions of former times are now fallen into disrepute.'[69]

Other writers of the period demonstrate similar vacillations between the discursive poles of 'Monkish Piles' and 'venerable ruin' and the competing visions of Gothic antiquity that each enshrined. In a journal entry of 19 August 1791 Frances Burney recorded a visit to the ruins of Glastonbury Abbey, Somerset, ambivalently phrasing her impressions in terms that are underpinned by her assumptions of their 'venerable' nature: 'These are the most elegant remains of monkish grandeur I have ever chanced to see,—the forms, designs, ornaments,—all that is left is in the highest perfection of Gothic beauty.'[70] Though she is 'quite bewitched with their antique beauty', these venerable ruins soon shade into a nursery of superstition, as Burney learns from a local tour guide the legend that circulates at Glastonbury around the healing properties of a magical well, a superstitious remainder in the landscape that seems to have escaped the extremes of Protestant reform.[71] 'What strange inventions and superstitions even the ruins of what had belonged to St. Dunstan can yet engender!' she exclaims—so overwhelming, in fact, that she quite forgets to enquire about the whereabouts of the Glastonbury Thorn, the other object of apocryphal Christian legend at the abbey.

William Gilpin's experiences at Glastonbury in *Observations on the Western Parts of England* (1798) were characterized by a similar oscillation. These architectural remains are 'venerable' insofar as they attest for Gilpin, as for Burgess and eventually for Anna Laetitia Aikin, to the education and maintenance of 400 children; the offering of hospitality to travellers; and the dispensing of charity to the needy and indigent; 'all this', Gilpin reasons, 'appears great and noble'.[72] 'On the other hand,' he argues in a startling change of direction,

---

[67] Aikin, 'On Monastic Institutions', pp. 90–1.   [68] Aikin, 'On Monastic Institutions', p. 117.
[69] Aikin, 'On Monastic Institutions', p. 117.
[70] Frances Burney, *Diary and Letters of Madame D'Arblay, Author of Evelina, Cecilia, &c. Edited by her Niece*, 7 vols (London: Henry Colburn, 1842), vol. 5, p. 246.
[71] Although Burney is not specific about this, she is in all likelihood referring to the nearby Chalice Well of popular legend.
[72] William Gilpin, *Observations on the Western Parts of England, Relative Chiefly to Picturesque Beauty* (London: Printed for T. Cadell Jun. and W. Davies, 1798), p. 138.

when we consider five hundred persons, bred up in indolence, and lost to the commonwealth; when we consider that these houses were the great nurseries of superstition, bigotry, and ignorance; the stews of sloth, stupidity, and perhaps intemperance; when we consider, that the education received in them had not the least tincture of useful learning, good manners, or true religion, but tended rather to vilify and disgrace the human mind; when we consider that the pilgrims and strangers who resorted thither, were idle vagabonds, who got nothing abroad that was equivalent to the occupations they left at home; and when we consider, lastly, that indiscriminate alms-giving is not real charity, but an avocation from labour and industry, checking every idea of exertion, and filling the mind with abject notions, we are led to acquiesce in the fate of these great foundations, and view their ruins, not only with a picturesque eye, but with moral and religious satisfaction.[73]

More than 'nurseries of superstition', Gilpin's Gothic abbeys are also the 'stews' of sloth, stupidity, and intemperance, the houses of false charity, callow learning, and dangerous economic inactivity. The anti-Catholicism of a writer such as John Aikin could curiously serve Gilpin's High Church Anglicanism well. Having surveyed both sides of the venerable ruin/monkish pile divide, Gilpin's picturesque aesthetic is troubled by an irrepressible memory of the latter. The only workable alternative, he suggests, is to exorcize ecclesiastical antiquities of their shameful and dishonourable past, appropriating them in the present as two-dimensional objects lacking in all points of historical and religious reference. While the histories that played themselves out in their interiors were the stuff of Protestant horror, their rugged, irregular exteriors, once abstracted, might be rendered pleasing to the Protestant picturesque eye. The matter, ultimately, hinged upon the difference between historical depth and spatial surface, between a building's interior and its exterior. Occluding the former so as to focus the Claude glass squarely on the latter, the aesthetic of the picturesque depended, as of old, upon a process of willed amnesia.

Fictional Expressions

Such shifts in perception, from those piles of monkish superstition to Gothic antiquity's venerable remains and back again, were by no means an exclusively topographical phenomenon. Indeed, the dynamic is crucial to understanding the ambivalences towards Catholicism, monasticism, and its architectural legacy that we see in the fiction of a writer such as Ann Radcliffe. Both poles of the discourse are brought to bear in the first appearance of an ecclesiastical ruin in Radcliffe's

[73] Gilpin, *Observations on the Western Parts of England*, pp. 138–9.

oeuvre, the description of the ruined abbey that the abducted Mary perceives on the Scottish landscape towards the end of *The Castles of Athlin and Dunbayne*: although it stands as 'a monument of mortality and of ancient superstition', its 'frowning majesty' also 'seemed to command silence and veneration'.[74] These ambivalences are amplified in *A Sicilian Romance*, when the fugitive heroine Julia, in flight from her patriarchal oppressors, makes of the monastery of St Augustin a temporary home. Insofar as the monastery's interiors provide her with a 'secure retreat', and the nuns who inhabit it a source of sweet and amiable conversation, St Augustin is a 'venerable' pile.[75] The Duke De Luovo enjoys similar hospitality and kindness during his temporary residence in a Sicilian monastery earlier in the narrative. Simultaneously, however, Radcliffe's narrator renders St Augustin in its external prospects as a nursery of monkish superstition, its 'large mass of Gothic architecture' of the twelfth century 'a proud monument of monkish superstition and princely magnificence'.[76] Her architectural imagination duly inspired by such associations, Julia responds with the penning of a poem, 'Superstition: An Ode', an act of literary creativity that is clearly motivated by the Radcliffean aesthetic of 'attendant circumstance', and which repeats the links between Gothic architecture and Catholic superstition that was germane throughout the century.[77] What is notable at this early point in Radcliffe's career, though, is the vague and imprecise nature of her architectural vocabulary: lacking in any discrimination between various styles or historical periods of Gothic, the description also conflates battlements and towers, structures more usually reserved for castles, with ecclesiastical buildings. Nonetheless, it is the 'sacred gloom' of the place that serves as a fitting emblem of the Catholic Middle Ages: even the stained-glass windows, Radcliffe, like Anna Laetitia Aikin, observes, show depictions of 'monkish fictions'.[78]

And so, the polarized terms of the discourse on ecclesiastical architecture inform the depiction of monasteries, abbeys, and convents throughout Radcliffe's major works. While these institutions, both ruined and complete, often embody a nightmarish past of superstition, oppression, and thwarted conjugal desire, they also often provide the full moral scope of Radcliffe's characters with hospitality, refuge, and security. In the positive functions that they fulfil, Radcliffe's monastic institutions embody many of the virtues that Aikin had enumerated in her essay on the topic, among them safety, chastity, sites of repentance, female companionship, employment, and much-needed retirement from a life of turmoil and loss. It is clear that Radcliffe had read the Aikins' *Miscellaneous Pieces* with considerable care: in addition to her echoing 'On Monastic Institutions', she directly alludes to, and rewrites, John Aikin's Gothic story 'Sir Bertrand, A Fragment' in her account

---

[74] Radcliffe, *The Castles of Athlin and Dunbayne*, p. 102.
[75] Radcliffe, *A Sicilian Romance*, p. 109.   [76] Radcliffe, *A Sicilian Romance*, p. 117.
[77] See Radcliffe's discussion of this in 'On the Supernatural in Poetry', *The New Monthly Magazine and Literary Journal* vol. 16, no.1 (1826): pp. 145–52.
[78] Radcliffe, *A Sicilian Romance*, p. 117.

of Emily's passage from Montoni's castle to Tuscany in the company of Bertrand in Volume 3 of *Udolpho*.[79]

What is particularly notable about the mature works, though, is the way in which they follow Gilpin's lead in superimposing the monkish pile/venerable ruin divide upon the difference between a building's interiors and exteriors. In *Udolpho*, for example, Blanche, recently released from the veil, is able to critique monastical existence on the basis of her first-hand experience of life inside a convent:

> 'Who could first invent convents!' said she, 'and who could first persuade people to go into them? and to make religion a pretence, too, where all that should inspire it, is so carefully shut out!...I never felt so much devotion, during the many dull years I was in the convent, as I have done in the few hours, that I have been here, where I need only look on all around me—to adore God in my inmost heart!'[80]

The divine not deigning to reside within them, convents are little more than nurseries of Catholic superstition. Shortly thereafter, however, when Blanche, her father, and Emily travel to the nearby monastery of St Claire, Radcliffe's description of the exterior of the partial ruin makes much of its 'venerable' nature as it lingers over the features of the edifice to observe 'the great grate and gothic window of the hall', 'the cloisters and the side of a chapel more remote', the 'venerable arch', and the 'majestic ruin'.[81] The monkish piles of history and lived personal experience might become the venerable ruins of the modern present only once they have been aesthetically reappropriated through Gilpin's picturesque frame. In *The Italian*, the difference between these two types of ecclesiastic structures becomes more pronounced. As I observed in Chapter 3, Radcliffe, apparently in response to those critics who accused her of anachronism and inaccuracy in *Udolpho*, suspends 'Gothic' as a term of architectural description in her next fiction. Though these buildings are nominally figured as classical or Italianate in design in *The Italian*, subtle intimations of the Gothic style nonetheless return in her depiction of ecclesiastical institutions, and this largely through the poetry that she cites to describe them. When Vivaldi first catches sight of the prisons of the Inquisition in Rome, for instance, the narrator describes their foreboding prospects and the gloomy prison guard before them as instances of 'Grim-visaged comfortless Despair', a line taken from Thomas Gray's address to the 'distant spires' and 'antique towers' of the Gothic Eton College Chapel in *An Ode on a Distant Prospect of Eton College* (1747).[82] Richard Bentley's tailpiece for

---

[79] Radcliffe, *The Mysteries of Udolpho*, pp. 407–10.
[80] Radcliffe, *The Mysteries of Udolpho*, p. 476.
[81] Radcliffe, *The Mysteries of Udolpho*, p. 482.
[82] Radcliffe, *The Italian*, p. 196. For the first edition of Gray's poem, see *An Ode on a Distant Prospect of Eton College* (London: Printed for R. Dodsley, 1747), p. 6.

Figure 5.2 Richard Bentley's tailpiece for Thomas Gray's 'Ode on a Distant Prospect of Eton College' published in *Designs by Mr R. Bentley, for Six Poems by Mr T. Gray* (1753). Courtesy of the Lewis Walpole Library, lwlpr16187.

the 1753 illustrated edition of Gray's poems, possibly the edition from which Radcliffe worked, depicts Eton's Gothic prospects clearly (see Figure 5.2). Classical architecture becomes architecturally and aesthetically 'Gothic' in *The Italian* through an act of poetic citation, and, as in her use of *capriccio* in *Udolpho*, Radcliffe relocates the English Gothic Eton to continental Europe. Of the many monastic institutions that populate the fiction, the Convent of San Stefano, in which Ellena di Rosalba is secreted after her abduction, and the Convent of Santa della Pietà, to which she thereafter retires, are the most important. The text relies heavily on the contrasts between the two: while San Stefano is a place of fear, coercion, imprisonment, and 'superstitious wonder', Santa della Pietà offers the heroine rest, safety, and asylum.[83] The ambivalences characterizing the presentation of abbeys and convents in the earlier fictions seem to have been separated out in *The Italian* into two distinct types of monastical institutions, the more favourable of the two founded, again, on the same constellation of values that

[83] Radcliffe, *The Italian*, p. 138.

Aikin had identified in 'On Monastical Institutions'. Here, in other words, Radcliffe's 'two-castle model' receives its ecclesiastical equivalent.

As critics have long noted, *The Italian* was, at least in part, Radcliffe's riposte to, and correction of, the excesses of Matthew Gregory Lewis's *The Monk* (1796) and other horrid fictions of the German, so-called 'male' Gothic school. Certainly, the contrasts between Radcliffe's picturesque, sometimes sentimental approach to monastic institutions and that of Lewis could not be starker. In *The Monk*, Lewis homophonically responds to the picturesque exteriors of the Convent of St Claire from *Udolpho* with the gloomy interiors of his own Convent of St Clare, in the fetid sepulchre beneath which Ambrosio and Matilda engage in acts of illicit sexuality and satanic conjuration. It is also within St Clare's vaulted sepulchres that the emaciated Sister Agnes and the corpse of her baby are eventually found, the sight of which provokes in Lorenzo the responses of horror, disgust, and pity.[84] Strongly influenced by Lewis, William Henry Ireland would put subterranean ecclesiastical space to similar use in his depiction of the Convent of Santa-Maria del Nova, Florence, in *The Abbess* (1799). Later, Charles Maturin would follow suit in the 'Tale of the Spaniard' in *Melmoth the Wanderer* (1820), the reluctant monk Alonzo Monçada's harrowing tale of confinement and torture within a Jesuit monastery. All three narratives are driven by the logic of disclosure, the revelation of ghastly Catholic horrors lurking behind seemingly picturesque ecclesiastical facades. As Maturin's Spaniard puts it, the experience of monastic life is 'like the wrong side of a tapestry, where we see only uncouth threads, and the harsh outlines, without the glow of the colours, the richness of the tissue, or the splendor of the embroidery, that renders the external surface so rich and dazzling; all this was carefully concealed'.[85] It is the task of the narrative to let this untidy finish gape. While their exteriors might be aesthetically beautiful and picturesque, their interiors harbour the stuff of horror.

Maturin, Anglican curate of St Peter's, Dublin, would consistently link Catholicism with the rhetoric of horror in his published *Sermons* (1819) and in his *Five Sermons, On the Errors of the Roman Catholic Church* (1826). In presenting their fictional convents, abbeys, and monasteries as sites of extreme horror, Lewis, Ireland, Maturin, and other exponents of Hoeveler's 'Gothic ideology' were drawing upon a tradition that, as I argued in Chapter 1, went as far back as Joseph Addison's essay 'No. 110' of 1711: the 'awfulness' of the ruined abbey that poured out its 'supernumerary horrors' upon everything in and around it, a turn of phrase that would be repeated in Robert Blair's *The Grave* (1743). The minor eighteenth-century poet Edward Jerningham did much to turn the 'supernumerary horrors'

---

[84] Matthew Lewis, *The Monk, A Romance*, ed. D. L. Macdonald and Kathleen Scherf (Peterborough, ON: Broadview Press, 2004), p. 303.
[85] Charles Maturin, *Melmoth the Wanderer*, ed. Douglas Grant, introd. Chris Baldick (Oxford: Oxford University Press, 1989), p. 76.

of graveyard verse of the 1740s into the vivid Gothic horrors of a Lewis or a Maturin. Though born into a wealthy landed Catholic family in Norfolk, and theologically trained at the English College, a Catholic seminary in Douai, France, Jerningham remained an ardent critic of the Catholic faith, later converting to Protestantism during the 1790s. Socially well connected, Jerningham enjoyed correspondence, friendship, and literary exchange with such important contemporary figures as Edmund Burke and Horace Walpole, seeing in the latter a mentor or a patron of sorts. In *An Elegy Written Among the Ruins of an Abbey* (1765), he turned his hand to the fashionable poetry of ecclesiastical ruin, describing, as in so many poems in this tradition, the dissolution of the monasteries as the felicitous vanquishing of 'tow'ring Superstition'.[86] As Michael Charlesworth has argued, the ruined abbey, in itself, was thought to embody the 'glories' of the English Reformation, and served the eighteenth century as metonym for the triumph of Protestantism over Catholicism.[87] This had been written into Whiggish, Protestant historiography of the Reformation ever since Bishop Gilbert Burnet's influential three-volume *The History of the Reformation of the Church of England* (1679–1714), the first fully documented account of King Henry's break from Rome and a response to Nicholas Sanders's questioning of the legitimacy of the Church of England in *De origine et progressu schismatio Anglicani libri tres* (1585; reissued in a new French translation in the mid-1670s).[88] The still officially Catholic Jerningham perpetuated these assumptions in his *Elegy*. Through a reworking of Addison, Blair, and Thomas Gray's *Elegy Written in a Country Churchyard* (1751), the darkened ruin in the poem becomes the site of unmitigated horror as a pack of wolves rushes into it to exhume and then devour the corpse of one Rufus, the abbey's erstwhile founder, that is buried within:

> When, horrid to relate! they burst the Tomb,
> And swift descending to the deepest Shade,
> Up-tore the shrouded Tenant from its Womb,
> And o'er the mangled Corse relentless prey'd.
> The paly Stars with dim reluctant Light,
> Like Tapers glimmer'd on their Orgies foul,
> While gliding Spectres scream'd with wild Affright,
> Re-echo'd loud by their tremendous Howl.[89]

Here, too, ecclesiastical ruin is the site of supernumerary horror, a clear echo of the work of Addison and Blair earlier in the century. It is not coincidental that

---

[86] Edward Jerningham, *An Elegy Written Among the Ruins of an Abbey*, 2nd edn (London: Printed for J. Dodsley, 1765), p. 5.
[87] Charlesworth, 'The ruined abbey: Picturesque and Gothic Values', p. 69.
[88] Martin Greig, 'Burnet, Gilbert (1643–1715)', *ODNB*, https://doi.org/10.1093/ref:odnb/4061 (accessed 13 October 2018).
[89] Jerningham, *An Elegy Written Among the Ruins of an Abbey*, p. 13.

Lewis would explicitly align himself with this tradition in *The Monk*, citing the extract in which Blair uses the phrase 'supernumerary horror' as an epigraph to the section in which the horrors of the sepulchre of St Clare are, indeed, the most vividly realized.[90] As Angela Wright has observed, however, Lewis's anti-Catholicism was as much indebted to Continental sources as it was to the English tradition: his presentation of the convent in *The Monk* is strongly influenced by the anti-clerical dramas that he attended in post-revolutionary Paris of the early 1790s, among them Benoît-Joseph Marsollier's *Camille, ou le souterrain* (1791) and Jacques-Marie Boutet de Monvel's *Les Victimes cloîtrées* (1791).[91]

From Romance to Antiquarianism

Radcliffe's departure from this tradition of Gothic writing in *The Italian* would become even more pronounced in her works that were published in four capacious volumes three years after her death. In addition to demonstrating the writer's ever-increasing remoteness from the sensationalism of her imitators, *Gaston De Blondeville*, 'St Alban's Abbey, A Metrical Tale', and their accompanying texts and journal entries also bear witness to a notable change in Radcliffe's own architectural imagination, one that might be summed up as the shift from romance, both the 'pure' romance of the earlier novels and the topographical romance of the *Journey*, to antiquarianism. While the first of these encoded responses to Gothic architecture that were technically imprecise and overtly imaginative, the second tempered and qualified these impressions with considerable antiquarian rigour and detail. As Rictor Norton has argued, 'St Alban's Abbey' was probably composed in 1808-9, following at least two day trips to the Cathedral and Abbey Church of St Alban, Hertfordshire, that Ann and her husband William appear to have made in 1802 and 1808.[92] The site was of particular significance for Gothic-architectural enthusiasts of the Radcliffes' ilk: the location of Britain's first Christian martyrdom, it also exhibited, as the endnotes to the poem confirm, 'the styles of architecture of several ages', from Roman, through the earliest Saxon, and down to later Tudor additions.[93] Historically, the abbey had played a strategic role in the first Battle of St Albans, the inaugurating event of the Wars of the Roses that began in May 1455. Despite the 'monkish' expectations conjured up by the poem's title, then, it is these military

---

[90] Lewis, *The Monk*, p. 228.
[91] Wright, *Britain, France and the Gothic, 1764-1820*, pp. 127-31.
[92] Norton, *Mistress of Udolpho*, p. 200.
[93] Ann Radcliffe, 'St Alban's Abbey, A Metrical Tale', in *Gaston De Blondeville; or, The Court of Henry III Keeping Festival in Ardenne, A Romance and St Alban's Abbey: A Metrical Tale; With Some Poetical Pieces*, 4 vols (London: Henry Colburn, 1826), vols 3-4 (vol. 4, p. 48).

exploits and their immediate consequences that the narrative explores, to the extent that St Albans comes to function more like a castle than a monastical pile.

In its form, arrangement, and subject matter, 'St Alban's Abbey' demonstrates the strong formative influence of the metrical romances of Walter Scott, particularly *The Lay of the Last Minstrel* (1805) and *Marmion* (1808). While it is well known that Scott was a reader of Radcliffe, critics have overlooked the extent to which Radcliffe read Scott. Thomas Noon Talfourd tells us that she 'devoured the earlier Scotch novels with all the avidity of youth, although she felt deeply a slighting expression in "Waverley" towards herself, which the author might have spared'.[94] Whereas the antiquarian Scott had intended the *Lay* as an illustration of 'the customs and manners which anciently prevailed on the Borders of England and Scotland', so Radcliffe explores in 'St Alban's Abbey' a vision of English clerical and military life in the fifteenth century.[95] Again like Scott, the opening invocation directly courts the 'Spirit of ancient days! who o'er these walls / Unseen and silent hold'st thy solemn state'; here, as elsewhere in the Gothic, it is primarily through architectural ruin that visions of Gothic antiquity might be accessed.[96] Canto I opens with an evocative description of the eponymous pile:

> Know ye that pale and ancient choir,
> Whose Norman tower lifts it's [*sic*] pinnacled spire?
> Where the long Abbey-aisle extends
> And battled roof o'er roof ascends;
> Cornered with buttresses shapely and small,
> That sheltered the Saint in canopied stall;
> And, lightened with hanging turrets fair,
> That so proudly their dental coronals wear,
> They blend with a holy, a warlike air,
> While they guard the Martyr's tomb beneath,
> And patient warriors, laid in death?[97]

Having traced, through a series of rhetorical questions, the pleasing view of St Albans's transept, its turrets, and its battlements under the light of 'the soft blue sky', the second stanza includes a sudden peripatetic shift when the persona notes that, for all their beauty, 'Yet lovelier far their forms appear / When they lift their heads in the moonlight air', a deliberate echo of the opening stanza of Canto Second in Scott's *Lay*: 'If thou would'st view fair Melrose aright, / Go visit it by the pale moonlight; / For the gay beams of lightsome day / Gild, but to flout, the ruins grey.'[98] Having learned from the Wizard of the North that ecclesiastical ruins are

---

[94] Talfourd, 'Memoir of the Life and Writings of Mrs Radcliffe', vol. 1, p. 99.
[95] Walter Scott, 'The Lay of the Last Minstrel', in *Scott: Poetical Works, With the Author's Introduction and Notes*, ed. J. Logie Robertson (London: Oxford University Press, 1971), pp. 1–88 (p. 1).
[96] Radcliffe, 'St Alban's Abbey', vol. 3, p. 91.   [97] Radcliffe, 'St Alban's Abbey', vol. 3, p, 93.
[98] Scott, 'The Lay of the Last Minstrel', p. 8.

244 GOTHIC ANTIQUITY

best viewed by moonlight, the Great Enchantress gives the remainder of the canto over to a description of St Albans by nightfall.

Radcliffe also appears to have looked to Scott's poetry as a model for the appropriate use and presentation of antiquarian material. As in the *Lay*, the endnotes to 'St Alban's Abbey', which run to some sixty-nine pages, 'authenticate' the foregoing verse with antiquarian detail derived from, among other sources, Peter Newcome's *The History of the Ancient and Royal Foundation, Called the Abbey of St Alban* (1793); Richard Gough's *British Topography* (1780); Browne Willis's *An History of the Mitred Parliamentary Abbies*; the thirteenth-century manuscripts of Matthew Paris; Thomas Warton's *The History of English Poetry* (1774–81); and Walpole's *Anecdotes of Painting in England*.[99] Norton is particularly dismissive of this antiquarian paraphernalia, claiming that Radcliffe's turn from Gothic romance to Gothic antiquarianism in 'St Alban's Abbey' brings with it a 'weakening' of the writer's imaginative powers, and that all that the poem ever amounts to is 'several hundred pages of turgid and morbid rhyming couplets'.[100] While there is indeed evidence to suggest that William had a hand in the endnotes' composition, this is not necessarily to conclude with Norton that *Gaston De Blondeville* and 'St Alban's Abbey' are the products of a collaboration between husband and wife, with William 'obviously at his wife's elbow for every antiquarian paragraph of the novel'.[101] Rather, they are best thought of as courageous, even feminist, forays into the masculine realms of antiquarian learning, a scholarly field that was almost exclusively the preserve of high-born gentlemen in the period.[102] In Radcliffe's posthumous works, we encounter the example of a woman of middling-class origins making a valiant approach upon masculine literary terrain, one that was presided over in the early nineteenth century by Scott the poet who, himself, had abandoned the 'feminine' impulses of his early Gothic endeavours in favour of the more 'masculine' spirit of antiquarian romance.[103]

In a less poetic strain, and as the endnotes indicate, Radcliffe's understanding of the architecture of St Albans was also heavily indebted to John Carter's *The Ancient Architecture of England* (1795–1814), a largely visual source of antiquarian engravings that seems to have supplemented her memory of the site when composing the poem back in London. In reflection of this, the architectural vocabulary employed here is much more archaeologically accurate than that encountered in the writer's earlier fictions. The verse distinguishes carefully

---

[99] For Scott's similar use of endnotes, see the first edition of *The Lay of the Last Minstrel: A Poem* (London: Printed for Longman, Hurst, Rees, and Orme; Edinburgh: James Ballantyne, 1805), pp. 195–319.
[100] Norton, *Mistress of Udolpho*, pp. 194, 200.
[101] Norton, *Mistress of Udolpho*, p. 195.
[102] On antiquarianism as an almost exclusively masculine pursuit in the period, see Sweet, *Antiquaries*, pp. 69–78.
[103] See Michael Gamer's argument in *Romanticism and the Gothic: Genre, Reception, and Canon Formation* (Cambridge: Cambridge University Press, 2000), pp. 163–200.

between different historical forms of the Gothic, and in a stanza such as the following, Radcliffe brings a remarkably close antiquarian eye to bear on the abbey's architectural features:

> St Cuthbert's Chapel had not lent
> Its wide screen then to veil the choir,
> Where now it bounds the nave's ascent
> With the carved niche and Gothic spire:
> Nor rose before St. Alban's shrine,
> In lofty state, as now is seen,
> The altar's more elaborate screen;
> Of fairy-filagree [sic] each line,
> Web-work each canopy and cell,
> Where many an imaged saint might dwell:
> Light are the flowery knots, that twine
> Round slender columns, clustered fine,
> That to the fretwork cornice go,
> Where flowers amid the foliage blow,
> And wheaten sheafs and roses spread,
> Spell of the Abbot and the King
> Who raised—to guard St. Alban's bed—
> This rich and glorious offering.[104]

This architecture is considerably different from the brooding, monolithic masses of the 'Saxon Gothic' in the earlier novels. Radcliffe's vision of the Middle Ages in the poem is equally nuanced, and what emerges here is not a dark Gothic past of darkness and superstition, but rather, as at the Chateau-le-Blanc in *Udolpho*, a 'white Gothic' age of 'merrie England', a time of music, vibrant colour, boar-roasting and feasting, minstrelsy, morris dancing, and tales of chivalry. The order, decorum, and social cohesiveness by which the past is characterized—aspects of which persist even amidst the chaos of the battle itself—is in keeping with large portions of the historical vision of *Gaston De Blondeville*, its companion piece. No monument to monkish superstition, St Albans Abbey is a venerable 'shrine of peace'.[105] Consequently, and unlike so many other poems about ecclesiastical ruin in the period, Radcliffe presents the dissolution of the monasteries not as the felicitous triumph of Protestantism over the errors of Catholicism, but as the savage and avaricious destruction of a beautiful, intricate, and sophisticated way of life: 'Next age, the latter Henry's bands / Each consecrated altar spoiled, / Seized on the Abbey's ample lands, / And recklessly for plunder toiled.'[106] It is for this

---

[104] Radcliffe, 'St Alban's Abbey', vol. 3, p. 339.
[105] Radcliffe, 'St Alban's Abbey', vol. 3, p. 133.
[106] Radcliffe, 'St Alban's Abbey', vol. 3, p. 126.

reason that, at the outset, she is able to quote a line from William Collins's 'Ode to Fear' (1747), exhorting her reader to engage before the ruined abbey in an imaginative act of architectural reconstruction: 'O come "with meek submitted thought," / With lifted eye, by Rapture taught, / And o'er your head the gloom shall rise / Of monkish chambers, still and wide, / As once they stood.'[107] As exemplified by Jerningham's *Elegy*, by far the majority of topographical writers and poets in the eighteenth century had much invested in the sight of ecclesiastical ruin. The radical nature of 'St Alban's Abbey', by contrast, lies in Radcliffe's decision to submit ecclesiastical ruin, without peril, to the process of rebuilding and completion through engaging her readers' architectural imaginations.

This move further aligns Radcliffe's poem with tensions that were evident in contemporary antiquarian writing. As 'venerable' objects, ruins often elicited from Protestant scholars of Gothic antiquity sometimes mournful, sometimes indignant outcries against the acts of architectural destruction wrought by Cromwell's dissolution of the monasteries, a process that, as Eamon Duffy's influential *The Stripping of the Altars* (1992) has shown, was particularly confusing and painful for English Catholics.[108] As Margaret Aston has argued, the cultural and psychological ramifications of the dissolution were far-reaching and quick to take effect, and no sooner had the physical institutions of Catholicism been laid to waste than figures such as Hugh Latimer, Francis Trigge, John Aubrey, and John Denham began to express their profound sense of loss and regret.[109] Alexandra Walsham has brought to light numerous examples of similar responses within the work of seventeenth- and early eighteenth-century British churchmen and antiquaries, from the first edition of Camden's *Britannia* (1586), through John Weever, to William Stukeley's *Itinerarium curiosum* (1724), showing in each instance how they articulated their concerns as a war against the forces of architectural 'sacrilege'.[110] As the vestiges of 'nurseries of superstition', however, ecclesiastical ruins simultaneously attested to the triumph of the Protestant faith, even owing their very existence to the larger historical processes of Reformation that self-identifying Protestants could only embrace. Nostalgia for the vanished Catholic past conflicted with a Whiggish religious history fashioned on the principles of progress and the implacable march of liberty. Simultaneously decrying iconoclastic acts of architectural destruction and celebrating the coming of the new and enlightened faith, Gothic antiquarians found themselves on the horns of a dilemma.

---

[107] Radcliffe, 'St Alban's Abbey', vol. 3, p. 100.
[108] See Eamon Duffy, *The Stripping of the Altars: Traditional Religion in England, 1400–1580* (New Haven and London: Yale University Press, 1992).
[109] Margaret Aston, 'English Ruins and English History: The Dissolution and the Sense of the Past', *Journal of the Warburg and Courtauld Institutes* vol. 36 (1973): pp. 231–55.
[110] Alexandra Walsham, *The Reformation of the Landscape: Religion, Identity, and Memory in Early Modern Britain and Ireland* (Oxford: Oxford University Press, 2011), pp. 273–86.

This paradox ran deeply throughout the eighteenth-century antiquarian tradition. Commenting on the despoiling of Abingdon Abbey, then in the county of Berkshire, Browne Willis famously argued that its 'pulling down and desecrating' was 'the chief Blemish of the Reformation, and what our Nation stands greatly censured for even by our own Authors'.[111] He underlined the point by citing from Denham's *Cooper's Hill* lines that do not appear in the first edition of 1642:

> Who sees these dismal Heaps, but would demand
> What barbarous Invader sackt the Land;
> But when one hears no *Goth*, no *Turk*, did bring
> This Desolation, but a Christian King;
> When nothing by the Name of Zeal appears,
> 'Twixt our best Actions, and the worst of theirs;
> What does he think our Sacrilege would spare,
> When such th' Effects of our Devotion are?[112]

King Henry and his team of despoilers were barbarous, sacrilegious Goths in all but name. The nascent Gothic-fictional imagination was quick to respond. As Alison Shell has argued, Willis's ghostly tale of the unfortunate fate of Walter Taylor, the infamous despoiler of the ruined Cistercian Abbey at Netley, is just one example of the antiquarian sacrilege narrative, a proto-Gothic form intended to discourage any further acts of architectural vandalism.[113] And yet, as neither a Catholic nor a Protestant Dissenter, Willis remained fervently committed to the Anglican Church: as his fellow antiquary Andrew Coltée Ducarel put it in an obituary published shortly after his death in 1760, 'He was strictly religious, without any Mixture of Superstition or Enthusiasm, and quite Exemplary in this Respect.'[114] Other antiquaries were similarly conflicted. Even as he praised 'the most laudable spirit of reformation' in *Anecdotes of British Topography* (1768), the Dissenter-turned-Anglican Richard Gough censured the violent 'spirit of avarice and outrage'—the physical acts of architectural vandalism—that accompanied it.[115] In James Bentham's *The History and Antiquities of the Conventual and Cathedral Church of Ely* (1771), these contrary impulses are still very much in place: even while observing the religious 'advancements' effected by the Reformation, Bentham chastises the agents of the dissolution for their 'sacrilegious avarice'.[116]

---

[111] Willis, *An History of the Mitred Parliamentary Abbies, and Conventual Cathedral Churches*, vol. 1, p. 2.

[112] Qtuoted in Willis, *An History of the Mitred Parliamentary Abbies, and Conventual Cathedral Churches*, vol. 1, p. 2.

[113] Alison Shell, *Oral Culture and Catholicism in Early Modern England* (Cambridge: Cambridge University Press, 2007), pp. 23–54.

[114] Andrew Coltée Ducarel, *Some Account of Browne Willis, Esq; L. L. D. late Senior Fellow of the Society of Antiquaries of London* (London, 1760), p. 6.

[115] Richard Gough, *Anecdotes of British Topography*, 2 vols (London: Printed by W. Richardson and S. Clarke, 1768), vol. 1, p. xxvi.

[116] Bentham, *The History and Antiquities of the Conventual and Cathedral Church of Ely*, p. 42.

Francis Grose was of much the same opinion in the first volume of *The Antiquities of England and Wales* (1772). Here, abbeys, monasteries, and other ecclesiastical buildings were to be valued both for their architectural beauty as well as for the important social functions they once fulfilled. While Grose describes the political and theological consequences of the Reformation as being 'of vast national benefit', he mourns the architectural destruction that the process occasioned: the 'furious zeal' with which the fine carvings and painted windows of the 'stately buildings and magnificent churches' were demolished suggests that those who directed the 'depredations' were 'actuated with an enmity to the fine arts, instead of a hatred to the popish superstition'.[117] Ecclesiastical ruins called forth in Protestant antiquaries complex sentimental responses of loss and exultation, nostalgia and recoil. At the very least, they prompted scholars wistfully to imagine a past in which the theological process of reformation had been achieved without the accompanying 'Gothic' acts of architectural vandalism.

Catholicism and the Gothic Revival

While Gothic fiction derived part of its effect by exploiting the assumption that Gothic architecture was an inherently benighted Catholic style, topographical writers such as Burgess, Aikin, and Gilpin worked hard to recuperate 'monkish piles' as instances of 'venerable ruin'. The shuttling between these discursive poles that I have traced in attitudes towards 'survivalist' forms of Gothic architecture, however, proved inadequate to the major Protestant exponents of the architectural Gothic Revival, for if a Catholic style was, indeed, to be resurrected and revivified in the enlightened present, it required a more decisive and confrontational approach to these tensions than an easy vacillation between them. Horace Walpole's rhetorical gestures are exemplary in this regard. Though inescapably a part of the reviled Catholic past, Gothic architecture, for Walpole, remained 'venerable' largely through his willingness to tolerate and indeed court and amplify the forces of ambivalence and contradiction at the heart of it. The examples of his use of the adjective 'venerable' in the context of discussions of Gothic architecture are numerous. Discussing the improvements that the genesis of the Gothic style had made upon the rounded arches of Saxon architecture, Walpole in the first volume of *Anecdotes of Painting in England* (1762) described the pointed arch, Gothic's most distinctive feature, as sufficient to render the buildings 'magnificent, yet genteel, vast, yet light, venerable and picturesque';[118] in the third volume of 1763, he castigated the destructiveness of Puritan factions during the English Civil War

---

[117] Francis Grose, *The Antiquities of England and Wales*, new edn, 8 vols (London: Printed for S. Hooper, 1772–6), vol. 1, pp. 104, 106.

[118] Walpole, *Anecdotes of Painting in England*, vol. 1, p. 107.

for deeming 'a venerable cathedral' to be as 'equally contradictory' to the Magna Carta as the Bible.[119]

Of course, the 'charming venerable Gothic' that he praised in a letter to George Montagu as early as 1748 found particular expression in his Gothicizing of Strawberry Hill, though his use of the style here was coupled with a considerable sensitivity to, and emphasis upon, its more negatively signifying, yet imaginatively richer, 'monkish' aspects.[120] Together with the Cloisters, the Tribune, and the Chapel in the Woods, it was the Hall or Paraclete that was one of Strawberry Hill's most self-consciously Catholic fixtures, a structure that, taking its name from the oratory founded by Peter Abelard in Ferreux-Quincey, France, had been immortalized for the eighteenth century by Alexander Pope in 'Eloisa to Abelard' (1717). As Walpole in 1747, having only recently leased Chopp'd Straw Hall from Mrs Chenevix, famously wrote, 'Pope's ghost is just now skimming under my window by a most poetical moonlight', one of many instances of his being drawn to the suburb of Twickenham precisely for its illustrious literary associations.[121] Strawberry's Paraclete was lit by a Gothic lantern that had been designed by Richard Bentley, and which, as Walpole wrote to Montagu in June 1753, 'casts the most venerable gloom on the stairs that was ever see since the days of Abelard'.[122] A month earlier, he had written to Horace Mann, thanking him profusely for having attempted to procure for him some 'Gothic remains from Rome' that were to be used in the refurbishment of Strawberry.[123] Doubting that 'Gothic remains' could ever be found in the Italian city of high classicism, though, Walpole responds with a gentle corrective: 'Sir, kind as you are about it, I perceive you have no idea what Gothic is; you have lived too long amidst true taste to understand venerable barbarism.'[124] Rejecting Mann's suggestions of a Gothic garden at Strawberry Hill, Walpole claims that 'Gothic is merely architecture', and resides in the 'satisfaction' that one derives from 'imprinting the gloomth of abbeys and cathedrals on one's house'.[125] The letter proceeds to illustrate the 'venerable barbarism' of the Gothic style through another telling description of the Paraclete: 'my house is so monastic', Walpole claims, 'that I have a little hall decked with long saints in lean arched windows and with taper columns, which we call the Paraclete, in memory of Eloisa's cloister'.[126] It is thus through the oxymoronic categories of 'venerable gloom', 'venerable barbarism', and 'gloomth'—a compound word formed of 'gloom' and 'warmth'—that Walpole was able to negotiate the discursive impasse at the heart of eighteenth-century perceptions of

---

[119] Walpole, *Anecdotes of Painting in England*, vol. 3, p. 1.
[120] Horace Walpole to George Montagu, 25 July 1748, *Correspondence*, vol. 9, p. 64.
[121] Horace Walpole to Henry Seymour Conway, 8 June 1747, *Correspondence*, vol. 37, p. 270.
[122] Horace Walpole to George Montagu, 11 June 1753, *Correspondence*, vol. 9, pp. 150–1.
[123] Horace Walpole to Horace Mann, 27 April 1753, *Correspondence*, vol. 20, p. 372.
[124] Horace Walpole to Horace Mann, 27 April 1753, *Correspondence*, vol. 20, p. 372.
[125] Horace Walpole to Horace Mann, 27 April 1753, *Correspondence*, vol. 20, p. 372.
[126] Horace Walpole to Horace Mann, 27 April 1753, *Correspondence*, vol. 20, p. 372.

Gothic architecture: though undoubtedly an example of Evelyn's and Wren's 'monkish piles' or Middleton's 'nurseries of superstition', the ecclesiastical Gothic could be retrieved as 'venerable barbarism' when it was enlisted in the service of modern Protestant domesticity. Once this had been achieved, Walpole could playfully sign himself in a letter to Montagu in 1764 as 'The Abbot of Strawberry', and in the second edition of *A Description* describe his house, via a line taken from Book the First of Pope's three-book *The Dunciad* (1728), as 'A Gothic Vatican of Greece and Rome'.[127]

References to Catholicism proliferate throughout the 1784 edition of *A Description*: upon entering the property via the great north gate, the first object to present itself to the visitor is 'a small oratory inclosed [sic] with iron rails'; in front, 'an altar, on which stands a saint in bronze'; 'open niches, and stone basins for holy water'; 'a small garden called the abbot's garden'; and 'a small cloyster' on the left.[128] Several objects in Walpole's extensive collection also derived from Catholic sources. Paul Sandby in *A Collection of Landscapes* (1777) registered the strongly Catholic feel to the place by accompanying his two views of Strawberry Hill with lines from Milton's evocative description of a Gothic cathedral in 'Il Penseroso': 'You are struck with an awe at entering it', Sandby writes, 'proceeding from "The high embowed roof, / And antique pillars' massy proof, / And storied windows richly dight, / Casting a dim, religious light"'.[129] Hannah More, in turn, described Strawberry Hill in July 1789 as a place 'whose Gothic towers and air of elder time so agreeably keep up the idea of haunted walks and popish spirits', while John Ferrar, during his visit in 1795, observed that 'The approach to the house through lofty trees, the embattled walls overgrown with ivy, the spiry pinnacles, the grave air of the building, give it all the appearance of an old abbey.'[130] Despite its castle-like aspects, Walpole clearly wished to foster the illusion that Strawberry Hill had been built on monastic foundations.[131] Thomas Rowlandson caricatured the Catholic atmosphere of Strawberry Hill on several occasions, including his watercolour of nuns at prayer before the altar in the Cabinet of 1805, and a procession of monks about to enter Walpole's home via the north entrance of c.1789 (see Figure 5.3).

The recuperative functions of oxymoron were coupled with Walpole's implementing of a careful distinction between the theological and the aesthetic legacies of the Catholic Gothic past. His primarily aesthetic responses to ecclesiastical architecture are illustrated in his effusive description of the ruins of Netley Abbey

---

[127] Horace Walpole to George Montagu, 18 June 1764, *Correspondence*, vol. 10, p. 127; Walpole, *A Description of the Villa of Mr Horace Walpole* (1784), p. iii.

[128] Walpole, *A Description of the Villa of Mr Horace Walpole* (1784), p. 2.

[129] Paul Sandby, *A Collection of Landscapes, Drawn By P. Sandby, Esq. R. A. and Engraved by Mr Rooker, and Mr Watts, with Descriptions* (London: Printed for G Kearsly, 1777), p. 16.

[130] Hannah More to Horace Walpole, 27 July 1789, *Correspondence*, vol. 31, p. 316; John Ferrar, *A Tour from Dublin to London, in 1795* (Dublin, 1796), p. 92.

[131] See Marion Harney, 'The visualisation of Strawberry Hill: A collusion of history and imagination', *Image [&] Narrative* vol. 18, no 3 (2017): pp. 30–45.

'VENERABLE RUIN' OR 'NURSERIES OF SUPERSTITION' 251

Figure 5.3 Thomas Rowlandson, *North Entrance of Strawberry Hill with a Procession of Monks* (c.1789). Courtesy of the Lewis Walpole Library, lwlpr25430.

as recorded in a letter to Richard Bentley in September 1755: 'In short, they are not the ruins of Netley, but of Paradise—Oh! the purple abbots, what a spot had they chosen to slumber in! The scene is so beautifully tranquil, yet so lively, that they seem only to have *retired into* the world.'[132] The 'purple abbots' with which Walpole imaginatively peoples Netley derive, again, from Pope, specifically his vision of monastic existence offered up in the lines, 'To happy Convents, bosom'd deep in vines, / Where slumber Abbots, purple as their wines', in Book IV of *The Dunciad in Four Books* (1743).[133] As this suggests, it was poetry, and not theology, that mediated Walpole's experience of 'real' ecclesiastical ruin. The distinction that Walpole imposed between Catholic theology and aesthetics was most clearly articulated in a postscript to a letter to William Cole in July 1778. Though he had been ordained as a deacon and then priest in the Church of England, Cole, in his own words, nurtured an 'old attachment to popery';[134] a strong opponent of the Protestant practice of clerical marriage, he had also intended earlier in his life to

---

[132] Horace Walpole to Richard Bentley, 18 September 1755, *Correspondence*, vol. 35, p. 251.
[133] Alexander Pope, *The Dunciad*, ed. James Sutherland, The Twickenham Edition of the Poems of Alexander Pope, Vol. V (London and New York, Routledge, 1963), ll. 301–2, p. 379. This line does not occur in the first, three-book edition of Pope's poem of 1728, just as the later edition renders the above-mentioned reference to 'A Gothic Vatican! of Greece and Rome' as 'A Gothic Library! of Greece and Rome'.
[134] William Cole to Horace Walpole, 11 February 1766, *Correspondence*, vol. 1, p. 105.

live among the English Benedictines at Paris, albeit without formally converting to Catholicism.[135] Registering his friend's lifelong pro-Catholic sympathies, Walpole wrote that 'I like Popery, as well as you, and have shown I do'.[136] The crucial difference, however, lay in what followed this assertion:

> I like it as I do chivalry and romance. They all furnish one with ideas and visions, which Presbyterianism does not. A Gothic church or convent fill [sic] one with romantic dreams—but for the mysterious, the Church in the abstract, it is a jargon that means nothing or a great deal too much, and I reject it and its apostles from Athanasius to Bishop Keene.[137]

Deconsecrated, secularized, and placed on a par with ancient chivalry and romance, Catholicism was for Walpole of aesthetic rather than metaphysical value. While reiterating the argument concerning the associative superiority of the Gothic style that he had made in the first volume of *Anecdotes of Painting*, Walpole's letter imposes a firm distinction between the aesthetic remains of Catholicism and its less-than-desirable theological underpinnings. As his responses to the Chapel at Chute's country house, The Vyne, Hampshire, indicate, he remained convinced that the sole value of Catholicism was its architectural superiority to Protestantism: 'At the Vine is the most heavenly chapel in the world; it only wants a few pictures to give it a true Catholic air—we are so conscious of the goodness of our Protestantism, that we don't care how things look.'[138] If ecclesiastical architecture was to be revived at all, this had to be achieved on the basis of its rich imaginative properties alone. A self-styled 'Protestant Goth', Walpole at Gloucester Cathedral was content to 'worship' a room in the Gothic style for its Protestant rather than its Catholic significance: the room in question was once inhabited by John Hooper, the Anglican Bishop of Gloucester and Worcestershire who was executed for heresy during the reign of Queen Mary I.[139]

This was a gesture repeated by several Protestant advocates of the Gothic in the eighteenth century. Though he was no admirer of Walpole and his work at Strawberry Hill, William Beckford was reported to have expressed similar claims in a posthumous recollection of the author that was published in *The New Monthly Magazine and Humorist* in November 1844. Now resident at Lansdown Crescent, Bath, the aged and reclusive Beckford had agreed to show the unnamed correspondent and his father round Lansdown Tower. The Catholic images on the walls of what looked somewhat like an oratory prompted the father to enquire of

---

[135] John D. Pickles, 'Cole, William (1714–1782)', *ODNB*, http://www.oxforddnb.com/view/article/5863 (accessed 23 March 2017).
[136] Horace Walpole to William Cole, 12 July 1778, *Correspondence*, vol. 2, p. 100.
[137] Horace Walpole to William Cole, 12 July 1778, *Correspondence*, vol. 2, p. 100.
[138] Horace Walpole to Horace Mann, 16 July 1755, *Correspondence*, vol. 20, p. 485.
[139] Horace Walpole to Richard Bentley, September 1753, *Correspondence*, vol. 35, p. 153.

their host his views on Roman Catholicism, Protestantism, and the differences between them, a question to which Beckford responded as follows:

> Why... the one is the opera and the other the dress rehearsal. Gracious God! the Roman Catholic religion is filled with fine stage effects, glittering crosses, censers, mitres, crosiers, dresses, candles, pictures, banners, processions, perfumes, dolls, and music, from the deep tones of the organ to the delightful squeakings of the pope's eunuchs.[140]

A spectacular, operatic performance, Catholicism for Beckford was primarily of aesthetic appeal. This comment provides some insight into his earlier decisions to build Fonthill Abbey in the Gothic style of James Wyatt from 1796 onwards, a building that self-consciously took much of its inspiration from his visits to the Gothic monasteries of the Grande Chartreuse, France, in 1778, and Batalha, Portugal, in 1794.[141] Joseph Farington visited Fonthill early on in its genesis, playfully observing in a diary entry of November 1798 that 'The Abbey [is] to be endowed, & Cathedral Service to be performed in the most splendid manner that the Protestant religion will admit.'[142] While remaining safely within the limits of Protestantism, Beckford exploited the Catholic associations of the Gothic to their limits. In 1823, John Rutter singled out Fonthill's Oratory as one of its most ecclesiastically suggestive rooms, claiming that 'It is a triumph which has never been achieved before in a less area than that of a cathedral, with all the aid of antiquity and religious association'; 'Art only has consecrated the spot,' he continued, 'and who will afterwards dare to dispute her divine right!'[143] Beckford's abbey was Catholic in every sense bar formal consecration, a feature that echoes Walpole's playful but revealing observation of 1759 that the Cabinet or Tribune at Strawberry Hill was to have about it 'all the air of a Catholic chapel—bar consecration!'[144] It was thus entirely fitting that, looking back on Christie's auctioning of the contents and collections of Fonthill Abbey in 1822, Beckford could claim that he had lost interest in his 'Holy Sepulchre' ever since its 'profanation' at the hands of a curious and mercenary public.[145]

Walpole and Beckford thus opened up the architectural terrain that would be occupied by Protestant practitioners of the Gothic, including John Ruskin and George Gilbert Scott, later in the nineteenth century, an issue that I shall explore

---

[140] Anon., 'Conversations with the Late William Beckford, Esq. No. V', *The New Monthly Magazine and Humorist*, 3rd part (1844): pp. 418-27 (pp. 419-20).
[141] Gemmett, *William Beckford's Fonthill*, pp. 26-7.
[142] Joseph Farington, *The Diary of Joseph Farington: Vol. III, September 1796-December 1798*, ed. Kenneth Garlick and Angus Macintyre (London and New Haven: Yale University Press, 1979), p. 916.
[143] John Rutter, *Delineations of Fonthill and Its Abbey* (London: Published by the Author, 1823), p. 35.
[144] Horace Walpole to Sir Horace Mann, 8 July 1759, *Correspondence*, vol. 21, p. 306.
[145] Quoted in Stephen Clarke, 'The Ruin of Fonthill: The Reputation and Influence of Beckford's Abbey', in *William Beckford and the New Millennium*, ed. Kenneth W. Graham and Kevin Berland (New York: AMS Press, 2004), pp. 181-203 (p. 185).

further in the Conclusion to this book. The one notable exception to Gothic Revivalists' retrieval of the aesthetics of the style from its Catholic underpinnings was John Milner, the antiquary and clergyman who championed the Gothic precisely for its religious meanings. Having trained, like Jerningham, for the Catholic priesthood at the English College of Douai, Milner returned to London, an ordained Catholic priest, in 1777.[146] In 1779, he was placed by Bishop Challoner at the mission in Winchester, a centre of Catholic recusancy since before the Civil War; in 1790, Milner was elected to the Society of Antiquaries of London. In 1792, only one year after a relief act that allowed for the first time since 1688 the public expression of Catholic worship, Milner oversaw the building of St Peter's Chapel, Winchester, a Gothic Revivalist construction that was built on the foundations of the insecure and incommodious church at which the Catholic community in the city had hitherto worshipped.[147] The building was conceptualized and designed, for the most part, by John Carter, that other zealot of the 'Gothic faith' with whom Milner had forged an important friendship. Though Carter was not officially a Catholic, he nurtured strong Catholic sympathies throughout his life: in his own words, he stood, religiously, somewhere 'between the Altar and the Communion-table'.[148] Together with Gough, he was often suspected by his fellow antiquaries to be part of a Popish cabal.[149] The works at St Peter's were financed by subscriptions from the congregation, by donations from wealthy friends, as well as by William Meader and Milner himself. On 5 December 1792, St Peter's Chapel was consecrated by Bishop Douglass to Our Lady, St Peter, St Birinus, and St Swithun.[150] Milner's 'Supplement' to the second volume of *The History Civil and Ecclesiastical, & Survey of the Antiquities, of Winchester* (1798–1801) paused to reflect on the use of the Gothic at St Peter's, a structure that, in his own words, turned its back upon 'the modern style of building churches and chapels' in favour of 'the models in this kind which have been left us by our religious ancestors'.[151] What results is a whimsical Gothic confection, what Milner describes as 'a light Gothic building, coated with stucco, resembling free stone, with mullioned windows, shelving buttresses, a parapet with open quatrefoils and crocketted [sic] pinnacles, terminating in gilt crosses'.[152]

In a context in which Catholic churches were either clandestinely built or disguised as domestic buildings, Milner's work at St Peter's was an audacious

---

[146] Judith F. Champ, 'Milner, John (1752–1826)', http://www.oxforddnb.com/view/article/18791 (accessed 3 April 2017).

[147] See Bridget Patten, *Catholicism and the Gothic Revival: John Milner and St Peter's Chapel, Winchester* (Hampshire Papers Committee, 2001).

[148] 'A True Englishman', 'Woodstock's Tomb', *GM*, 78 (1808), II, pp. 1165–7 (p. 1166n).

[149] For an account of Carter's complex relationship with Catholicism, see Crook, *John Carter and the Mind of the Gothic Revival*, pp. 58–9.

[150] Patten, *Catholicism and the Gothic Revival*, p. 1.

[151] John Milner, *The History Civil and Ecclesiastical, & Survey of the Antiquities, of Winchester*, 2 vols (Winchester: Printed and Sold by Jas. Robbins, 1798–1801), vol. 2, p. 230.

[152] Milner, *The History Civil and Ecclesiastical, & Survey of the Antiquities, of Winchester*, vol. 2, p. 233.

exercise in English Catholic visibility. As his later antiquarian writings indicate, his choice of the Gothic was theologically motivated, for it was through this that he sought to forge distinct continuities between the faith of the Middle Ages and the practices of modern Catholicism. As such, and as Rosemary Hill has argued, Milner was a formative influence on the work of A. W. N. Pugin in the 1830s and 1840s.[153] The Gothic at St Peter's Chapel, he argued in *The History Civil and Ecclesiastical, & Survey of the Antiquities, of Winchester*, was central to the act of Catholic worship, a controversial claim to which John Sturges critically responded in *Reflections on the Principles and Institutions of Popery* (1799). Milner repeated these claims in *An Inquiry into Certain Vulgar Opinions Concerning the Catholic Inhabitants and the Antiquities of Ireland* (1808).[154] Here, the Gothic was said to have been 'invented' and 'perfected' for religious reasons, that is to say, 'for augmenting the solemnity of divine worship, and exciting the attention, awe, and devotion to those who assisted at it'.[155] For all his theological differences from Walpole, these observations are couched in a deliberate echoing of Walpole's claims in *Anecdotes of Painting*, namely that 'It is difficult for the noblest Grecian temple to convey half so many impressions to the mind, as a cathedral does of the best Gothic taste.'[156] In Milner's version, though, it is religion and not 'taste' that is the primary consideration: 'who will say that the paragon of modern art and magnificence, St. Paul's Cathedral, disposes his mind for prayer and contemplation in the same degree that York, Lincoln, and Winchester Cathedrals do?'[157] With this important modification and caveat, Milner appropriates for Catholicism Walpole's claim that Westminster Abbey, though 'stripped of it's [sic] altars and shrines', is 'nearer converting one to popery than all the regular pageantry of Roman domes'.[158] For Walpole, Gothic churches inspire 'superstition'; for Milner, they encourage those who worship within them to true and authentic acts of Catholic devotion.

England's Enlightened Catholics

Gothic for Milner was inherently Catholic, pious, and venerable, and he thus remained largely unaffected by the anxieties around architectural nomenclature that had plagued so many of his contemporaries. As he explained in 1808, 'I own

---

[153] Rosemary Hill, '"Ivi'd ruins of forlorn Grace Dieu": Catholics, Romantics and late Georgian Gothic', in *Gothic Architecture and its Meanings, 1550–1830*, ed. Michael Hall (Reading: Spire Books Ltd in association with the Georgian Group, 2002), pp. 159–84.

[154] See Milner, *The History Civil and Ecclesiastical, & Survey of the Antiquities, of Winchester*, vol. 2, p. 230.

[155] John Milner, *An Inquiry into Certain Vulgar Opinions Concerning the Catholic Inhabitants and the Antiquities of Ireland* (London: Printed and Published by Keating, Brown, and Co., 1808), p. 254.

[156] Walpole, *Anecdotes of Painting*, vol. 1, p. 107.

[157] Milner, *An Inquiry into Certain Vulgar Opinions*, p. 254.

[158] Walpole, *Anecdotes of Painting*, vol. 1, p. 108.

the word Gothic does not raise my stomach in the same degree as it does those of some of my friends', primarily since it 'does not convey any such disgraceful ideas at present, and the style itself is generally admired'.[159] Milner, however, is a notable exception, for, as I argued in the Introduction, it was not possible for many Protestant admirers of Gothic architecture to maintain quite so sanguine a disposition in relation to the Catholic associations conjured up by the term 'Gothic' itself—tellingly, the activities of those antiquaries who studied the Gothic past's architectural remains were often tainted by aspersions of popery, the material 'relics' with which they dealt as mystical as the remains and personal effects of a Catholic saint.[160]

And yet, one of the greatest consolations within Protestant conceptualizations of the antique Gothic past was the belief that it was precisely within such 'nurseries of superstition' that the 'seeds' of the Reformation first began to germinate: as William Camden put it in Britannia, the monasteries of the nation, though overgrown with 'weeds' in later ages, were the 'seed-gardens from whence Christian Religion and good learning were propagated over this isle'.[161] From the mid-sixteenth century onwards, this historical vision often centred around the figure of John Wyclif, the controversial, even 'heretical', fourteenth-century Oxford-based scholastic philosopher, theologian, and biblical exegete who challenged a number of the core practices and theological principles of the then-universal Catholic church. In his opposition to 'idolatry' broadly construed, the veneration of the saints, monasticism, and the belief in literal transubstantiation, Wyclif was an English Protestant *avant la lettre*, he and his Lollard followers, in Anne Hudson's words, exponents of the 'premature Reformation' nearly two centuries before the fact.[162] For later English Protestants, Wyclif was nothing less than a cherished source of light in an otherwise benighted Gothic past. As John Foxe, echoing John Bale in *Illustrium maioris Britanniae scriptorium, hoc est, Angliae, Cambriae ac Scotiae Summarium* (1548), wrote in *Actes and Monuments of these Latter and Perilous Dayes* (1563), 'euen as the morning starre being in the middest of a cloud, and as the mone being full in her course, & as the bright bemes of the sonne: so dooth he shine & glitter in the temple and church of God'.[163] Eighteenth-century editions of Foxe published under the more familiar title of *The Book of Martyrs* repeated these metaphors, with one from 1747–8 claiming that 'In those times of

---

[159] Milner, *An Inquiry into Certain Vulgar Opinions*, p. 253.
[160] See Walsham, *The Reformation of the Landscape*, p. 294.
[161] This is taken from Philemon Holland's English translation of 1610 in *Britain, or A Chorographicall Description of the Most Flourishing Kingdomes, England, Scotland, and Ireland, and Islands Adjoining, out of the Depths of Antiquitie* (London: Printed at Eliot's Court Press, 1610), 'The Author to the Reader'.
[162] Anne Hudson, *The Premature Reformation: Wycliffite Texts and Lollard History* (Oxford: Clarendon Press, 1988).
[163] John Foxe, *Actes and Monuments of these Latter and Perilous Dayes* (London: Printed by John Day, 1563), p. 137.

gross darkness, ignorance, trouble and confusion there seemed to be not one spark of gospel doctrine left in its purity, till Wickliff by God's providence came forth'; through Wyclif's ministry, 'the Lord awakened and roused the world, which had for many years been plunged, and even drowned in erroneous doctrine and immoral living'.[164] The 'translatio imperii ad Teutonicos', a particular version of history that had been set in place during the Reformation, drew strong analogies between the collapse of the Roman Empire and the Reformation's rejection of Rome's religious authority.[165] By this way of thinking, the Gothic sacking of Rome was replayed so many centuries later in European humanist reformers' vanquishing of Catholicism, an historical double vision that allowed for the absorption of religious history by eighteenth-century political myth. Accordingly, James Thomson presented Wyclif as the light-bearing precursor to the Reformation in Part Four of *Liberty* (1736), a historical moment in which 'The returning Light, / That first thro' WICKLIFF streak'd the *Priestly Gloom*, / Now burst in open Day'.[166] Viscount Bolingbroke similarly enlisted Wyclif in his Tory appropriation of Gothic historiography in *Remarks on the History of England*: 'WICKLIFFE', he wrote, arose to dispel the 'magick Charm' of clerical corruption, to 'undraw the Veil of this pretended Sanctuary; and to expose the Horrors and Trifles, which lurk'd beneath it, to publick View, Indignation and Contempt.'[167] Wyclif was to Catholicism what the Goths were to ancient Rome. David Hume celebrated Wyclif in similar terms in *The History of England*: as the first English cleric to insist on the authority of the scriptures and to question the belief in transubstantiation, the merit of monastic vows, the materiality of the Church, and the supremacy of the Church of Rome, Wyclif 'spread the doctrine of reformation' in England long before the reformers of the sixteenth century; he thus 'has the honour of being the first person in Europe, that publicly called in question those principles, which had universally passed for certain and undisputed during so many ages'.[168]

Such historiographic claims worked their way into eighteenth-century perceptions of Gothic architecture, for 'monkish piles' could be reframed as 'venerable ruins' if one considered that it was here that the views and opinions of proto-Protestant reformers the likes of Wyclif were first nurtured. In 'The Ruin'd Abby; or, The Effects of Superstition' (1743), a Whiggish poem charting the progress of English religious history from the Catholic Middle Ages to the Protestant

---

[164] John Foxe, *The Book of Martyrs: or, The History of the Church, from the Beginning of Christianity to the Conclusion of the Reign of Queen Mary I*, 2 vols (London: Printed for John Lewis, 1747–48), vol. 1, p. 252.
[165] See Kliger, *The Goths in England*, pp. 33–4.
[166] James Thomson, *Britain: Being the Fourth Part of Liberty, A Poem* (London: Printed for A. Millar, 1736), ll. 903–5, p. 49.
[167] Viscount Henry St John Bolingbroke, *Remarks on the History of England. From the Minutes of Humphry Oldcastle*, Esq. (London: Printed for R. Francklin, 1743), p. 61.
[168] David Hume, *The History of England from the Invasion of Julius Caesar to the Revolution in 1688*, foreword by William B. Todd, 6 vols (Indianapolis: Liberty Fund, 1983), vol. 2, p. 326.

Georgian present, William Shenstone, like Jerningham and many others before and after him, described British ecclesiastical ruins as the 'opulent abodes' of superstition. The home of the lustful priest and 'perjur'd monk', the site of 'Roman magic' and 'the pensive gloom which superstition loves', abbeys are vestiges of the 'inglorious days' of Catholicism, and every measure of Evelyn's 'Monkish Piles'.[169] But it is into this Gothic darkness that the 'Bold WICKLIFF' spontaneously bursts, irradiating the 'religious gloom' with the radiant light of reason and truth:

> Hail honour'd WICKLIFF! enterprising sage!
> An Epicurus in the cause of truth!
> For 'tis not radiant suns, the jovial hours
> Of youthful spring, an ether all serene,
> Nor all the verdure of CAMPANIA'S vales,
> Can chase religious gloom! 'Tis reason, thought,
> The light, the radiance that pervades the soul,
> And sheds its beams on heav'n's mysterious way![170]

Though his light 'but glimmer'd' before 'again / Error prevail'd', Shenstone hails Wyclif as evidence of the fact that Britain's religious past was not solely one of darkness and superstitious error. Much the same pertained to *The Lives of John Wickliff* (1765), the biography of Wyclif and later Lollards that William Gilpin, himself descending from a line of proto-Protestant reformers, published the following year. Gilpin's study is prefaced with 'The House of Superstition. A Vision', a poem by Thomas Denton, the writer and Church of England rector of Ashtead in Surrey. The unruined 'Gothic dome' that the poem describes is the place where 'SUPERSTITION holds her dreary reign', its dark interiors inhabited by Ignorance, Error, Prejudice, and misplaced Zeal. Again, it was within this darkness that 'Wicliff the first [sic] appeared, and led the croud, / And in his hand a lighted torch he bore, / To drive the gloom of superstition's cloud / And all corruption's mazes to explore.'[171] Gilpin continues in this vein throughout his biography, lauding his subject's constant inveigling against the dogmas of the established Church in order to conclude that 'Wicliff was in religion, what Bacon was afterwards in science; the great detecter [sic] of those arts and glosses, which the barbarism of ages had drawn together to obscure the mind of man'.[172] Ecclesiastical ruins were thus not only 'nurseries of superstition' but also the 'venerable' abodes of proto-Protestant reformers. Albeit without naming Wyclif

---

[169] Though written in 1743, Shenstone's poem was first published in *The Works in Verse and Prose, of William Shenstone, Esq.*, 2 vols (London: Printed for R. and J. Dodlsey, 1764), vol. 1, pp. 308–21.
[170] Shenstone, 'The Ruin'd Abby', vol. 1, p. 318.
[171] Denton's poem is included in the prefatory material to William Gilpin's *The Lives of John Wickliff; And of the Most Eminent of His Disciplines; Lord Cobham, John Huss, Jerome of Prague, and Zisca* (London: Printed for J. Robson, 1765), pp. 5–10.
[172] Gilpin, *The Lives of John Wickliff*, p. 57.

in particular, Anna Laetitia Aikin suggested as much when she sought to retrieve the memory of ecclesiastical architecture's positive values in 'On Monastic Institutions':

> The church was reformed from within, not from without; and like the silk-worm, when ripened in their cells to mature vigour and perfection, they pierced the cloud themselves had spun, and within which they had so long been enveloped.[173]

A germinating seed, a bearer of light, a metamorphosing, brightly coloured butterfly: John Wyclif played an important role within eighteenth-century perceptions of the Dark Ages and, through this, conceptualizations of the meanings of Gothic architectural ruin. Breaching the divide between the benighted Catholic past and post-Reformation modernity, Wyclif provided for both Anglican and Dissenting traditions historical proof that the nation bore an innately Protestant sensibility and a long-standing suspicion towards Catholicism. Representations of ecclesiastical ruins in Gothic fiction and poetry, then, were not uniformly engaged in the perpetuation of Hoeveler's anti-Catholic 'Gothic ideology', but were also used as sites for the projection of a fantasy of the enlightened, proto-Protestant Catholic.

More immediately to the period, it was, once again, Alexander Pope who served for Protestants of the age as another salutary example of the 'enlightened' English Catholic, and part of the reason, no doubt, for Walpole's considerable investment in his work. At first glance, Walpole the Whiggish Protestant Goth's lifelong interest in the work of Pope the Catholic Tory is, indeed, curious: though no supporter of the Old Pretender and the restoration of the Stuart line of kings, Pope was what Richard Braverman has termed an 'emotional Jacobite', and in the three-book *The Dunciad* he mobilized a powerful critique of the 'Gothic' literary and political cultures of Hanoverian Whiggism.[174] David Womersley has shown, though, that political and religious differences between Whigs and Tories in the period did not preclude the possibilities of convivial intellectual and aesthetic exchange.[175] Other Protestant Whigs were enamoured of Pope and his work, too: in the veritable 'Whig Pantheon' that was William Kent's Temple of British Worthies at Stowe, Cobham placed a bust of Pope alongside one of the Whig MP Sir John Barnard, celebrating both as living heroes of sorts.[176]

As Chester Chapin has pointed out, Pope himself looked back to the sixteenth-century Dutch Catholic priest and humanist scholar Desiderius Erasmus as 'an

---

[173] Aikin, 'On Monastic Institutions', p. 106.
[174] Richard Braverman, '"Dunce the Second Reigns Like Dunce the First": The Gothic Bequest in the "Dunciad"', *ELH* vol. 62, no. 4 (winter 1995): pp. 863–82.
[175] David Womersley, 'Introduction', in *Cultures of Whiggism: New Essays on English Literature and Culture in the Long Eighteenth Century*, ed. David Womersley, assisted by Paddy Bullard and Abigail Williams (Newark: University of Delaware Press, 2005), pp. 9–26 (pp. 11–12).
[176] Robinson, *Temples of Delight*, pp. 90–1.

exemplar of an enlightened Christianity, an apostle of moderation, tolerance, charity, and a foe to bigotry, obscurantism, and sectarian animosity'.[177] While resisting conversion to the reformed religion, Erasmus had sought to transform Catholicism from within, critiquing across such texts as *Handbook for the Christian Faith* (1504) and *The Praise of Folly* (1511) the superstitions of the Church and such key Catholic practices as monasticism and the requirement of clerical celibacy. Pope's own Erasmianism is most clearly expressed in his depiction of the superstitions of the early Catholic Church in *An Essay on Criticism* (1711): after the fall of the Roman Empire, Pope notes,

> With *Tyranny*, then *Superstition* join'd,
> As that the *Body*, this enslav'd the *Mind*;
> Much was *Believ'd*, but little *understood*,
> And to be *dull* was constru'd to be *good*;
> A second Deluge Learning thus o'er-run,
> And the *Monks* finish'd what the *Goths* begun.[178]

In their presentation of medieval Roman Catholicism as the religion of 'Gothic' darkness, it is hardly surprisingly that these lines caused considerable consternation among Pope's Catholic readers; by the same token, however, such declamations endeared the Catholic poet to eighteenth-century Whiggish Protestants. Like Protestant perceptions of Wyclif, Pope figures Erasmus in the succeeding lines as illuminating this superstitious gloom with the light of truth and reason: 'At length, *Erasmus*, that *great, injur'd* Name, / (The *Glory* of the Priesthood, and the *Shame!*) / *Stemm'd* the *wild Torrent* of a *barb'rous Age*, / And drove those *Holy Vandals* off the Stage.'[179]

Pope would continue in this anti-clerical tradition in 'Eloisa to Abelard' (1717), his heroic epistle that was inspired by John Hughes's English translation of the letters of Abelard to Eloisa of 1713.[180] In this poem, twelfth-century Catholicism is depicted as a force of imperious sexual and emotional repression, one that, in its insistence upon clerical celibacy, subjects its devotees to a tragic existence of melancholia and perpetual yearning. What is particularly striking is the depiction of architectural space. Strongly influenced by the melancholy mood of Gray's *Elegy* and by Milton's presentation of ruined Gothic architecture in 'Il Penseroso',

---

[177] Chester Chapin, 'Alexander Pope: Erasmian Catholic', *Eighteenth-Century Studies*, vol. 6, no. 4 (summer 1973): pp. 411–30 (p. 424).
[178] Alexander Pope, 'An Essay on Criticism', in *Pastoral Poetry and An Essay on Criticism*, ed. E. Audra and Aubrey Williams, The Twickenham Edition of the Poems of Alexander Pope, Vol. I (London and New York: Routledge, 1993), pp. 195–326 (ll. 687–92, pp. 317–18).
[179] Pope, 'An Essay on Criticism', ll. 693–6, pp. 318–19.
[180] See *Letters of Abelard and Heloise. To which is Prefix'd A Particular Account of their Lives, Amours, and Misfortunes, Extracted Chiefly from Monsieur Bayle. Translated from the French* (London: Printed for J. Watts, 1713).

Pope presents the architectural surroundings of Eloisa's convent as spaces of enforced solitude and lugubrious rumination:

> In these deep solitudes and awful cells,
> Where heav'nly pensive, contemplation dwells,
> And ever-musing melancholy reigns;
> What means this tumult in a Vestal's veins?[181]

The spirit of melancholy seems to hover above these 'awful cells' as if it were a cloud. 'Lost in a convent's solitary gloom', Eloisa is the victim of a 'stern religion' that 'quench'd' passion's 'unwilling flame'; immured behind 'Relentless walls' whose 'darksom round contains / Repentant sighs, and voluntary pains', she and her fellow nuns live a paradoxical life of elected imprisonment.[182] Architecture has a crucial role to play in sealing Eloisa's fate, and although Pope does not make use of the word, it is clear that the convent is 'Gothic' in style and design: 'These moss-grown domes with spiry turrets crown'd, / Where awful arches make a noon-day night, / And the dim windows shed a solemn light.'[183] As Joseph Warton observed, the painter seeking to represent some of the most vivid descriptions in the poem 'might place Eloisa in the long ile [sic] of a great Gothic church', over her head—like Bentley's Gothic lantern at Strawberry Hill—a lamp 'whose dim and dismal ray should afford only light enough to make darkness visible'.[184]

In 'Eloisa to Abelard' Pope thus gave expression not to what Purves has taken to be a 'sentimental' image of cloistered life but a negative representation that strongly asserted monasticism's numerous drawbacks: isolation, imprisonment, and a perpetual struggle between the life of the spirit and the desires of the flesh.[185] For his Protestant readers, this was a sign of the Catholic poet's enlightenment, his ability to see through the errors of his own faith. Well beyond his naming of the Hall at Strawberry Hill as the 'Paraclete', Horace Walpole was particularly enamoured of Pope's depiction of conventual life in 'Eloisa to Abelard'. His numerous annotations in his personal copy of the poem as published in the first volume of *The Works of Alexander Pope, Esq* (1743) indicate something of the intensity with which he read and reread it.[186] As critics have pointed out, the poem duly became central to the Gothic-fictional aesthetic: Gillian Beer sees echoes of it throughout the female Gothic tradition, while Anne Williams has described 'Eloisa to Abelard'

---

[181] Alexander Pope, 'Eloisa to Abelard', in *The Rape of the Lock and Other Poems*, ed. Geoffrey Tillotson, The Twickenham Edition of the Poems of Alexander Pope, Vol. II (London and New York: Routledge, 1993), pp. 291–349 (ll. 1–4, p. 319).
[182] Pope, 'Eloisa to Abelard', ll. 37–40, p. 322; ll. 17–24, p. 320.
[183] Pope, 'Eloisa to Abelard', ll. 141–4, p. 331.
[184] Joseph Warton, *An Essay on the Genius and Writings of Pope*, 4th edn, corrected, 2 vols (London: Printed for J. Dodsley, 1782), vol. 1, p. 339–40.
[185] See Maria Purves's reading of the poem in *The Gothic and Catholicism*, pp. 70–1.
[186] For Walpole's heavily annotated copy, see Volume I of *The Works of Alexander Pope, Esq* (London: Printed for Henry Lintot, 1743), pp. 175–90, LWL, 49 2453.

as the symbolic 'mother' of *The Castle of Otranto*.[187] Though deriving ultimately from classical sources, particularly Ovid's *Heroides* and Horace's *Epistles*, Pope's poem exemplified the hybridity of what William Fitzgerald calls 'Augustan Gothic', and, as such, was eagerly appropriated by exponents of the Gothic imagination.[188]

In the hands of other Protestant writers, 'Eloisa to Abelard' could be put to even stronger anti-Catholic uses in their responses to ruined Gothic abbeys. One such example is Edward Hamley, who reworked it several times across his collection of *Sonnets* from 1789.[189] In 'Sonnet XVII, Written in the Ruins of a Monastery', the opening quatrain joyfully celebrates, in by now familiar terms, the English Reformation and the dissolution of the monasteries as the vanquishing of Catholic fear and superstition by the reasonable powers of the Established Church:

> Blest be the day, when superstitious Fear
> And holy Fraud receiv'd their fatal wound,
> For cloyster'd Guilt's eternal fall renown'd,
> To Freedom, Reason, and religion dear![190]

When Hamley addresses a more specific ruined monastery in 'Sonnet LVII, Written in Netley Abbey, Near Southampton', this anti-Catholicism is amplified.[191] In a rewriting of 'Eloisa to Abelard', the persona's flight of fancy fixates upon the fate of a virgin nun, one who has been subject to a veritable 'live burial' within the Abbey's walls:

> How oft the Virgin in her stony cell
> To the slow moaning of the midnight bell
> Responsive sigh'd, recalling those sweet days,
> When free she led the dance's sprightly maze,
> With many a youthful friend she lov'd full well.[192]

As in so much anti-Catholic discourse of the period, Hamley presents Catholic vows of celibacy as unnatural obstacles to the expression of the young nun's warm romantic affection for her suitor, as she, like Eloisa before her, pines away with the memory of 'Love's enchanting joys', 'rememb'ring all his winning charms, / That fail would bear her to her Lover's arms'. Hamley returned to the same subject six years later, including his longer 'Reflections in Netley Abbey' in his collection

---

[187] See Gillian Beer, '"Our unnatural No-voice": The Heroic Epistle, Pope, and Women's Gothic', *The Yearbook of English Studies* vol. 12 (1982): pp. 125–51, and Williams, *Art of Darkness*, p. 50.

[188] See William Fitzgerald, 'Augustan Gothic: Alexander Pope Reads Ovid', in *Augustan Poetry and the Irrational*, ed. Philip Hardie (Oxford: Oxford University Press, 2016), pp. 187–98.

[189] Edward Hamley, *Sonnets* (London: G. G. J. and J. Robinson, 1789).

[190] Hamley, *Sonnets*, p. 21.

[191] Hamley, *Sonnets*, p. 61. For a full account of literary and touristic responses to the ruins of Netley Abbey in the period, see Dale Townshend, 'Ruins, Romance and the Rise of Gothic Tourism: The Case of Netley Abbey, 1750–1830', *Journal for Eighteenth-Century Studies* vol. 37, issue 3 (September 2014): pp. 377–94.

[192] Hamley, *Sonnets*, p. 61.

Poems of Various Kinds in 1795, and providing here a masculine retelling of Pope's poem of thwarted desire and affection. Here, too, the life of Catholic piety is figured as life imprisonment, in which a lovesick monk, consumed with memories of his beloved, miserably sees through the remainder of his days.[193] In Hamley and other minor eighteenth-century poets of ecclesiastical ruin, the musings of Pope the Erasmian Catholic are appropriated to vehemently anti-Catholic ends.

Enlightened Catholicism and Gothic Romance

Poignantly aware of the examples of Wyclif and Pope, Gothic fictions of the late eighteenth century almost routinely include within them characters who, though notionally Catholic, are possessed with sufficient insight to perceive the errors of their own faith. Lorenzo in *The Monk* and the Superior of the Convent of Santa della Pieta in *The Italian* are just two of many examples: Lorenzo's 'good sense' renders him all too aware of 'the artifices of the monks, and the gross absurdity of their miracles, wonders, and superstitious reliques', while Radcliffe's Superior, though outwardly conforming to the customs of the 'Roman church', does not suppose 'a faith in all of them to be necessary to salvation'.[194] The issue became more urgent, however, when Gothic writers set their fictions not in Catholic southern Europe but in either real or imagined monastical institutions in 'Gothic' Britain. Here, what critics have addressed as the trope of the 'good Catholic' that curiously surfaces in a largely anti-Catholic fictional tradition assumes far greater significance. Like John Wyclif, their very existence within the annals of the dark and benighted Gothic past went some way towards ameliorating the hiatus in national history that the Reformation occasioned, forging, through this, the fantasy of a continuous and unbroken line of proto-Protestant and Protestant belief that coincided closely with the political myth of Gothic origins. William Hutchinson's important but critically neglected early Gothic romance *The Hermitage: A British Story* (1771) signifies in its subtitle its interests in ancient national history. Though it is set in an unspecified time during which the 'first vestiges of the Reformation had not yet taken place in this kingdom', its two main characters are, like Wyclif, English Protestants in all but name.[195] The enlightened Periander and his son Astianax are engaged in continuous conflict with the treacherous priest, Father Peter, a Catholic cleric who oversees a life of vice and luxury at the nearby monastery of St Benedict, itself a symbol of 'the liberty which

---

[193] Edward Hamley, *Poems of Various Kinds* (London: Printed by J. W. Myers for T. Cadell and W. Davies, 1795), pp. 37–9.
[194] Lewis, *The Monk*, p. 294; Radcliffe, *The Italian*, p. 300.
[195] William Hutchinson, *The Hermitage: A British Story* (York: Printed by C. Etherington, for the Author, 1771), p. 4.

these times of bigotry afforded to the churchmen'.[196] Directly inspired by *Otranto*, Hutchinson's narrative includes several episodes that are designed to illustrate the workings of Catholic superstition, including an animated suit of armour and a magical onyx crucifix that, as in Conyers Middleton and Walpole, cries tears of blood—all testament, in fact, to a Gothic past of hypocrisy, avarice, vengeance, magic, superstition, and darkness. To this prevailing miasma, however, Astianax is curiously immune, and in a revealing moment of free indirect discourse he mentally anticipates the Reformation and dissolution of the monasteries long before the actual historical event:

> My prophetic mind presages to me many degradations of the church... The insolence of priesthood will exist to the last verge; till at length the total dissolution of these monasteries, these convents, these cathedrals and colleges, like shackles on the hand of liberty, worn in ages of supine indolence, will be torn off; and all the pompous acclamations of a choir of priests, will change for that most acceptable service, the sighings of a contrite heart.[197]

In *The Hermitage*, the anti-Catholic discourse of later Protestant reformers is repeatedly put into the mouths of notionally Catholic Britons, as if to illustrate that the national past had always been Protestant, and Catholicism only a temporary interruption of a much older religious tradition.

It thus follows that, when Hutchinson turned his hand to the writing of topography, the dissolution was not solely the felicitous vanquishing of Catholic darkness but also, somewhat more ambivalently, the unfortunate destruction of an originally pious way of life. Standing before the ruins of Lanercost ('Lenercost') Priory, now in Cumbria, Hutchinson in the revised and illustrated edition of *An Excursion to the Lakes, in Westmoreland and Cumberland* (1774) of 1776 records a rich, associative reverie that pre-empts Radcliffe's later responses to the ruins at Furness. 'Imagination', he writes, 'is immediately figured, from conceptions of the rites which once hallowed the place;—where piety has breathed the acceptable prayer, and devotion poured forth her energy, witnessed and approved by angels.'[198] If this indicates a positive conceptualization of the Catholic past, Hutchinson's subsequent reflections make clear his conviction that it was the Reformation and dissolution that violently put paid to it: 'The benevolent mind turns away from ideas of those horrid crimes, which, through the corruption of men, polluted these holy mansions; and will not yield to the sable characters, which would blot out all pleasing visions.'[199] As in Radcliffe's presentation of the

---

[196] Hutchinson, *The Hermitage*, p. 18.
[197] Hutchinson, *The Hermitage*, pp. 51–3.
[198] William Hutchinson, *An Excursion to the Lakes in Westmoreland and Cumberland; With a Tour Through Part of the Northern Counties in the Years 1773 and 1774*, 2nd edn (London: Printed for J. Wilkie, 1776), p. 268.
[199] Hutchinson, *An Excursion to the Lakes in Westmoreland and Cumberland*, p. 268.

dissolution in 'St Alban's Abbey', this is a poignant example of the mournful nostalgia of the Protestant Gothic that Milbank has so extensively charted.[200] 'All reformation has been attended with an extravagance of bigotry,' Hutchinson writes, and while assuring his readers that he remains 'an enemy to superstition and its images', he claims that he admires 'the artist, wherever I discover him, be it in the works of the heathen, the catholic, or reformer, without regarding any mistaken application of the work'.[201] The anonymous Gothic fiction *St Bernard's Priory: An Old English Tale* (1786) presented ancient 'Gothic' times in a comparable fashion: though the narrative is set during the twelfth-century reign of King Henry II, the ruined abbey of its title looms large over the action, as if to suggest that England had always been Protestant, its abbeys, monasteries, and priories already in a state of reform-driven ruination.[202] Such architectural details in early Gothic fictions, in Hoeveler's words, 'elide the very specific historical act carried out by Henry VIII and place the ruined Gothic abbey in the service of a transhistorical fantasy'.[203] Enlightened, rational, and anticlerical to boot: the Catholics that inhabit these fictions are the very opposite of that family of superstition-peddling Catholics from the north of England who are held responsible for trafficking in Counter-Reformation superstitions in the first Preface to *The Castle of Otranto*.

Richard Warner, another topographer-turned-Gothic romancer and the friend and protégé of William Gilpin, achieved much the same in *Netley Abbey: A Gothic Story*, a two-volume fiction that was published simultaneously in Southampton by the author and in London by the Minerva Press in 1795.[204] In his earlier *Topographical Remarks, Relating to the South-Western Parts of Hampshire* (1793), Warner's description of Beaulieu Abbey, Hampshire, the neighbouring institution whence the monks at Netley came, had negatively figured the Catholic Middle Ages as a time of superstition, sensuality, and indulgence.[205] Such views were given fictional expression in *Netley Abbey*, a virulently anti-Catholic tale involving supernatural occurrence, mysteriously changing portraits, incestuous sexuality, and cross-gendered disguise, the influence of which is clearly seen in Lewis's treatment of similar themes in *The Monk* one year later. As it is eventually revealed, the monks in residence at Netley have been complicit in the machinations of the villain, Sir Hildebrand, in converting portions of its holy interiors into a prison for the incarceration and torture of Agnes Warren, the object of Sir Hildebrand's incestuous designs. Within this dark and superstitious Catholic past,

---

[200] Milbank, *God and the Gothic*, pp. 40–61.
[201] Hutchinson, *An Excursion to the Lakes in Westmoreland and Cumberland*, p. 281.
[202] See Anon., *St Bernard's Priory: An Old English Tale* (London: Printed for the Authoress, 1786).
[203] Hoeveler, *The Gothic Ideology*, p. 286, n. 1.
[204] Richard Warner, *Netley Abbey: A Gothic Story*, 2 vols (London: Printed for William Lane at the Minerva Press, 1795).
[205] Richard Warner, *Topographical Remarks, Relating to the South-Western Parts of Hampshire: To Which is Added a Descriptive Poem*, 2 vols (London: Printed for R. Blamire, 1793), vol. 1, pp. 275–6.

though, Warner recovers the salutary presence of proto-Protestant consciousness when the notionally Catholic hero pauses to reflect on the numerous vices to which the monastical pile has been witness:

> Edward viewed these various proofs of human folly and superstition with pity and contempt; 'strange,' thought he, 'that man should so perversely heap upon himself unnecessary discomfort; and wilfully mistake the purposes for which he was created! Can the voluntary infliction of painful penances and unnatural mortifications be pleasing in the eye of that all-gracious being who rejoices only in the happiness of his creatures? Or can the empty pomp of solitary devotion atone for the neglect of those duties to each other, which we were born to fulfil?'[206]

In the tradition of John Wyclif and Alexander Pope, Warner's hero is an enlightened English Catholic who clearly sees the errors of his own faith. Turning from topography and fiction to current politics, Warner would later give unrestrained vent to his anti-Catholicism in an acerbic reaction to the anticipated emancipation of Catholics in 1829, publishing shortly before the passing of the Act an inflammatory pamphlet entitled *Catholic Emancipation, Incompatible with the Safety of the Established Religion, Liberty, Laws, and Protestant Succession, of the British Empire* (1829). Here, too, metaphors of Gothic architecture resound with the political resonances that I outlined in the previous chapter: if the 'BRITISH CONSTITUTION in CHURCH and STATE' is an ancient Gothic pile that, though its foundations had been laid earlier, was consolidated with the Protestant settlement of 1688, the emancipation of the nation's benighted Catholics is a possibility that is 'pregnant with *future* ruin'.[207] For Warner and others of his persuasion, the forces of a benighted Gothic antiquity are in danger of returning in the modern, enlightened present. As I argue in the Conclusion to this book, these fears would become all the more real in the public architectural debates that were precipitated in Britain by the burning down of the Houses of Parliament in October 1834.

---

[206] Warner, *Netley Abbey*, vol. 1, pp. 149–50.
[207] Richard Warner, *Catholic Emancipation, Incompatible with the Safety of the Established Religion, Liberty, Laws, and Protestant Succession, of the British Empire* (London: C. J. G. & F. Rivington, 1829), p. 3.

6
Antiquarian Gothic Romance
Castles, Ruins, and Visions of Gothic Antiquity

As my discussion of William Hutchinson, Richard Warner, and Ann Radcliffe in 'St Alban's Abbey' in the previous chapter implies, topography in eighteenth- and early nineteenth-century Britain constituted more than the kinds of picturesque, poetic descriptions of real-life ruins and landscapes that, as I argued in Chapter 3, we see taking shape in the domestic sections of Radcliffe's *Journey*. In a much more precise sense, topography was also the quasi-scientific practice of describing a particular place, building, ruin, city, town, manor, or parish, the detailed and accurate delineation of any locality that was most closely associated with antiquarianism in the period. As the eighteenth century gave way to the nineteenth, so several Gothic writers came enthusiastically to participate in this more exacting conceptualization of the topographical endeavour, jettisoning the 'castles in the air'—those imaginary castles of southern Europe and Britain—and turning instead to the 'real' Gothic architectural antiquities that they perceived around them as setting and subject matter for their narratives. What results, I want to argue in this chapter, is the curious, oxymoronic category of the 'antiquarian romance', a strain of Gothic writing that, even as it peddled its hyperbolic, highly fanciful tales, self-consciously aspired towards the rigour and facticity of the antiquarian topographical method. Qualifying the inveterate, Georg Lukács-derived assumption that the historical novel arose, *ex nihilo* and fully formed, with the publication of Walter Scott's *Waverley* in 1814, critics such as Ruth Mack, Richard Maxwell, Anne H. Stevens, Devoney Looser, and Fiona Price have drawn attention to the extensive corpus of historical fictions in Britain and Europe that predated this moment.[1] While it is tempting to regard the romances that I explore in this chapter as examples of this tradition, they are not historical novels in the same way that, say, Thomas Leland's *Longsword, Earl of Salisbury* (1762) might be said to be. In place of the 'real' historical events and personages that Leland explores—at the very least, his hero is based on William Longespée, 3rd Earl of Salisbury and illegitimate son of Henry II—these are fictions that are

---

[1] See Mack, *Literary Historicity*; Richard Maxwell, *The Historical Novel in Europe, 1650–1950* (Cambridge: Cambridge University Press, 2009); Anne H. Stevens, *British Historical Fiction Before Scott* (Houndmills: Palgrave Macmillan, 2010); Devoney Looser, *British Women Writers and the Writing of History, 1670–1820* (Baltimore and London: Johns Hopkins University Press, 2000); and Price, *Reinventing Liberty*.

Gothic Antiquity: History, Romance, and the Architectural Imagination, 1760–1840. Dale Townshend, Oxford University Press (2019). © Dale Townshend.
DOI: 10.1093/oso/9780198845669.001.0001

self-consciously written in the romance mode and feature, as such, characters and events that have little or no relation to what Leland referred to as the work of 'the antient English historians'.[2] The designation 'antiquarian romance' describes the particularities of this subgenre particularly well, and serves to distinguish a discrete body of texts from what Montague Summers and other early critics tended to designate as the 'Historical Gothic'.[3]

First and foremost, then, the antiquarian romance is a Gothic tale that is set within a 'real' or extant Gothic architectural ruin across Britain; though the stories that the antiquarian romance tells are entirely imaginary, these fictions nonetheless cultivate certain similarities with the topographical tradition, anchoring the Gothic architectural structures that inspire them in information gleaned from topographical tomes. Exploring some of the formal and thematic continuities between antiquarian topographical writing and Gothic fictions set in extant British ruins, this chapter elaborates upon, and in some senses qualifies, Katie Trumpener's observation that much Romantic-era fiction takes off from the antiquarian interest in vernacular antiquities with which it was contemporary.[4] As I show, the relationship between fiction and antiquarianism that this called into being was seldom a happy one. But the chapter also addresses a few notable instances in which early nineteenth-century antiquaries themselves, often to disastrous effects, made recourse to the form of popular romance as a means of further disseminating their arcane architectural findings. Focusing on the ways in which a particular topographical site inspired the writing of antiquarian romance, the argument then turns to consider some of the many texts written in, about, and to the Gothic ruins of Kenilworth Castle, Warwickshire, addressing specifically the ways in which these material remains served as portals to so many different imaginative, politically charged recreations of Britain's Gothic past.

Antiquarian Gothic Topography

It was the antiquary Richard Gough who, in the last four decades of the eighteenth century, most enthusiastically enjoined Britons to appreciate, study, record, draw, and write about their own Gothic architectural inheritance. Elected to the Society of Antiquaries in 1767, Gough would be nominated as Director in 1771, a position that he held until December 1797.[5] Even as he charted a national spirit of

---

[2] Thomas Leland, *Longsword, Earl of Salisbury: An Historical Romance*, 2 vols (London: Printed for W. Johnston, 1762), vol. 1, 'Advertisement'.

[3] See Summers, *The Gothic Quest*, pp. 153–201, and Devendra P. Varma, *The Gothic Flame* (London: Arthur Barker, 1957), pp. 74–84.

[4] Katie Trumpener, *Bardic Nationalism: The Romantic Novel and the British Empire* (Princeton, NJ: Princeton University Press, 1997).

[5] R. H. Sweet, 'Gough, Richard (1735–1809)', *ODNB* <http://www.oxforddnb.com/view/article/11141> (accessed 6 September 2016).

antiquarian enquiry that went back as far as John Leland, Gough in *Anecdotes of British Topography* (1768) bemoaned the attitudes of ignorance that prevailed among the English in relation to the architectural relics of their native Gothic past. Instead of seeking to understand and preserve the architecture of 'our forefathers' in 'their own country', antiquaries of the day, he lamented, 'penetrate the wilds of Europe, and the desarts [sic] of Asia and Africa, for the remains of Grecian, Roman, and earlier architecture'.[6] Gough intensified this campaign in his two-volume *British Topography* of 1780, a collection that is useful in gauging what the eighteenth century meant by the term 'topography', the breadth and extent of its focus, and its relations to Gothic architecture. At its most fundamental, topography constituted the field of 'geographical description', though one in which architectural ruins took precedence over the description of natural landscape.[7] More accurately, topography was the place at which the disciplines of geography and history intersected: a concern with the physical layout of a particular site or space coincided with an interest in its temporal and historical dimensions. In contrast to the soaring narratives of eighteenth-century philosophical history, though, topography necessitated a close engagement with material culture, demanding an empirical approach to the physical remains of antiquity that could then be used as 'proof' or 'evidence' for the practice of historical conjecture and supposition. Comprising 'surveys of kingdoms, principalities, and provinces', as well as 'descriptions of a few particular cities, towns, churches, religious houses, and other monuments', topography was a particularly capacious category, and yet, within it, descriptions, drawings, and written records of the ruined remains of Gothic antiquity were paramount.[8] Aiming at making both natives and foreigners of the land 'acquainted with its remote antiquities', Gough promoted topography as an exercise in historical education on a grand, national scale.[9] These nationalistic leanings, however, were offset by a privileging of the local within the topographical enterprise, an interest that often extended no further outwards than the nearest town, parish, region, or county.

Conceived as a bulwark against the passage of time, the topographer's drawing and description of local ruins were mooted by Gough as a means of conserving them. Although, as John Frew has argued, earlier antiquaries such as Browne Willis and William Stukeley had expressed concerns for the conservation of ancient buildings, it is really to Gough whom we should look as the late eighteenth

---

[6] Gough, *Anecdotes of British Topography*, vol. 1, pp. xx–xxi.
[7] Richard Gough, *British Topography; or, An Historical Account of What Has Been Done for Illustrating the Topographical Antiquities of Great Britain and Ireland*, 2 vols (London: Printed for T. Payne and Son, and J. Nichols, 1780), vol. 1, p. i.
[8] Gough, *British Topography*, vol. 1, p. i.
[9] Gough, *British Topography*, vol. 1, p. xx.

century's primary exponent of architectural preservationism.[10] Situating himself within a longer tradition, Gough in *British Topography* singled out for commendation the picturesque perspectives of, among others, the architect and watercolourist Thomas Sandby, Samuel and Nathaniel Buck, Francis Grose, and George Vertue, all British artists and antiquaries who, in the spirit of conservation, had done much to capture images of the country's crumbling Gothic remains. Gough's praise was well considered, for in their proposals for publishing by subscription two collections of engravings of the ruins of the counties of Wiltshire, Gloucestershire, and Monmouthshire, and Norfolk, Suffolk, and Essex, in 1732 and 1737 respectively, brothers Samuel and Nathaniel Buck foregrounded their preservationist agenda by claiming that the illustration of 'those valuable Structures' that are now 'mould'ring in Ruins' was a means of preserving the '*History* of the former State of this *Island*' and transmitting to 'Posterity' those things 'which must otherwise by irretrievably lost'.[11] Paul Sandy's engravings were informed by a similar preservationist impulse, as were Francis Grose's undertakings in *The Antiquities of England and Wales* (1772).[12] Having discussed the slighting of castles by republican factions during the English Civil War, for instance, Grose noted in the first volume of his study that, ever since then, castles in England 'have been abandoned to the mercy of time, weather, and the most unsparing hands of avaricious men'; plundering the nation's ruined castles for their materials, such individuals have 'deprived' their countrymen of the 'remains of antiquity', the architectural relics, he claims, that are so essential to the 'dignity' of a nation.[13]

This became a familiar cry in antiquarian writing of the period, and one that ran throughout the work of Edward King, Paul Sandby, and others.[14] In the first four decades of the nineteenth century, it was most enthusiastically championed by John Britton, the prolific and indefatigable topographer of England's Gothic monuments across such series as *The Beauties of Wiltshire* (1801–25); several tomes in the twenty-seven-volume *The Beauties of England and Wales* series that he produced with Edward Wedlake Brayley from 1801 onwards; the multivolume *The Architectural Antiquities of Great Britain* (1807–27); his magnum opus,

---

[10] Frew, 'Richard Gough, James Wyatt, and Late 18th-Century Preservation'. As Frew points out, Gough published two letters in *The Gentleman's Magazine* in 1786 and 1788 respectively, the second of which might be read as 'the first coherent preservationist manifesto' (p. 367).

[11] See Samuel Buck, *Proposals for Publishing by Subscription, Twenty Four Perspective Views, of the Present State of the Most Noted Abbies, Religious Foundations, Castles, and Other Remains of Antiquity; in the Counties of Wiltshire, Gloucester, and Monmouth* (London, 1732), and *Proposals for Publishing by Subscription, Twenty Four Perspective Views, of the Present State of the Most Noted Abbies, Religious Foundations, Castles, and Other Remains of Antiquity, in Norfolk, Suffolk, and Essex* (London, 1737).

[12] See Paul Sandby, *The Virtuosi's Museum; Containing Select Views, in England, Scotland, and Ireland* (London: Printed for G. Kearsly, 1778).

[13] Grose, *The Antiquities of England and Wales*, vol. 1, pp. 13–14.

[14] See Edward King, *Observations on Ancient Castles* (London: Printed by John Nichols, 1782), p. 3.

Cathedral Antiquities of England (1814–35); and other topographical works.[15] As the architect George Cooper in *Architectural Reliques* (1807), a collection of etchings and aquatints of ruined Gothic castles and abbeys across Britain, argued, it was the arts that could best preserve 'accurate memorials' of the nation's hastily decaying monuments: the printing press could record 'the descriptions and admeasurements, the proportions and the history', the 'pencil and the graver [*sic*] delineate the actual effect and appearance' of every remaining ruin.[16] It was such technological advancements that drove Richard Gough's *Sepulchral Monuments of Great Britain* (1786–96; introductory volume published in 1799), his major quasi-scientific conservationist intervention that, as Noah Heringman has shown, depended largely on Gough's collaborations with the self-educated draftsman Jacob Schnebbelie and the semi-official engraver to the Society of Antiquaries James Basire the Elder.[17] Similar impulses informed the publication of capacious illustrations of ancient Gothic monuments, many of them by John Carter, in the Society of Antiquaries' *Vetusta Monumenta* series (1718–1906), as well as Schnebbelie's cheaper, less ambitious, and unfinished *The Antiquaries Museum* (1791; posthumously completed and edited by Richard Gough and John Nichols in 1800).

And yet, the assumption that, of all the arts, it was literature in particular that could play a crucial conservationist role was a pervasive one, and one that went at least as far back as Shakespeare's offering up of poetic inscription as consolation for the passage of time in the couplet of Sonnet 65, 'Since brass, nor stone, nor earth, nor boundless sea': 'Oh none, unless this miracle have might, / That in black ink my love may still shine bright'.[18] Similar claims concerning the importance of poetry to architectural preservation run throughout Edmund Spenser's *Complaints* (1591), particularly in his early translations of Joachim du Bellay's *Les Antiquités de Rome* and *Songe* (1558). In 'The Ruines of Time', for example, Spenser implicitly offers his own verse as a means through which the crumbling ruins of Verulam in England and the Eternal City of Rome might achieve immortality. Well aware of these literary antecedents, Gough cited a portion of 'The Ruines of Rome' in his Preface to *British Topography*, thereby putting Spenser's classicism in the poem to use in his defence of the preservation of British Gothic antiquities.[19]

---

[15] For a useful overview of Britton's career, see J. Mordaunt Crook, 'John Britton and the Genesis of the Gothic Revival', in *Concerning Architecture: Essays on Architectural Writers and Writing Presented to Nikolaus Pevsner*, ed. John Summerson (London: Allen Lane, 1968), pp. 98–119.

[16] George Cooper, *Architectural Reliques; or, The Present State of the Most Celebrated Remains of Ancient British Architecture and Sculpture* (London: Printed for the Author by J. Barfield, 1807), p. 3.

[17] See Heringman, *Sciences of Antiquity*, pp. 231–80.

[18] This is quoted from Edmond Malone's definitive eighteenth-century edition of Shakespeare's Sonnets, in *The Plays and Poems of William Shakespeare*, 10 vols (London: Printed by H. Baldwin for J. Rivington and Sons, L. Davis, B. White and Son, T. Longman, S. Law et al, 1790), vol. 1, pp. 245–7.

[19] Edmund Spenser, 'The Ruines of Rome. By Bellay', in *The Works of Spenser*, 6 vols (London: Printed for J. and R. Tonson and S. Draper, 1750), vol. 5, pp. 223–36 (pp. 235–6).

The cry for architectural preservation, of course, is a manifestation of the spirit of 'heritage' that has characterized Western attitudes towards the material and immaterial remains of the past in post-World War II society. Although, as Astrid Swenson has cautioned, the term 'heritage' is anachronistic within the context of late eighteenth-century Britain and Europe, the period, in its frequent cries for the 'preservation' of 'ancient monuments', nonetheless witnessed the birth of this concept.[20] Indeed, if, as Rodney Harrison has argued, post-1972 notions of heritage uniformly depend upon a sense of modernity and its rupture with the past, an impending sense of threat and loss, systems of classification and ordering, and the impulse towards conservation, these are all elements that feature in the antiquarian topographies of late-Enlightenment Britain.[21] As fictions such as Elizabeth Bonhôte's *Bungay Castle* (1796), Edward Montague's *The Castle of Berry Pomeroy* (1806), and *The Castle of Tynemouth* (1806) and *Brougham Castle* (1816) by Jane Harvey indicate, antiquarian romances—Gothic romances set in some of the extant ruined castles of eighteenth-century Britain—participated in this mindset, too, and thus constitute, like the topographical descriptions with which they were contemporary, an important moment in the 'prehistory' of modern heritage, an instance of what Swenson has called 'heritage consciousness "*avant la lettre*"'.[22] Later, in the Victorian period, it was a writer such as William Harrison Ainsworth who would draw most strongly upon literature's ability to preserve ancient architecture, including in the Preface to his historical romance *The Tower of London* (1840) a poignant *cri de coeur* to this effect.

Such cries were frequently to be heard in earlier Gothic fictions. Returning to Bungay Castle, Suffolk, later in her life, Elizabeth Bonhôte observed with some consternation that the castle's ruins, some of them converted into makeshift cottages, had become the dwelling place of the rural poor. Contemplating how she might 'reverse the order of things, and render them as lovely and beautiful in age, as they were grand and magnificent before time had robbed them of those envied and valuable properties which it cannot restore', she turns to a resource that is closest to hand, maintaining that she has been 'furnished for this employment with no other materials than the scanty portion her own imagination afforded'.[23] Offering up romance as a means of vanquishing the depredations of time, Bonhôte loosely returns in the narrative to the Barons' Wars of the thirteenth century, for 'then it was that *Bungay Castle* reared its proud towers and battlements aloft', its 'massy walls' standing in 'gloomy and majestic grandeur' as if in defiance of 'every design formed against them by man, and to the more

---

[20] See Astrid Swenson's argument in *The Rise of Heritage: Preserving the Past in France, Germany and England, 1789-1914* (Cambridge: Cambridge University Press, 2013).
[21] See Rodney Harrison, *Heritage: Critical Approaches* (Abingdon: Routledge, 2013), pp. 13–67.
[22] Swenson, *The Rise of Heritage*, p. 28.
[23] Bonhôte, *Bungay Castle*, vol. 1, pp. xii–xiii, xiv.

certain influence of all-conquering time'.[24] As in so many other topographies and antiquarian romances, the architectural imagination that is urged into action by the sight of a ruined castle tends always towards completion, passing beyond the scene of present dilapidation in order to imagine the pile in its original, unruined state. This move was crucial to the antiquarian tradition, and a continuation of the imaginative turn that Angus Vine has identified within sixteenth- and seventeenth-century antiquarian practice: the dynamic, recuperative, and resurrective tendency to restore ruins imaginatively to their former splendour, as if as a means of defying the depredations of time.[25] Though it originated in the work of Petrarch and other early modern Italian humanists, this impulse was still present in the study of antiquities a century later. In *A Treatise on the Study of Antiquities* (1782), Thomas Pownall had argued that if the antiquary were to avoid the charge of being always confined to the mundane orders of the material relic—the remains of Francis Bacon's 'shipwreck of history'—his mind ought to aspire towards the larger, complete, yet lost historical realms to which the fragment attested, all the while avoiding the 'seductions of fancy'—the building of those 'castles in the air'— to which antiquaries were often said to be prone.[26] In a similar fashion, what Bonhôte's Introduction had emotively described as a 'mere heap of unconnected ruins' becomes in the narrative a redoubtable Gothic edifice that is not only an 'object of desire' to the 'proud and aspiring barons', but even, it has been said, 'to contending kings'.[27] Moving well beyond the discourse of preservation, though, Bonhôte also effects in *Bungay Castle* a full-scale act of imaginative architectural restoration, championing through her architectural preoccupations a return to the splendours of thirteenth-century England in a move that is ideologically inseparable from the conservative politics that she expresses throughout the novel.

Motivated by a similar topographical impulse, Edward Montague began *The Castle of Berry Pomeroy* (1806) on a note that stressed his commitment to retrieving the ruins of the eponymous castle in Dorset from oblivion: 'In the west of England are yet to be seen the ruins of Berry Pomeroy Castle, formerly a place of great strength, but now, like the proud ancient possessors, almost forgotten, and daily mingling with the dust.'[28] But it was the Gateshead-born travel writer, poet, children's author, and Gothic romancer Jane Harvey who most enthusiastically responded to the topographical call to write about, and in so doing preserve, the Gothic antiquities of nearby and familiar locales. In the Preface to *The Castle of Tynemouth* (1806), Harvey attempted to negotiate her way through

---

[24] Bonhôte, *Bungay Castle*, vol. 1, p. 2.
[25] See Vine, *In Defiance of Time*, particularly the discussion of the work of Thomas Coryate, pp. 139–68.
[26] Thomas Pownall, *A Treatise on the Study of Antiquities as the Commentary to Historical Learning* (London: Printed for J. Dodsley, 1782), pp. 39, 3–6.
[27] Bonhôte, *Bungay Castle*, vol. 1, pp. xi, 2.
[28] Edward Montague, *The Castle of Berry Pomeroy*, 2 vols (London: Printed at the Minerva Press for Lane, Newman, and Co., 1806), vol. 1, p. 1.

the impasse that was the history/romance divide by maintaining that it was through topography, the strict observance of 'geographical accuracy' and the 'localities of place', that the tensions between the 'integrity, truth and candour' of the historian and the 'work of imagination' of the romancer might be resolved.[29] Accordingly, the Preface to the novel expresses an indebtedness to the topographical descriptions of William Hutchinson in *A View of Northumberland with an Excursion to the Abbey of Mailross [sic] in Scotland* (c.1778) and John Brand's *The History and Antiquities of the Town and County of the Town of Newcastle upon Tyne* (1789). Compressing the information contained in both studies, Harvey, in the fashion of a topographer herself, also resorts to the firsthand, empirical information about Tynemouth Castle that she has been able to glean through information collected 'on the spot, or elsewhere'.[30] The first chapter of the narrative that follows is a standard topographical description of the ruin and adjacent priory: the 'history' and 'curious remains' of the 'venerable priory' afford 'an ample field for conjecture and inquiry' to those 'who love to contemplate the monuments' and 'search into the records of past ages', while the 'natural grandeur' and the 'bold, majestic, and sublime scenery' of the site 'must ever delight the mind, and inspire it with noble sentiments'.[31]

Much the same applies to *Brougham Castle* (1816), Harvey's Gothic romance set in and around the 'extensive ruins' of the titular pile that was then located on the border of Westmorland. Harvey expresses affinities with the topographer's preservationist agenda early on in the novel, but even as she does so, she moves beyond the concern with present ruin in order to describe the castle in its former state, for, 'To describe the shattered remains of Brougham Castle, as they now stand,' she reasons, 'would convey little pleasure to the reader.'[32] Though inspired by ruin, the architectural imagination aspires towards completion; as in *Bungay Castle*, preservationism is merely a preamble to an imaginative act of reconstruction. Here, though, it is Ann Radcliffe more than any antiquarian source that dominates the narrative. Citing the evocative but factually erroneous description of Brougham that Radcliffe had offered in her *Journey*, the narrator observes that the site is 'rendered more interesting by having been occasionally the residence of the humane and generous Sir Philip Sydney [sic]', who had 'only to look from the windows of this once-noble edifice to see his own Arcadia spreading on every side'.[33] Repeating Radcliffe's tendency in the *Journey* to render the English landscape in terms identical to those employed in her Gothic fictions, Harvey too renders the Lake District as the enchanted ground of romance, a compound of

[29] Harvey, *The Castle of Tynemouth*, vol. 1, pp. i–ii.
[30] Harvey, *The Castle of Tynemouth*, vol. 1, p. viii.
[31] Harvey, *The Castle of Tynemouth*, vol. 1, p. 6.
[32] Jane Harvey, *Brougham Castle: A Novel*, 2 vols (London: Printed at the Minerva Press for A. K. Newman and Co., 1816), vol. 1, pp. 6–7.
[33] Harvey, *Brougham Castle*, vol. 1, p. 5.

pleasure and horror, beauty and sublimity that is best expressed through the remark of Charles Avison that William Gilpin and Radcliffe herself had later cited: 'Here is beauty indeed—beauty lying in the lap of horror'.[34]

It is seemingly in an attempt at counterbalancing the flighty turns of romance that Harvey's narrative is supported, authenticated, and qualified by the use of footnotes, a paratextual apparatus that, as Anthony Grafton, Susan Manning, and Rosemary Sweet have pointed out, was a feature particular to antiquarian writing in the period.[35] The first volume, for instance, includes lengthy footnotes that explain the origins of local lore and legend and the history of Brougham, while the second references such literary sources as Gilpin's citing of Avison in his *Observations* of 1786.[36] In locating themselves in extant Gothic ruins, and supporting their narrative with empirical facts and information concerning local antiquities, Gothic romances aspire towards the scholarly rigour and objectivity of antiquarian topography, a tendency that is particularly well illustrated in the later fiction of T. J. Horsley Curties. Of course, the imaginary piles to be found in Curties's earlier works neither warranted nor required anchorage in topographical evidence and historical fact. But when Curties sets about the writing of a lengthy romance set against the backdrop of the English Civil War in his penultimate novel, *St Botolph's Priory* (1806), the now self-consciously 'historical romancer' feels it necessary to supplement his narrative with footnotes of relevant historical and antiquarian detail. Historical facts, some of them taken from Hume's *The History of England*, are used to authenticate developments of the plot and character in Volumes 1 and 2, and when the action turns to Carisbrooke Castle, Curties cites in footnotes, among other sources, Richard Worsley's topographical study *The History of the Isle of Wight* (1781).[37] These predominate in the fourth volume, in which, having abandoned the largely imaginary landscapes on the Isle of Wight of the earlier sections, Curties accounts the regicide of King Charles I at the hands of the fiction's arch-villain, Oliver Cromwell.

Early Gothic fictions set in real-life Gothic ruins habitually place themselves in a particular relation to orality, setting out to record the oral traditions in storytelling, local lore, and popular superstition that circulated around these Gothic buildings as if motivated by the desire to preserve them. Bonhôte, for example, notes how, in early youth, she had listened at the ruins with 'pleased and captured

---

[34] Harvey, *Brougham Castle*, vol. 2, p. 200.

[35] See Anthony Grafton, *The Footnote: A Curious History* (Cambridge, Mass.: Harvard University Press, 1997); Susan Manning, 'Antiquarianism, the Scottish Science of Man, and the Emergence of Modern Disciplinarity', in *Scotland and the Borders of Romanticism*, ed. Leith Davis, Ian Duncan, and Janet Sorensen (Cambridge: Cambridge University Press, 2004), pp. 57–76; and Sweet, *Antiquaries*, pp. 7–8. For an account of how footnotes, together with other paratextual apparatuses, worked their way into historical fiction between 1762 and 1813, see Stevens, *British Historical Fiction before Scott*, pp. 97–107.

[36] See Harvey, *Brougham Castle*, vol. 1, pp. 98–100, 115; and vol. 2, p. 200.

[37] See T. J. Horsley Curties, *St Botolph's Priory; or, The Sable Mask. An Historic Romance*, 5 vols, (London: J. F. Hughes, 1806), vol. 4, p. 110.

attention' to the 'unaccountable tales related by the old and superstitious, and considered as real by herself and her inexperienced companions'.[38] One such tale concerns 'the ghost of an ancient warrior, clad in armour', who took his nightly turns around the ruin, while, in another, a 'lovely female form' of a spectre had been seen to glide around the castle, prior to disappearing on the very spot where it was imagined that her lover had been slain.[39] Edward Montague, too, looked back to an oral tradition of storytelling in claiming of Berry Pomeroy that 'Many are the dark deeds said to have been perpetrated within its walls', of which the 'yet blood-stained stones and flitting shades that nightly hover over their sad remains, entombed amongst the ruins, or buried without, sepulchral rites' are but 'sad mementos'.[40] Having recounted the histories of the guilt-stricken Lady Elinor de Fortebrand and the Abbot Bertrand at the outset, Montague's narrator notes that 'Such are the reports which the neighbouring peasantry have handed down to their offspring, and who, to this day, relate to the traveller the sad tales.'[41] While, following the Radcliffean example, Harvey and Bonhôte ultimately vanquish these popular beliefs in spectres through the contrivances of the explained supernatural, the ending of Montague's fiction leaves them very much in place. Either way, such texts look back to the oral tales of working-class superstition that circulated around ruined Gothic piles, the same stories of the servants that had driven Joseph Addison to the imaginary ruined abbey in Worcestershire in his essay in *The Spectator* in July 1711.

Although Thomas Percy had confined his sources for his assemblage of Gothic literary antiquities in the *Reliques* to printed and manuscript texts, other literary antiquarians of the age, including James Macpherson in his collection of Celtic verse in *Fragments of Ancient Poetry* (1760), worked with largely oral material. Throughout Macpherson's Ossianic poetry, ghostliness is a persistent theme. Recalling the work of the literary antiquarian, Gothic antiquarian romances are bound up in a dynamic of double preservation, collecting and recording in print the oral tales of the supernatural that had circulated around ruined Gothic piles in the same gesture that they seek to record, preserve, and transmit the memory of the ruins themselves. It is this that links them with the often more ambivalent attitudes towards popular superstitions witnessed in much contemporary antiquarian writing. For, albeit in a very controlled and particular way, antiquaries too often expressed an interest in recording popular tales of the supernatural. John Aubrey's *Miscellanies* (1696), for example, included a chapter on apparitions, a compilation of several notable instances of haunting and ghost-seeing, from classical antiquity through to his seventeenth-century present; while some of the accounts Aubrey claims to have derived from William Dugdale, others he seems to

---

[38] Bonhôte, *Bungay Castle*, vol. 1, p. ix.   [39] Bonhôte, *Bungay Castle*, vol. 1, p. x.
[40] Montague, *The Castle of Berry Pomeroy*, vol. 1, pp. 1–2.
[41] Montague, *The Castle of Berry Pomeroy*, vol. 1, p. 4.

have experienced at first hand.[42] Later, Henry Bourne's *Antiquitates vulgares* (1725) brought the urbane gaze of the antiquary to bear on the oral tradition of folklore and superstition, recording and explaining across his study such practices of the 'common people' as death and burial rituals; fears concerning the midnight appearance of evil spirits; haunted houses and their exorcism; belief in fairies and hobgoblins; and fireside tales of spirits and apparitions.[43] Strongly Lockean in its orientation, Bourne's study aimed to vanquish the hold that such superstitions had on the working classes, often through tracing them back to the 'evil' practices of heathenism and the benighted beliefs of the Catholic past. John Brand's reprinting, revision, and extension of Bourne in *Observations on Popular Antiquities* (1777) was motivated by a similar objective. In *A Provincial Glossary, with a Collection of Local Proverbs and Popular Superstitions* (1787), however, Francis Grose jettisoned the tendency to explain away working-class superstition as the residue of the dark, monkish past by committing himself merely to the impartial recording of supernatural beliefs both present and 'formerly current in this country'.[44] Suspending the judgements of earlier writers, Grose in his extended account of local and national superstitions—ghosts, witches, sorcerers, witchcraft, fairies, second sight, soothsaying, omens, charms, and other 'miscellaneous superstitions'—actually countenances a belief in the supernatural, even going so far as to distinguish without the slightest trace of scepticism a particularly English version of the supernatural from the French, German, and Spanish varieties: 'Dragging chains', he argues, 'Is not the fashion of English Ghosts; chains and black vestments being chiefly the accoutrements of foreign spectres, seen in arbitrary governments: dead or alive, English spirits are free.'[45] As I have argued in this book, ghosts were an important aspect of England's 'Gothic' cultural and political inheritance, and had been embraced as such since at least William Temple's essay 'Of Poetry' (1690). But they were a crucial part of the popular superstitions of Scotland, too, particularly as witnessed in Walter Scott's *Minstrelsy of the Scottish Border* (1802) and, more anthropologically, in Anne Grant's *Essays on the Superstitions of the Highlanders of Scotland* (1811). Famously, Grose commissioned Robert Burns to write 'Tam o'Shanter', a comic poem about the haunting of Alloway Church, South Ayrshire, in c.1790; the poem was first published in the *Edinburgh Herald* in March 1791, and then reprinted in a lengthy footnote in the second volume of Grose's *The Antiquities of Scotland* (1791)

---

[42] John Aubrey, *Miscellanies* (London: Printed for Edward Castle, 1696), pp. 59–82.
[43] Henry Bourne, *Antiquitates Vulgares; or, The Antiquities of the Common People* (Newcastle: Printed by J. White for the Author, 1725).
[44] Francis Grose, *A Provincial Glossary, with a Collection of Local Proverbs and Popular Superstitions* (London: Printed for S. Hooper, 1787), p. 6.
[45] Grose, *A Provincial Glossary*, p. 10.

shortly thereafter.[46] Grose framed the inclusion of Burns's poem as a gesture of cultural preservation, claiming that 'Diverse stories of these horrid rites are still current.'[47] Conserving the ruins as much as the supernatural lore that accrete around them, early Gothic fictions deliberately courted affinities with literary antiquarianism and antiquarian topography as a means of grounding and authenticating the apocryphal, somewhat illegitimate histories that they narrated.

Antiquarianism and the Problem of Romance

If this suggests an easy relation of reciprocity and exchange between romance and antiquarian practice, it is important to remember that, in principle, the two remained vigorously opposed. At the very least, they were intended for two very different class-based readerships, the elite and educated writers and readers of antiquarian studies on the one hand, and the middle- and lower-class producers and consumers of fictional romance on the other. While several articles published in *Archaeologia* were devoted to careful debates concerning the origins of 'romance' as both a term and an object of literary enquiry, the scientific aspirations of antiquarianism required that the imaginative spirit of romance be strenuously excluded.[48] The aim of antiquarian scholarship, the inaugural issue of *Archaeologia* made clear, had always been 'either to separate falshood [sic] from truth, and traditions from evidence, to establish what had probability for its basis, or to explode what rested only in the vanity of the inventors and propagators'.[49] Providing the evidence upon which history could depend, antiquarianism aimed at the generation of truth, that is, not 'a mere narrative taken up at random and embellished with poetic diction, but a regular and elaborate inquiry into every ancient record and proof, that can elucidate or establish them'.[50] In *The Antiquary* (1816), Walter Scott registered the tensions between antiquarianism and imaginative fiction in having Jonathan Oldbuck adopt a position of scepticism towards the superstitious lore surrounding the Green Chamber, the supposedly haunted bedroom at his home at Monkbarns in

---

[46] See Hamish Mathison and Angela Wright, 'The Haunting of Britain's Ruins', in *Writing Britain's Ruins*, ed. Michael Carter, Peter N. Lindfield, and Dale Townshend (London: British Library, 2017), pp. 210–28.

[47] Francis Grose, *The Antiquities of Scotland*, 2 vols (London: Printed for S. Hooper, 1791), vol. 2, p. 199.

[48] For examples of discussions of romance as word and object among eighteenth-century antiquaries, see 'Remarks on the word *Romance*. By the Rev. Mr Bowles, FSA. In a Letter to the Secretary. Read January 8, 1778', *Archaeologia* vol. V (1779): pp. 267–71, and 'On the Origin of the word Romance; by the Rev. Mr Drake. In a Letter to the Secretary', *Archaeologia* vol. IV (1786): pp. 142–8. For an account of the scientific aspirations of Romantic-era antiquarian practice, see Heringman, *Sciences of Antiquity*.

[49] See 'Introduction: Containing an Historical Account of the Origins and Establishment of the Society of Antiquaries', *Archaeologia*, vol. 1 (1770): pp. i–xliii (p. i).

[50] 'Introduction: Containing an Historical Account of the Origins and Establishment of the Society of Antiquaries': p. ii.

which his friend William Lovel spends the night. This episode, as Fiona Robertson has pointed out, is deeply charged with romance's imaginative possibilities.[51] Highly intertextual by nature, it is a reworking of Ludovico's experiences in the haunted chamber in *The Mysteries of Udolpho*, an episode in Radcliffe's fiction that Scott particularly admired, and a scenario to which he would return in 'The Tapestried Chamber; or, The Lady in the Sacque' in 1829. The supernatural contents of Lovel's dreams also recall those of his namesake Edmund Lovel in the haunted apartments of the castle in Reeve's *The Old English Baron*, as well as the portentous dreams of the heroine Adeline in Radcliffe's *The Romance of the Forest*. But for the misogynistic Oldbuck, the romantic rumour of ghostly activity at Monkbarns is merely evidence of the 'childish nonsense' that is peddled by his sister Griselda, even while he takes particular pride in his collection of antique literary objects and displays a tapestried representation of 'The Marriage of Sir Gawaine', a ballad included in Percy's *Reliques*, on the wall of his study.[52] Later, Oldbuck dismisses 'The Fortunes of Martin Waldeck', the German tale of spectral conjuration that is retold by Isabella Wardour, as 'trumpery' and 'ridiculous legend'; though it might be 'the fashion' to 'admire those extravagant fictions', Oldbuck, in distinction from Grose's emphasis upon national English superstition, reworks lines from Mathias's *The Pursuits of Literature* to claim that 'I bear an English heart, / Unused at ghosts and rattling bones to start'.[53] If ghosts are to be spoken of at all, they ought to be approached in the spirit of cold and objective rationalism that is epitomized for Oldbuck by John Aubrey's account of spectres and other occult phenomena in his *Miscellanies*.[54]

Two examples of the deliberate fusion of the generic properties of antiquarian writing with those of popular romance illustrate the fractious relationship between the two modes particularly well. Thomas Pownall's *An Antiquarian Romance* (written in 1782; published in 1795) turned the tables on conjectural history by adopting the furthest reaches of antiquity—that remote realm characteristically dismissed by historians such as Hume as the place of mere romantic speculation and conjecture as the legitimate object of scholarly enquiry. The Preface to the text turns upon a canny exploitation of architectural metaphor. Just as the antiquary pieced together dispersed and broken fragments of buildings so as to restore them in some degree to their former splendour, so the historian built his histories on the sometimes scant traces of the remaining textual evidence. Both, Pownall maintained, were comparable with the work of the romancer, since he or she too worked conjecturally with the 'fragments and remnants of a system, which once had actual existence, but of which the fragments now lie scattered and

---

[51] Fiona Robertson, 'Romance and the Romantic Novel: Sir Walter Scott', in *A Companion to Romance: From Classical to Contemporary*, ed. Corinne Saunders (Oxford: Blackwell Publishing, 2007), pp. 287–304 (p. 288).
[52] Walter Scott, *The Antiquary*, ed. Nicola J. Watson (New York: Oxford University Press, 2002), p. 95.
[53] Scott, *The Antiquary*, p. 180.   [54] Scott, *The Antiquary*, pp. 90–1.

neglected, partly buried in oblivion, and partly smothered and over-grown with the weeds of fable'.[55] Thus daringly drawing parallels between history, antiquarianism, and the writing of romance, Pownall's study focused on the *Cymri, Cimmerii,* or *Cimbri*, the aboriginal inhabitants of Europe from which such nations as the Goths, Danes, Picts, Scythians, Saxons, and Jutes were all said to have descended. Evidence is continuously marshalled to confirm historical conjecture, with Pownall seeking to dispel fables and myths as he proceeds; his study, he claims, should in this respect be regarded as 'a plain clue to that labyrinth [of antique history], which learning had rendered so perplexed'.[56] Despite the promises of its title, though, *An Antiquarian Romance* is hardly the populist form that it presents itself as being. Instead, it bears all the marks of inaccessible antiquarian scholarship, consisting, as it does, of elaborate genealogies, complex etymological analyses, detailed geographical description, and copious footnotes.

Pownall's foray into romance-writing was nothing short of disastrous. The review of *An Antiquarian Romance* that was published in *The Monthly Review* was, at best, measured, the account in *The Gentleman's Magazine* somewhat damming.[57] But the full impact of Pownall's text fell on the Society of Antiquaries and the author's relationship to it. The Reverend Edward Ledwich read his reply to Pownall, 'A Dissertation on the Religion of the Druids', at the Society in November 1784; this was subsequently published in *Archaeologia* in 1785, and thereafter summarized and endorsed in *The Critical Review* and *The Monthly Review*.[58] In addition to Pownall's account of Druidical religion, it was his scandalous recourse to conjectural methods of reasoning to which Ledwich took such exception. Dismissing it as 'literary pharmacy', 'literary trifling', and a dangerous admixture of 'truth and conjecture', Ledwich felt the urge to reassert the distinctions between history, antiquarianism, and romance that Pownall had so carelessly flouted.[59] What made the affair especially galling was that Pownall himself had sought to juxtapose the antiquarian method with 'incomprehensible romance' in his earlier *A Treatise on the Study of Antiquities*. As Sweet's account of the debacle has pointed out, Pownall was increasingly isolated from the Society of Antiquaries from this moment onwards.[60] This is not without echoes of antiquarian reactions to Walpole's *Historic Doubts* that I discussed in the Introduction to this book: as both men had learned to their peril, the divide between fiction and

---

[55] Thomas Pownall, *An Antiquarian Romance, Endeavouring to Mark a Line, By Which The Most Ancient People, and the Processions of the Earliest Inhabitants of Europe, May be Investigated* (London: Printed by and for John Nichols, 1795), p. xlii.

[56] Pownall, *An Antiquarian Romance*, p. 184.

[57] See 'Article VIII', in *The Monthly Review* (August 1795): pp. 413-17, and the review published in *GM*, 2nd series, vol. LXV, part 1 (February 1795); pp. 139-40.

[58] See Edward Ledwich, 'A Dissertation on the Religion of the Druids. Addressed to Governor Pownall', *Archaeologia* vol. 3 (1785): pp. 303-22.

[59] Ledwich, 'A Dissertation on the Religion of the Druids', pp. 304, 311, 304.

[60] See Sweet, *Antiquaries*, pp. 25-6.

rigorous antiquarian learning could not be breached without the severest of consequences.

Though it ultimately turned out to be more professionally productive than catastrophic, Walter Scott's involvement in the completion and publication of Joseph Strutt's *Queenhoo-Hall, A Romance* (1808) underlined for the writer a similar lesson. A prolific antiquary and engraver, Strutt was the author of, among other scholarly works, *The Regal and Ecclesiastical Antiquities of England* (1771); *The Chronicle of England* (1779); *A Complete View of the Dress and Habits of the People of England* (1796–9); and *The Sports and Pastimes of the People of England* (1801).[61] Towards the end of his career, he embarked upon the writing of *Queenhoo-Hall*, a romance set in and around the eponymous manor house at Tewin, Hertfordshire, the architectural portal through which he set out to access, through narrative and story, the habits, pastimes, sports, costumes, and beliefs that prevailed there during the 'Gothic' times of the reign of Henry VI. Notions of Gothic pertain to the fiction's contents, too, for, in intending his work as a means of disseminating, popularizing, and rendering less 'dry' the antiquarian research that he had published elsewhere, Strutt made pointed use of what by now were the established conventions of Gothic romance, including a preoccupation with orality and the superstitious beliefs of the lower orders; necromancy; ghosts; witchcraft; Catholic indiscretion; and spectral conjuration. These come together powerfully in the history of Lady Emma that takes up much of the second volume, an interpolated narrative that reads as a tale of terror very much in the tradition of Radcliffe. At the time of Strutt's death in October 1802, however, the narrative was left incomplete, and in 1807 John Murray passed the manuscript on to Walter Scott who, by this time, had achieved poetic fame with *The Lay of the Last Minstrel* (1805), was shortly to publish *Marmion* (1808) with Constable, Miller, and Murray, and was already privately at work on what would eventually become the early sections of *Waverley*. Drawing the text to a hasty conclusion, Scott added two final chapters, and together with Strutt's drama *Ancient Times, Queenhoo-Hall, A Romance* was published in four volumes by Murray in London and Constable in Edinburgh in 1808. In by-now familiar ways, the 'Advertisement' for the work defensively figured Scott the unnamed editor's involvement in architectural terms: Strutt's original was merely 'the outline and main plan of his building, without the gothic façade, which should have given a character to the whole', but if the editor had failed in the end to furnish his readers with the absent edifice, this was because it could not have been achieved without a full-scale act of rewriting.[62]

---

[61] For an account of the antiquarian practice and methodology of Strutt, see Ina Ferris, 'Unhinging the Past: Joseph Strutt and the Antiquarian Poetics of the Piece', in *Romantic Antiquarianism*, ed. Noah Heringman and Crystal B. Lake, *Romantic Circles Praxis* (June 2014): http://www.rc.umd.edu/praxis/antiquarianism/praxis.antiquarianism.2014.ferris.html (accessed 18 January 2018).

[62] Joseph Strutt, *Queenhoo-Hall, A Romance; and Ancient Times, A Drama*, 4 vols (Edinburgh: Archibald Constable and Co.; London: John Murray, 1808), vol. 1.

Upon publication, *Queenhoo-Hall* garnered mixed reactions. An article in *The Critical Review* began with a nod of approval to what the fiction, in principle, had set out achieve, claiming that while it 'does not frequently happen that we are called upon to estimate in the same manner the merits of deep and laborious research and those of imagination and fancy', there remains 'every reason to wish that union a circumstance of more frequent occurrence'.[63] The generic merging of romance and antiquarian knowledge, the reviewer went on, was an effective way of ensuring that the reader's attention remained engaged during an otherwise potentially arduous process of didactic instruction, one of the advantages of the romance mode that Clara Reeve had discussed in *The Progress of Romance*. Apparently unsuspecting of the fact that the unnamed 'editor' of Strutt's work was Walter Scott, this reviewer singled out aspects of Scott's *Marmion*, published earlier that same year, as a good though not entirely problem-free example of the literary treatment of antiquities. 'But when the writer [of *Marmion*] breathes from the heat of battle and leads us away from his dying hero only to show us the Gothic characters inscribed on the tomb of Sybill [sic] Grey,' the reviewer continued, 'we are most properly offended and tempted, at the moment, to exclaim, "This is the very vice of antiquarian pedantry!"'[64] *Queenhoo-Hall* too, then, suffered from the same 'vice of antiquarian pedantry' that the reviewer had identified in *Marmion*, the review concluding with a denouncement of it as 'tedious performance' with momentary glimpses of 'amusing and characteristic bits'.[65]

Though excoriating, the critique was not necessarily unfair, for the antiquarian details concerning the sports, recreations, clothing, and beliefs of the Gothic past that Strutt includes not in footnotes but in the body of the text do, indeed, seem to weigh down the narrative with an accumulation of information that turns out to be inimical to the work of fiction-making. Simply put, *Queenhoo-Hall* wears the mantle of antiquarian learning too heavily, and this prevents the narrative from ever scaling the imaginative heights that readers and reviewers expected of the romance mode. As the mention of *Marmion* made clear, though, Scott, for some of his readers, was narrowly in danger of committing the same error. As Francis Jeffrey's review of *Marmion* in *The Edinburgh Review* put it, Scott's poetic romance contained 'more tedious and flat passages, and more ostentation of historical and antiquarian lore' than *The Lay of the Last Minstrel*.[66] For Jeffrey, Scott in *Marmion* was overly preoccupied with the imitation of 'obsolete extravagance, and in the representation of manners and sentiments in which none of his

---

[63] Review of *Queenhoo-Hall* in *The Critical Review*, 3rd series, vol. 14, no. 4 (August 1808): pp. 406–9 (p. 406).
[64] Review of *Queenhoo-Hall* in *The Critical Review*, p. 407.
[65] Review of *Queenhoo-Hall* in *The Critical Review*, p. 409.
[66] [Francis Jeffrey], 'Art. I: Review of Walter Scott's *Marmion*', *The Edinburgh Review* vol. 13 (April 1808): pp. 1–35 (p. 2).

readers can be supposed to take much interest, except the few who can judge of their exactness'.[67]

The quasi-scientific leanings and generic features of antiquarian scholarship, as many reviews and essays of the period made clear, were not welcome in the realms of poetry and imaginative fiction. As John and Anna Laetitia Aikin's essay 'On Romances, an Imitation' (1773) argued, while romance enjoyed universal appeal, antiquarianism, like theology and geometry, could 'only hope to please those whom a conformity of disposition has engaged in similar pursuits'.[68] Critical responses to the novels of Horsley Curties, in particular, sounded this note continuously. 'More abbeys, with "battlement ramparts" and "heavy *Gothic* pillars of the *Saxon* order"!' complained a reviewer of *Ancient Records* (1801); given the inaccuracies and anachronisms in which the fiction nonetheless abounded, the review facetiously proposed that Curties improve his antiquarian learning by penning a tract entitled *A Treatise on the Mode of Posting in the Thirteenth and Fourteenth Centuries*.[69] Sarah Green in *Romance Readers and Romance Writers* (1810) similarly presented Curties as a dull antiquary who inflicted upon his readers interminable and 'intolerably dull and tiresome' tomes.[70] In the particular case of Scott's poem, the overfondness for antiquarian learning sat uneasily with a romance that, with equal regret, Jeffrey held to be too 'Gothic' in style, too filled with 'the machinery of a bad German novel'.[71] The vaulted subterranean chamber, the monks, smoking tapers, stern abbots, and haughty prioresses described during the immurement of Constance de Beverley in Lindisfarne Priory in Canto II of *Marmion*, Jeffrey claimed, 'are all images borrowed from the novels of Mrs. Radcliffe and her imitators'; 'the public', he concluded, 'has now supped full of this sort of horrors [*sic*]; or, if any effect is still to be produced by their exhibition, it may certainly be produced at too cheap a rate, to be worthy the ambition of a poet of original imagination'.[72]

Scott recounted his involvement with *Queenhoo-Hall* in the 'General Preface' to the so-called Magnum Opus edition of his novels in 1829, noting how discouraged he had been by its 'indifferent reception'.[73] By this time, however, the reasons for this had become abundantly clear: 'by rendering his language too ancient, and displaying his antiquarian knowledge too liberally, the ingenious author had

---

[67] [Jeffrey], 'Art. I: Review of Walter Scott's *Marmion*', p. 5.

[68] J. and A. L. Aikin, 'On Romances, an Imitation', in *Miscellaneous Pieces, in Prose* (London: Printed for J. Johnson, 1773), pp. 39–46 (p. 40).

[69] Review of T. J. Horsley Curties's *Ancient Records* (1801), *The Critical Review* vol. xxxii (June 1801): p. 232.

[70] Sarah Green, *Romance Readers and Romance Writers: A Satirical Novel*, 3 vols (London: Printed for T. Hoookham, Jnr and E. T. Hookham, 1810), vol. 1, p. vi.

[71] [Jeffrey],'Art. I: Review of Walter Scott's *Marmion*', p. 9.

[72] [Jeffrey], 'Art. I: Review of Walter Scott's *Marmion*', p. 9.

[73] Walter Scott, 'General Preface', in *Introduction and Notes from the Magnum Opus: Waverley to A Legend of the Wars of Montrose*, ed. J. H. Alexander, with P.D. Garside and Claire Lamont (Edinburgh: Edinburgh University Press, 2012), pp. 8–22 (p. 13).

raised up an obstacle to his own success', shipwrecking himself on the very rocks of antiquarian knowledge that he had sought to bring to light.[74] Addressing himself too exclusively to the antiquary, Strutt had alienated the popular readership that he set out to engage. Jeffrey's critique of *Marmion* had driven these lessons even closer to home. If Scott had learned one thing from the experience, though, it was that antiquarian findings had to be communicated through a literary work that was 'more light and obvious to general comprehension' than Strutt's had been. From now on, Anne H. Stevens observes, the writer could not afford to overlook the importance of balancing 'historical detail and modern interest' in his fictions.[75] An important and, indeed, formative moment in the genesis of the historical novelist, Scott's work on *Queenhoo-Hall* would lead to his return to the manuscript of *Waverley*, this time with a commitment to redressing Strutt's misjudging of fictional style and content. By the time of the publication of *Ivanhoe* in 1820, Scott could articulate through the authorial persona of Laurence Templeton a cogent manifesto for his literary practice, prefacing the novel with a 'Dedicatory Epistle' that made clear his fiction's difference from the antiquarianism of the Rev. Dr Dryasdust, F.A.S. and Oldbuck, his Scottish friend. His foray into 'the domestic antiquities of England' in *Ivanhoe*, he was well aware, was unlikely to please the tastes of the 'severer' or 'more grave' antiquary insofar as it depended strongly on an 'intermingling' of fiction and truth, a deliberate 'polluting' of the 'well of history' with modern, imaginative inventions.[76] Abandoning the archaic language, idiom, and register of *Queenhoo-Hall*, Scott expressed here a commitment to a style that was accessible and modern. Strutt's readers, by contrast, had been 'much trammelled by the repulsive dryness of mere antiquity', and in this manner, 'a man of talent, and of great antiquarian erudition' had 'limited the popularity of his work, by excluding from it every thing which was not sufficiently obsolete to be altogether forgotten and unintelligible'.[77]

If this recalls Horace Walpole's determination to distance himself from the 'dry' antiquarianism of his day that I discussed earlier in this book, it is a parallel of which Scott was well aware, for together with the modernizing gestures of the antiquary George Ellis in his *Specimens of Early English Metrical Romances* (1805), Scott in the 'Dedicatory Epistle' to *Ivanhoe* cites Walpole as his major literary example and precedent. But the similarities between Scott and Walpole do not end there, and in a fascinating turn Scott adopts a revealing architectural metaphor as descriptive of his own creative practice: 'It is my comfort, that errors of this kind will escape the general class of readers, and that I may share in the ill-deserved applause of those architects, who, in their modern Gothic, do not hesitate to

---

[74] Scott, 'General Preface', p. 13.
[75] Stevens, *British Historical Fiction Before Scott*, p. 147.
[76] Walter Scott, *Ivanhoe: A Romance*, ed. Ian Duncan (Oxford: Oxford University Press, 1996), pp. 13–17.
[77] Scott, *Ivanhoe*, p. 18.

introduce, without rule or method, ornaments proper to different styles and to different periods of the art.'[78] That is, refining the long-standing sense of himself as an 'aerial architect', Scott here figures himself as one who would be glad to share in the 'ill-deserved applause' accorded to architects of 'modern Gothic' forms. Again, the Walpolean connection was paramount, for Scott, in his 1811 Introduction to Ballantyne's edition of *Otranto*, saw both Walpole's fiction and his home as an expression of 'modern Gothic' sensibilities.[79] As Scott well knew, though, 'modern Gothic', more than being a neutral term of description, was the opprobrious appellation through which antiquaries and architectural traditionalists habitually dismissed the Gothic Revivalist architecture of their day, what they took to be the tasteless and historically inaccurate intermingling of different architectural styles that they witnessed at Strawberry Hill, Fonthill Abbey, and in so many other 'debased' modern architectural constructions.

The negative associations of architecture in the 'modern Gothic' style in the period cannot be overemphasized. As Peter N. Lindfield has pointed out, the epithet was coined by Richard Neve in 1739 as a means of rejecting the frivolity, imaginative excess, and stylistic incongruities of the revived Gothic style.[80] As such, it encompassed much Gothic Revivalist architecture of the eighteenth century, including the suturing of Gothic and classical forms that we encounter in William Kent and Batty Langley; the rococo Gothic of Richard Bentley, James Paine, Thomas Chippendale, and Sanderson Miller; and the merging of Gothic and neoclassical forms in Robert Adam and James Wyatt.[81] Equally deserving of the moniker were the curious Oriental/Gothic hybrids of William and John Halfpenny in *Chinese and Gothic Architecture Properly Ornamented* (1752) and *The Country Gentleman's Pocket Companion* (1756), or the uncomfortable merging of the classical and the Gothic in Thomas Collins Overton's *The Temple Builder's Most Useful Companion* (1766). Often composed of jarring assemblages of incompatible modes and idioms, eighteenth-century Gothic Revivalist architecture was an impure form, and it was this stylistic irregularity that 'modern Gothic' was used to signify. As a term of aesthetic judgement, it remained current later in the period, too. In 1796, and in the midst of his work on the Bank of England, London, John Soane was deeply offended to learn from the architect Richard Jupp that James Wyatt, himself a notorious dabbler in the 'modern Gothic', had read out to a gathering of distinguished architects a poem entitled *The Modern Goth* (1788), a satire by one Norris on Soane and his distinctive brand of classicism that began with the lines, 'GLORY to thee, great artist, soul of taste! / For mending pigsties when a plank's misplaced'.[82] In its original context, the poem referenced Soane's removal of the cupola of the Rotunda in the course of his

---

[78] Scott, *Ivanhoe*, p. 21.   [79] Scott, 'Introduction', p. xii.
[80] Lindfield, *Georgian Gothic*, p. 42.   [81] See Lindfield, *Georgian Gothic*.
[82] *The Modern Goth. [A Satire in Verse on Sir John Soane. By-Norris]* (London, 1788), ll. 1–2.

remodelling of the Bank, an act that was seen to replay the ancient Goths' sacking of Rome. Wyatt revived *The Modern Goth* some eight years later, circulating it among Fellows at New College, Oxford; brought thus to light, Norris's poem was subsequently republished in *The Observer* in October 1796. As Gillian Darley has pointed out, the poem contained nothing that was particularly damaging, yet the slight of being called a 'modern Goth' was enough for Soane to pursue the matter to the courts of libel.[83] In his *Memoirs* of almost forty years later, Soane was still smarting at the insult: 'it was a black joke,' he bitterly recalled, yet one that was entirely in keeping with the character of Wyatt, its rebarbative teller.[84] The anonymous poem *Metrical Remarks on Modern Castles and Cottages, and Architecture in General* (1813) included an equally satirical treatment of the taste for the 'modern Gothic', the contemporary bastardization, it claimed, of the 'genuine' and 'authentic' Gothic style:

> Loaded with mass of tower or round or square,
> The new-built CASTLE shows its borrowed air,
> Aping old Conway's or Caernarvon's pride;
> Its only Likeness, that the rifted side,
> And gaping fissure of disjointed wall,
> Proclaim it nodding quickly to its fall.[85]

John Carter would add his voice to the attack in his regular columns in *The Gentleman's Magazine* between 1797 and 1817, variously dismissing modern Gothic forms as 'the fantastic order of architecture', 'this *farrago* of architecture', or 'a half-begotten, misshapen "congestion", called "Gothic architecture revived"'.[86] Despite his earlier having collaborated with Walpole on the visual recording of his home, Carter by 1801 was now content to cite Strawberry Hill, together with Fonthill Abbey, as the epitome of this monstrous style. Such are the attitudes upon which Scott knowingly draws when he has Jonathan Oldbuck, a keen promoter of 'ancient' Gothic architecture, frequently express his distaste for the 'modern Gothic' of his day. His taste in ecclesiastical architecture, Oldbuck, with reference to Thomas Warton's typology, makes clear during a particularly tiresome peroration, runs from the 'massive Saxon' to the 'florid Gothic', abruptly stopping short at the 'evils' of the 'mixed and composite' styles that took effect in the reign of James I.[87] In the 'Dedicatory Epistle' to *Ivanhoe*, however, Scott adopts

---

[83] Darley, *John Soane*, pp. 132-3.
[84] Soane, *Memoirs of the Professional Life of an Architect*, p. 29.
[85] Anon., *Metrical Remarks on Modern Castles and Cottages, and Architecture in General* (London: Printed for J. Nunn, 1813), p. 21.
[86] See J. C., 'The Fantastic Order of Architecture', *GM* 72 (1802), II, pp. 719-21; 'An Architect', 'Pursuits vii', *GM* lxix (1799), I, pp. 92-4 (p. 93); and 'An Architect', 'Pursuits xxxv', *GM* 71 (1801), I, pp. 413-18 (p. 417).
[87] Scott, *The Antiquary*, p. 182.

the unorthodox, whimsical, and invariably anachronistic mixture of styles characteristic of the 'modern Gothic' as a metaphor for his own craft.[88]

Scott's choice of metaphor was as much a clever riposte to Jeffrey as a means of marking his difference from the stultifying antiquarianism of Oldbuck. As Susan Manning has argued, Jeffrey had employed a revealing distinction between the historian, on the one hand, and the antiquary, on the other, in his review of John Millar's *An Historical View of the English Government* (1803) in *The Edinburgh Review* in October 1803.[89] As I argued in Chapter 4, this was a common distinction in the period, and worked its way into writers as diverse as John Dart and Edmund Burke: while antiquaries were often confined solely to the order of ruins, historians such as Millar for Jeffrey were better conceived as architects insofar as they were able to move beyond the material relic so as to produce 'the plan and elevation of the original fabric', enabling their readers 'to trace the connexions of the shattered fragments, and to determine the primitive form and denomination of all the disfigured masses that lay before us'.[90] This distinction between the antiquary and the higher-minded architect was replayed in Scott's comparative review of George Ellis's *Specimens of Early English Metrical Romances* (1805) and Joseph Ritson's *Ancient English Metrical Romances* (1802) in *The Edinburgh Review* in January 1806. Ellis's work, Scott here observed, 'sufficiently illustrates his superior skill as an antiquary', for, although he brought to light fewer literary materials than Ritson, 'it is evidently because he wished to be an architect, not a mere collector of stones and rubbish'.[91] To compound matters further, Jeffrey's review of *Marmion* had claimed that 'To write a modern romance of chivalry', as Scott had done, 'seems to be much such [sic] a fantasy as to build a modern abbey, or an English pagoda', a barb no doubt directed at Scott's description of his imagination as an evanescent Gothic pile in the Introduction to Canto First of *Marmion*.[92] The passage in Scott's poem is not without allusions to the disappearing palaces of Shakespeare's Prospero:

> The vision of enchantment's past:
> Like frostwork in the morning ray,
> The fancied fabric melts away;

---

[88] For more on Scott's 'cavalier' attitude towards anachronism in the 'Dedicatory Epistle' to *Ivanhoe*, see Graham Tulloch, 'Imagining the Middle Ages and Renaissance in *Ivanhoe* and *Kenilworth*', in *Approaches to Teaching Scott's Waverley Novels*, ed. Evan Gottlieb and Ian Duncan (New York: Modern Language Association of America, 2009), pp. 164–9.

[89] See Susan Manning, 'Walter Scott, Antiquarianism and the Political Discourse of the *Edinburgh Review*, 1802–11', in *British Romanticism and the Edinburgh Review: Bicentenary Essays*, ed. Massimiliano Demata and Duncan Wu (Houndmills: Palgrave Macmillan, 2002), pp. 102–23 (pp. 108–9).

[90] Quoted in Manning, 'Walter Scott, Antiquarianism and the Political Discourse of the *Edinburgh Review*, 1802–11', p. 108.

[91] [Walter Scott], 'Art. Vi. Review of George Ellis's *Specimens of Early English Metrical Romances* and Joseph Ritson's *Ancient English Metrical Romances*', *The Edinburgh Review* vol. 7, no. 14 (January 1806): pp. 387–413 (p. 413).

[92] [Jeffrey],'Art. I: Review of Walter Scott's *Marmion*', p. 5.

> Each Gothic arch, memorial-stone,
> And long, dim, lofty aisle, are gone;
> And lingering last, deception dear,
> The choir's high sounds die on my ear.[93]

Embracing Jeffrey's metaphor of modern Gothic and Orientalist architecture while refusing its negative associations, Scott employs it as a guiding image for his craft. If what resulted were, indeed, the castles in the air to which he later referred in his journal, these fabrications were self-consciously Gothic Revivalist in design. Invigorating 'dry antiquity' with imaginative fiction, the historical novel was a corrective to the antiquarian romances of writers such as Strutt, a careful bringing together of the Romantic popular interest in national antiquities with the commercial imperatives of the literary marketplace.[94] It is to an account of how other writers negotiated the relationship between antiquarianism and romance that this chapter now turns.

Visions of Gothic Antiquity at Kenilworth Castle

As I argued in the Introduction, the Scottish antiquary John Pinkerton in an article published in *The Gentleman's Magazine* in 1788 bemoaned the fact that antiquarianism had taken a 'visionary turn', an imaginative predisposition that uncomfortably aligned it with the dreams and visions of the romancer. His point was well made, for, in addition to being objects of interest in their own right, the ruins of Gothic castles, abbeys, towers, and other ancient fortifications were regarded by antiquaries as portals to the vanished Gothic past, as points of entry into a much larger, richer, and arguably more important vanished historical realm. As Edward King in the 1782 edition of *Observations on Ancient Castles* argued, the 'attentive examination' of castle ruins 'may help us to form clearer ideas of some of the most important parts of history; and may also make us understand more fully the gradual progress of the arts'.[95] Francis Grose had argued much the same in the first volume of *The Antiquities of England and Wales*, while the architect George Cooper expressed similar claims in *Architectural Reliques* of 1807: 'If we would know even the general state of the wealth and power, or the political strength of our ancestors, the best documents in proof of them are the monuments they have left us of their industry and their art, their

---

[93] Walter Scott, 'Marmion', in *Scott: Poetical Works, With the Author's Introduction and Notes*, ed. J. Logie Robertson (London: Oxford University Press, 1971), pp. 89–206 (p. 92).
[94] See Ina Ferris, 'Scott's Authorship and Book Culture', in *The Edinburgh Companion to Sir Walter Scott*, ed. Fiona Robertson (Edinburgh: Edinburgh University Press, 2012), pp. 9–21.
[95] King, *Observations on Ancient Castles*, p. 4.

works of military defence, of piety, and of public gratitude.'[96] Ruins prompted in the antiquaries who sketched, traced, and studied them visionary acts of historical reconstruction, not only of the piles in their original state but of the remote historical past that they were thought to incarnate and embody.

There is perhaps no clearer example of this visionary turn than in the numerous texts that were prompted and inspired by the Gothic ruins of Kenilworth Castle, Warwickshire, in the eighteenth and nineteenth centuries. In Dialogue III of his *Moral and Political Dialogues* (1759), Richard Hurd staged an imaginary philosophical exchange between Robert Digby, John Arbuthnot, and Joseph Addison when the three visited the ruins of Kenilworth Castle in the summer of 1716.[97] Armed with a copy of William Dugdale's *The Antiquities of Warwickshire* (1656), the visitors, Hurd's commentary observes, sought at the ruins to 'indulge to the utmost the several reflexions which such scenes are apt to inspire', an observation that locates the scenario firmly within the aesthetic of architectural associationism that I explored in Chapter 1.[98] Digby soon fades from the account as Addison and Arbuthnot begin to engage one another in rigorous Socratic exchange on the precise nature of the Gothic past to which the ruins before them attest. Though he begins his discourse with a passionate and nostalgic paean to the Elizabethan age of tilts and tournaments, torches and minstrelsy, feasting and revelry to which the castle once was home, Addison's Whiggish vision rapidly assumes a much darker tone: the ruins of Kenilworth, he claims, ultimately bear witness to 'the prosperous tyranny of those wretched times', an association that contrasts sharply with 'the happiness we enjoy under a juster and more equal government' in the present.[99] As the discussion continues, so Addison's position becomes clearer: as in his earlier dismissals of the Gothic, these ruins bring to mind nothing but 'the memory of barbarous manners and a despotic government' and 'pride and indolence of the old nobility': no sentimental 'Golden Age' of Queen Elizabeth, this, but a dark 'Gothic' past of barbarism, tyranny, violence, and class-based oppression.[100]

Having declared his 'pure love of antiquity', the Tory Arbuthnot is alarmed at the 'political indignation' of his interlocutor, for his, it soon becomes clear, is a very different vision, one that countenances nothing but 'the acknowledged virtues of that princess and the wisdom of her government'.[101] The Gothic past for Arbuthnot is one of hospitality, genius, and sovereign beneficence, a long-faded age of simplicity and innocence that, unsullied by the vice of modern luxury,

---

[96] Cooper, *Architectural Reliques*, p. iii.
[97] Richard Hurd, 'Dialogue III. On the Golden Age of Queen Elizabeth: Between the Hon. Robert Digby Dr Arbuthnot, and Mr Addison', in *Moral and Political Dialogues: Being the Substance of Several Conversations Between Divers Eminent Persons of the Past and Present Age* (London. Printed for A. Millar, W. Thurlbourne, and J. Woodyer, 1759), pp. 93–126.
[98] Hurd, 'Dialogue III', p. 95.   [99] Hurd, 'Dialogue III', p. 99.
[100] Hurd, 'Dialogue III', pp. 102, 104.   [101] Hurd, 'Dialogue III', pp. 100, 96, 100.

allowed the gentle rhythms of rural industry to flourish. Arbuthnot's version of history is strongly informed by a sense of colour, pageantry, and spectacle, and drawing on George Gascoigne's description of Elizabeth I's visit to Kenilworth in 1575 in *The Princely Pleasures at Kenelworth [sic] Castle* (1587), he patriotically defends the age as one of 'Gothic Tilts and Tournaments', the spirit of chivalry a veritable light in the 'dark ages'.[102] Quick off the mark, Addison responds with a quip that foregrounds the age-old negative associations of the term 'Gothic' as the marker of things barbaric, uncivilized, and unenlightened: Arbuthnot's vision, for him, is a sentimental fiction, a 'jumble of *Gothic* romance and pagan fable', chivalry the fruit of Gothic fierceness that emerged from the tribe's 'original rudeness and brutality'.[103] Though the third dialogue breaks off inconclusively, the support that Hurd offers for Arbuthnot's Tory position is clear, and as he would explore in more detail in his *Letters on Chivalry and Romance* three years later, the Gothic past was one of extraordinary creative richness and vitality that, like the institutions of chivalry and romance, demanded recuperation at whatever the cost.

This exchange between exponents of vastly divergent and politically opposing impressions of Gothic antiquity would be repeated in Ann Radcliffe's *Gaston De Blondeville* (written 1802/3; published 1826) and Walter Scott's *Kenilworth* (1821), two antiquarian fictions that, like those discussed above, located themselves precariously at the interface between romance and the antiquarian interest in ruined Gothic castles. In the autumn of 1802, Thomas Noon Talfourd's 'Memoir of the Life and Writings of Mrs Radcliffe' notes, Ann Radcliffe and her husband, William, made a journey to Leicester and Warwick, returning to their home in London via Woodstock and Oxford. Of the three architectural sites that the couple visited on this tour—the baroque opulence of John Vanbrugh and Nicholas Hawksmoor at Blenheim Palace; Warwick Castle; and the majestic Gothic ruins at Kenilworth—it was the latter that seemed to have left the most striking impression upon Radcliffe. As did her account of her imaginative reveries in the ruins of Furness Abbey in the *Journey*, the extracts from Radcliffe's travel journal included in Talfourd's 'Memoir' articulate a very clear link between scenes of Gothic architectural ruin at Kenilworth and the onset of imaginative activity. 'They spoke at once to the imagination,' she writes, 'with the force and simplicity of truth, the nothingness and brevity of this life': 'generations have beheld us and passed away', the ruins portentously proclaim, 'as you now behold us, and shall pass away: they thought of the generations before them, as you now think of them, and as future ages shall think of you'.[104] The rhetorical term for this is

---

[102] Hurd, 'Dialogue III', p. 107.   [103] Hurd, 'Dialogue III', pp. 117–18, 114.
[104] These extracts from Radcliffe's travel journal are reprinted in Thomas Noon Talfourd, 'Memoir of the Life and Writings of Mrs Radcliffe', in Anne [sic] Radcliffe, *Gaston De Blondeville; or, The Court of Henry III Keeping Festival in Ardenne, A Romance and St Alban's Abbey: A Metrical Tale; With Some Poetical Pieces* 4 vols (London: Henry Colburn, 1826), vol. 1, pp. 1–130 (p. 58).

prosopopoeia, the attribution of speech to an inanimate object, a trope that occurs frequently in literary responses to ruins in the period.[105] Thus personified, Kenilworth Castle recites a version of Shakespeare's Sonnet 55, albeit one in which the Bard's conceptualization of time and monumentalization has been reversed and reconfigured: here, it is not the lines of a poem—'this powerful rhyme'—that outlive the depredations of 'sluttish time' so much as the masonry or 'unswept stone' of the ruins of Kenilworth themselves.

As Norton has argued, the Introduction that frames *Gaston*, including the portion that was extracted in the *New Monthly Magazine* as 'On the Supernatural in Poetry' in 1826, probably postdates the writing of the novel in 1802/3 by over a decade.[106] Even so, Radcliffe writes her own experiences at Kenilworth in 1802 into the character of Mr Willoughton, one of the Introduction's two fictional interlocutors. Like Radcliffe, so Willoughton too claims to hear in the castle's ruins a sombre message of mortality 'spoken' to the dead, the living and the yet-to-be-born: 'Generations have beheld us and passed away, as you now behold us, and shall pass away. They have thought of the generations before their time, as you now think of them, and as future ones shall think of you.'[107] Radcliffe's self-fictionalizing here is not without a modicum of parody. In response to Mr Simpson's good-humoured gibe that Willoughton, in all his Shakespearean, historical, and architectural enthusiasm, is little more than a 'painful antiquary', Willoughton responds with a revealing pronouncement: however remote, such 'picturesque visions' as these are capable of awakening 'a peculiar kind of interest' and 'sentiment no less delightful', both of which 'render antiquity, of all studies, the least liable to the epithet of dry'.[108] For Willoughton as for Radcliffe, Walpole, and Scott, 'Antiquity', particularly the antique past of Gothic ruin, is 'one of the favourite regions of poetry'. Though the sceptical Simpson replies with the question that appears as the epigraph to this book—'Who ever thought of looking for a muse in an old castle?'—the narrator's position is clear: for Radcliffe, as for her fictional mouthpiece, old castles do, indeed, serve as the source and inspiration for literary composition.[109] Such is the architectural imagination as Radcliffe theorizes it in the Introduction to *Gaston De Blondeville*.

But if an old castle is a muse, Radcliffe is also at pains in this piece to explore the problems by which the architectural imagination is beset, suggesting that architecture's inspirational qualities are easily missed and attenuated, and the flights of architectural fancy often threatened by the challenges of a much more prosaic political and historical reality. In gazing upon the Castle, Willoughton's mind is

---

[105] For an account of prosopopoeia and architectural aesthetics, see John Dixon Hunt, 'Folly in the Garden', *The Hopkins Review* vol. 1, no. 2 (spring 2008): pp. 262–72.
[106] Norton, *Mistress of Udolpho*, p. 185.
[107] Radcliffe, *Gaston De Blondeville*, vol. 1, p. 21.
[108] Radcliffe, *Gaston De Blondeville*, vol. 1, p. 47.
[109] Radcliffe, *Gaston De Blondeville*, vol. 1, p. 47.

'crowded' with historical associations that combine to form a 'new train of ideas', generating a romance of Gothic antiquity that has been prompted by the castle's connections with the noble line of English sovereigns: this site, he well knows, has served as both a prison and a royal palace, the same pile in which Edward II suffered the humiliations of Mortimer and in which Leicester entertained Queen Elizabeth with 'princely splendour'.[110] His reverie is abruptly ruptured, though, by a number of indigent peasant children who flock towards his chaise: at this moment, 'a sense of real life broke in upon him', and the 'visions of quiet solitude and of venerable antiquity... in an instant, dispersed'.[111] To his further dismay, the ruin has been brutally stripped of the 'customs of former times': the gateway to the castle has been closed up, the tower is no longer accessible to visitors, there is no portcullis hanging in the arched entrance, and the building has been defiled by the hand of modern improvement.

As it dawns upon Willoughton that something more than the passage of time is responsible for the castle's ruinous state, so a tall, thin stranger enters the scene to confirm his suspicions: 'that part was pulled down by Cromwell's soldiers,' he gestures, 'and, if they had more time on their side, they would have pulled it all down; as it was, they did a mort of mischief'.[112] With this disclosure, the ruins assume urgent historical and political meanings. Once a Royalist stronghold against the concentration of parliamentarian forces at Warwick Castle, Kenilworth had been 'slighted' by a parliamentary decree of 1649, a strategy of deliberate architectural demolition that sought to render this and other fortifications across Wales, the English Midlands, and Yorkshire unusable to the Royalist cause.[113] In the present, the ruins thus bear the scars of historical trauma: the ravages of the republican cause; the bloody combat of the English Civil War; and, most urgently, the taint of regicide. Even with his familiar reluctance to engage with a ruin's political history, William Gilpin had registered as much when he visited Kenilworth in 1772: though 'magnificent', the ruins were incapable of furnishing 'a good picture' primarily because they so cogently displayed the signs of political and historical process.[114] Resisting the interruption of his reverie, Radcliffe's Gilpinian Willoughton takes momentary refuge in the consolations of picturesque vision, adopting an aesthetic stance in which the beauty of the ruin's composition is his sole consideration. But when the stranger returns to the subject of Cromwell, Willoughton is forced into a heartfelt denunciation of any aspect of

---

[110] Radcliffe, *Gaston De Blondeville*, vol. 1, p. 5.
[111] Radcliffe, *Gaston De Blondeville*, vol. 1, p. 6.
[112] Radcliffe, *Gaston De Blondeville*, vol. 1, p. 7.
[113] For an account of the extensive slighting of Kenilworth by Colonel Hawkesworth, see John Goodall, *The English Castle, 1066-1650* (New Haven and London: Yale University Press, 2011), pp. 489–90.
[114] Gilpin, *Observations, Relative Chiefly to Picturesque Beauty, Made in the Year 1772, on Several Parts of England; Particularly the Mountains, and Lakes of Cumberland and Westmoreland*, vol. 1, pp. 40–2.

political history that does not conform to his comfortable version of the splendid Gothic past. 'What had the venerable scenes of Kenilworth to do with politics, or freedom?' he expostulates, 'if even the leaders in political agitations have a better taste themselves than to destroy, for the mere sake of destruction, they let the envy and malice of their followers rage away against whatsoever is beautiful, or grand.'[115] As Radcliffe describes it through Willoughton, the architectural imagination eschews politics in favour of a 'beautiful' and picturesque version of Gothic antiquity.

Buying from the stranger three ancient documents that once belonged to the monks in the nearby monastery of Black Canons, Willoughton returns to the inn to read 'A Boke, Conteynynge a trew chronique of what passed at Killingworth'. An English translation of a Norman text made only marginally more readable by Willoughton's editorial interventions, this is *Gaston De Blondeville* itself, a 'Trew Chronique' that, however marvellous its subject matter, self-consciously displays the markers of antiquarian learning, including linguistic archaism, interpolated songs and ballads, and the lengthy endnotes, each taken from erudite antiquarian tomes and each vouching for the accuracy of the events, personages, and objects described.[116] The text displays all of the tensions and paradoxes of the antiquarian romance that I have explored above: ghostly, highly imaginative subject matter coupled with the authenticating gestures of scholarly knowledge, some of it gleaned from an eighteenth-century edition of John Leland's *Collectanea*. But despite this paraphernalia, *Gaston* remains a fiction very much of modern provenance. Set in or around 1256, during the reign of Henry III of England (1216–72), the narrative returns to a time before Henry granted Kenilworth Castle to Simon de Montfort, and prior to de Montfort's notorious turning against the king and his use of the castle as the centre for resistance to the sovereign during the Second Barons' War (1263–7). At the centre of the tale lies an urgent plea for justice when, interrupting the impending festivities of Henry III and Eleanor of Provence, a stranger, the Bristol merchant Hugh Woodreeve, arrives at Kenilworth, demanding redress for the murder of kinsman Reginald de Folville three years earlier. Woodreeve points to Gaston, the king's favourite knight, as Folville's murderer, but doubting the veracity of his witnesses and deeming the accusation itself slanderous, Henry imprisons the merchant in one of the castle's towers. From this moment, Gaston is plagued by visions of a strange and menacing apparition, while events at the castle assume an ever more supernatural air. Read by those who oppose Woodreeve as evidence of his earlier dealings in magic, the ghostly messenger goes unheeded by the king. Persisting in their persecution of the merchant, Henry and his supporters find him guilty of necromancy and perjury and sentence him to death. This state of affairs persists until, during a spectacular

---

[115] Radcliffe, *Gaston De Blondeville*, vol. 1, p. 25.
[116] For an account of these sources, see Norton, *Mistress of Udolpho*, p. 280.

tournament, the ghost returns on a black charger as an armour-clad knight with fire in his eyes, demanding, at once, reprieve for the innocent Woodreeve and the punishment of Gaston, his kinsman's murderer. Gaston's sudden death is shortly followed by the death of his duplicitous accomplice, the Prior of Saint Mary; Henry, in turn, is eventually made to see the error of his ways, and Woodreeve is given reprieve. No longer the prerogative of the sovereign, justice in *Gaston de Blondeville* has been effectively dispensed by a spectre.

As this synopsis suggests, aspects of the narrative are deeply anachronistic in relation to its thirteenth-century setting: Gaston's and Henry's ghostly visions directly recall those of the guilty Macbeth during the banquet scene, while the play within a play that performs Gaston's guilt before him is taken from *Hamlet*. More crucially, the scenario in which one who is favoured by a king stands accused of murder by an outsider is a reworking of a fiction of a much more recent date, Harriet Lee's *Kruitzner; or, The German's Tale*, a story in the fourth volume of Harriet and Sophia Lee's *Canterbury Tales* (1797–1805) that was published by Radcliffe's erstwhile publishers, G. G. and J Robinson, in 1801, and which is best remembered today as the source for Byron's tragedy *Werner* (1822). In a moment of crisis in Lee's narrative, a Hungarian stranger arrives at Kruitzner's castle, accusing Kruitzner's son, Conrad, of the murder of Baron Stralenheim. In his demand for justice, the Hungarian resembles Radcliffe's Woodreeve, and Conrad, 'a darling, an almost adored son', Gaston himself.[117] Though he admits to the crime, Conrad, as Radcliffe's Gaston does of Henry, demands that the Hungarian be permanently silenced. While there is no ghost in the narrative other than those spectres that haunt Kruitzner's guilty conscience, Radcliffe appears to have derived her sense of a wronged party's difficult quest for justice from Lee's popular and influential text. At least one reviewer in 1826 was struck by the similarities between them, noting of *Gaston* that 'There is a strong resemblance, between the general outline of the story and that Miss Harriet Lee's celebrated tale of Kruitzner.'[118]

More than a fascinating textual detail, however, this interruption of a more recent fiction into a text otherwise concerned with thirteenth-century English history is an instance of what Jeremy Tambling has provocatively called 'deliberate anachronism', a device that effectively shuttles *Gaston* into the early nineteenth-century present and raising the question, as it does so, of whether the architectural imagination as Radcliffe theorizes it through Willoughton can ever be, or remain, an ahistorical, apolitical faculty solely preoccupied with the picturesque beauties of a Gothic ruin.[119] For in its concerns with the ghostly supplement of a failing

---

[117] Harriet Lee, 'Kruitzner; or, The German's Tale', in *Canterbury Tales, Volume the Fourth*, by Harriet Lee (London: Printed for G. and J. Robinson, 1801), pp. 3–368 (p. 345).
[118] 'Art. VI. Mrs Radcliffe's Posthumous Works', *The Monthly Review* (May–August 1826): vol. 2, pp. 280–93 (p. 284).
[119] Jeremy Tambling, *On Anachronism* (Manchester: Manchester University Press, 2010), pp. 1–6.

legal system, in its account of a form of justice that is not exacted by the sovereign but delivered from a spectral messenger as if from the outside, *Gaston De Blondeville* negotiates a pressing political issue that was at the heart of British politics in the last decade of the eighteenth century. Reading *Gaston* more as a 'Trew Chronique' of the 1790s than the mid-thirteenth century of its setting, Frances Chiu has convincingly pointed out the extent to which the rhetoric of reformist and radical writers of post-revolutionary England infiltrates the text, arguing that Radcliffe, in keeping with this tradition, offers up in *Gaston* an 'oblique criticism' of the oppressive regime of William Pitt the Younger.[120] Angela Wright, similarly, has read the text as an 'indirect rebuke' of Edmund Burke's reading of the French Revolution as a tragicomic drama in his *Reflections on the Revolution in France* (1790).[121] For Claudia Johnson, the ordeal that Woodreeve suffers at the hands of a biased legal system in *Gaston* recalls the plight of the eponymous character in Godwin's *Caleb Williams* (1794), an intertextual echo that aligns Radcliffe with the radicalism of Godwin's *An Enquiry Concerning Political Justice* (1793).[122] But perhaps Radcliffe's political interventions run even deeper than this, for, like Hurd's Addison before her, she aims her imaginative powers in *Gaston* directly at the pervasive myth of Gothic origins, shaking at its foundations a powerful political ideology that had shaped the Whig political agenda in England since the end of the seventeenth century.

This is both an extension and an intensification of the political meanings of Gothic architecture that Radcliffe, as I showed in Chapter 3, had explored throughout her earlier fiction. The politics of this narrative becomes particularly clear when it is placed alongside perceptions of Henry III that were current in the late eighteenth and early nineteenth centuries. As the revised edition of Hume's *The History of England* of 1778 made clear, the reign of Henry III witnessed the consolidation of the British constitution in its most recognizable and modern of forms. Commenting on the range of political innovations that the monarch set in place, Hume claimed that Henry's charters 'were the peculiar favourites of the English nation, and esteemed the most sacred rampart to national liberty and independence'.[123] The Gothic system of balance between Parliament and the monarch, Hume continues, was perfected during Henry's reign: securing the rights 'of all orders of men', he also established the foundational principles of the English constitutional monarchy, an 'original contract' that 'both limited the

---

[120] Frances A. Chiu, 'Introduction', in *Gaston De Blondeville; or, The Court of Henry III Keeping Festival in Ardenne*, by Ann Radcliffe, ed. Frances Chiu (Chicago: Valancourt Books, 2006), pp. vii–xxxviii (p. xxii).
[121] Wright, *Britain, France and the Gothic, 1764–1820*, p. 116.
[122] See William Godwin, *An Enquiry Concerning Political Justice*, ed. Mark Philp (Oxford: Oxford University Press, 2013), pp. 219–22; Claudia L. Johnson, *Equivocal Beings: Politics, Gender, and Sentimentality in the 1790s* (Chicago and London: University of Chicago Press, 1995), p. 137.
[123] Hume, *The History of England*, vol. 2, p. 6.

authority of the king' and 'ensured the conditional allegiance of his subjects'.[124] This was a particularly generous assessment on behalf of the Tory, Scottish Hume, one who often adopts in the *History* an attitude of scepticism towards the Whiggish, English myth of Gothic origins. Although he is specifically referring here to Henry's ratification of the Great Charter and the Charter of the Forest, Hume's emphasis upon the securing of 'the rights of all orders of men' carried for the eighteenth-century understanding of the Gothic past other, more fundamental associations, too. As James Thomson had noted in his paean to British freedom in Book IV of *Liberty* (1736), 'The Commons are generally thought to have been first represented in Parliament towards the end of *Henry* the third's Reign.'[125] 'Till then,' Thomson continued, 'History makes no Mention of them; whence a very strong Argument may be drawn, to fix the Original of the House of Commons to that Era.'[126] Though its foundations had been sketched out, through the barons' checking of royal prerogative, by Magna Carta of 1215, the spirit of British liberty was thus thought to have achieved one of its fundamental components—the representation of the commoners—under Henry's rule.

The myth of Henry III as the consolidator of ancient English liberties assumed other forms too. In a panel of the engraving that he produced for the title page of William Dugdale's *Monasticon Anglicanum* (1655–73), Wenceslaus Hollar depicted Henry III engaged in the act of re-endorsing the terms of Magna Carta, the charter to which his father, King John, had originally committed (see Figure 6.1).[127] These claims to Henry III's reinstatement of the original terms of the ancient constitution continued to circulate in the nineteenth century, and were repeated in Sharon Turner's work on the history of England during the Middle Ages. For the eighteenth and early nineteenth centuries, the period in English history to which Radcliffe in *Gaston* returns thus marked that crucial period in which the system of Gothic liberties, if not actually initiated, were set more firmly in place, consolidated, and formally enshrined, a perception that ran concurrently with the belief in the Norman Yoke.

As Radcliffe envisages him, Henry III is no sovereign tyrant. Rejecting the suggestion that Woodreeve be subject to a trial by ordeal, a 'barbaric' legal process that relied upon the extraction of extreme physical pain, the king defends the virtues of trial by jury, a much more moderate judicial practice that was said to have been imported into Britain with the arrival of the Goths. It is over this Gothic legal system that the king presides on the sixth day of the action, as a jury and several witnesses assemble in the White Hall of Kenilworth Castle. When the first

---

[124] Hume, *The History of England*, vol. 2, p. 7.
[125] Thomson, *Britain; Being the Fourth Part of Liberty, a Poem*, p. 44n.
[126] Thomson, *Britain; Being the Fourth Part of Liberty, a Poem*, p. 44n.
[127] For the identification of Henry III in this engraving, and for a detailed reading of the political import of the title page, see Margery Corbett, 'The Title-Page and Illustrations to the *Monasticon Anglicanum*, 1655–1673', *The Antiquaries Journal* vol. 67 issue 1 (March 1987): pp. 102–10.

Figure 6.1 Detail from Wenceslaus Hollar's title page for William Dugdale's *Monasticon Anglicanum* (1655), depicting Henry III re-endorsing the Magna Carta. Courtesy of Yale Center for British Art, Paul Mellon Collection, S 29.7 Folio A.

jury finds Woodreeve innocent of the accusations of witchcraft and slander, the prior, complicit in the murder from the start, insists that a second jury be formed and a second trial commenced. It is when this second jury finds Woodreeve guilty that the king's integrity begins to falter: while Prince Edward and the Archbishop of York can perceive Woodreeve's innocence for what it is, Henry's favouritism towards Gaston blinds him to the truth. His objectivity compromised by the favour in which he holds others, Radcliffe's Henry demonstrates the same weakness of partiality and favouritism that Hume had identified in the monarch. Addressing the system of sovereignty in general, Godwin had issued a similar caution in *Political Justice*. At its point of installation, then, the Gothic system of values in *Gaston* is plagued by a number of faults and weaknesses: while the power of the sovereign may indeed be dutifully held in check by the measures of the people, this does not render legality invulnerable to the miscarriage of justice. Moreover, and despite contemporary historiographic claims to the contrary, Henry's juridical system does not naturally incorporate or extend to commoners the likes of Woodreeve. Radcliffe in *Gaston* exposes a fundamental bias at the heart of the Whiggish myth, what Sean Silver has described as its neglect of anyone 'who was not a freeholder, including the masses of disenfranchised British men and women, agricultural leaseholders or wage-labourers who in the end had no representation under the Gothic system of government'.[128] Although the Whiggish Robert Molesworth in 1705 had claimed that ancient Gothic constitutionalism comprised 'the Three Estates of King (or Queen) Lords and Commons', Radcliffe in the plight of Woodreeve points to the elision or marginalization of the 'middling sorts', the class to which she herself belonged.[129] The possibility also remains that the ultimate object of Radcliffe's critique is Magna Carta itself: with the exception of Clause 41, an assertion of foreign merchants' rights to enter and exit England freely in their pursuit of business, the charter makes no mention of this emergent sector of medieval society, which existed outside of the three divinely ordained estates of the church, the nobility, and the peasantry. Most crucially, Henry's Gothic political system bears no natural or inevitable relation to justice, a glaring infringement of Magna Carta's 40th clause: '*Nulli vendemus, nulli negabimus, aut differemus, rectum aut justitiam*' (To no one will [or would] we sell, to no one will [or would] we deny or delay, right or justice').[130] Though the sheath of Henry's sword bears upon it, inscribed in rubies, the words 'Truth and Right', it is 'justice', the term to which Woodreeve makes his original appeal, that is ominously missing.[131] Tellingly, though, this is the word that appears on the sword carried by the ghostly knight on the charger: his is a 'a sword of strange shape, unknown in our tournays; which, as some nigh affirmed, bore on the scabbard, in characters of fire, the words 'Justice!''[132] Radcliffe supplements the lack at the heart of Gothic jurisprudence with her first and only recourse to a 'real' ghost.[133]

Though the architectural imagination as it is conceptualized through Willoughton is one of anodyne, apolitical escapism into the antique past, Radcliffe in the body of the text puts the same imaginative faculty to pointed political use, to the extent that the Introduction reads as a disclaimer for the text that follows it: the ruins of Kenilworth Castle call up a vision of Gothic antiquity that challenges liberal Whiggism at its point of installation. As Fiona Price's reading of *Gaston* has pointed out, it is just such an interrogation of the principles of ancient constitutionalism that aligns Radcliffe with Walpole, Reeve, Lee, and other exponents of historical fiction before Walter Scott.[134] What distinguishes Radcliffe, though, is that she elects to do this through taking issue with that Whiggish 'Constitutional

---

[128] Silver, 'The Politics of Gothic Historiography, 1660–1800', p. 9.
[129] Molesworth, *An Account of Denmark*, p. 174.
[130] *Magna Carta*, with a new Commentary by David Carpenter (London: Penguin Books, 2015), p. 52.
[131] Radcliffe, *Gaston De Blondeville*, vol. 1, p. 90.
[132] Radcliffe, *Gaston De Blondeville*, vol. 2, pp. 379–80.
[133] For an engaging account of how the complex logic of supplementarity pertains to *Gaston*, see Chaplin, *Gothic and the Rule of Law, 1764–1820*, pp. 116–24.
[134] See Price, *Reinventing Liberty*, pp. 46–54.

Sort of Reverence' that the sight of an ancient 'Gothick hall' evoked in the writer of that article in *Common Sense* in 1739.

Walter Scott's Compromise

The belated publication of Radcliffe's final fiction meant that, when James Ballantyne reissued five of her novels in Volume 10 of the 'Novelist's Library' series in 1824, *Gaston De Blondeville* was not included. Consequently, Walter Scott demonstrated no knowledge of the text in his 'Prefatory Memoir to Mrs Ann Radcliffe', the introduction to the Ballantyne edition that would later be reprinted in *Lives of the Novelists* (1825). Nonetheless, it is clear that his own fictional responses to Kenilworth's ruins were strongly conditioned by the Gothic aesthetic, not only as represented by Radcliffe's other novels but also by Sophia Lee's *The Recess* (1783–5), portions of which are set in the same castle.

Like Radcliffe, Scott's exposure to Kenilworth was empirical and immediate. As John Gibson Lockhart's *Memoirs of the Life of Sir Walter Scott, Bart.* (1837–8) recounts, Scott, in a small group that included his cousin and travelling companion John Scott and the English theatre manager and renowned comic actor Charles Mathews, visited the Castles of Kenilworth and Warwick upon his return from the war-torn Continent in mid-September 1815.[135] As the more detailed account of this journey that John Scott provides in his *Journal of a Tour to Waterloo and Paris* (1842) recounts, the three men, having dined with Lord Byron the evening before, left London early on the morning of 15 September en route to Scott's home at Abbotsford; making particularly good time, the travellers reached Leamington and then Warwick Castle, a distance of some 90 miles, on the same day. From there, they journeyed a short distance to Kenilworth, where, together with a certain Mr Hall, they took in the prospect of the castle's ruins. 'This I believe', John Scott notes, 'was not Scott's first visit to those ruins, he examined them however very minutely, alluding frequently to the extreme state of decay into which they had fallen, and to the vast extent of the castle of which they gave evidence.'[136] When Mrs Anne Jackson Mathews, the wife of Charles Mathews, recounted her husband's visit to Kenilworth in the company of Scott in *Memoirs of Charles Mathews, Comedian* (1838–9), she made much of Mathews's account of Scott's animated responses to the relics: 'On my husband's return home he described to me and others the effect Kenilworth produced upon Mr. Walter Scott, whose delight and enthusiasm led him to make several remarkable

---

[135] John Gibson Lockhart, *Memoirs of the Life of Sir Walter Scott, Bart.*, 7 vols (Edinburgh: Robert Cadell; London: John Murray and Whittaker and Co., 1837–8), vol. 3, p. 373.
[136] John Scott, *Journal of a Tour to Waterloo and Paris, in Company with Sir Walter Scott in 1815* (London: Saunders and Otley, 1842), p. 256.

observations while surveying these splendid ruins, all of which were indelibly impressed upon Mr. Mathews's memory.'[137] Indeed, so great an impression did Scott's effusions leave that when *Kenilworth: A Romance* was published in January 1821, Mathews and the others present on the occasion of Scott's visit in 1815 were left in little doubt as to who the mysterious 'Author of "Waverley," "Ivanhoe," &c' of the title page was: 'if any evidence was then necessary to prove who the *Great Unknown* was,' Mrs Mathews claims, 'the fact of those very phrases, and the precise quotations appearing in the Romance when it was published, was enough to settle the point with those to whom they had been repeated.'[138]

An architectural palimpsest, Kenilworth Castle in Scott's novel provides a still-legible record of English history on its walls, including material traces of the Clinton family, Henry III, Edward II, Roger Mortimer, and Simon de Montfort and the Barons' Wars. It is also a record of the nation's architectural styles insofar as it presents 'on its different fronts magnificent specimens of every species of castellated architecture, from the Conquest to the reign of Elizabeth, with the appropriate style and ornaments of each'.[139] Its primary functions in the narrative, however, are not historical but imaginative and literary: as it did for Hurd's Arbuthnot and Radcliffe, Kenilworth serves as the site for the projection of a fantasy of the venerable Gothic past, one in which the conventions of romance are present from the very start. When the Countess of Leicester enters it, she observes in the architecture several references to the court of King Arthur; in appearance, the warder of the pile is much like Colbrand the Giant from *Guy of Warwick* or Ascapart, Bevis of Hampton's mythological adversary.[140] As one reviewer of the novel thus observed, 'Kenilworth castle, which is one of the most picturesque and interesting ruins in the kingdom, is the grand theatre of this Romance.'[141] As a particularly theatrical space, Kenilworth becomes the site of three multisensory performances that take up much of the middle sections of the narrative. The first of these, a spectacle in which the Arthurian Lady of the Lake appears on a floating island, occurs on the evening of 9 July 1575, when Queen Elizabeth, having arrived at Dudley's castle, enters the chase. Here, the novel expresses the early nineteenth-century revival of interest in Arthurian myth and legend. Scott abruptly cuts his description short, though, referring his readers to its source in Robert Langham's or Laneham's 'A Letter', an antiquarian resource that Scott consulted in the first volume of John Nichols's *The Progresses, and Public Processions, of Queen*

---

[137] Anne Jackson Mathews, *Memoirs of Charles Mathews, Comedian*, 4 vols (London: Richard Bentley, 1838–9), vol. 2, p. 378.
[138] Mathews, *Memoirs of Charles Mathews, Comedian*, vol. 2, p. 378.
[139] Walter Scott, *Kenilworth: A Romance*, ed. and introd. J. H. Alexander (London: Penguin, 1999), p. 263. This edition of the text is a revised and updated version of the edition that Alexander prepared for the Edinburgh Edition of the Waverly Novels in 1993, and is based on the first edition of the novel from 1821.
[140] Scott, *Kenilworth*, pp. 259, 260.
[141] Review of Walter Scott's *Kenilworth*, *GM* (March 1821): pp. 246–53 (p. 247).

Elizabeth (1788). Laneham's 'Letter' draws sharply into focus the particular vision of Gothic antiquity that Scott here is seeking to evoke:

> And fyrst, who that considerz unto the stately seat of *Kenelwoorth Castl*, the rare beauty of bilding that his Honor hath avaunced; all of the hard quarry stone: every room so spacious, so well belighted, and so hy roofed within: so seemly too sight by du proportion without: a day tyme, on every side so glittering by glasse; a nights, by continuall brighnesse of candel, fyre, and torch-light, transparent thro the lyghtsome wyndz, az it wear the *Egiptian Pharos* relucent untoo all the Alexandrian coast.[142]

Couched in metaphors of light, visibility, and dazzling brightness, Laneham's description enshrines a sense of the white Gothic in the festivities at Kenilworth. The second spectacle in the narrative is one of Scott's own invention, and one for which readers of *Ivanhoe* of the previous year would have been well prepared. Here, four groups of players perform an elaborate quadrille, each group representing 'one of the various nations by which England had at different times been occupied': the aboriginal Britons; the Romans; the ancient Saxons or Goths; and the Normans. Though their dance enacts a past of conflict, it is union and harmony that is the ultimate outcome, as Elizabeth declares that 'no single one of these celebrated nations could claim pre-eminence over the others', since each has 'contributed to form the Englishman of her own time'.[143] Here, Scott's novel shares in the stadial conceptualization of history to which he had given expression in *Ivanhoe*, in this way completing, as Stephen Arata has argued, the work of exploring the 'mongrel' origins of the nation that the novelist had begun earlier.[144]

During the third spectacle, Scott returns to his antiquarian sources in Laneham, Gascoigne, and others in order to mount a re-enactment of the Danish invasions of England from AD 997 onwards. Of the three displays in the novel, this is the most satirically handled, for not only does it critique the tendencies towards exaggeration in Scott's sources, but it also returns to the sense of the fabrication and empty performance of history conjured up in the description of some of the castle's architectural details: the 'mere pageants composed of paste-board and buckram' of England's Arthurian past that the Countess of Leicester observes on the battlements.[145] In the Magnum Opus edition of the novel in 1831, Scott, in a note to Chapter 17, would criticize Laneham's 'Letter' as being 'written in a style of the most intolerable affectation', deriding the author as a 'small man in office'

---

[142] John Nichols, *The Progresses, and Public Processions, of Queen Elizabeth*, 2 vols (London. Printed by and for the Editor, 1788), vol. 1, p. 42.
[143] Scott, *Kenilworth*, p. 351.
[144] See Stephen Arata, 'Scott's Pageants: The Example of *Kenilworth*', *Studies in Romanticism* vol. 40, no. 1 (spring 2001): pp. 99–107.
[145] Scott, *Kenilworth*, p. 259.

filled with 'conceit and self-importance' and 'as great a coxcomb as ever blotted paper'.[146] But evidence of his reservations with his sources are apparent in the 1821 edition of the text too. For, in place of Laneham's humourlessness, this third spectacle is theatrical to the point of being ludicrous, with oversized hobby horses, the stuff of 'morrice-dance [sic]' and dramatic entertainment, taking the place of real horses, their riders even more 'incongruous and ridiculous'.[147] The array of the warriors, too, is 'ludicrous enough', and their weapons, though 'formidable enough to deal sound blows', are 'long alder-poles instead of lances, and sound cudgels for swords'.[148] More 'anti-masque, or burlesque' than the stately pageant described in its antiquarian sources, this staging of the conflict between the Saxons and the Danes rapidly descends into farce as the rails defending the ledges of the bridge on which it is enacted give way, cooling off the 'hot courage' of the combatants in the lake beneath.[149] Though the novel appears to appropriate the ruins of Kenilworth for the projection of a romance of splendid Gothic antiquity remarkably similar to that of Hurd's Dr Arbuthnot, Scott subtly undermines this vision through foregrounding its basis in pasteboard and buckram, inauthentic performance and sheer buffoonery.

Overlooking these intimations of a hollow theatricality at work in the festivities at Kenilworth, several early readers applauded the novel for what they took to be its vivid account of a particularly noble period in English history. A critic in *The Gentleman's Magazine*, for instance, picked up on the highly visual nature of Scott's pageantry in describing the novel as a rousing 'panorama of the age of Elizabeth', while another response in *The Monthly Review* commended the author's ability to evoke, in the present, an almost 'living' sense of the Elizabethan past, 'that golden period' that was 'the good old time of Elizabeth'.[150] Modern-day critics have tended to echo these impressions. For Arata, for instance, the success and enormous popularity of the novel throughout the nineteenth century was largely attributable to its heightened sense of 'spectacle'.[151] As Michael Dobson and Nicola J. Watson have argued, Scott in *Kenilworth* had effectively retrieved Elizabeth I from the sentimental representation she had received in earlier Gothic fictions in order to evoke a sense of 'the never-never land of Merrie England', the 'velvety meadows', 'royal oaks', 'Christmas cheer', 'quaffed October ales', 'moated

---

[146] Walter Scott, *Introduction and Notes from the Magnum Opus: Waverley to A Legend of the Wars of Montrose*, ed. J. H. Alexander, with P.D. Garside and Claire Lamont (Edinburgh: Edinburgh University Press, 2012), pp. 121–3.

[147] Scott, *Kenilworth*, p. 363.   [148] Scott, *Kenilworth*, p. 363.

[149] Scott, *Kenilworth*, pp. 363, 364.

[150] See, respectively, the review of Walter Scott's *Kenilworth*, GM, vol. 91, part 1 (January–June 1821) pp. 246–53 (p. 253), and 'Art. III', *The Monthly Review* 2nd series, vol. 94 (February 1821): pp. 146–61 (p. 148).

[151] Arata, 'Scott's Pageants', p. 99.

castle', 'lofty turrets', and 'chivalry' of 'bonny old England' so powerfully evoked in at least one contemporary review.[152]

These are certainly sound observations, but they do not adequately account for what several critics identified in the novel: a darker, more tragic and disturbing strain that pulsed beneath Scott's rendition of Kenilworth's Elizabethan splendour. 'The key-note of the tale is sad,' remarked the same critic in *The Monthly Review*, 'and its vibrations sound heavily in contrast to the noise of unfeeling pomp, festive gladness, and gorgeous parade, which is heard in the stately halls and pleasant bowers of that renowned castle.'[153] The contrasts in sight, sound, and tone mentioned here are revealing, and point directly to the tale of Amy Robsart at Cumnor Hall with which the novel opens and closes. Indeed, there is an alternative architectural imagination at work in *Kenilworth*, a vision of the past that, while familiarly called up in relation to architectural form, undercuts the 'gorgeous parade' at Kenilworth with a harrowing tale of solitude, 'gloom', and 'confinement'. In Lukács's reading of Scott, literary character is said to function as an embodiment of history, with each of the novelist's fictions portraying 'the struggles and antagonisms of history by means of characters who...always represent social trends and historical forces'.[154] As the example of *Kenilworth* suggests, though, the same might be said of Scott's Gothic architecture: though Kenilworth Castle generates a fiction of 'merry England', this is rivalled by an alternative romance that is called into being by Cumnor Hall, an ancient Gothic pile that figures prominently in the narrative's opening and closing sequences.

Indeed, the Castles of Kenilworth and Warwick were not the only architectural topics of conversation that passed between John and Walter Scott on the day of their visit in September 1815. Bidding farewell to Mr Mathews, John, Walter, and Mr Hall, so John Scott's *Journal* relates, left Kenilworth for Derby, on the outskirts of which the celebrated poet, descrying a 'good example of an English manor house' set in a fine park, was overcome by a train of poetic associations:

'Now there,' said Scott, 'is a fine specimen of an ancient hall,—quite an English scene, not much picturesque beauty about it, but so soft and rich, with that hospitable old mansion embosomed among those old woods;—there is a verse of a ballad by Meikle [*sic*], that seems to me to picture such a scene admirably:

The dews of summer night did fall,
    The moon, sweet regent of the sky,
Silver'd the walls of Cumnor hall,
    And many an oak that grew thereby,

---

[152] Michael Dobson and Nicola J. Watson, *England's Elizabeth: An Afterlife in Fame and Fantasy* (Oxford: Oxford University Press, 2002), p. 150. For the original review, see 'Art. III', *The Monthly Review* (February 1821): p. 158.
[153] 'Art. III', *The Monthly Review* (February 1821): p. 158.
[154] Georg Lukács, *The Historical Novel*, trans. Hannah and Stanley Mitchell (Harmondsworth: Penguin, 1976), p. 33.

This stanza is an old favourite of mine, and often occurs to me when I see an old place like that.'[155]

Prompted by the powers of architectural association, Scott remembers and recites the opening stanza of 'Cumnor Hall', the popular ballad by William Julius Mickle that was first published in Thomas Evans's antiquarian collection *Old Ballads, Historical and Narrative* (1777), his poetic supplement to Percy's *Reliques*. Mickle's ballad immortalized for the later eighteenth century the Gothic façades of Cumnor Hall (or Place), Berkshire (now Oxfordshire), the grand residential home attached to the Benedictine monastery of Abingdon that had been built during the early fourteenth century by the monks of Abingdon Abbey, and which had served as the country seat or rectory of the Abbot of Abingdon since around 1330. As the apocryphal tale goes, it was at Cumnor Hall that Amy Robsart, married to Dudley in 1550, had met her mysterious death on 8 September 1560, purportedly by falling down a flight of stairs within the vast pile and breaking her neck. Despite the official verdict of death by accident, it was soon thereafter rumoured that Dudley, with the assistance of his gentleman-retainer Sir Richard Verney, was responsible for Amy's murder, a suspicion that seemed all the more plausible in the light of Dudley's vaulting ambition and ever-growing intimacy with the queen.

As Hugh Usher Tighe's *An Historical Account of Cumner [sic]* (1821) notes, Cumnor Hall had been demolished by its then owner, the Earl of Abingdon, in 1810, some five years before Scott's visit. What drove its demolition, though, was the local superstitious belief that the pile was haunted by the ghost of the murdered Amy Robsart:

> The apparition was said to appear in the form of a young and beautiful woman, superbly attired, and was mostly seen on the steps, the immediate scene of the barbarous act. The tradition of the place relates, that the ghost was at last removed from the house, and laid to rest in a pond at a short distance from it.[156]

As Alfred Darling Bartlett later described it, the memory of Lady Dudley's melancholy end 'was revived among the ignorant villagers, whose imaginations conjured up forms and horrors before unheard of; and hence arose the legendary tales, that have descended to the present day'.[157] Like the Gothic ruins that prompted the antiquarian romances discussed above, Cumnor Hall was the focus of local popular oral superstitions, a reiteration of the coupling of ruined

---

[155] Scott, *Journal of a Tour to Waterloo and Paris*, pp. 257-8.
[156] Hugh Usher Tighe, *An Historical Account of Cumner [sic]; With Some Particulars of the Traditions Respecting the Death of the Countess of Leicester* (Oxford: Printed and Sold by Munday and Slatter, 1821), p. 21.
[157] Alfred Darling Bartlett, *An Historical and Descriptive Account of Cumnor Place, Berks, with Biographical Notices of the Lady Amy Dudley and of Anthony Forster, Esq.* (Oxford and London: John Henry Parker, 1850), p. 9.

architecture and ghostliness that Addison had addressed over a century earlier. It is the supernaturalism of these tales that Mickle's ballad records, particularly in the recurrent references to ghostly activity in the concluding stanzas. As the final quatrain reads, 'Full manye a traveller oft hath sigh'd / And pensive wepte the countess' falle, / As wand'ring onwards they've espied / The haunted tow'rs of Cumnor Halle.'[158] In the fashion of an antiquarian Gothic romancer, Scott puts the ballad to work in Kenilworth in the construction of an inset narrative that is aesthetically 'Gothic' in atmosphere and tone, a ghostly, imaginative supplement, perhaps, to the 'dry' antiquarian details about Cumnor that he gleaned from Elias Ashmole's The Antiquities of Berkshire (1710).[159]

With its heavy stonework, shafted windows, and ivy-strewn walls, Cumnor Place in Scott's novel bears a 'monastic front' and an 'old superstitious foundation' that reaches back to its Catholic past.[160] With its studded, iron-bolted door that would not be out of place in a country jail, Cumnor has everything of 'a melancholy, secluded, and monastic appearance' about it, and when Michael Lambourne and Edmund Tressilian first approach it, they are struck by its casting of 'a gloom over the scene' and its making of a 'proportional impression' on the mind of those who visited it.[161] An imaginary reconstruction of the demolished building from Bartlett's An Historical and Descriptive Account of Cumnor Place, Berks. (1850) clearly illustrates its architectural and literary Gothicism (see Figure 6.2). As Lambourne and Tressilian soon learn, the interiors of Cumnor are as dark and foreboding as its façade. Self-appointed knights in service of the lady who is imprisoned there, the two men make sense of their surroundings through the language and generic conventions of romance, with Lambourne resolving 'to thwack giant, dragon, or magician' for the sake of Robsart's deliverance and Tressilian regarding Varney as 'as dangerous a monster as ever a knight-adventurer encountered in the old story books'.[162] If the descriptions of Cumnor rely heavily upon Gothic-fictional conventions, there is a further aspect of the pile's architecture that makes more specific allusion to the mode: the luxurious, finely decorated suite of apartments into which Amy is moved is a reiteration of the cloying, Orientalized luxury of the 'enchanted' apartments of the Marquis de Montalt in which Adeline is imprisoned in The Romance of the Forest, rooms that are themselves strongly indebted to Busirane's enchanted castle in the Faerie Queene as well as the allegorically charged architecture of John Bunyan's The Pilgrim's Progress.

---

[158] See 'Cumnor Hall', in Old Ballads, Historical and Narrative, With Some of Modern Date, ed. T. Evans, 4 vols (London: Printed for T. Evans, 1777), vol. 4, pp. 130–5 (p. 135).
[159] Ashmole's standard antiquarian account makes no reference to supernatural activity at Cumnor. See The Antiquities of Berkshire, 3 vols (London: Printed for Edmund Curll, 1719), vol. 1, pp. 149–54.
[160] Scott, Kenilworth, pp. 22, 41.   [161] Scott, Kenilworth, p. 21.
[162] Scott, Kenilworth, p. 16.

WEST SIDE OF THE QUADRANGLE OF CUMNOR PLACE.

Figure 6.2 Engraving of Cumnor Place from Alfred Darling Bartlett, *An Historical and Descriptive Account of Cumnor Place, Berks, with Biographical Notices of the Lady Amy Dudley and of Anthony Forster, Esq.* (1850). Alamy, Image ID: PN5235.

These two romances of the historical past—the white, Tory Gothic of the spectacles at Kenilworth, and the dark Gothic romance of Cumnor Hall—combine and interact when Amy, refusing to pose as Varney's wife, goes to Kenilworth in order to take up her rightful position alongside her husband. At this moment, her experience recalls that of Sophia Lee's Matilda, the heroine who pursues her lover Dudley to Kenilworth in the first volume of *The Recess*; as Fiona Robertson has shown, Gothic romance, here and elsewhere, is integral to Scott's narration of national history.[163] Amy's first impressions of 'those grey and massive towers' betray a response that is 'far different' from others, and directly recall the melancholy awe that Emily St Aubert experiences when she first glimpses Udolpho, a scene in the novel that Scott would later commend.[164] Absorbing and

---

[163] See Fiona Robertson's argument in *Legitimate Histories: Scott, Gothic, and the Authorities of Fiction* (Oxford: Clarendon Press, 1994). For other accounts of Scott's use of Gothic, see Ian Duncan, 'Walter Scott, James Hogg, and Scottish Gothic', in *A New Companion to the Gothic*, ed. David Punter (Oxford: Blackwell, 2012), pp. 123–34, and Fiona Robertson, 'Gothic Scott', in *Scottish Gothic: An Edinburgh Companion*, ed. Carol Margaret Davison and Monica Germanà (Edinburgh: Edinburgh University Press 2017), pp. 103–14.

[164] Scott, *Kenilworth*, p. 225.

throwing into relief the full Gothic implications of Leicester's intentions towards the queen, the plot that recounts the experiences of Amy Robsart at Kenilworth shadows the brightness, pomp, and spectacle of the white Gothic with a darker tale of terror, suffering, and anxiety. In their turn, these competing visions of the past are strongly gendered, the romance of Kenilworth answering to the 'rough masculine spirit' of King Henry VIII to which Elizabeth is heir, and Amy's narrative to the realm of the feminine.[165] Upon her return to Cumnor towards the novel's end, the script of feminine suffering comes back into its own, assuming increasingly Gothic-fictional proportions as Amy is confined to the chamber that is effectively a place of incarceration. In a moment of tragic inevitability, Tressilian arrives too late for effective intervention, and, plunging via the trapdoor outside her bedroom door into an abyss below, Amy meets her death at the hands of Forster and Varney. Varney commits suicide, and the fate of Forster, though initially unknown, is intimated in the tales of ghostly activity that begin to circulate around Cumnor shortly after the catastrophe. As further investigation reveals, however, these sounds are not of supernatural origin but the death agonies of Forster himself. If this seems like a version of Radcliffe's 'explained supernatural' that Scott elsewhere derided, the closing moments of the novel assert a persistent, interminable ghostliness that cannot be rationally explained away: locked in deep melancholy, Tressilian remains 'haunted' by the image of his dead lover, and, in citing the last two stanzas of Mickle's ballad, the novel's close returns the reader to 'The haunted towers of Cumnor-Hall' encountered at the outset.

Confronted with these two competing visions of Gothic antiquity, nineteenth-century adaptors of Scott's novel had no choice but to choose one of the two stories: W. Oxberry focused for the most part on the festivities at the castle in *Kenilworth; A Melo-Drama* (1824), while Elijah Barwell Impey retold the sad Robsart plot in his tragedy *Cumnor; or, The Bugle-Horn* (1822). For many contemporary readers, the structural and thematic interruption of 'authentic' Elizabethan history by a dark, apocryphal romance of feminine suffering was only one instance of a broader split or division in the fiction. One of the few negative reviews that *Kenilworth* received claimed that the Amy Robsart tale 'encroaches, as it appears to us, somewhat too rudely upon the severe, we had almost said the consecrated and exclusive province, of our National Annals'.[166] Gothic romance had usurped the place of authentic and legitimate history. A reviewer in *The Gentleman's Magazine* in March 1821 concurred, though couching his critique in terms that boldly confronted the novel's Gothic elements. 'In the same degree as the wonderful Tales of Mrs. Ratcliffe [*sic*] eclipsed all

---

[165] Scott, *Kenilworth*, p. 365.
[166] Review of Walter Scott's *Kenilworth* in *The British Review* vol. 17, no. 33 (March 1821): pp. 216–29 (p. 218).

contemporary productions in fertility of invention', so 'The Author of Waverley may be considered as the founder of a new school'.[167] The novel at hand, however, challenged this distinction between Scott and Radcliffe, history and romance by too heavy a reliance on sensation and sentiment: 'the productions of the Ratcliffe [sic] school', the reviewer regretfully concluded, 'must ever present their beauties and allurements'.[168] Yet if there was one thing upon which Scott remained insistent, it was that history and romance, far from being irreconcilable opposites, were complementary to the point of being indistinguishable. As he put it in 'An Essay on Romance' (1824), 'Romance and real history have the same common origin.' While romance ought to maintain 'as long as possible' the 'mask of veracity', history, particularly the historical chronicles of the past, participates to such a high degree in the features of romance that, taken together, they constitute a hybrid form, and may be termed either 'romantic histories' or 'historical romances' according to 'the proportion in which their truth is debased by fiction, or their fiction mingled with truth'.[169] It is difficult not to hear in these observations echoes of the claims that Walpole had made to the same effect so many years earlier.

Critics have often commented upon what seem to be Scott's deliberate, self-conscious forays into historical inaccuracy in *Kenilworth*. Queen Elizabeth, for instance, expresses a fondness for Shakespeare's history plays, while the story at various moments alludes to *Othello*, *King Lear*, and *Macbeth*. As in *Gaston*, the use of Shakespeare is anachronistic within the context of the novel's setting: in 1575, Shakespeare was only 11 years old. More trenchantly, the death of Amy Robsart occurred in September 1560, almost fifteen years prior to Elizabeth's Kenilworth visit. Violating linear chronology, Scott seems intentionally to draw the two narratives into direct confrontation with one another, a gesture, it is clear, that was licensed by the architectural metaphor of the 'modern Gothic' that he employed in the 'Dedicatory Epistle' to *Ivanhoe* barely a year before. Like his own craft, the 'modern Gothic' was composed of disparate architectural styles gleaned from vastly different periods. As Scott's experience with *Queenhoo-Hall* had taught him, too dogged an adherence to historical truth on the romance-writer's behalf made for dry and stultifying reading. If the modern writer, he reiterated in his account of *The Old English Baron* in *Lives of the Novelists*, were faced with a stark choice between pleasing his readers of 'the modern world' and pandering to the rigours of 'the rigid antiquary', he ought always to 'sacrifice the last to the first object'.[170] Unlike Reeve, though, who had presented her tale of the Middle Ages in language and costume more appropriate to the seventeenth

---

[167] Review of Walter Scott's *Kenilworth*, GM, vol. 91, part 1 (January–June 1821): p. 246.
[168] Review of Walter Scott's *Kenilworth*, GM, vol. 91, part 1 (January–June 1821): p. 247.
[169] Walter Scott, 'An Essay on Romance', in *Essays on Chivalry, Romance, and the Drama*, by Walter Scott (Edinburgh: Robert Cadell; London: Whittaker and Co., 1834), pp. 127–216 (p. 134).
[170] Walter Scott, *Lives of the Novelists*, 2 vols (Philadelphia: H. C. Carey and I. Lee, et al.; New York: Collins and Hannay, 1825), vol. 1, p. 170.

century, Scott had at least confined his anachronisms to elements that all issued out of the same 'Gothic' past, however capaciously conceived. In interrupting the story of royal pageantry at Kenilworth with a tale of haunting that was not contemporary to it, Scott was also critiquing or at least tempering the complacent, self-congratulatory vision of Gothic antiquity that he found in antiquarian records such as Laneham, a sentiment that would align him in some ways with Radcliffe's more overtly political stance in *Gaston*.

Whatever Scott's reasons for these deliberate historical anachronisms, one thing remains clear: his architectural imagination was inspired more by the remains of Cumnor Hall than it was by the ruins of Kenilworth Castle when he visited both sites in the autumn of 1815. As Lockhart noted, Archibald Constable wanted Scott to write a tale about Queen Elizabeth as a companion piece to his account of the character and times of Mary Stuart in *The Abbot* (1820). Agreeing to the challenge, Scott 'immediately expressed his willingness to 'take up his own old favourite', the legend of Meikle's [sic] ballad', wishing to call his novel, like the ballad, *Cumnor-Hall*.[171] This initial choice seems to have been carefully considered, for as the introductory chapter to *Waverley* indicates, Scott was acutely attuned to the Gothic expectations that a novel's title was likely to evoke:

> Had I, for example, announced in my frontispiece, 'Waverley, a Tale of other Days,' must not every novel reader have anticipated a castle scarce less than that of Udolpho, of which the eastern wing had long been uninhabited, and the keys either lost or consigned to the care of some aged butler or housekeeper, whose trembling steps, about the middle of the second volume, were doomed to guide the hero, or heroine, to the ruinous precincts?[172]

His letters suggest something of the alacrity with which he set out. In a letter of September 1820, he requested Constable to send him a copy of all the passages about Cumnor already published in Daniel and Samuel Lysons' multivolume *Magna Britannia* (1806–22) and any other information about the village that occurred to him.[173] Manuscript sources, too, indicate that, knowing his abiding interest in the subject, Scott's friends continued to send him information about, and images of, Cumnor for several years after the novel was first published.[174] With regards to the novel's title, however, Constable had different plans, and conceding to his publisher's wishes, Scott duly compromised, substituting *Kenilworth* for his preferred title of *Cumnor Hall*. Although the correspondence

---

[171] Lockhart, *Memoirs of the Life of Sir Walter Scott, Bart.*, vol. 5, p. 28.
[172] Walter Scott, *Waverley; or, 'Tis Sixty Years Since*, ed. Claire Lamont (Oxford: Oxford University Press, 1986), p. 3.
[173] Herbert Grierson, ed., *The Letters of Sir Walter Scott*, 12 vols (London: Constable, 1932–7), vol. 6, pp. 226–7.
[174] See the Millgate Union Catalogue of Walter Scott Correspondence, National Library of Scotland, MS 3914/17–18 (dated 1830; from Charles Kirkpatrick Sharpe) and MS 3907/155–59 (dated 1828; from Mary Anne Hughes).

between Constable and Scott on the matter of the novel's title no longer exists, it is tempting to think that what was really at stake was the problem of Gothic romance: since the Hall was commonly known to be haunted, the title *Cumnor Hall* could not but have conjured up expectations of a Gothic romance in the tradition of Ann Radcliffe—inappropriate fare, as Constable perhaps saw it, for the purveyor of authentic historical fiction. Even as he acknowledged its inspiration in the Magnum Opus edition of the novel, Scott himself eventually came to distance *Kenilworth* from its source in Mickle's ballad, dismissing it and poems of its ilk as the stuff of 'immature taste', the relics of 'a period in youth when the mere power of numbers has a more strong effect on ear and imagination, than in more advanced life'.[175] Though in all senses 'foundational' to the narrative, ghostly orality would be covered over by the fabrications of a more mature imaginative construction, although one that remained indebted to the anachronistic combinations of the 'modern Gothic' architectural style. It was thus towards the princely splendours of Kenilworth that Scott's architectural imagination aspired, disavowing the very romance of superstitious association that had set the construction of 'aerial architecture' in place.

---

[175] See *Introduction and Notes from the Magnum Opus: Waverley to A Legend of the Wars of Montrose*, p. 114.

Conclusion: From the Gothic to the Medieval
Historiography, Romanticism, and the Trajectories of the Architectural Imagination

'On reaching the water-side, a spectacle at once sublime and appalling burst upon my eye,' a correspondent in *The Gentleman's Magazine* in November 1834 breathlessly related; 'St. Stephen's Chapel in flames, with the House of Lords a little further to the south, and (the sensation which I felt at the sight as an antiquary and a British subject, I shall not easily forget) the gable of Westminster Hall, contiguous to the fire, apparently alight in two or three places!'[1] This contribution by one A. J. K. claimed to provide an eyewitness account of the devastating fire at the Palace of Westminster, London, that began on the evening of Thursday, 16 October 1834. Despite the correspondent's commitment to providing an objective report from an 'unexaggerated point of view', the description of the spectacle continues, as if without choice, in the following dramatic and hyperbolic terms:

> This Hall (realizing the visions of the romantic age) its huge proportions, its rich wrought and stupendous roof, were about to yield to the devouring element, and to lie a shapeless mass of ruins smouldering in the dust! I felt as if a link would be burst asunder in my national existence, and that the history of my native land was about to become, by the loss of this silent but existing witness, a dream of dimly shadowed actors and events.[2]

The loss of an impartial witness to the onset of modernity; the destruction of the stony embodiment of 'the visions of the romantic age'; and the disappearance of an empirical guarantor of a noble national past, without which history is merely a romance or a shadowy dream: the burning down of the Palace of Westminster in 1834 threatened this British antiquary with the erasure of a sense of selfhood, history, and nationhood alike.

---

[1] A. J. K., 'Conflagration of the Two Houses of Parliament (*with a Plan*)', *GM* (Nov. 1834): pp. 477–80 (p. 477).
[2] A. J. K., 'Conflagration of the Two Houses of Parliament': p. 477.

Gothic Antiquity: History, Romance, and the Architectural Imagination, 1760–1840. Dale Townshend, Oxford University Press (2019). © Dale Townshend.
DOI: 10.1093/oso/9780198845669.001.0001

Raging from approximately 6 p.m. on 14 October until 6 a.m. the following morning, the fire struck at the literal and symbolic centre of British political, economic, and legal existence. By 1834, there had been a royal palace at Westminster for 800 years or more, the history of the site reaching as far back as Edward the Confessor (reigned 1042–66) and conceivably even earlier.[3] Though it had ceased to function as a permanent royal residence, the palace, more commonly known as the Houses of Parliament, was, and had long been, home to all of the major executive functions of the British government, including the Exchequer, Chancery, and the legal system. By 1834, it was also increasingly the venue at which Parliament, that great political structure of 'Gothic' antecedents, convened. While the destruction of governmental parchments and records was alarming enough, many, including the author of this letter in *The Gentleman's Magazine*, were equally concerned by the architectural devastation that was revealed by the smoky light of dawn the following day. A ramshackle assemblage of passages, annexes, additions, and alterations by this time the palace undoubtedly was: Christopher Wren had extended it in 1707 so as to accommodate Scottish MPs after the Acts of Union; together with the surrounding buildings, James Wyatt had altered it in his signature 'modern Gothic' style following the Act of Union with Ireland in 1801; and John Soane had incorporated a number of Grecian additions in his capacity as an architect in His Majesty's Office of Works. At Westminster, William Blackstone's sense of the British constitution as an old Gothic castle 'fitted up for a modern inhabitant' was as literal as it was symbolic. Alongside these modern alterations stood the ancient Westminster Hall and St Stephen's Chapel, the former, by virtue of the vastness of its hammer-beam roof alone, celebrated as 'The wonder unrivalled of Europe, the palladium of the English monarchy', the latter, a thirteenth-century royal chapel-turned-chamber for the House of Commons.[4] While Westminster Hall survived the fire, the Painted Chamber, the priceless Armada tapestries, the House of Lords, the House of Commons and its library, and, most painfully, St Stephen's Chapel, were all but destroyed; those portions of its walls that remained, badly charred, above the Chapel of St Mary Undercroft in the crypt were demolished in 1835.

Visible for miles around London, the blaze was watched with awe and consternation by thousands of spectators, among them such prominent and soon-to-be prominent figures as the Prime Minister Lord Melbourne; the young Augustus Welby Northmore Pugin; the architect Charles Barry; possibly the young Charles Dickens; the artists Clarkson Stanfield, J. M. W. Turner, and John Constable; Thomas Carlyle; and King William IV and his consort, Adelaide of Saxe-Meiningen.

---

[3] For an account of the early history of the Palace of Westminster, see John Goodall, 'The Medieval Palace of Westminster', in *The Houses of Parliament: History, Art, Architecture*, ed. David Cannadine, Dorian Church et al. (London: Merrell Publishers, 2000), pp. 49–67.

[4] A. J. K., 'Conflagration of the Two Houses of Parliament': p. 477.

For at least one of these onlookers, though, the fire was a welcome event, a crucible for the purification of what, through years of piecemeal additions, had become a modern Gothic monstrosity. As A. W. N. Pugin wrote to Edward James Willson some three weeks later,

> there is nothing much to regret & a great deal to rejoice in. a vast quantity of Soanes mixtures & Wyatts heresies have been effectually consigned to oblivion. oh it was a glorious sight to see his composition mullions & cement pinncles [sic] & battlements flying & cracking While his 2.6 turrets were smoking [sic] Like so many manufactoring chimnies till the heat shivered them into a thousand peices [sic].[5]

For Pugin, the fire constituted somewhat of an architectural purge: while ancient and 'true' Gothic architecture represented endurance and strength, the modern additions of Soane and Wyatt were trifling embellishments mercifully doomed to obliteration. It is this sense of Gothic 'purification' that I wish to explore by way of conclusion to this book. The destruction and subsequent rebuilding of the Houses of Parliament in the 'reformed' Gothic style of A. W. N. Pugin and Charles Barry, I argue, marked the formal installation of what I have termed in this study the white Gothic: a particular conceptualization of the noble and venerable Gothic past as embodied in, represented by, and accessed through the Gothic architectural style. This was the consolidation of cultural processes that had been at work through much of the eighteenth century, an impulse that gathered particular momentum in architectural, historiographic, and literary discourses and practices in the first four decades of the nineteenth. As cultural conceptualizations of the Gothic 'Dark Ages' gradually ceded to notions of the 'medieval', so architectural theorists, historians, and aestheticians formalized and refined extant understandings of medieval England's architecture. The term 'Gothic', once so freighted with negative significations, lost currency, either to be replaced by less pejorative synonyms or fundamentally altered and recuperated as the positive cipher of a noble, English architectural tradition. Moreover, even as they continued to represent, respond to, and muse about real and imaginary architectural forms, the major exponents of British romanticism adopted a critical stance in relation to the associative paradigm, a move that shook the architectural imagination to its foundations. This assault was only intensified by the theories of Gothic architecture advanced by A. W. N. Pugin and John Ruskin. No longer solely a figure of creativity and sublime genius who invited comparisons with other artists, writers, and poets, the architect himself became one of the nineteenth century's new professionals, a significant discursive and institutional shift that severed many of

---

[5] A. W. N. Pugin to Edward James Willson, 6 November 1834, *The Collected Letters of A.W. N. Pugin, Vol I: 1830–1842*, ed. with notes and introd. Margaret Belcher (Oxford: Oxford University Press, 2001), pp. 41–3 (p. 42).

the continuities between the architect and the writer that I have explored in this book. The destruction and gradual reconstruction of the Palace of Westminster, I argue, was the greatest symbolic expression of these changes.

The Fire's Immediate Aftermath

Caroline Shenton has exhaustively charted the range of sentimental, political, and cultural responses that the 1834 fire provoked, be they of Tory or Whig persuasion, pro-establishment or radical, lofty or scurrilous.[6] Coming only two years after the Great Reform Act of 1832 and the Poor Law Amendment Act of earlier that same year, the fire was, for some, an act of self-destruction on the part of a Parliament that had quite outdone itself, for others, just deserts for these Acts' amelioration of the plight of the indigent and disenfranchised.[7] As David Cannadine has pointed out, British radicals and progressives celebrated the destruction as both timely and opportune, since it 'swept away the ramshackle and inefficient buildings that were the physical embodiment of the world of "old corruption," the end of which had already been portended in the legislation passed in 1832'.[8] Echoes of the debates concerning acts of literal and symbolic demolition, improvement, and rebuilding that, as I argued in Chapter 4, raged throughout Britain during the 1790s would not have been lost on those old enough to remember them. Journalists cynically saw in the acts of firefighting allegorical representations of the nation's futile battle against the powers of governmental bureaucracy and inertia, while those of a more suspicious bent read in the event uncanny similarities with the Gunpowder Plot of 1605.[9] Predictably, conspiracy theories abounded, including the possibility of arson, and fears of a takeover by the increasing number of Irish immigrants in London in possible collusion with recently emancipated Catholics. Others, like a second writer in *The Gentleman's Magazine* in November 1834, were far less paranoid in their speculations, claiming, in an 'authenticated statement' that followed the first letter, that while 'The origin of the fire could not with certainty be ascertained', the 'most probable account' was that it had 'originated in the flues used for warming the House of Lords, which had been unusually heated by a large fire made by the burning of the old wooden Exchequer tallies, and which had been improperly entrusted by the clerk of the works to a workman named Cross'.[10] Indeed, as the final report on

---

[6] Caroline Shenton, *The Day Parliament Burned Down* (Oxford: Oxford University Press, 2012).
[7] Shenton, *The Day Parliament Burned Down*, pp. 2–3.
[8] David Cannadine, 'The Palace of Westminster as Palace of Varieties', in *The Houses of Parliament: History, Art, Architecture*, ed. David Cannadine, Dorian Church et al. (London: Merrell Publishers, 2000), pp. 11–29 (p. 13).
[9] Shenton, *The Day Parliament Burned Down*, pp. 102–3.
[10] Anon., 'Brief and Authenticated Statement', *GM* (Nov. 1834): pp. 480–3 (p. 482).

the disaster in November 1836 ruled, the fire had been caused not by subterfuge or radical discontent but by the negligence of Joshua Cross and Patrick Furlong, two Irish immigrants who, acting under the instruction of the Clerk of Works, had set about burning the piles of disused wooden tallies in the coal furnaces beneath the House of Lords chamber.[11]

Alarmed by the damage, Edward Wedlake Brayley and John Britton set to work on *The History of the Ancient Palace and Late Houses of Parliament at Westminster* (1836), an antiquarian study of the old building that tried to capture, in words and engraved images, all that had been lost. The spirit of preservation that began in earlier periods, and which would be of such significance to nineteenth-century architectural developments, had been galvanized.[12] Like the political debates in Britain provoked by the fall of the Bastille forty-five years earlier, national attention turned almost immediately to the prospect of reconstruction. Tories wished for the rebuilding of the palace on the original site according to the same architectural principles expressed in the nearby Westminster Hall and Abbey; Whigs favoured rebuilding at Westminster but wanted a more modern and progressive approach to the appointment of the architect; and radicals desired the construction of an entirely new building far away from the contaminations of the past.[13] In the preference that he expressed for the Gothic style, the correspondent in *The Gentleman's Magazine* ventriloquized Edmund Burke's figuring of British political values as an ancient Gothic edifice in *Reflections on the Revolution in France*—even if, in this particular instance, the flame of chivalry had alarmingly achieved too literal a manifestation. To rebuild in the Gothic style, the writer claimed, would be to resurrect the Burkean 'Gothic' values for which the building stood. John Soane set about the repair of the Old Palace at Westminster shortly after the fire. When Robert Smirke, who had initially been commissioned with the drawing up of plans for the rebuilding, presented them to the new Prime Minister Sir Robert Peel in early 1835, Peel, in a campaign headed up by the disgruntled Tory MP Sir Edward Cust, was accused of nepotism and Smirke of opportunism.[14] The design and plans for the remodelling were now to be decided upon through an open competition, and to this end a Commons Select Committee was appointed in March 1835.[15] The competition was announced in July 1835, and

---

[11] Shenton, *The Day Parliament Burned Down*, p. 240.

[12] For more on nineteenth-century architectural preservation, see Michael Thompson, *Ruins Reused: Changing Attitudes to Ruins Since the Late Eighteenth Century* (Norfolk: Heritage Marketing and Publications, 2006), and Simon Thurley, *Men from the Ministry: How Britain Saved Its Heritage* (New Haven and London: Yale University Press, 2013).

[13] See Caroline Shenton, *Mr Barry's War: Rebuilding the Houses of Parliament After the Great Fire of 1834* (Oxford: Oxford University Press, 2016), p. 13, and Andrea Frederickson, 'Parliament's Genius Loci: The Politics of Place after the 1834 Fire', in *The Houses of Parliament: History, Art, Architecture*, ed. David Cannadine, Dorian Church et al. (London: Merrell Publishers, 2000), pp. 99–111.

[14] See Shenton, *Mr Barry's War*, p. 11.

[15] For a detailed account of the competition, see M. H. Port, *The Houses of Parliament* (New Haven and London: Yale University Press, 1976), pp. 20–52.

the closing date for the submission of entries set for 1 December of the same year. The committee's stipulation that all tendered designs be in the 'national' architectural style—that is, either the Elizabethan or the Gothic—was as much a fulfilment of the wishes of the writer in *The Gentleman's Magazine* as an expression of the political conservatism of the 1830s. For, as Cannadine has argued, the new palace was intended 'to articulate a hierarchical image of the social and political order, stressing venerable authority, providential subordination and true conservative principles'—that is, the very antithesis of the classical style, in all its associations with the 'rootless anarchy and national enmity of revolutionary France' or republican America.[16] Of the ninety-seven submitted entries, a Royal Commission, comprising Charles Hanbury Tracy, the Hon. Thomas Liddell, George Vivian, and Sir Edward Cust himself, judged the anonymous design number 64, by Charles Barry with drawings executed by A.W. N. Pugin, to be the winner, and the results of the competition were publicly announced in February 1836.

Gothic Romance in the Battle of the Styles

Even before the results of the competition were known, the mere possibility that rebuilding could proceed according to Gothic principles was enough to pre-empt what architectural historians have described as the Battle of the Styles, an urgent pamphlet war between defenders of the Gothic style and some of its most vociferous opponents. Bernard Porter has provided a searching account of how the debates concerning the perceived aesthetic and political differences between the Gothic and the classical played themselves out around three particularly contested sites in London during the nineteenth century: the Houses of Parliament in Westminster (1835–c.1860); the British Foreign Office in Whitehall (1855–61); and the Law Courts in the Strand (1874–82).[17] Less acknowledged, though, is the extent to which, in relation to the new palace at Westminster, both sides of the argument looked to literature—the Gothic aesthetic as it was manifested in the romances of Walpole, Radcliffe, Scott, Mary Shelley, and many others—as either justification for, or evidential proof against, the Gothic as an appropriate national style. The debates also point towards what would become a priority for Auguste Charles Pugin and his son Augustus Welby Northmore Pugin, John Ruskin, and other Gothic Revivalists of the nineteenth century: the need to cleanse or purge Gothic architecture of its long-standing connections with Gothic romance, restituting instead a national idiom that was authentic,

---

[16] Cannadine, 'The Palace of Westminster as Palace of Varieties', p. 12.
[17] See Bernard Porter, *The Battle of the Styles: Society, Culture and the Design of a new Foreign Office, 1855–61* (New York: Continuum, 2011).

grounded, and freed of architectural whimsy. A survey of the tracts from the Battle of the Styles is useful, too, in understanding what the term 'Gothic' by 1835 had come to mean, an endeavour that, in turn, reveals that what was really at stake in the dispute over the rebuilding of the Houses of Parliament was the conflict between the two competing conceptualizations of the Gothic past that I have explored throughout this book: Gothic antiquity as an age of darkness and barbarism or an epoch of literal and metaphorical enlightenment.

Motivated, perhaps, by the desire to promote and defend the designs that his father, James Hakewill, had entered in the open competition, the architectural commentator Arthur William Hakewill was one of the first publicly to declare his repugnance for the Gothic in his pamphlet *Thoughts Upon the Style of Architecture to be Adopted in Rebuilding the Houses of Parliament* (1835). Recalling Wren's argument in *Parentalia*, Hakewill regarded the Gothic merely as 'the means of perpetuating the memory of a period of comparative barbarism', a style that was rapidly becoming obsolete and one that was utterly 'unsuited' to 'the prevailing sentiment of an age so enlightened' as the present.[18] The intellectual darkness out of which Gothic arose, he continued, is thoroughly at odds with 'all those attributes of an enlightened period' that 'exert such visible influence over the manners of the present generation'.[19] A more becoming mirror of modernity, one that is consistent with 'the present refined state of society', is Greek or modern Italian architecture, both styles that, incorporating within them allusions to the monumental architecture of ancient Rome, are designated 'under the generic term of Classic architecture'.[20] The Elgin Marbles, brought to England from Athens, much to Lord Byron's chagrin, between 1801 and 1805, and bought from Lord Elgin by Parliament in 1816, ought thus to serve as 'stumbling *blocks* to the whole nation' otherwise caught up in the taste for Gothic architecture; a Gothic Houses of Parliament, by contrast, would constitute 'a palpable instance of owl-like stumbling in the broad light of day'.[21] While the Gothic's 'monstrous' properties embody a past age of darkness and barbarism, the balance and symmetry of classicism, 'free from gloom' and thoroughly coeval with the rise and progress of the arts and sciences in Greece and Italy, incarnate an age of enlightenment.[22] Resisting the associationist tradition that had long extolled the ability of Gothic to conjure up visions in the perceiver's consciousness, Hakewill's tract confrontationally condemned the style for being 'comparatively so inferior and so limited in

---

[18] Arthur William Hakewill, *Thoughts Upon the Style of Architecture to be Adopted in Rebuilding the Houses of Parliament* (London: John Weale, 1835), pp. 7–8.
[19] Hakewill, *Thoughts Upon the Style of Architecture*, p. 8.
[20] Hakewill, *Thoughts Upon the Style of Architecture*, p. 12.
[21] Hakewill, *Thoughts Upon the Style of Architecture*, pp. 15, 16.
[22] Hakewill, *Thoughts Upon the Style of Architecture*, pp. 19, 12.

its powers over the mind' and 'so powerless in its appeal to the sympathetic emotions of the heart'.[23]

It was Hakewill's dismissal of the Gothic's affective and imaginative appeal to which the young and as yet undistinguished A. W. N. Pugin responded in *A Letter to A. W. Hakewill, Architect* (1835). Billing himself as a 'jealous professor' of the 'noble style of architecture termed Gothic', Pugin, here in line with earlier writers like Walpole, makes a courageous assertion of a Gothic building's superlative imaginative potential, arguing that 'the grandeur of their masses—the exquisite finish of their details—their bold and scientific construction—the light, and at the same time solid, manner in which they are erected' collectively contribute 'to fill the mind of the beholder with admiration, and a profound veneration for the skill and perseverance of the ages in which they were produced'.[24] Though Pugin's use of the word 'light' in this instance is as an indicator of weight rather than vision, his tract turns upon a careful dismissal of Hakewill's sense of Gothic antiquity as an epoch of darkness, and the promotion, instead, of the Middle Ages as an age of enlightenment: at the very least, the sheer magnitude of a Gothic cathedral attests to the skill and perseverance of the craftsmen who built it. Where evocations of antiquity are concerned, the architecture of St Paul's Cathedral, London, presents itself as a case in point: without hesitation, Pugin pronounces Wren's rebuilding of old St Paul's in the classical style in the wake of that other disastrous fire of 1666 to be 'greatly inferior' to 'many of those stupendous Cathedrals which will for ever immortalise the architects of the middle ages'.[25] For Pugin, the promotion of the Gothic ultimately amounted to a matter of national taste, and revising Hakewill's metaphor of the Gothic building as a noxious 'weed' among the 'flowers' of the Greek school, his tract asserted the quintessentially English nature of the style: 'in lieu of borrowing our architecture from foreign climes, we possess buildings whose character is more suited to our country and climate'.[26]

Benjamin Ferrey, the one-time draftsman under the tutorship of A. W. N. Pugin's father Auguste Charles Pugin and later biographer of both father and son, entered the fray with the publication of his *Answer, to 'Thoughts on Rebuilding the Houses of Parliament'* (1835). Like Pugin, Ferrey refutes Hakewill's sense of the Gothic past as an age of barbarism and darkness by pointing out that, as the remains of such buildings as the Roman Colosseum attest, classical antiquity was by no means an era of 'bliss and peace, liberty and happiness', but one of violent sport and pagan ritual.[27] Opposing Hakewill, the Gothic for Ferrey is as 'fully deserving' of consideration as

---

[23] Hakewill, *Thoughts Upon the Style of Architecture*, pp. 13, 9.
[24] A. Welby Pugin, *A Letter to A. W. Hakewill, Architect, in Answer to His Reflections on the Style for Rebuilding the Houses of Parliament* (Salisbury: Printed and Published for the Author by W. B. Brodie and Co., 1835).
[25] Pugin, *A Letter to A. W. Hakewill, Architect*, p. 7.
[26] Pugin, *A Letter to A. W. Hakewill, Architect*, pp. 13–14.
[27] Benjamin Ferrey, *Answer, to 'Thoughts on Rebuilding the Houses of Parliament'* (London: John Weale, 1835), p. 8.

the architecture of 'this enlightened age': originating in an age of cultural greatness, the Gothic style was perfectly suited to the modern present, the classical, by contrast, only to 'the objects and times they recorded'.[28] Such views, however, were scant defence against the tide of anti-Gothic vitriol that issued from the press in the wake of the news that it was Charles Barry's Gothic designs for the new building that had been selected over all other entries. Shortly after the announcement, William Richard Hamilton expressed his disappointment with the competition's outcome, as well as his continued support for Greek and Roman classicism, in three public letters addressed to Thomas Bruce, 7th Earl of Elgin, then Trustee of the British Museum. Hamilton, an English diplomat and antiquary, had earlier, under the direction of Elgin, travelled to Egypt in the wake of the Battle of Alexandria, seizing from the French the Rosetta Stone and overseeing its transportation to London. In 1802, again under the direction of the earl, Hamilton had superintended the collection and removal to England of the Elgin Marbles from the Parthenon in Athens. Predictably, Hamilton took a firmly classicist stance in the stylistic debate of 1835–6. Deeming in his first pamphlet the original stipulation that all designs be in either the Gothic or the Elizabethan styles to be, in itself, restrictive, Hamilton echoes the reservations of Hakewill in describing the Gothic as the 'style of bygone days', the architecture of a dark and superstitious past 'in which the cultivation of the fine arts had made comparatively small progress'.[29] Setting out a teleological narrative in which the architecture of any given nation inevitably progresses across time from the deformed to the beautiful, the barbarian to the civilized, the meretriciously ornamented to the simple and elegant, Hamilton, like Hakewill before him, regards architecture as 'a mirror of the improvement of science in various periods', one in which the antiquary 'who visits our cathedrals' is likely only ever to catch a fleeting glimpse of the darkness of the Catholic past.[30] Threatening the architectural progress wrought by the dissolution of the monasteries, and witnessed thereafter in the Italianate impulses of the Tudor period, the Palladianism of Inigo Jones; the English baroque classicism of Christopher Wren; the quasi-neo-Palladianism of the early eighteenth century; and the neoclassicism and Greek revival of the later eighteenth century, the return of the Gothic style is likely to plunge the nation back into the barbarism and superstition of the Middle Ages. A Gothic Houses of Parliament, Hamilton opines, stands in grave danger of tampering with the evolutionary narratives of history, of 'confounding times and usages', and effectively converting 'our public buildings into architectural romances'.[31] To refashion in the Gothic is to turn national history into a fanciful fiction, one that, in its 'modern disregard of properties', is dangerously close to the architectural experiment of 'an amateur of great celebrity' who has 'lately built

---

[28] Ferrey, *Answer*, pp. 10, 13.
[29] William Richard Hamilton, *Letter from W. R. Hamilton, To the Earl of Elgin, on the New Houses of Parliament*, 2nd edn (London: John Weale, 1836), p. 4.
[30] Hamilton, *Letter*, p. 5.   [31] Hamilton, *Letter*, p. 5.

himself a Gothic house, in which each of the three architectural sides presents a distinct character'.[32]

The 'amateur celebrity' to whom Hamilton here refers is eventually identified when, towards the end of the tract, he places the blame for the revival of interest in the Gothic style squarely at the door of Horace Walpole and his home at Strawberry Hill:

> And yet there is but little doubt that this temporary rage for Gothic architecture would never have controuled [sic] the talents and taste of the English of the last or present century, if it had not been for the singular notions of one individual, an ingenious trifler, as Gibbon calls him, the late Horace Earl of Orford, who in the indulgence of a peculiar fancy in ornamenting an insignificant villa, and from a desire to give birth to a new fashion, employed a long life, and the influence he possessed amongst the upper classes of society, to introduce a passion for what he styled the charming venerable Gothic.[33]

More recently, he claims, the 'delusional' taste for Gothic architecture has been further promoted by the novels of Walter Scott, 'the magical creations' of the Waverley novels, with all their 'irregular and fanciful combinations of turrets', 'painted windows and grotesque sculpture, oriels and buttresses', appealing to their readers' 'feudal and ancestral recollections'.[34] For Hamilton, to rebuild so iconic a structure as the new palace in the Gothic idiom was in danger of contaminating the teleological trajectories of history with the romances of Walpole and Scott, inflicting upon the nation a ghastly example of the much-reviled 'modern Gothic'.

Buoyed up by the approval with which his first letter to Elgin was met, Hamilton published his *Second Letter* a few months later. In this pamphlet, his critique of what he terms the 'Gothomania' of contemporary taste is based upon a conflation of architectural and literary values similar to those that he had employed earlier: while the Grecian style is akin to a mimetic form governed by the ideals of truth, beauty, and verisimilitude, the wild, unruly, and excessively imaginative nature of the Gothic is of the order of romance.[35] Although he offers a surprisingly positive assessment of the origin and development of the Gothic in Europe—these buildings, he notes, 'rose in gorgeous magnificence' in the place of Roman ruin—it is a style for Hamilton that remains inseparable from the abhorrent Catholic past: as 'striking remnants of Popery', Gothic structures manifest all the excessive dedication of 'Catholic times'.[36] As this suggests, variations on John Evelyn's 1664 dismissal of the Gothic's 'monkish piles' were still current in Britain

---

[32] Hamilton, *Letter*, p. 5.   [33] Hamilton, *Letter*, pp. 7–8.   [34] Hamilton, *Letter*, pp. 7–8.
[35] William Richard Hamilton, *Second Letter from W. R. Hamilton, Esq. To the Earl of Elgin, on the Propriety of Adopting the Greek Style of Architecture in the Construction of the New Houses of Parliament* (London: John Weale, 1836), p. 3.
[36] Hamilton, *Second Letter*, pp. 11, 14.

some 170 years later, and even following the Roman Catholic Relief Act of 1829. The ecclesiastical functions of the Gothic, Hamilton claimed, were unsuited to the secular, political, and economic needs of the present, for the 'cumbrous and dark piles' of the Middle Ages might only ever serve as reminders 'of the times of ignorance' and darkness, effecting a recidivist return to the dark days of 'chivalry and superstition'.[37] 'At a period of time, when the greatest exertions are making to get rid of all preconceived notions handed down to us from a Gothic ancestry,' he emotively writes, a Gothic palace at Westminster could only ever produce 'an humble copy of the gloomy mansions of our forefathers'.[38] Without the pure and simple lines of the Grecian as a template, a rebuilding of the palace in the Gothic mode would result in a monstrous combination of incongruities, drawing inspiration from several medieval buildings across the country and combing them into a 'conglomeration of heterogeneous parts' that incarnated all manner of 'horrors and deformities'.[39] The claim is underscored by notions of the 'modern Gothic' that I addressed in Chapter 6: the Gothic/classical hybrids of Kent and Langley; the merging of rococo and Gothic styles in Bentley, Paine, Chippendale, and Miller; and the fusion of Gothic and neoclassical forms in the work of Adam and Wyatt. Though his sense of the monstrosity of architectural hybridity ultimately derives from the classicism of Horace's *Ars Poetica*, Hamilton couches his invective against Gothic architecture in terms that, following the publication of Mary Shelley's *Frankenstein* in 1818, had become synonymous with the conventions of Gothic fiction. That is, the piecemeal suturings of the Creature's body served as an appropriate metaphor for the architectural experiments of the eighteenth-century Gothic Revival.

In his second letter to Elgin, Hamilton invoked, if only to contradict, Samuel Taylor Coleridge's views on Gothic architecture that had been published in *The Literary Remains of Samuel Taylor Coleridge* (1836) earlier that same year. The first volume of Henry Nelson Coleridge's edition of selections of his uncle's works contained transcriptions, by members of the public in attendance, of the lectures that the poet had presented in 1818. In Lecture I, 'General Character of the Gothic Mind in the Middle Ages', Coleridge drew upon earlier accounts of the sublimity of Gothic architecture, but supplemented them with ideas that he had gleaned in the interim from his reading of Immanuel Kant.[40] While claiming that the contemplation of 'the works of [classical] antique art excites a feeling of elevated beauty, and exalted notions of the human self', Coleridge argued that a Gothic building was both distinct and superior insofar as it 'impresses the beholder with a

---

[37] Hamilton, *Second Letter*, pp. 23, 30, 23, 18.
[38] Hamilton, *Second Letter*, p. 52.   [39] Hamilton, *Second Letter*, p. 52.
[40] For more on Coleridge and Kant, see, among other studies, Paul Hamilton, *Coleridge and German Philosophy: The Poet in the Land of Logic* (London: Bloomsbury, 2007), and Monika Class, *Coleridge and Kantian Ideas in England, 1796–1817* (London: Bloomsbury, 2012).

sense of self-annihilation'.[41] The consciousness of the perceiver rapidly becomes one with the Gothic structure that it perceives, the individual becoming, 'as it were, a part of the work contemplated'.[42] With the individual parts of a building combining into a perfect whole, the plan of which is 'not distinct from the execution', Gothic architecture for Coleridge is, by its very nature, moral, the embodiment in stone of the Protestant sublime: 'A Gothic cathedral', he writes, 'is the petrefaction [sic] of our religion.'[43]

In Lecture II, 'General Character of the Gothic Literature and Art', Coleridge made his indebtedness to both Burkean and Kantian distinctions between the sublime and the beautiful more explicit, describing classical Greek architecture as a manifestation of the beautiful and Gothic architecture, through the sense of subjective annihilation that it imposes, as a source of sublimity. His comments replay the commonplace contrasting of the classical and the Gothic that, as I have shown in this book, structured much architectural thought in the eighteenth and early nineteenth centuries:

> The Greek art is beautiful. When I enter a Greek church, my eye is charmed, and my mind elated; I feel exalted, and proud that I am a man. But the Gothic art is sublime. On entering a cathedral, I am filled with devotion and with awe; I am lost to the actualities that surround me, and my whole being expands into the infinite; earth and air, nature and art, all swell up into eternity, and the only sensible impression left, is, 'that I am nothing!'[44]

Coleridge's reference to infinity here is significant, and again registers the influence of Kant's account of the mathematical sublime in *Critique of Judgement* (1790). As Henry Nelson Coleridge in *Specimens of the Table Talk of the Late Samuel Taylor Coleridge* (1835) recorded the poet as saying in 1833, 'The principle of the Gothic architecture is Infinity made imaginable.'[45] In Coleridge's understanding of the architectural sublime, a Burkean emphasis upon obscurity had given way to Kantian boundlessness and infinity. 'It is no doubt a sublimer effort of genius than the Greek style,' Coleridge in *Table Talk* continued, 'but it depends much more upon execution for its effect. I was more than ever impressed with the marvellous sublimity and transcendant [sic] beauty of King's College Chapel.'[46] The juxtaposition of Grecian beauty with Gothic sublimity continues throughout

---

[41] Samuel Taylor Coleridge, 'Lecture I: General Character of the Gothic Mind in the Middle Ages', in *The Literary Remains of Samuel Taylor Coleridge*, ed. Henry Nelson Coleridge, 4 vols (London: William Pickering, 1836), vol. 1, pp. 67–9 (pp. 68–9).

[42] Coleridge, 'Lecture I', p. 68.   [43] Coleridge, 'Lecture I', p. 69.

[44] Samuel Taylor Coleridge, 'Lecture II: General Character of the Gothic Literature and Art', in *The Literary Remains of Samuel Taylor Coleridge*, ed. Henry Nelson Coleridge, 4 vols (London: William Pickering, 1836), vol. 1, pp. 70–8 (p. 71).

[45] Henry Nelson Coleridge, ed., *Specimens of the Table Talk of the Late Samuel Taylor Coleridge*, 2 vols (London: John Murray, 1835), vol. 2, p. 199.

[46] Coleridge, ed., *Table Talk*, vol. 2, pp. 199–200.

Lecture II, too, but it is when Coleridge turns to a comparison of the literatures of the two traditions that his support for the Gothic becomes particularly apparent: while, in Homer, one might encounter a poem 'perfect in its form', and descriptive visions brought gratifyingly to life before one, it is to the 'Gothic' literature of the Middle Ages that one ought to look for any stirring emotional effects: 'if I wish my feelings to be affected, if I wish my heart to be touched,' he asserts, 'if I wish to melt into sentiment and tenderness, I must turn to the heroic songs of the Goths, to the poetry of the middle ages'.[47]

To encounter in so admired a figure as the recently deceased Coleridge a strong defence of the Gothic style was, to the classicist position, nothing short of alarming, and one to which Hamilton in his second letter to Elgin responded through a willed misreading of the poet's argument. Fixing on Coleridge's sense of Grecian beauty in the second lecture while overlooking his celebration of Gothic sublimity, Hamilton disingenuously co-opts Coleridge for the classicist cause, maintaining that even 'the intellectual Coleridge' concedes that 'it is the Greek art, which is the beautiful', and that, 'within the Greek building' and not the Gothic 'his eye was charmed, and his mind elated, that he felt exalted, and proud that he was a man'.[48] While, in a Gothic building the infinite variety of the 'grotesques' within and without capture and preoccupy Coleridge's mind as distinct and separate entities, in a Grecian building, Hamilton, misleadingly citing the poet's view on the Pantheon, continues, 'the whole is perceived in a perceived [sic] harmony, which composes it; and as the parts preserve each its distinct individuality, each being essentially a whole in itself, the result is simple beauty, or beauty simply'.[49]

Hamilton's opposition to a Gothic Houses of Parliament took an even greater literary turn in his final publication in the furore, *Third Letter from W. R. Hamilton Esq. To The Earl of Elgin* (1837). Reiterating his earlier arguments, Hamilton's third tract argued that the ecclesiastical style of the Middle Ages was both inappropriate for modern, secular politics, and likely to occasion a regressive return to the 'monkish times' from which they sprang.[50] Advocating the clear lines and symmetries of the Grecian over the Gothic's 'mass of grotesque buttresses', Hamilton's third letter stages another confrontation with the arch-defender of the Gothic style, Horace Walpole.[51] In a letter to George Montagu on 31 October 1760, Walpole, self-consciously aware of himself as the founder of 'a new sect' of Gothic 'followers', had articulated a major principle behind the early Gothic Revival, namely that, in place of the slavish imitation of classical precedent, the task at hand was one of

---

[47] Coleridge, 'Lecture II', p. 72.
[48] Hamilton, *Second Letter*, p. 22.   [49] Hamilton, *Second Letter*, p. 22.
[50] William Richard Hamilton, *Third Letter from W. R. Hamilton, Esq. To The Earl of Elgin, on the Propriety of Adopting the Greek Style of Architecture in Preference to the Gothic, in the Construction of the New Houses of Parliament* (London: John Weale, 1837), p. 6.
[51] Hamilton, *Third Letter*, p. 7.

creative and imaginative construction, albeit undertaken according to sound Gothic principles: 'We are a thousand times a greater nation than the Grecians,' he exhorts, 'why are we to imitate them! Our sense is as great, our follies greater; sure we have all the pretensions to superiority.'[52] In 1837, the currency of Walpole's words was assured by their publication in the second volume of *Correspondence of Horace Walpole with George Montagu Esq.*, a new edition of which had been published in the same year in which Hamilton penned his third letter. Against this assertion of the Gothic architect's imaginative powers, Hamilton defends the neoclassical principle of *imitatio* while arguing that, contrary to the claims of many, Gothic is not quintessentially English in nature. Appalled at the nation's election 'to dig up from the tomb of Gothic barbarism modes which have been for centuries exploded, and whims, fancies and extravagancies, which monkish ignorance and ambitious superstition alone could have given rise to', Hamilton's rhetoric, this time with greater forcefulness, again echoes the work of Victor in *Frankenstein*, the revised edition of which had been published by Henry Colburn and Richard Bentley in 1831.[53] The allusion becomes even more pronounced in his apocalyptic vision of the Gothic monstrosities that the sordid activities of the charnel house are likely to set loose upon the world:

> Soon as the eyes of the public are opened to the unsightliness of the Gothic monster we are to have, the recriminations which will not be spared, will fall upon the head of the originators of the scheme; and they, conscious that they were guided in this voluntary and gratuitous production of evil, by local and insufficient consideration, that they all knew what was right, but that they were induced to prefer the crooked to the straight path, will blush for their mistake, and wonder how they could have been so misguided.[54]

This was, indeed, a curious architectural appropriation of a Gothic fiction that, as I elaborate below, ultimately had very little to say about Gothic architecture at all.

Hamilton, however, was not the first architectural critic to appropriate *Frankenstein* as a means of expressing his distaste for the 'monstrosity' of the reanimated 'modern Gothic' style. Earlier, and in the face of similar criticisms, John Rutter in his *Delineations of Fonthill and Its Abbey* (1823) was defensively led to assure his readers that 'The Abbey is no *Frankenstein*, built up of the actual head of one individual, the arms of another, and the body of a third, forming a disgusting and unnatural whole.'[55] Later, in a letter to the editor of *The Pall Mall Gazette* in March 1872, John Ruskin reflected upon the influence of his defence of Venetian Gothic architecture in *The Stones of Venice* and elsewhere, describing the numerous

---

[52] *Correspondence of Horace Walpole with George Montagu, Esq.*, new edn, 3 vols (London: Henry Colburn, 1837), vol. 2, p. 45.
[53] Hamilton, *Third Letter*, pp. 3–4. [54] Hamilton, *Third Letter*, p. 18.
[55] Rutter, *Delineations of Fonthill and Its Abbey*, p. 64.

Revivalist Gothic buildings that had sprung up in and around London as 'the accursed Frankenstein monsters of, *indirectly*, my own creation'.[56]

For Hamilton in 1837, the reanimation of a moribund Gothic style at Westminster was an evil, guilt-inducing act of monstrous, Frankensteinian proportions, the monster's hybrid body an appropriate metaphor for revivalist architectural impurity. Well beyond its affinities with Frankenstein's monster, a Gothic palace at Westminster is a sign of folly, the fruits of a diseased imagination, a miscarriage of true creative genius that is indistinguishable in form and structure from the irrational, intricate, and confused narratives of Gothic romance: faced with the current vogue for the Gothic, Hamilton ominously observes, classical art 'has to renew the fight against a revived race of romancers, who like the schoolmen of old...would now give us forms without reason, complexity for precision, confusion instead of harmony, and tawdriness for simplicity'.[57] A romance in stone, a Gothic building inflicts upon those who perceive it varieties of the madness induced in the readers of imaginative fiction, for in the highly ornamented Gothic style in which 'there is a crowded succession of part', the 'variety itself becomes sameness, and the mind is bewildered in a forest of sweets'.[58] The English nation ought thus to be no more willing to rebuild according to Gothic principles than to return to the dark and monkish times represented in ancient chronicles and modern Gothic romances alike. Though 'we like to read the chronicles of those times, even in the imperfect language in which they were written, nor do we repudiate them, however distorted and exaggerated by the romancer and the novelist', we do not, he insists, 'wish to revive the one, or to live in the other'.[59]

Hamilton's biases against the Gothic style were most energetically challenged in Colonel Julian Jackson's *Observations on A Letter from W. R. Hamilton, ESQ. To the Earl of Elgin, on the New Houses of Parliament* (1837). Here, Jackson systematically examined each of Hamilton's claims, taking particular issue with the two related assumptions that the Gothic was not a native or vernacular mode, and that, as a civil and secular building, the Houses of Parliament ought not to be remodelled according to what was ostensibly an ecclesiastical style. For Jackson, the Gothic, in contrast to the classicism of Jones, Wren, and Chambers, is not only quintessentially English, but also capable of inspiring in those who perceive it a patriotic sentiment that is almost indistinguishable from religious devotion: though by no means a place of divine worship, Parliament 'is an edifice in which the affairs of the state are discussed,—in which its laws are framed: it is, or should be, the rallying-place of patriotism; and patriotic feeling, if not strictly a

---

[56] John Ruskin, *Arrows of the Chace; Being a Collection of Scattered Letters Published Chiefly in the Daily Newspapers, 1840–1880: Volume I* (New York: John Wiley & Sons, 1881), p. 156.
[57] Hamilton, *Third Letter*, p. 39.   [58] Hamilton, *Third Letter*, p. 12.
[59] Hamilton, *Third Letter*, p. 14.

religious feeling, is very nearly allied to it'.[60] If the Gothic is infinitely superior to the Grecian, this is primarily because the former 'is more national', and inspiring of 'more patriotic reminiscences'.[61]

If Gothic is 'eminently English in every respect', it is because Jackson, against Hamilton, recruits to his use of the term a range of positive, even utopian, meanings, among them the historical, the architectural, and the political:

> It is the architecture of our history and our romance. Our kings of old held court in Gothic structures. In buildings of a similar character our British barons held their lordly revels, or, in times of feudal warfare, aided by their kinsmen and valiant vassals, withstood the assaults of rival chiefs. In Gothic halls, our ancestors met in council to frame laws and weigh affairs of state. The set of every great event of England's olden time is connected in some way or other with the pointed arch.[62]

It is in elaborating on the claim that 'our very romance is of Gothic connexion' that Jackson draws a bold link between English nationality, Gothic architecture, and the Gothic fictions of Walpole, Radcliffe, Lewis, and Scott:

> Murders, ghosts, midnight noises, banditti, persecuted damsels, high-born dames, and gentle pages, knights, and squires, and all the tales of wonder that charmed us in our early youth, are connected in our minds with Gothic vaults, and keeps, and watch-towers, and dungeons, and subterranean passages, and oriel windows, and latticed casements; and, though certainly no reason this of itself to warrant a preference of Gothic architecture for a house of parliament, it goes to prove that we are intimate with Gothic forms, and that they constitute in our minds very positively, though perhaps unconsciously, a connecting link in that great chain of associations which bind us still more closely to our country.[63]

For Hamilton, it was Gothic architecture's associations with Gothic fiction that made of a modern Gothic structure at Westminster a dangerous, madness-inducing architectural 'romance'; for Jackson, by contrast, it is precisely its connection with Gothic romance that makes Gothic architecture suitable for the rebuilding of the new Parliament. Regularly encountered in the stories that we consume as children, Gothic buildings 'are like old friends', and it is this intimacy and familiarity that make the style not only 'more national than any other', but the most 'appropriate' for the building in question.[64] If the act of Gothic remodelling is to result in those architectural romances against which Hamilton had cautioned, Jackson claims that an architecture 'founded on whim and caprice' is more likely

---

[60] J. R. Jackson, *Observations on A Letter from W. R. Hamilton, ESQ. To the Earl of Elgin, on the New Houses of Parliament* (London: John Weale, Architectural Library, 1837), p. 13.
[61] Jackson, *Observations*, p. 13.   [62] Jackson, *Observations*, p. 17.
[63] Jackson, *Observations*, p. 17.
[64] Jackson, *Observations*, pp. 17, 18.

to come of the Grecian than the Gothic.[65] And if Walpole and Scott are, indeed, responsible for the revival of Gothic architecture, it is only insofar as 'the Earl of Orford merely re-instated a primitive taste' that had 'been for a while dethroned by fashion'; by the same token, Scott's Waverley novels appeal to 'every one susceptible of old English feeling', and it is this that makes the Gothic 'justly dear to us'.[66] While the 'lax principles' and 'licentiousness' of Gothic Revival architecture may, indeed, have 'produced many monsters', 'frightfully ugly buildings' are also to be found among buildings of the Grecian school; even so, Jackson concludes, the character of the British nation is more Germanic than Hellenic, to the extent that 'the gloomy broodings of a Byron' are more highly relished by British readers than the 'flowery flights of Anacreontic [Thomas] Moore'.[67] The Battle of the Styles of the mid-1830s was inseparable from the deeper and more pressing concern with the nature of the antique past and its relation to the present. Literature and literary aesthetics, as I have shown, were central to these questions.

Architecture and Historiography: from the Gothic to the Medieval

The pamphlet war that I have outlined above began long before the building of the New Palace of Westminster had even begun. As Alexandra Wedgwood, Rosemary Hill, Caroline Shenton, and others have shown, the process of rebuilding between 1840 and 1860 was hardly less vexed, but a gargantuan and drawn-out process fraught with practical difficulties, setbacks, criticisms, financial troubles, delays, rivalries, and personal tensions.[68] Though neither A. W. N. Pugin nor Barry lived to see its completion—Pugin had died, young, overworked, and psychotic, in 1852, and Barry died in 1860, just ten days before the Union Jack was first flown from the recently completed Victoria Tower on 22 May—the nineteenth century's grandest and most ambitious architectural project was more or less completed by 1860, albeit, in Shenton's words, at 'three times over budget and 16 years behind schedule'.[69] Guidebooks to the site published between 1849 (two years after the rebuilt House of Lords was first used, and by which time most of the structure was in place) and 1862 indicate that the cultural meanings of Gothic architecture had shifted considerably. The Old Palace, one guidebook of 1849

---

[65] Jackson, *Observations*, p. 22.
[66] Jackson, *Observations*, pp. 36, 30, 30.   [67] Jackson, *Observations*, pp. 31, 36.
[68] See Alexandra Wedgwood, 'The New Palace of Westminster', in *The Houses of Parliament: History, Art, Architecture*, ed. David Cannadine, Dorian Church et al. (London: Merrell Publishers, 2000), pp. 113–35, and 'The New Palace of Westminster' in *Pugin: A Gothic Passion*, ed. Paul Atterbury and Clive Wainwright (New Haven and London: Yale University Press, in association with the Victoria & Albert Museum, 1994), pp. 219–36; Rosemary Hill, *God's Architect: Pugin and the Building of Romantic Britain* (London: Penguin Books, 2008); and Shenton, *Mr Barry's War*.
[69] See Shenton, *Mr Barry's War*, p. 5.

noted, was 'ill ventilated and unwholesome', but the new structure was a glorious place of light and air.[70] Henry T. Ryde's *A History of the Palace of Westminster* (1849) similarly drew comparisons between the new and old piles by invoking Soane's unheeded warning of 1822, namely that the 'narrow, gloomy, and unhealthy' passages and interiors of the Old Palace were a dangerous 'assemblage of combustible materials', a treacherous hazard waiting to burst into flame.[71] The original structure, Ryde wrote, was 'confined and incommodious', a desultory 'piece of patchwork' of subsequent additions and improvements that, like Macbeth's castle, was 'cabined, cribbed, confined'; the New Palace, by contrast, was a refreshing symphony of light, air, and spatial expanse.[72] In 1856, the author of another guidebook concurred: the original palace was 'confined and incommodious', the New Palace a 'magnificent Structure' that affords, for the first time, 'a place of meeting for the Parliament worthy of England'.[73] Visitors to the Peers' Lobby, one guide claimed, could not help but be struck by its magnificence, for 'the decorations, both architectural and pictorial, are extremely elegant and appropriate'.[74]

The politics of the new building was especially pronounced, for the gilded interiors and fixtures of the House of Lords were said to 'unite in forming a scene of Royal magnificence as brilliant as it is unequalled'.[75] The subjects of the frescos adorning its interior walls, a guidebook of 1862 claimed, personify the themes of 'Religion, Justice, and the Spirit of Chivalry', with other planned additions ideally corresponding with these so as to express 'the relation of the Sovereign to the Church, to the Law, and as the foundation of power, to the State'.[76] Though a style that was once most closely (though not exclusively) associated with the Whiggish appeal to ancient British liberties, the Gothic of the new Houses of Parliament was firmly Tory in political orientation, the power that it represented biased in favour of the interests of the economic and political elite.[77] By 1834, that is, Edmund Burke's Old Whiggish defence of 'Gothic' precedent had been co-opted by the Tory cause. Thus, for all the solicitations expressed by the likes of Hamilton, the act of Gothic rebuilding had brought about neither a horrifying actualization of Gothic romance nor a regressive return to a savage and dark Catholic age. Rather, just as Pugin had hoped it might, the fire

---

[70] Anon., *A Description of the New Palace of Westminster*, 3rd edn (London: W. Warrington & Son, 1849), p. 2.
[71] See Soane, *Memoirs of the Professional Life of an Architect*, p. 57.
[72] Henry T. Ryde, *A History of the Palace of Westminster* (London: Warrington & Son, 1849), p. 53.
[73] Anon., *A Descriptive Account of the Palace of Westminster* (London: Warrington & Co., 1856), p. 5.
[74] Anon., *A Description of the New Palace of Westminster*, p. 5.
[75] Anon., *A Description of the New Palace of Westminster*, p. 8.
[76] Anon., *The New Palace of Westminster* (London: Warrington & Co., 1862), p. 8.
[77] See David Cannadine's argument in 'The Palace of Westminster as Palace of Varieties'.

had proved to be a crucible of sorts, the rebuilding in a 'purified' Gothic style the cultural instantiation of the white Gothic.

It was, indeed, to a glorious, chivalrous, emphatically Protestant past of 'merrie England' to which the New Palace self-consciously referred: a description of the Peers' Library in 1856 claimed that 'we could quite fancy ourselves in one of those artistic and lordly apartments of olden time, once to be found in the old mansions of Henry's and Elizabeth's time such as [Frederick] Nash or [George] Cattermole delights to paint, but few of which known now remain in their pristine state'; the carpeting, statuary, furnishings, and tapestries together form a 'tout ensemble' that, more than the Gothic of the exterior, carries the imagination of the perceiver back 'to those old times of feudal magnificence, in the style of which both the Old Palace at Westminster has been conceived, and which is so properly valued as our only really national style of architecture'.[78] In a word, the Gothic past represented at Westminster by England's national architectural style had become 'medieval', the rebuilt palace one of the most cogent and iconic manifestations of this cultural strand in mid-nineteenth-century Britain.

As I argued in the previous chapter, Walter Scott made frequent allusion to Arthurian legend in his staging of the white Gothic at Kenilworth Castle. Indeed, a revived interest in Arthurianism was central to nineteenth-century medievalism, and was spearheaded by three new editions of Thomas Malory's long-out-of-print *Le Mort d'Arthur* (1485) in 1816–17: Alexander Chalmers's two-volume *The History of the Renowned Prince Arthur, King of Britain* (1816); Joseph Haslewood's three-volume *La Mort D'Arthur* (1816); and William Upcott's two-volume *The Byrth, Lyf, and Actes of Kyng Arthur* with an extended introduction by Robert Southey (1817). At the suggestion of Prince Albert, William Dyce was commissioned in 1848 to produce seven frescos on Arthurian themes for the Robing Room in the New Palace, an undertaking that the artist, working with Southey's edition as his primary source, duly fulfilled.[79] In these, its official—and self-consciously masculine—manifestations, Arthurianism radically reinvented the Gothic past, substituting its horrors, its darkness, and its ghosts with myths of glorious chivalry and sovereign devotion.[80]

As scholars have pointed out, the 1840s, the decade in which the work at Westminster commenced, marked the zenith of medievalism in Britain and

---

[78] Anon., *A Descriptive Account of the Palace of Westminster*, pp. 34, 45.
[79] See Debra N. Mancoff, 'Myth and Monarchy: Chivalric Legends for the Victorian Age', in *The Houses of Parliament: History, Art, Architecture*, ed. David Cannadine, Dorian Church et al. (London: Merrell Publishers, 2000), pp. 241–51, and T. S. R. Boase, 'The Decoration of the New Palace at Westminster, 1841–1863', *Journal of the Warburg and Courtauld Institutes* vol. 17, no. 3 (1954): pp. 319–58.
[80] As Katie Garner has pointed out, however, the distinction between Arthurianism and the Gothic is not an absolute one, for several women writers of the 1790s had drawn the two together in fashioning a distinctive form of 'Gothic Arthurianism'. See Katie Garner, *Romantic Women Writers and Arthurian Legend: The Quest for Knowledge* (London: Palgrave Macmillan, 2017), pp. 69–114.

mainland Europe. Michael Alexander, for instance, has shown how the Romantic medievalism of Coleridge, Scott, and John Keats culminated in the sympathies for medieval Catholicism expressed by John Keble, John Henry Newman, Edward Pusey, and other exponents of the Oxford Movement (1833–45); in A. W. N. Pugin's defence of medieval faith and architecture in *Contrasts* (1836); in the nostalgia of Thomas Carlyle in *Past and Present* (1843); in Benjamin Disraeli's novels of the 1840s; and in John Ruskin's *The Stones of Venice* (1851–3).[81] Surveying the same territory, David Matthews has described the period 1839 to 1851—the 'long decade' that runs from the Eglinton Tournament in Ayrshire to Pugin's Mediæval Court at the Great Exhibition's Crystal Palace, London—as 'the conclusive phase' of Victorian medievalism, an unprecedented eleven-year span that also witnessed the founding of the Cambridge Camden Society (later the Ecclesiological Society) and the Oxford Architectural Society; Pugin's commencement of work at St Chad's Church, Birmingham, and the publication of his *Apology for the Revival of Christian Architecture in England* (1843); Alfred, Lord Tennyson's 'Morte d'Arthur' (1842) and Edward Bulwer Lytton's *The Last of the Barons* (1843); Eugène Viollet-le-Duc's restoration of Sainte-Chapelle and the Cathedral of Notre Dame, Paris; Ruskin's *The Seven Lamps of Architecture* (1849); the founding of the Pre-Raphaelite Brotherhood in 1848; and the publication of an English translation of Friedrich von Schlegel's 'An Essay on Gothic Architecture' (1849).[82] It was also during this decade that the noun 'medievalism' was first used, a term that pejoratively referred initially to the Catholic sympathies of High Church Anglicanism, Tractarianism, or the Oxford Movement: gradually superseded by the 'medieval', 'Gothic' retained its currency largely as a specialized term of architectural and literary description.[83]

It is worth returning to what the *OED* lists as the first recorded usage of the adjectival 'medieval' in order to gauge the connotations that the term was originally intended to mobilize. It was in the second, enlarged edition of his *British Monachism* (1817) that the Protestant antiquary Thomas Dudley Fosbrooke (or Fosbroke) proposed 'to illustrate mediæval customs upon mediæval principles', an undertaking, he claimed, that was motivated by the assumption that 'contemporary ideas'—that is, historical ideas particular to the age being studied—are 'requisite' to accurate historical comprehension and elucidation.[84] In his careful avoidance of the pitfalls of historical presentism, Fosbrooke's endeavours recall those of Alexander Pope, John Hughes, and Richard Hurd, all of whom, as I argued in Chapter 2 of this book, variously sought to approach the architecture

---

[81] Michael Alexander, *Medievalism: The Middle Ages in Modern England* (New Haven: Yale University Press, 2007), pp. 25–104.

[82] Matthews, *Medievalism*, pp. x, 55–9.

[83] See Matthews, *Medievalism*, pp. 51–3, and David Matthews, 'From Mediaeval to Medievalism: A New Semantic History', *The Review of English Studies* vol. 62, no. 257 (November 2011): pp. 695–715.

[84] Thomas Dudley Fosbrooke, *British Monachism; or, Manners and Customs of the Monks and Nuns of England*, 2nd edn (London: Printed by and for John Nichols, Son, and Bentley, 1817), p. vi.

of the Middle Ages on its own terms, striving to employ appropriately 'Gothic' critical and aesthetic standards that were unhindered by the biases and presuppositions of the neoclassical present. But what is novel about Fosbrooke's study is that it achieves this impartiality through a careful replacement of the term 'Gothic' with 'mediæval', a substitution that is consistent with his intention to provide a revisionist account of British Catholicism that is unhindered by the 'morbid propensities' of many an earlier scholar. Through his careful avoidance of the term 'Gothic' across both the first and second editions of *British Monachism*, Fosbrooke strives for greater historical objectivity, avoiding the term's historical associations with savagery, barbarity, and darkness and replacing it with the more neutral coinage 'mediæval'.[85] To be sure, his presentation of Catholicism in the study is hardly positive: as of old, monks are 'luxurious', 'debauched', and prone to 'bigoted superstition', while popery 'manifestly implies tenacity of obsolete barbarism'.[86] Furthermore, the term 'Gothic' returned in the second edition of *British Monachism* when Fosbrooke appended to it *The Economy of Monastic Life*, his lengthy poem of c.1795 that includes reflections on the connections between the Catholic faith and Gothic architecture. As in Anna Laetitia Aikin, Thomas Warton, John Soane, and others, Gothic architecture, in its labyrinthine gloom, is the material accomplice to Catholicism's superstitious ways, 'The riddling art that charm'd the Gothic mind'.[87] Nonetheless, Fosbrooke never designates the Middle Ages themselves as 'Gothic', reserving it instead as a term of architectural description, a deliberate and noteworthy suspension that is illustrative of a larger cultural shift in conceptualizations of Britain's antique past in the first three decades of the nineteenth century. As Matthews points out, Fosbrooke would subsequently play an important role in popularizing the term, both in his contributions to *The Gentleman's Magazine* and in the title of his multivolume *Encyclopædia of Antiquities, and Elements of Archaeology, Classical and Mediæval* (1825). When, during the later 1830s, the complementary term 'Renaissance' entered common parlance—the *OED* lists Catherine Gore's *The Diary of Désennuyée* (1836) as the first recorded use of the word in print, rapidly followed by a number of other instances in the same decade—'Gothic antiquity', that capacious yet monolithic category that had governed historical reasoning in Britain from the late seventeenth century onwards, fractured into two smaller, discrete epochs.

Fosbrooke's work on 'mediæval' Catholicism saw its architectural equivalent in Thomas Rickman's *An Attempt to Discriminate the Styles of English Architecture, from the Conquest to the Reformation* (1817) of the same year. In its title alone, Rickman's study is noteworthy, for the architecture of the Middle Ages, hitherto

---

[85] See, too, David Matthews's argument in 'From Mediaeval to Medievalism'.
[86] Fosbrooke, *British Monachism*, p. vii.
[87] Thomas Dudley Fosbroke, *The Economy of Monastic Life: A Poem* (Gloucester: Printed by R. Raikes, and Sold by R. Faulder, 1795?), p. 35.

almost uniformly described as 'Gothic', is here designated as 'English', a crucial shift that is informed by a strong nationalist imperative. As I argued at the outset of this book, the naming of Gothic architecture as such had long been a source of contention for its antiquarian defendants. Rickman confronts the same problem early on in his study, claiming that 'It may, however, be proper here to offer a few remarks on the use of the term English, as applied to that mode of building usually called the Gothic, and by some the pointed architecture.'[88] If 'English architecture' is a more appropriate term it is partly (though, admittedly, inconclusively) because so-called 'Gothic' architecture was first produced in England by English architects. Less contentiously, Rickman continues, the ancient architecture of Britain is best referred to as 'English' because it is distinguished from other national styles by 'pure simplicity and boldness of composition', and is thus 'of a very different character' from the 'Gothic' architecture to be found in Italy, Flanders, France, Spain, and Germany. A more refined and context-specific alternative to 'Gothic', Rickman's 'English architecture' brought to this hitherto largely homogeneous category of architectural description a process of refinement and internal differentiation. This characterizes other aspects of his study, too, for, dismissing the various 'orders' of Gothic as they had been theorized by Batty Langley, Thomas Warton, and others, Rickman conclusively articulated the various types of English architecture across historical time, providing a critical vocabulary that is still in use today: the Norman; Early English; Decorated English; and Perpendicular styles. Saxon Gothic, that curious category that had been of such significance to Gray, Warton, Walpole, Radcliffe, and others in the eighteenth century, summarily dissolved as a term of Gothic architectural reasoning with Rickman's insistence that those examples of Saxon architecture thought to remain were really of Norman origin. In *An Inquiry into the Origin and Influence of Gothic Architecture* of 1819, William Gunn would coin the category of the Romanesque, a discrete architectural style that, itself, would become the object of a nineteenth-century revival.[89] Identified, discriminated, internally differentiated, and rendered fully legible, Rickman's English architecture bears almost no relation to the massy piers and gloomy, monkish piles of the previous century, a consideration that, as in Fosbrooke, was in no small part facilitated by his suspension of the injurious term 'Gothic'.

One year later, Coleridge voiced his opposition to the assumption that Gothic antiquity was an age of national savagery and darkness in 'General Character of the Gothic Literature and Art', an observation that makes Hamilton's

---

[88] Thomas Rickman, *An Attempt to Discriminate the Styles of English Architecture, from the Conquest to the Reformation, Preceded by a Sketch of the Grecian and Roman Orders, with Notices of Nearly Five Hundred English Buildings* (London: Longman, Hurst, Rees, Orme, and Brown, 1817), p. 37.

[89] See J. B. Bullen, 'The Romanesque Revival in Britain, 1800–1840: William Gunn, William Whewell, and Edmund Sharpe', *Architectural History* vol. 47 (2004): pp. 139–58.

appropriations of his arguments to anti-Gothic ends in 1836 seem all the more disingenuous. In this lecture, Coleridge praised the Anglo-Saxon king, Alfred the Great, as the very model of fortitude, perseverance, mercy, and justice, seeing in his instituting of trial by jury one of the greatest achievements of the Middle Ages. 'I gaze upon it as the immortal symbol of that age,' he nostalgically muses, 'an age called indeed dark'; 'but how could that age be considered dark,' he continues, 'which solved the difficult problem of universal liberty, freed man from the shackles of tyranny, and subjected his actions to the decision of twelve of his fellow countrymen?'[90] For all the connotations of its name, the 'Gothic' system of trial by jury, alone, attested for Coleridge to an epoch of justice, liberty, and enlightenment, compared to which Grecian models of legislature are merely a 'meteor' that 'blazed for a short time, and then sank into eternal darkness'.[91]

Albeit in theological ways that ran counter to the by now Anglican Coleridge, the young A. W. N. Pugin mounted a similar interrogation of the darkness of the Middle Ages in *Contrasts* (1836). As Hill has pointed out, Pugin's way in *Contrasts* had in some senses been prepared by the work of earlier architects: in stressing the Gothic style's inherently Christian meanings, John Britton's *The Architectural Antiquities of Great Britain* (1807–27) was the architectural equivalent to Scott's *Waverley*, while in a discreet footnote to the text that he provided for Volume I of A. C. and A. W. N. Pugin's *Examples of Gothic Architecture* (1831), the Catholic Edward Willson had advanced the claim that Gothic was best described as 'Catholic Architecture'.[92] Pugin's views on architecture also marked the consolidation of the theories of John Milner that I addressed in Chapter 5. While critiquing the 'wretched' and 'degraded' state of contemporary architectural practice, his argument in *Contrasts* turns on a series of visual oppositions, the plates in the appendix juxtaposing a selection of fourteenth- and fifteenth-century buildings with their inferior, less desirable modern equivalents—another example, no doubt, of the spirit of comparison that John Stuart Mill in 1831 had taken to be the 'dominant idea' of the age.[93] Much of Pugin's polemic recalls that of Coleridge in 'Character of the Gothic Mind in the Middle Ages', particularly his conceptualization of the theological sublimity of Gothic ecclesiastical architecture in his claim that a Gothic cathedral is the 'petrefaction [*sic*] of our religion'. But for the now officially Catholic Pugin, it is Coleridge's assumption of a shared Protestantism that is subject to revision, as he turns to celebrate 'those stupendous

---

[90] Coleridge, 'Lecture II', p. 74.   [91] Coleridge, 'Lecture II', p. 74.
[92] Hill, *God's Architect*, pp. 51, 98. For Willson's original comment, see A. C. Pugin, E. J. Willson, and A. W. N. Pugin, *Examples of Gothic Architecture*, 3 vols (London: Henry G. Bohn, 1831–6), vol. 1, p. xiv.
[93] John Stuart Mill, *The Collected Works of John Stuart Mill, Volume XXII: Newspaper Writings December 1822–July 1831 Part I*, ed. Ann P. Robson and John M. Robson, introd. Ann P. Robson and John M. Robson (Toronto: University of Toronto Press; London: Routledge and Kegan Paul, 1986), p. 228.

Ecclesiastical Edifices of the Middle Ages' as the embodiment and first cause of a specifically Catholic version of the sublime:

> It is, indeed, a sacred place; and well does the fabric bespeak its destined purpose: the eye is carried up and lost in the height of the vaulting and the intricacy of the ailes [sic]; the rich and varied hues of the stained windows, the modulated light, the gleam of the tapers, the richness of the altars, the venerable images of the departed just,—all alike conspire to fill the mind with veneration for the place, and to make it feel the sublimity of Christian worship.[94]

Built by men motivated more by piety than personal gain, and in a pre-Reformation age yet untouched by the scourge of religious sectarianism, Gothic architecture for Pugin speaks volubly of an epoch of Catholic religious devotion. By this way of reckoning, the English Reformation and dissolution of the monasteries marked not the felicitous obliteration of the 'nurseries of superstition' of previous centuries but the lamentable destruction of noble Gothic edifices and places of pious monastical existence. An organic, spiritual, and intricately structured way of life had been replaced by a Protestant age of strident individualism and tasteless architectural improvement. His sense of the many unfortunate consequences, architectural and otherwise, of the English Reformation reverberates strongly with the arguments of the Catholic priest and historian John Lingard in *A History of England* (1819–30) and William Cobbett's use of Lingard in *A History of the Protestant 'Reformation', in England and Ireland* (1824–7), both of whom had sought to revise the Protestant biases seen in earlier histories, from the work of Bishop Burnet onwards. It thus stands to reason why Pugin's ideas, in time, would initially be received with such enthusiasm by the Oxford Movement, although this was to cool considerably as time wore on.[95] Throughout *Contrasts*, in fact, the Catholic Middle Ages are figured as a favourable alternative to the modern industrial present, a site of medievalist fantasy into which one could understandably wish to retreat. The only way of reversing the encroachments of modernity, Pugin argues, is to restore the revived Gothic style to its originally Catholic meanings, for "Tis they alone that can restore Gothic architecture to its former glorious state'.[96] Without the requisite spiritual sensibility, all work executed in the Gothic style 'will be a tame and heartless copy'—aesthetically 'Catholic' architectural experiments that, like Walpole's Strawberry Hill, might superficially be 'true as the mechanisms of the style goes', yet are, in reality, 'utterly

---

[94] A. W. N. Pugin, *Contrasts; a Parallel Between the Noble Edifices of the Fourteenth and Fifteenth Centuries, and Similar Buildings of the Present Day; Shewing the Present Decay of Taste: Accompanied by Appropriate Text* (London: Printed for the Author, and Published by Him, at St Marie's Grange, near Wiltshire, 1836), p. 2.

[95] On Pugin's complex relationship with the Oxford Movement, See Hill, *God's Architect*, pp. 120, 224, 338–9.

[96] Pugin, *Contrasts*, p. 22.

wanting' in that authentic religious sentiment that distinguishes true ancient architectural design.[97]

Pugin repeated these arguments with greater vehemence in *An Apology for a Work Entitled 'Contrasts'* (1837) one year later, controversially insisting that all edifying art was inherently Catholic by nature; that the Protestant Reformation had resulted in the destruction of art, an irreverence towards religion, and the loss of all noble sentiments; and that the deplorable state of contemporary art was solely attributable to the lack of Catholic sentiment informing it.[98] In the second, enlarged edition of *Contrasts* of 1841, he revised the claims of earlier writers such as Conyers Middleton and Walpole in order audaciously to couple pagan and Protestant architecture, underscoring the juxtaposition of buildings in the earlier edition through the addition of more images. Though not uncontested, such bold assertions of the Gothic's innately Catholic meanings would remain in place until John Ruskin, taking up the challenge that Walpole and Beckford had faced earlier, recuperated the Gothic style for evangelical Protestantism in Volume II of *The Stones of Venice* in 1853. As he put it in his essay 'The Nature of Gothic', the 'rigidity' of the style attested to 'the very temper which has been thought most adverse to it, the Protestant spirit of self-dependence and inquiry'.[99] His use of Venetian examples in the piece notwithstanding, it was through Ruskin's privileging of the Gothic's northern, Protestant credentials over the Catholicism of Italian High Renaissance art that he was able to retrieve something of the style's moral values. What Carlyle, through reference to a line from Shakespeare's *As You Like It*, famously called Ruskin's '*Sermons* in Stones' were resolutely Protestant in nature, a tendency that would be repeated in the work of George Gilbert Scott, that other 'Protestant Goth' of the nineteenth century.[100] And in place of the ecclesiastical basis of Pugin's conceptualization of Gothic, Ruskin continuously asserted the style's suitability to civic use.

Ruskin's opposition to Pugin's Catholicism would culminate in the attack on 'Romanist Modern Art' appended to *The Stones of Venice*, as well as in his well-known dislike for the New Palace of Westminster.[101] Though Gothic architecture, for Ruskin, fitted more with his sense of a wondrous 'medieval' than 'Gothic' past,

---

[97] Pugin, *Contrasts*, p. 22.
[98] See A. W. N. Pugin, *An Apology for a work Entitled 'Contrasts'; Being a Defence of the Assertions Advanced in that Publication, Against the Various Attacks Lately Made Upon It* (Birmingham: Printed for the Author by R. P. Stone and Son, 1837).
[99] John Ruskin, 'The Nature of Gothic', in *Library Edition*, vol. 10, pp. 180–269 (p. 242). For a discussion of Ruskin's ethical, Protestant response to the Gothic style, and how it differs from the more aesthetic responses of the nineteenth century, see David Spurr, *Architecture and Modern Literature* (Ann Arbor: University of Michigan Press, 2012), pp. 113–23.
[100] See David R. Sorensen, 'Ruskin and Carlyle', in *The Cambridge Companion to John Ruskin*, ed. Francis O'Gorman (Cambridge: Cambridge University Press, 2015), pp. 189–201 (p. 191).
[101] For an account of the complex relationship between Pugin and Ruskin, and particularly the intellectual sources that both men shared, see Rosemary Hill, 'Ruskin and Pugin', in *Ruskin & Architecture*, ed. Rebecca Daniels and Geoff Brandwood (Reading: Spire Books, 2003), pp. 223–45.

it nonetheless retained the darkness and shadows, the savageness and monstrosity with which previous centuries had imbued it through the quality of the grotesque, that crucial category of aesthetic experience in nineteenth-century culture.[102] He both celebrated and formalized his understanding of the 'grotesque' nature of Gothic in *The Stones of Venice*, situating its signature 'tendency to delight in fantastic and ludicrous, as well as in sublime, images' alongside the characteristics of savageness, changefulness, naturalism, rigidity, and redundancy.[103] It is hardly surprising that it is this particular quality of Gothic architecture that Victorian Gothic fictions most commonly foreground, from the 'quantity of grotesque carving' lavished over the front of the eponymous house in Emily Brontë's *Wuthering Heights* (1847), through the 'old stone lions and grotesque monsters' that bristle and snarl at Chesney Wold in Charles Dickens's *Bleak House* (1852–3), to the 'demoniacal grotesques in which the cynical and ghastly fancy of old Gothic carving delights' referenced in Sheridan Le Fanu's *Carmilla* (1872). There are few if any equivalent applications of the term 'grotesque' to Gothic architecture in Gothic fictions and architectural studies of the eighteenth century: when William Wrighte applied the adjective to his account of the Gothic in *Grotesque Architecture; or, Rural Amusement* (1767), he used it in the now-obsolete sense of picturesque irregularity (*OED*, 2b), and not as the name for the style's hybrid, monstrous appeal.

Though its architecture was grotesque, the medieval period itself was now more likely to be construed as a time of literal light and figurative enlightenment than one of savagery, darkness, and superstition. Henry Hallam had paved the way for this reassessment of the past in his *View of the State of Europe During the Middle Ages* (1818), a crucial moment in the genesis of what Herbert Butterfield has influentially termed the 'Whig interpretation of history'.[104] In 1844, Samuel Roffey Maitland published *The Dark Ages*, a series of essays on the religion and literature of the ninth, tenth, eleventh, and twelfth centuries that he had originally published in *The British Magazine* between March 1835 and February 1838. Though born into a Dissenting family, Maitland was ordained as a deacon in the Church of England in 1821, becoming Curate of St Edmund's, Norwich, thereafter; without ever formally joining it, he expressed sympathies with the Oxford Movement, and is best remembered today for his critique of a new edition of Foxe's *Acts and Monuments* that was published in stages from 1837 onwards.[105] The title of *The*

---

[102] For a good account of the importance of the grotesque to nineteenth-century culture, see Colin Trodd, Paul Barlow and David Amigoni, eds, *Victorian Culture and the Idea of the Grotesque* (Aldershot: Ashgate, 1999).
[103] Ruskin, 'The Nature of Gothic', p. 239.
[104] See Herbert Butterfield, *The Whig Interpretation of History* (New York and London: W. W. Norton, 1965).
[105] D. Andrew Penny, 'Maitland, Samuel Roffey (1792–1866)', *ODNB* (Oxford: Oxford University Press, 2004), http://www.oxforddnb.com/view/article/17834 (accessed 24 July 2017).

Dark Ages is ironically inflected, for what Maitland aims to argue is that the Middle Ages—here tellingly termed 'mediæval' and not 'Gothic'—are only 'dark' insofar as modern scholars have routinely adopted an attitude of ignorance and willed blindness in relation to them. Darkness, he provocatively claims, 'is quite a different thing from shutting the eyes', and we 'have no right to complain that we can see but little until we have used due diligence to see what we can'—a criticism that he directs at the earlier histories of William Robertson and John Jortin.[106] Undoubtedly, he concedes, the people of the so-called 'dark ages' knew 'nothing of many things which are familiar to us, and which we deem essential to our comfort, and almost to our existence'; 'but still', he insists, 'I doubt whether, even in this point of view, they were so entirely dark as some would have us suppose'.[107] Metaphorically, the darkness of the past is merely the consequence of us having spent far too long in the light; once we have acclimatized ourselves to it, and surveyed its manifold achievements in learning, art, and literature, we are likely to realize that the medieval past barely answers to the adjective 'dark' at all. A misnomer born of modern ignorance, 'the dark ages' is also the fabrication of Gothic romance, the past as it had been consistently misrepresented in and by popular literature from *The Castle of Otranto* onwards: Maitland's aim in part is to address the reader 'who has formed his idea of the dark ages only from some modern popular writers', providing antiquarian proof as a means of combatting those 'extremely false' impressions that 'have been handed about from one popular writer to another'.[108] As it did for Pugin, purification plays an important role in this act of historiographic revision, for in order to be recuperated as an age of light, the medieval age had to be cleansed or purged of its representations in the pages of Gothic fiction, a reiteration of the same dilemma that, as I have argued, John Carter faced in relation to the Gothic drama some three decades earlier.

This is not to say that, by the late 1830s, 'Gothic' antiquity had been completely replaced and superseded by a 'medieval' past of literal and figural light. Jacob Burckhardt, for one, juxtaposed a benighted Gothic past with the rejuvenated classicism of fourteenth- and fifteenth-century Italy in *The Civilization of the Renaissance in Italy* (1860). But it is to say that, in the work of Fosbrooke, Rickman, Pugin, Coleridge, Ruskin, Maitland, and others, popular and historiographic assumptions about the darkness of the Gothic past had, by 1840, been subject to interrogation and considerable revision. The emergent spirit of Victorian medievalism, we might say, penetrated the darkness upon which the Gothic fictional aesthetic often (though not uniformly) depended, shaking, as it did so, the Gothic architectural imagination to its foundations.

---

[106] S. R. Maitland, *The Dark Ages; A Series of Essays, Intended to Illustrate the State of Religion and Literature in the Ninth, Tenth, Eleventh, and Twelfth Centuries* (London: Printed for J. G. F. & J. Rivington, 1844), p. 2.
[107] Maitland, *The Dark Ages*, p. 2.   [108] Maitland, *The Dark Ages*, pp. 8, 7.

Romanticism, Architecture, and the Ends of Associationism

This dismantling was intensified in other ways by the early exponents of British romanticism, when Wordsworth and Coleridge countered associationism with their theories of the poetic imagination. In the Preface to *Poems by William Wordsworth* of 1815, Wordsworth had acknowledged a certain continuity between fancy and the imagination even as he theorized the differences between them, claiming that 'To aggregate and to associate, to evoke and to combine, belong as well to the Imagination as to the Fancy'.[109] But while fancy remains ever confined to, and bound by, the laws of association, Wordsworth maintains that it is the peculiar power of the imagination to shape, rework, and refashion all the information derived from the empirical world of impressions and ideas: 'She recoils from every thing but the plastic, the pliant, and the indefinite.'[110] Tim Fulford has drawn attention to just how extraordinary this moment in 1815 was: 'Imagination' had not featured significantly in the 1800 Preface to the two-volume *Lyrical Ballads*, and did not register in the *Poems, in Two Volumes* of 1807; although Coleridge had invoked the concept in his lectures, he was yet to publish his extended account of it in *Biographia Literaria* (1817). In 1815, Fulford claims, imagination served Wordsworth in this, his first collected edition, as a means of poetic reinvigoration, self-reinvention, and self-valorization.[111] In *Biographia Literaria*, Coleridge took a more decisive approach to the differences between Wordsworth's two creative principles, arguing that fancy and imagination, far from being interchangeable with one another, were 'two distinct and widely different faculties'.[112] His theory relies as much on a turning away from his earlier allegiances to the associationism of David Hartley as it does on the influence of A. W. Schlegel. As Coleridge defines them, fancy is a passive, mechanical, material, and association-dependent effect, the imagination an active, 'esemplastic', transcendent, and organic cause, 'the living power and prime agent of all human perception' and 'a repetition in the finite mind of the eternal act of creation in the infinite I AM'.[113] If fancy is playful, unregulated, chaotic, unpredictable, and resolutely popular, the imagination is grounded, disciplined, and transcendental, as well as the marker of sound aesthetic taste and judgement—the distinction itself the product of a cultural 'fanciphobia' that reached back to William Duff, Dugald

---

[109] William Wordsworth, 'Preface', in *Poems by William Wordsworth: Including Lyrical Ballads, and the Miscellaneous Pieces of the Author*, 2 vols (London: Printed for Longman, Hurst, Rees, Orme, and Brown, 1815), vol. 1, pp. vii–xliii (p. xxxiii).

[110] Wordsworth, 'Preface', p. xxxiii.

[111] Tim Fulford, *Wordsworth's Poetry, 1815–1845* (Philadelphia: University of Pennsylvania Press, 2019), pp. 11–19.

[112] Samuel Taylor Coleridge, 'Biographia Literaria; or, Biographical Sketches of my Literary Life and Opinions', in *Samuel Taylor Coleridge: The Major Works*, ed. H. J. Jackson (Oxford and New York: Oxford University Press, 2000), pp. 155–482 (p. 203).

[113] Coleridge, 'Biographia Literaria', p. 313.

Stewart, and other aestheticians of the eighteenth century.[114] But as I have argued throughout this book, the literary Gothic imagination depended upon nothing if not the power of architectural form to conjure up imaginative visions in the perceiving mind, an association-based aesthetic that ran from Addison's critique of Locke at the beginning of the century, through the work of Gerard, Chambers, Walpole, Beckford, and others, and into Soane. With Wordsworth and Coleridge's formalization of the differences between fancy and the imagination, however, the architectural imagination, its follies, and the florid mental romances that it engendered were relegated to the realm of fancy, an inferior aesthetic category in which romanticism, not coincidentally, also habitually located Gothic fiction.[115] As even the best-known examples demonstrate, it was the Gothic mode's dependence upon the fancies bred and nurtured by association that provoked the Romantics' particular displeasure, from Coleridge's stinging review of *The Monk* in *The Critical Review* of February 1797, through his dismissal of Gothic as a 'mental camera obscura' in a footnote to Chapter III of *Biographia Literaria*, to Wordsworth's denunciation of the 'frantic novels, sickly and stupid German Tragedies, and deluges of idle and extravagant stories in verse' in the Preface to the two-volume edition of *Lyrical Ballads* in 1800.[116]

Wordsworth's aim to 'counteract' this 'degrading thirst after outrageous stimulation' is made especially clear in his use of Gothic architecture in *Lyrical Ballads*, most notably in 'Tintern Abbey'. This Cistercian ruin is not the haunted, monkish pile at the centre of a frantic plot about the Catholic past and the terrors of the French Revolution that we encounter in Sophia Ziegenhirt's *The Orphan of Tintern Abbey* (1816), a Gothic romance that was published by William Lane's Minerva Press, but rather the quiet, picturesque prompt of memory and personal reflection.[117] The persona in Wordsworth's poem has already moved beyond the world of empirical associations and into the idealist reaches of the Romantic imagination, for here, the 'eye and ear' are not merely mirrors to the influx of sensory perceptions but, instead, simultaneously 'create' and 'perceive' the world around them.[118] Similarly, Furness Abbey as it is described in Book Second of the

---

[114] See Jeffrey C. Robinson *Unfettering Poetry: The Fancy in British Romanticism* (New York: Palgrave Macmillan, 2006), pp. 1–21, 25–48.

[115] As Robinson claims, romanticism, despite its apparent 'Fanciphobia', produces a radical poetry and poetics of fancy, inaugurating an aesthetic impulse that extends up to experimental modernism in the twentieth century. See Robinson, *Unfettering Poetry*.

[116] See Samuel Taylor Coleridge's review of *The Monk*, *Critical Review* series 2, vol. 19 (February 1797): pp. 194–200, in *Coleridge's Miscellaneous Criticism*, ed. Thomas Middleton Raysor (Cambridge: Harvard University Press, 1936), pp. 370–8 (p. 374); Coleridge, 'Biographia Literaria', p. 182; and William Wordsworth, 'Preface to *Lyrical Ballads* (1800)', in *Lyrical Ballads, 1798 and 1800*, ed. Michael Gamer and Dahlia Porter (Peterborough, ON: Broadview, 2008), pp. 171–87 (pp. 174, 177).

[117] Wordsworth, 'Preface to *Lyrical Ballads* (1800)', p. 177.

[118] William Wordsworth, 'Lines Written a Few Miles Above Tintern Abbey, On Revisiting the Banks of the Wye During a Tour, July 13, 1798', in *Lyrical Ballads, 1798 and 1800*, ed. Michael Gamer and Dahlia Porter (Peterborough, ON: Broadview, 2008), pp. 142–7 (p. 145, ll. 107–8).

1805 *The Prelude* is not the richly associative object that had inspired Radcliffe's vision of a procession of ghostly monks in the *Journey* but a serene, 'holy' scene that serves as 'The safeguard for repose and quietness':

> a structure famed
> Beyond its neighbourhood, the antique walls
> Of that large abbey which within the Vale
> Of nightshade, to St Mary's honour built,
> Stands yet, a mouldering pile with fractured arch,
> Belfry, and images, and living trees—
> A holy scene.[119]

Though Radcliffe's descriptions of the Lake District and its ruins, as I argued in Chapter 3, had been consistently cited in guidebooks to the region well into the 1830s, the fifth and definitive edition of Wordsworth's own *A Guide through the District of the Lakes* (1835) makes no mention of De Quincey's Great Enchantress. The omission reads somewhat like deliberate avoidance.

The two poetical illustrations by Letitia Elizabeth Landon (L. E. L.) that were included in Fisher's *Drawing Room Scrap-Book* in the 1830s similarly mark their difference from the architectural imagination of Gothic romance. In the first of these, 'Furness Abbey, In the Vale of Nightshade, Lancashire' (1832), this 'holy shrine' becomes the object of the persona's profound and melancholic nostalgia, the ruins figured as a pious, quiet, and contemplative retreat and a welcome antidote to the cares and concerns of the present. Not insignificantly, Landon alludes to, but in that gesture substantially rewrites, Alexander Pope's sense of the fleshly deprivations of monastical existence in 'Eloisa to Abelard': 'I think of the days we are living now, / and I sigh for those of the veil and the vow.'[120] Landon's persona yearns for a return to a life of chastity, poverty, and obedience, and not the consummation of thwarted romantic and sexual desire. In 'Chapter-House, Furness Abbey' (1835), Landon translated and reworked Charles Augustin Sainte-Beuve's epistle to the twelfth-century Fontenay Abbey in Burgundy, France, again presenting Furness as a place of absolute tranquillity and rest, a balm of silence and solitude in a world of wearying activity and woe.[121]

Wordsworth wrote two further sonnets about Furness Abbey in c.1840 and 1845. As in Landon's poems, what is striking about the first of these is the way in which the vivid associations of the Gothic romancer have been replaced by a

---

[119] William Wordsworth, *The Prelude, 1799, 1805, 1850*, ed. Jonathan Wordsworth, M. H. Abrams, and Stephen Gill (New York and London: W. W. Norton & Co., 1979), pp. 71–3, ll. 102–21.

[120] L. E. L. [Letitia Elizabeth Landon], 'Furness Abbey, In the Vale of Nightshade, Lancashire', in *Fisher's Drawing Room Scrap-Book, with Poetical Illustrations by L. E. L.* (London: Fisher, Son, and Jackson, 1832), p. 18.

[121] See L. E. L. [Letitia Elizabeth Landon], 'Chapter-House, Furness Abbey', in *Fisher's Drawing Room Scrap Book; With Poetical Illustrations by L. E. L.* (London: H. Fisher, R. Fisher, & P. Jackson, 1835), pp. 49–50.

grounded and much more realistic attempt at natural and topographical description: 'See how her [Nature's] Ivy clasps the sacred Ruin / Fall to prevent or beautify decay; / And, on the mouldered walls, how bright, how gay, / The flowers in pearly dews their bloom renewing!'[122] In the second sonnet, Wordsworth extends his earlier evocations of the 'holy' or 'sacred' nature of the abbey to describe a scene in which ordinary workmen retire at noon into the ruin, spontaneously experiencing there the pervasive 'sacredness' that, despite the dissolution two centuries earlier, has persisted through time: 'All seem to feel the spirit of the place, / And by the general reverence God is praised.'[123] No Gothic monument to the monkish superstitions of the past, this, but a picturesque object of contemplation that imposes upon those who perceive it in the present intimations of its venerable, time-honoured, and, though deconsecrated, always unmistakably Protestant sacredness.

And so Wordsworth's preoccupations with Gothic architectural form continue throughout his oeuvre, from his early descriptions of the Grand Chartreuse in *Descriptive Sketches* (1793), through 'Tintern Abbey', the Salisbury Plain poems (1793–1842), the 1805 *Prelude*, and into *The Excursion* (1814) and the representation of Bolton Priory, Yorkshire, in *The White Doe of Rylstone* (1815). Taking his cue from Wordsworth's description of his oeuvre in the Preface to *The Excursion* as a 'gothic Church' comprising 'little Cells, Oratories, and sepulchral Recesses', Tom Duggett has usefully explored the culture of 'Gothic Romanticism' in Britain from the mid-1790s to the early 1830s, a purified, English, Protestant literary and political tradition that was often given symbolic architectural expression in the work of Wordsworth, Coleridge, and Robert Southey.[124] If his oeuvre was a Gothic church, Wordsworth the poet was, by implication, an architect, a return to the metaphors of original genius that reached far back into the eighteenth century. But in order for this metaphor to take effect, Gothic architecture had to be stripped of its associations with the 'Gothic' romances of Walpole, Radcliffe, and Scott—a problem that, as I have argued, confronted other defenders of the Gothic style in the period too.[125]

There is no clearer illustration of the difference between the Romantic imagination and Gothic architectural imagination of the previous century than in *Ecclesiastical Sketches* (1822), Wordsworth's sonnet sequence that recounts, albeit

[122] William Wordsworth, 'At Furness Abbey [c. 1840]', in *Last Poems, 1821–1850*, ed. Jared Curties, with Apryl Lea Denny-Ferris and Jillian Heydt-Stevenson, The Cornell Wordsworth (Ithaca and London: Cornell University Press, 1999), p. 350, ll. 5–8.

[123] Wordsworth, 'At Furness Abbey [1845]', in *Last Poems, 1821–1850*, p. 397, ll. 11–12.

[124] William Wordsworth, *The Excursion*, ed. Sally Bushell, James A. Butler, and Michael C. Jaye, assisted by David Garcia, The Cornell Wordsworth (Ithaca, NY, and London: Cornell University Press, 2007), p. 38; Tom Duggett, *Gothic Romanticism: Architecture, Politics, and Literary Form* (New York: Palgrave Macmillan, 2010).

[125] Duggett, *Gothic Romanticism*, pp. 12–13. See, too, Duggett's argument in 'Gothic Forms of Time: Architecture, Romanticism, Medievalism', in *Romantic Gothic: An Edinburgh Companion*, ed. Angela Wright and Dale Townshend (Edinburgh: Edinburgh University Press, 2016), pp. 339–60.

with a number of significant omissions, the religious history of England from its pagan origins onwards. His choice of the sonnet form here is, in itself, significant: as Fulford has shown, it marked a self-conscious return on Wordsworth's behalf to the religious and poetic tradition of John Milton, John Donne, and George Herbert, a turning away from the Jacobin contents and form of the earlier verse and an embrace of the public and poetic establishment.[126] Elaborating upon the architectural metaphor of *The Excursion*, the sonnet, Fulford continues, was an architectural form in itself, a kind of room, oratory, or cell that offered the poet containment and respite from the pressures of poetic liberty—even if, having experienced its limitations, Wordsworth would subsequently abandon it. But his use of the sonnet was also a response to the Gothic, a tradition from which the poet of *Ecclesiastical Sketches* subtly distanced himself by employing the form in its Petrarchan and not its English, Shakespearean, Spenserian, or 'Gothic' varieties. We know that the collection was directly inspired by the 'Catholic Question' when, in 1820, Wordsworth made a visit to the site of a new church being built by Sir George Beaumont, a strong opponent of Catholic Emancipation. Accordingly, Parts I and II entertain topics that are ripe for Gothic-fictional appropriation, particularly in their exploration of England's pre-Reformation past. The life of Catholic monasticism described in Part I is one in which 'Monks abide / In cloistered privacy'; an abandoned hermitage in Sonnet XXII is at least potentially the site of a haunting ('Fit haunts of shapes whose glorious equipage / Perchance would throng my dreams'); and in Sonnet XXXVIII, papal authority is ominously figured as 'A ghostly Domination'.[127] In line with the anti-Catholic ruin poetry that I surveyed in Chapter 5, 'Cistertian [sic] Monastery', the opening sonnet to Part II, describes a familiar scene of monkish superstition, before proceeding to explore such topics as 'Corruptions of the Higher Clergy', 'Abuse of Monastic Power', 'Monastic Voluptuousness', and 'Dissolution of the Monasteries'. As Mark Canuel has observed, *Ecclesiastical Sketches* is vehemently anti-Catholic in places, ameliorated only by the fact that Wordsworth directs his ire in the sequence towards other, Dissenting forms of Christianity, too.[128]

Fulford sees in this something of Wordsworth's apostasy, his retreat from the support for Catholic emancipation that he offered during the 1790s. And yet, while these sections of the *Ecclesiastical Sketches* appear to perpetuate that familiar sense of Catholic establishments as the 'nurseries of superstition', they never realize this with quite the same intensity as a Shenstone, Jerningham, Lewis, Ireland, or Maturin, not even in 'Imaginative Regrets', a poem about the haunting of an ecclesiastical building that had fallen with the dissolution: 'But from the

---

[126] Fulford, *Wordsworth's Poetry, 1815–1845*, pp. 214–28.

[127] William Wordsworth, 'Ecclesiastical Sketches', in *Sonnet Series and Itinerary Poems*, ed. Geoffrey Jackson, The Cornell Wordsworth (Ithaca and London: Cornell University Press, 2004), pp. 125–347 (Part I, Sonnet XXI, ll. 5–6; Part I, Sonnet XXII, ll. 8–9; Part I, Sonnet XXXVIII, l. 4).

[128] Canuel, *Religion, Toleration, and British Writing, 1790–1830*, p. 199.

ghostly Tenants of the wind, / Demons and Spirits, many a dolorous groan / Issues for that dominion overthrown.'[129] Instead, the movement of the sequence is towards unity and religious reconciliation, a healing of the breach between Catholics and Protestants that had opened up with the Reformation, and which had widened through political and religious events in England ever since. 'Old Abbeys', Sonnet XVII from Part III, even provides an answer to the muted anti-Catholicism of the earlier sections in extending to 'MONASTIC DOMES' the spirit of national toleration and forgiveness. The lines recall the 'holiness' of Furness Abbey in the 1805 *Prelude*: 'Once ye were holy, ye are holy still; / Your spirit freely let me drink and live!'[130] They also look forward to Wordsworth's preoccupations with 'holy' space in his second sonnet about Furness Abbey in 1845. Architecturally, the sequence culminates in an apparently non-partisan (yet always firmly Protestant) celebration of what Wordsworth describes as 'this immense / And glorious Work of fine Intelligence!', the architecture of King's College Chapel, Cambridge, a structure that was routinely celebrated, neutrally and without much political and religious investment, by numerous exponents of the eighteenth- and nineteenth-century Gothic Revival. Stripped bare of the rich associations that it had been given by the architectural imagination of the Gothic romancer, Gothic architecture is once again purged, purified, and installed as a sign of enduring piety in Wordsworth's retelling of national religious history. When, in a later poem such as 'St Bees' (1835), Wordsworth presented ancient Catholic monasticism as a sound and legitimate basis for life in a modern Protestant seminary, the poet expressed views that were consistent with those of John Keble, Edward Pusey, John Henry Newman, and other exponents of the Oxford Movement in the 1803s.[131]

Other Romantic novelists and second-generation Romantic poets responded to the architectural imagination of Gothic writing with a greater sense of levity, playfulness, and wit, and this far beyond the well-known example of *Northanger Abbey* that I discussed in Chapter 4. Like Austen's novel, the fiction of Thomas Love Peacock actively courted the architectural associations of Gothic romance in such evocative titles as *Headlong Hall* (1816), *Nightmare Abbey* (1818), and *Crotchet Castle* (1831). But Peacock's narratives habitually frustrate rather than gratify these Gothic expectations, replacing romantic flights of fancy with rational, dialogic discourses on matters of contemporary taste and manners. As a reviewer of *Nightmare Abbey* in *The Tickler* in 1818 noted, 'whoever takes up Nightmare Abbey, in the hope of finding a novel of *exquisite horror*, and *terrific mystery*, will be disappointed. It is, in fact, a spirited satire upon the popular follies of the age, in

---

[129] Wordsworth, 'Ecclesiastical Sketches', Part II, Sonnet XX, ll. 3–5.
[130] Wordsworth, 'Ecclesiastical Sketches', Part III, Sonnet XVII, ll. 13–14.
[131] See Tonya Moutray, 'Remodeling Catholic Ruins in William Wordsworth's Poetry', *European Romantic Review* vol. 22, no. 6 (Dec. 2011): pp. 819–31.

which leading topics and varied opinions are discussed, in the form of dialogue, by the *dramatis personæ*.'[132] Indeed, Peacock, far from penning a Gothic fiction in *Nightmare Abbey*, sets out to expose the Gothic romancer's characteristic relation to architecture as one of self-conscious pretentiousness in and through Scythrop Glowry, a satirical portrait of his friend Percy Bysshe Shelley. Inspired by Radcliffe, Charlotte Dacre, and other Gothic writers, the young Shelley had exploited the imaginative hold of architecture in his Gothic juvenilia, particularly in his presentation of the ruined abbey and the eponymous castle in which the action culminates in *St Irvyne; or, The Rosicrucian* (1811). We see, in this, something of Shelley's own characterization of his boyish self in stanza 5 of 'Hymn to Intellectual Beauty' (written 1816; published 1817): 'While yet a boy I sought for ghosts, and sped / Through many a listening chamber, cave and ruin / And starlight wood, with fearful steps pursuing / Hopes of high talk with the departed dead.'[133] Peacock registers Shelley's early susceptibility to the fanciful lure of Gothic ruins in having Scythrop inhabit a ruinous, ivy-covered, and owl-inhabited tower on the south-eastern side of Nightmare Abbey, itself a gloomy 'castellated abbey' that recalls Walpole's fusion of the castle and ecclesiastical styles at Strawberry Hill.[134] Scythrop, it soon becomes clear, is one of those romantic devotees of the Gothic edifice that Lewis had invoked in the Prologue to *The Castle Spectre* (1797; 1798), but which had been gently satirized in the fashion of the 'votaress of romance' invoked in *The Age* in 1810:

> He wandered about the ample pile, or along the garden-terrace, with 'his cogitative faculties immersed in cogibundity of cogitation'. The terrace terminated at the south-western tower, which, as we have said, was ruinous and full of owls. Here would Scythrop take his evening seat, on a fallen fragment of mossy stone, with his back resting against the ruined wall,—a thick canopy of ivy, with an owl on it, over his head,—and the Sorrows of Werther in his hand.[135]

The line from Henry Carey's *Chrononhotonthologos* (1734)—a burlesque of heroic tragedy and a satire upon Robert Walpole—that Peacock quotes here is underscored shortly thereafter through a return to a familiar metaphor: drinking from a skull, wholly enamoured of Gothic ruins, and sleeping with a copy of Carl Grosse's *Horrid Mysteries* (1796) beneath his pillow, Scythrop is prone to erecting 'many castles in the air', peopling them 'with secret tribunals, and bands of illuminati' and 'ghastly confederates holding midnight conventions in subterranean caves'.[136] Painfully alert to the sensory impressions of the place, he becomes enslaved to the

---

[132] This review is reprinted in Thomas Love Peacock, *Nightmare Abbey*, ed. Lisa Vargo (Peterborough, Ontario: Broadview, 2007), pp. 137–8.
[133] Percy Bysshe Shelley, 'Hymn to Intellectual Beauty', in *Romanticism: An Anthology with CD-ROM, Second Edition*, ed. Duncan Wu (Oxford: Blackwell, 1998), pp. 841–3 (p. 842, ll. 49–52).
[134] Peacock, *Nightmare Abbey*, p. 51.   [135] Peacock, *Nightmare Abbey*, p. 56.
[136] Peacock, *Nightmare Abbey*, pp. 56, 57.

powers of architectural association, responding to the requisite reverberations, footsteps, and hollow echoes at Nightmare Abbey with 'a mood most sympathetically tragic'.[137] Scythrop's romantic excesses persist in his relationship with the appropriately named 'Stella', the alias of the runaway daughter Celinda Toobad, as he indulgently fashions 'castles in the air' while his beloved piles further 'towers and turrets on the imaginary edifices'.[138] Matters are drawn to a bathetic climax when those in residence at the abbey, including the Coleridgean Mr Flosky, come to believe that it is haunted. When the supernatural is humorously explained away, the Gothic architectural imagination is reduced, as in Austen, to error, irrationality, and folly.

In *Frankenstein* of the same year, Mary Shelley would effect a subtle but significant shift away from the architectural associationism of earlier Gothic romance even as she set out in the text to fashion a story that, as she later put it, would 'rival' those 'which had 'excited [her] to the task'—Jean-Baptiste Benoît Eyriès's French translation of a selection of German Gothic tales in *Fantasmagoriana* (1812).[139] Prompted, perhaps, by her parents' scepticism towards both 'survivalist' and 'revivalist' forms of the Gothic, Shelley jettisoned the historical settings and their attendant architectural trappings of the Gothic mode in order to contemplate the vision of a nightmarish present and future; the narrative's movement into enlightened, republican Geneva in the unspecified year 17— meant that it could safely dispense with the architectural markers of the dark and distant past. To be sure, *Frankenstein* is not entirely devoid of reference to the Gothic style.[140] One thinks here of the 'gloomy prison-chamber' into which the innocent Justine is thrown, her forced yet false confession of guilt clearly replaying the predicament of Vivaldi in the dungeons of the Inquisition in Radcliffe's *The Italian*.[141] The dungeon in which the Turkish merchant is imprisoned recalls the numerous dungeons and cells that we encounter in Godwin and Wollstonecraft, while the Irish prison in which Victor is incarcerated after the death of Henry Clerval references the Gothic architecture of Byron's *The Prisoner of Chillon* (1816) and the Shelleys' own account of the dungeons beneath the Castle of Chillon in their *History of a Six Weeks' Tour* (1817). The novel is also shot through with the revolutionary discourse of ruin and deliberate ruination that had been advocated by Wollstonecraft and other radicals during the 1790s, from the Creature's eavesdropping on Felix's reading of Volney's *Les Ruines* to Safie, through to Victor's and the Creature's respective wishes to wreak destruction on the buildings, people, and institutions that surround them.[142] Though, at moments such as these, Shelley's text seems highly aware of the architectural imagination of Gothic writing—a mode that Mary and Percy read extensively

---

[137] Peacock, *Nightmare Abbey*, p. 59. [138] Peacock, *Nightmare Abbey*, p. 105.
[139] Shelley, *Frankenstein*, p. 175. [140] Shelley, *Frankenstein*, pp. 117–18.
[141] Shelley, *Frankenstein*, p. 60. [142] See Shelley, *Frankenstein*, pp. 100, 138, 170.

between 1814 and 1818, and which, more immediately, was strongly invoked in several stories in *Fantasmagoriana*—not one is realized with the intensity and detail that we would routinely encounter in Gothic romance, drama, and poetry. Although architectural debates after 1818, as I have shown, frequently invoked Shelley's text, it ultimately had very little to say about Gothic architecture itself.

Instead, *Frankenstein* continuously celebrates in relation to architecture the powers of the idealist imagination, the ability of the human mind not only passively to reflect but also to construct lofty structures of its own devising. These powers assume particularly architectural forms when the Creature, speaking of the rustic shepherd's hut in which he first takes shelter, notes that 'it presented to me then as exquisite and divine a retreat as Pandæmonium appeared to the daemons of hell after their sufferings in the lake of fire'.[143] Here, Shelley alludes to Satan's speech in Book I of *Paradise Lost*: 'The mind is its own place, and in itself / Can make a heaven of hell, a hell of heaven.'[144] The Creature repeats this claim when he sets up home in the low hovel beside the De Lacey Cottage: making of this 'kennel' an 'agreeable asylum', this becomes 'indeed a paradise, compared to the bleak forest, my former residence, the rain-dropping branches, and dank earth'.[145] Later, when he is freed from prison, Victor too claims that the structuring effects of consciousness have the power completely to override architecture's associative chains, observing that 'to me the walls of a dungeon or a palace were alike hateful', and that 'a prison was as welcome a residence as the divinest scene in nature'.[146] The mind in *Frankenstein* is no longer the passive receptacle of the empirical world of experience, but a power that forms and structures that experience itself.

In a short poem of c.1817, John Keats had little to say about the associations evoked by Gothic architecture beyond that 'The Gothic looks solemn'.[147] Inspired by a visit to the ruins of Lincluden Priory, Dumfries, in July 1818, however, Keats in the winter of 1819 would draft and rework 'The Eve of St Agnes' (1820), a Spenserian poem about popular superstition and the defiant energies of young romantic and sexual love.[148] Here, the imaginative appeal of Gothic architecture takes precedence. Pausing over such details as the sculptures of knights and ladies in the chapel, the 'carved angels' in the masonry, and the heraldry, stained glass, and 'triple-arch'd' casements in Madeline's bedchamber, the persona ties Gothic architecture closely into the appeal of 'old romance' and 'faery fancy'.[149] But what

---

[143] Shelley, *Frankenstein*, p. 75.
[144] John Milton, *Paradise Lost*, ed. Alastair Fowler (London and New York: Longman, 1971), Book I, ll. 254–5.
[145] Shelley, *Frankenstein*, p. 76.   [146] Shelley, *Frankenstein*, p. 139.
[147] John Keats, 'The Gothic looks solemn', in *John Keats: Complete Poems*, ed. Jack Stillinger (Cambridge, MA, and London: Harvard University Press, 1982), p. 62, l. 1.
[148] For an account of Keats and Lincluden Priory, see Nicholas Roe, *John Keats: A New Life* (New Haven and London: Yale University Press, 2012), pp. 241–2.
[149] John Keats, 'The Eve of St Agnes', in *John Keats: Complete Poems*, ed. Jack Stillinger (Cambridge, MA, and London: Harvard University Press, 1982), pp. 229–39 (ll. 34, 28).

emerges in 'The Eve of St Agnes', as in its companion piece 'The Eve of St. Mark' (written 1819; published 1848), is not a sensationalist 'Gothic' narrative but a short, poetic 'medievalist' romance in the tradition of the 'Provençal Tale' from Radcliffe's *Udolpho* and other white Gothic texts: tellingly, the darker, more disturbing aspects of the Gothic past are relegated to the troubling dreams of those who remain behind in the Gothic pile from which Madeline and Porphyro flee: 'That night the Baron dreamt of many a woe, / And all his warrior-guests, with shade and form / Of witch, and demon, and large coffin-worm, / Were long be-nightmar'd.'[150] In *A Defence of Poetry* (written 1821; posthumously published 1840), Percy Shelley moved away from the associationism of his youth in order to advance an account of the poetic imagination as a far more active, productive, and synthesizing force.[151] In the Piranesian nightmares of De Quincey's Opium Eater in 1821, classical architecture was Gothicized and internalized as the cipher of the troubled Romantic psyche. Byron, for his part, would parody the ghostly associations evoked by Gothic architecture in the Black Friar episode from the Norman Cantos (Cantos XVI and XVII) of *Don Juan* (1824), playfully using the Gothic setting of the Amundevilles' 'improved' Norman Abbey—often said to be based on his own home at Newstead—as the setting for an unfinished, anticlimactic, and ultimately inconclusive tale of the explained supernatural.

Romantic poets subjected the architectural imagination of earlier Gothic writing to continuous parody, subversion, and critique. Peacock returned to the question of the architectural imagination in his later conversational novel *Crotchet Castle* (1831), here undertaking with castles what he had achieved with ecclesiastical architecture in *Nightmare Abbey*. In a satirical treatment of the revivalist taste for the Gothic, Ebenezer Mac Crotchet retires to his castellated villa in the Thames Valley, concealing his Scottish and Jewish ancestry by renaming himself E. M. Crotchet and embracing at Crotchet Castle the 'English' Gothic architectural style. It is through the aptly named Mr Chainmail, though, that Peacock most satirizes the literary and architectural impulses of the early Gothic Revival. A young gentleman with 'very antiquated tastes', Chainmail is fond of 'old poetry' and reads deeply in 'monkish literature'.[152] More acutely, he ardently defends, against the opinions of Mr Mac Quedy, the antique English past as everything that I have designated in this book as the white Gothic: a past of liberty and Magna Carta, beef and ale, Robin Hood and the Jolly Pinder of Wakefield, heraldry, chivalry, honour, falconry, minstrelsy, and splendid Gothic architecture, all of which culminated, he claims, in the twelfth century during the reign of King Richard I. Though some have the impudence to call it 'dark', Gothic antiquity for

---

[150] Keats, 'The Eve of St Agnes', ll. 372-4.
[151] See Bryan Keith Shelley, 'The Synthetic Imagination: Shelley and Associationism', *The Wordsworth Circle* vol. 14, issue 1 (winter 1983): pp. 68-73.
[152] Thomas Love Peacock, 'Crotchet Castle', in *Novels of Thomas Love Peacock*, introd. J. B. Priestley and notes by Barbara Lloyd Evans (London: Pan Books, 1967), pp. 257-359 (p. 288).

him is anything but benighted. In an exchange that recalls that between Addison and Arbuthnot before the ruins of Kenilworth in Hurd's *Dialogues*, Mac Quedy vehemently disagrees:

> No, nor was it. It was a period of brutality, ignorance, fanaticism, and tyranny; when the land was covered with castles, and every castle contained a gang of banditti, headed by a titled robber, who levied contributions with fire and sword; plundering, torturing, ravishing, burying his captives in loathsome dungeons, and broiling them on gridirons, to force from them the surrender of every particle of treasure which he suspected them of possessing; and fighting every now and then with the neighbouring lords, his conterminal bandits, for the right of marauding on the boundaries.[153]

These references to castles, banditti, torture, and loathsome dungeons indicate that Mac Quedy's impressions of the 'Dark Ages' have been forged on a familiarity with popular Gothic romance, a tendency against which Maitland in *The Dark Ages* would later caution. For Mac Quedy, in fact, even Walter Scott's renditions of life in twelfth-century England in *Ivanhoe* are far too sanguine, and border on false and sentimental idealization, whereas for Mr Chainmail, they do not go far enough in paying tribute to just how splendid that Gothic past was.

Unlike Hurd, Peacock's intention at this point is not to take sides, but to satirize the very debate around the nature of Gothic antiquity itself: as I have shown, the question was continuously pondered throughout the period 1760 to 1840. Towards the end of the novel, Peacock turns his satirical gaze upon Chainmail's Gothic architectural imagination. While sitting on a rock near the base of a ruined castle, he is depicted as 'calling up the forms of past ages on the wall of an ivied tower', shades of the 'castles in the air' imagined by the Shelleyan Scythrop in the earlier text.[154] Overly susceptible to the romantic reveries set in place by the associations elicited by the ruin, Chainmail begins to frame his experience as a Radcliffean romance, making of the corpulent, rubicund Susannah Touchandgo, herself already a parody of a Gothic heroine, a pale, sylph-like creature who is, at once, his 'lady of the lake' and his 'enchantress of the ruined castle'.[155] The episode reads very much like the tale of the Black Friar in *Don Juan*, with its equally voluptuous Duchess of Fitz-Fulke assuming the role of Lewis's Bleeding Nun in order to seduce Byron's hero. In search of his flighty beloved, Chainmail haunts the ruin like a ghost, the episode self-consciously fuelled by all the effusiveness and balladry of Radcliffe. Through such heightened and laughter-inducing fictionality, the architectural imagination is once again reduced to folly, the same frivolous capacity that is embodied in the *faux* Gothic battlements of Chainmail Hall in which the pair, having married, eventually settle, presiding there over a ludicrous

---

[153] Peacock, 'Crotchet Castle', p. 314. [154] Peacock, 'Crotchet Castle', p. 330.
[155] Peacock, 'Crotchet Castle', p. 333.

exaggeration of Christmas festivities all executed according to Burkean 'Gothic customary' at the novel's end.

John Ruskin would rephrase the Romantic critique of associationism in terms that were more naturally oriented towards architectural practice and appreciation. In a lecture on 'Turner and His Works' that he delivered in Edinburgh in November 1853, he commended Ann Radcliffe for her absorption of the spirit of natural sublimity that had first been visually expressed in the paintings of Claude, Poussin, and Rosa. Tracking the developments of this impulse in subsequent writers, Ruskin turns to the poetry and fiction of Walter Scott, pausing to celebrate the writer for his 'touching and affectionate appreciation of the Gothic architecture, in which alone he found the elements of natural beauty seized by art'.[156] Scott's descriptions of Melrose Abbey in *The Lay of the Last Minstrel* and Holy Island Cathedral in *Marmion*, together with the 'ideal' or imaginary abbeys of *The Monastery* (1820) and *The Antiquary* (1816) and the 'real' castles of Caerlaverock and Lochleven in *Guy Mannering* (1815) and *The Abbot* (1820), remain for Ruskin 'the staple possessions and text-books of all travellers, not so much for their beauty or accuracy, as for their *exactly expressing that degree of feeling with which most men in this century can sympathise*'.[157]

If this reads like an affirmation of the Gothic's associative appeal over a concern with archaeological accuracy, it is a position from which Ruskin would subsequently recant. Reflecting on, and partly revising, his earlier work in *The Poetry of Architecture* (1837–8), his account of memory in the first edition of *The Seven Lamps of Architecture* (1849), *The Stones of Venice* (1851–3), and his architectural lectures, Ruskin in the 1855 Preface to the second edition of *The Seven Lamps* outlined an important anatomy of architectural response, one in which the aesthetics of associationism suffered further theoretical relegation. Having investigated the emotions that are 'generally felt' by 'well-educated people respecting various forms of good architecture', he articulates a hierarchically arranged taxonomy of architectural response: 'Sentimental Admiration'; 'Proud Admiration'; 'Workmanly Admiration'; and 'Artistical and Rational Admiration'.[158] It is the first of these categories that is of interest here, for it is through this that Ruskin groups together the architectural associations that had informed the production of Gothic romance, drama, and poetry from Addison onwards:

> The kind of feeling which most travellers experience on first entering a cathedral by torchlight, and hearing a chant from concealed choristers; or in visiting a

---

[156] John Ruskin, 'Lecture III: On Turner and His Works', in *Library Edition* (1903–12), vol. 12, pp. 102–33 (p. 121).
[157] Ruskin, 'Lecture III: On Turner and His Works', vol. 12, p. 121.
[158] John Ruskin, 'Author's Preface to the Second Edition of *The Seven Lamps of Architecture*', *Library Edition*, (1903–12), vol. 8, pp. 7–14 (pp. 7–8).

ruined abbey by moonlight, or any building with which interesting associations are connected, at that time when they can hardly see it.[159]

Less sophisticated than all other responses, the Gothic architectural imagination is 'excitable in nearly all persons', its effects generated by 'a certain amount of darkness and slow music in a minor key'.[160] That it had important functions is undoubtable. But even in its highest manifestations—Scott's celebrated descriptions of Melrose in *The Lay* and Glasgow Cathedral in *Rob Roy* (1817)—it is the 'sentimental admiration' of architecture that blinds Scott to the differences between, say, the 'true Gothic' at Glasgow and the 'false Gothic' (or Scottish baronial) at Abbotsford. Undiscriminating in its fancies, associationism overlooks the important differences between 'true' medieval architecture and the bastardized forms of the 'modern Gothic', indiscriminately making of any architectural structure the occasion for romance. 'As a critical faculty', Ruskin concludes, 'I found it was hardly to be taken into consideration in any reasoning on the higher merits of architecture.'[161]

Seemingly, his critique was almost immediately effective. When Charles Locke Eastlake published his seminal *A History of the Gothic Revival* in 1872, he abruptly terminated an account of the positive role that *Marmion* and *The Lay* had played in 'encouraging a national taste for Mediæval architecture' with a blunt rejection of the associationist paradigm: 'The time may perhaps have now arrived when the popular mind can dispense with the spell of association, and learn to admire Gothic for its intrinsic beauty.'[162] The differences, in Stephen Clarke's terms, between the 'written' and 'built' Gothic had been formally enshrined in architectural history.[163] Thus it was that Kenneth Clark in *The Gothic Revival* (1928) could confidently make the claim that I explored in the Preface to this study: that there is no perceivable relation between 'Gothic novels' and 'Gothic buildings', and that to suggest otherwise is sheer folly. It is my hope that the argument of *Gothic Antiquity* has convincingly proved the opposite. However the term was understood, and regardless of whether it was embraced or disavowed, 'Gothic Story' was central to British architectural practice and debate in the late eighteenth and early nineteenth centuries.

The Gothic Revival as it was self-consciously practised and theorized by Pugin the Elder and Younger, Ruskin, Eastlake, and others in the mid- to late decades of the nineteenth century did everything in its power to distance itself from the cultural material that I have explored throughout this book: the profound,

---

[159] Ruskin, 'Author's Preface to the Second Edition of *The Seven Lamps of Architecture*', vol. 8, pp. 7–8.
[160] Ruskin, 'Author's Preface to the Second Edition of *The Seven Lamps of Architecture*', vol. 8, p. 9.
[161] Ruskin, 'Author's Preface to the Second Edition of *The Seven Lamps of Architecture*', vol. 8, p. 9.
[162] Eastlake, *A History of the Gothic Revival*, p. 115.
[163] Clarke, 'Abbeys Real and Imagined: Northanger Abbey, Fonthill, and Aspects of the Gothic Revival'.

imaginative re-evaluation of the art and architecture of the Gothic past that, though certainly present earlier in both 'survivalist' and 'revivalist' forms, came to particular prominence in Britain from around 1760 onwards, and assumed both literary and architectural manifestations in the work of Walpole and Beckford, Radcliffe, Lewis, and their contemporaries, and into the poetry and fiction of Walter Scott. By the second decade of nineteenth century, Walpole's literary and architectural reputation was in sharp decline. William Hazlitt's unsigned review of *Letters from the Hon. Horace Walpole, to George Montagu, Esq.* (1818) in *The Edinburgh Review* characterized the author as an effete gossip who revelled at Strawberry Hill 'in a world of chests, cabinets, commodes, tables, boxes, turrets, stands, old printing, and old china', letting his visitors and the readers of his letters loose 'at once amongst all the frippery and folly of the last two centuries'.[164] In an 1833 review of *Letters of Horace Walpole, Earl of Orford, to Sir Horace Mann* (1833), a vicious ad hominem attack that would seal Walpole's reputation for much of the nineteenth century, Thomas Babington Macaulay claimed that the author had frittered away a long life in decorating 'a grotesque house with piecrust battlements', creating for himself an overfilled cabinet of curiosities to house an arcane collection of engravings, antique chimney-boards, and odd gauntlets.[165] William Beckford's fate was no less ignominious: in *The London Magazine* in November 1822, William Hazlitt dismissed Fonthill Abbey and its collections as 'a desart [sic] of magnificence, a glittering waste of laborious idleness, a cathedral turned into a toy-shop, an immense Museum of all that is most curious and costly, and, at the same time, most worthless, in the productions of art and nature'.[166]

Similar sentiments were expressed across nineteenth-century Gothic architectural tracts. A deep-seated contempt for everything that Walpole's work at Strawberry Hill had come to represent for later devotees of medieval architecture runs throughout the text that Willson prepared for A. C. Pugin's two-volume *Specimens of Gothic Architecture* (1821–3). In their disregard for historical accuracy and consistency, 'many builders, miscalled architects', Willson writes, have 'committed egregious blunders, and have jumbled together, in one design, not only the styles of different ages, but mixtures of castellated, domestic, and ecclesiastical architecture'—a clear reference to the playful vacillation between these various modes at Strawberry Hill that I discussed in Chapter 2.[167] Such 'licentious' departures from original rules had been responsible for the 'execrable Gothic of Batty Langley', the same tradition of amateur revivalism in which

---

[164] [William Hazlitt], 'Art. IV', *The Edinburgh Review* no. 61 (December 1818): pp. 80–93 (p. 81).
[165] [Thomas Babington Macaulay], 'Art. XI', *The Edinburgh Review* no. 117 (October 1833): pp. 227–58 (p. 228).
[166] William Hazlitt, 'Fonthill Abbey', in *Criticisms on Art; and Sketches of the Picture Galleries of England* (London: John Templeman, 1843), pp. 284–99 (p. 284).
[167] A. C. Pugin, *Specimens of Gothic Architecture Selected from Various Ancient Edifices in England*, 2 vols (London: J. Taylor, 1821), vol. 1, Preface.

Pugin locates Walpole. While tasteless in and of themselves, these and other irresponsible approximations of the 'modern Gothic' also bring original, surviving Gothic forms into disrepute. While acknowledging Walpole's contribution to restoring Gothic taste, *Specimens of Gothic Architecture* ultimately denounces Walpole's project as 'a heap of inconsistencies, and altogether a mere toy', harshly concluding that 'His imitations at Strawberry-Hill are hardly to be called Architecture' at all.[168] Once authenticated, grounded, and truthfully and accurately executed, the Gothic might only be applied to modern buildings according to a seemingly paradoxical principle of 'true simulation': 'By a judicious attention to appropriate models, a modern residence, of whatever size of character, may be constructed in the Gothic style, without departing from sound principles of taste.'[169]

A. W. N. Pugin proceeded in a similar fashion in *The True Principles of Pointed or Christian Architecture* (1841), a critique of the 'deceptions' and 'illusions' of the 'modern Gothic' of the previous century that is often more emotive than that of his father: 'What absurdities, what anomalies, what utter contradictions do not the builders of modern castles perpetrate! How many portcullises which will not lower down, and drawbridges which will not draw up!—how many loop-holes in turrets so small that the most diminutive sweep could not ascend them!'[170] While scornfully anticipating the sham Gothic of Mr Wemmick's castle in Dickens's *Great Expectations* (1860-1), this passage also looks back to Strawberry Hill and Fonthill Abbey, both Gothic confections, for Pugin, that gratuitously sported interiors in which 'every thing is crocketed with angular projections, innumerable mitres, sharp ornaments, and turreted extremities'. As he bitterly but humorously concludes, 'A man who remains any length of time in a modern Gothic room, and escapes without being wounded by some of its minutiae, may consider himself extremely fortunate.'[171] For Pugin, the Gothic experiments of Walpole and Beckford violated the 'true principles' of the 'Christian' or 'Pointed' style, their attempts at divorcing a Catholic aesthetic from its deeper religious meanings indicative of the designers' self-indulgence. Buildings that, like Strawberry and Fonthill, 'had been raised somewhat in the guise of the solemn architecture of religion and antiquity', reveal themselves to be 'a mere toy, built to suit the caprice of a wealthy individual, and devoted to luxury'.[172] Pugin's revived Gothic, by contrast, was one of truth, integrity, and a profound respect for the style's original

---

[168] Pugin, *Specimens of Gothic Architecture*, vol. 1, pp. xiv, xv.
[169] Pugin, *Specimens of Gothic Architecture*, vol. 2, pp. xxi–xxii.
[170] A. W. N. Pugin, *The True Principles of Pointed or Christian Architecture: Set Forth in Two Lectures Delivered at St Marie's, Oscott* (London: John Weale, 1841), p. 58.
[171] Pugin, *The True Principles of Pointed or Christian Architecture*, p. 40.
[172] Pugin, *The True Principles of Pointed or Christian Architecture*, p. 59.

Catholic theological significance.[173] As the Victorian period saw it, the Gothic Revival itself was thus not one long continuous process that began the century before, but split rather definitively into two distinct phases, with Walpole ignominiously at the head of the first, and Pugin the Elder and Younger leading the second. With the dismissal of the Gothic of the previous century as child's play, the future of Gothic Revivalism belonged to more sober-minded (but by no means whimsy-free) architects the likes of William Butterfield, George Edmund Street, and George Gilbert Scott.

In time, architectural historians of the late nineteenth and early twentieth centuries would express a similar repugnance for all Gothic Revivalist architecture prior to Pugin and Ruskin through a calculated use of the term 'Gothick', a deliberate linguistic archaism that was intended to signify the frivolousness, sentimental antiquarianism, and misplaced archaeological rigour of earlier practitioners.[174] In *A History of the Gothic Revival* Eastlake used this spelling to mark his contempt for the work of Thomas and Batty Langley, differentiating it in this way from the respectable 'Gothic' of Pugin and Barry. As I pointed out in the Preface, a similar distinction between the playful and irresponsible 'Gothick' of Walpole and buildings of the later, more reliable 'Gothic' Revival runs throughout Kenneth Clark's *The Gothic Revival*. For Clark, 'Gothick' was the preserve of the brothers Langley, William Halfpenny, Robert Chambers, Walpole, Beckford, and Wyatt, 'Gothic' the more respectable terrain of Pugin. H. M. Colvin returned to the problem in 'Gothic Survival and Gothick Revival', arguing that, despite a few occasions of overlap, the persistence of medieval 'Gothic' styles well into the eighteenth century was distinct from the 'Gothick' of revivalists such as Walpole.[175] What was once rejected as 'Gothic' was now dismissed by early architectural historians as 'Gothick'; as of old, the appreciation and critical reception of, by now, largely 'medieval' architecture was dependent upon the terms used to name it.

Coda: The Architect as New Professional

The differences between the classical and Gothic styles were not the only topics to be debated in the pamphlet war that ensued over the building of the New Palace of Westminster in 1835–7. In such tracts as Edward Cust's *An Apology for the Architectural Monstrosities of London* (1835) and T. Juvara's *Strictures on*

---

[173] For an attempt at situating Pugin's work in relation to the earlier Gothic Revival, see S. Lang, 'The Principles of the Gothic Revival in England', *Journal of the Society of Architectural Historians* vol. 25, no. 4 (Dec. 1966): pp. 240–67.
[174] See Michael Hall, 'Introduction', in *Gothic Architecture and its Meanings, 1550–1830*, ed. Michael Hall (Reading, Spire Books, 2002), pp. 7–24 (p. 11).
[175] Colvin, 'Gothic Survival and Gothick Revival': pp. 91–8.

Architectural Monstrosities (1835), both sides of the argument also expressed strong opinions regarding the role and identity of the architect, the levels of his autonomy and accountability to others, and, related to that, the age-old question of whether his work was best to be thought of as a science or an art. As the titles of these tracts suggest, Victor's lack of accountability to others in *Frankenstein* was central to the dispute. In and around 1834, these were particularly topical concerns: the year of the fire at Westminster also marked the founding of the Institute of British Architects of London, an establishment that received its royal charter in 1837, thereafter becoming known as the Royal Institute of British Architects of London, and, after 1892, the Royal Institute of British Architects (RIBA). The establishment of RIBA marked a crucial moment in the history of British architecture insofar as it constituted the first step in the professionalization of the role and function of the architect and his work, a process that would be continued with the introduction of compulsory qualifying examinations for institutional membership from 1882; the establishment of full-time academic architectural courses at London Universities from 1895; the appointment of the RIBA Board of Architectural Education in 1904 and 1922; and the Architects' Registration Acts of 1931 and 1938.[176] Prior to this, and as I argued at the outset of this book, the title of 'architect' was one that was often freely and loosely appropriated, the eighteenth century being the great age of architectural amateurism or John Wilton-Ely's 'gentleman architects'. As the first professional architectural institute, however, RIBA aimed to regulate and control entry into the profession. Distinguishing and separating out, through a process of institutional inclusion and exclusion, the role of the architect from that of the builder, mason, surveyor, engineer, and other participants in the building process, RIBA distanced the practice of architecture from the more material aspects of construction, an elision of labour that was both in keeping with, and significantly intensified by, the rapid industrialization of the first half of the nineteenth century.

There is no doubt that these changes were driven by the discourse of the sister arts, that classically derived claim that architecture was an art form akin to those of painting, sculpture, music, and poetry. Distinct from the common workmen of the building trade, the architect, as of old, was a man of imaginative genius, his work the original creation of his superior imaginative abilities. Accordingly, RIBA remained firmly of the opinion that Charles Barry, the Institute's Vice President, ought to be allowed to exercise his creative genius at Westminster wholly unhindered by the interventions and opinions of others: '[W]e ardently hope, that in the erection of our intended Houses of Parliament, the Architect will be left to the free

---

[176] See, for example, Mark Crinson and Jules Lubbock, *Architecture: Art of Profession?* (1994), and Spiro Kostof, ed., *The Architect: Chapters in the History of the Profession* (New York: Oxford University Press, 1977).

exercise of his own judgment, uncontrolled and unshackled in matters of art by the opinion of others.'[177] As artist, the architect was an autonomous entity who was answerable only to himself. Unlike authors and other professional artists, however, he lacked professional standing and adequate legal protection, and it was these aspects of architectural practice that the formation of the Institute was intended to redress.

In one sense, this appears to be just another iteration of the assumptions that I have explored throughout this study: an assertion of the architect's artistic identity; a refusal to impose any absolute distinction between architecture, literature, and other forms of creativity; and the institutional recognition, assertion, and protection of the power and autonomy of the architect-as-creative-genius, comparable in its way to the contemporary debates around perpetual literary copyright. Upon closer inspection, however, the professionalization of the practice of architecture marked yet another instance of the dismantling of the key terms of the Gothic architectural imagination. Putting paid to the creative amateurism of the eighteenth century, professionalization was an obstacle to that easy transition from literature to architecture and back again that we see in the life and works of Walpole and Beckford. Placing between writers such as Scott, Radcliffe, and Wordsworth, all of whom had once asserted the affinities between their literary craft and the practice of architecture, a formal system of training, examination, and accreditation, professionalization paradoxically separated off architecture from all the other arts.

It thus seems especially fitting that nineteenth-century Gothic architects vehemently resisted professionalization. For a start, the anonymity of the medieval architect meant that he could not be easily accommodated by the celebrity culture that professionalism engendered. Pugin had included a bitter invective against professionalization towards the end of *Contrasts*, and included an engraving of a medieval scholar-turned-architect in a scriptorium as the frontispiece to *True Principles*, a defiant assertion of a deliberately archaic architectural identity that also affirmed Gothic architecture's ultimately Catholic origins (see Figure 7.1).[178] Ruskin was similarly suspicious of his culture's aggrandizement of the new architectural professional, and in 'The Nature of Gothic' argued that 'The painter should grind his own colours; the architect work in the mason's yard with his men.'[179] Under Ruskin's influence, William Morris and the Arts and Crafts Movement would reaffirm the importance of masonry and craftsmanship to architectural practice, their socialist visions self-consciously reviving medieval models of community and production. Still, the march of modernity was implacable. The translation in 1836 of Gotthold Ephraim Lessing's critique of the equivalences between painting and poetry in *Laocoön* (1766) further alienated the sister arts from one

---

[177] P. F. Robinson, 'Report of the Council', *Transactions of the Institute of British Architects of London, Sessions 1835–36*, vol. 1, part 1 (1836): pp. xxiii–xxx (p. xxv).
[178] See Pugin, *Contrasts*, p. 34.   [179] John Ruskin, 'The Nature of Gothic', p. 201.

Figure 7.1 Frontispiece to A. W. N. Pugin's *The True Principles of Pointed or Christian Architecture: Set Forth in Two Lectures Delivered at St. Marie's, Oscott* (1841). Courtesy of Yale Center for British Art, Paul Mellon Collection, NA440 P9 1841 copy 2.

another, urging a reassessment of their apparent similarities. Through these and other discursive and institutional changes from the mid-1830s onwards, the relationship between literature and architecture, two creative forms of expression that, for over a century, were seen as interchangeable forms of creative expression, was thoroughly reconfigured, and reorganized along very different lines.

Select Bibliography

All quoted sources are referenced in full in the footnotes to the text. Rather than repeat that information here, this select bibliography lists only longer works, and for the most part excludes duplicate editions of the same text, as well as short historical reviews and articles.

Acosta, Ana M., 'Hotbeds of Popery: Convents in the English Literary Imagination', *Eighteenth-Century Fiction* vol. 50, no. 3-4 (July 2003): pp. 615-42.

Addison, Joseph, *Remarks on Several Parts of Italy, &c. in the Years 1701, 1702, 1703* (London: Printed for Jacob Tonson, 1705).

Addison, Joseph, *The Drummer; or, The Haunted House, A Comedy* (London: Printed for Jacob Tonson, 1716).

Addison, Joseph, *The Works of the Late Right Honourable Joseph Addison, Esq*, 4 vols (Birmingham: Printed by John Baskerville for J. and R. Tonson, 1761).

Addison, Joseph, *Critical Essays from The Spectator, With Four Essays by Richard Steele*, ed. Donald F. Bond (Oxford: Clarendon Press, 1970).

Aikin, John, 'Letter XXIV. On Ruins', in *Letters from A Father to His Son, on Various Topics, Relative to Literature and the Conduct of Life, Written in the Years 1792 and 1793* (London: Printed for J. Johnson, 1793), pp. 262-73.

Aikin, J., and A. L., *Miscellaneous Pieces, in Prose* (London: Printed for J. Johnson, 1773).

Akenside, Mark, *The Pleasures of Imagination. A Poem in Three Books* (London, 1744).

Aldrich, Megan, *Gothic Revival* (London: Phaidon Press, 1994).

Aldrich, Megan, 'Gothic Sensibility: The Early Years of the Gothic Revival', in *A.W.N. Pugin: Master of Gothic Revival*, ed. Paul Atterbury (New Haven and London: Yale University Press, 1995), pp. 13-30.

Alexander, Boyd, ed., *The Journal of William Beckford in Portugal & Spain, 1787-1788*, 2nd edn (Stroud: Non Such Publishing, 2006).

Alexander, Michael, *Medievalism: The Middle Ages in Modern England* (New Haven: Yale University Press, 2007).

Alison, Archibald, *Essays on the Nature and Principles of Taste* (London: Printed for J. J. G. and G. Robinson; Edinburgh: Bell & Bradfute, 1790).

Ames, Dianne S., 'Strawberry Hill: Architecture of the "As If"', *Studies in Eighteenth-Century Culture* 8 (1979): pp. 351-63.

Andrews, Malcolm, *The Search for the Picturesque: Landscape Aesthetics and Tourism in Britain, 1760-1800* (Aldershot: Scolar Press, 1990).

Andrews, Miles Peter, *The Castle of Wonders* [1786?], M.S. Larpent Collection, No. 752. Henry E. Huntington Library and Art Gallery, San Marino, CA.

Andrews, Miles Peter, *The Songs, Recitatives, Airs, Duets, Trios, and Choruses, Introduced in the Pantomime Entertainment of the Enchanted Castle, as Performed at the Theatre-Royal, Covent-Garden* (London: Printed for the Author, 1786).

Andrews, Miles Peter, *The Mysteries of the Castle: A Dramatic Tale, in Three Acts* (London: Printed by W. Woodfall for T. N. Longman, 1795).

Anon., '*Common Sense*, Dec. 15, no. 150', *GM* vol. 9 (Dec. 1739): pp. 640-2.

Anon., *The Art of Architecture, A Poem. In Imitation of Horace's Art of Poetry* (London: Printed for R. Dodsley, 1742).
Anon., *An Essay on the Qualifications and Duties of an Architect, &c. With Some Useful Hints for the Young Architect or Surveyor* (London: Printed for the Author, 1773).
Anon., *St Bernard's Priory: An Old English Tale* (London: Printed for the Authoress, 1786).
Anon. [A Jacobin Novelist], 'Terrorist System of Novel-Writing', *The Monthly Magazine*, vol. IV, no. xxi (Aug. 1797): pp. 102–4.
Anon., 'Terrorist Novel Writing', in *Spirit of the Public Journals for 1797* (London: Printed for R. Phillips, 1798), pp. 223–5.
Anon., 'The Female Castle-Builder. A Picture from Real Life', *Flowers of Literature for 1801 and 1802*, vol. 1 (1803): pp. 215–17.
Anon., 'Castle-Building, An Elegy', in *English Minstrelsy. Being a Selection of Fugitive Poetry from the Best English Authors; With Some Original Pieces Hitherto Unpublished*, 2 vols (Edinburgh: Printed for John Ballantyne and Co.; Manners and Miller; and Brown and Crombie; London: John Murray, 1810).
Anon., *The Age; A Poem: Moral, Political, and Metaphysical* (London: Printed for Vernor, Hood, and Sharpe, 1810).
Anon., *Metrical Remarks on Modern Castles and Cottages, and Architecture in General* (London: Printed for J. Nunn, 1813).
Anon., 'Conversations with the Late William Beckford, Esq. No. V', *The New Monthly Magazine and Humorist*, 3rd part (1844): pp. 418–27.
Anon., *A Description of the New Palace of Westminster*, 3rd edn (London: W. Warrington & Son, 1849).
Anon., *A Descriptive Account of the Palace of Westminster* (London: Warrington & Co., 1856).
Anon., *The New Palace of Westminster* (London: Warrington & Co., 1862).
Anon., *The Age of Folly: A Poem* (London: Printed for the Author, n.d.).
Arata, Stephen, 'Scott's Pageants: The Example of *Kenilworth*', *Studies in Romanticism* vol. 40, no. 1 (spring 2001): pp. 99–107.
Archer, John, 'The Beginnings of Association in British Architectural Esthetics', *Eighteenth-Century Studies* vol. 16, no. 3 (spring 1983): pp. 241–64.
Archer, John, *The Literature of British Domestic Architecture, 1715–1842* (Cambridge, MA, and London: MIT Press, 1985).
Ariosto, Ludovico, *Orlando Furioso, By Ludovico Ariosto. Translated from the Italian, by William Huggins, Esq.*, 2nd edn, 2 vols (London: James Rivington and James Fletcher; Surrey: John Cook, 1757).
Ashmole, Elias, *The Antiquities of Berkshire*, 3 vols (London: Printed for Edmund Curll, 1719).
Astley, Stephen, *Robert Adam's Castles* (London: The Soane Gallery, 2000).
Aston, Margaret, 'English Ruins and English History: The Dissolution and the Sense of the Past', *Journal of the Warburg and Courtauld Institutes* vol. 36 (1973): pp. 231–55.
Aubin, Robert Arnold, *Topographical Poetry in Eighteenth-Century England* (New York: Modern Languages Association of America, 1936).
Aubrey, John, *Miscellanies* (London: Printed for Edward Castle, 1696).
Auslander, Leora, *Cultural Revolutions: Everyday Life and Politics in Britain, North America, and France* (Berkeley: University of California Press, 2009).
Austen, Jane, *Northanger Abbey, Lady Susan, The Watsons, and Sanditon*, ed. John Davie and introd. Terry Castle (Oxford and New York: Oxford University Press, 1990).
Bakhtin, Mikhail Mikhailovich, 'Forms of Time and of the Chronotope in the Novel: Notes toward a Historical Poetics', in M. M. Bakhtin, *The Dialogic Imagination: Four Essays*,

trans. M. Holquist and Caryl Emerson (Austin: University of Texas Press, 1981), pp. 84–258.
Ballantyne, Andrew, 'Genealogy of the Picturesque', *British Journal of Aesthetics* vol. 32, no. 4 (Oct. 1992): pp. 320–9.
Bann, Stephen, *Romanticism and the Rise of History* (New York: Twayne, 1995).
Bannerman, Anne, *Tales of Superstition and Chivalry* (London: Printed for Vernor and Hood, by James Swan, 1802).
Barbauld, Anna Laetitia, 'Mrs Radcliffe', in *The British Novelists, With An Essay, and Prefaces Biographical and Critical, Vol. XLIII* (London: Printed for F. C. and J. Rivington et al., 1820), pp. i–viii.
Barchas, Janine, *Matters of Fact in Jane Austen: History, Location, and Celebrity* (Baltimore: Johns Hopkins University Press, 2012).
Barnett, S. J., *Idol Temples and Crafty Priests: The Origins of Enlightenment Anticlericalism* (New York: St Martin's Press, 1999).
Bartlett, Alfred Darling, *An Historical and Descriptive Account of Cumnor Place, Berks, with Biographical Notices of the Lady Amy Dudley and of Anthony Forster, Esq.* (Oxford and London: John Henry Parker, 1850).
Bayer-Berenbaum, Linda, *The Gothic Imagination: Expansion in Gothic Literature and Art* (Cranbury, NJ, London, and Mississauga, ON: Associated University Presses, 1982).
Beattie, James, *Dissertations Moral and Critical* (London: Printed for W. Strahan and T. Cadell; Edinburgh: Printed for W. Creech, 1783).
Beckford, William, *The Long Story* (c.1777), Bodleian Library, Oxford, MS. Beckford c. 46.
Beckford, William, *Fonthill Foreshadowed* (c.1777–8), Bodleian Library, Oxford, MS. Beckford d. 9.
Beckford, William, *Fragments of an English Tour* (1779), Bodleian Library, Oxford, MS Beckford d.3, fols 10–18.
Beckford, William, *Dreams, Waking Thoughts, and Incidents, In a Series of Letters, from Various Parts of Europe* (London: Printed for J. Johnson and P. Elmsly, 1783).
Beckford, William, *Italy; With Sketches of Spain and Portugal*, 2 vols (London: Richard Bentley, 1834).
Beckford, William, *Recollections of an Excursion to the Monasteries of Alcobaça and Batalha* (London: Richard Bentley, 1835).
Beer, Gillian, '"Our unnatural No-voice": The Heroic Epistle, Pope, and Women's Gothic', *The Yearbook of English Studies* vol. 12 (1982): pp. 125–51.
Belsham, William, *Historic Memoir on the French Revolution* (London: Printed for C. Dilly, 1791).
Bennett, Mark, 'Gothic Travels', in *Romantic Gothic: An Edinburgh Companion*, ed. Angela Wright and Dale Townshend (Edinburgh: Edinburgh University Press, 2016), pp. 224–46.
Bentham, James, *The History and Antiquities of the Conventual and Cathedral Church of Ely* (Cambridge: Printed at the University Press, 1771).
Bentham, Jeremy, *A Fragment on Government; Being an Examination of what is Delivered, on the Subject of Government in General, in the Introduction to Sir William Blackstone's Commentaries* (London: Printed for T. Payne, P. Elmsly, and E. Brooke, 1776).
Bernstein, Susan, *Housing Problems: Writing and Architecture in Goethe, Walpole, Freud, and Heidegger* (Stanford, CA: Stanford University Press, 2008).
Betham, Matilda, *Poems* (London: Printed for J. Hatchard, 1808).
Bingham, Neil, Clare Carolin, Peter Cook, and Rob Wilson, *Fantasy Architecture, 1500–2036* (London: Hayward Gallery Publishing, 2004).

Birkhead, Edith, *The Tale of Terror: A Study of the Gothic Romance* (London: Constable and Co., 1921).
Blackstone, William, *Commentaries on the Laws of England*, 4 vols (Oxford: Clarendon Press, 1765–9).
Blair, Hugh, *Lectures on Rhetoric and Belles Lettres*, 3 vols (Dublin: Printed for Messrs Whitestone, Colles, Burnet, et al., 1783).
Blair, Robert, *The Grave: A Poem* (London: Printed for M. Cooper, 1743).
Blank, Antje, '"Things as They Were": The Gothic of Real Life in Charlotte Smith's *The Emigrants* and *The Banished Man*', *Women's Writing* vol. 16, issue 1 (2009): pp. 78–93.
Boase, T. S. R., 'The Decoration of the New Palace at Westminster, 1841–1863', *Journal of the Warburg and Courtauld Institutes* vol. 17, no. 3 (1954): pp. 319–58.
Bolingbroke, Viscount Henry St John, *A Dissertation Upon Parties; In Several Letters to Caleb D'Anvers* (London: Printed by H. Haines, 1735).
Bolingbroke, Viscount Henry St John, *Remarks on the History of England. From the Minutes of Humphy Oldcastle, Esq.* (London: Printed for R. Francklin, 1743).
Bonhôte, Elizabeth, *Bungay Castle: A Novel*, 2 vols (London: Printed for William Lane at the Minerva Press, 1796).
Botting, Fred, 'In Gothic Darkly: Heterotopia, History, Culture', in *A New Companion to the Gothic*, ed. David Punter (Oxford: Blackwell, 2012), pp. 13–24.
Bourne, Henry, *Antiquitates Vulgares; or, The Antiquities of the Common People* (Newcastle: Printed by J. White for the Author, 1725).
Bradley, Simon, 'The Englishness of Gothic: Theories and Interpretations from William Gilpin to J. H. Parker', *Architectural History* vol. 45 (2002): pp. 325–46.
Braverman, Richard, '"Dunce the Second Reigns Like Dunce the First": The Gothic Bequest in the "Dunciad"', *ELH* vol. 62, no. 4 (winter 1995): pp. 863–82.
Briggs, Martin S., *Goths and Vandals: A Study of the Destruction, Neglect and Preservation of Historical Buildings in England* (London: Constable, 1952).
Bromwich, David, 'Burke, *Reflections on the Revolution in France*', in *The Cambridge Companion to British Literature of the French Revolution in the 1790s*, ed. Pamela Clemit (Cambridge: Cambridge University Press, 2011), pp. 16–30.
Brooks, Chris, *The Gothic Revival* (London: Phaidon Press, 1999).
Brydone, Patrick, *A Tour Through Sicily and Malta. In A Series of Letters to William Beckford, Esq.*, 2 vols (London: Printed for W. Strahan and T. Cadell, 1773).
Buck, Samuel, *Proposals for Publishing by Subscription, Twenty Four Perspective Views, of the Present State of the Most Noted Abbies, Religious Foundations, Castles, and Other Remains of Antiquity; in the Counties of Wiltshire, Gloucester, and Monmouth* (London, 1732).
Buck, Samuel, *Proposals for Publishing by Subscription, Twenty Four Perspective Views, of the Present State of the Most Noted Abbies, Religious Foundations, Castles, and Other Remains of Antiquity, in Norfolk, Suffolk, and Essex* (London, 1737).
Bullen, J. B., 'The Romanesque Revival in Britain, 1800–1840: William Gunn, William Whewell, and Edmund Sharpe', *Architectural History* vol. 47 (2004): pp. 139–58.
Burgess, Thomas, *An Essay on the Study of Antiquities* (Oxford, 1780).
Burke, Edmund, *A Philosophical Enquiry into the Origin of Our Ideas of the Sublime and Beautiful* (London: Printed for R. and J. Dodsley, 1757).
Burke, Edmund, *Reflections on the Revolution in France, and on the Proceedings in Certain Societies in London Relative to that Event* (London: Printed for J. Dodsley, 1790).
Burke, Edmund, *Thoughts on the Prospect of a Regicide Peace, in a Series of Letters* (London: Printed for J. Owen, 1796).

Burney, Frances, *Memoirs of Doctor Burney, Arranged from his own Manuscripts, from Family Papers, and from Personal Recollections*, 3 vols (London: Edward Moxon, 1832).

Burney, Frances, *Diary and Letters of Madame D'Arblay, Author of Evelina, Cecilia, &c. Edited by her Niece*, 7 vols (London: Henry Colburn, 1842).

Butler, Marilyn, 'Introduction', in *Northanger Abbey*, by Jane Austen, ed. M. Butler (London: Penguin, 2003), pp. xi–l.

Butterfield, Herbert, *The Whig Interpretation of History* (New York and London: W. W. Norton, 1965).

Camden, William, *Britain, or A Chorographicall Description of the Most Flourishing Kingdomes, England, Scotland, and Ireland, and Islands Adjoining, out of the Depths of Antiquitie*, trans. Philemon Holland (London: Printed at Eliot's Court Press, 1610).

Cannadine, David, 'The Palace of Westminster as Palace of Varieties', in *The Houses of Parliament: History, Art, Architecture*, ed. D. Cannadine, Dorian Church et al. (London: Merrell Publishers, 2000), pp. 11–29.

Canuel, Mark, *Religion, Toleration and British Writing, 1790–1830* (Cambridge: Cambridge University Press, 2002).

Carso, Kerry Dean, *American Gothic Art and Architecture in the Age of Romantic Literature* (Cardiff: University of Wales Press, 2014).

Carter, John, *Pursuits of Antiquaries, During the Years 1791, 1793, 1794, 1795, 1796, 1797, 1798, 1799. In Four Parts. A Merry Ballad. To the Ancient Tune of 'When we were not over wise'* (c.1803). King's College London, Archives, Leathes MS 7/5.

Carter, John *Occurrences in the Life, and Memorandums Relating to the Professional Persuits [sic] of J. C.* (1817), King's College London, Archives, Leathes MS 7/4.1.

Chalcraft, Anna, *A Paper House: Horace Walpole at Strawberry Hill* (London: Highgate Publications, 1998).

Chalcraft, Anna, and Judith Viscardi, *Visiting Strawberry Hill: An Analysis of the Eton Copy of 'The Description of the Villa'* (Wimbledon: Chalcraft & Viscardi, 2005).

Chambers, William, *A Treatise on Civil Architecture, in which the Principles of that Art are Laid Down, and Illustrated by Plates, Accurately Designed, and Elegantly Engraved by the Best Hands* (London: Printed for the Author by J. Haberkorn, 1759).

Chapin, Chester, 'Alexander Pope: Erasmian Catholic', *Eighteenth-Century Studies*, vol. 6, no. 4 (summer 1973): pp. 411–30.

Chaplin, Sue, *Gothic and the Rule of Law, 1764–1820* (Basingstoke and New York: Palgrave Macmillan, 2007).

Charlesworth, Michael, 'The Ruined Abbey: Picturesque and Gothic Values', in *The Politics of the Picturesque: Literature, Landscape and Aesthetics Since 1770*, ed. Stephen Copley and Peter Garside (Cambridge: Cambridge University Press, 1994), pp. 63–79.

Charlesworth, Michael, ed., *The Gothic Revival 1720–1870*, 3 vols (Mountfield: Helm Information, 2002).

Cheeke, Stephen, *Writing for Art: The Aesthetics of Ekphrasis* (Manchester and New York: Manchester University Press, 2008).

Chiu, Frances A., 'Faulty Towers: Reform, Radicalism and the Gothic Castle, 1760–1800', *Romanticism on the Net* no. 44 (Nov. 2006): https://www.erudit.org/fr/revues/ron/2006-n44-ron1433/013996ar/ (accessed 5 June 2017).

Chiu, Frances A., 'Introduction', in *Gaston De Blondeville; or, The Court of Henry III Keeping Festival in Ardenne*, by Ann Radcliffe, ed. F. A. Chiu (Chicago: Valancourt Books, 2006), pp. vii–xxxviii.

Clark, Kenneth, *The Gothic Revival: An Essay in the History of Taste*, 2nd edn (Harmondsworth: Penguin Books, 1962).

Clarke, James, *A Survey of the Lakes of Cumberland, Westmorland, and Lancashire* (London: Printed for the Author, 1789).
Clarke, Stephen, 'Abbeys Real and Imagined: Northanger Abbey, Fonthill, and Aspects of the Gothic Revival', *Persuasions* 20 (1998): pp. 93-105.
Clarke, Stephen, 'The Ruin of Fonthill: The Reputation and Influence of Beckford's Abbey', in *William Beckford and the New Millennium*, ed. Kenneth W. Graham and Kevin Berland (New York: AMS Press, 2004), pp. 181-203.
Clarke, Stephen, 'Horace Walpole's Architectural Taste', in *Horace Walpole: Beyond The Castle of Otranto*, ed. Peter Sabor (New York: AMS Press, 2009), pp. 233-44.
Clarke, Stephen, '"Lord God! Jesus! What a House!": Describing and Visiting Strawberry Hill', *Journal for Eighteenth-Century Studies* vol. 33, no. 1 (2010): pp. 357-80.
Clarke, Stephen, *The Strawberry Hill Press & Its Printing House: An Account and an Iconography* (New Haven and London: Yale University Press, 2011).
Class, Monika, *Coleridge and Kantian Ideas in England, 1796-1817* (London: Bloomsbury, 2012).
Clery, E. J., ed., *The Castle of Otranto* (Oxford: Oxford University Press, 1996).
Clery, E. J., 'The genesis of "Gothic" fiction', in *The Cambridge Companion to Gothic Fiction*, ed. Jerrold E. Hogle (Cambridge: Cambridge University Press, 2002), pp. 21-40.
Clery, E. J., *Eighteen Hundred and Eleven: Poetry, Protest and Economic Crisis* (Cambridge: Cambridge University Press, 2017).
Clery, E. J., and Robert Miles, eds, *Gothic Documents: A Sourcebook, 1700-1820* (Manchester: Manchester University Press, 2000).
Clifford, Frances, *The Ruins of Tivoli; A Romance*, 4 vols (London: J. F. Hughes, 1810).
Coke, Edward, *The Third Part of the Institutes of the Laws of England: Concerning High Treason, and Other Pleas of the Crown, and Criminall Causes* (London: Printed by M. Flesher, for W. Lee and D. Pakerman, 1644).
Coleridge, Henry Nelson, ed., *Specimens of the Table Talk of the Late Samuel Taylor Coleridge*, 2 vols (London: John Murray, 1835).
Coleridge, Samuel Taylor, *The Literary Remains of Samuel Taylor Coleridge*, ed. Henry Nelson Coleridge, 4 vols (London: William Pickering, 1836).
Coleridge, Samuel Taylor, 'Biographia Literaria; or, Biographical Sketches of my Literary Life and Opinions', in *Samuel Taylor Coleridge: The Major Works*, ed. H. J. Jackson (Oxford and New York: Oxford University Press, 2000), pp. 155-482.
Colley, Linda, *Britons: Forging the Nation 1707-1837*, 2nd edn (New Haven and London: Yale University Press, 2005).
Collins, William, *Odes on Several Descriptive and Allegoric Subjects* (London: Printed for A. Millar, 1747).
Colman, George, and David Garrick, *The Clandestine Marriage, A Comedy* (London: Printed for P. Becket and P. A. De Hondt; R. Baldwin; and T. Davies, 1766).
Colvin, H. M., 'Gothic Survival and Gothick Revival', *The Architectural Review* vol. 103 (1948): pp. 91-9.
Colvin, H. M., 'Aubrey's *Chronologia Architectonica*', in *Concerning Architecture: Essays on Architectural Writers and Writing Presented to Nikolaus Pevsner*, ed. John Summerson (London: Allen Lane, 1968), pp. 1-12.
Combe, William, *The Tour of Dr Syntax in Search of the Picturesque: A Poem* (London: R. Ackermann's Repository of Arts, 1812).
Cook, Alexander, 'Reading Revolution: Towards a History of the Volney Vogue in England', in *Anglo-French Attitudes: Comparisons and Transfers between English and*

French Intellectuals Since the Eighteenth Century, ed. Christophe Charle, Julien Vincent, and Jay Winter (Manchester: Manchester University Press, 2007), pp. 125–46.

Cooper, George, *Architectural Reliques; or, The Present State of the Most Celebrated Remains of Ancient British Architecture and Sculpture* (London: Printed for the Author by J. Barfield, 1807).

Corbett, Margery, 'The Title-Page and Illustrations to the *Monasticon Anglicanum*, 1655–1673', *The Antiquaries Journal* vol. 67, issue 1 (Mar. 1987): pp. 102–10.

Cox, Oliver, 'An Oxford College and the Eighteenth-Century Gothic Revival', *Oxoniensia* vol. 77 (2012): pp. 117–35.

Coykendall, Abby, 'Chance Enlightenments, Choice Superstitions: Walpole's Historic Doubts and Enlightenment Historicism', *The Eighteenth Century* vol. 54, no. 1 (spring 2013): pp. 53–70.

Crary, Jonathan, *Techniques of the Observer: On Vision and Modernity in the Nineteenth Century* (Cambridge, Mass., and London: MIT Press, 1992).

Crinson, Mark, and Jules Lubbock, *Architecture: Art of Profession? Three Hundred Years of Architectural Education in Britain* (Manchester: Manchester University Press, 1994).

Crook, J. Mordaunt, 'John Britton and the Genesis of the Gothic Revival', in *Concerning Architecture: Essays on Architectural Writers and Writing Presented to Nikolaus Pevsner*, ed. John Summerson (London: Allen Lane, 1968), pp. 98–119.

Crook, J. Mordaunt, *John Carter and the Mind of the Gothic Revival* (London: The Society of Antiquaries of London, 1995).

Cross, J. C., 'Halloween; or, The Castles of Athlin and Dunbaye', in *Circusiana; or, A Collection of the Most Favourable Ballets, Spectacles, Melo-Drames, &c. Performed at the Royal Circus, St George's Field*, 2 vols (London: Lackington, Allen, and Co., 1809), vol. 2, pp. 185–230.

'Cumnor Hall', in *Old Ballads, Historical and Narrative, With Some of Modern Date*, ed. T. Evans, 4 vols (London: Printed for T. Evans, 1777), vol. 4, pp. 130–5.

Cunningham, Allan, *Biographical and Critical History of the British Literature of the Last Fifty Years* (Paris: Baudry's Foreign Library, 1834).

Curties, T. J. Horsley, *Ancient Records; or, The Abbey of Saint Oswythe*, 4 vols (London: Printed at the Minerva Press, 1801).

Curties, T. J. Horsley, *St Botolph's Priory; or, The Sable Mask. An Historic Romance*, 5 vols, (London: J. F. Hughes, 1806).

Dale, Antony, *James Wyatt, Architect: 1746–1813* (Oxford: B. Blackwell, 1936).

Darley, Gillian, *John Soane: An Accidental Romantic* (New Haven and London: Yale University Press, 1999).

Dart, John, *Westmonasterium; or, The History and Antiquities of the Abbey Church of St Peters, Westminster* (London: Printed and Sold by James Cole, et al., [1723]).

Davison, Carol Margaret, *Gothic Literature 1764–1824* (Cardiff: University of Wales Press, 2009).

Davison, Carol Margaret, 'Gothic Architectonics: The Poetics and Politics of Gothic Space', *Papers on Language and Literature* vol. 46 (2010): pp. 136–63.

De Beer, E. S., 'Gothic: Origin and Diffusion of the Term; The Idea of Style in Architecture', *Journal of the Warburg and Courtauld Institutes* vol. 11 (1948): pp. 143–62.

DeLamotte, Eugenia C., *Perils of the Night: A Feminist Study of Nineteenth-Century Gothic* (New York and Oxford: Oxford University Press, 1990).

DeLucia, JoEllen, 'From the Female Gothic to a Feminist Theory of History: Ann Radcliffe and the Scottish Enlightenment', *The Eighteenth Century* vol. 50, no. 1 (spring 2009): pp. 101–15.

DeLucia, JoEllen, 'Transnational Aesthetics in Ann Radcliffe's *A Journey Made in the Summer of 1794* (1795)', in *Ann Radcliffe, Romanticism and the Gothic*, ed. Dale Townshend and Angela Wright (Cambridge: Cambridge University Press, 2014), pp. 135–50.

Dennis, John, *The Advancement and Reformation of Modern Poetry. A Critical Discourse. In Two Parts* (London: Printed for Richard Parker, 1701).

Dent, John, *The Bastille: A Musical Entertainment of One Act*, 2nd edn (London: Printed for W. Lowndes, 1790).

Dent, Jonathan, *Sinister Histories: Gothic Novels and Representations of the Past, From Horace Walpole to Mary Wollstonecraft* (Manchester: Manchester University Press, 2016).

De Quincey, Thomas, *The Works of Thomas De Quincey, Vol. II: Confessions of an English Opium-Eater, 1821–1856*, ed. Grevel Lindop (London: Pickering & Chatto, 2000).

Dew, Ben, and Fiona Price, eds, *Historical Writing in Britain, 1688–1830: Visions of History* (Houndmills: Palgrave Macmillan, 2014).

D'Ezio, Marianna, '"As like As Peppermint Water is to Good French Brandy": Ann Radcliffe and Hester Lynch Salusbury (Thrale) Piozzi', *Women's Writing* vol. 22 no. 3, (July 2015): pp. 343–54.

Dickins, Lilian, and Mary Stanton, eds, *An Eighteenth-Century Correspondence [...] to Sanderson Miller, Esq. of Radway*, (London: John Murray, 1910).

Dobson, Michael, and Nicola J. Watson, *England's Elizabeth: An Afterlife in Fame and Fantasy* (Oxford: Oxford University Press, 2002).

Doerksen, Teri, 'Framing the Narrative: Illustration and Pictorial Prose in Burney and Radcliffe', in *Book Illustration in the Long Eighteenth Century: Reconfiguring the Visual Periphery of the Text*, ed. Christina Ionescu (Newcastle upon Tyne: Cambridge Scholars Publishing, 2011), pp. 463–500.

Douglas, James, *The History of Julia d'Haumont: or, The Eventful Connection of the House of Montmelian with that of d'Haumont*, 2 vols (London: Printed for G. Cawthorn, 1797).

Drake, Nathan, 'Number XX ["The Abbey of Clunedale"]', in *Literary Hours; or, Sketches Critical and Narrative*, 3 vols (London: Printed by J. Burkitt, 1798), vol. 1, pp. 325–44.

Drake, Nathan, *Essays, Biographical, Critical, and Historical, Illustrative of the Rambler, Adventurer, and Idler [...]*, 2 vols (London: Printed by J. Seeley for W. Suttaby, 1810).

Ducarel, Andrew Coltée, *Some Account of Browne Willis, Esq; L. L. D. late Senior Fellow of the Society of Antiquaries of London* (London, 1760).

Duckworth, Alistair M., *The Improvement of the Estate: A Study of Jane Austen's Novels* (Baltimore and London: The Johns Hopkins University Press, 1971).

Duff, David, 'Burke and Paine: Contrasts', in *The Cambridge Companion to British Literature of the French Revolution in the 1790s*, ed. Pamela Clemit (Cambridge: Cambridge University Press, 2011), pp. 47–70.

Duff, William, *An Essay on Original Genius; And its Various Modes of Exertion in Philosophy and the Fine Arts, Particularly in Poetry* (London: Printed for Edward and Charles Dilly, 1767).

Duffy, Eamon, *The Stripping of the Altars: Traditional Religion in England, 1400–1580* (New Haven and London: Yale University Press, 1992).

Dugdale, William, *Monasticon Anglicanum; or, The History of the Ancient Abbies, and other Monasteries, Hospitals, Cathedral and Collegiate Churches in England and Wales. With Divers French, Irish, and Scotch Monasteries formerly Relating to England*, 3 vols (London: Printed for Sam Keble, 1693).

Duggett, Tom, *Gothic Romanticism: Architecture, Politics, and Literary Form* (New York: Palgrave Macmillan, 2010).

Duggett, Tom, 'Gothic Forms of Time: Architecture, Romanticism, Medievalism', in *Romantic Gothic: An Edinburgh Companion*, ed. Angela Wright and Dale Townshend (Edinburgh: Edinburgh University Press, 2016), pp. 339-60.

Duncan, Ian, *Modern Romance and the Transformations of the Novel: The Gothic, Scott, Dickens* (Cambridge: Cambridge University Press, 1992).

Duncan, Ian, 'Walter Scott, James Hogg, and Scottish Gothic', in *A New Companion to the Gothic*, ed. David Punter (Oxford: Blackwell, 2012), pp. 123-34.

Dunlop, John, *A History of Fiction: Being a Critical Account of the Most Celebrated Prose Works of Fiction, from the Earliest Greek Romances to the Novels of the Present Age*, 3 vols (London: Longman, Hurst, Rees, Orme, and Brown, 1816).

During, Simon, *Modern Enchantments: The Cultural Power of Secular Magic* (Cambridge, Mass., and London: Harvard University Press, 2002).

Dussinger, John A., 'Middleton, Conyers (1683-1750)', *Oxford Dictionary of National Biography*, http://www.oxforddnb.com/view/article/18669 (accessed 16 March 2017).

Dyer, George, 'On the Use of Topography in Poetry', in *Poetics; or, A Series of Poems, and Disquisitions on Poetry*, 2 vols (London: Printed for J. Johnson and Co., 1812), vol. 2, pp. 112-23.

Eastlake, Charles L., *A History of the Gothic Revival* (London: Longmans, Green, and Co., 1872).

Engravings from the Drawings of the Late Rev. William Warren Porter, Fellow of St. John's College, Oxford (London: Printed by J. Tyler, 1806).

Essays on Gothic Architecture, by the Rev. T. Warton, Rev. J. Bentham, Captain Grose, and the Rev. J. Milner (London: Printed by S. Gosnell for J. Taylor, 1800).

Evans, Joan, *A History of the Society of Antiquaries* (Oxford: Oxford University Press, 1956).

Evelyn, John, trans., *A Parallel of the Ancient Architecture with the Modern in a Collection of Ten Principal Authors who have Written Upon the Five Orders [...]* (London: Printed by Thomas Roycroft for John Place, 1664).

Evelyn, John, *An Account of Architects and Architecture, Together with an Historical, Etymological Explanation of Certain Terms, Particularly Affected by Architects* (London, 1706).

Fairer, David, '*The Faerie Queene* and Eighteenth-century Spenserianism', in *A Companion to Romance: From Classical to Contemporary*, ed. Corinne Saunders (Oxford: Blackwell Publishing, 2007), pp. 197-215.

Farington, Joseph, *The Diary of Joseph Farington: Vol. III, September 1796-December 1798*, ed. Kenneth Garlick and Angus Macintyre (London and New Haven: Yale University Press, 1979).

Fay, Elizabeth, *Romantic Medievalism: History and the Romantic Literary Ideal* (Basingstoke: Palgrave Macmillan, 2002).

Fenn, Ellenor, *The Female Guardian* (London: Printed and Sold by John Marshall and Co., 1784).

Fermanis, Porscha, and John Regan, eds, *Rethinking British Romantic History, 1770-1845* (Oxford: Oxford University Press, 2014).

Ferrar, John, *A Tour from Dublin to London, in 1795* (Dublin, 1796).

Ferrey, Benjamin, *Answer, to 'Thoughts on Rebuilding the Houses of Parliament* (London: John Weale, 1835).

Ferris, Ina, 'Scott's Authorship and Book Culture', in *The Edinburgh Companion to Sir Walter Scott*, ed. Fiona Robertson (Edinburgh: Edinburgh University Press, 2012), pp. 9-21.

Ferris, Ina, 'Unhinging the Past: Joseph Strutt and the Antiquarian Poetics of the Piece', in *Romantic Antiquarianism*, ed. Noah Heringman and Crystal B. Lake, *Romantic Circles Praxis* (June 2014): http://www.rc.umd.edu/praxis/antiquarianism/praxis.antiquarianism. 2014.ferris.html (accessed 18 January 2018).

Ferry, Kathryn, *Lacock, Wiltshire* (Swindon: The National Trust, 2013).

Fletcher, Loraine, 'Charlotte Smith's Emblematic Castles', *Critical Survey* vol. 4, no. 1 (1992): pp. 3–8.

Fothergill, Brian, *Beckford of Fonthill* (London: Faber & Faber, 1979).

Fosbroke, Thomas Dudley, *The Economy of Monastic Life: A Poem* (Gloucester: Printed by R. Raikes, and Sold by R. Faulder, 1795?).

Fosbrooke, Thomas Dudley, *British Monachism; or, Manners and Customs of the Monks and Nuns of England*, 2nd edn (London: Printed by and for John Nichols, Son, and Bentley, 1817).

Foxe, John, *Actes and Monuments of these Latter and Perilous Dayes* (London: Printed by John Day, 1563).

Frank, Frederick S., ed., *The Castle of Otranto and The Mysterious Mother, A Tragedy* (Peterborough, Ont.: Broadview, 2003).

Frankl, Paul, *The Gothic: Literary Source and Interpretations through Eight Centuries* (Princeton, NJ: Princeton University Press, 1960).

Frederickson, Andrea, 'Parliament's Genius Loci: The Politics of Place after the 1834 Fire', in *The Houses of Parliament: History, Art, Architecture*, ed. David Cannadine, Dorian Church, et al. (London: Merrell Publishers, 2000), pp. 99–111.

Frew, John M., 'Richard Gough, James Wyatt, and Late 18th-Century Preservation', *The Journal of the Society of Architectural Historians* vol. 38, no. 4 (Dec. 1979): pp. 366–74.

Frew, John M., 'Some Observations on James Wyatt's Gothic Style 1790–1797', *The Journal of the Society of Architectural Historians* vol. 41, no. 2 (May 1982): pp. 144–9.

Frew, John, and Carey Wallace, 'Thomas Pitt, Portugal and the Gothic Cult of Batalha', *The Burlington Magazine* vol. 128, no. 1001 (Aug. 1986), pp. 579–85.

Fulford, Tim, *Wordsworth's Poetry, 1815–1845* (Philadelphia: University of Pennsylvania Press, 2019).

Gamer, Michael, *Romanticism and the Gothic: Genre, Reception, and Canon Formation* (Cambridge: Cambridge University Press, 2000).

Gamer, Michael, ed., *The Castle of Otranto* (London: Penguin, 2001).

Garner, Katie, *Romantic Women Writers and Arthurian Legend: The Quest for Knowledge* (London: Palgrave Macmillan, 2017).

Gemmett, Robert J., *William Beckford's Fonthill: Architecture, Landscape and the Arts* (Oxford and Charleston, SC: Fonthill Media Limited, 2016).

Gephardt, Katarina, *The Idea of Europe in British Travel Narratives, 1789–1914* (Farnham: Ashgate, 2014), pp. 48–59.

Gerard, Alexander, *An Essay on Taste [...] With Three Dissertations on the Same Subject by Mr De Voltaire, Mr D'Alembert, Mr De Montesquieu* (London: Printed for A. Millar; Edinburgh: Printed for A. Kincaid and J. Bell, 1759).

Gerard, Alexander, *An Essay on Genius* (London: Printed for W. Strahan; T. Cadell; Edinburgh: W. Creech, 1774).

Germann, Georg, *Gothic Revival in Europe and Britain: Sources, Influences and Ideas*, trans. Gerald Onn (London: Lund Humphries with the Architectural Association, 1972).

Gerrard, Christine, '*The Castle of Indolence* and the Opposition to Walpole', *The Review of English Studies* vol. 41, no. 161 (Feb. 1990): pp. 45–64.

Gerrard, Christine, *The Patriot Opposition to Walpole: Politics, Poetry, and National Myth, 1725-1742* (Oxford: Clarendon Press, 1994).

Gilbert, Sandra M., and Susan Gubar, *The Madwoman in the Attic: The Woman Writer and the Nineteenth-Century Literary Imagination* (New Haven and London: Yale University Press, 1979).

Gilpin, William, *The Lives of John Wickliff; And of the Most Eminent of His Disciplines; Lord Cobham, John Huss, Jerome of Prague, and Zisca* (London: Printed for J. Robson, 1765).

Gilpin, William, *Observations on the River Wye, and Several Parts of South Wales, &c. Relative Chiefly to Picturesque Beauty; Made in the Summer of the Year 1770* (London: Printed for R. Blamire, 1782).

Gilpin, William, *Observations, Relative Chiefly to Picturesque Beauty, Made in the Year 1772, on Several Parts of England; Particularly the Mountains, and Lakes of Cumberland and Westmoreland*, 2 vols (London: Printed for R. Blamire, 1786).

Gilpin, William, *Three Essays: On Picturesque Beauty; On Picturesque Travel; And On Sketching Landscape: To Which is Added A Poem, On Landscape Painting* (London: Printed for R. Blamire, 1792).

Gilpin, William, *Observations on the Western Parts of England, Relative Chiefly to Picturesque Beauty* (London: Printed for T. Cadell Jun. and W. Davies, 1798).

Girouard, Mark, *The Return to Camelot: Chivalry and the English Gentleman* (New Haven and London: Yale University Press, 1981).

Godwin, William, *Life of Geoffrey Chaucer, Early English Poet*, 2nd edn, 4 vols (London: Printed by T. Davison for Richard Phillips, 1804).

Godwin, William, *Caleb Williams; or, Things as They Are*, ed. and introd. Maurice Hindle (London: Penguin Books, 1988).

Godwin, William, *An Enquiry Concerning Political Justice*, ed. Mark Philp (Oxford: Oxford University Press, 2013).

Goldgar, Bertrand A., *Walpole and the Wits: The Relation of Politics to Literature, 1722-1742* (Lincoln and London: University of Nebraska Press, 1972).

Goodall, John, 'The Medieval Palace of Westminster', in *The Houses of Parliament: History, Art, Architecture*, ed. David Cannadine, Dorian Church, et al. (London: Merrell Publishers, 2000), pp. 49-67.

Goodall, John, *The English Castle, 1066-1650* (New Haven and London: Yale University Press, 2011).

Gottlieb, Evan, 'No Place Like Home: From Local to Global (and Back Again) in the Gothic Novel', in *Representing Place in British Literature and Culture, 1660-1830: From Local to Global* (Aldershot: Ashgate, 2013), pp. 85-102.

Gough, Richard, *Anecdotes of British Topography*, 2 vols (London: Printed by W. Richardson and S. Clarke, 1768).

Gough, Richard, *British Topography; or, An Historical Account of What Has Been Done for Illustrating the Topographical Antiquities of Great Britain and Ireland*, 2 vols (London: Printed for T. Payne and Son, and J. Nichols, 1780).

Grafton, Anthony, *The Footnote: A Curious History* (Cambridge, Mass.: Harvard University Press, 1997).

Graves, Michael, 'Foreword', in *The Architectural Capriccio: Memory, Fantasy and Invention*, ed. Lucien Steil (Farnham: Ashgate, 2014), pp. xxxix-l.

Graves, Richard, *The Spiritual Quixote; or, The Summer's Ramble of Mr Geoffry [sic] Wildgoose, A Comic Romance*, 3 vols (London: Printed for J. Dodsley, 1773).

Gray, Thomas, *Thomas Gray's Commonplace Book* (c.1736-71), 3 vols, Pembroke College Library, Cambridge, CB1-3.

368 SELECT BIBLIOGRAPHY

Gray, Thomas, *An Ode on a Distant Prospect of Eton College* (London: Printed for R. Dodsley, 1747).
Gray, Thomas, 'A Long Story', in *Designs by Mr R. Bentley, for Six Poems by Mr T. Gray* (London: Printed for R. Dodsley, 1753), pp. 14–23.
Gray, Thomas, *The Poems of Mr Gray. To Which are Prefixed Memoirs of his Life and Writings by W. Mason, M.A.* (York: Printed by A. Ward, 1775).
Green, Sarah, *Romance Readers and Romance Writers: A Satirical Novel*, 3 vols (London: Printed for T. Hoookham, Jnr and E. T. Hookham, 1810).
Greig, Martin, 'Burnet, Gilbert (1643–1715)', *ODNB*, https://doi-org.ezproxy.mmu.ac.uk/10.1093/ref:odnb/4061 (accessed 13 October 2018).
Grierson, Herbert, ed., *The Letters of Sir Walter Scott*, 12 vols (London: Constable, 1932–7).
Groom, Nick, *The Making of Percy's Reliques* (Oxford: Clarendon Press, 1999).
Groom, Nick, *The Gothic: A Very Short Introduction* (Oxford: Oxford University Press, 2012).
Grose, Francis, *The Antiquities of England and Wales*, new edn, 8 vols (London: Printed for S. Hooper, 1772–6).
Grose, Francis, *A Provincial Glossary, with a Collection of Local Proverbs and Popular Superstitions* (London: Printed for S. Hooper, 1787).
Grose, Francis, *The Antiquities of Scotland*, 2 vols (London: Printed for S. Hooper, 1791).
Grundy, Isobel, 'Anna Letitia Barbauld: A Unitarian Poetics?', in *Anna Letitia Barbauld: New Perspectives*, ed. William McCarthy and Olivia Murphy (Lewisburg: Bucknell University Press, 2014), pp. 59–81.
Guillery, Peter, and Michael Snodin, 'Strawberry Hill: Building and Site', *Architectural History* 38 (1995): pp. 102–28.
Guydickens, Frederick William, *An Answer to Mr Horace Walpole's Late Work, Entitled Historic Doubts on the Reign and Life of King Richard the Third; Or, An Attempt to Confute Him from His Own Arguments* (London: Printed for B. White, 1768).
Haggerty, George E., 'Strawberry Hill: Friendship and Taste', in *Horace Walpole's Strawberry Hill*, ed. Michael Snodin with the assistance of Cynthia Roman (New Haven and London: Yale University Press, 2009), pp. 75–85.
Hakewill, Arthur William, *Thoughts Upon the Style of Architecture to be Adopted in Rebuilding the Houses of Parliament* (London: John Weale, 1835).
Hall, Michael, 'Introduction', in *Gothic Architecture and its Meanings, 1550–1830*, ed. M. Hall (Reading: Spire Books, 2002), pp. 7–24.
Halmi, Nicholas, 'Ruins Without a Past', *Essays in Romanticism* vol. 18 (2011): pp. 7–27.
Hamilton, Paul, *Coleridge and German Philosophy: The Poet in the Land of Logic* (London: Bloomsbury, 2007).
Hamilton, William Richard, *Letter from W. R. Hamilton, To the Earl of Elgin, on the New Houses of Parliament*, 2nd edn (London: John Weale, 1836).
Hamilton, William Richard, *Second Letter from W. R. Hamilton, Esq. To the Earl of Elgin, on the Propriety of Adopting the Greek Style of Architecture in the Construction of the New Houses of Parliament* (London: John Weale, 1836).
Hamilton, William Richard, *Third Letter from W. R. Hamilton, Esq. To The Earl of Elgin, on the Propriety of Adopting the Greek Style of Architecture in Preference to the Gothic, in the Construction of the New Houses of Parliament* (London: John Weale, 1837).
Hamley, Edward, *Sonnets* (London: G. G. J. and J. Robinson, 1789).
Hamley, Edward, *Poems of Various Kinds* (London: Printed by J. W. Myers for T. Cadell and W. Davies, 1795).

Hammond, P. W., 'Introduction', in *Historic Doubts on the Life and Reign of Richard the Third, Including the Supplement, Reply, Short Observations and Postscript*, by Horace Walpole, ed. P. W. Hammond (Gloucester: Alan Sutton, 1987), pp. vii–xxiii.
Harley, Mrs M., *The Castle of Mowbray, An English Romance* (London: Printed for C. Stalker and H. Setchell, 1788).
Harney, Marion, *Place-making for the Imagination: Horace Walpole and Strawberry Hill* (Farnham: Ashgate, 2013).
Harney, Marion, 'The visualisation of Strawberry Hill: A collusion of history and imagination', *Image [&] Narrative* vol. 18, no 3 (2017): pp. 30–45.
Harrington, Kevin, *Changing Ideas on Architecture in the Encyclopédie, 1750–1776* (Ann Arbor, MI: UMI Research Press, 1985).
Harrison, Rodney, *Heritage: Critical Approaches* (Abingdon: Routledge, 2013).
Hart, Vaughan, *Sir John Vanbrugh: Storyteller in Stone* (New Haven and London: Yale University Press, 2008).
Hart, Vaughan, and Peter Hicks, *Palladio's Rome: A Translation of Andrea Palladio's Two Guidebooks to Rome* (New Haven and London: Yale University Press, 2009).
Harvey, Jane, *The Castle of Tynemouth. A Tale*, 2 vols (London: Printed for Longman, Hurst, Rees, & Orme; and Vernor, Hood, and Sharp, 1806).
Harvey, Jane, *Brougham Castle: A Novel*, 2 vols (London: Printed at the Minerva Press for A. K. Newman and Co., 1816).
Haydon, Colin, *Anti-Catholicism in Eighteenth-Century England, c. 1714–80: A Political and Social Study* (Manchester and New York: Manchester University Press, 1993).
Hazen, A. T., *A Bibliography of Horace Walpole* (New Haven: Yale University Press, 1948).
Hazen, Allen T., *A Catalogue of Horace Walpole's Library. With Horace Walpole's Library by Wilmarth Sheldon Lewis*, 3 vols (New Haven and London: Yale University Press, 1969).
Hazlitt, William, *Lectures on the English Comic Writers* (London: Printed for Taylor and Hessey, 1819).
Headley, Gwyn, and Wim Meulenkamp, *Follies: A National Trust Guide* (London: Jonathan Cape, 1986).
Heringman, Noah, *Sciences of Antiquity: Romantic Antiquarianism, Natural History, and Knowledge Work* (Oxford: Oxford University Press, 2013).
Hill, Rosemary, '"Ivi'd ruins of forlorn Grace Dieu": Catholics, Romantics and late Georgian Gothic', in *Gothic Architecture and its Meanings, 1550–1830*, ed. Michael Hall (Reading: Spire Books Ltd in association with the Georgian Group, 2002), pp. 159–84.
Hill, Rosemary, 'Ruskin and Pugin', in *Ruskin & Architecture*, ed. Rebecca Daniels and Geoff Brandwood (Reading: Spire Books, 2003), pp. 223–45.
Hill, Rosemary, *God's Architect: Pugin and the Building of Romantic Britain* (London: Penguin Books, 2008).
Hobbes, Thomas, 'The Answer of Mr Hobbes to Sir Will. D'Avenant's Preface Before Gondibert', in *The Preface to Gondibert, An Heroic Poem* (Paris: Chez Matthieu Guillemot, 1650), pp. 129–64.
Hoeveler, Diane Long, *The Gothic Ideology: Religious Hysteria and Anti-Catholicism in British Popular Fiction, 1780–1880* (Cardiff: University of Wales Press, 2014).
Hoeveler, Diane Long, 'The Heroine, the Abbey and Popular Romantic Textuality', in *Ann Radcliffe, Romanticism and the Gothic*, ed. Dale Townshend and Angela Wright (Cambridge: Cambridge University Press, 2014), pp. 100–16.
Hogle, Jerrold E., 'The Restless Labyrinth: Cryptonomy in the Gothic Novel', *Arizona Quarterly* no. 36 (1980): pp. 330–58.

Home, Henry Lord Kames, *Elements of Criticism*, 3 vols (London: Printed for A. Millar; Edinburgh: A. Kincaid and J. Bell, 1762).

Home, John, *Douglas. A Tragedy. By Mr Home. Marked with the Variations in the Manager's Book, at the Theatre Royal in Covent Garden* (London: Printed for T. Lowndes, T. Nicholl, and S. Bladon, 1784).

Hudson, Anne, *The Premature Reformation: Wycliffite Texts and Lollard History* (Oxford: Clarendon Press, 1988).

Hughes, John, ed.,*The Works of Mr Edmund Spenser*, 6 vols (London: Printed for Jacob Tonson, 1715).

Hughes, William, David Punter, and Andrew Smith, eds, *The Encyclopedia of the Gothic*, 2 vols (Oxford: Wiley-Blackwell, 2013).

Hume, David, *A Treatise of Human Nature: Being an Attempt to Introduce the Experimental Method of Reasoning into Moral Subjects*, 3 vols (London: Printed for John Noon, 1739-40).

Hume, David, *The History of England from the Invasion of Julius Caesar to the Revolution in 1688*, foreword by William B. Todd, 6 vols (Indianapolis: Liberty Fund, 1983).

Hunt, John Dixon, 'Folly in the Garden', *The Hopkins Review* vol. 1, no. 2 (spring 2008): pp. 272-62.

Hunt, Leigh, *A Book for a Corner; or, Selections in Prose and Verse from Authors the Best Suited to that Mode of Enjoyment* (London: Chapman & Hall, 1849).

Hurd, Richard, *Moral and Political Dialogues: Being the Substance of Several Conversations Between Divers Eminent Persons of the Past and Present Age* (London: Printed for A. Millar, W. Thurlbourne, and J. Woodyer, 1759).

Hurd, Richard, *Letters on Chivalry and Romance* (London: Printed for A. Millar; Cambridge: Printed for W. Thurlbourn and J. Woodyer, 1762).

Hutcheson, Francis, *An Essay on the Nature and Conduct of the Passions and Affections. With Illustrations on the Moral Sense*, 2nd edn (London: Printed for James and John Knapton and John Crownfield et al., 1730).

Hutchinson, William, *The Hermitage: A British Story* (York: Printed by C. Etherington, for the Author, 1771).

Hutchinson, William, *An Excursion to the Lakes in Westmoreland and Cumberland; With a Tour Through Part of the Northern Counties in the Years 1773 and 1774*, 2nd edn (London: Printed for J. Wilkie, 1776).

Iddon, John, *Strawberry Hill & Horace Walpole: Essential Guide* (London: Scala, 2011).

'Introduction: Containing an Historical Account of the Origins and Establishment of the Society of Antiquaries', *Archaeologia*, vol. 1 (1770): pp. i–xliii.

Jackson, J. R.,*Observations on A Letter from W. R. Hamilton, ESQ. To the Earl of Elgin, on the New Houses of Parliament* (London: John Weale, Architectural Library, 1837).

Jacob, Hildebrand, *Of the Sister Arts; An Essay* (London: Printed for William Lewis, 1734).

Jacobs, Edward H., *Accidental Migrations: An Archaeology of Gothic Discourse* (Lewisburg: Bucknell University Press; London: Associated University Presses, 2000).

Jephson, Robert, *The Count of Narbonne. A Tragedy. As it is Acted at the Theatre Royal in Covent Garden* (London: Printed for T. Cadell, 1781).

Jerningham, Edward, *An Elegy Written Among the Ruins of an Abbey*, 2nd edn (London: Printed for J. Dodsley, 1765).

Jestin, Loftus, *The Answer to the Lyre: Richard Bentley's Illustrations from Thomas Gray's Poems* (Philadelphia: University of Pennsylvania Press, 1990).

Johnson, Claudia L., *Equivocal Beings: Politics, Gender, and Sentimentality in the 1790s* (Chicago and London: University of Chicago Press, 1995).

Johnson, Samuel, *A Dictionary of the English Language*, 2 vols (London: Printed by W. Strahan for J. and P. Knapton, and T. and T. Longman; C. Hitch and L. Hawes; A Millar; and R. J. Dodsley, 1755-6).

Johnson, Samuel, *The Lives of the Most Eminent English Poets; With Critical Observations on their Works*, 2nd edn, 4 vols (London: Printed for C. Bathurst et al., 1783).

Johnston, Arthur, *Enchanted Ground: The Study of Medieval Romance in the Eighteenth Century* (London: The Athlone Press, 1964).

Jones, Barbara, *Follies & Grottoes*, 2nd edn (London: Constable and Co., 1974).

Jones, David Annwn, *Gothic Effigy: A Guide to Dark Visibilities* (Manchester: Manchester University Press, 2018).

Jones, Vivien, '"The coquetry of nature": Politics and the Picturesque in Women's Fiction', in *The Politics of the Picturesque: Literature, Landscape and Aesthetics Since 1770*, ed. Stephen Copley and Peter Garside (Cambridge: Cambridge University Press, 1994), pp. 120-44.

Jung, C. G., *Contributions to Analytical Psychology*, trans. H. G. and Cary F. Baynes (New York: Harcourt Brace, 1928).

Kahane, Claire, 'Gothic Mirrors and Feminine Identity', *The Centennial Review* vol. 24, no. 1 (winter 1980): pp. 43-64.

Kalter, Barrett, 'DIY Gothic: Thomas Gray and the Medieval Revival', *ELH* vol. 70, no. 4 (winter 2003): pp. 989-1019.

Kalter, Barrett, *Modern Antiques: The Material Past in England, 1660-1780* (Lewisburg: Bucknell University Press, 2012).

Karatani, Kojin, *Architecture as Metaphor: Language, Number, Money*, trans. Sabo Kohso and ed. Michael Speaks (Cambridge, Mass.: MIT Press, 1995).

Kaul, Suvir, *Poems of Nation, Anthems of Empire: English Verse in the Long Eighteenth Century* (Charlottesville and London: University Press of Virginia, 2000).

Keats, John, *John Keats: Complete Poems*, ed. Jack Stillinger (Cambridge, MA, and London: Harvard University Press, 1982).

Kelly, Gary, *English Fiction of the Romantic Period, 1789-1830* (London and New York: Longman, 1989).

Kennedy, Deborah, 'The Ruined Abbey in the Eighteenth Century', *Philological Quarterly* vol. 80, no. 4 (Fall 2001): pp. 503-20.

Ketton-Cremer, R. W., *Horace Walpole, A Biography*, 3rd edn (Northampton: John Dickens & Co. Ltd, 1964).

King, Edward, *Observations on Ancient Castles* (London: Printed by John Nichols, 1782).

Klein, Lawrence E., 'Joseph Addison's Whiggism', in *'Cultures of Whiggism': New Essays on English Literature and Culture in the Long Eighteenth Century*, ed. David Womersley, assisted by Paddy Bullard and Abigail Williams (Newark: University of Delaware Press, 2005), pp. 108-26.

Kliger, Samuel, *The Goths in England: A Study in Seventeenth and Eighteenth Century Thought* (Cambridge, Mass.: Harvard University Press, 1952).

Kostof, Spiro, ed., *The Architect: Chapters in the History of the Profession* (New York: Oxford University Press, 1977).

Kramnick, Isaac, *Bolingbroke and His Circle: The Politics of Nostalgia in the Age of Walpole* (Cambridge, Mass.: Harvard University Press, 1968).

Labbe, Jacqueline M., 'Introduction', in *The Old Manor House*, by Charlotte Smith, ed. J. M. Labbe (Peterborough, ON: Broadview Press, 2002), pp. 9-29.

Lamont, Claire, 'Domestic Architecture', in *Jane Austen in Context*, ed. Janet Todd (Cambridge: Cambridge University Press, 2005), pp. 225-33.

Lang, S., 'The Principles of the Gothic Revival in England', *Journal of the Society of Architectural Historians* vol. 25, no. 4 (Dec. 1966): pp. 240–67.

Langley, Batty, and Thomas Langley, *Ancient Architecture, Restored and Improved, by a Great Variety of Grand and Usefull Designs, Entirely New, in the Gothick Mode for the Ornamenting of Buildings and Gardens* (London, 1742).

Lee, Harriet, 'Kruitzner; or, The German's Tale', in *Canterbury Tales, Volume the Fourth*, by Harriet Lee (London: Printed for G. and J. Robinson, 1801), pp. 3–368.

L. E. L. [Letitia Elizabeth Landon], 'Furness Abbey, In the Vale of Nightshade, Lancashire', in *Fisher's Drawing Room Scrap-Book, with Poetical Illustrations by L. E. L.* (London: Fisher, Son, and Jackson, 1832), p. 18.

L. E. L. [Letitia Elizabeth Landon], 'Chapter-House, Furness Abbey', in *Fisher's Drawing Room Scrap Book; With Poetical Illustrations by L. E. L.* (London: H. Fisher, R. Fisher, & P. Jackson, 1835), pp. 49–50.

Leland, Thomas, *Longsword, Earl of Salisbury: An Historical Romance*, 2 vols (London: Printed for W. Johnston, 1762).

Letters of Abelard and Heloise. To which is Prefix'd A Particular Account of their Lives, Amours, and Misfortunes, Extracted Chiefly from Monsieur Bayle. Translated from the French (London: Printed for J. Watts, 1713).

Levey, Michael, '"The Enchanted Castle" by Claude: Subject, Significance and Interpretation', *The Burlington Magazine* vol. 130, no. 1028 (Nov. 1988), pp. 812–20.

Levine, William, 'Collins, Thomson, and the Whig Progress of Liberty', *Studies in English Literature, 1500–1900* vol. 34, no. 3 (summer 1994): pp. 553–77.

Lewis, Matthew Gregory, *The Castle Spectre: A Drama* (London: Printed for J. Bell, 1798).

Lewis, Matthew, *The Monk, A Romance*, ed. D. L. Macdonald and Kathleen Scherf (Peterborough, ON: Broadview Press, 2004).

Lewis, Michael J., *The Gothic Revival* (London: Thames & Hudson, 2002).

Lewis, W. S., ed., *A Note Book of Horace Walpole* (New York: William Edwin Rudge, 1927), Lewis Walpole Library, 575 927 3 Copy 1.

Lewis, W. S., 'The Genesis of Strawberry Hill', *Metropolitan Museum Studies* vol. 5, no. 1 (Aug. 1934): pp. 57–92.

Lewis, W. S., ed., *The Yale Edition of Horace Walpole's Correspondence*, 48 vols (New Haven: Yale University Press, 1937–83).

Lewis, Wilmarth S., 'Horace Walpole, Antiquary', in *Essays Presented to Sir Lewis Namier*, ed. Richard Pares and A. J. P. Taylor (London: Macmillan, 1956), pp. 178–203.

Lewis, W. S., 'Introduction', in *The Castle of Otranto, A Gothic Story*, by Horace Walpole, ed. and introd. W. S. Lewis (London: Oxford University Press, 1964), pp. vii–xvi.

Lewis, Wilmarth Sheldon, *One Man's Education* (New York: Alfred A. Knopf, 1968).

Lewis, Wilmarth S., *Rescuing Horace Walpole* (New Haven and London: Yale University Press, 1978).

Liddell, Henry, *The Wizard of the North; The Vampire Bride; and Other Poems* (Edinburgh: William Blackwood; London: T. Cadell, 1833).

Lindfield, Peter N., *Georgian Gothic: Medievalist Architecture, Furniture and Interiors, 1730–1840* (Woodbridge: Boydell Press, 2016).

Lindfield, Peter N., 'Heraldry and the Architectural Imagination: John Carter's Visualisation of *The Castle of Otranto*', *The Antiquaries Journal* vol. 96 (2016): pp. 291–313.

Lindfield, Peter N., 'Imagining the Undefined Castle in *The Castle of Otranto*: Engravings and Interpretations', *Image [&] Narrative* vol. 18, no. 3 (2017): pp. 45–62.

Lindfield, Peter N., and Dale Townshend, 'Reading *Vathek* and Fonthill Abbey: William Beckford's Architectural Imagination', in *Fonthill Recovered: A Cultural History*, ed. Caroline Dakers (London: UCL Press, 2018), pp. 284–301.

Locke, John, *Some Thoughts Concerning Education*, 5th enlarged edn (London: Printed for A. and J. Churchill, 1705).

Locke, John, *An Essay Concerning Humane Understanding. In Four Books* (London: Printed for Awnsham and John Churchill; and Samuel Manship, 1706).

Lockhart, John Gibson, *Memoirs of the Life of Sir Walter Scott, Bart.*, 7 vols (Edinburgh: Robert Cadell; London: John Murray and Whittaker and Co., 1837–8).

Longueil, Alfred E., 'The Word "Gothic" in Eighteenth Century Criticism', *Modern Language Notes* 38, no. 8 (Dec. 1923): pp. 453–60.

Looser, Devoney, *British Women Writers and the Writing of History, 1670–1820* (Baltimore and London: Johns Hopkins University Press, 2000).

Lowenthal, David, *The Past is a Foreign Country, Revisited* (Cambridge: Cambridge University Press, 2015).

Lukacher, Brian, *Joseph Gandy: An Architectural Visionary in Georgian England* (New York: Thames & Hudson Inc., 2006).

Lukács, Georg, *The Historical Novel*, trans. Hannah and Stanley Mitchell (Harmondsworth: Penguin, 1976).

Lüsebrink, Hans-Jürgen, and Rolf Reichardt, *The Bastille: A History of a Symbol of Despotism and Freedom*, trans. Norbert Schürer (Durham and London: Duke University Press, 1997).

Lydenberg, Robin, 'Gothic Architecture and Fiction: A Survey of Critical Responses', *The Centennial Review* vol. 22 (1978): pp. 95–109.

Macaulay, Catharine, *Observations on the Reflections of the Right Hon. Edmund Burke, on the Revolution in France, in a Letter to the Right Hon. The Earl of Stanhope* (London: Printed for C. Dilly, 1790).

McCarthy, Michael, 'Sir Roger Newdigate: Drawings for Copt Hall, Essex, and Arbury Hall, Warwickshire', *Architectural History* vol. 16 (1973): pp. 26–88.

McCarthy, Michael, *The Origins of the Gothic Revival* (New Haven and London: Yale University Press, 1987).

McEvoy, Emma, *Gothic Tourism* (Basingstoke: Palgrave Macmillan, 2016).

McIntyre, Clara, *Ann Radcliffe in Relation to her Time* (New Haven and London: Yale University Press, 1920).

McIntyre, Clara F., 'Were the "Gothic Novels" Gothic?', *PMLA* vol. 36, no. 4 (Dec. 1921): pp. 644–67.

Mack, Ruth, *Literary Historicity: Literature and Historical Experience in Eighteenth- Century Britain* (Stanford: Stanford University Press, 2009).

Mack, Ruth, 'Paper Castle, Paper Collection: Walpole's Extra-Illustrated Copy of the Description of Strawberry Hill', in *Horace Walpole's Strawberry Hill*, ed. Michael Snodin with the assistance of Cynthia Roman (New Haven and London: Yale University Press, 2009), pp. 107–15.

McMillan, Dorothy, 'The Secrets of Ann Radcliffe's English Travels', in *Romantic Geographies: Discourses of Travel, 1775–1844*, ed. Amanda Gilroy (Manchester: Manchester University Press, 2000), pp. 51–67.

Madoff, Mark, 'The Useful Myth of Gothic Ancestry', *Studies in Eighteenth-Century Culture* vol. 8 (1979): pp. 337–50.

Magna Carta, with a new Commentary by David Carpenter (London: Penguin Books, 2015).

Maitland, S. R., *The Dark Ages; A Series of Essays, Intended to Illustrate the State of Religion and Literature in the Ninth, Tenth, Eleventh, and Twelfth Centuries* (London: Printed for J. G. F. & J. Rivington, 1844).

Malone, Edmond, ed., *The Plays and Poems of William Shakespeare*, 10 vols (London: Printed by H. Baldwin for J. Rivington and Sons, L. Davis, B. White and Son, T. Longman, S. Law, et al., 1790).

Mancoff, Debra N., 'Myth and Monarchy: Chivalric Legends for the Victorian Age', in *The Houses of Parliament: History, Art, Architecture*, ed. David Cannadine, Dorian Church, et al. (London: Merrell Publishers, 2000), pp. 241–51.

Manners, George, *Edgar; or, Caledonian Feuds. A Tragedy* (London: Printed for Tipper and Richards, 1806).

Manning, Susan, 'Walter Scott, Antiquarianism and the Political Discourse of the *Edinburgh Review*, 1802–11', in *British Romanticism and the Edinburgh Review: Bicentenary Essays*, ed. Massimiliano Demata and Duncan Wu (Houndmills: Palgrave Macmillan, 2002), pp. 102–23.

Manning, Susan, 'Antiquarianism, the Scottish Science of Man, and the Emergence of Modern Disciplinarity', in *Scotland and the Borders of Romanticism*, ed. Leith Davis, Ian Duncan, and Janet Sorensen (Cambridge: Cambridge University Press, 2004), pp. 57–76.

Mant, Richard, *The Poetical Works of the Late Thomas Warton, BD, Volume I*, 5th edn (Oxford: Printed at the University Press, for W. Hanwell and J. Parker; London: F. and C. Rivington, 1802).

Masters, Robert, *Some Remarks on Mr Walpole's Historic Doubts on the Life and Reign of King Richard the Third* (London: Printed by W. Bowyer and J. Nichols, 1772).

Mathews, Anne Jackson, *Memoirs of Charles Mathews, Comedian*, 4 vols (London: Richard Bentley, 1838–9).

Mathias, Thomas James, *The Pursuits of Literature: A Satirical Poem in Four Dialogues. With Notes*, 8th edn (London: Printed for T. Becket, 1798).

Mathison, Hamish, and Angela Wright, 'The Haunting of Britain's Ruins', in *Writing Britain's Ruins*, ed. Michael Carter, Peter N. Lindfield, and Dale Townshend (London: British Library, 2017), pp. 210–28.

Matthews, Carol, 'Architecture in Blackstone's Life and *Commentaries*', in *Blackstone and his Commentaries*, ed. Wilfrid Prest (Oxford and Portland, OR: Hart Press, 2009), pp. 15–34.

Matthews, David, 'From Mediaeval to Medievalism: A New Semantic History', *The Review of English Studies* vol. 62, no. 257 (Nov. 2011): pp. 695–715.

Matthews, David, *Medievalism: A Critical History* (Cambridge: D. S. Brewer, 2015).

Maturin, Charles, *Melmoth the Wanderer*, ed. Douglas Grant, introd. Chris Baldick (Oxford: Oxford University Press, 1989).

Maxwell, Richard, *The Historical Novel in Europe, 1650–1950* (Cambridge: Cambridge University Press, 2009).

Mayernick, David, 'Meaning and Purpose of the *Capriccio*', in *The Architectural Capriccio: Memory, Fantasy and Invention*, ed. Lucien Steil (Farnham: Ashgate, 2014), pp. 5–16.

Maynard, Luke R. J., 'A Forgotten Enchantment: The Silenced Princess, the Andalusian Warlord, and the Rescued Conclusion of "Sir Bertrand"', *Eighteenth-Century Fiction* vol. 23, no. 1 (Fall 2010): pp. 141–62.

Meehan, Michael, *Liberty and Poetics in Eighteenth-Century England* (London and Sydney: Croom Helm, 1986).

Melville, Lewis, *The Life and Letters of William Beckford of Fonthill* (London: William Heinemann, 1910).

Michasiw, Kim Ian, 'Nine Revisionist Theses on the Picturesque', *Representations* no. 38 (spring 1992): pp. 76-100.

Middleton, Conyers, *A Letter from Rome, Showing an Exact Conformity between Popery and Paganism; or, The Religion of the Present Romans to be Derived Entirely from that of Their Heathen Ancestors* (London: Printed for W. Innys, 1729).

Middleton, Conyers, *The History of the Life of M. Tullius Cicero*, 3 vols (London: Printed for W. Innys and R. Manby, 1741).

Middleton, Robin, 'Chambers, W. "A Treatise on Civil Architecture", London 1759', in *Sir William Chambers*, ed. Michael Snodin (London: V&A Publications, 1996), pp. 68-76.

Milbank, Alison, 'Introduction', in *A Sicilian Romance* by Ann Radcliffe, ed. A. Milbank (Oxford: Oxford University Press, 1993), pp. viii-xxviii.

Milbank, Alison, 'Introduction', in *The Castles of Athlin and Dunbayne* by Ann Radcliffe, ed. A. Milbank (Oxford: Oxford University Press, 1995), pp. vii-xxiv.

Milbank, Alison, 'Ways of Seeing in Ann Radcliffe's Early Fiction: *The Castles of Athlin and Dunbayne* (1789) and *A Sicilian Romance* (1790)', in *Ann Radcliffe, Romanticism and the Gothic*, ed. Dale Townshend and Angela Wright (Cambridge: Cambridge University Press, 2014), pp. 85-99.

Milbank, Alison, *God and the Gothic: Religion, Romance, and Reality in the English Literary Tradition* (Oxford: Oxford University Press, 2018).

Miles, Robert, *Gothic Writing, 1750-1820: A Genealogy* (London: Routledge, 1993).

Miles, Robert, *Ann Radcliffe: The Great Enchantress* (Manchester: Manchester University Press, 1995).

Mill, John Stuart, *The Collected Works of John Stuart Mill, Volume XXII: Newspaper Writings December 1822-July 1831 Part I*, ed. Ann P. Robson and John M. Robson, introd. A. P. Robson and J. M. Robson (Toronto: University of Toronto Press; London: Routledge & Kegan Paul, 1986).

Milner, John, *A Dissertation on the Modern Style of Altering Antient Cathedrals, As Exemplified in the Cathedral of Salisbury* (London: Printed by and For J. Nichols, 1798).

Milner, John, *The History Civil and Ecclesiastical, & Survey of the Antiquities, of Winchester*, 2 vols (Winchester: Printed and Sold by Jas. Robbins, 1798-1801).

Milner, John, *An Inquiry into Certain Vulgar Opinions Concerning the Catholic Inhabitants and the Antiquities of Ireland* (London: Printed and Published by Keating, Brown, and Co., 1808).

Milton, John, *Paradise Lost*, ed. Alastair Fowler (London and New York: Longman, 1971).

The Modern Goth. [A Satire in Verse on Sir John Soane. By-Norris] (London, 1788).

Molesworth, Robert, *An Account of Denmark, With Francogallia and Some Considerations for the Promoting of Agriculture and Employing the Poor*, ed. and introd. Justin Champion (Indianapolis: Liberty Fund, 2011), p. 174.

Mommsen, Theodore E., 'Petrarch's Conception of the "Dark Ages"', *Speculum* vol. 7, no. 2 (Apr. 1942): pp. 226-42.

Montague, Edward, *The Castle of Berry Pomeroy*, 2 vols (London: Printed at the Minerva Press for Lane, Newman, and Co., 1806).

Moore, Roger E., *Jane Austen and the Reformation: Remembering the Sacred Landscape* (Abingdon and New York: Routledge, 2016).

More, Hannah, *Village Politics. Addressed to all the Mechanics, Journeymen, and Day Labourers, in Great Britain*, 2nd edn (London: Printed for and Sold by F. and C. Rivington, 1792).

Morrissey, Lee, *From the Temple to the Castle: An Architectural History of British Literature, 1660-1760* (Charlottesville and London: University Press of Virginia, 1999).

Moutray, Tonya, 'Remodeling Catholic Ruins in William Wordsworth's Poetry', *European Romantic Review* vol. 22, no. 6 (Dec. 2011): pp. 819–31.
Mowl, Timothy, *Horace Walpole, the Great Outsider* (London: John Murray, 1996).
Mullett, Michael, *Catholics in Britain and Ireland, 1558–1829* (London: Macmillan, 1988).
Myrone, Martin and Lucy Peltz, eds, *Producing the Past: Aspects of Antiquarian Culture and Practice, 1700–1850* (Aldershot: Ashgate, 1999).
Nasmyth, James, *James Nasmyth, Engineer: An Autobiography*, ed. Samuel Smiles (London: John Murray, 1883).
Nichols, John, *The Progresses, and Public Processions, of Queen Elizabeth*, 2 vols (London: Printed by and for the Editor, 1788).
Norman, E. R., *Anti-Catholicism in Victorian England* (London: Allen & Unwin, 1968).
Norton, Rictor, *Mistress of Udolpho: The Life of Ann Radcliffe* (London: Leicester University Press, 1999).
Norton, Rictor, ed., *Gothic Readings: The First Wave, 1764–1840* (London: Leicester University Press, 2000).
Norton, Rictor, 'Ann Radcliffe, The Shakespeare of Romance Writers', in *Shakespearean Gothic*, ed. Christy Desmet and Anne Williams (Cardiff: University of Wales Press, 2009), pp. 37–59.
O'Brien, Karen, *Narratives of Enlightenment: Cosmopolitan History from Voltaire to Gibbon* (Cambridge: Cambridge University Press, 1997).
Otto, Peter, '"Where am I, and what?" – Architecture, Environment, and the Transformation of Experience in Radcliffe's *The Mysteries of Udolpho*', *European Romantic Review* vol. 25, no. 3 (2014): pp. 299–308.
Oxford Dictionary of National Biography (Oxford: Oxford University Press, 2018).
Oxford English Dictionary (Oxford: Oxford University Press, 2018).
Paine, Thomas, *Rights of Man: Being an Answer to Mr Burke's Attack on the French Revolution* (London: Printed for J. Johnson, 1791).
Palin, William, 'J. M. Gandy's Composite Views for John Soane', in *The Architectural Capriccio: Memory, Fantasy and Invention*, ed. Lucien Steil (Farnham: Ashgate, 2014), pp. 99–115.
Parris, Leslie, *The Loyd Collection of Paintings and Drawings at Betterton House, Lockinge near Wantage, Berkshire* (London: Bradbury Agnew Press, 1967), pp. 7–10.
Patten, Bridget, *Catholicism and the Gothic Revival: John Milner and St Peter's Chapel, Winchester* (Hampshire Papers Committee, 2001).
Peacock, Thomas Love, 'Crotchet Castle', in *Novels of Thomas Love Peacock*, introd. J. B. Priestley and notes by Barbara Lloyd Evans (London: Pan Books, 1967), pp. 257–359.
Peacock, Thomas Love, *Nightmare Abbey*, ed. Lisa Vargo (Peterborough, ON: Broadview, 2007).
Pearce, Susan, ed., *Visions of Antiquity: The Society of Antiquaries of London, 1707–2007* (London: The Society of Antiquaries of London, 2007).
Peardon, Thomas Preston, *The Transition in English Historical Writing, 1760–1830* (New York: Columbia University Press, 1933).
Penny, Andrew D.,'Maitland, Samuel Roffey (1792–1866)', *Oxford Dictionary of National Biography* (Oxford: Oxford University Press, 2004), http://www.oxforddnb.com/view/article/17834 (accessed 24 July 2017).
Perovic, Sonja, 'Lyricist in Britain; Empiricist in France: Volney's Divided Legacy', in *Historical Writing in Britain, 1688–1830: Visions of History*, ed. Ben Dew and Fiona Price (Houndmills: Palgrave Macmillan, 2014), pp. 127–44.

SELECT BIBLIOGRAPHY 377

Pevsner, Nikolaus, 'The Architectural Setting of Jane Austen's Novels', *Journal of the Warburg and Courtauld Institutes* vol. 31 (1968): pp. 404–22.

Pevsner, Nikolaus, 'Walpole and Essex', in *Some Architectural Writers of the Nineteenth Century*, by N. Pevsner (Oxford: Clarendon Press, 1972), pp. 1–8.

Phillips, Mark Salber, *Society and Sentiment: Genres of Historical Writing in Britain, 1740–1820* (Princeton, NJ: Princeton University Press, 2000).

Pickles, John D., 'Cole, William (1714–1782)', *Oxford Dictionary of National Biography*, http://www.oxforddnb.com/view/article/5863 (accessed 23 March 2017).

Piggott, Stuart, *Ruins in a Landscape: Essays in Antiquarianism* (Edinburgh: Edinburgh University Press, 1976).

Piozzi, Hester Lynch, *Observations and Reflections Made in the Course of a Journey through France, Italy, and Germany*, 2 vols (London: Printed for A. Strahan and T. Cadell, 1789).

Pocock, J. G. A., *The Ancient Constitution and the Feudal Law: A Study of English Historical Thought in the Seventeenth Century, A Reissue with a Retrospect* (Cambridge: Cambridge University Press, 1987).

Pope, Alexander, ed., *The Works of Shakespear*, 6 vols (London: Printed for Jacob Tonson, 1725).

Pope, Alexander, *The Works of Alexander Pope, Esq* (London: Printed for Henry Lintot, 1743), pp. 175–90, LWL, 49 2453.

Pope, Alexander, *The Dunciad*, ed. James Sutherland, The Twickenham Edition of the Poems of Alexander Pope, Vol. V (London and New York, Routledge, 1963).

Pope, Alexander, 'An Essay on Criticism', in *Pastoral Poetry and An Essay on Criticism*, ed. E. Audra and Aubrey Williams, The Twickenham Edition of the Poems of Alexander Pope, Vol. I (London and New York: Routledge, 1993), pp. 195–326.

Pope, Alexander, 'Eloisa to Abelard', in *The Rape of the Lock and Other Poems*, ed. Geoffrey Tillotson, The Twickenham Edition of the Poems of Alexander Pope, Vol. II (London and New York: Routledge, 1993), pp. 291–349.

Port, M. H., *The Houses of Parliament* (New Haven and London: Yale University Press, 1976).

Porter, Bernard, *The Battle of the Styles: Society, Culture and the Design of a new Foreign Office, 1855–61* (New York: Continuum, 2011).

Porter, David, 'From Chinese to Goth: Walpole and the Repudiation of Chinoiserie', *Eighteenth-Century Life* vol. 23, no. 1 (Feb. 1999): pp. 46–58.

Pownall, Thomas, *A Treatise on the Study of Antiquities as the Commentary to Historical Learning* (London: Printed for J. Dodsley, 1782).

Pownall, Thomas, *An Antiquarian Romance, Endeavouring to Mark a Line, By Which The Most Ancient People, and the Processions of the Earliest Inhabitants of Europe, May be Investigated* (London: Printed by and for John Nichols, 1795).

Prest, Wilfrid, 'Blackstone as Architect: Constructing the *Commentaries*', *Yale Journal of Law and the Humanities* vol. 15 (2003): pp. 103–33.

Price, Fiona, *Reinventing Liberty: Nation, Commerce and the Historical Novel from Walpole to Scott* (Edinburgh: Edinburgh University Press, 2016).

Pugin, A. C., *Specimens of Gothic Architecture Selected from Various Ancient Edifices in England*, 2 vols (London: J. Taylor, 1821).

Pugin, A. C., E. J. Willson, and A. W. N. Pugin, *Examples of Gothic Architecture*, 3 vols (London: Henry G. Bohn, 1831–6).

Pugin, A. Welby [A. W. N.], *A Letter to A. W. Hakewill, Architect, in Answer to His Reflections on the Style for Rebuilding the Houses of Parliament* (Salisbury: Printed and Published for the Author by W. B. Brodie and Co., 1835).

Pugin, A. W. N., *Contrasts; a Parallel Between the Noble Edifices of the Fourteenth and Fifteenth Centuries, and Similar Buildings of the Present Day; Shewing the Present Decay of Taste: Accompanied by Appropriate Text* (London: Printed for the Author, and Published by Him, at St Marie's Grange, near Wiltshire, 1836).

Pugin, A. W. N., *An Apology for a work Entitled 'Contrasts'; Being a Defence of the Assertions Advanced in that Publication, Against the Various Attacks Lately Made Upon It* (Birmingham: Printed for the Author by R. P. Stone and Son, 1837).

Pugin, A. W. N., *The True Principles of Pointed or Christian Architecture: Set Forth in Two Lectures Delivered at St Marie's, Oscott* (London: John Weale, 1841).

Pugin, A. W. N., *The Collected Letters of A.W. N. Pugin, Vol I: 1830–1842*, ed. with notes and intro. by Margaret Belcher (Oxford: Oxford University Press, 2001).

Punter, David, *The Literature of Terror: A History of Gothic Fictions from 1765 to the Present Day* (London and New York: Longman, 1980).

Punter, David, and Glennis Byron, *The Gothic* (Oxford: Blackwell, 2004).

Purves, Maria, *The Gothic and Catholicism: Religion, Cultural Exchange and the Popular Novel, 1785–1829* (Cardiff: University of Wales Press, 2009).

Radcliffe, Ann, *A Journey Made in the Summer of 1794 Through Holland and the Western Frontier of Germany, With a Return Down the Rhine: To Which are Added Observations During a Tour to the Lakes of Lancashire, Westmoreland, and Cumberland* (London: G. G. and J. Robinson, 1795).

Radcliffe, Ann, *Gaston De Blondeville; or, The Court of Henry III Keeping Festival in Ardenne, A Romance and St Alban's Abbey: A Metrical Tale; With Some Poetical Pieces*, 4 vols (London: Henry Colburn, 1826).

Radcliffe, Ann, 'On the Supernatural in Poetry', *The New Monthly Magazine and Literary Journal* vol. 16, no. 1 (1826): pp. 145–52.

Radcliffe, Ann, 'St Alban's Abbey', in *Gaston De Blondeville; or, The Court of Henry III Keeping Festival in Ardenne, A Romance and St Alban's Abbey: A Metrical Tale; With Some Poetical Pieces* 4 vols (London: Henry Colburn, 1826), vols 3–4.

Radcliffe, Ann, *The Romance of the Forest*, ed. Chloe Chard (Oxford: Oxford University Press, 1986).

Radcliffe, Ann, *The Italian; or, The Confessional of the Black Penitents, a Romance*, ed. Frederick Garber (Oxford and New York: Oxford University Press, 1992).

Radcliffe, Ann, *A Sicilian Romance*, ed. Alison Milbank, (Oxford: Oxford University Press, 1993).

Radcliffe, Ann, *The Castles of Athlin and Dunbayne*, ed. Alison Milbank, (Oxford: Oxford University Press, 1995).

Radcliffe, Ann, *The Mysteries of Udolpho, A Romance; Interspersed with Some Pieces of Poetry*, ed. Bonamy Dobrée, intro. and notes by Terry Castle (Oxford: Oxford University Press, 1998).

Railo, Eino, *The Haunted Castle: A Study of the Elements of English Romanticism* (London: George Routledge & Sons, 1927).

Ramsay, Allan, *A Dialogue on Taste*, 2nd edn (London, 1762).

Reeve, Clara, *The Progress of Romance, Through Times, Countries, and Manners; With Remarks on the Good and Bad Effects of It, On Them Respectively; In a Course of Evening Conversations*, 2 vols (Colchester: Printed by W. Keymer, 1785).

Reeve, Clara, *The Old English Baron*, ed. James Trainer, with intro. and notes by James Watt, 2nd edn (Oxford: Oxford University Press, 2008).

Reeve, Matthew M., 'Dickie Bateman and the Gothicization of Old Windsor: Gothic Architecture and Sexuality in the Circle of Horace Walpole', *Architectural History* 56 (Jan. 2013): pp. 97–131.

Reeve, Matthew M., 'Gothic Architecture, Sexuality, and License at Horace Walpole's Strawberry Hill', *Art Bulletin* 95, no. 3 (Sept. 2013): pp. 411-39.

Reeve, Matthew M., '"A Gothic Vatican of Greece and Rome": Horace Walpole, Strawberry Hill, and the Narratives of Gothic', in *Tributes to Pierre du Prey: Architecture and the Classical Tradition, from Pliny to Posterity*, ed. M. M. Reeve (New York: Harvey Miller, 2014), pp. 185-98.

Reeve, Matthew M., and Peter N. Lindfield, '"A Child of Strawberry": Thomas Barrett and Lee Priory, Kent', *The Burlington Magazine*, CLVII, Dec. 2015, pp. 836-842.

Repton, Humphry, with the assistance of John Adey Repton, *Fragments on the Theory and Practice of Landscape Gardening. Including Some Remarks on Grecian and Gothic Architecture, Collected from Various Manuscripts* (London: Printed by T. Bensley and Son for J. Taylor, 1816).

Reynolds, Joshua, and Edmond Malone, 'The True Idea of Beauty' in *The Works of Sir Joshua Reynolds: Containing his Discourses, Idlers, A Journey to Flanders and Holland (Now First Published), and his Commentary on Du Fresnoy's 'Art of Painting'* (Cambridge: Cambridge University Press, 2014), pp. 357-62.

Reynolds, Nicole, 'Gothic and the Architectural Imagination', in *The Gothic World*, ed. Glennis Byron and Dale Townshend (Abingdon and New York: Routledge, 2014), pp. 85-97.

Rhodes, Ebenezer, *Peak Scenery; or, The Derbyshire Tourist*, 2nd edn (London: Printed for Longman, Hurst, Rees, Orme, Brown, and Green, 1824).

Rickman, Thomas, *An Attempt to Discriminate the Styles of English Architecture, from the Conquest to the Reformation, Preceded by a Sketch of the Grecian and Roman Orders, with Notices of Nearly Five Hundred English Buildings* (London: Longman, Hurst, Rees, Orme, and Brown, 1817).

Roberts, Marion, 'Thomas Gray's Contribution to the Study of Medieval Architecture', *Architectural History* vol. 36 (1993): pp. 49-68.

Robertson, Fiona, *Legitimate Histories: Scott, Gothic, and the Authorities of Fiction* (Oxford: Clarendon Press, 1994).

Robertson, Fiona, 'Romance and the Romantic Novel: Sir Walter Scott', in *A Companion to Romance: From Classical to Contemporary*, ed. Corinne Saunders (Oxford: Blackwell Publishing, 2007), pp. 287-304.

Robertson, Fiona, 'Gothic Scott', in *Scottish Gothic: An Edinburgh Companion*, ed. Carol Margaret Davison and Monica Germanà (Edinburgh: Edinburgh University Press 2017), pp. 103-14.

Robinson, Jeffrey C., *Unfettering Poetry: The Fancy in British Romanticism* (New York: Palgrave Macmillan, 2006).

Robinson, John Martin, *Temples of Delight: Stowe Landscape Gardens* (London: George Philip and the National Trust, 1990).

Robinson, John Martin, *James Wyatt: Architect to George III* (New Haven and London: Yale University Press, 2011).

Roe, Nicholas, *John Keats: A New Life* (New Haven and London: Yale University Press, 2012).

Rogers, Samuel, *The Pleasures of Memory, A Poem* (London: Printed by J. Davis and sold by T. Cadell, 1792).

Rounce, Adam, 'Akenside's Clamours for Liberty', in *'Cultures of Whiggism': New Essays on English Literature and Culture in the Long Eighteenth Century*, ed. David Womersley, assisted by Paddy Bullard and Abigail Williams (Newark: University of Delaware Press, 2005), pp. 216-33.

Ruskin, John, *Arrows of the Chace; Being a Collection of Scattered Letters Published Chiefly in the Daily Newspapers, 1840-1880: Volume I* (New York: John Wiley & Sons, 1881).

Ruskin, John, *Library Edition: The Works of John Ruskin*, 39 vols, ed. E. T. Cook and Alexander Wedderburn (London: George Allen; New York: Longmans, Green, and Co., 1903–12).

Russell, Gillian, *The Theatres of War: Performance, Politics, and Society, 1793–1815* (Oxford: Clarendon Press, 1995).

Rutter, John, *Delineations of Fonthill and Its Abbey* (London: Published by the Author, 1823).

Ryde, Henry T., *A History of the Palace of Westminster* (London: Warrington & Son, 1849).

Rymer, Thomas, *The Tragedies of the Last Age Consider'd and Examin'd by the Practice of the Ancient, and by the Commonsense of All Ages* (London: Printed for Richard Tonson, 1678).

Sabor, Peter, ed., *Horace Walpole: The Critical Heritage* (London and New York: Routledge & Kegan Paul, 1987).

Sabor, Peter, 'Medieval Revival and the Gothic', in *The Cambridge History of Literary Criticism, Vol. IV: The Eighteenth Century*, ed. H. B. Nisbet and Claude Rawson (Cambridge: Cambridge University Press, 1997), pp. 470–88.

Sadleir, Michael, *The Northanger Novels: A Footnote to Jane Austen*, The English Association Pamphlet no. 6 (Oxford: Oxford University Press, 1927).

Sage, Victor, *Horror Fiction in the Protestant Tradition* (Houndmills: Macmillan Press, 1988).

Sage, Victor, 'Gothic Revival', in *The Handbook of the Gothic*, 2nd edn, ed. Marie Mulvey-Roberts (Houndmills: Palgrave Macmillan, 2009), pp. 156–69.

Sagharchi, Alireza, 'Introduction', in *The Architectural Capriccio: Memory, Fantasy and Invention*, ed. Lucien Steil (Farnham: Ashgate, 2014), pp. lxv–lxxiv.

Saglia, Diego, *Poetic Castles in Spain: British Romanticism and Figurations of Iberia* (Amsterdam and Atlanta, GA: Rodopi, 2000).

Sandby, Paul, *A Collection of Landscapes, Drawn By P. Sandby, Esq. R. A. and Engraved by Mr Rooker, and Mr Watts, with Descriptions* (London: Printed for G Kearsly, 1777).

Sandby, Paul, *The Virtuosi's Museum; Containing Select Views, in England, Scotland, and Ireland* (London: Printed for G. Kearsly, 1778).

Sawyer, Sean, '"The Baseless Fabric of a Vision": Civic Architecture and Pictorial Representation at Sir John Soane's Museum', in *The Built Surface, Vol. I: Architecture and the Pictorial Arts from Antiquity to the Enlightenment*, ed. Christy Anderson (Aldershot: Ashgate, 2002), pp. 260–77.

Scarborough, Dorothy, *The Supernatural in Modern English Fiction* (New York and London: G. P. Putnam's Sons, 1917).

Schürer, Norbert, 'The Storming of the Bastille in English Newspapers', *Eighteenth- Century Life* vol. 29, no. 1 (winter 2005): pp. 50–81.

Scott, John, *Journal of a Tour to Waterloo and Paris, in Company with Sir Walter Scott in 1815* (London: Saunders and Otley, 1842).

Scott, Walter, *The Lay of the Last Minstrel: A Poem* (London: Printed for Longman, Hurst, Rees, and Orme; Edinburgh: James Ballantyne, 1805).

Scott, Walter, 'Introduction', in *The Castle of Otranto; A Gothic Story*, by Horace Walpole (Edinburgh: Printed by James Ballantyne and Co; London: Hurst, Rees, Orme, and Brown, 1811), pp. iii–xxxvi.

Scott, Walter, 'Prefatory Memoir to Mrs Ann Radcliffe', in *The Novels of Mrs Ann Radcliffe [...] Complete in One Volume. To Which is Prefixed, A Memoir of the Life of the Author* (London: Hurst, Robinson, and Co.; Printed at Edinburgh by James Ballantyne and Co., 1824), pp. i–xxxix.

Scott, Walter, *Lives of the Novelists*, 2 vols (Philadelphia: H. C. Carey and I. Lee, et al.; New York: Collins and Hannay, 1825).

Scott, Walter, 'An Essay on Romance', in *Essays on Chivalry, Romance, and the Drama*, by W. Scott (Edinburgh: Robert Cadell; London: Whittaker and Co., 1834), pp. 127–216.

Scott, Walter, *Scott: Poetical Works, With the Author's Introduction and Notes*, ed. J. Logie Robertson (London: Oxford University Press, 1971).

Scott, Walter, *Waverley; or, 'Tis Sixty Years Since*, ed. Claire Lamont (Oxford: Oxford University Press, 1986).

Scott, Walter, *Ivanhoe: A Romance*, ed. Ian Duncan (Oxford: Oxford University Press, 1996), p. 13–17.

Scott, Walter, *The Journal of Sir Walter Scott*, ed. and introd. W. E. K. Anderson (Edinburgh: Canongate Books, 1998).

Scott, Walter, *Kenilworth: A Romance*, ed. and introd. J. H. Alexander (London: Penguin, 1999).

Scott, Walter, *The Antiquary*, ed. Nicola J. Watson (New York: Oxford University Press, 2002).

Scott, Walter, 'General Preface', in *Introduction and Notes from the Magnum Opus: Waverley to A Legend of the Wars of Montrose*, ed. J. H. Alexander, with P. D. Garside and Claire Lamont (Edinburgh: Edinburgh University Press, 2012), pp. 8–22.

Scott, Walter, *Introduction and Notes from the Magnum Opus: Waverley to A Legend of the Wars of Montrose*, ed. J. H. Alexander, with P. D. Garside and Claire Lamont (Edinburgh: Edinburgh University Press, 2012).

Shaftesbury, Anthony Ashley Cooper, Earl of, *Characteristicks of Men, Manners, Opinions, Times*, 3 vols (London: Printed by John Darby, 1711).

Shakespeare, William, *The Norton Shakespeare, Based on the Oxford Edition*, 2nd edn, ed. Stephen Greenblatt, Walter Cohen, Jean E. Howard, and Katharine Eisaman Maus, with an essay by Andrew Gurr (New York and London: W. W. Norton & Co., 2005).

Shapira, Yael, 'Shakespeare, *The Castle of Otranto*, and the Problem of the Corpse on the Eighteenth-Century Stage', *Eighteenth-Century Life* vol. 6, no. 1 (winter 2012): pp. 1–29.

Shell, Alison, *Oral Culture and Catholicism in Early Modern England* (Cambridge: Cambridge University Press, 2007).

Shell, Alison, 'John Soane, Bardolater', in *'The Cloud-Capped Towers': Shakespeare in Soane's Architectural Imagination* (London: The Sir John Soane's Museum, 2016), pp. 19–27.

Shelley, Mary, *Frankenstein; or, The Modern Prometheus: The 1818 Text*, ed. Nick Groom (Oxford: Oxford University Press, 2018).

Shenstone, William, *The Works in Verse and Prose, of William Shenstone, Esq.*, 2 vols (London: Printed for R. and J. Dodsley, 1764).

Shenton, Caroline, *The Day Parliament Burned Down* (Oxford: Oxford University Press, 2012).

Shenton, Caroline, *Mr Barry's War: Rebuilding the Houses of Parliament After the Great Fire of 1834* (Oxford: Oxford University Press, 2016).

Silver, Sean R., 'Visiting Strawberry Hill: Horace Walpole's Gothic Historiography', *Eighteenth-Century Fiction* vol. 21, no. 4 (summer 2009): pp. 535–64.

Silver, Sean, 'The Politics of Gothic Historiography, 1660–1800', in *The Gothic World*, ed. Glennis Byron and Dale Townshend (Abingdon and New York: Routledge, 2014), pp. 3–14.

Simmons, Clare A., *Popular Medievalism in Romantic-Era Britain* (New York: Palgrave Macmillan, 2011).

Skilton, David, 'Tourists at the Ruins of London: The Metropolis and the Struggle for Empire', *Cercles* vol. 17 (2007): pp. 93-119.

Smith, Charlotte, *The Banished Man, A Novel*, 4 vols (London: Printed for T. Cadell Jnr and W. Davies, 1794).

Smith, Charlotte, *Desmond*, ed. Antje Blank and Janet Todd (Peterborough, ON: Broadview Press, 2001).

Smith, Charlotte, *The Old Manor House*, ed. Jacqueline M. Labbe (Peterborough, ON: Broadview Press, 2002).

Smith, R. J., *The Gothic Bequest: Medieval Institutions in British Thought, 1688-1863* (Cambridge: Cambridge University Press, 2002).

Smith, Roland M., 'Chaucer's "Castle in Spain"', *Modern Language Notes* vol. 60, no. 1 (Jan. 1945): pp. 39-40.

Smith, Warren H., *Architectural Design on English Title-Pages* (London: Bibliographical Society, 1933).

Smith, Warren Hunting, *Architecture in English Fiction*, Yale Studies in English, Vol. LXXXIII (New Haven: Yale University Press; Oxford: Oxford University Press, 1934).

Smith, Warren Hunting, 'Strawberry Hill and Otranto', *The Times Literary Supplement*, Sat., 23 May 1936, p. 440.

Snodin, Michael, 'Going to Strawberry Hill', in *Horace Walpole's Strawberry Hill*, ed. M. Snodin, with the assistance of Cynthia Roman (New Haven and London: Yale University Press, 2009), pp. 15-57.

Snodin, Michael, ed., with the assistance of Cynthia Roman, *Horace Walpole's Strawberry Hill* (New Haven and London: Yale University Press, 2009).

Soane, John, *Plans, Elevations, and Perspective Views, of Pitzhanger Manor-House, and of the Ruins of an Edifice of Roman Architecture, Situated on the Border of Ealing Green, with a Description of the Ancient and Present State of the Manor-House, in a Letter to a Friend* (London: J. Moyes, 1802).

Soane, John, *Memoirs of the Professional Life of an Architect, Between the Years 1768 and 1835. Written by Himself* (London: Privately Printed by James Moyes, 1835).

Soane, John, 'Crude Hints Towards a History of my House', ed. Helen Dorey, in *Visions of Ruin: Architectural Fantasies & Designs for Garden Follies, with 'Crude Hints Towards a History of My House'* (London: The Soane Gallery, 1999), pp. 53-78.

Soane, John, *Crude Hints Towards a History of My House* (1812), MS in the John Soane's Museum Archive, Soane Case 31.

Soane, John, Miscellaneous Manuscripts Concerning the Fake Ruins at Pitzhanger (1802), John Soane's Museum Archive, MS 7/G/4/2-MS 7/G/4/5.

Sorensen, David R., 'Ruskin and Carlyle', in *The Cambridge Companion to John Ruskin*, ed. Francis O'Gorman (Cambridge: Cambridge University Press, 2015), pp. 189-201.

Southey, Robert, 'Poor Mary, The Maid of the Inn', in *An Apology for Tales of Terror*, ed. Walter Scott (Kelso: Printed at the Mail Office, 1799), pp. 19-26.

The Spectator, 10th edn, 9 vols (London: Tonson, 1729), Lewis Walpole Library, 49 1860, v. 1-9.

Spenser, Edmund, 'The Ruines of Rome. By Bellay', in *The Works of Spenser*, 6 vols (London: Printed for J. and R. Tonson and S. Draper, 1750), vol. 5, pp. 223-36.

Spenser, Edmund, *The Faerie Queene. By Edmund Spenser [...] Adorn'd with thirty- two Copper-Plates, from the Original Drawings of the late W. Kent, Esq; Architect and principal Painter to his Majesty*, 3 vols (London: Printed for J. Brindsley and S. Wright, 1751).

Spurr, David, *Architecture and Modern Literature* (Ann Arbor: University of Michigan Press, 2012).

Steil, Lucien, 'Preface', in *The Architectural Capriccio: Memory, Fantasy and Invention*, ed. L. Steil (Farnham: Ashgate, 2014), pp. li–lviii.

Stevens, Anne H., *British Historical Fiction Before Scott* (Houndmills: Palgrave Macmillan, 2010).

Stevenson, William, ed., *A Supplement to the First Edition of Mr Bentham's History and Antiquities of the Cathedral & Conventual Church of Ely* (Norwich: Printed by and for Stevenson, Matchett, and Stevenson, 1817).

Stewart, David, 'Political Ruins: Gothic Sham Ruins and the '45', *Journal of the Society of Architectural Historians* vol. 55, no. 4 (Dec. 1996): pp. 400–11.

Stewart, Donald R., 'James Essex', *The Architectural Review* (Nov. 1950): pp. 317–21.

Stone, Francis, *An Examination of the Right Hon. Edmund Burke's Reflections on the Revolution in France* (London: Sold by G. C. J. and J. Robinson, J. Johnson, et al, 1792).

Strachey, Lytton, *Characters and Commentaries* (New York: Harcourt, Brace and Company, 1933).

Strutt, Joseph, *Queenhoo-Hall, A Romance; and Ancient Times, A Drama*, 4 vols (Edinburgh: Archibald Constable and Co.; London: John Murray, 1808).

Summers, Montague, 'Introduction', in Horace Walpole, *The Castle of Otranto and The Mysterious Mother*, ed. M. Summers (London: Constable, 1924), pp. xi–lvii.

Summers, Montague, 'Architecture and the Gothic Novel', *Architectural Design and Construction* vol. 2, no. 2 (Dec. 1931): pp. 78–81.

Summers, Montague, *The Gothic Quest: A History of the Gothic Novel* (London: The Fortune Press, 1938).

Summerson, John, *The Classical Language of Architecture* (London: Methuen & Co., 1963).

Sweet, R. H., 'Gough, Richard (1735–1809)', *Oxford Dictionary of National Biography*, http://www.oxforddnb.com/view/article/11141 (accessed 6 September 2016).

Sweet, Rosemary, *Antiquaries: The Discovery of the Past in Eighteenth-Century Britain* (London and New York: Hambledon & London, 2004).

Sweet, Rosemary, *Cities and the Grand Tour: The British in Italy, c. 1690–1820* (Cambridge: Cambridge University Press, 2012).

Sweet, Rosemary, 'Gothic Antiquarianism in the Eighteenth Century', in *The Gothic World*, ed. Glennis Byron and Dale Townshend (Abingdon and New York: Routledge, 2014), pp. 15–26.

Swenson, Astrid, *The Rise of Heritage: Preserving the Past in France, Germany and England, 1789–1914* (Cambridge: Cambridge University Press, 2013).

Swinburne, Henry, *Travels in the Two Sicilies, by Henry Swiburne, Esq. in 1777, 1778, 1779, and 1780*, 2nd ed., 4 vols (London: Printed by J. Nichols, for T. Cadell and P. Elmsly, 1790).

Switzer, Stephen, *The Nobleman, Gentleman, and Gardener's Recreation; or, An Introduction to Gardening, Planting, Agriculture, and Other Business and Pleasures of a Country Life* (London: Printed for B. Barker and C. King, 1715).

Talfourd, Thomas Noon, 'Memoir of the Life and Writings of Mrs Radcliffe', in Anne [sic] Radcliffe, *Gaston De Blondeville; or, The Court of Henry III Keeping Festival in Ardenne, A Romance and St Alban's Abbey: A Metrical Tale; With Some Poetical Pieces* 4 vols (London: Henry Colburn, 1826), vol. 1, pp. 1–130.

Tambling, Jeremy, *On Anachronism* (Manchester: Manchester University Press, 2010).

Tarr, Mary Muriel, *Catholicism in Gothic Fiction: A Study of the Nature and Function of Catholic Materials in Gothic Fiction in England, 1762–1820* (Washington: Catholic University of America Press, 1946).

Tasso, Torquato, *Jerusalem Delivered; An Heroic Poem: Translated from the Italian of Torquato Tasso, by John Hoole*, 2 vols (London: Printed and sold by J. Dodsley,

P. Vaillant, T. Davies et al; Oxford: D. Prince; Cambridge: W. Thurlbourn and J. Woodver, 1763).
Taylor, George, *The French Revolution and the London Stage, 1789-1805* (Cambridge: Cambridge University Press, 2000).
Temple, William, *Miscellanea: The Second Part. In Four Essays*, 2nd edn (London: Printed by J. R. for Ri. and Ra. Simpson, 1690).
Thelwall, John, *The Rights of Nature, Against the Usurpations of Establishments*, 2nd edn (London: Published by H. D. Symonds and J. March, Norwich, 1796).
Thelwall, John, *Rights of Nature, Against the Usurpations of Establishments. Part the Second* (London: Published by H. D. Symonds and J. March, Norwich, 1796).
Thomas, Edward, *A Literary Pilgrim in England* (Oxford: Oxford University Press, 1980).
Thomas, Peter D. G. and Roger Newdigate, 'Sir Roger Newdigate's Essays on Party, c. 1760', *The English Historical Review* vol. 102, no. 403 (Apr. 1987): pp. 394–400.
Thompson, Michael, *Ruins Reused: Changing Attitudes to Ruins Since the Late Eighteenth Century* (Norfolk: Heritage Marketing and Publications, 2006).
Thomson, James, *Britain: Being the Fourth Part of Liberty, A Poem* (London: Printed for A. Millar, 1736).
Thomson, James, *The Castle of Indolence: An Allegorical Poem. Written in Imitation of Spenser* (London: Printed for A. Millar, 1748).
Thurley, Simon, *Men from the Ministry: How Britain Saved Its Heritage* (New Haven and London: Yale University Press, 2013).
Tighe, Hugh Usher, *An Historical Account of Cumner [sic]; With Some Particulars of the Traditions Respecting the Death of the Countess of Leicester* (Oxford: Printed and Sold by Munday and Slatter, 1821).
Tompkins, J. M. S., 'Introduction', in Devendra P. Varma, *The Gothic Flame, Being a History of the Gothic Novel in England: Its Origins, Efflorescence, Disintegration, and Residuary Influences* (London: Arthur Barker: 1957), pp. xi–xv.
Tompkins, J. M. S., *The Popular Novel in England 1770-1800*, 2nd edn (Lincoln: University of Nebraska Press, 1961).
Townshend, Dale, 'Royalist Historiography in T. J Horsley Curties's *Ethelwina; or, The House of Fitz-Auburne* (1799), *Gothic Studies* vol. 14, no. 1 (May 2012): pp. 57–73.
Townshend, Dale, 'T. I. Horsley Curties, Romance, and the Gift of Death', *European Romantic Review* vol. 24, issue 1 (2013): pp. 23–42.
Townshend, Dale, 'Architecture and the Romance of Gothic Remains: John Carter and *The Gentleman's Magazine*, 1797–1817', in *Gothic and the Everyday: Living Gothic*, ed. Lorna Piatti-Farnell and Maria Beville (Houndmills: Palgrave Macmillan, 2014) pp. 173–94.
Townshend, Dale, 'Ruins, Romance and the Rise of Gothic Tourism: The Case of Netley Abbey, 1750–1830', *Journal for Eighteenth-Century Studies* vol. 37, issue 3 (Sept. 2014): pp. 377–94.
Townshend, Dale, 'The Aesthetics of Ruin', in *Writing Britain's Ruins*, ed. Michael Carter, Peter N. Lindfield, and D. Townshend (London: British Library Publishing, 2017), pp. 83–115.
Townshend, Dale, and Angela Wright, 'Gothic and Romantic Engagements: The Critical Reception of Ann Radcliffe, 1789–1850', in *Ann Radcliffe, Romanticism and the Gothic*, ed. D. Townshend and A. Wright (Cambridge: Cambridge University Press, 2014), pp. 3–32.
Toynbee, Paget, 'Horace Walpole's Journals of Visits to Country Seats', in *The Sixteenth Volume of the Walpole Society, 1927-1928* (Oxford: Printed for the Walpole Society by John Johnson at the University Press, 1928).

Trodd, Colin, Paul Barlow, and David Amigoni, eds, *Victorian Culture and the Idea of the Grotesque* (Aldershot: Ashgate, 1999).

Trumpener, Katie, *Bardic Nationalism: The Romantic Novel and the British Empire* (Princeton, NJ: Princeton University Press, 1997).

Tulloch, Graham, 'Imagining the Middle Ages and Renaissance in *Ivanhoe* and *Kenilworth*', in *Approaches to Teaching Scott's Waverley Novels*, ed. Evan Gottlieb and Ian Duncan (New York: Modern Language Association of America, 2009), pp. 164-9.

Tyack, Geoffrey, 'The Folly and the Mausoleum', *Country Life* vol. 183, issue 16 (20 Apr. 1989): pp. 215-20.

Tyack, Nicholas, ed., *England's Long Reformation, 1500-1800* (Abingdon and New York: Routledge, 1998).

Varma, Devendra P., *The Gothic Flame: Being a History of the Gothic Novel in England* (London: Arthur Barker, 1957).

Vasari, Giorgio, *The Lives of the Artists*, trans. Julia Conaway Bondanella and Peter Bondanella (Oxford: Oxford University Press, 2008).

Vidler, Anthony, *The Architectural Uncanny: Essays in the Modern Unhomely* (Cambridge, MA, and London: MIT Press, 1992).

Vine, Angus, *In Defiance of Time: Antiquarian Writing in Early Modern England* (Oxford: Oxford University Press, 2010).

Wallace, Peter G., *The Long European Reformation: Religion, Political Conflict, and the Search for Conformity, 1350-1750*, 2nd edn (Houndmills: Palgrave Macmillan, 2012).

Walpole, Horace, *Short Notes of the Life of Horatio Walpole, Youngest Son of Robert Walpole Earl of Orford, and of Catherine Shorter, his First Wife* (c.1746-1779), Lewis Walpole Library, MSS vol. 149.

Walpole, Horace, 'Patapan; or, The Little White Dog: A Tale from Fontaine' (1749), Lewis Walpole Library, Folio 49 2616 II MS, fols 93-112.

Walpole, Horace, *Book of Materials, 1759*, Lewis Walpole Library, 49 2615.

Walpole, Horace, *Book of Materials, 1775*, Lewis Walpole Library, 49 2615.

Walpole, Horace, *Anecdotes of Painting in England; With Some Account of the Principal Artists; And Incidental Notes on Other Arts; Collected by the Late Mr George Vertue; and Now Digested and Published from His Original MSS*, 4 vols (Strawberry Hill: Printed by Thomas Farmer, 1762-71 [1780]).

Walpole, Horace, *Historic Doubts on the Life and Reign of King Richard the Third* (London: Printed for J. Dodsley, 1768).

Walpole, Horace, *A Description of the Villa of Horace Walpole, Youngest Son of Sir Robert Walpole Earl of Orford, at Strawberry-Hill, Near Twickenham. With an Inventory of the Furniture, Pictures, Curiosities, &c.* (Strawberry Hill: Printed by Thomas Kirgate, 1774).

Walpole, Horace, *A Description of the Villa of Horace Walpole, Youngest Son of Sir Robert Walpole Earl of Orford, at Strawberry-Hill, Near Twickenham. With an Inventory of the Furniture, Pictures, Curiosities*, &c, 2nd edn (Strawberry Hill: Printed by Thomas Kirgate, 1784).

Walpole, Horace, *Hieroglyphic Tales* (Strawberry Hill: Printed by Thomas Kirgate, 1785).

Walpole, Horace, *The Works of Horatio Walpole, Earl of Orford*, 5 vols (London: Printed for G. G. and J. Robinson, and J. Edwards, 1798).

Walpole, Horace, 'The Mysterious Mother: A Tragedy', in *Five Romantic Plays, 1768-1821*, ed. Paul Baines and Edward Burns (New York: Oxford University Press, 2000), pp. 1-69.

Walpole, Horace, *The Castle of Otranto*, ed. Nick Groom (Oxford: Oxford University Press, 2014).

Walpole, Horace, *Sermon on the Use and Abuse of Painting* (1742), Lewis Walpole Library, Folio 49 2616 II MS.

Walsham, Alexandra, *The Reformation of the Landscape: Religion, Identity, and Memory in Early Modern Britain and Ireland* (Oxford: Oxford University Press, 2011).

Walton, John K., and Jason Wood, eds, *The Making of a Cultural Landscape: The English Lake District as a Tourist Destination, 1750–2010* (Farnham: Ashgate, 2013).

Warburton, William, ed., *The Works of Alexander Pope, Esq*, 9 vols (London: Printed for A. Millar, J. and R. Tonson, et al., 1760).

Warburton, William, ed., *The Works of Alexander Pope, Esq., Vol. IV. Containing His Satires, etc.*, (London: Printed for C. Bathurst, W. Strahan, J. and F. Rivington, et al., 1770).

Warner, Richard, *Topographical Remarks, Relating to the South-Western Parts of Hampshire: To Which is Added a Descriptive Poem*, 2 vols (London: Printed for R. Blamire, 1793).

Warner, Richard, *Netley Abbey: A Gothic Story*, 2 vols (London: Printed for William Lane at the Minerva Press, 1795).

Warner, Richard, *Catholic Emancipation, Incompatible with the Safety of the Established Religion, Liberty, Laws, and Protestant Succession, of the British Empire* (London: C. J. G. & F. Rivington, 1829).

Warton, Thomas, *The Pleasures of Melancholy. A Poem* (London: Printed for R. Dodsley, 1747).

Warton, Thomas, *Observations on The Fairy Queen of Spenser*, 2nd edn, 2 vols (London: Printed for R. and J. Dodsley; Oxford: Printed for J. Fletcher, 1762), Lewis Walpole Library, 48 1840.

Warton, Joseph, *An Essay on the Genius and Writings of Pope*, 4th edn, corrected, 2 vols (London: Printed for J. Dodsley, 1782).

Warton, Thomas, *Verses on Sir Joshua Reynolds's Painted Window at New-College Oxford* (London: Printed for J. Dodsley, 1782).

Watkin, David, 'Built Ruins: The Hermitage as a Retreat', in *Visions of Ruin: Architectural Fantasies and Designs for Garden Follies, with 'Crude Hints Towards a History of My House' by John Soane* (London: The Soane Gallery, 1999), pp. 5-14.

Watkin, David, ed., *Sir John Soane: The Royal Academy Lectures* (Cambridge: Cambridge University Press, 2000).

Watt, Ian, 'Time and the Family in the Gothic Novel: *The Castle of Otranto*', *Eighteenth-Century Life* vol. 10, no. 3 (1986): pp. 159–71.

Watt, James, *Contesting the Gothic: Fiction, Genre and Cultural Conflict, 1764–1832* (Cambridge: Cambridge University Press, 1999).

Watt, James, 'Gothic', in *The Cambridge Companion to English Literature, 1740–1830*, ed. Thomas Keymer and Jon Mee (Cambridge: Cambridge University Press, 2004), pp. 119–37.

Watt, James, 'Ann Radcliffe and Politics', in *Ann Radcliffe, Romanticism and the Gothic*, ed. Dale Townshend and Angela Wright (Cambridge: Cambridge University Press, 2014), pp. 67–82.

Webster, John, *The Duchess of Malfi*, ed. Elizabeth M. Brennan (New York: W. W. Norton & Co., 1986).

Wedgwood, Alexandra, 'The New Palace of Westminster' in *Pugin: A Gothic Passion*, ed. Paul Atterbury and Clive Wainwright (New Haven and London: Yale University Press, in association with the Victorian & Albert Museum, 1994), pp. 219–36.

Wedgwood, Alexandra, 'The New Palace of Westminster', in *The Houses of Parliament: History, Art, Architecture*, ed. David Cannadine, Dorian Church, et al. (London: Merrell Publishers, 2000), pp. 113–35.

West, Gilbert, *The Institution of the Order of the Garter. A Dramatick Poem* (London: Printed for R. Dodsley, 1742).
Whately, Thomas, *Observations on Modern Gardening, Illustrated by Descriptions* (London: Printed for T. Payne, 1770).
Whittington, G. D., *An Historical Survey of the Ecclesiastical Antiquities of France; With a View to Illustrate the Rise and Progress of Gothic Architecture in Europe* (London: Printed by T. Bensley for J. Taylor, 1809).
Williams, Abigail, *Poetry and the Creation of a Whig Literary Culture* (Oxford: Oxford University Press, 2005).
Williams, Anne, *Art of Darkness: A Poetics of Gothic* (Chicago and London: University of Chicago Press, 1995).
Williams, Anne, 'Reading Walpole Reading Shakespeare', in *Shakespearean Gothic*, ed. Christy Desmet and A. Williams (Cardiff: University of Wales Press, 2009), pp. 13–36.
Williams, Helen Maria, 'To Dr Moore', in *Romantic Women Poets, 1770–1838: An Anthology*, ed. Andrew Ashfield (Manchester and New York: Manchester University Press, 1998), pp. 74–6.
Willis, Browne, *An History of the Mitred Parliamentary Abbies, and Conventual Cathedral Churches*, 2 vols (London: Printed by W. Bowyer for R. Gosling, 1718–19).
Wilson, Michael, *Claude, The Enchanted Castle* (London: The National Gallery, 1982).
Wilton-Ely, John, 'The Rise of the Professional Architect in England', in *The Architect: Chapters in the History of the Profession*, ed. Spiro Kostof (New York: Oxford University Press, 1977), pp. 180–208.
Wilton-Ely, John, 'Gingerbread and sippets of embroidery': Horace Walpole and Robert Adam', *Eighteenth-Century Life* vol. 25, no. 2 (spring 2001): pp. 147–69.
Wilton-Ely, John, 'Style and Serendipity: Adam, Walpole and Strawberry Hill', *The British Art Journal* vol. 11, no. 3 (spring 2011): pp. 3–14.
Wollstonecraft, Mary, *A Vindication of the Rights of Men; in a Letter to the Right Honourable Edmund Burke; Occasioned by his Reflections on the Revolution in France* (London: Printed for J. Johnson, 1790).
Wollstonecraft, Mary, *An Historical and Moral View of the Progress of the French Revolution*, 2 vols (London: Printed for J. Johnson, 1794).
Wollstonecraft, Mary, *Mary and The Wrongs of Woman*, ed. Gary Kelly (Oxford: Oxford University Press, 1998).
Womersley, David, 'Introduction', in *Cultures of Whiggism: New Essays on English Literature and Culture in the Long Eighteenth Century*, ed. D. Womersley, assisted by Paddy Bullard and Abigail Williams (Newark: University of Delaware Press, 2005), pp. 9–26.
Wood, Jason, 'Furness Abbey: A Century and a Half in the Tourists' Gaze', in *The Making of a Cultural Landscape: The English Lake District as a Tourist Destination, 1750–2010*, ed. John K. Walton and J. Wood (Farnham: Ashgate, 2013), pp. 220–40.
Woodward, Christopher, 'Scenes from the Future', in *Visions of Ruin: Architectural Fantasies and Designs for Garden Follies, with 'Crude Hints Towards a History of My House' by John Soane* (London: The Soane Gallery, 1999), pp. 15–50.
Woodward, Christopher, *In Ruins* (London: Vintage, 2002).
Wordsworth, William, 'Preface', in *Poems by William Wordsworth: Including Lyrical Ballads, and the Miscellaneous Pieces of the Author*, 2 vols (London: Printed for Longman, Hurst, Rees, Orme, and Brown, 1815), vol. 1, pp. vii–xliii.
Wordsworth, William, *The Prelude, 1799, 1805, 1850*, ed. Jonathan Wordsworth, M. H. Abrams, and Stephen Gill (New York and London: W. W. Norton & Co., 1979).

Wordsworth, William, *Last Poems, 1821-1850*, ed. Jared Curties, with the assistance of Apryl Lea Denny-Ferris and Jillian Heydt-Stevenson, The Cornell Wordsworth (Ithaca and London: Cornell University Press, 1999).

Wordsworth, William, 'Ecclesiastical Sketches', in *Sonnet Series and Itinerary Poems*, ed. Geoffrey Jackson, The Cornell Wordsworth (Ithaca and London: Cornell University Press, 2004), pp. 125-347.

Wordsworth, William, *The Excursion*, ed. Sally Bushell, James A. Butler, and Michael C. Jaye, assisted by David Garcia, The Cornell Wordsworth (Ithaca, NY, and London: Cornell University Press, 2007).

Wordsworth, William, *Lyrical Ballads, 1798 and 1800*, ed. Michael Gamer and Dahlia Porter (Peterborough, ON: Broadview, 2008).

The Works of Anna Laetitia Barbauld, with a Memoir by Lucy Aikin, 2 vols (London: Printed for Longman, Hurst, Rees, Orme, Brown, and Green, 1825).

Worsley, Giles, 'The Origins of the Gothic Revival: A Reappraisal: The Alexander Prize Essay', *Transactions of the Royal Historical Society* vol. 3 (1993): pp. 105-50.

Wotton, Henry, *The Elements of Architecture* (London: Printed by John Bill, 1624).

Wren Jnr, Christopher, *Parentalia: Or, Memoirs of the Family of the Wrens* (London: Printed for T. Osborn and R. Dodsley, 1750).

Wright, Angela, 'Inspiration, Toleration and Relocation in Ann Radcliffe's *A Journey Made in the Summer of 1794, Through Holland and the Western Frontier of Germany* (1795)', in *Romantic Localities: Europe Writes Place*, ed. Christoph Bode and Jacqueline Labbe (London: Pickering & Chatto, 2010), pp. 131-43.

Wright, Angela, 'The Fickle Fortunes of Chivalry in Eighteenth-Century Gothic', *Gothic Studies*, vol. 14, no. 1 (May 2012): pp. 47-56.

Wright, Angela, *Britain, France and the Gothic, 1764-1820: The Import of Terror* (Cambridge: Cambridge University Press, 2013).

Wright, Angela, 'The Gothic', in *The Cambridge Companion to Women's Writing in the Romantic Period*, ed. Devoney Looser (Cambridge: Cambridge University Press, 2015), pp. 58-72.

Yearsley, Ann, *Poems on Several Occasions*, 3rd edn (London: Printed for T. Cadell, 1785).

Young, Edward, *Conjectures on Original Composition, in a Letter to the Author of Sir Charles Grandison* (London: Printed for A Millar, and R. and J. Dodsley, 1759).

Zuckert, Rachel, 'The Associative Sublime: Gerard, Kames, Alison, and Stewart', in *The Sublime: From Antiquity to the Present*, ed. Timothy M. Costelloe (Cambridge: Cambridge University Press, 2012), pp. 64-76.

Index

Note: Figures are indicated by an italic '*f*' following the page number.

For the benefit of digital users, indexed terms that span two pages (e.g., 52–53) may, on occasion, appear on only one of those pages.

abbesses 221–2
abbeys 168–9, 184, 221–2, 238–41
Acts of Union (1707) 230–1
Adam, Robert 59–60, 192–3
   Landscape Fantasy Showing Castles and a Domed City, A (c.1777–87) 167
   Picturesque Compositions (1782) 167
Addison, Joseph 9–10, 191–2, 289–90
   Cato, A Tragedy (1712–13) 49
   Drummer, The (1716) 50–1
   'No. 110' (1711) 49–52, 240–1
   Remarks on Several Parts of Italy (1705; 1726) 48–9, 54–5, 61–2
   Spectator, The, articles published in 47–8, 51–4, 61–2, 275–6
   'Taste and the Pleasures of the Imagination' (1711–1712) 47–8, 51–2, 61–2
Age of Folly, The (Anon., n.d.) 17–18
Age, The (Anon., 1810) 12
Aikin, Anna Laetitia (Mrs Anna Laetitia Barbauld) 127–8, 132–3
   Eighteen Hundred and Eleven (1812) 166
   Miscellaneous Pieces, in Prose (with Aikin, J., 1773) 127–8, 231–5, 237–8, 283
   'On Monastic Institutions' (1773) 231–5, 237–8, 258–9
Aikin, John
   'Letter XXIV. On Ruins' (1793) 233
   Miscellaneous Pieces, in Prose (with Aikin, A. L., 1773) 127–8, 231–5, 237–8, 283
   'Sir Bertrand: A Fragment' 127–8, 237–8
   Treatise on the Situation, Manners, and Inhabitants of Germany, A (1777) 5–6
Ainsworth, William Harrison, *Tower of London, The* (1840) 272
Akenside, Mark, *Pleasures of Imagination, The* (1744) 52–5, 86–7, 191–2
Alcobaça, monastery of 85–6
Alfred the Great, King 332–3
Alison, Archibald, *Essays on the Nature and Principles of Taste* (1790) 69–71, 144, 180–1

Allston, Washington 147–8
Amadis of Gaul (Anon., 1508) 104–5, 108, 112–13
Andrews, James Pettit 125–6
Andrews, Miles Peter
   Enchanted Castle, The (*Castle of Wonders*) (1786) 126n.173, 129
   Mysteries of the Castle, The (1795) 153–5
Anglo-Saxons 5–6, 168–70, 223–4, 332–3
anti-Catholicism 221–2, 241–2, 256–7, 259
   and literature 48–51, 221–2, 232–4, 262–6, 341–2
   see also monasteries, dissolution of; Reformation, the
anti-French sentiment 195–6
antiquarianism/antiquaries 4–5, 25–6, 30, 139–40
   and conservation 1, 203–4
   and fiction 268, 278, 288, 290–1, 293–4; *see also* antiquarian romance
   and restoration 185–6, 195–6, 268–73, 315–16
   and romance 23–4, 268–9, 278–9, 288, 290–1
   and ruins, studying 223–4, 230–1, 288–9
   scholarly/literary 23–4, 27–8, 244, 275–80, 283, 293–4, 353
   and topography 171–2, 267–8
   see also antiquarian romance
antiquarian romance 267–8, 272–3, 278
apparitions *see* ghosts/spectral beings
Arbury Hall, Warwickshire 191–2
Arbuthnot, John 289–90
Archaeologia 26–7
arches
   pointed 'Norman' style 63–4, 68–9, 248–9
   round 'Saxon' style 68–9
architect, the 355–6
   artistic identity/cultural position of 15–17, 19–22, 354–5
   gendered notions of 14–15
   and genius 14–15, 54–5, 71–2, 354–5
   and professional training 15–17, 313–14, 353–6
architectural training, professionalization of 313–14, 353–6

Ariosto, Ludovico 103–4
  Orlando Furioso (1516) 104–5, 108–11,
    114–15, 120–2
Aristotle, *Poetics* (*c*.335 BC) 22–3
Arthurian myth/legend 300–2, 329
artist-architect, the 15–17; *see also* architect, the
Art of Architecture, The (Anon., 1742) 19–20
Arts and Crafts Movement 355–6
Arville Castle (Anon., 1795) 156–7
Ashmole, Elias, *Antiquities of Berkshire, The*
    (1710) 304–5
associationism 46–8, 69–70
  and architectural theory and practice 45–6,
    60–3, 70–1, 144–6, 171–2, 289
  and Gothic architectural styles 144–6, 231–2,
    291–2, 345–6, 349–50
  and history 75–6, 231–2
  and literature 80–1, 89, 144–6, 345–6
  scepticism towards 46–7, 55, 75–8, 349
Aubrey, John
  Chronologia Architectonica (1670s) 4–5
  Miscellanies (1696) 276–9
Austen, Jane 182–4, 209–10
  Northanger Abbey (1818) 179–84

Bacon, Francis, *Advancement of Learning, The*
    (1605) 20–2
Bacon, Nathaniel, *Historicall Discourse..., An*
    (1647–51) 5–6
Baillie, Joanna, *De Montfort* (1798) 31–2
Baillie, John, *Essay on the Sublime, An*
    (1747) 52–3
Bannerman, Anne, *Tales of Superstition and
    Chivalry* (1802) 11–12
barbarism 32–8, 44, 106, 289, 317–18
  and Middle Ages, association with 31–2, 39,
    318–20
Barbauld, Anna Laetitia *see* Aikin, Anna Laetitia
Barrett, Thomas 125–6
Barry, Charles 312–14, 327–8
  Westminster, Palace of, rebuild plans 315–16,
    318–20, 354–5
Bartlett, Alfred Darling, *Historical and
    Descriptive Account of Cumnor Place,
    Berks., An* (1850) 305, 306*f*
Bastille, fall of the (1789) 137–9, 182, 201–3, 207–8
  British responses to 202–5, 211–12
Batalha, monastery of 85–7
Bateman, Richard ('Dickie') 125–6
'Battle of the Styles' 71–2, 316–20, 326–7
Bayliss, John, *Mysteries of Udolpho, The*
    (1804) 153–5
Beattie, James, *Dissertations Moral and Critical*
    (1783) 72–4, 144

Beauclerk, Diana 123–5
  Faerie Queene, The (Book III, 1781),
    illustration from 113–14, 114*f*
Beaulieu Abbey, Hampshire 265–6
Beauty
  and classical architecture 78, 322–3
  and Gothic architecture 74–5, 78, 292–3
  and the sublime 69–71
Beckford, William 45–6, 78, 139–40, 350–1
  architectural space, imaginative responses
    to 79–81, 83–5
  books owned by 79
  Dreams, Waking Thoughts, and Incidents
    (1783) 80–3, 84*f*
  European travels 81–6
  Fragments of an English Tour (1779) 79–81
  Italy; With Sketches of Spain and Portugal
    (1834) 83–6
  journals 85
  *Recollections of an Excursion to the
    Monasteries of Alcobaça and Batalha*
    (1835) 85–7
  'The Transport of Pleasure' (*c*.1777–8) 88
  Vathek (1786) 88, 129–30
  Vision, The ('The Long Story', *c*.1777) 87–8
  see also 'Conversations with the Late
    William Beckford'
Belsham, William 203–5
Bentham, James, *History and Antiquities of the
    Conventual and Cathedral Church at Ely,
    The* (1771) 38, 68–9, 247–8
Bentham, Jeremy, *Fragment on Government, A*
    (1776) 200–1, 208
Bentham, John, *Essays on Gothic Architecture*
    (1800) 167–8
Bentley, Richard 125–6, 250–2
  *Designs by Mr R. Bentley, for Six Poems by
    Mr T. Gray* (1753), illustrations
    from 134–5, 135*f*, 238–40, 239*f*
  Strawberry Hill, design work at 125–6, 249–50
Bernard, Scrope 187–8
Bingham, Lavinia 93–4
Birch, George 122–3
Birrell, Andrew 42–4, 94–6
Blackstone, William 198–201, 312
  Abridgment of Architecture, An (1743) 198
  Commentaries on the Laws of England
    (1765–9) 197–8, 200
  Elements of Architecture (1746–7) 198
Blair, Hugh, *Lectures on Rhetoric and Belles
    Lettres* (1783) 22–3
Blair, Robert, *Grave, The* (1743) 51–2
Blondel, Jacques-François, *Cours d'architecture*
    (1771–7) 19–20

Bonhôte, Elizabeth 275-6
　Bungay Castle (1796) 157-8, 272-3
book illustrations 133-5, 147-55
Bourne, Henry, *Antiquitates vulgares* (1725) 276-8
Boyle, Richard, 3rd Earl of Burlington 191-2
Boyse, Samuel, 'The Triumph of Nature'
　(1742) 6-8
Brakspear, Harold 187-8
Brand, John, *History and Antiquities of the Town
　and County of the Town of Newcastle upon
　Tyne, The* (1789) 273-4
Brayley, Edward Wedlake (with Britton, J.),
　*History of the Ancient Palace and Late
　Houses of Parliament at Westminster, The*
　(1836) 315-16
Britain, history of 36-7, 293-6, 300-2
　'Gothic' 4-10, 30, 182, 215-16, 268-9
　Protestant 263-5
　Roman 4-5, 67-8
　see also England
Britton, John 269-70
　Architectural Antiquities of Great Britain, The
　　(1807-27) 167-8, 333-4
　*History of the Ancient Palace and Late Houses
　of Parliament at Westminster, The* (with
　Brayley, E. W., 1836) 315-16
Brontë, Emily, *Wuthering Heights* (1847) 335-6
Brooke, Frances, *History of Lady Julia
　Mandeville, The* (1763) 85
Brougham Castle, Westmorland 174-5, 272,
　274-5
Brydone, Patrick, *Tour Through Sicily and Malta,
　A* (1773) 139-40
Buck, Samuel and Nathaniel 269-70
Bull, Richard 94-6
Burckhardt, Jacob, *Civilization of the Renaissance
　in Italy, The* (1860) 337
Burgess, Thomas, *Essay on the Study of
　Antiquities, An* (1780) 4-5, 230-1
Burghley House, Lincolnshire 109-10
Burke, Edmund 204-8
　Philosophical Enquiry..., *A* (1757) 55
　Reflections on the Revolution in France
　　(1790) 201-5, 217-18, 294-5, 315-16
　Thoughts on the Prospect of a Regicide Peace
　　(1796) 207-8
Burlington House, Piccadilly, London 191-2
Burnet, Bishop Gilbert, *History of the
　Reformation of the Church of England,
　The* (1679-1714) 240-1
Burney, Frances 92-3, 235
Burns, Robert, 'Tam o'Shanter' 276-8
Burrell, Lady, 'Lines Sent to Mr Walpole'
　(1790) 123-5

Burton, Richard, *Anatomy of Melancholy, The*
　(1621) 155-6
Byron, Lord (George Gordon) 187-8, 345-6
　Don Juan (1819-24) 346-7

Calvinism 233-4
Cambridge University 99, 102; *see also* King's
　College Chapel, Cambridge
camera obscura 76-8
Campbell, Archibald 190-1
Campbell, Colen, *Vitruvius Britannicus*
　(1725-25) 4-5
Canterbury Cathedral 81, 83-5
'Capability' Brown, Lancelot 185-6
capriccios 164-7, 169-70, 170*f*
Carey, Henry, *Chrononhotonthologos*
　(1734) 344-5
Carlyle, Thomas 335
　Past and Present (1843) 329-30
Carter, John 185-6
　Ancient Architecture of England, The
　　(1795-1814) 244-5
　architectural journalism of 1-3, 9-10, 18-19,
　　31-2, 35, 37-8, 195-6
　Catholic sympathies of 253-4
　*Entry of Prince Frederick into the Castle of
　Otranto, The* (watercolour, 1817) 39-42,
　40*f*, 93-4
　Gentleman's Magazine, The, publication in
　　1, 18-19, 31-2, 35, 37-8, 194-7, 286-7
　Occurrences in the Life (1817) 39-41
　Pursuits of Antiquaries (c.1803) 34-6
　St Peter's Chapel, Winchester (design)
　　253-5
　sites of architectural interest, visits to 1-3,
　　8-9, 35-6
　South View of the Castle of Otranto (n.d.)
　　94-6, 95*f*
　Specimens of Ancient Sculpture and Painting
　　(1786) 39-41
　theatrical reviews by 31-3
　Vetusta Monumenta series (1718-1906),
　　illustrations for 270-1
　Walpole, working for 39-41, 40*f*
　Wyatt, responses to the work of 192-5
Carver, Elizabeth, *Horrors of Oakendale Abbey,
　The* (1797) 182-4
castellations/castellated architecture 100-1,
　191-2, 233, 300-1, 351-2
Castle Conwy, North Wales 11-12, 31-2
Castle Howard, Yorkshire 190-1
Castle of Udolpho, The (Anon., 1808) 153-5
castles 143-4, 174-5
　dungeons of 2-3, 8-9

castles (*cont.*)
  enchanted 107, 117–22, 127–30, 158, 163–5, 167–70, 219
  haunted 107, 140–1
  and patriarchal authority, expressions of 140–3, 145–6
  and literature 145–6, 153–5, 272, 290–1, 300–1, 303
  metaphor, use as 197–201, 208
  paintings/artworks of 147–55
  ruins of 4–5, 269–70, 272–5, 290–1
  and the sublime 144–6
  see also 'castles in the air'; 'two-castle model'
'castles in the air' 13–14, 117–18, 135–6, 155, 164–5, 203–4, 272–3, 288
Castles of Athlin and Dunbayne, The (Anon., 1789) *see under* Radcliffe, Ann
Catholic Emancipation Act (1829) 221–2
Catholics/Catholicism 82–3, 168–9, 240–1, 252
  and art 335
  and idolatry 226–30
  and literature 221–2, 263–4
  and the Gothic Revival 248, 334–5
  and gothic style, association with 36–8, 42–4, 66–7, 71–2, 184, 224–5, 230–3, 250, 330–1, 333–5
  medieval 260–1, 320–1
  and nostalgia 246, 264–5
  perceived pagan origins of 225–30
  and superstition 225–6, 228, 232–3, 263–6, 318–21, 330–1
  see also anti-Catholicism
Celts 4–5
Cervantes, Miguel de, *Don Quixote* (1605–15) 112–13, 155–6
Chalmers, Alexander, *History of the Renowned Prince Arthur, The* (1816) 329
Chambers, William 79
  Dissertation on Oriental Gardening, A (1772) 62, 79
  Treatise on Civil Architecture, A (1759) 55–6, 58–60, 62
Chambray, Roland Fréart de 36–7
'*chateaux en Espagne*' 155–7
Chaucer, Geoffrey 104–5
  House of Fame, The (*c*.1379–80) 155–6
  Life of Geoffrey Chaucer (Godwin, 1804) 11–12
Chinese styles 81–3, 89–90
chivalry 41–2, 215–19, 250–2, 289–90
Chopp'd Straw Hall *see* Strawberry Hill, Twickenham
Chute, John 125–6, 252

Cirencester Park, Gloucestershire: Alfred's Hall 160–1, 191–2
Clarke, Anne Melicent 42–4, 94–6
Clarke, James, *Survey of the Lakes of Cumberland, Westmorland, and Lancashire, A* (1789) 174–5
Clark, Kenneth, *Gothic Revival, The* (1928) 350, 353
classical orders 64–5; *see also* Greek architecture, ancient; Roman architecture, ancient
classical styles 54–5, 144–5, 171–2, 188–9
  and beauty 81–2, 143–4, 322–3
  and culture 78, 139–40
  and Gothic styles, in comparison with 45–6, 48–9, 58–63, 71–5, 103–5, 145–6, 180–1, 198, 318
  and Gothic styles, merging with 67, 193–4, 285–6, 320–1; *see also* 'modern Gothic' style
  grandeur of 48, 104–5, 143–4
  and interiors 189
  and the sublime 55–7, 72–4, 322–3
  see also Battle of the Styles
classicism 19–20, 36–7, 81–2, 325
  and architecture 48–9, 51–2, 56–9, 64–5, 71–2, 322–3; *see also* classical styles
  and literature/myth 82–3, 322–3
  and politics 191–2
  see also Battle of the Styles
Claude glass 76–7, 236
Claude Lorrain ('Claude') 164–5, 349
  Landscape with Psyche... (1664) 152–3
Clifford, Frances, *Ruins of Tivoli, The* (1810) 51–2
Cobbett, William, *History of the Protestant 'Reformation', A* (1824–7) 334–5
Codrington library, All Souls College, Oxford 198
Coke, Edward, *Third Part of the Institutes of the Laws of England, The* (1644) 184
Coke, Lady Mary 92, 113–14
Coleridge, Samuel Taylor 169–71, 338–9
  Biographia Literaria 338–9
  'General Character of the Gothic Literature and Art' (1818) 332–3
  'General Character of the Gothic Mind in the Middle Ages' (1818) 321–2
  Literary Remains of Samuel Taylor Coleridge (1836) 321–3
  Table Talk (1835) 322–3
Cole, William 26–8, 63–4, 102, 122–3, 226, 250–2
Collins, William
  'Ode to Fear' (1747) 245–6
  'To Liberty' (1747) 6–8, 198–9

Colman the Younger, George, *Feudal Times* (1799) 31–2
Combermere Abbey, Cheshire 187–8
Combe, William, *Tour of Dr Syntax in Search of the Picturesque, The* (1812) 75–6
conservatism 211–13, 219–20
Constable, Archibald 309–10
convents 238–42
'Conversations with the Late William Beckford' (1844) 252–3
Conway, Henry Seymour 108, 117–18
Cooper, Anthony Ashley, 3rd Earl of Shaftesbury, *Advancement and Reformation of Modern Poetry, The* (1701) 72–4
Cooper, George, *Architectural Reliques* (1807) 269–70, 288–9
Corneille, Pierre, *Horace* (1640) 6–8
Costes, Gauthier de, *Cléopâtre* (1648) 108
Cotton, Robert 187–8
Cotton, Stapleton 187–8
Couchman, Henry 191–2
country houses *see* domestic architecture
craftsman-architect, the 15–17; *see also* architect, the
Craftsman, The 6–8
Craven, Lady Elizabeth 93–4
Cross, John, *Halloween* (1799) 136–7
Culloden Tower, Richmond, North Yorkshire 190–1
Cumnor Hall, Berkshire (now Oxfordshire) 304–7, 309–10
Cunningham, Allan, *Biographical and Critical History* (1834) 133–5
Curties, T. J. Horsley 157, 209–10
  Ancient Records (1801) 185–9, 209–10, 283
  Ethelwina (1799) 209–10
  Monk of Udolpho, The (1807) 153–5
  St Botolph's Priory (1806) 275
Cust, Edward, *Apology for the Architectural Monstrosities of London, An* (1835) 353–4

Damer, Anne Seymour 123–5
Danes 5–6, 279–80
'Dark Ages' 35, 259, 289–90, 313–14, 336–7, 348
darkness 317–21, 335–6
  fear of the 46–7, 50–1, 55
  and the Middle Ages 35, 39, 318–20, 336–7
  and the supernatural 46–7, 50–1
Dart, John, *Westmonasterium* (1723) 203–4
Davenant, William, *Preface to Gondibert* (1650) 112–13
De Chassebœuf, Constantin-François, comte de Volney, *Les Ruines* (1791) 207–8

demolition/destruction 81–2, 186–7, 193–4, 196–7, 200–1, 292–3, 304, 314–15
  and revolution 201–5, 207–9
  see also Bastille, fall of the; 'improvements', architectural; Westminster, Palace of
Denham, John, *Cooper's Hill* (1642) 172–3, 247
Dennis, John, *Advancement and Reformation of Modern Poetry, The* (1701) 72–4
Dent, John, *Bastille, The* (1790) 202–3
Denton, Thomas, 'The House of Superstition' (1765) 258–9
De Quincey, Thomas 131–2, 178, 346–7
destruction *see* demolition/destruction
Dickens, Charles
  Bleak House (1852–3) 335–6
  Great Expectations (1860–1) 352–3
Diderot, Denis, and Alembert, Jean le Rond d', *Encyclopédie* (1751–72) 19–22, 21f
Digby, Robert 289
domestic architecture 125–6, 187–9, 219–20
Donnington Grove, Berkshire 125–6
Douglas, James, *History of Julia d'Haumont, The* (1797) 153–5
Downton Castle, Herefordshire 189
Drake, Nathan, 'The Abbey of Clunedale' (1798) 51–2
drawing 1, 268–70, 288–9; *see also* painting
Drayton, Michael, *Poly-Olbion* (1612; 1622) 172–3
dreams 103
Ducarel, Andrew Coltée, *Anglo-Norman Antiquities Considered* (1767) 168–9
Duff, William, *Essay on Original Genius, An* (1767) 14–15
Duffet, Thomas, *Mock Tempest, The* (1674) 122n.151
Dugdale, William
  Antiquities of Warwickshire, The (1656) 289
  History of St Pauls Cathedral in London, A (1658) 4–5, 115–17
  Monasticon Anglicanum (1655–73) 4–5, 223–4, 296, 297f
Dunlop, John 134–5
Durham Cathedral 193–5
Dyce, William 329
Dyer, George, *Poetics* (1812) 163–4

Eastlake, Charles Locke, *History of the Gothic Revival, A* (1872) 330, 353
Eccardt, John Giles, *Conyers Middleton* 226–8, 227f
ecclesiastical architecture 100–1, 252
  and anti-Catholicism 260–3

ecclesiastical architecture (*cont.*)
  and Catholicism 71–2, 168–9, 184, 221–2, 230–1, 233, 247–8, 257–8
  and country houses, reworking as 187–8
  and literature 175–6, 186, 221–2, 236–8, 260–263
  and supernatural terror 51–2, 240–2
  and superstition 228, 232–4, 236–7, 246, 257–259, 275–6
  veneration, as objects of 4–5, 223–5, 230–2, 234–5, 238–40, 245–6, 258–9
  see also monasteries/monastic buildings; ruins, architectural
Edgeworth, Maria 159–60
  Castle Rackrent (1800) 158
ekphrasis 133–4, 152–3
Elgin Marbles, the 317–20
Elizabeth I, Queen of England 302–3, 308–9
Ellis, George, *Specimens of Early English Metrical Romances* (1805) 287
empiricism 45–6, 76–8
enchantment 110–11, 113–14, 123–5
  and castles 107, 117–22, 127–30, 158, 163–5, 167–70, 219
England 4–10, 67–8, 167–8, 176–7, 182, 268–9, 325–7, 329, 331–2; *see also* Britain, history of
Enquiry into the Origin of the Human Appetites and Affections, An (Anon., 1747) 52–3
Erasmus, Desiderius 259–60
Essay on the Qualifications and Duties of an Architect, An (Anon., 1773) 15–17
Essex, James 38, 63–4
Eton College 238–40, 239*f*
Evelyn, John 86–7, 320–1
  Account of Architects and Architecture, An (1706/1723) 36–7, 224–5
  dismissal of Gothic styles ('Monkish Piles') 224–5, 231–2, 234–5, 238–40
  Parallel of the Antient Architecture with the Modern, A (1664) 36–7
Eyriès, Jean-Baptiste Benoît, *Fantasmagoriana* (1812) 345–6

'fancy' 14–15, 18, 26–7, 52–3, 338–9; *see also* imagination
Farington, Joseph 253
Farleigh Hungerford estate, Bath 182–4
Fawley Court, Buckinghamshire 160–1
'The Female Castle-Builder' (Anon., 1801–1802) 159
Fenn, Ellenor, *Female Guardian, The* (1784) 128–9

Ferrey, Benjamin, *Answer, to 'Thoughts on Rebuilding the Houses of Parliament'* (1835) 318–20
Fletcher, Phineas, *Purple Island, The* (1633) 119–20
follies, architectural 17–18, 160–2, 179–80, 190–191
'folly' 17–18, 99–100, 179–80, 325
Fonthill Abbey 253, 286–7, 324–5, 350–3
Fonthill Splendens 85, 88
fortifications, ruins of 4–5; *see also* ruins, architectural
Fosbrooke, Thomas Dudley, *British Monachism* (1817) 39, 330–1
Foxe, John, *Actes and Monuments* (later *Book of Martyrs, The*) (1563) 256–7
Fox Talbot, William Henry 187–8
France 168
  as a literary setting 107–8, 168–9
  post-revolutionary 137–9, 155–6, 182, 195–6, 201–2, 206–7
  see also anti-French sentiment; Bastille, fall of the; French Revolution
Frances, Sophia, *Nun of Misericordia, The* (1807) 9–10
'Frankenstein' (critical use of term) *see* 'modern Gothic' style
Freeman, John 160–1
French Revolution (1789) 137–9, 155–6, 182, 201–5, 214
Frogmore, Berkshire 192–3
Furness Abbey, Lancashire (now Cumbria) 131–2, 174–6, 339–43

Gandy, Joseph Michael 162–3, 166
  Architectural Ruins–a Vision (1832) 162–3
gardening *see* landscape gardening
Garrick, David and Colman the Elder, George, *Clandestine Marriage, The* (1766) 160–1
Gellée, Claude *see* Claude Lorrain
gender politics 140–3; *see also* patriarchal authority, architectural expressions of
genius 14–15, 17, 31–2, 54–5, 61–2, 71–2, 139–140, 341
Gentleman's Magazine, The 8–9, 33, 160–1, 197, 280–1, 288–9, 307–8, 311–12, 314–16, 330–331
  Carter's writing published in 1, 18–19, 31–2, 35, 37–8, 194–7, 286–7
'gentleman architects' 15–17, 353–4
George III, King of England 192–3, 208
Gerard, Alexander
  Essay on Genius, An (1774) 14–15

Essay on Taste, An (1759) 14–15, 55–8, 58*f*, 145
Germany, architecture of 36–7, 81, 331–2
Gheeraerts the Younger, Marcus, *Henry Cary, 1st Viscount Falkland* (*c*.1603) 93–4
ghosts/spectral beings 304–5
  and the imagination 50–1
  and story-telling 46–7, 276–8, 304–5
  visions of (within Gothic architectural spaces/ruins) 2–3, 8–9, 35–6, 50–1, 78–81
Gibbon, Edward, *History of the Decline and Fall of the Roman Empire, The* (1776–89) 5–6, 38
Gibbs, James: Temple of Liberty, Stowe 6–8
Gilbert Scott, George 335
Gilpin, William 45–6, 74–6, 188–9, 292–3
  Essay on Prints, An (1768) 74–5
  Glastonbury Abbey, Somerset (drawing) 76*f*
  Lives of John Wickliff, The (1765) 258–9
  Observations on the River Wye (1782) 78
  Observations on the Western Parts of England... (1798) 75–6, 235–6
  Observations Relative Chiefly to Picturesque Beauty (1786) 167–8, 176–7, 275
  Three Essays (1792) 74–7
Glastonbury Abbey, Somerset 76*f*, 235
Gloucester Cathedral 252
Godwin, William 345–6
  Enquiry Concerning Political Justice, An (1793) 294–5
  Caleb Williams (1794) 215–16, 294–5
  Life of Geoffrey Chaucer (1804) 11–12, 215–216
  'Of History and Romance' (1797) 215–16
'Gothic balance' 5–6
'Gothic bequest' 182, 215–16
'Gothick' 19–20, 36–8, 64–5, 72–4, 353
Gothic Revival, the 208, 248–9, 323–4, 326–7, 350–3
  and Catholicism 248
  and Protestantism 252–6
Gothic Revivalist architecture 33, 190–1, 199–200, 316–17, 324–5
  and Catholicism 236
  critics of 353
  and domestic/country houses 125–6, 187–8
  and literature 115–17, 123–5, 284–5, 288, 316–17
  and Strawberry Hill 39–41, 90–1, 125–6
  see also 'modern Gothic' style
Gothic romance 103–6, 155–6, 275, 325
  conventions of 8–9, 112–13, 281, 305
  and history 307–10

  negative responses to 156–8
  see also antiquarian romance; 'castles in the air'
'Goths', Germanic 5–6, 224–5, 247, 279–80, 296–8
Gough, Richard 185–6, 194–5, 268–9
  Anecdotes of British Topography (1768) 247–8, 268–9
  British Topography (1780) 244, 268–71
  Sepulchral Monuments of Great Britain (1786–96) 269–70
grandeur 48, 55–6, 104–5, 141–4
grand tour, the 67–8, 102, 164–5, 168
Grant, Anne, *Essays on the Superstitions of the Highlanders of Scotland* (1811) 276–8
Graves, Richard, *Spiritual Quixote, The* (1773) 17–18
Gray, Thomas 122–3
  Elegy Written in a Country Churchyard (1751) 240–1
  'Gothica Architectura' (*Commonplace Book*, *c*.1736–71) 67–9
  on Grand Tour 67–8
  Journal of a Visit to the Lake District in 1769 (1775) 175
  'A Long Story' (*Designs by Mr R. Bentley, for Six Poems by Mr T. Gray*, 1753) 134–5
  'Ode for Music' (1769) 176
  Ode on a Distant Prospect of Eton College, An (1747) 238–40, 239*f*
Greatheed, Bertie 42–4
Greek architecture, ancient 48, 62–5, 71–2, 74–75, 323
Greene, Robert, *Historie of Orlando Furioso, The* (1594) 155–6
Green, Sarah, *Romance Readers and Romance Writers* (1810) 283
Grose, Francis
  Antiquities of England and Wales, The (1772) 247–8, 269–70, 288–9
  Antiquities of Scotland, The (1791) 276–8
  Essays on Gothic Architecture (1800) 167–8
  Provincial Glossary, A (1787) 276–8
grotesque, the 320, 323, 335–6
Grove House ('The Priory'), Old Windsor 125–6
Gunn, William, *Inquiry into the Origin and Influence of Gothic Architecture, An* (1819) 331–2
Guydickens, Frederick William 26–7

Hakewell, Arthur William, *Thoughts Upon the Style of Architecture to be Adopted in Rebuilding the Houses of Parliament* 317–320

Halesowen Priory (folly), The Leasowes, Halesowen 17–18, 190–1
Halfpenny, William and John, *Chinese and Gothic Architecture Properly Ornamented* (1752) 285–6
Hallam, Henry, *View of the State of Europe During the Middle Ages* (1818) 336–7
Hamilton, William Richard 326–7
 first pamphlet (1836) 318–20
 Second Letter (1836) 320–3
 Third Letter (1837) 323–5
Hamley, Edward
 'Reflections in Netley Abbey' (1795) 262–3
 Sonnets (1789–) 262–3
Handel, George Frideric, *Armida* (1711) 109–10
Harding, George Perfect 42–4, 43f
Hardwick Hall, Derbyshire 174–5
Hartley, David 338–9
 Observations on Man... (1749) 55
Harvey, Jane
 Brougham Castle (1816) 272, 274–5
 Castle of Tynemouth, The (1806) 158, 272–4
Haslewood, Joseph, *La Mort D'Arthur* (1816) 329
Hawksmoor, Nicholas 198
Hazlitt, William 74–5, 180–1, 350–1
 Lectures on the English Comic Writers (1819) 131–2
Henley, Samuel 129–30
Henry III, King of England 293–8, 297f
heraldry 41–2
heritage 272, 315–16; *see also* 'improvements', architectural; preservation, architectural; restoration
historical inaccuracy 31–2, 168, 238–40, 308–9; *see also* 'modern Gothic' style
'historiography'/historical writing 22–5, 29–30, 171–2, 273–4
history/historians 75–6, 215–16, 231–2, 303
 and antiquarianism/antiquaries, comparison with 203–4, 279–80, 287
 and romance 23–5, 29–30, 215–16, 273–4, 278–81, 291–2, 307–10
 and ruins 223–5, 234–5, 288–93
 and truth 24–5, 29–30, 283–4, 308–9, 351–2
 see also 'historiography'/historical writing
Hobbes, Thomas 112–13
Hollar, Wenceslaus, Henry III re-endorsing the Magna Carta 296, 297f
Home, Henry, Lord Kames 188–9
 Elements of Criticism (1762) 72–4
Home, John, *Douglas: A Tragedy* (1756) 136–7
Hooper, John (Bishop of Gloucester and Worcestershire) 252

Horace, *Ars Poetica* (c.19 BC) 18–19
horror 2–3, 51–2, 240–2
Houghton Hall, Norfolk 118–19, 191–2
Houses of Parliament *see* Westminster, Palace of
Hughes, John 104–5
human existence, transience of 117–18, 122–3
Hume, David 29–30
 History of England, The (1754–61; 1778) 256–7, 295–6
 Treatise of Human Nature, A (1739) 52–3, 159
Hunt, Leigh 132–3
Hurd, Richard 106, 112–13
 Letters on Chivalry and Romance (1762) 103–6, 123–5, 289–90
 Moral and Political Dialogues (1759) 106, 289
Hutcheson, Francis, *Essay on the Nature and Conduct of the Passions and Affections, An* (1728) 52–3
Hutchinson, William
 Excursion to the Lakes, An (1774; rev. 1776) 264–5
 Hermitage, The (1771) 263–4
 View of Northumberland, A (c.1778) 273–4

idealism 87–8
idolatry 226–30
imagination 20–2, 338–9, 346–7
 and Gothic architecture, responses to 60–1, 70–1, 79–81, 145–6, 180–1, 290–5, 349–50
 and landscape painting 76–7, 164–5
 theories of the 47–54, 69–70
 see also associationism; *capriccios*; romance
imitatio 323–4
Impey, Elijah Barwell, *Cumnor; or, The Bugle-Horn* (1822) 307–8
imprisonment 82–3, 111, 113–14, 129, 136–7, 140–1, 204–5, 262–3, 345–6
'improvements', architectural 181–7, 314–15
 destructive, regarded as 193–4, 216–18
 metaphor, use as 196–204
 and modernization 188–9, 212, 219–20
Ireland, William Henry 240–1
 Abbess, The (1799) 240
Italy
 classical architecture of 81–3, 171–2, 317–18
 and literature 107–9, 168–9, 171
 see also Otranto, Castello di; Rome; Sicily; Venice

Jackson, Julian, *Observations on A Letter from W. R. Hamilton* (1837) 325–7
Jacob, Hildebrand, *Of the Sister Arts* (1734) 18–20

Jacobites/Jacobitism 190-1, 259
Jeffrey, Edward, *Otranto* (1796) 96-7, 96n.28, 97f
Jeffrey, Francis: book reviews 282-4, 287
Jephson, Robert 127
Count of Narbonne, The (1781) 126-7
Jerningham, Edward, *Elegy Written Among the Ruins of an Abbey, An* (1765) 240-2
Johnson, Samuel
Dictionary of the English Language, A (1755-6) 3
Lives of the Most Eminent English Poets, The (1779-81) 172-3
Johnston, Arthur 23-4
Jones, Inigo 19-20, 36-7, 318-20
Jordanes, *Getica* (c.AD 551) 5-6
Jutes 5-6, 279-80
Juvara, T., *Strictures on Architectural Monstrosities* (1835) 353-4

Kant, Immanuel 321-2
Critique of Judgement (1790) 322-3
Critique of Pure Reason (1781) 88
Keats, John 346-7
'Eve of St Agnes, The' (1820) 346-7
Keene, Henry 191-2
Kelly, Isabella, *Baron's Daughter, The* (1802) 9-10
Kenilworth Castle, Warwickshire 148-9, 172-3, 288, 299
and 'white Gothic' 301, 305-7
Kent, William
Faerie Queene, The (1751), illustrations to 112-13
Stowe, Buckinghamshire, work at 160-1, 191-2, 259
Ker, Anne, *Adeline St Julian* (1800) 9-10
Kerrich, Thomas, 'Some Observations on the Gothic Buildings Abroad...' (1812) 168
King, Edward, *Observations on Ancient Castles* (1782) 288-9
King's College Chapel, Cambridge 41-2, 102, 129-30, 342-3
Knight, Richard Payne 189
Analytical Inquiry into the Principles of Taste, An (1805) 72-4
Landscape, The (1794) 72-4

Lacock Abbey, Wiltshire 187-8
Lake District, the 176-8, 274-5
Landon, Letitia Elizabeth
'Chapter-House, Furness Abbey' (1835) 340
'Furness Abbey, In the Vale of Nightshade, Lancashire' (1832) 340

landscape gardening 72-4, 89-90, 160-1, 191-2
landscape painting, tradition of 76-7, 164-6; see also *capriccios*
Laneham, Robert *see* Langham, Robert
Lanercost ('Lenercost') Priory, Cumbria 264-5
Langham, Robert, 'A Letter' (1788) 300-2
Langley, Batty, *Ancient Architecture Restored, and Improved* (1741-2) 64-5
Lansdown Tower, Bath 86-7, 252-3
Lathom, Francis, *Castle of Ollada, The* (1795) 153-5
Le Fanu, Sheridan, *Carmilla* (1872) 335-6
Leasowes, The, Halesowen 17-18, 190-1
Ledwich, Reverend Edward 280-1
Lee, Harriet, *Kruitzner* (1797-1805) 294
Lee Priory, Kent 125-6
Lee, Sophia, *Recess, The* (1783-5) 23-4, 172-3, 299, 306-7
Leland, Thomas, *Longsword, Earl of Salisbury* (1762) 23-4, 267-8
Lessing, Gotthold Ephraim, *Laocoön* (1766) 19-20, 355-6
Lettice, John 79-80, 82-3
Lewis, Matthew 31-2, 240-1
Adelmorn, the Outlaw (1801) 31-2
Castle Spectre, The (1797/98) 10-12, 31-2
Monk, The (1796) 240-2, 263-4
Lewis, W. S. 98-9
'The Genesis of Strawberry Hill' (1934) 97-8
One Man's Education (1968) 98-9
Rescuing Horace Walpole (1978) 122-3
Lichfield Cathedral 193-4
Lincluden Priory, Dumfries 346-7
Lingard, John, *History of England, A* (1819-30) 334-5
Llandaff Cathedral, Cardiff 2-3
Locke, John 52-3, 55
Essay Concerning Humane [sic] Understanding, An (1690; 1700) 46-7, 50-51
Some Thoughts Concerning Education (1693; 1705) 46-7
Lovibond, Edward, 'On Rebuilding Combe Neville' (1785) 6-8
'Loyalist Gothic' 172-3
Lyson, Samuel, *Remains of Two Temples...* (1802) 161-2
Lytton, Edward Bulwer, *Last of the Barons, The* (1843) 329-30

Macaulay, Catharine 204-7
Macaulay, Thomas Babington 350-1
Macpherson, James, *Fragments of Ancient Poetry* (1760) 276-8

magic 110–11; *see also* enchantment; supernatural, the
magic-lantern shows 76–8
Magna Carta 296–8, 297f
Maitland, Samuel Roffey, *Dark Ages, The* (1844) 336–7
Malory, Thomas, *Le Mort d'Arthur* (1485) 329
Manners, George, *Edgar; or, Caledonian Feuds* (1806) 139–40
Mann, Horace 117–20, 249–50
Marlow, William, *Capriccio* (c.1795) 169–70
Marmontel, Jean-François, *Les Yncas* (1777) 29–30
Marshall, James, *Ruins, The* (1792) 207–8
Marshal, William *see* Walpole, Horace
Mason, William 67–8, 100–1
  English Garden, The (1772–81) 72–4
  'Unconnected Thoughts on Gardening' (1764) 72–4
Masters, Robert, Reverend Mr 26–7
Mathews, Charles 299–300
Mathias, T. J. 131–2
  Works of Thomas Gray, The (1814) 67–9
Maturin, Charles
  Five Sermons (1826) 240–1
  Melmoth the Wanderer (1820):'Tale of the Spaniard' 240
  Sermons (1819) 240–1
medieval romance 23–4, 33, 41–2, 107, 117, 245–6
medievalism 33–4, 39, 41–2, 313–14, 329–31, 337
Melville, Lewis, *Life and Letters of William Beckford of Fonthill, The* (1910) 79
memento mori, ruins as 141–3
'memory' 20–2, 52–3, 72–4, 276–8, 339–40, 349; *see also* associationism
Metrical Remarks on Modern Castles and Cottages (Anon., 1813) 285–6
Mickle, William Julius, 'Cumnor Hall' (1777) 304, 306–7, 309–10
Middle Ages 31–2, 39, 318–20
  architects/architecture of 89, 355–6
  and barbarism, perceptions of 31–2, 39, 318–20
  and enlightenment, perceptions of 318, 332–7
  literature 23–4, 33, 41–2, 245–6
  see also medievalism
Middleton, Conyers 226–8, 227f
  History of the Life of M. Tullius Cicero, The (1741) 225–6
  Letter from Rome, A (1729) 225–30
  and Horace Walpole, influence on 226–30
Miller, Sanderson 187–8, 191–2

Milles, Jeremiah, Reverend Doctor 26–7
Milner, John 194–5, 253–6
  Dissertation on the Modern Style of Altering Antient Cathedrals, A (1798) 38
  Essays on Gothic Architecture (1800) 167–8
  History Civil and Ecclesiastical, & Survey of the Antiquities, of Winchester, The (1798–1801) 253–5
  Inquiry into Certain Vulgar Opinions Concerning the Catholic Inhabitants and the Antiquities of Ireland, An (1808) 254–5
Milton, John 103–4
  Comus (1634) 104–5, 120–2
  'Il Penseroso' (1645) 66–7, 137–8, 250
  Paradise Lost (1667; 1674) 104–5, 159–60, 346
minstrelsy 41–2
'modern Gothic' style 193–4, 284–7, 308–10, 350
  critics of 320–1, 324–5, 351–3
Molesworth, Robert
  'The Principles of a Real Whig' (1705) 6–8
  Account of Denmark, An (1705) 296–8
monasteries, dissolution of (1536–41) 168–9, 223–4, 240–1, 245–8, 262, 264–5, 334–5
monastic buildings/monasteries 222–3, 230–1, 233–5, 238–41
  and literature 184, 221–2, 233–4, 236–42, 260–2
  see also ruins, architectural
monasticism 341–3
  and anti-Catholic literature 260–2
  and celibacy 260–3
  isolation/imprisonment of 260–3
monks 35–6, 221–2, 233–4, 265–6
  processions of 175–6, 250, 251f
Montague, Edward, *Castle of Berry Pomeroy, The* (1806) 272–6
Montague, Elizabeth 189
Montagu, George 27–8, 91–2, 119–20, 323–4
Moore, George, *Grasville Abbey* (1793–7) 182–4
More, Hannah, *Village Politics* (1792) 209
Morris, William 355–6
Müntz, Johann Heinrich 125–6
Murphy, James, *Travels in Portugal* (1795) 86–7
music 18–20; *see also* sister arts, the

Nasmyth, James, etching of Castle of Udolpho (1854) 149–50, 149f
nationalism 4–5, 167–8, 195–6, 326–7, 331–2
neoclassicism/neoclassical aesthetics 55, 59–61, 192–3, 318–20, 323–4; *see also* classical styles; classicism
Nether Winchendon, Buckinghamshire 187–8

Netley Abbey, Hampshire 9–10, 118, 250–2, 262, 265–6
Neve, Richard 285–6
Newdigate, Sir Roger 191–2
  'Essays on Party' (c.1760) 198–9
Newstead Abbey, Nottinghamshire 187–8
Norman architecture 37–8, 63–4, 67–9, 71–2, 331–2
Norris (?), *Modern Goth, The* (1788) 285–6
nostalgia 33, 222–3, 234–5, 246, 264–5
Nugent, Thomas, *Spirit of Laws, The* (transl., 1750) 5–6

Oldbuck, Jonathan 286–7
oral traditions
  and storytelling 275–8, 304–5
  and superstition 275–8, 304–5
Oriental styles 81–2, 89–90, 285–6
Otranto, Castello di 93–6, 95f; *see also* Walpole, Horace
Overton, Thomas Collins, *Temple Builder's Most Useful Companion, The* (1766) 285–6
Oxberry, W., *Kenilworth; A Melo-Drama* (1824) 307–8
Oxford Movement (1833–45) 329–30, 334–7, 342–3

Paganism
  and Catholicism 225–30
  and Classical associations 82–3, 103–4
pageantry 289–90, 301–3
Paine, Thomas, *Rights of Man* (1791) 204–5, 209
painting 18–20, 74–7; *see also* landscape painting, tradition of; sister arts, the
palaces 143–4
Palladian style 46–7, 89–90, 143–4, 188–9, 191–2, 318–20
Palladio, Andrea 81–2, 165–6, 191–2
Palmer, John, *Haunted Cavern, The* (1795) 156–7, 182–4
Pantheon, Oxford St, London 192–3
'paper house' metaphor (Strawberry Hill) 115–17, 125–6
Parsons, Eliza, *Castle of Wolfenbach, The* (1793) 172–3
patriarchal authority, architectural expressions of 140–3, 145–6
patriotism 325–6
Peacock, James 15–17
Peacock, Thomas Love
  Crotchet Castle (1831) 347–9
  Nightmare Abbey (1818) 343–5
Percy, Thomas
  Northern Antiquities (1770) 5–6

Reliques of Ancient English Poetry (1765) 23–4, 133–4, 278–9
Pevsner, Nikolaus 182–4
Phantoms of the Cloister (Anon., 1795) 9–10
Philistor *see* Pinkerton, John
philosophers 17
picturesque, the 4–5, 74–8
  and historical association, disregard for 74–6, 236, 292–5
  and landscape art 74–7
  and landscape gardening 72–4
Pinkerton, John 33, 288–9
  Dissertation on the Origin and Progress of the Scythians or Goths, A (1787) 5–6
  Inquiry into the History of Scotland, An (1789) 28–9
Piozzi, Hester, *Observations and Reflections...* (1789) 143–5
Piranesi, Giovanni Battista
  Carceri d'Invenzione (1750) 82–3, 167
  Grotteschi (1750) 167
Pitzhanger Manor, Ealing 161–2
Plato
  Republic, The (c. 380 BC) 17
  Symposium, The (385–370 BC) 17
plays 31–2, 126–8, 136–7
pleasure 69–70
  aesthetic of 14–15, 47–51, 53–4, 58–9
  and classical architecture 57, 62–3
  and imagination 53–4
poetry 6–8, 18–22
  topographical 13–14, 163–4, 172–3
  see also sister arts, the
politics/political systems 5–6, 137–9, 196–204; *see also* revolution; Tory politics/politicians; Whigs/Whiggism
Pope, Alexander 249–50, 259–60
  Dunciad, The (1728; 1743) 249–52, 259
  'Eloisa to Abelard' (1717) 260–2, 340
  Essay on Criticism, An (1711) 259–60
  Works of Shakespear, The (1725) 104–5
Portchester Castle, Hampshire 2–3, 8–9
Porter, William Warren, *Castle of Udolpho* (1790s) 148f
Poussin, Nicolas 164–5, 349
Pownall, Thomas
  Antiquarian Romance, An (1782; 1795) 279–81
  Treatise on the Study of Antiquities, A (1782) 272–3, 280–1
Pre-Raphaelite Brotherhood 329–30
preservation, architectural 185–7, 195, 269–72, 274–5, 315–16; *see also* 'improvements', architectural

Price, Uvedale, *Essay on the Picturesque, An* (1794) 72–4
Priestley, Joseph 233
Protestants/Protestantism 36–7, 42–4, 263–5, 335, 340–1
  and architectural writing 224–5
  and Gothic architectural style, opinions on 224–5
  and the Gothic Revival 252–6
  and reformers 168–9, 240–1, 263–4; *see also* Reformation, the
Pugin, A. C., *Specimens of Gothic Architecture* (1821–3) 351–2
Pugin, A. W. N. 254–5, 312–14, 327–8, 355–6
  Apology for a Work Entitled 'Contrasts', An (1837) 335
  Contrasts (1836/1841) 329–30, 333–5, 355–6
  Letter to A. W. Hakewill, Architect, A (1835) 318
  True Principles of Pointed or Christian Architecture, The (1841) 352–3, 355–6, 356*f*
  Westminster, Palace of, rebuild plans 315–16

Raby Castle, County Durham 35–6
Radcliffe, Ann 8–9, 57–8, 58*f*, 129–30, 145, 167–8, 210–11, 349
  and antiquarianism 242–6
  Castles of Athlin and Dunbayne, The (1789) 136–8, 236–7
  contemporary criticism of 131–5, 169–71, 173, 178
  ecclesiastical architecture in her works 236–40
  enchanted castles in her works 129–30, 158, 163–5, 167–70
  Gaston De Blondeville (1826) 13, 171, 210–11, 242–6, 290–9
  Italian, The (1797) 133–4, 171–4, 238–40, 263–4
  Journey Made in the Summer of 1794, A (1795) 131–2, 171, 173–8, 274–5
  Mysteries of Udolpho, The (1794) 9–10, 133–4, 143–6, 148*f*, 149*f*, 151*f*, 153–5, 163–4, 168–70, 176–7, 237–40, 278–9, 306–7
  'On the Supernatural in Poetry' (1826) 145, 291
  and politics 137–9, 294–6
  and romance 242–3, 307–8
  Romance of the Forest, The (1791) 182–4, 187–9, 278–9
  'St Alban's Abbey' (1826) 171, 242–6
  Sicilian Romance, A (1790) 138–43, 236–7
  travel journal 290–1

  visits to sites of architectural interest 173–7, 290–1
  and Walter Scott, influence of 243–4
Ramsay, Allan, *Dialogue on Taste, A* (1755; 1762) 70–1
Rastell, John, *Dialogue Concerning Heresies* (1529) 42–4
Ratcliffe, Eliza, *Mysterious Baron, The* (1808) 9–10
'reason' 20–2, 57, 202, 206, 257–8, 260
Reeve, Clara
  Old English Baron, The (1778; prev. *Champion of Virtue, The*, 1777) 9–10, 127–8, 172–3, 278–9
  Progress of Romance, The (1785) 112–13, 158–9
Reformation, the 240–1, 246–8, 256–7, 262, 264–5, 334–5, 342–3; *see also* monasteries, dissolution of
'Renaissance' 330–1
renovations 180–5, 188–9, 195, 212, 219–20
Repton, Humphry
  Fragments on the Theory and Practice of Landscape Gardening (1816) 188–9
  Observations on the Theory and Practice of Landscape Gardening (1805) 72–4
restoration 185–6, 195–6, 272–3; *see also* preservation, architectural; renovations
Reveley, Willey, *South West view of the Castle of Otranto, Italy* (1785) 93–6, 95*f*
revolution 155–6, 207–8; *see also* French Revolution
Reynolds, Joshua 66–7, 70–1
Rhodes, Ebenezer, *Peak Scenery* (1819) 163–4
Richardson, Samuel 22–3
Rickman, Thomas, *Attempt to Discriminate the Styles of English Architecture, An* (1817) 64–5, 86–7, 331–2
Ritson, Joseph, *Ancient English Metrical Romances* (1802) 287
Robsart, Amy, death of 304–5
Roman architecture, ancient 36–7, 48, 51–2, 62–8, 71–2, 82–3, 171, 317–18
romance 22–4, 103–4, 159–60, 206–7, 214–15, 320–1
  and antiquarianism 268–9, 288, 290–1
  conventions of 128–9, 281
  and gender 22–3, 159, 206–7
  and Gothic architectural ruins 176, 272, 291–2
  and history/historical writing 23–5, 29–30, 171–2, 215–16, 273–4, 278–81, 291–2, 307–8
  and the imagination 47–8, 176–7, 250–2, 273–4, 278–9, 300–1

and the Middle Ages 23-4, 33, 41-2, 107, 117, 245-6
  see also antiquarian romance
Romanesque architecture 68-9, 168-9, 331-2
romantic fiction 179-80, 272, 275, 291; *see also* antiquarian romance; Gothic romance
romanticism 74-7, 313-14, 338; *see also* antiquarian romance; Gothic romance; medieval romance; romance
Rome 171, 225-6
  Colosseum 82-3
  Pantheon 82-3
  St Peter's 48-9, 82-3, 225-6
Rome, religious authority of (Catholicism) 256-7
Rosa, Salvator 164-5, 167, 349
Rowlandson, Thomas, *North Entrance of Strawberry Hill with a Procession of Monks, c.*1789 250, 251f
Royal Academy of Arts, London 15-17, 66-7, 71-2, 162-3, 232-3
Royal Institute of British Architects (RIBA) 15-17, 353-4
royalism 195-6
ruins, architectural 4-5, 184, 186, 206-8, 221-5, 234-5, 240-1, 245-6, 289-91
  and beauty 74-5, 78
  and Catholicism 71-2, 168-9, 184, 230-1, 233, 257-8
  and grandeur 141-3
  and history 223-5, 234-5, 288-93
  evoking horror/terror 2-3, 51-2, 240-2
  and the imagination 50-1, 72-4, 252
  and literature 168-9, 175-6, 179-80, 272, 275-6, 289-93
  ornamental use of 72-4; *see also* follies, architectural
  and superstition 228, 232-4, 236-7, 246, 257-9, 275-6
  as 'venerable' objects 246, 248-50, 256-9
  see also demolition; restoration
ruins, sham *see* follies, architectural
Ruskin, John 313-14, 349
  'The Nature of Gothic' 335, 355-6
  Seven Lamps of Architecture, The (1849/1855) 329-30, 349-50
  Stones of Venice, The (1851-3) 324-5, 329-30, 335-6
Rutter, John 253
  Delineations of Fonthill and Its Abbey (1823) 324-5
Ryde, Henry T., *History of the Palace of Westminster, A* (1849) 327-8
Rymer, Thomas, *Tragedies of the Last Age, The* (1678) 104-5

Sage, Victor, *Horror Fiction in the Protestant Tradition* (1988) 221-2
Salisbury Cathedral 194
Sandby, Paul 167
  Collection of Landscapes, A (1777) 250
Sandby, Thomas 269-70
Sanders, Nicholas, *De origine et progressu schismatio Anglicani libri tres* (1585) 240-1
Sandleford Priory, Berkshire 189
Saxon Gothic style 68-9, 148-9, 168-70, 331-2
Saxons 5-6, 23-4, 279-80
Schlegel, August Wilhelm 338-9
  Course of Lectures on Dramatic Art and Literature, A (1815) 74-5
Schlegel, Friedrich von, 'An Essay on Gothic Architecture' (1849) 329-30
Scotland 4-5, 28-9, 136-7, 276-8
Scott, John, *Journal of a Tour to Waterloo and Paris* (1842) 299-300, 303-4
Scott, Walter 134, 147-8, 159-60, 163-4, 243-4, 281, 283-4, 286-7, 299, 326-7, 350
  Abbot, The (1820) 349
  Ancient Times, Queenhoo-Hall, A Romance (1808) 281-4
  'An Essay on Romance' (1824) 307-8
  Antiquary, The (1816) 278-9, 349
  Apology for Tales of Terror, An (1799) 51-2
  Castle of Otranto, introduction to (1811) 99-100
  English Minstrelsy (1810) 14-15, 159-60
  Guy Mannering (1815) 349
  Ivanhoe (1820) 283-4, 286-7, 308-9
  journal (1829) 159-60
  Kenilworth (1821) 290-1, 299-310
  Kenilworth and Warwick castles, visits to (1815) 299-301, 309
  Lay of the Last Minstrel, The (1805) 243-4, 349-50
  Lives of the Novelists (1825) 299
  Marmion (1808) 282-4, 287-8, 349-50
  Minstrelsy of the Scottish Border (1802) 276-8
  Monastery, The 349
  'Prefatory Memoir to Mrs Ann Radcliffe' 133-4
  Waverley 309, 326-7
Seabright, Sir Thomas 125-6
Shakespeare, William 9-10, 25-6, 50-1, 103-5, 271, 290-1, 308-9
  Hamlet [*c.*1600] 104-5, 107, 294
  Macbeth [*c.*1606] 104-5, 294
  Midsummer Night's Dream, A [*c.*1594-6] 104-5, 156-7
  Tempest, The (*c.*1611) 122-5, 129, 152-3, 155-7, 162-3
'Sharawaggi' 89-90

Shelley, Mary, *Frankenstein* (1818; 1831) 159–60, 320–1, 323–5, 345–6, 353–4
Shelley, Percy Bysshe 345–6
  Defence of Poetry, A (1821/1840) 346–7
  St Irvyne (1811) 343–4
Shenstone, William 17–18
  'Unconnected Thoughts on Gardening' (1764) 72–4
  'The Ruin'd Abby' (1743) 257–9
Shotover Park, Oxfordshire 190–1
Sicily 139–40
sister arts, the 18–22, 41–2, 58–9, 71–2, 354–6
sketching *see* drawing
Smirke, Robert 315–16
Smith, Charlotte 147–8, 172–3
  Banished Man, The (1794) 157, 219–20
  Desmond (1792) 211–15, 218–20
  Emigrants, The (1793) 214
  Emmeline (1788) 157–8, 172–3
  Old Manor House, The (1794) 216–20
Smith, Warren Hunting 98–9
  Architecture in English Fiction (1934) 98–9
  'Strawberry Hill and Otranto' (1936) 99
Soane, John 71–2
  Bank of England, remodelling of the 285–6
  Crude Hints Towards an History of My House in Lincoln's Inn Field (1812) 166
  Description of Three Designs for the Two Houses of Parliament... (1835) 162–3
  homes/residences of 161–3
  Memoirs of the Professional Life of an Architect (1835) 161–2, 285–6
  Plans, Elevations, and Perspective Views, of Pitzhanger Manor-House (1833) 161–2
  Westminster, Palace of, work on the 312–16
Society of Antiquaries of London, the 26–7, 270–1, 280–1
Southey, Robert, 'Poor Mary, The Maid of the Inn' (1799) 51–2
spectacle 123–5, 300–3
Spectator, The 47–8, 51–4, 61–2, 275–6
spectral beings *see* ghosts/spectral beings
Spenser, Edmund
  Complaints (1591) 271
  Faerie Queene, The (1590–6) 64–7, 104–5, 112–15, 114*f*, 119–22
Spiller, James 162n.129
St Albans Abbey, Hertfordshire 242–6
St Bernard's Priory (Anon., 1786) 264–5
St George's Chapel, Windsor: restoration of (1787) 192–3
St John, Henry, 1st Viscount Bolingbroke
  Dissertation Upon Parties, A (1735) 6–8

'Remarks on the History of England...' (1730–1) 6–8
Remarks on the History of England (1743) 256–7
St Paul's Cathedral, London 115–17, 169–70, 170*f*, 318
St Peter's Chapel, Winchester 253–5
St Peter's Church, Wallingford, Oxfordshire 198
Stoke Manor House, Stock Park, Buckinghamshire 134–5, 135*f*
Stone, Francis 203–4
Stoneleigh Abbey, Warwickshire 182–4
Stowe, Buckinghamshire
  Temple of Ancient Virtue 191–2
  Temple of Liberty 6–8, 190–1
  Temple of British Worthies 259
Strawberry Hill, Twickenham 39–41, 62–3, 89–92, 115
  artworks displayed at 93–4, 115–19, 226–8, 250
  books/library at 108–10, 112–13, 115–19, 226–8
  and Castle of Otranto, suggested as inspiration for 91–4, 96–103, 115–17
  construction/architectural remodelling of 59–60, 100–1, 115–17, 250
  critics of 286–7, 350–3
  as an 'enchanted castle' 120–2, 128–9
  influence of 125–6
  paintings/drawings of 96–7, 115–17, 120, 250, 251*f*
  paper, decorative use of 115–18
  Paraclete (Hall) 249–50, 261–2
  and 'white Gothic' 123–5
Strutt, Joseph, *Queenhoo-Hall* (1808) 281–4
Stuart, Gilbert, *Historicall Dissertation..., An* (1768) 5–6
Sturges, John, *Reflections on the Principles and Institutions of Popery* (1799) 254–5
sublime, the, experience of 55–6, 144–6
  and Gothic architectural styles 41–2, 57–8, 70–1, 143–6, 322, 333–4
  and literature 322–3, 349
sublime, the, theories of
  and beauty 69–71
  and classical (Grecian) style 55–7, 72–4, 322–3
  and gothic style 41–2, 57–8, 70–1, 143–6, 322, 333–4
Summers, Montague, *Gothic Quest, The* (1938) 221–2
supernatural, the 35–6, 46–7, 50–1, 78, 99–100
  and classical culture 78

and literature 9–10, 218
and oral storytelling 9–10, 46–7, 276–8, 304–5
see also ecclesiastical architecture
superstition
  and Catholicism 225–6, 228, 232–3, 263–6, 318–21, 330–1
  and ecclesiastical buildings 228, 232–4, 236–7, 246, 257–9
  and oral storytelling traditions 275–8, 304–5
  and ruins 275–6
Swinburne, Henry, *Travels in the Two Sicilies* (1783–1785/1790) 139–40
Switzer, Stephen, *Nobleman, Gentleman, and Gardener's Recreation, The* (1715) 72–4

Tacitus, Cornelius, *Germania* (c.AD 98) 5–6
Talbot, John Ivory 187–8
Talfourd, Thomas Noon 132–3
  'Memoir of the Life and Writings of Mrs Radcliffe' 290–1
Tarr, Mary Muriel, *Catholicism in Gothic Fiction* (1946) 221–2
Tasso, Torquato 103–4
  Jerusalem Delivered (1763) 106, 109–12, 114–15, 120–2, 152–3
  La Gerusalemme liberata (1581) 104–5, 108–10
Taste
  and aesthetics 55–7, 69–70, 254–5
  and Classical architecture 62–3
  and Gothic architecture 61–2, 318
Taylor, Robert 198
Temple, Richard, Viscount Cobham 6–8
Temple, William
  Introduction to the History of England, An (1695) 5–6
  'Of Heroick Virtue' (1690) 5–6
  'Of Poetry' (1690) 72–4
  'Upon the Gardens of Epicurus' (1685) 89–90
Tennyson, Alfred, Lord, 'Morte d'Arthur' (1842) 329–30
terror 2–3, 51–2, 55, 240–2
'Terrorist Novel Writing' 9–11
theatre/theatrical productions 31–3, 153–5, 202; *see also* plays
Thelwall, John, *Rights of Nature, The* (1796) 207–8
Thomson, James
  Castle of Indolence, The (1748) 120–2, 155–6
  Liberty (1735–6) 5–6, 256–7, 295–6
  Winter (1726) 5–6
Tighe, Hugh Usher, *Historical Account of Cumner [sic], An* (1821) 304
Tintern Abbey, Monmouthshire 35–6, 339–40

Tomkins, J. M. S., *Popular Novel in England, 1700–1800, The* (1932) 221–2
'topographical Gothic' 171–3, 176–7
topography 267–9
  and antiquarianism 171–2, 267–8
  and drawings/illustrations, use of 268–70
  and literature 13–14, 163–4, 171–7, 182–4, 245–6, 248–9, 264–6, 268
  see also poetry
Tory politics/politicians 4–8, 182, 191–2, 195, 295–6, 328–9
Trinity College, Cambridge 99
Tuck, Mary, *Durston Castle* (1804) 9–10
Turner, Sharon, *History of the Anglo-Saxons, The* (1799–1805) 5–6
'two-castle model' 136–8, 150, 151*f*, 238–40
Tyrrell, James 190–1
  Bibliotheca politica (1692–4) 5–6
  General History of England, The (1699) 5–6

Upcott, William, *Byrth, Lyf, and Actes of Kyng Arthur, The* (1817) 329

Vanbrugh, John 51–2, 59–60, 160–1, 290–1
Vasari, Giorgio, *Lives of the Artists, The* (1549–50; 1568) 36–7
veneration, buildings as subjects of 4–5, 223–4, 230–2, 234–5, 248–50, 256–9
Venice 82–3, 143–4, 169–70, 170*f*, 324–5
Verstegan, Richard, *Restitution of Decayed Intelligence, A* (1605) 5–6
Vertue, George 269–70
Viollet-le-Duc, Eugène 329–30
Virgil, *Aeneid* (29–19 BC) 78
Vitruvius, *De architectura* (c.15BC) 6–8, 46
Vivarès, François and Woollett, William, *Enchanted Castle, The* (1782) 152–3, 153*f*
Volney, comte de, *Les Ruines* (1791) 166
Vortigern 5–6
Vyne, The, Hampshire 125–6, 252

Wales 1, 4–5, 292–3
Walker, George, *Haunted Castle, The* (1794) 172–3
Walpole, Horace 59, 102, 117–18, 122–3, 191–2, 194, 323–4, 350–1
  Aedes Walpoliana (1747) 118–19
  Anecdotes of Painting in England (1762–71; 1780) 12, 27–8, 59–66, 71–2, 79–80, 89–90, 248–9, 254–5
  'Anecdotes Relating to Dr Conyers Middleton' (1740) 226–8
  and anti-Catholicism 228–30
  and antiquarianism 27–8

Walpole, Horace (*cont.*)
  architectural tastes of 59–61, 248–50
  Book of Materials (c.1759; c.1775) 61–3, 65–6, 70–1
  Castle of Otranto, The (1764; 1765) 3, 9–10, 27–8, 30, 39–44, 39f, 61, 89–91, 106–7, 115, 122–3, 126–30, 229–30; *see also* Otranto, Italy
  Catalogue of the Royal and Noble Authors of England, A (1758) 29–30
  and Catholicism, appreciation of aesthetic value of 226–8, 250–3
  collections of 27–9, 93–4, 115–19, 226–8, 250
  critics of 126–30, 229–30
  Description of the Villa of Mr Horace Walpole, A (1774; 1784) 39–41, 92–6, 118, 122–3, 249–50
  and ecclesiastical architecture, responses to 248–52
  'Epistle from Florence' (1740) 226–9
  Hieroglyphic Tales (1785) 27, 29–30, 118n.134
  Historic Doubts on the Life and Reign of King Richard the Third (1768) 24–7, 29–30, 280–1
  letters 98–102, 117–18, 166, 249–52
  literary influence of 126–7, 129–30, 284–5
  Miscellaneous Antiquities (1772) 27
  Mysterious Mother, The (1768) 229–30
  'Patapan' (1749) 109–10
  pseudonym, use of a (William Marshal) 91–2, 100–2, 112–13
  reading habits 108–10, 112–13, 115–19, 226–8
  Sermon on Painting (1742) 226–8
  Short Notes of the Life of Horatio Walpole (c.1746–79) 63–4, 102
  Society of Antiquaries fellowship 25–7
  travels/tours of 102, 109–10
  Works of Horatio Walpole, The (1798) 26–7, 29–30, 61, 93–6, 118, 228
  see also Strawberry Hill, Twickenham
Walpole, Robert 120–2, 191–2, 226
Warburton, William (Bishop of Gloucester), *Works of Alexander Pope, The* (1751; 1760) 63–4
Ware, Isaac, *Complete Body of Architecture, A* (1756) 4–5
Warner, Richard
  Catholic Emancipation (1829) 266
  Netley Abbey (1795) 9–10, 265–6
  Topographical Remarks (1793) 265–6
Warton, Thomas
  Essays on Gothic Architecture (1800) 167–8
  History of English Poetry, The (1774) 23–4

  Observations on the Fairy Queen of Spenser (1754; 1762) 64–7, 104–5, 114–15, 119–20
  Pleasures of Melancholy, The (1747) 176
  Verses on Sir Joshua Reynolds's Painted Window at New-College Oxford (1782) 66–7, 86–7, 198–9, 232–3
Warwick Castle, Warwickshire 148–9, 290–1, 299–300
Webster, John, *Duchess of Malfi, The* (1613–14) 50–2, 223–4
West, Gilbert, *Institution of the Order of the Garter* (1742) 6–8
Westminster Abbey, London 35–7
Westminster, Palace of
  destruction by fire (1834) 311–14
  remodelling of (post-1834) 315–17, 323–4, 327–9, 353–4
West, Thomas, *Antiquities of Furness, The* (1774) 175
Whately, Thomas, *Observations on Modern Gardening* (1770) 72–4
Whigs/Whiggism 6–8, 49, 54–5, 65–6, 72–4, 182, 190–2, 296–8, 328–9
White Castle, Monmouthshire 1–2, 8–9
'white Gothic' 33–6, 39, 41–2, 123–5, 150, 151f, 196–7, 209–10, 245–6, 301, 305–7, 313–14, 328–9, 347–8
Whitehead, William 190–1
White, James, *Earl Strongbow* (1789) 172–3
Whittington, G. D., *Historical Survey of the Ecclesiastical Antiquities of France, An* (1809) 168
Whitton Park, Middlesex 190–1
Williams, Helen Maria
  'The Bastille, A Vision' (1790) 212–13
  'To Dr Moore' (1792) 212–13
Willis, Browne 244, 247–8
Willson, Edward 333–4
Wollstonecraft, Mary 345–6
  Maria (1798) 158, 206–7
  Vindication of the Rights of Men, A (1790) 206
  Vindication of the Rights of Woman, A (1792) 206–7
women, oppression of 140–1, 145–6, 210–11
Woollett, William *see* Vivarès, François
Wordsworth, William 341
  Ecclesiastical Sketches (1822) 341–3
  Furness Abbey sonnets 340–1
  Guide Through the District of the Lakes, A (1835) 178, 340
  'Imaginative Regrets' 342–3
  Lyrical Ballads (1798; 1800) 338–40
  'Tintern Abbey' 339–40

Poems by William Wordsworth (1815) 338–9
Prelude, The (1805) 339–40, 342–3
'St Bees' (1835) 342–3
Worsley, Richard, *History of the Isle of Wight, The* (1781) 275
Wotton, Henry, *Elements of Architecture, The* (1624) 46
Wren, Christopher 312, 318–20
Parentalia (1750) 36–7, 225, 317–18
Wrighte, William, *Grotesque Architecture* (1767) 335–6
Wyatt, James 125–6, 192–4, 285–6, 312–14

Wyatville, Jeffry 192–3
Wyclif, John 256–9

Yearsley, Ann, *Otranto* (1784) 123–5
Yorke, Mrs, *Haunted Palace, The* (1801) 172–3
York Minster, York 79–80
Young, Edward, *Conjectures on Original Composition* (1759) 14–15, 131–2

Ziegenhirt, Sophia, *Orphan of Tintern Abbey, The* (1816) 339–40
Zouch, Reverend Henry 106